CHICAGO

Rising from the Prairie

BY RICHARD CAHAN

First Edition
Copyright©2000
by Heritage Media Corporation
All inquiries should be addressed to Heritage Media Corp.

ISBN: 1-886483-46-9

Library of Congress Card Catalog Number: 00-103659

Writer and Photo Editor: Richard Cahan

Publisher: C.E. Parks

Editor-in-Chief: Lori M. Parks

VP/National Sales Manager: Ray Spagnuolo

VP/Corporate Development: Bart Barica

CFO: Randall Peterson

Managing Editor: Betsy Baxter Blondin

Production Manager: Deborah Sherwood

Art Director: Gina Mancini

Senior Designer: Susie Passons

Project Editor: John Woodward

Coordinating Editors: Renee Kim, Betsy Lelja, Elizabeth Lex, Sara Rufner, Mary Ann Stabile, Adriane Wessels

Production Staff: Jeff Caton, Brad Hartman, Dave Hermstead, Marianne Mackey, Jay Kennedy, John Leyva, Gavin Rattman, Charlie Silvia

Profile Writers: Kathleen Burke, Sheree R. Curry, Jerry Detra, Silvia Kucenas Foti, Nina M. Gadomski, Jennifer Kales, Nicole M. Neal, Janice Rosenberg, Bill Rush, Debi Schepers, Karen Schwartz, Rosanne M. Ullman, James Alfred Van Dellen

Human Resources Manager: Ellen Ruby

Administration: Juan Diaz, Debbie Hunter, Azalea Maes, Majka Penner, Scott Reid, Patrick Rucker, Cory Sottek

Project Manager: Michael Klein

Project Coordinators: Robin Martino, Randy Block Petersen, Paul Shandling, Jill Wettersten

Published by

Heritage Media Corp.

Corporate Office:
6354 Corte del Abeto, Suite B
Carlsbad, California 92009
www.heritagemedia.com

Local address:
Three First National Plaza
70 West Madison, Suite 1400
Chicago, IL 60602

Printed in cooperation with the Landmarks Preservation Council of Illinois — www.landmarks.org

Printed by Heritage Media Corp. in the United States of America

This book was inspired and formed by a group of people I greatly value and trust. Aaron Cahan spent the summer with me gathering photographs from all over the country. Mark Jacob and Cate Cahan helped me write and edit the text. Kenan Heise and Tim Samuelson offered many ideas and checked historical facts. Ken Burkhart, Torry Bruno and Jack Miller provided invaluable photos.

Many thanks to the Chicago Historical Society, which maintains a most comfortable and wonderful library. This book was completed because many outstanding historians have found Chicago to be a worthwhile subject. I hope it adds to the literature and lore of my hometown.

Acknowledgments

For my children, Elissa, Claire, Aaron and Glenn

If the 20th century was an American century in a global sense, it was the century of Chicago in an American sense.

Perhaps no city better defines America or is more American than Chicago. In the 20th century, Chicago rode the booming tide of industrialism, saw its manufacturing base shrivel and then reinvented itself as a corporate and high-tech center for a new era. In the 20th century, Chicago struggled with the same problems as other American cities, but emerged at the end of the century as the nation's most vibrant and exciting city. In the 20th century, Chicago was saddled with Hollywood stereotypes associated with gangsters but recast itself as the home of real-life heros Michael Jordan and Sammy Sosa.

Now, as we begin a new century of hope and promise, Chicago welcomes the challenges and opportunities that lie ahead. Chicagoans have always been optimistic and unflappable. When

A Message from the Mayor

By Mayor Richard M. Daley

a great fire leveled much of Chicago in 1871, Chicagoans rebuilt with a passion that defined their city. In the years following the fire, Chicago built the world's first skyscraper. The city became known for its stunning skyline, now recognized around the world. On clear days, even lifelong Chicagoans stop to marvel at the city's downtown, set against the sprawling natural beauty of Lake Michigan.

Chicagoans are fiercely proud of their heritage and of the city's firsts and number ones. Three of the world's tallest buildings are in Chicago: the Sears Tower, Aon Building and John Hancock Center. Chicago is the nation's transportation center and has one of the world's busiest airports, O'Hare International. It has the world's largest public library, largest cookie and cracker factory, and largest population of Poles outside of Poland. And among other things, Chicago produced the first elevated railway, roller skates, zippers, pinball game and McDonald's restaurant.

Chicago has also long been home to some of the world's largest and most prominent companies. The second half of this book profiles a number of them. McDonald's Corporation, Motorola, Sears Roebuck, United Airlines and Quaker Oats are just a few of the Chicago-area companies that are household names. With its robust economy and educated work force, Chicago has become one of the nation's most desirable locations for business. And we are working hard to attract new companies, particularly the high-tech and Internet-based companies that will define our modern, global economy.

As Chicago begins the 21st century, there is much to be proud of. In recent years — through an unprecedented investment in our neighborhoods — the city has undergone a renaissance comparable to the rebuilding effort that followed the great fire of 1871. Just 10 years ago, Chicagoans were uneasy about what the future held for their city. But working together, we have revived the city and changed its destiny once again, building a new sense of community, hope and pride in the process.

Chicago is a city of neighborhoods, and in the past decade, we have invested billions of dollars to improve the quality of life in our communities. We have invested in parks, libraries, public schools, police stations, firehouses and city infrastructure improvements such as new streets, sidewalks, alleys and sewers. Throughout the city, new medians, trees, flowers and landscaping have brought a softer feel to the city. Downtown, a beautiful new park is taking shape, dedicated to the spirit of the new millennium. New businesses are investing in our neighborhoods. The downtown business district is thriving. And families who once would have chosen to live in the suburbs are opting to make their lives in the city.

But perhaps the single most important initiative we have undertaken in recent years is our effort to rebuild and reform our public schools. Chicago has become a national model for urban school reform. We addressed the physical needs of our school system, investing over $2 billion to build new schools and to rebuild, refurbish and replace aging buildings. We also demanded account-ability from students, teachers, administrators and parents. We ended social promotions, got the community involved in the schools, instituted a back-to-basics approach to the curriculum, required more homework, brought stability to the system through better management and created alternative schools. Our work has paid off. Test scores, attendance and graduation rates are climbing. And in every neighborhood in the city, you can feel a sense of pride in the public schools that hasn't been felt in decades.

Much work remains to be done. We must continue to improve our public schools if we intend to keep and attract families to our neighborhoods and prepare the next generation of leaders for our city and nation. We must continue to improve Chicago's infrastructure and raise the quality of life in our neighborhoods. And we must continue to find new ways to create economic opportunity for everyone.

Chicago begins the 21st century with a strong sense of itself, its history, its place in the world and its destiny. As we accept the challenges and seize the opportunities of this new era, Chicagoans are proud that their city remains and will always be what poet Carl Sandburg called the "City of the Big Shoulders." ∎

Table of Contents

Table of Contents

continued

In *Chicago: Rising From the Prairie*, Richard Cahan appropriately and engagingly portrays the Metropolis of the Midwest as both a place and an idea. He shows us Chicago as a young city, one that was organized as a town in 1833 with a population of 350 pioneers (in contrast to its long-established American Indian population, which that year had to sign a treaty to leave the area).

The author lists many of Chicago's proud firsts that occurred at a time when other cities of the world were hundreds if not thousands of years old and had populations in the hundreds of thousands if not millions.

Richard Cahan tells the city's story, treating the Great Chicago Fire of 1871 as dramatically as it deserves, using on-the-scene reporting rather than a dry recitation of the property and

Foreword

By Kenan Heise
Noted Chicago author, historian and journalist

long forgotten buildings destroyed. The aftermath of the fire was a great rebirth and renewal of the young city that had grown up haphazardly and recklessly. Cahan tells of thought, invention and imagination replacing impulse, especially as the youthful town discovered a new architecture — an American one.

Chicago found immense success, rapidly making millions of dollars for its entrepreneurs and jobs for the multitude of immigrants attracted from around the world.

The city's fast growth created not only opportunity but also problems. Its people met the latter with extraordinary and refreshing resourcefulness. We are shown a Chicago literally lifted out of the mud with handscrews, resilient from its fire and using its architectural discoveries to build upward as well as outward.

The facts of Chicago's growth and development remain forever interesting and the author does them justice not only in the text, but also with a plethora of illustrations that show the deft hand of a man who served well as the picture editor of a major Chicago metropolitan newspaper.

Still, it is in the unraveling of Chicago as an idea that Richard Cahan and this book perform the highest service. To those with only disdain for the White City, Chicago would seem a rather distasteful and frightening place, full of gangsters and imbued with a second-rate, forgettable and often uncouth style.

This is emphatically not the Chicago Richard Cahan has unveiled. He shows us a world-class city teeming with creativity, imagination and inventiveness — a very uncommon city, deeply proud of who it is rather than who it pretends to be.

Eschewing the aesthetes and the elites, he uses the eyes of those alive to beauty and possibility to view Chicago. The people he introduces include the politically and legally heroic figures John Peter Altgeld and Clarence Darrow, the architecturally imaginative Louis Sullivan and Frank Lloyd Wright, the deeply humanitarian Jane Addams, and the refreshingly literary Margaret Anderson, Ben Hecht and Richard Wright.

For once, a history of the city brings into sharp focus the contributions of African-Americans, principally by highlighting the careers and person of Robert S. Abbott, founder of the *Chicago Defender*.

The book does not ignore Chicago's gangsters, racial conflicts, political imbroglios and smelly stockyards but includes them as part of a self-image that helps the city from becoming pretentious.

This is a refreshing book that honestly, intelligently and cheerfully celebrates Chicago. ■

Chicago has been a trading hub for its whole history. At first, its development depended upon the waterway connections from its pivotal location on Lake Michigan. By the 1850s, the railroad networks ensured Chicago's position as the crucial transportation link between the vast resources of the West and the nation's urban markets to the east and south. But Chicago was a crossroads not only of goods, but of ideas as well. It attracted those who were young, restless, inventive, determined, daring, hard-working, ambitious, and pragmatic. Some say it is the quintessential American city.

Above all, Chicago is known for its architecture, for its pride in construction, for its skill in knowing how to make things. Here on the flat Midwestern prairie, buildings *are* the topography and the revolutionary high-rise form known as the "skyscraper" achieved its early expression. Chicago continues to be a laboratory for modern architecture today.

Introduction

By Judith Paine McBrien
President, Landmarks Preservation Council of Illinois

Skyscrapers were not even the first structural innovation born in Chicago. Clever carpenters in the 1830s began to frame houses by nailing lightweight lumber studs together instead of joining huge timbers one to another in a slow, cumbersome process. Housing could be built faster and cheaper than ever before, thus changing how — and how many — people could be easily sheltered. This "balloon frame" system is ubiquitous today, seen on construction sites throughout the world.

Perhaps more than other cities then, Chicago's identity was forged by its ability to build fast, well and tall. This tradition of quality construction and design has become a key part of the city's ethos. As noted architect Bertrand Goldberg once said, "There is a reason for Frank Lloyd Wright being in Chicago. There is a reason for Louis Sullivan being in Chicago… It is a profound tradition we are continuing with. You don't dare *not* do the best you can."

The Landmarks Preservation Council of Illinois (LPCI) began 30 years ago with a mission to save Chicago's architectural heritage. It focused first on the buildings of the Chicago Loop that represented examples of the "Chicago School of Architecture," the early starting points for modern architecture. These structures show confidence in developing not only a new way of building, but also a new American style independent of European decorative formulas.

Slowly but surely the appreciation for Chicago's heritage has grown, due in part, to LPCI's strong, consistent voice. In the early days particularly, it was not always a popular voice. However, today the buildings LPCI worked so hard to preserve — the Marquette Building, the Chicago Theater and the Reliance Building to name just a few — are among those buildings that millions of tourists come to visit each year. These visitors contribute tens of millions of dollars to city coffers and bring international prestige to the city. Chicago's architecture continues to tell the story of Chicago better than anything else.

The Landmarks Preservation Council is pleased to sponsor this book, *Chicago: Rising From the Prairie*, because we support promoting a better understanding of Chicago's remarkable history and spirit. The book introduces readers to some of the characters, companies and events that transformed Chicago from a frontier outpost to an international city in less than a century. Think of it: When Gurdon Hubbard first came to Illinois in 1818, there was no town or city, only small Fort Dearborn. When he died in 1886, Chicago had grown to become one of the largest cities in the world.

The young city's most cataclysmic event, the Great Chicago Fire of 1871, is described firsthand in the following pages by a young widow trying to save her children. The fire was both good and bad for the city. It was a horrifying inferno but when it was over, citizens were determined to survive and to thrive. The destruction of the central city also created the opportunity for talented young architects to work. Louis Sullivan, William LeBaron Jenney, and John Root all moved to Chicago to develop their professional careers. The buildings they built came to be known as the Chicago School of Architecture.

Chicago always seems to have envisioned itself as a great city. But it was also an instant city. Its population of 300,000 in 1871 reached almost two million persons by the early 1900s. It attracted thousands of immigrants and others from around the country and the world. The chaos, crowding and working conditions resulted in major social unrest and strife evident in race riots and the notorious Haymarket Affair. However, those problems inspired others to work even harder for equal opportunities, more parks and better education.

The famous *1909 Plan of Chicago* by Daniel Burnham and Edward Bennett made tangible some of these dreams for a better city and is still a blueprint for thoughtful development nearly a century later. In the 1920s, Chicago was a city of culture; it was a city of crime. Carl Sandburg worked here but so did Al Capone. Bronzeville became a flourishing neighborhood as the Great Migration brought thousands of African-Americans to Chicago from the south. The 1933-34 "Century of Progress" Fair showcased Chicago's accomplishments to the world as had the World's Columbian Exposition 50 years before.

The next decades saw Chicago's growth slow and the city endure the Great Depression and World War II. Gradually in the late 1950s the city picked up its pace and renewed itself once again, although many chose to live, if not work, in the suburbs. Today, the children of those who moved out of Chicago are returning because of the vitality of Chicago's cultural and neighborhood life, the proximity of amenities such as the great lakefront parks and the buzz of new businesses. Some of the newest Internet enterprises can be found in some of Chicago's oldest buildings.

Throughout this recent period, LPCI has played a crucial role in educating people about the history of their city and the importance of preserving its heritage. And it will continue to do so. These historic structures belong not just to Chicago, but to the world they transformed. ∎

Chicago's Landmarks Portfolio

This section contains a selection of buildings designated as landmarks in one of the nation's greatest architectural cities. The photos were taken over the decades between the 1930s and the 1990s, and the buildings are denoted by their original names. Many of these buildings have been altered and changed, but they endure.

Portfolio photographs except opposite image provided by the Landmarks Preservation Council of Illinois and the City of Chicago's Commission on Chicago Landmarks

CORNICE, PIER CAPITALS AND
CONTINUOUS HEAD ORNAMENT
NOW REMOVED · RECON-
STRUCTION FROM ORIGINAL
PLANS OF BUILDING IN THE
POSSESSION OF SCHMIDT,
GARDEN & ERIKSON — ARCH-
ITECTS, CHICAGO, ILLINOIS.

EIGHTH FLOOR

SEVENTH FLOOR

SIXTH FLOOR

FIFTH FLOOR

FOURTH FLOOR

THIRD FLOOR

SECOND FLOOR

FIRST FLOOR

NOTE: THIS ENTRANCE
EXISTING.

BASEMENT FLOOR

81'-0¼"

NORTH ELEVATION

SCALE : ⅛" = 1'-0"

NOTE: THE GROUND FLOOR ELEVATION IS DRAWN AS
ORIGINALLY BUILT WITH THE RECONSTRUCTION
BEING MADE FROM ORIGINAL PLANS OF THE
BUILDING AND AN EARLY PHOTOGRAPH TAKEN
BY CHICAGO ARCHITECTURAL PHOTOGRAPHING CO.

CHICAGO PROJECT II 1964
ROBERT E. FELIN, J REX ROGGENPOHL, DEL.

UNDER DIRECTION OF UNITED STATES DEPARTMENT OF THE INTERIOR
NATIONAL PARK SERVICE, BRANCH OF PLANS AND DESIGN

NAME OF STRUCTURE
CHAPIN AND GORE BUILDING
65 EAST ADAMS STREET
CHICAGO, ILLINOIS

SURVEY NO.

HISTORIC AMERICAN
BUILDINGS SURVEY
SHEET 3 OF 3 SHEETS

(Top) Glessner House, 1800 South Prairie Avenue   (Bottom) Goldblatt's Building, 333 South State Street *Photo by Jane Smith*

26

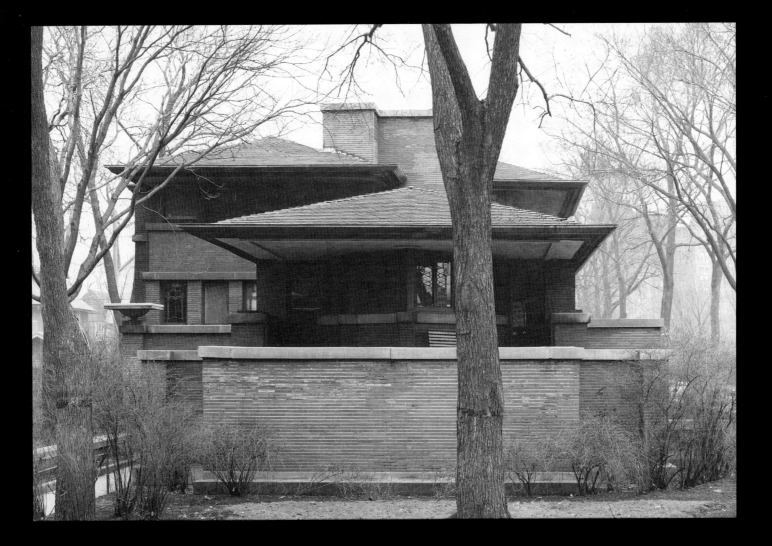

Wrigley Building (left), 400 and 410 North Michigan Avenue, and Tribune Tower, 435 North Michigan Avenue *Photo by Hedrich-Blessing*

(Left) Howe House, 10233 South Wood Street *Photo by Mati Maldre* (Right) Pattern Block House, 2314 West 111th Place *Photo by Bob Thall*

South Michigan Avenue Streetwall *Photo by Mark Hallett*

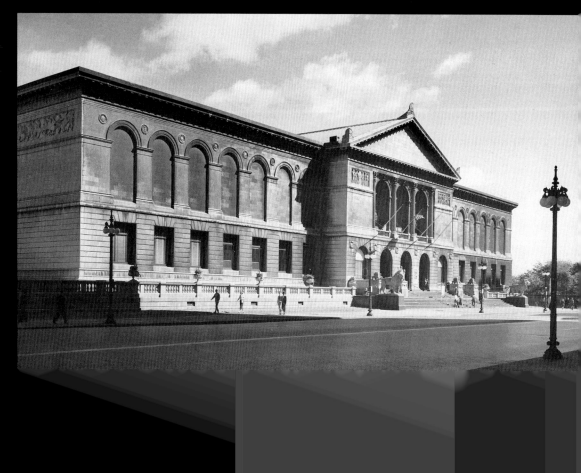

Prologue

The remnants of old Chicago are all around.

Plant and animal fossils, bones and arrowheads are stored in museums. Quarries and moraines show the work of the Ice Age. Streets honor the American Indians and pioneers who settled here first.

Miami Avenue is named after one of Chicago's Indian tribes. Caldwell Avenue recalls Billy Caldwell, the Potawatomi who helped make peace between the Indians and settlers. Blackhawk Street recognizes the wily Sauk Indian chief, and Dearborn Street honors Gen. Henry Dearborn, who ordered construction of the city's first fort.

Blue Island and Stony Island were once actual islands that rose out of sprawling Lake Chicago. Ridge Avenue and the Calumet Sag Channel follow the rises and valleys of receding glaciers.

Chicago's early history is all around — but only if we look.

The city's oldest monument, a limestone marker from 1822, stands in a field at State Line Road and 103rd Street. Installed well before Chicago was a town, it locates the Illinois-Indiana border. A cedar cross on the 2600 block of South Damen, just north of the Chicago River, was placed to honor Father Jacques Marquette, the first European explorer.

"We have seen nothing like this river we enter as regards its fertility of soil, its prairies and woods; its cattle, elk, deer, wildcats, bustards, swans, ducks, parakeets, and even beaver," wrote Marquette on crossing the Chicago portage on the Illinois River in 1673.

How much has changed. How much to remember.

A plaque at the corner of Rogers Avenue and Clark Street on the far North Side establishes where the Indian Boundary Line was drawn during the early 1800s. Nearby, at Rogers and Kilbourn avenues, a tablet shows the site of the Old Treaty Elm. "This tree which stood here until 1933 marked the northern boundary of the Fort Dearborn Reservation, the trail to Lake Geneva, the center of Billy Caldwell's (Chief Sauganash) reservation and the site of the Indian Treaty of 1835."

A tablet on the Michigan Avenue bridge over the Chicago River refers to a more primitive history.

It reads: "This river, originally flowing eastward from the prairie homeland of the Potawatomi and other Indian tribes, into Lake Michigan, linked the waters of the

Old Kinzie mansion in 1832
History of Chicago by Alfred T. Andreas

Atlantic, the St. Lawrence and the Great Lakes with those of the Illinois, the Mississippi and the Gulf of Mexico. From 1673, commerce and civilization flowed through this natural waterway from the seaboard to the heart of the continent."

Chicago's unique geography has stamped its destiny. At the base of Lake Michigan and in the heart of the fertile Midwest, Chicago was suited to become one of America's thriving trading centers and the nation's major transportation hub.

The Michigan Avenue Bridge is at the very center of the history that follows. Literally, the bridge connects the city's North and South sides. Symbolically, the bridge spans the ages, for it is here — near the mouth of the Chicago River — that the story of modern Chicago begins.

Words on the bridge honor early explorers Sieur de La Salle and Henri de Tonti, "Who passed through this river on their way to the Mississippi" in December 1681. They followed Marquette and Louis Jolliet.

A bronze plaque just north of the bridge reads: "Near this site stood Kinzie Mansion 1784-1832, home of Pointe Du Saible, Le Mai, and John Kinzie."

Jean Baptiste Point duSable (as his name is most often spelled) settled north of the river, establishing a large farm and home and opening a trading post during the last decade or so of the 18th century. Of African descent, duSable lived with his Indian wife, Catherine, and two children. He sold his estate in 1800 and moved to Missouri, where he suffered financial losses. He died in poverty but is remembered as the first non-Indian settler in the city we know today.

A plaque at the south end of the bridge recalls Chicago's founding fort. It reads: "Fort Dearborn served as the major western garrison of the United States until destroyed during an Indian uprising in August of 1812. A second fort, erected on the same site in 1816, was demolished in 1856."

The first Fort Dearborn was constructed to stake a claim in territory deeded to the United States in the Louisiana Purchase. Capt. John Whistler and six soldiers began work on August 17, 1803, and completed work late in the year.

Nine years later U.S. Army officials ordered the Fort Dearborn garrison to evacuate. They worried about a

possible Indian uprising. On August 15, 1812, some 600 Indians set up an ambush as the soldiers and their families headed south along the Lake Michigan beach on their way to refuge in Fort Wayne, Indiana. Sixty-six troopers and 20

civilians, including six women and 12 children, were killed. Others were taken captive. The fort was torched.

Fort Dearborn is represented by one of four stars on the municipal flag. The other stars are for the Chicago Fire of 1871, the Columbian Exposition of 1893 and A Century of Progress Exposition of 1933.

The stars and stripes of the city flag tell the story of Chicago. The white stripes represent the North Side, West Side and South Side. The blue stripes symbolize Lake Michigan, the Chicago River and the Great Canal.

But that is only the historic and physical slant of the story. Chicago is made up of millions of people who have been marked and who have left their marks on this great city at the edge of the prairie.

This is their story.

Chicago in 1779, showing the cabin of Jean Baptiste Point duSable
History of Chicago by Alfred T. Andreas

Old Fort Dearborn on the south bank of the Chicago River in 1803
History of Chicago by Alfred T. Andreas

"The Second Fort Dearborn" by Dwight Benton *Chicago Historical Society*

Gurdon S. Hubbard

"*Looking north, I saw the whitewashed buildings of Fort Dearborn sparkling in the sunshine, our boats with flags flying, and oars keeping time to the cheering boat song. I was spellbound and amazed at the beautiful scene before me.*"

— *The Autobiography of Gurdon Saltonstall Hubbard*

Chapter One
1830–1871

Image on opposite page from *History of Chicago* by Alfred T. Andreas

1

In 1818, the year that Illinois became a state, Gurdon S. Hubbard made his entrance into the wilderness settlement that 19 years later would become the city of Chicago

Hubbard, 16, was born in Vermont. He had signed up to work for John Jacob Astor's American Fur Company in Montreal. He left there for the wilds of the Northwest in May of that year, reached the company's Mackinac Island headquarters at the top of Michigan in early July and left for Chicago and Illinois in mid-September. The trip was difficult. The birch bark canoes carried heavy loads of freight. On lakes or rivers, Hubbard and his mates could make 40 miles on a good day. Under sail, with favorable winds, the boats could make 75 miles a day. But while portaging, the traders were often limited to a couple hundred yards of progress.

Young Gurdon Hubbard from an 1830 miniature Chicago Historical Society

"We started at dawn," Hubbard wrote years later about the day he reached Chicago. "The morning was calm and bright, and we, in our holiday attire, with flags flying, completed the last 12 miles of our lake voyage. Arriving at Douglas Grove, where the prairie could be seen through the oak woods, I landed, and climbing a tree, gazed in admiration on the first prairie I had ever seen. The waving grass, intermingling with a rich profusion of wild flowers, was the most beautiful sight I had ever gazed upon. In the distance the grove of Blue Island loomed up, beyond it the timber on the Desplaines River, while to give animation to the scene, a herd of wild deer appeared, and a pair of red foxes emerged from the grass within gunshot of me."

In the distance, Hubbard saw Fort Dearborn, the outpost that had been overrun by Indians only six years earlier. The fort had been rebuilt at the same site, just south of the Chicago River and just west of Lake Michigan." I took the trail leading to the fort, and, on my arrival, found our party camped on the north side of the river, near what is now State Street. A soldier ferried me across the river in a canoe, and thus I made my first entry into Chicago, October 1, 1818."

Hubbard was met by John Kinzie and his family, who had moved to a home across the river from Fort Dearborn

in 1804. After repairing their boats, they headed down the South Branch of the Chicago River. Portaging several miles southwest of the present-day neighborhood of Bridgeport was particularly difficult. They had to cross Mud Lake to the Aux Plaines River, which soon after became known as the Des Plaines River.

"The mud was very deep, and along the edge of the lake grew tall grass and wild rice, often reaching above a man's head, and so strong and dense it was almost impossible to walk through them," Hubbard wrote. The empty boats were pulled up the channel or jerked through the mud for three straight days. Tons of supplies and goods were carried on the backs of the traders.

"Those who waded through the mud frequently sank to their waist, and at times were forced to cling to the side of the boat to prevent going over their heads; after reaching the end and camping for the night came the task of ridding themselves from the blood suckers," he wrote.

Eventually, Hubbard and the traders completed the portage and made it through the Illinois and Mississippi rivers, down a trade route that Indians had long used. During the next 16 years, Hubbard became the most successful trader in the Northwest. He would head to the interiors of Illinois or Michigan during the winters to buy and barter with the Indians and would return to Mackinac during the summers to package and send furs back to the East. Only 20 people lived in Chicago when he made that first trip. When he died in 1888, more than 1 million lived in the city near the shore.

Gurdon S. Hubbard was as responsible as any early pioneer for what Chicago became. In 1827, when the Winnebago Indians in the area threatened to unite with other tribes and attack Chicago, Hubbard rode his horse 125 miles through Indian country to muster a militia. "No textbook heralds to a rising generation the fame of Gurdon Hubbard's ride to Danville to bring troops to imperiled Chicago," wrote historian Milo M. Quaife." Yet, in comparison with it, the midnight ride of Paul Revere was merest child play."

In 1835 a bystander described Hubbard to author E.O. Gale: "Why, that is the proprietor of the warehouse, Gurdon S. Hubbard. He is just as nature labeled him. He can outrun or outwalk any Indian, takes difficulties as you would dessert after dinner, seems to hanker after them, is as true as steel, with a heart as tender as any woman's. He is worth five hundred ordinary men to any town."

Hubbard started Chicago's first meatpacking businesses and ran the largest packinghouse in the West for decades. He built the city's first brick building and served as a director of Chicago's first bank. He wrote the city's first insurance policy and purchased the city's first fire engine. He set up the first water-works, built hotels, was instrumental in the creation of the Illinois & Michigan Canal, made a fortune in real estate, ran a steamboat line and helped nominate his friend, Abraham Lincoln, at the 1860 Republican convention in Chicago.

Hubbard seemed to have a hand in just about every historical event during Chicago's early years. On September 8, 1860, Hubbard's steamer, the *Lady Elgin*, was rammed by the schooner *Augusta* about 10 miles off the shore of Lake Michigan north of Chicago. The *Augusta* limped into port while the *Lady Elgin* sank. It was one of the worst disasters in Great Lakes shipping history. About 300 people were lost at sea; only a few were saved. Hubbard rushed to the beach but knew it was too late to help. He was exonerated of any blame but always felt guilty that the *Lady Elgin* did not have more lifeboats.

In 1861 Hubbard took a leadership role on the Union Defense Committee to raise money for men and equipment for the cause only days after Fort Sumter fell. Hubbard helped form the Second Board of Trade Regiment and served as captain for a short time. Ten years later, Hubbard took a leadership role in saving neighbors and friends in the Great Chicago Fire.

But Hubbard had a secret. During the 1820s he married a Potawatomi woman named Watseka, the niece of an Indian chief. Because of her beauty and the way she comported herself, Watseka was known within her community as "Princess Watseka." She and Hubbard loved and were loyal to each other for several years. The couple had two daughters. The first died at childbirth and the second at 8 months. The two deaths put a strain on the relationship. Watseka refused to leave her people and Hubbard refused to abandon his.

By the late 1820s it was obvious that the fur-trading business was disintegrating. New white settlers did not understand Indian ways; they were trading whiskey for furs and land. And American Indians did not understand white law or the one-sided treaties they were signing.

In 1830 Hubbard returned to the East to pay a visit to his mother. He must have frightened his family; he spoke Potawatomi, wore buckskins and was comfortable sleeping in a teepee. But, as his 1830 portrait indicates, Hubbard returned to his roots. He cut his hair and bought a suit before returning to Illinois. In 1831 he married the sister of a Danville friend. He was elected to the Illinois General Assembly and finally moved to Chicago for good in 1834.

His Indian days were over, but he likely never told his new wife or his son about his Indian love. Watseka moved with the Potawatomis west of the Mississippi River in 1834 after the tribe was forced out of Illinois. She apparently visited Chicago before the move but was not acknowledged by Hubbard.

Their story was symbolic of the early years of Chicago.

Chicago is really two great cities — the gangly, frontier town that was the gateway to the Great West and the rebuilt colossus that we know today.

Chicago's industrious pioneers raised the city from the mud and constructed a booming, freewheeling outpost

The Indian princess Watseka, Hubbard's first wife, portrait by Laura Hunt Eaton on display at the Watseka Public Library

known as the "City in a Garden." From its port and canals to its primitive and mighty railroads, Chicago built its reputation early as a transportation hub and became the home of many of the country's most vital industries.

The roots of modern Chicago stretch back to 1830 when it was surveyed and platted. James Thompson mapped out a town just west of the Fort Dearborn reservation and less than one-half square mile, bounded by Kinzie on the north, Madison on the south, Desplaines on the west and State on the east. The surveyor drew a uniform grid of 58 blocks, and gave street names —

James Thompson's Plan of 1830 — this map helped define downtown Chicago.
History of Chicago by Alfred T. Andreas

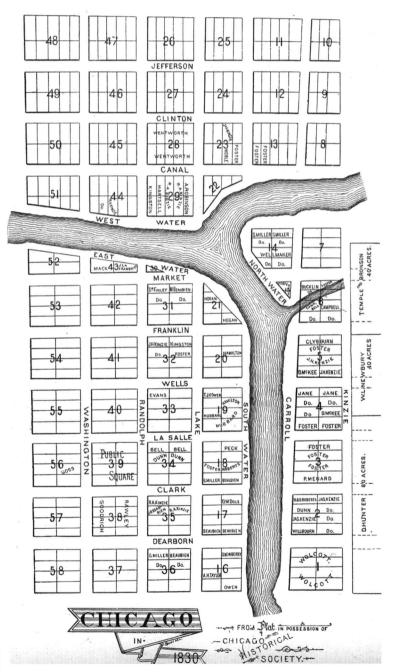

South Water, Lake, Randolph, Washington, Dearborn, Clark, LaSalle, Wells, Franklin — that we use today. The term "Block 37," still used to denote an undeveloped parcel in the heart of the Loop, was Thompson's Block 37. His map is one of the most important documents in Chicago history.

Once platted, Chicago started showing evidence of becoming a community. A lighthouse was built and bridges were constructed across the Chicago River. A drugstore opened and a slaughterhouse was established. The *Chicago Democrat* began publication and the First Presbyterian Church was built. In 1831 Cook County was organized and a post office was started. Deeds were recorded and wills were filed. In 1832 a street leading to Lake Michigan, Water Street, was laid out and a Sunday school was organized in a small frame building on the Fort Dearborn reservation.

Chicago was organized as a town in 1833 with a population of 350 and incorporated as a city in 1837. It's not clear how the city got its name. Historian Joseph Kirkland offered 16 possibilities in his 1892 book *The Story of Chicago*. None of the explanations are definitive. Chicago may have been a word based on the name of an Indian chief, but the most popular explanation is that the name comes from an Indian word meaning "wild onion" or "garlic" or "skunk." It has the connotation of "powerful."

More than a century later, historian John F. Swenson wrote that the name Chicago actually comes from chicagoua, a native garlic plant that grew along the south bank of Lake Michigan. The series of rivers that flowed near the bank was also sometimes called chicagoua. The name, Chicago, was later used as the mouth of the Chicago River, where Fort Dearborn was used.

"English accounts tracing the name to a 'wild onion' date from after 1800, when different groups of Indians, mainly Potawatomi, had displaced the original Miami. In the Potawatomi language, chicago meant both the native garlic and the wild onion," Swenson wrote.

Gurdon Hubbard moved to Chicago permanently in 1834, the last year before American Indians were removed from Chicago.

Chicago in 1833 — color illustration from 1903

The Treaty of Greenville had long ago opened Indian land at the mouth of the Chicago River to the United States. The Winnebagos relinquished all land south and east of the Wisconsin and Fox rivers in 1832 and the following year the Treaty of Chicago called for the Potawatomi, Chippewa and Ottawa Indians to cede all territory in Illinois and Wisconsin in return for annuities (2 cents per acre) and land in the Kansas territory. The last Indian tribes living in the Chicago area left for the West in the mid-1830s. After collecting blankets, pots and their final cash payments, they held a raucous whiskey party in the streets of Chicago on their final days, while the white settlers cowered behind locked doors. Then they left, never to return.

As the threat of Indians lessened, the city became a popular destination for people and for Western culture. Three hundred new residents arrived in one week in May 1834. A drawbridge was built across the river at Dearborn Street. The first piano was moved into town and the first professional public entertainment was staged. With people came problems. A Sunday closing law was passed, carrying with it a $5 fine for anybody keeping open a tippling house or grocery store. The board of trustees prohibited gambling and the firing of guns in town. The first murder trial was held that year.

Two major cemeteries, one north of the city and one south, were started in 1835. The first public school

building, a temporary structure, was constructed and the volunteer fire department was established. Chicago was booming and land speculation ran wild. In three years, a choice 80-by-100-foot parcel soared in value from $100 to $15,000. Hubbard sold property he bought for $67 in 1830 for $96,700. Buy by the yard, sell by the foot became a credo for land speculators, whose run continued until the financial Panic of 1837.

By 1836 Chicagoans were already looking back at bygone days. Troops were permanently withdrawn from Fort Dearborn, marking an end to Chicago's frontier past. John Calhoun, editor of the *Democrat*, gave a farewell speech that year about his three years at the paper. "Instead of 600 inhabitants, which Chicago then contained, there are now as many thousands," Calhoun said. "In place of log cottages we see spacious and elegant buildings. On every side we witness the progress of real and substantial improvement."

Chicago was incorporated as a city in 1837. The city charter created a system of government with a mayor and six aldermen. Businessman and promoter William Ogden was elected as the city's mayor. From the start, Chicago was informally divided three ways: the North Division, north of the Chicago River's east branch, the South Division, south of the branch, and the West Division, west of the northern and southern branches. The first census showed a population of 4,170.

Chicago in 1845,
shown from the west
*History of Chicago
by Alfred T. Andreas*

Chicago in 1845,
shown from the west
*History of Chicago
by Alfred T. Andreas*

These early years were a particular challenge to Chicagoans. Many businesses crashed during the Panic of 1837 and the council issued scrip. The city suffered through cholera and malaria epidemics in 1838. Being a Western town, there was a shortage of marriageable women. A correspondent wrote to the *New York Star*: "Interesting women are in demand here. I understand that when the steamboats arrive from Buffalo and Detroit that nearly all business is suspended; and crowds of desolate, rich young bachelors flock to the pier and stand ready to catch the girls as they land."

By 1839 Chicago was starting to assert itself as a transportation hub. Work on the Illinois and Michigan Canal had begun. A regular steamboat line was established between Chicago and Buffalo, New York, and a 160-mile stagecoach run between Chicago and Galena in western Illinois opened for business. The two-day trip cost $12.50.

More people meant more amenities and more laws. Dearborn Park, later renamed Grant Park, opened that year, and the first daily paper, the *Chicago Daily American*, was published. Fort Dearborn was divided into town lots and offered for sale. The Common Council started passing rules that infuriated some. Billiard tables and nine-pin alleys were prohibited, and lot owners were told they must build sidewalks of stone, brick or wood. That was the reality of city life.

In 1840 Chicago had a population of 4,479, spread across about 10 square miles. This was the decade in

The McCormick
Reaper Works
produced farm
machines that tamed
the Great Plains.
*History of Chicago
by Alfred T. Andreas*

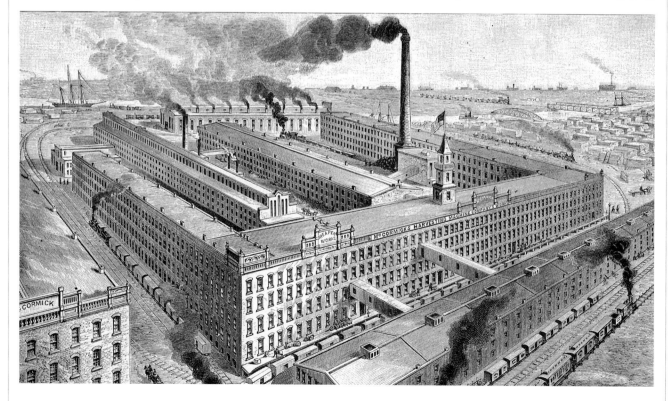

which many of city's major institutions and businesses were established. A city hall was built and floating bridges were built across Clark and Wells streets. The first general hospital was opened and the first permanent theater was opened. Chicago's first permanent school building was constructed due to the efforts of Ira Miltmore. The school cost $7,500. Its official name was Dearborn School, but some called it "Miltmore's Folly." Mayor August Garrett thought the school was too large; he wanted to use the building for an insane asylum instead.

Many mainstay Chicago businesses started in the 40s. Joseph T. Ryerson and Son started manufacturing iron, steel and machinery. The first cattle yards were opened as Gurdon Hubbard joined with Archibald Clybourn to slaughter and pack cattle for eastern markets. The Board of Trade, a key part of the commodities industry for 150 years, opened, too. Chicago businesses from that era still thrive. The year 1847 is the founding date of three ongoing companies: The Chicago Title and Trust, the Chicago Daily Tribune and the McCormick Reaper Works. The *Tribune* published its first edition on June 10. When Cyrus Hall McCormick moved his machine manufacturing company to Chicago, he claimed that his reaper could harvest up to 10 acres a day, in an era when a farmer with a scythe could harvest only two. The company eventually became International Harvester and later Navistar.

The city's early religious institutions began to take root. Three churches were formed in 1833 — a Catholic, a Presbyterian and a Baptist. St. Peter's Catholic Church was organized in 1842 and the following year was the start of an important city tradition — the celebration of St. Patrick's Day. Jews, most escaping persecution in Germany, arrived in Chicago during these years. In 1848 the first synagogue was established. It was called Kehilath Anshe Maarev, Congregation of the Men of the West.

Chicago staked its claim as a transportation center when the Illinois & Michigan Canal opened for navigation in 1848. Started in 1836, the I & M was one of the last great transportation canals built in the nation. The northeast terminus of the canal was at Bridgeport, a Chicago southwest side neighborhood first known as Hardscrabble. The canal, a dream promoted by Chicago pioneers for decades, began its operations when the freighter General Fry took dignitaries and a brass band down to Lockport. The canal ran through 16 locks from Chicago to the downstate city of LaSalle on the Illinois River. From there, boats could navigate to the Mississippi River and eventually connect with New Orleans and the Gulf of Mexico.

The flood of 1849 was one of the city's first natural disasters. *History of Chicago by Alfred T. Andreas*

With locks made of timber, stone and mortar, the canal completed a link between the East and the Great Lakes with the Mississippi Valley. Chicago was the fulcrum. The canal, which operated until 1933, made shipping between regions much cheaper and sparked manufacturing. Timber was shipped from Michigan, corn from the Midwest. Cotton moved up from the South. And quarry stone from Downstate Illinois was shipped around the country.

By the late 1840s Chicago was losing some of its residents to the lure of the West. Gold was discovered in 1848 and the California Gold Rush of 1849 positioned Chicago as a center for western emigrants. Wagons and wagon covers were built and pistols and bowie knives were in high demand. Even canal boats left with families on their way West.

By 1850 the city's population reached 30,000. Chicago was becoming an urban center. The city grew in 1851, extending its western border to Western Avenue, making it 13.5 square miles. It grew again in 1853, extending its northern border to Fullerton and southern limits to 31st Street. The city continued to shed its frontier past. Frink and Walker dissolved its stage coach service. Chicago built a sewer system, created a police department and established a street numbering system. Chicago High, the city's first high school, opened in 1856. In the midst of urbanization, city planners started recognizing the importance of parks. Union Park was planned as a park "with lake and rustic bridge and gliding swans." The biggest change during the decade perhaps came at the start, when streets were lit for the first time — by gas lamps. "Night was transformed into a mimic of day," wrote a contemporary.

Culture, too, was coming to Cow Town. The first opera, Bellini's *La Sonnambula*, was presented on July 30, 1850. The night after the opening performance, the theater

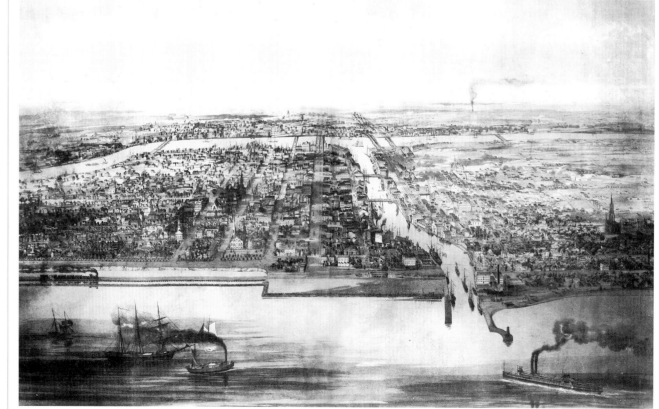

Old block house and lighthouse in 1857 and the last remains of the second Fort Dearborn
History of Chicago by Alfred T. Andreas

Second Cook County Courthouse, before the third story was added — this daguerreotype was by Alexander Hesler.
History of Chicago by Alfred T. Andreas

was demolished by fire, making this the city's shortest opera season in history. Later that year, the Philharmonic Society was established. The symphony performed for 18 years.

The Southern Plank Road, following State Street several miles south of the city, was constructed in 1850. The Northwestern Plank Road (now known as Milwaukee Avenue) had been built the previous year and the Southwestern Plank Road (Ogden Avenue) was completed in 1848.

By the end of the decade, most of the streets were planked in pine in an attempt to pull Chicago out of the mud. The city council's major concern during the decade was raising the street levels to control flooding and muddy conditions on streets and sidewalks. Streets were so muddy that residents put up signs on mud patches that read "No bottom," "team underneath," "This way to China" and "stage dropped through." At one spot, a hat was placed atop the mud and marked "Man lost." It was so wet on State Street that guests at the Tremont House hotel used to sit on the porch and take potshots at the ducks in the street. The street-raising

Chicago City Railway tickets
History of Chicago by Alfred T. Andreas

project was awesome. The Briggs Hotel, five stories tall and weighing 22,000 tons, was lifted 4.5 feet, with a new foundation built underneath — and it stayed open for business the entire time. George Pullman, later to build the famed company town called Pullman, was a leader of this engineering feat, stationing hundreds of men around buildings and lifting them by the use of large hand screws. The project took decades to complete.

Railroads, which became the key to Chicago's growth, got their start during the late 1840s and came into their own during the 50s. The Pioneer, a used locomotive, sailed to Chicago on a vessel from New York, made its first run from Chicago on November 20, 1848. The 10-mile trip over the Galena and Chicago Union Railroad to the Des Plaines River was without fanfare. A farmer met the train and sold oxen and load of wheat before the train was turned and headed back.

In 1850 the Galena line was the only railroad in or out of Chicago. The Illinois Central Railroad as well as the Chicago and Milwaukee Railroad were granted charters in 1851. The Illinois Central laid tracks on stilts east of Michigan Avenue. The Michigan Central Railroad connected Chicago to Detroit and points east. In 1854 the Chicago, Rock Island and Pacific Railroad was the first to reach the Mississippi River from Lake Michigan. The Rock Island's arrival at the banks was marked by fanfare. The trip guaranteed the destiny and success of Chicago, for it showed that Chicago — not St. Louis — would become the railroad gateway to the West. A year later, the Rock Island built a 1,535-foot-long bridge across the mighty Mississippi into Iowa and Chicago's direct connection to the West was complete.

By 1856 there were 10 lines with 58 passenger trains and 38 freight trains arriving or departing the city daily. The battle over land rights to lay rail tracks could be fierce. At the area now known as Grand Crossing, the Michigan Southern Railroad refused to let the Illinois Central cross at grade. So the

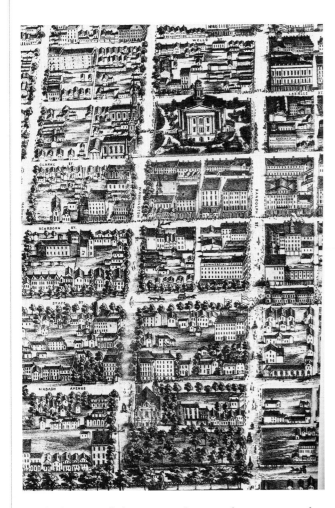

IC had its track layers sneak onto the site at night, overpower a guard and lay track before daybreak. By 1856 the IC was also running the first suburban trains, connecting Chicago and suburban Hyde Park with four round trips daily and operating passenger trains all the way to Cairo. How far that lonesome whistle had come in less than a decade.

The black population of Chicago numbered only about 500 in 1850, but African-Americans help provide a new insight to all Chicagoans as the nation plunged toward the Civil War. Anti-slavery meetings were held frequently during the late 1850s. The first passengers on the Underground Railroad had arrived in the city in 1839. Seven years later, two runaway slaves were captured and taken before a judge. Blacks passed the two slaves down the stairs into the arms of friends before they could be taken back into slavery. In 1850 members of the African Methodist Episcopal Church deplored the passage of the federal Fugitive

Slave Law, which set harsh penalties for anyone aiding runaway slaves. The Common Council met that year and resolved that the law was cruel and unjust and that it should not be respected. The following year, a runaway slave from Missouri, Morris Johnson, was arrested and tried. He was freed by the courts.

"Viewed through the lens of the Civil War, Chicago was a contradiction," wrote Theodore J. Karamanski, in *Rally 'Round the Flag*. Before 1860 the city was routinely denounced by Southerners as a 'nigger lovin' town' and a 'sink hole of abolitionism.' Yet during the war Chicago was often described as a 'hotbed' of antiwar dissent.'"

Levi D. Boone of the Know-Nothing Party was elected mayor in 1854. He immediately declared that only native-born Americans could become policemen, incensing the Irish especially, since many were on the force. Boone then took aim at the Germans. He viewed beer drinking as un-American, since it was most popular among the city's German immigrants. He raided closed saloons on Sunday (only those that served beer; the ones that served good old American whiskey somehow stayed open). Boone's crackdown sparked street unrest that was called "the lager beer riots."

By the 1850s the city was developing a furious reputation as a city of sin. Wrote one journalist, in 1855: "Men are getting rich faster, and living higher and doing more business and drinking more and going to the devil by a shorter road in Chicago than at any place I have ever seen out west." During the following year, it was reported Chicagoans supported 100 public and 400 private prostitutes, with 110 public houses of ill fame.

Colorful Mayor Long John Wentworth took aim at the Sands, a red-light district on the North Side along the

View of City Hall, Courthouse and Public Square in 1857
Chicago Historical Society

Clark Street in 1857
History of Chicago by Alfred T. Andreas

Results of John Wentworth's raid on vice district in The Sands
History of Chicago by Alfred T. Andreas

lake in 1857. At a bordello called Freddie Webster's, one of the prostitutes was said to have been neither sober nor clothed in three years. She died in March 1857 from what the coroner called "intemperance." The next month, Wentworth gave the tavern/bordellos a deadline to leave the area or have their buildings put to the torch. To back up his threat, he sent the volunteer fire department to the area. Most of the male habitues of the Sands were away at a dogfight at the time, and the woman left the area without a fight. After they departed, some of the rickety buildings were hooked up to chains and pulled down by a team of horses. Several of the remaining buildings were set afire. It's unclear whether the prostitutes set the fires out of spite as they left or whether the buildings were torched by firefighters who wanted a little practice.

The battle between good and evil has been a major theme in Chicago history. During the 1850s the Chicago Temperance Society was formed to encourage total abstinence and the Magdalene Asylum was opened. This was a place established for unfortunate females to go to abandon their course of degradation. Despite these efforts, sin held sway. By 1858, according to one count, Chicago had 70 churches and 541 saloons.

By 1860 the city's population was nearly 110,000. Early Chicago was a foreign mecca: more than half of its residents had been born outside the United States.

Germans and Irish constituted the bulk of the early immigrants. Germans settled just north and south of the Chicago River and in Bridgeport. The Irish, driven to America because of the Great Famine of the 1840s and to Chicago because of East Coast persecution, settled along the east bank of the river, close to what is now called the Loop, and in Bridgeport. They settled near the stockyards and the docks, where they found work. But the city was still dominated by "Yankees," native-born Protestants who had migrated from the East. Although they made up a small minority, the urban elite held the money and power in the city.

The first half of the decade revolved around a domestic issue, the War Between the States. Despite its location far from most of the battlefields, Chicago played an important role in the Civil War. The two leading presidential candidates in the 1860 election, Stephen A. Douglas and Abraham Lincoln, had strong Chicago ties. Douglas was the Democratic flag-bearer who later rallied the city behind the Union cause. Lincoln won the Republican convention in large part due to Chicago backers. They nominated the Springfield lawyer at the Chicago convention held in a temporary wooden hall called the Wigwam.

Ironically, two major anti-Union figures also had Chicago ties. Jefferson Davis, president of the

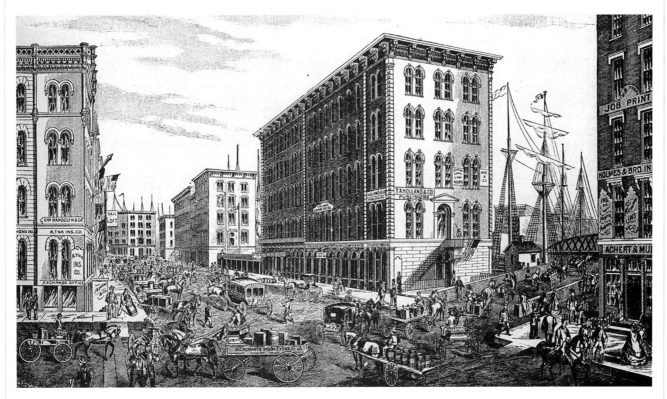

Clark and South Water streets about 1860
History of Chicago
by Alfred T. Andreas

Troops were offered money to join the Civil War before the draft was announced.

Confederacy, visited Fort Dearborn in 1829 as a lieutenant in the army looking for deserters. Later, he advised the Army Corps of Engineers on the location for the rebuilt mouth of the Chicago River. John Wilkes Booth, Lincoln's assassin, was the talk of the town when he appeared on stage in 1862. He was the city's most popular actor after starring as the vicious Richard III.

The opening of the war, the South's attack on Fort Sumter in the harbor of Charleston, South Carolina, on April 12, 1861, prompted Chicago Mayor John Wentworth to close public offices. U.S. flags were ordered displayed in honor of Major Robert Anderson, who had attempted to defend the fort against heavy bombardment.

After Lincoln called for troops, Gen. H.K. Swift, a Chicago banker, headed to downstate Cairo with 872 men, 46 horses and guns. By May 1861, 13 Chicago companies were in service and 23 were in reserve. Chicago was transformed by the war; the city became a major supplier. It was in a good location, far enough from the action to be spared damage, but connected directly by

railroads and waterways. As in other Northern cities, tailors turned out uniforms, shoemakers made boots and women sewed flannel shirts. The meat-packing factories, iron makers and railroad car companies grew to meet the demand of the Union war machine. Following the war, these companies were on such good footing that they could continue to grow.

The war also opened Chicago's conscience. A few months after Fort Sumter, the school board voted 6-3 to admit a black student to the city high school.

Camp Douglas, a military camp named after Stephen A. Douglas, was established in 1861 at Cottage Grove on the South Side as a major center for incoming soldiers from the Midwest. The following year, 7,000 Confederates captured at Fort Donelson were sent to Camp Douglas for imprisonment. The POW camp was a foul place, and a curiosity for thousands of Chicagoans who traveled there to see and talk to the Johnny Rebs. But, overcrowding and unsanitary conditions led to high mortality. In the last three years of the war, more than 6,000 Confederate POWs died out of 20,000 held at the camp.

Aerial view of Camp Douglas, a holding facility for Confederate soldiers built on the South Side
History of Chicago by Alfred T. Andreas

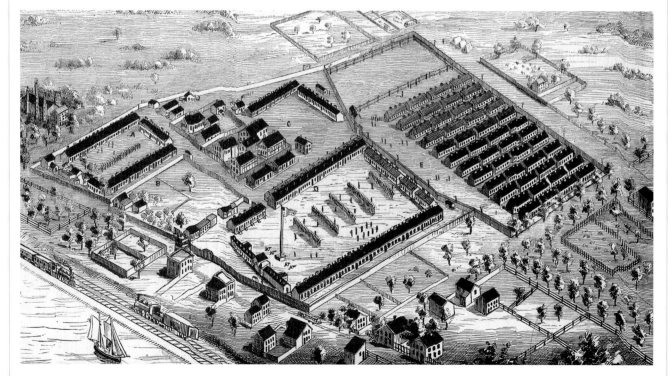

News of Gen. Robert E. Lee's surrender to Gen. Ulysses S. Grant on April 9, 1865, reached Chicago the following evening. It was met with a 100-gun salute and the roar of cannons. Gurdon Hubbard attended Chicago's "grand review" when regiments returned to the city later that year. The toll of the war was apparent: the 88th Illinois Regiment came back with 209 out of its original 900 strong and the 89th Illinois Regiment returned with 300 out of 900. Hubbard, who had raised a company and served as captain for a short while, found his troops to congratulate them. In all, Chicago sent 15,000 soldiers. About 4,000, including the sons of many of the city's most prominent citizens, never returned.

Abraham Lincoln's body was brought to Chicago on May 1, 1865. A special depot was built to receive his funeral train. Following a long, somber procession, Lincoln's body lay in state in the courthouse rotunda for two days before heading off for its final trip to Springfield. The name of North Side Park was changed to Lincoln Park. Douglas Park and Logan Square were named after Civil War leaders, too.

Not all life revolved around the war during the 1860s. The city was divided into 16 wards in 1863 and the mayoral term was lengthened from one to two years. The southern boundary of the city was extended to 39th street that year and the western boundary was extended to Crawford Avenue in 1869.

During the mid-1860s, a tunnel was built 60 feet deep and two miles into Lake Michigan to gather fresher drinking water. Lake water was tainted by waste dumped into the Chicago River, which fed into the lake. A new water tower and pumping station were completed in 1869 near Michigan and Chicago avenues.

On the other side of town, the Union Stock Yards opened in 1865 with room for 20,000 cattle, 75,000 hogs, 20,000 sheep. When the wind was wrong, the scent was quite annoying to people downtown.

With the war over, Chicago once again started building. Developer Potter Palmer bought three-fourths of a mile along State Street and transformed the area into a hotel and retail mecca that included the Field, Leiter & Co. store and the Palmer House hotel. Palmer was the first to base his business policy on the slogan that "The Customer Is Right."

Washington Street tunnel beneath the Chicago River
History of Chicago
by Alfred T. Andreas

The Water Tower was completed in 1869. It conceals a stand-pipe 138 feet high.
History of Chicago
by Alfred T. Andreas

Promoter Uranis H. Crosby built one of the city's finest pieces of architecture, the Crosby Opera House, financed by raffle tickets. The winner of the raffle was supposed to win ownership of the $600,000 theater. But after the drawing was held, he was revealed to be an out-of-towner who immediately sold the building back to Crosby for $200,000. Other raffle ticket holders were not amused, and Crosby skipped town ahead of the lynch mob, leaving ownership of the building to his brother. (The opera house was destroyed in the Great Fire of 1871.)

City attitudes started changing after the war. Seances and fortune telling were the rage. Liberal ideas started taking root. The German Workingmen's Association spoke out in favor of an eight-hour work day in 1867. The state legislature voted to make eight hours a legal day's work, unless other arrangements were specified. A meat inspection system was ordered for the Stock Yards in 1868. Later that year, the Bennett College of Eclectic Medicine and Surgery became the first medical school to admit women.

The idea of parks also a firm hold. The phrase City in a Garden was based on private plots, not public parks. "The behemoth Trade swallows up everything," wrote the *Tribune* in 1853. "Still we say parks — give us public parks. They are the 'lungs of the metropolis.' Let us breathe or we and our children die." Small public places for neighborhoods were built during the 1850s, and in 1863 the area that would be known as Lincoln Park was denoted as a park. In 1869 the legislature made laws to build boulevards and major parks around the city. Landscape architect Frederick Law Olmsted, who had designed New York City's Central Park, came to the area to begin designing the suburb of Riverside. Chicago's green space had been defined.

By the end of the decade, Chicago had become one of the nation's busiest ports. Docks lined the river and lake traffic caused backups on land. Some 27 bridges spanned the river and in 1869 the Washington Street tunnel under the Chicago River formally opened. It was the first river tunnel constructed in the United States.

Chicago was connected to the Pacific Ocean on May 10, 1869, when the last spike of California gold was driven into the soil near Promontory, Utah. The transcontinental railroad was complete. Chicagoans filled the streets in joy. Chicago was now the center, and the heart, of the nation.

Crosby's Opera House, one of the city's first grand buildings
History of Chicago by Alfred T. Andreas

"Memories of the Chicago Fire of 1871" by Julia Lemos *Chicago Historical Society*

W. D. Kerfoot

"Everything gone but wife, children & energy."

— *Sign installed the morning of October 10, 1871, on "Kerfoot's Block," the first business structure*

built following the fire. The wood shanty, on Washington between Dearborn and Clark streets,

became a symbol of the city's determination to rebuild.

Chapter Two
1871–1880

Image on opposite page *from* History of Chicago *by Alfred T. Andreas*

Chicago was forever defined by the great fire that swept the city on October 8th, 9th and 10th in 1871. The fire gave Chicago a chance to be reborn.

"About 9 o'clock that evening, my baby was asleep and I began to get ready to retire," wrote Julia Lemos about that night. "Our cottage had front shutters, solid without slats in them, so when shut, the room was in complete darkness. I pulled the shutters to close them, but there was such a strong wind blowing, that I had to pull hard to close them. I said out loud, Oh what a wind. It would be bad if there was a fire — I did not know then, but the fire had already started on the west side."

Lemos' words were written in 1918 to describe a painting she completed depicting the scene from her bedroom window. The view is powerful — even 130 years later — for it shows neighbors gathering their families and belongings in the wake of the fire as it approached the North District.

"I retired," Lemos wrote, "but about five o'clock in the morning was woke up by a rumbling noise, so as I was awake I got up and threw open the shutters. I thought I was dreaming, the whole street was crowded with people, just getting up?

"I said yes, what is the matter? The sky was reflecting fire, she said the city has been burning all night, and the fire is coming to the north side."

Nobody can understand Chicago unless they understand the fire.

The frontier village of Chicago was poised for greatness on that Sunday night in 1871. The Great Chicago Fire put an end to the City in a Garden and shaped the Chicago of today. The calamity wiped out the best parts of the frontier metropolis but created opportunity and attracted the best and brightest to rebuild. Only three years after the city lay in ruins, it was obvious that Chicago would attain a greater destiny.

The pre-fire Chicago was a flawed wonder. The *Stranger's City Directory*, published by a morning newspaper, said Chicago had "more gambling halls than any city with the same number of churches, more rats to the square yard, and worst evening papers than any city in the union."

Its greatest liability, however, was that it was a city built of kindling. Barn fires were common and city rules against the use of candles and lamps in barns were largely ignored. The city was especially liable to fires because of the invention of balloon frame construction, a wooden framing system forming the structure of most of Chicago's buildings. Lumber dealer George Snow invented the type of building in 1832. With lumber as a chief commodity, the balloon frame made construction easy and inexpensive. It was one of the major reasons the city was built so quickly and one of the reasons the city burned so easily.

Balloon framing was not the chief cause of the fire's severity. It was a matter of high winds and a

Chicago in 1871, just prior to the Great Fire
Harper's Weekly

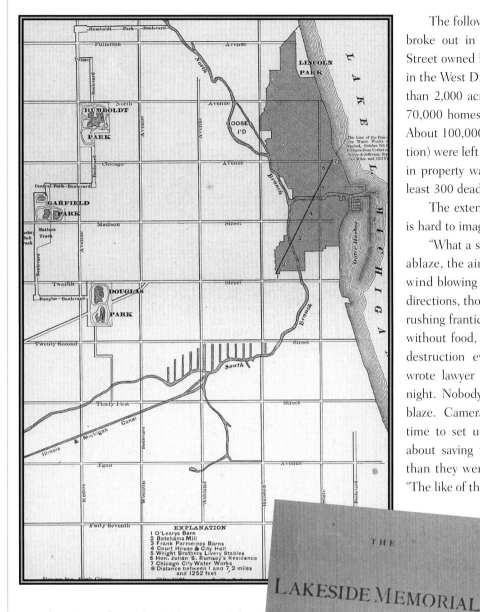

The following night, at about 9 o'clock, fire broke out in the cow barn at 137 DeKoven Street owned by Patrick and Catherine O'Leary in the West District. The fire stormed over more than 2,000 acres of the dry city, burning about 70,000 homes, 1,600 stores and 600 factories. About 100,000 people (one-third of the population) were left homeless and about $200 million in property was destroyed. The human toll: at least 300 dead.

The extent and physical impact of the fire is hard to imagine.

"What a sight: a sea of fire, the heavens all ablaze, the air filled with burning embers, the wind blowing fiercely & tossing fire brands in all directions, thousands upon thousands of people rushing frantically about, burned out of shelter, without food, the rich of yesterday poor today, destruction everywhere — is it not awful?" wrote lawyer Jonas Hutchinson the following night. Nobody took photographs of the actual blaze. Cameras were cumbersome and took time to set up. People were more concerned about saving their lives and their belongings than they were about documenting the event. "The like of this sight since Sodom & Gomorrah has never met human vision. No pen can tell what a ruin this is."

For a century the consensus was that Mrs. O'Leary's cow kicked over a lantern in the barn, sparking the Great Chicago Fire. Mrs. O'Leary has been cleared over and over again. At least there is no direct evidence linking her or the cow to the fire. But as the *Chicago Evening Journal* once wrote, she has never been cleared from the "verdict of history." Modern suspicions are that the fire might have been started by O'Leary's neighbor, 'Peg Leg' Sullivan, who lost his wooden leg in the fire. There is even a strange theory that the fire was caused by a

proliferation of combustible materials. The combination of wind and extreme heat made almost everything burn, melt or disintegrate.

A fire in 1870 destroyed $2.5 million in property and caused several deaths. A blaze in September 1871 caused $3 million in damage, and a fire on October 7, 1871, burned $1 million in property. That evening, author George Francis Train told a crowd of onlookers: "This is the last public address that will be delivered within these walls! A terrible calamity is impending over the City of Chicago! More I cannot say; more I dare not utter."

Title page from the
book *Through the
Flames and Beyond*

101

Bird's-eye view of the fire at the Chicago River *Harper's Weekly*

played virtually no role in the Great Fire. Containing the fire was like containing the wind, as one contemporary observed.

By the time the first engines arrived, fire had consumed about five or six barns in the O'Leary neighborhood. In the first hour the fire was contained to the O'Leary block, but then the wind blew the fire northeast to a district of lumberyards and an Irish shantytown. It jumped the South Branch of the Chicago River eastward at about midnight, igniting the huge Parmelee Omnibus and Stage Company at the southeast corner of Jackson and Franklin and torching the municipal gasworks.

fiery meteor shower (since another huge fire — the worst in U.S. history — started almost the same hour in the northern Wisconsin town of Peshtigo, 200 miles north).

Whoever or whatever was to blame, a small fire on Chicago's Near West Side quickly became a large one, fed by a strong wind that carried burning cinders from rooftop to rooftop. The fire department, hampered by communication problems and already exhausted by the large fire the night before, was simply overmatched. It

Aided by fuel and feeding on its own energy and a huge wind that the fire itself helped create, the fire was a mile wide heading toward the business district. The pine-planked streets and wooden sidewalks provided a direct thoroughfare for the fire to move through town. So

People head north on Randolph Street Bridge. *Harper's Weekly*

People trapped on the roof begin to pray as fire nears.

Panic at Clark and
Randolph streets
*Leslie's
Illustrated Weekly*

intense was its heat that the fire created spontaneous combustion in front of it. By now the "fireproof" buildings downtown could not withstand the blaze. The fire melted the iron and dissolved the mortar. Brick was peeled off the walls, exposing wooden rafters and tarpaper roofs. Within a few hours the fire had swept through most of downtown, freeing prisoners in the jail and ravaging the $1 million courthouse. The courthouse bell, which had been clanging calls of distress for hours, dropped at 2:05 a.m.

The flames swept northward, crossing the State Street Bridge to the North Division at 1:30 a.m. and setting a stable on fire by 2:30 a.m. At times the blaze was spreading through a block in less than 60 seconds.

The fire blackened Chicagoans. Most were forced to leave in the middle of the night wearing bedclothes. Some tried to save belongings; most abandoned them. Chaos was everywhere. Residents filled the city's 12 bridges. Many went to the beaches and parks near Lake Michigan, eventually being forced into the water. Some men buried their wives and children in wet sand along the shore, leaving breathing holes to keep them alive. Some fled into the lake, wading and watching their city burn. Some left by boat.

"Imagine the scene of the horrid drama," wrote A.T. Andreas, "No possibility of escape — a raging fury at the rear, a pitiless expanse of lake front — a small area filled with human creatures, maddened animals, delicate and refined women, pure and innocent children; the aged, the infirm, the weak, the dying, the despairing; young girls, whose artless lives were unfamiliar with even the name of crime; men of well-ordered lives and Christian minds; brutes in human form, who were not only ready to do acts of crime, but whose polluting wickedness was rank and cast off prison-fumes upon the air. All kinds and conditions and grades of life — all forms of death, from calm and peaceful passing to a welcome rest to that which follows in the train of vicious deeds."

In less than seven hours flames traveled to the water works, more than two miles northeast of the O'Leary barn. The new Water Tower and pumping station, off Chicago Avenue, was the city's last hope, for it controlled the city's water supply. The buildings were considered fireproof, built in an isolated area of stone battlements and turrets with a slate roof. They did stand up to the fire, but within a short while, the pumping station machinery ground to a halt. Chicago had no more water —and the fire would have to work its way out.

Julia Lemos, a widow, had recently put four of her children in an institution where they could be raised and protected. She was trying to earn a living with a lithography company to support her family. After being alerted by her neighbor, she ran to the back room of her North Side home and woke her father and mother.

"Father ran around shaking his hands," she wrote, "the children, the children, I must go for them, he said. I said no, you stay here and take care of mother and the baby, then I ran to the asylum, they were moving there up north to another building, the matron said my children would be all right, and wanted me to leave them, but I insisted on taking them, and had to bring them with ragged clothes on, though I had given good clothes when I took them there, but I was thankful to get them in any way. My youngest boy had to go with me without a hat, as it was all confusion there."

Lemos' text is detailed and, though written 47 years after the fire, still breathless.

"Well we got home and I gave the children breakfast, then father said I should go to the landlord next door and ask him to return to me the $12 I had given him for rent in advance, as we were going to be burnt out, and I was a widow with all that family, he refused to give me back the money, but was an expressman and had a wagon, he said that he had been moving their household goods up north on the prairie, and that he would move one load of my things for that money, which he did, things we would need at first, but all our best things had to burn.

"I had a trunk with papers valuable to the family and my best clothes, and father had a large trunk with papers of value and mother's and his best clothes. His name was on the outside of his trunk and my name was on my trunk also, then there was a mattress and a feather bed and other things put

on the wagon, and it went off. We did not know if we could find the things again, by that time the fire was advancing on us, I wanted to leave the house, but father said, O, the wind will change. People were still running in crowds past our house, I stood with my baby in my arms and the other children beside me, when a woman running past with three children said to me, Madam, ain't you going to save those children, that started me."

Lemos told her father she was leaving the house at once.

"Mother put some bread and a pound of coffee in a valise, then she took a small tin kettle — father came out of the house, with his hunting dog, which was worth $25 on a chain, his gun and a large round cloak he wore those days, then he locked the door, and put the key in his pocket, we always laughed about that afterwards — then we started away with the crowd and went way up north till we came to prairies, where people had moved their goods."

The fire roared through the North Division, taking with it most every building north of the river —including the huge home of Gurdon S. Hubbard on LaSalle Street. Hubbard's third wife, Mary Ann, was combing her hair in the second-floor dressing room of the couple's ivy-covered mansion when she looked south and saw the conflagration. She woke her husband, but he dismissed her at first. Soon after, he awoke and drove his mother-in-law to safety on the West Side. He returned and found his house filled with neighbors, friends and refugees who counted on Hubbard in times of emergency. The

The Sands, near Lake Michigan, was a haven for many escaping the fire.

Hubbards served food and soaked the mansion's roof in water in the hopes of saving the house, but it burned to the ground shortly after daybreak.

Hubbard, who had lost his meatpacking company to fire in 1868, lost his house in the Great Chicago Fire and 800 pages of manuscripts that he had written about his life. Hubbard had invested heavily in insurance companies and had written thousands of policies before the fire. He went deep into debt, but worked five years to pay off the insurance claims and his obligations. He persevered and ended up selling off real estate and living a comfortable, yet more modest, life.

It was in the prairies that Lemos found herself and her family.

"We found our goods and trunks in a pile by themselves, by that time it was getting late in the afternoon," she wrote in 1918. "The children were very tired as we all were, father took the mattress and laid the children on it and the feather bed and covered them with his large cloak, they got asleep for about an hour, when word came that we would have to run again.

"The fire was on us, the wind blew the blazing boards for a long distance and set fire to all the goods on the prairie. A dry goods store on the corner of Wells and North Avenue had their stock here, and the fire ran along the long grass too, we had no rain for a long time, and everything was very dry. I had to wake the children up, and we had to run again, and leave everything to burn, this time we felt the heat on our backs when we ran, like when one stands with the back to a grate fire.

"Well we ran a good way North, then father thought we were safe and we stopped, then the sky was clouding up and getting dark, there was an old board fence where we were and father pulled four boards off, and laid them on the grass and laid three of the children on them and covered them with his large cloak again, but my oldest child, a boy about 9 years old stayed with me. I set on the grass holding the baby, and the boy laid his head on my lap and went to sleep, then it was dark, and from where I was sitting I could see a circle of fire at a distance, then I saw a church steeple topple over in the flames.

"Just then my boy woke up, and began to sob, I said Willie, mama is here, do not cry. He said yes but Mama, Isn't this the Last Day? You see, he had been to Sunday school and heard about the Day of Judgment — the end of the world, Well it was getting very dark, then it began to rain, a pouring rain, I said to father it will kill those children to sleep in that rain. Poor old man, he said, I have done all I can."

The rain that fell late in the evening of October 10 and a shifting wind put an end to the fire's fury. The blaze had spread as far north as Fullerton Avenue and as far west as Halsted. Ironically, the West Division, where the fire started, suffered least — only 500 structures were destroyed and even the O'Learys' house (south of the fire) was spared. The South Division, which included downtown, and the North Division suffered far more damage. The North Side lost 13,000 buildings; only 500 were left standing. The fire's exact path of destruction was hard to figure — some isolated homes caught fire while a few

The Merchants Insurance Building, at the corner of Washington and LaSalle streets, in ruins Stereoview by W.E. Bowman, Tory Bruno Collection

homes in dense neighborhoods remained unscathed.

About 120 bodies were found but hundreds more remain missing. Several were killed on the Division Street bridge. People were crushed against the railings as they headed to the West Side.

The Lemos family found shelter the first night after the fire on a nearby farm and slept in a shed. The following morning, October 11, Lemos' father and mother returned to the prairie to see if their trunks had survived.

"By and by they came back and told me that everything that was stored on the prairie was burned," Julia Lemos wrote. "We had a mattress and a feather bed, all that remained of that was a few feathers flying in the air. A policeman saw father hunting around, and asked him what he was looking for. Father told him we had goods there, and among them were two trunks, but he could not find the remains of them.

"The policeman asked him, what names were on the outside of the trunks, father said his name Eustace Wyszynski was on one, and my name Mrs. Julia Lemos was on the other. The policeman said, here they are, and he pointed to a mound of earth, then he took a spade and dug them out. He told father he was there when the fire reached the goods, and saw the trunks and thought they were of value, so he covered them with the ground, so the fire passed over them. People have said it was a miracle, as everything else was burned. Then father got a man with a

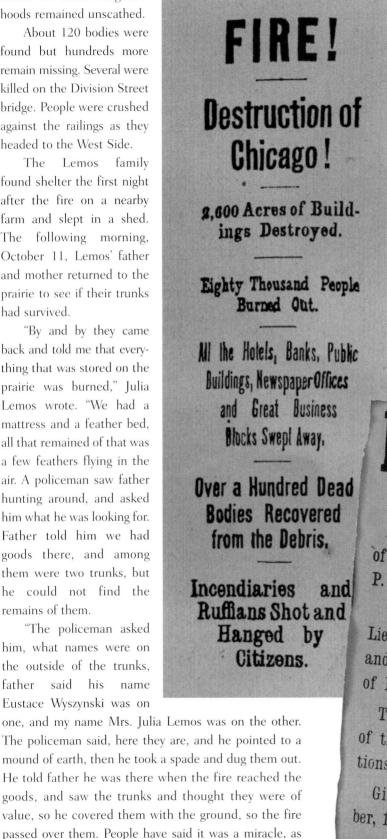

FIRE!

Destruction of Chicago!

2,600 Acres of Buildings Destroyed.

Eighty Thousand People Burned Out.

All the Hotels, Banks, Public Buildings, Newspaper Offices and Great Business Blocks Swept Away,

Over a Hundred Dead Bodies Recovered from the Debris.

Incendiaries and Ruffians Shot and Hanged by Citizens.

wheelbarrow to take them in the basement of a church which was opened for the refugees, then father came after us, and we all went to the church."

They found shelter for several days in a crowded German Lutheran church on North Sedgwick. The children slept in the first two pews and the government sent wagons of provisions for the refugees.

"Then father told me that the government was giving free passes on the railroads, so people could go to their friends and that he could take us to New York to my aunt there. As all the firms I worked for were burned I knew it would be very long before I would have work to support the family, but might get working in New York, so I told father to get the pass and we would go.

"The next morning he went after the pass. While he was gone there was a great commotion, every one ran to the church

Chicago Tribune from October 11, 1871 — some of these front-page stories were not true.

Announcement by Lt. Gen. Philip Henry Sheridan on October 11, 1871

PROCLAMATION!

The preservation of the good order and peace of the city is hereby entrusted to Lieut. General P. H. Sheridan, U. S. Army.

The Police will act in conjunction with the Lieut. General in the preservation of the peace and quiet of the city, and the Superintendent of Police will consult with him to that end.

The intent hereof being to preserve the peace of the city, without interfering with the functions of the City Government.

Given under my hand this 11th day of October, 1871.

R. B. MASON, Mayor.

doors and looked out, so I went to see what was the matter. There was a crowd in the middle of the street dragging a man along with a rope around his neck, they were going to hang him, he had been caught setting fire for robbery, that frightened me, and I said we will leave Chicago at once, I would be afraid to have my children on the street."

Julia's father sold his hunting dog to the church janitor in exchange for a wagon ride to the train. The family, with its two trunks, rode through the charred city. The streetcar tracks had been warped. Rowdies stood around the wagon in a threatening manner but the family made it to the station and took the train with several refugees to New York City and points east. Other passengers gave cake and candy to the children. Julia got a job as a lithographer three days after arriving in New York. The family lived with relatives but returned to Chicago 18 months later. Julia got her old job back at the lithograph establishment.

"We have remained here ever since."

After the flames subsided, the first efforts turned to helping the homeless and the suffering. On Tuesday, October 11, the *New York Herald* wrote about the city's major challenge. "Fifty thousand men, women, and children huddled together like so many wild animals; helpless children asking for bread; heart-broken parents, who know not which way to turn or what to say."

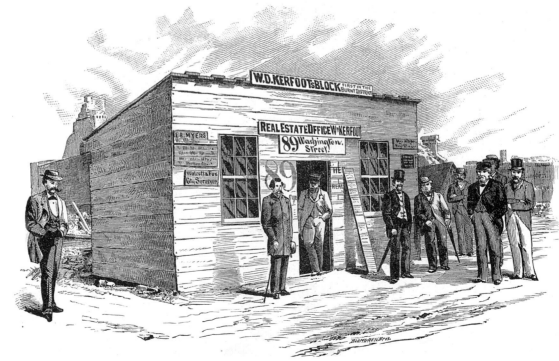

Rebuilding Chicago, from *Harper's Weekly*, shows the corner of Lake and LaSalle streets, looking toward the lake.

Drawing of Drexel
Boulevard in the 1870s
Chicago Historical Society

Order and control was one of the first orders of business. Lt. General Philip Henry Sheridan, whose home had been destroyed by the fire, was asked immediately by Mayor Roswell B. Mason and city elders to take charge of security of the fallen city. At first the Civil War hero resisted, but he soon brought five companies of infantry to Chicago, establishing strict curfews and instituting martial law. Sheridan and his troops were dismissed later in the month after a prominent attorney was shot and killed after the curfew.

The other priority was relief for the homeless. About $5 million in donations flooded into the city, including $1 million from foreign countries (half of it from England; $145.91 from Russia). Of the 100,000 homeless, about 20,000 left Chicago and 15,000 were taken in by friends or relatives. That left about 13,000 homeless families.

The last building ignited on Tuesday morning and lumber was delivered Tuesday afternoon. The "Great Rebuilding," as it was known, actually started the previous day, October 10, when real estate agent W.D. Kerfoot erected a wooden shanty and reopened his real estate business with the sign: "Everything gone but wife, children, and energy." The sign symbolized the spirit that overtook the city.

"And then came the first thoughts of rebuilding," wrote Andreas, whose 1886 *History of Chicago* chronicled the struggle. "It was a dreary waste of tottering walls and smoldering ruins to look upon, and enough to almost discourage the stoutest heart. But courage revived, and soon — before the embers were cold — hundreds of men began to venture around where had stood their stores and offices, and to search for safes, books and papers."

"Chicago Shall Rise Again" was the lead editorial in the first paper after the fire, on October 11. At first it was thought that rebuilding Chicago would take 20 years, but the job was mostly accomplished in three years. Architects and workmen came from all over the country, attracted by the challenge and by the opportunity to make money. Debris was hauled and dumped in the lake, creating new land along Chicago's lakefront.

Bridges and viaducts were the first structures to be rebuilt, but that took time. For three months after the fire, the LaSalle Street tunnel was the only direct connection between the North and South Sides of the city.

There was never much doubt that the city would rise from the ashes. Chicago was already the nation's transportation center. Railroad lines and waterways were damaged but working. The Union Stock Yards were untouched. About half of the $196 million in losses was covered by insurance, although many insurance companies became insolvent following the fire.

"All felt, all knew, and all said, the city must be rebuilt," Andreas wrote. "The vast railroad, and lake and commercial interests of such a great business center demanded it; the generous confidence of the capitalists of the Eastern cities gave assurance of help in so costly an undertaking. Delay was impossible."

A week after the fire, carpenters built 100 warehouses to serve as temporary homes of retail and wholesale stores. Shanties for the homeless were built, too. Schools reopened on October 23. The waterworks pumps started running October 27. The winter did not slow construction. The first major brick building, the Central Union Block, was completed by mid-December. Bonfires to warm the mortar and workers were everywhere.

"The walls of more than three hundred of the better class of brick and stone buildings are already rising in the South Division — rising even in midwinter, when masons are driven to cover in every other city north of 35 degrees. Who thinks of using a trowel all through the winter months in New York, Boston, St. Louis, or even Cincinnati?" asked William A. Croffut in the January 1872 issue of *Lakeside Monthly*.

The Grand Pacific Hotel was started before plans were even complete. New public buildings such as the post office, custom house, courthouse and jail were started in 1872 and built as fire proof as possible. LaSalle Street, known for its magnificent office buildings, was rebuilt to

be even more magnificent. The new Chicago was starting to take shape. By February most of the 100,000 homeless had been relocated and new workers were moving in to the city. Mementos from the fire, about 500,000 bells made from old Court House bell, were sold.

"There has been but one parallel to the mighty creation recorded in Genesis. That parallel is the rebuilding of Chicago in 12 months," proclaimed a real estate monthly on the first anniversary of the fire.

Six months later, by early 1873, few remnants of the fire were visible. The city was reborn despite increased labor and material costs and the financial panic that gripped the nation that year. The Grand Pacific Hotel opened on the site of the Pacific Hotel, which had been finished just before the fire. A rebuilt Palmer House, with a barbershop studded with silver dollars, opened that year, too, as the first wholly fireproof hotel. The destroyed McCormick Reaper plant was relocated to the South Side.

"By the first days of 1874, the people of Chicago occupied a rebuilt metropolis," wrote historian Karen Sawislak. "Though the physical losses caused by the Fire had been erased, there is no way to account for the emotional or financial scars that doubtless continued

The Chicago Public Library — the city's library system was established when Great Britain donated more than 17,000 books after the Great Chicago Fire. The library's own building opened in 1897.

to mark the lives of thousands of individuals and families. Yet it seems clear that by this time the more regular patterns of urban life and politics had been restored."

Chicago's population was nearly 300,000 spread over 35 square miles in 1870. By the following year the city's population had increased to 325,000. Amazingly the population increased once again to 367,000 in 1872, indicating that nothing — not even the fire that leveled much of the city — would stand in the way of growth.

New rules were adopted in an attempt to make the city less prone to future fires. In November 1871 the city council prohibited wooden buildings in a newly enlarged fire zone. Joseph Medill, an editor of the *Tribune*, left the paper to win election as the mayor on the Fire-proof ticket. The city reorganized the fire department and increased the water supply. The council also required all buildings four stories or taller to have metallic ladders or fire escapes.

The business center, which doubled in size, was rebuilt as the most fire resistant in America. The new all-brick fire zone pushed poor people away from downtown. The fire routed the black neighborhood just south of the Loop. Russian and Polish Jews were forced west to enlarge the Maxwell Street neighborhood. And the enlarged commercial district pushed the city's wealthy elite out of the central business district. When retailer Marshall Field moved to Prairie Avenue, about two miles south of downtown, others followed, creating Chicago's first Gold Coast.

Life — generally — went on. The finest billiard hall in the world opened opposite the courthouse in 1873. The can-can craze hit Chicago in 1875, and women were told to be more decent. Gambling dens, quiet for two years, were in full swing by the end of the decade. The Chicago White Stockings, the National League baseball team, stopped playing in 1872 and 1873 because of the fire but resumed their bid for the pennant the following year. The team would eventually become known as the Cubs.

The Chicago Public Library and Cook County Hospital opened during the decade. The Lincoln Park Zoo was started with the purchase of a $10 bear cub. Bell Telephone Company was chartered and the Art Institute was incorporated. Montgomery Ward opened the world's first mail-order business in the loft of a Chicago barn. Merchants, feeling threatened, sometimes got the catalogs intercepted at post offices, forcing Ward to mail out the catalogs in plain brown paper envelopes for a time.

Did the fire ultimately benefit Chicago? For those who lived through that terrifying 24 hours, the question is unthinkable. As Lemos' account shows, the fire was etched on the minds of Chicagoans for as long as they lived. But the fire also broke barriers, if even for only a matter of hours. The wealthy and poor, bluebloods and immigrants, ran through the streets together, spent nights together in the parks and depended on each other. Order was quickly restored and the city's subgroups — ethnic, racial and classes — were separated again and put back into place. But that experience, too, was etched on the minds of Chicagoans.

The struggle and idealism that resulted from those days were felt by the city for decades. Chicago became a center for labor, democratic ideals and anarchistic thought. That, too, was a legacy of the Great Fire.

A check from 1855 shows that Chicago was developing into a mercantile center.

Prairie Avenue and 12th Street
History of Chicago by Alfred T. Andreas

"World's Columbian Exposition of 1893" by H.D. Nichols *Chicago Historical Society*

John Peter Altgeld

"Does clubbing a man reform him? Does brutal treatment elevate his thoughts?"

— John Peter Altgeld in **Our Penal Machinery and Its Victims**, 1886

Chapter Three
1880–1900

3

In the spring of 1893 attorney Clarence Darrow paid a visit to newly elected Gov. John Peter Altgeld. Altgeld had helped inspire Darrow to move to Chicago and Darrow had encouraged Altgeld to run for state office. They both admired each other's work.

But Darrow was disappointed. Darrow had counted on the governor to act quickly after his inauguration and commute the sentences of the three remaining Haymarket anarchists. Hundreds had been injured in the Haymarket Riot of 1886 which resulted from a confrontation between police and striking workers. In 1887 four of the Haymarket defendants were hanged for their involvement in the riot. One committed suicide. Defendants Samuel Fielden and Michael Schwab received life sentences and Oscar Neebe was sentenced to 15 years in prison.

Altgeld had never talked publicly about the Haymarket case, but his record gave Darrow reasons for hope. Altgeld was known to be fair as a judge in the Cook County Superior Court. In the early 1880s Altgeld showed his sensitivity to injustice and a fondness for the

Haymarket drawing by Mitchell Siporin
Haymarket Scrapbook

THE MARTYRS & THEIR MOVEMENT

plight of labor in his book *Our Penal Machinery and Its Victims.* "Does clubbing a man reform him?" Altgeld asked. "Does brutal treatment elevate his thoughts?" In 1891, after police broke up a union meeting in Turner Hall by clubbing union members and shooting one man dead, Altgeld wrote the city police chief: "It is an axiom of the law that mere talk, no matter how abusive, does not constitute a crime."

The Haymarket defendants had been charged with murder and conspiracy, but the charges were directed toward their "mere talk." The person who tossed the bomb that killed eight police officers during the Haymarket Riot was never found. The eight anarchists who were arrested were writers, speakers and organizers. They were never connected to the bomb thrower; they were indicted on the theory that they had incited violence. So Darrow, much aware of Altgeld's past beliefs, expected that he would pardon the three living Haymarket anarchists soon after his January 10, 1893, inauguration.

Altgeld was so sick when he took over that he could not finish his inauguration address. He had been thrown from his horse that day as he rode to the State Capitol in Springfield. After 10 days in bed Altgeld asked for the complete judicial record of the Haymarket case. He headed South to recuperate and was presented with a petition signed by thousands of residents urging executive clemency. The petitions argued that the Haymarket trio had been punished enough.

But for months Altgeld remained silent, which prompted Darrow's visit.

"Go tell your friends that when I am ready I will act," he told a surprised Darrow in Springfield. "I don't know how I will act, but I will do what I think is right.

"We have been friends for a long time," Altgeld continued. "You seem impatient; of course I know how you feel; I don't want to offend you or lose your friendship, but this responsibility is mine, and I shall shoulder it. I have not yet examined the record. I have opinions about it. It is a big job. When I do examine it I will do what I believe to be right, no matter what that is."

Darrow told Altgeld that the decision to free the defendants would not be met with great hostility. Altgeld disagreed.

"But don't deceive yourself," he warned Darrow. "If I conclude to pardon these men it will not meet with the approval you expect; let me tell you that from that day I will be a dead man."

THE CHICAGO ANARCHISTS OF 1886:

Adolph Fischer	Louis Lingg	August Spies
Michael Schwab	Lucy E. Parsons	Samuel Fielden
Albert R. Parsons		Oscar Neebe

birth but an alien by temperament and sympathies. He has apparently not a drop of pure American blood in his veins." Decades later John F. Kennedy included Altgeld in his *Profiles In Courage.*

Altgeld's pardon message was 60 pages long.

"Upon the question of having been punished enough, I will simply say that if the defendants had a fair trial, and nothing has developed since to show that they were not guilty of the crime charged in the indictment, then there ought to be no executive interference, for no punishment under our laws could be too severe.

"Government must defend itself; life and property must be protected, and the law and order must be maintained; murder must be punished, and if the defendants are guilty of murder, either committed by their own hands or by some one else acting on their advice, then, if they have had a fair trial, there should be in this case no executive interference. The soil of America is not adapted to the growth of anarchy. While our institutions are not free from injustice, they are still the best that have yet been devised, and therefore must be maintained."

Altgeld concluded that the trial was unfair.

The jury was packed, he wrote. Instead of drawing names out of a box, a special bailiff was appointed to find potential jurors. The bailiff bragged that he would manage the case.

"Nearly every juror called stated that he had read and talked about the matter, and believed what he had heard and read, and had formed and expressed an opinion, and still held it, as to the guilt or innocence of the defendants; that he was prejudiced against them; that the prejudice was deep-rooted, and that it would require evidence to remove that prejudice."

The 12 jurors that were finally appointed — after all the defense objections were used — were of the same general character, Altgeld wrote.

Altgeld also argued that no connection was ever shown between the defendants and the bomb thrower. "Again, it is shown here that the bomb was, in all probability, thrown by someone

Altgeld could have commuted the sentences to time served. The three defendants would be released and Altgeld — who had hopes to serve as a U.S. senator — could have escaped the brunt of criticism. But he told a friend: "No man has the right to allow his ambition to stand in the way of the performance of a simple act of justice."

On June 26 Altgeld gave Samuel Fielden, Oscar Neebe and Michael Schwab an absolute pardon, restoring their innocence. The three men were released that day.

The pardons put an end to Altgeld's political career. The *Chicago Tribune* declared that Altgeld, a German immigrant, had shown himself to be "not merely an alien by

THE CHICAGO RIOT

A RECORD OF THE errible Scenes of May 4, 1886.

Chicago and New York:
BELFORD, CLARKE & CO.,
1886.

Illustrations from *The Lives, Crimes and Convictions of the Eight Chicago Anarchists and Bomb Throwers* published just after the 1887 trial

Cover of a popular book on the Haymarket Riot *Haymarket Scrapbook*

Dearborn Station
*History of Chicago by
Alfred T. Andreas*

Carriages wait for
supplies on
South Water Street,
east of Franklin.

seeking personal revenge; that a course had been pursued by authorities which would naturally cause this; that for a number of years prior to the Haymarket affair there had been labor troubles, and in several cases a number of laboring people, guilty of no offense, had been shot down in cold blood by Pinkerton men, and none of the murderers were brought to justice."

Finally Altgeld criticized the presiding judge, Joseph E. Gary, saying that Gary incorrectly tried all eight together,

that he manipulated the trial, made insinuating remarks to the jury and ruled consistently against the defendants.

Because he had gone beyond commuting the prisoners' sentences and attacked the judicial system, Altgeld left himself open to attack. The reaction was immediate. First he was called an anarchist, a strange label for a man who had served as a prosecutor, judge and had made his fortune as a real estate developer. Altgeld, the first foreign-born governor of Illinois, was called "an alien himself" by the *Washington Post* and criticized by most every major newspaper in the country. He became known for decades as John Pardon Altgeld.

"He fearlessly and knowingly bared his devoted head to the fiercest, most vindictive criticism ever heaped upon a public man, because he loved justice and dared to do the right," Darrow later said about Altgeld.

The governor never talked publicly about the case again. He reportedly told an associate, "You are younger than I and will live to see my pardon of the anarchists justified." History has proven Altgeld correct. His pardon statement is considered an

Chicago Board of Trade, erected in 1887
History of Chicago by Alfred T. Andreas

important document in judicial history and it righted the wrongs of an era when hysteria ruled.

Chicago came of age during the last two decades of the 19th century. The world's great architects came here, creating the world's first skyscrapers. Railroads converged here, connecting Chicago to the civilized east and Wild West. And Chicago's great institutions — such as retail and catalog stores, the stockyards and the steel industries — began to make their mark. The city was rebuilt bigger and better than before.

The city's population was 503,000 in 1880 and doubled to more than 1 million in 1890, making Chicago the nation's second city. It almost doubled again by the turn of the century. The city annexed surrounding areas, increasing in size from 36 square miles in 1888 to 185 square miles by 1893.

But Chicago was still a town wrestling with its frontier past and cosmopolitan potential. During the early 1880s Buffalo Bill Cody gave riding and roping exhibitions. Chicago bar owner Mickey Finn slipped knockout powder into drinks, then rifled patrons' pockets and dumped them in the street. But thousands of carriages filled the boulevards on Sunday afternoons and cable cars started running down State Street. Business was booming. Apartments were often fully rented before building was

complete. "I adore Chicago," said famed actress Sarah Bernhardt, who made appearances at the McVickers Theater. "It is the pulse of America."

By the mid-1880s the great financial center developed on LaSalle Street when the Board of Trade Building was relocated there. State Street became a retail center. Lawyers, stockbrokers, grain dealers and doctors all carved out their little neighborhood.

The fire, which had wiped the central city virtually clean, heralded a new age as Chicago rose phoenix-like on a grander vision by young, ingenious builders from all over the nation. Civil War architects and engineers such as William Le Baron Jenney and William Sooey Smith were attracted by the challenge of Chicago's soft soil and by the fact that the town had no building tradition. They would set the style.

Demand for commercial space in Chicago's expanding downtown area soon outstripped available land. Clearly the only way to go was up. To maximize their land, real estate brokers pressed architects and engineers to find a way to do it. Combining beauty and functional utility, a distinctive new style of architecture evolved, which is often known as the "Chicago School." The leaders of the movement, William LeBaron Jenney, Louis Sullivan, John Wellborn Root, Daniel Burnham and others were more than stylists.

The Auditorium Building was the tallest in Chicago when it was built in 1887.

Stereograph from 1893 shows one of Chicago's crowded streets.

It was Jenney who started Chicago's parade of sky-scrapers. With his nine-story Home Insurance Building, constructed in the 1880s, Jenney demonstrated that buildings could soar to the sky with walls, floors and everything in it supported by a slender internal skeleton of iron or steel. People could be whisked to the highest floors on the wings of high-speed elevators. No longer did buildings need to hunker close to the earth, built stone-by-stone like pyramids. With the skyscraper Chicago created its own monuments to immortality.

Louis Sullivan gave artistic expression to the skyscraper. Sullivan, the idealist, was born and mostly raised in Boston. He was attracted to Chicago because of its lofty elms, oaks and willows, spectacular church spires and grain elevators. He walked miles every day to see what remained undestroyed from the garden city of the past and decided that this was the place for him. "This remnant scene of ruin is a prophesy," he later wrote. He started work in Jenney's office in 1873. He joined Dankmar Adler in 1880 and three years later became Adler's partner. Sullivan's architecture career spanned five decades.

Root's career was much shorter; he died of pneumonia in 1891. Root was a cigar-and-brandy man who was able to combine his clients' needs with fine architecture. He was an artistic genius who could design massive business centers such as the Rookery Building with a deft touch that married business and art.

"We struck the home trail now, and in a few hours we're in that astonishing Chicago — a city where they are always rubbing the lamp and fetching up the genii and contriving and achieving new impossibilities," wrote Mark Twain in his 1883 *Life on the Mississippi*. "It is hopeless for the occasional visitor to try to keep up with Chicago — she outgrows his prophecies faster than he can make them. She is always a novelty; for she is never the Chicago you saw when you passed through the last time."

Between 1885 and 1892, 21 skyscrapers were built in the Loop. "There is nothing on earth like it since Egypt built the pyramids," wrote British painter John Lauery years later. Chicago journalist John J. Flynn wrote as early as 1890 that the city's architecture made it special.

"The traveled stranger, to whom the great cities of the world are familiar, however he may become impressed with the manners and customs of our people, or with the methods of doing business, and however loath he may be to admit the justice of our claims to preeminence in other respects, must acknowledge that this is the best city in the universe to-day," Flynn wrote.

"For nearly twenty years, or since the great fire of 1871 swept over the business center of the city, and laid it in ruins, architecture in Chicago has been steadily marching forward, until we are enabled in 1891 to point out some of the grandest achievements of the art to be found on the face of the earth."

Marshall Field, George Pullman and other capitalists such as Potter Palmer played an important role in shaping Chicago during these decades. Their confidence and their money helped rebuild Chicago. Retailer Field opened his namesake store on State Street. Railroad-car

A woodcut promotes the *Daily News*, which sold for 1 cent a day.

A bomb explodes at Haymarket Market on May 4, 1886. *Anarchy and Anarchists by Michael J. Schaack*

maker Pullman opened his namesake company town on 3,500 acres south of the city. It was a city based on an idealistic vision that he could work in harmony with his laborers. Real estate magnate Potter Palmer built his namesake mansion. The Potter Palmer home defined North Lake Shore Drive. Before that the Prairie Avenue District on the South Side had been the place where the rich built their homes. Palmer and his wife, Bertha, set a new trend that established the Gold Coast with their mansion, designed to look like a European castle. Once costs soared past $1 million, Palmer asked not to be told the final tally. The place was indeed a castle — even close friends were required to make a written request to visit.

As the barons got richer, the masses became more discontent. Strikes became common — from the tanners to the horseshoers, from cigar makers to brick laborers. In the summer of 1877 labor trouble boiled over in Chicago, the result of a national railroad strike caused by pay cuts. Trainmen walked off their jobs and rioters tore up tracks and railroad equipment. Chicago police, militia and the U.S. cavalry were called to quell the disturbances. More than 20 strikers were killed and 60 injured in a week of violence.

The pot simmered until the Haymarket Riot in 1886. The major issue, which had been paramount to activists since the late 1860s, was the adoption of an eight-hour workday. The world's first May Day celebration was followed on May 3 by a riot at the McCormick Harvester Plant. One worker was killed as police broke up pickets. More than 50 pickets and police officers were injured.

The following day, May 4, activists held a meeting at Haymarket Square, just west of the business district, to

denounce what had occurred at the harvester plant. As police moved in to break up the meeting, a bomb exploded, killing seven officers and injuring dozens. Police and protesters drew their weapons. Hundreds were injured by gunfire. It was never determined how many protesters were killed or wounded. And nobody ever determined who threw the bomb.

Anarchists arms, red flags, literature and their newspaper, *Arbeiter Zeitung*, were seized during the first weeks of May. Albert R. Parsons, one of the anarchist leaders, went into hiding, but eventually gave himself up. Eight anarchists were charged with planting the ideas for the murderous act. In the wake of the Haymarket Riot, the federal government built Fort Sheridan to add security to the city.

Nina Van Zandt, a society woman, married anarchist August Spies in jail. The marriage was later called illegal. The State Supreme Court sustained the sentences of the Haymarket Five later that year and four — including Parsons and Spies — were hanged in 1887. Louis Lingg had a bomb smuggled into jail and detonated it while it was in his mouth.

Gurdon S. Hubbard died in 1886 at age 84. "The congregation was an assemblage such as is seldom gathered in this or any other city," reported the *Chicago Times*. "It was a sea of white heads, representing men who had come to Chicago when there was no Chicago, and have lived to see the results they began."

Hubbard was buried with honor and fanfare at Graceland Cemetery, the final resting place of many Chicago leaders. His final decade was productive. In 1875, at the age of 73, he took a nostalgic trip down Hubbard's Trail, his trading route to downstate Iroquois County, with family friend Henry Hamilton. When they visited the trading town that was renamed Watseka, Hubbard talked briefly about the Indian princess and promised to recount all of his memories. But he never did. In 1878 Hubbard learned that Watseka had died in Council Bluffs, Iowa. Hubbard started rewriting his

Chicago: Rising from the Prairie

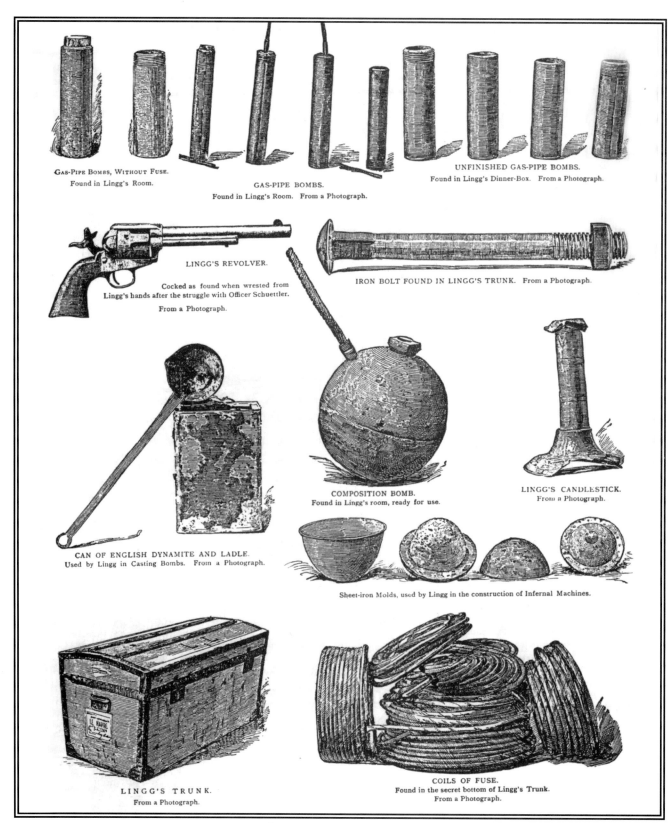

GAS-PIPE BOMBS, WITHOUT FUSE.
Found in Lingg's Room.

GAS-PIPE BOMBS.
Found in Lingg's Room. From a Photograph.

UNFINISHED GAS-PIPE BOMBS.
Found in Lingg's Dinner-Box. From a Photograph.

LINGG'S REVOLVER.
Cocked as found when wrested from Lingg's hands after the struggle with Officer Schuettler.
From a Photograph.

IRON BOLT FOUND IN LINGG'S TRUNK. From a Photograph.

CAN OF ENGLISH DYNAMITE AND LADLE.
Used by Lingg in Casting Bombs. From a Photograph.

COMPOSITION BOMB.
Found in Lingg's room, ready for use.

LINGG'S CANDLESTICK.
From a Photograph.

Sheet-iron Molds, used by Lingg in the construction of Infernal Machines.

LINGG'S TRUNK.
From a Photograph.

COILS OF FUSE.
Found in the secret bottom of Lingg's Trunk.
From a Photograph.

Items found in the possession of Louis Lingg
Anarchy and Anarchists by Michael J. Schaack

126

recollections in 1879, but became ill and only completed 107 pages. He did not mention Watseka.

Hubbard became critically ill in 1883 and had his left eye removed the following year. "True to his Indian training he resolutely refused an anesthetic or to let anyone hold his hands," wrote Hamilton of Hubbard. "He simply lay down without a murmur or tremor and let doctors cut out his eye."

In 1888 Carson, Pirie, Scott and Company moved its retail store downtown. Lincoln Park purchased an elephant, camel, lioness, two leopards, two Bengal tigers, an ibex, a zebu and a llama from Barnum and Bailey to enlarge its zoo. Louis Sullivan and Dankmar Adler were building an architectural gem, the Auditorium Building, and located their own offices on the top floor to demonstrate their confidence that the world's tallest building wouldn't fall down, as some had predicted.

The building, which opened in 1889, helped make Michigan Avenue a great street of culture. Later, the Fine Arts Building and the Art Institute to the north, made "Boul Mich" the finest street in the world. According to artist Ralph Fletcher Seymour, it created "a district wherein the musicians, artists, book lovers, actors, dancers and craftsmen gathered and established themselves."

By 1899 Chicago was much more than Michigan Avenue. Here is how Carrie Meeber saw the city when she arrived that year in Theodore Dreiser's classic novel *Sister Carrie*:

"Chicago's… many and growing commercial opportunities gave it widespread fame, which made it a giant magnet, drawing to itself, from all quarters, the hopeful and the hopeless — those who had their fortune yet to make and those whose fortunes and affairs had reached a disastrous climax elsewhere… The sound of the hammer engaged upon the erection of new structures was

everywhere heard. Great industries were moving in. The huge railroad corporations had seized upon vast tracts of land for transfer and shipping purposes. Streetcar lines had been extended far out into the open country in anticipation of rapid growth… There were regions open to the sweeping winds and rain, which were lighted throughout the night with long, blinking lines of gas lamps, fluttering in the wind. Narrow boardwalks extended out, passing here a house, and there a store, at far intervals, eventually ending in the open prairie."

Chicago did offer a second chance to many newcomers, but like all American cities of that age, it implanted a rigid caste system. "The entire metropolitan center possessed a high and mighty air calculated to overawe

Art Institute façade — the present building was constructed between 1893 and 1910.

(Far left) Michigan Avenue looking north from 26th Street

A Hull House postcard on which the sender wrote in 1908: "I thought you would be interested in this picture. It is in the ghetto, a poor district of Chicago."

Poster promoting modern Chicago in the 1890s
Chicago Historical Society

and abash the common applicant, and to keep the gulf between poverty and success seem both wide and deep," wrote Dreiser.

Enter Jane Addams, a young woman from the northern Illinois town of Rockford who rented a few rooms in Hull House, a former residence more recently used as a secondhand furniture store, and began working at that gulf, tending to the city's poor and improving the conditions of the industrial districts. In 1889 she began a career of service that would make her one of the most admired social workers in history. By 1890 Addams' Hull House, at the corner of Halsted and Polk streets, was playing host to 2,000 people every week. With Ellen Gates Starr, she added about 12 buildings to her settlement house, providing an art gallery, music school, employment bureau, nursery school, library, gymnasium, baths, classes and clubs. Addams, who was one of the most respected women of her generation, shared the Nobel Peace Prize in 1931.

Boom times helped metropolitan Chicago grow. Developers of Morgan Park, then a distant suburb but now an established and aged city neighborhood, touted the place as "semi-mountainous" because it was 100 feet above the level of Lake Michigan. In the midst of the Midwest flatlands, the developers described "the oak-shaded heights of the Blue Island plateau."

The city expanded, too, as voters in areas around Chicago voted to join the city. In 1889 the city annexed the town of Jefferson, the city of Lake View, the town of Lake and the village of Hyde Park. More than 200,000 lived in the new territory.

The city was taking shape. The Chicago Symphony Orchestra was formed, with German immigrant Theodore Thomas leading it into prominence. Provident Hospital and Training School, a South Side hospital for African Americans, was opened by Dr. Daniel Hale Williams, a black physician who performed the first surgery to suture the human heart. Plans for the Art Institute were approved and a building permit was issued for the Newberry Library. Ground was broken for the Alley Elevated and Standard Oil announced plans to erect the greatest oil refinery in the world.

John J. Flynn's guides to the city during the early 1890s smack of boosterism, but they speak of the pride many Chicagoans felt.

"Not in the Arabian nights' Entertainments, though bathed in all the glorious colorings of Oriental fancy, is there a tale which surpasses in wonder the plain, unvarnished history of Chicago," Flynn wrote. "Chicago is one of the wonders of modern times. Her progress amazes mankind. There is not on record an achievement of human intellect, skill and industry that will bear comparison with the transformation of a dismal swamp, in the midst of a trackless desert, within the span of a human life, into one of the mightiest and grandest cities on the globe."

Garfield Bathing Pavilion around 1900
W.H. Jackson & Co.,
Kenneth C. Burkhart
Collection

Flynn's *Guide* points out what was best about this Chicago. His tour of Lake Shore Drive gives us a sense of the city's elegance. "This is the grandest boulevard drive in Chicago. Beginning at the North Side Water-Works on Pine street it skirts the lake to the northern extremities of Lincoln Park, where it connects with Sheridan Road, which is nearly completed for 25 miles along the north shore. Before reaching the park some of the most magnificent mansions in the city are passed on the left. On the right is a fringe of sward, dotted with flower-beds and covered with beautiful foliage in the summer months. The lake beats against an embankment to the right, and frequently the spray is dashed across the flower-beds when the sea is high. Reaching the park you pass through beautiful avenues until you strike the Drive again."

But Chicago could be a scary place. Railroads, which built the city, posed a great threat to daily life. Journalist

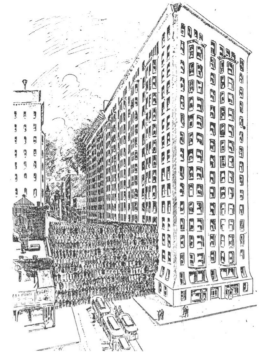

William T. Stead wrote that the city was tied in the merciless grip of the mechanized beast. "If a stranger's first impression of Chicago is that of the barbarous gridironed streets, his second is that of the multitude of mutilated people whom he sees on crutches. Excepting immediately after a great war, I have never seen so many mutilated fragments of humanity as one finds in Chicago. Dealers in artificial limbs and crutches ought to be able to do a better business in Chicago than in any other city I have ever visited."

Trains were not the city's only menace. The typhoid death rage reached alarming levels during the 1890s as city fathers worried about the quality of drinking water. Local newspapers published maps daily showing areas of the city that needed to boil their drinking water.

Graft was a problem too: In 1890, 26 men were indicted for election fraud. In 1891 City Hall employees were required to contribute 5 percent of their monthly

Train stations were crowded and plentiful in Chicago. *Chicago Historical Society*

salary to re-elect Mayor D.C. Cregier. After visiting, Chicago, Rudyard Kipling blasted the city as being uncivilized. "Having seen it, I urgently desire never to see it again. It is inhabited by savages."

Contrast that to Chicago's attempt to become a cultural center. Leading the way was Potter Palmer's wife, Bertha Honore Palmer, who was the queen of Chicago society from the 1870s until World War I. She became interested in French impressionism

The Union Stock Yards during the late 1890s could accommodate 25,000 head of cattle, 14,000 sheep and 150,000 hogs. *Keystone stereograph Torry Bruno Collection*

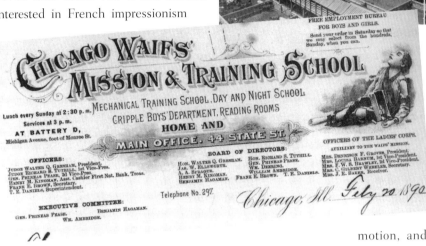

Calling card of a free employment bureau for boys and girls

$35 million. "The good Lord gave me the money I have. Could I withhold it from Chicago?" he asked.

The first president was William Rainey Harper, an esteemed Yale linguistics professor who headed the national Chautauqua Association. Amos Alonzo Stagg signed on as football coach. Stagg would later invent the shift, the man in motion, and the end-around play. He was also the first university athletic director to receive full faculty status.

during the late 1880s, when the painters were still considered revolutionaries and their art was considered junk. She met Claude Monet in 1891 and bought 22 of his paintings. She also showed the work of Monet and Manet, Pissarro, Degas and other impressionists at the 1993 World's Columbian Exposition. Their work caused a sensation worldwide. She filled her Lake Shore Drive castle with the art, showing them in tiers. She and most of her friends willed the paintings — and work done by Cezanne, Gauguin, Van Gogh, Toulouse-Lautrec and Seurat — to the new Art Institute, which remains as the home of one of the world's greatest collections.

"What is art?" she said. "I cannot argue with Lorado Taft who is a pundit, but in my limited conception it is the work of some genius graced with extraordinary proclivities not given to ordinary mortals. Speaking of art, my husband can spit over a freight car."

Meanwhile culture was coming to the South Side: Ground was broken for the first University of Chicago buildings in 1891. Marshall Field gave 10 acres of land near Ellis and 56th for the proposed school and John D. Rockefeller contributed $600,000 to firmly establish the University of Chicago. He would eventually contribute

University of Chicago postcard — the university was founded in 1891.

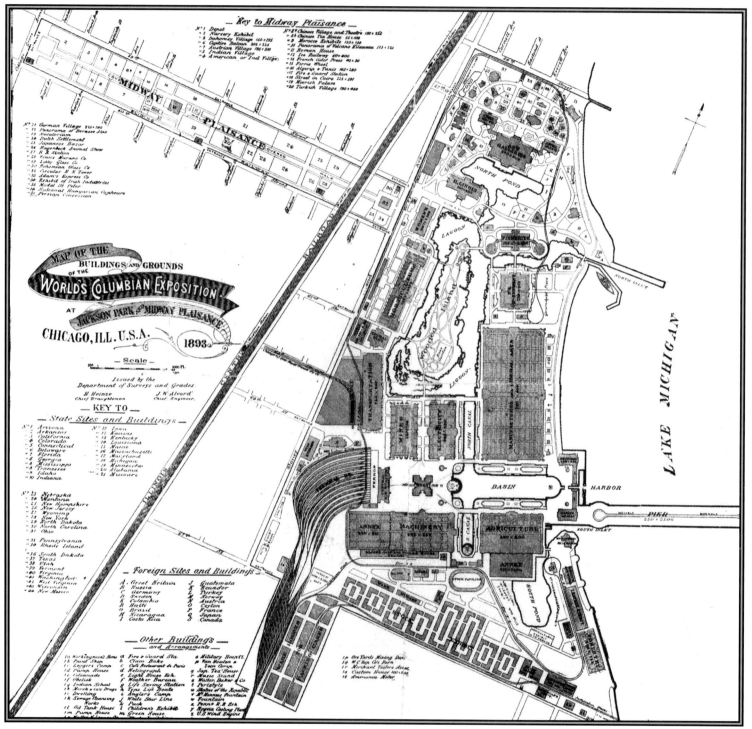

Map of World's Columbian Exposition

"Great is Administration and Great her Glory, Chicago's World Fair." The Administration Building was located just west of the Basin. *B.W. Kilburn stereograph, Kenneth C. Burkhart Collection*

Chicago was selected as the site of the next World's Fair despite protests from other U.S. cities. The nickname "The Windy City" was born in 1890 during the world's fair debate when *New York Sun* editor Charles Dana wrote that Chicago was full of blowhards.

"Don't pay any attention to the nonsensical claims of that Windy City," Dana wrote. "Its people couldn't build a world's fair if they won it." In truth, there are quite a few U.S. cities windier than Chicago, although Chicago's winter wind is impressive enough to have its own nickname, "The Hawk."

It seemed Dana might prove prophetic the following year. Architects John Root and his partner, Daniel Burnham, were appointed to oversee the architecture of the fair. After touring a group of New York architects around the proposed Jackson Park site, Root became ill. Burnham rushed to his side and stayed with him for three days until he died.

"I have worked, I have schemed and dreamed to make us the greatest architects in the world — I have made him see it and kept him at it and now he dies," Burnham said. "Damn! damn! damn!"

The World's Columbian Exposition was built to showcase Chicago's virtues. It was opened on May 1, 1893, by President Grover Cleveland, who pressed an electric key to start the wheels in the Manufacturers Building turning. Drapery fell from a gilded statue of the republic and the great South Side fair was born. It was known as "The White City" — a grouping of majestic classical structures that enthralled many but disgusted architect Louis Sullivan, whose modernistic, original Transportation Building stood in contrast to the rest. The White City remained white because the burning of soft coal was banned nearby.

"The Surging Sea of Humanity at the opening of the Columbia Exposition" in 1893 *B.W. Kilburn stereograph, Kenneth C. Burkhart Collection*

Gallery of Fine Arts, also called the Art Palace at the World's Fair, was later remodeled into the
Museum of Science and Industry.

Novelist Henry Blake Fuller called the fair the "city's graduation day." The fair attracted 27 million visitors — nearly half the country's population. Among the guests were Archduke Ferdinand (whose assassination in 1914 would spark World War I) and her royal highness, the Infanta Eulalia of Spain, who insulted Bertha Palmer by referring to her as "my innkeeper's wife." (The Infanta was staying at Palmer House.) Among the entertainers was an Egyptian dancer named Fahreda Mahzar, known as "Little Egypt." She wore a full, semi-transparent skirt and modest underwear. One Chicago police officer said that when she danced "you could see every muscle in her body at the same time."

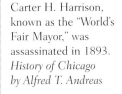

Another star was the Ferris wheel. Thousands of people, paying 50 cents each, filled the 36 cars of George Ferris' invention and took a ride on the giant wheel, 250 feet in diameter. The ride was disassembled after the fair and rebuilt near the North Side intersection of Clark and Wrightwood. But hard times kept attendance down and the Ferris wheel was taken down by the turn of the century. It was reassembled at the St. Louis Worlds Fair in 1904 and junked two years later.

The year 1893 was especially newsworthy. It was the year that Gov. John Peter Altgeld pardoned the three Haymarket anarchists and that Mayor Carter H. Harrison was assassinated at the doorsteps of his home. Harrison was shot by a man who thought he should have been appointed as the city's chief lawyer.

Regular service started on the Lake Street L in 1893 and the Art Institute building was opened. Lake Shore Drive was renamed Palmer Drive, but the new name never became popular.

But not all was well with Chicago. The Depression of 1893 caused a surge in unemployment. Soup kitchens were filled and the corridors of city hall were filled with sleeping, homeless Chicagoans. It was also the year that Ida B. Wells, a black Southerner campaigning to prevent lynchings, moved to Chicago to continue her crusade.

Her life was in danger in Memphis because of murder threats by white racists.

In 1894 British reformer William Thomas Stead published his book about corruption, *If Christ Came to Chicago*. The nonfiction book sold 100,000 copies in the first week.

"If Chicago is to be the Capital of Civilization, it is indispensable that she should at least be able to show that every resident within her limits enjoyed every advantage which intelligent and public-spirited administration has secured for the people elsewhere," Stead wrote. He asserted that only two of the 68 Chicago aldermen were not taking bribes. However, it's likely that the main source of the book's popularity was his detailed description of Chicago's prostitution industry.

Carter H. Harrison, known as the "World's Fair Mayor," was assassinated in 1893. *History of Chicago by Alfred T. Andreas*

Drawings of Siegel, Cooper & Co. in 1891 include millinery and cloak departments.

DREXEL FOUNTAIN.

Parks in Chicago

ANT MEMORIAL.

Metropolitan
Elevated Railroad
bridge at Van Buren
about 1900

Also in 1894, workers at the Pullman railroad car factory went on strike after he reduced their wages but not the rent he was charging them to live in his company town. George Pullman, who was incensed that his workers would join a union, refused to negotiate. "The workers have nothing to do with the amount they receive; that is solely the business of the company," said the palace-car prince.

Despite warnings by the mayor and Gov. Altgeld, President Cleveland sent federal troops to Chicago to put down the violence. By the time order was restored, 13 people had been killed. Union leader Eugene Debs was arrested and charged with criminal conspiracy for not ending the strike. He served 163 days at a jail in Woodstock, Illinois. The strike was broken but that did little to reduce animosities.

The Town of Pullman was annexed by Chicago in 1889, but George Pullman continued to operate the town until he was ordered by the court to sell off the town following the strike.

Fire destroyed some of the remaining World's Fair buildings in 1894. The first public beaches were opened and the first bloomers were seen in Chicago. Reform was just around the corner — but still, around the corner. Michael "Hinky Dink" Kenna, a political kingpin of the Levee red-light district, may have been surprised when his gambling den on the second floor of his saloon was closed. He reopened in the basement.

Hinky Dink was more of a character than a criminal — but Chicago had its share of criminals. None were more notorious than a pharmacist named Herman Mudgett, alias Henry H. Holmes, "The Monster of 63rd Street," who admitted killing 27 people and was suspected of killing 23 more. Holmes built a huge South Side mansion with trap doors, concealed stairways, a torture chamber, a gas chamber, acid vats and a room lined in asbestos and equipped with a blowtorch. Holmes reportedly did experiments on people to see whether their bodies could be stretched to twice their original length. Among his suspected victims were the children of friends and visitors to the Columbian Exposition who rented rooms in his house. Holmes was hanged.

The nation's first movie studio opened in 1895. The Selig Polyscope Company, founded by William N. Selig, featured Western star Tom Mix. By 1910 one-fifth of the world's movie production was in Chicago, much of it at another Chicago studio, Essanay Studios (pronounced S&A, named after owners George Spoor and Gilbert M. Anderson), which possessed such stars as Wallace Beery, Gloria Swanson, Francis X. Bushman and for a time Charlie Chaplin. Chicago had a ready supply of actors: In 1910 there were about 4,000 actors and 3,500 vaudevillians listed in Chicago. But alas, by the second decade of the century, the industry found the Southern California climate more conducive to movie production.

The end of the 19th century was the end of an innocent era. In 1896 a jury ruled that baseball could be played on Sunday; each member of the Chicago Baseball Club, including Cap Anson, had been fined $3. In 1898 the height of buildings was limited by ordinance to 10 stories or 130 feet and in 1899 the Board of Education established kindergartens in public schools.

But the last years also presaged a new century. The first elevated trains ran around the Loop and the first public play yard was opened. The Public Library at Randolph and Michigan, now known as the Cultural Center, was dedicated, and the Juvenile Court of Cook County was established. Carter H. Harrison Jr., the son of the assassinated mayor, was elected mayor in 1897. As his father had, he would be elected as mayor for five terms.

George Pullman died of a heart attack that year. His coffin was secured with railroad iron encased in concrete to prevent the many who hated him from defiling his crypt.

As the century came to a close, the *Chicago Tribune* estimated that about 300 millionaires lived in Chicago.

But all was far from golden. A score of people jumped to their death from a tall, arched, scenic archway over the Lincoln Park lagoon known as the "Suicide Bridge." It was eventually dismantled. And in 1899 the Chicago River caught fire. The oil, grease and gas dumped in the river fed the fire, and the 50-foot flames scorched and burned the Kinzie Street bridge.

Chicago continued to grow and modernize. Two major inventions — the telephone and the automobile — were about to change the nature of Chicago and cities everywhere. As the century closed, a franchise was granted to the Illinois Telephone and Telegraph Company and the first cars were demonstrated on the city streets. Chicago was ready for modern times.

Alson Skinner Clark's 1906 painting "Coffee House"

"Grain elevators, Goose Island" by George Demont Otis *Chicago Historical Society*

Margaret Anderson

"*Chicago: enchanted ground to me from the moment Lake Michigan entered the train windows. I would make my beautiful life here. A city without a lake wouldn't have done.*"

— Margaret Anderson in *My Thirty Years' War*

Chapter Four
1900–1917

Photo on opposite page by Man Ray

4

Margaret Anderson came to Chicago, looking to escape her "boring" college life at Western College for Women in Oxford, Ohio, and her suffocating, affluent family home in Columbus, Indiana. She arrived in 1906. The city forever changed her, as she changed it.

A beautiful, charmingly manipulative young woman, Margaret yearned above everything else to have an exciting life. She always knew what she wanted: "The great thing to learn about life is, first, not to do what you don't want to do, and second, to do what you want to do," she wrote. Even as a child, Margaret decided that her life would be beautiful and different as no other life had been.

After three years of studying music in college — where she mainly listened to music that she talked other students

State Street, in the heart of the downtown shopping district during the early 1900s
Keystone View stereograph, Kenneth C. Burkhart Collection

144

or teachers into playing for her — Margaret, over the protests of her mother, convinced her father to travel with her to Chicago. From the first moment, she was enchanted. She loved Michigan Avenue and Orchestra Hall, the Art Institute and Lake Michigan. And she loved the undercurrent of possibility, as writers and artists were drawn to this Midwestern city by an unexplainable feeling that something important was about to happen there.

In Chicago's Left Bank, Alson J. Smith wrote of these early years of the new century: "It was only natural that when the rebuilding (after the Great Fire) began, the area in the immediate vicinity of the old water tower should be dubbed 'Towertown'. And, like the arch in New York's Washington Square and the golden dome of Sacre Coeur on Montmartre, that tower was destined to cast a long shadow over the world of arts and letters.

"In the years between 1912 and 1924, it was a geographical center of what was perhaps the most vital literary and artistic upsurge in the history of the country," Smith wrote. "In those years corn-fed hopefuls from all over the Midwest flowed into the free-and-easy bohemia of the gigantic abattoir by Lake Michigan. They came to read their poems to Harriet Monroe in the studio at 543 Cass Street, to study under Lorado Taft at the Art Institute, and to chase fire engines for Henry Justin Smith and the *Chicago Daily News* in return for the privilege of rubbing shoulders in the city room with Carl Sandburg and Ben Hecht."

And before long, they were coming for Margaret Anderson. Margaret had found her way to the Fine Arts Building on South Michigan Avenue. The picturesque building was a rabbit warren of studios, literary offices and her favorite bookstore, Browne's, on the seventh floor.

A motor bus is pictured on Michigan Boulevard, now Michigan Avenue, which has long been the city's most elite street.

(Far left) The Fine Arts Building was built in 1886 as the Studebaker building.

Lorado Taft's "Fountain of Time" in Washington Park

145

"The Chicago March" sheet music from 1909

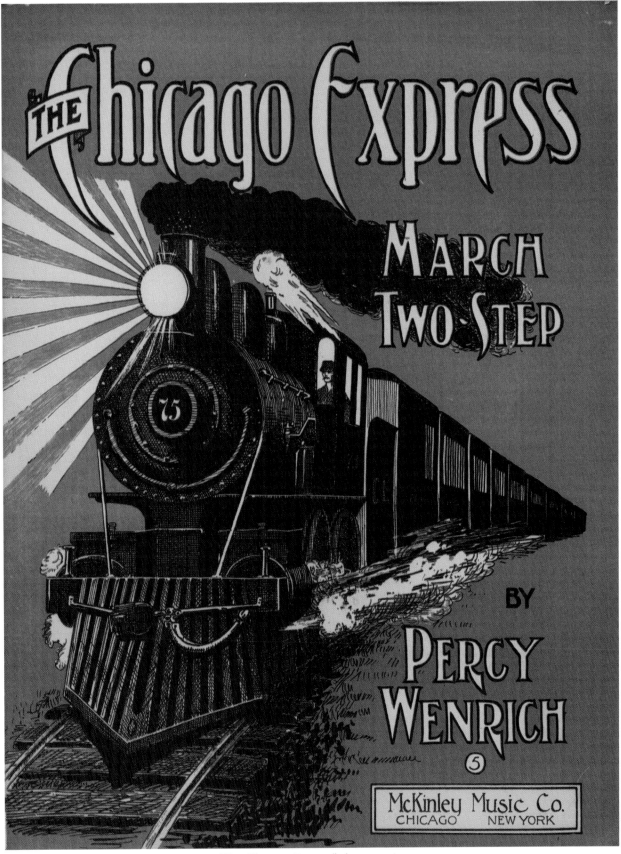

"The Chicago Express" sheet music

Of these early years in Chicago, Anderson later wrote: "Back in Chicago I began a marvelous life as literary editor. And I came to love Chicago as one only loves chosen — or lost — cities. I knew it in every aspect — dirt, smoke, noise, heat, cold, wind, mist, rain, sleet, snow. I walked on Michigan Boulevard on winter afternoons

when the wind was such a tempest and the snow so icy that ropes were stretched along the buildings to keep pedestrians from falling. On white misty winter mornings at six o'clock, I used to walk the ten miles from Wilson Avenue to Congress Street for the simple pleasure in the exercise and the chocolate at Child's afterward. I was always pretending that I was a poor working-girl, always forgetting that I was really poor — also a working girl."

As writer Sherwood Anderson wrote of these years, "You gave a lot of queer and isolated people a sudden sense of each other. Something started..." The Chicago Literary Renaissance began. From roughly 1912 until 1924, the young city on the prairie was the center of arts because of the creative literary activity in and around the Fine Arts Building.

Anderson had lost her job reviewing books for a religious magazine because she gave an enthusiastic review to Theodore Dreiser's *Sister Carrie,* which was questioned by religious groups as giving an immoral message to young people. So Margaret got a job at Browne's bookstore in the Fine Arts Building and spent much of her time around Floyd Dell, who was the editor of *The Chicago Evening Post's* literary section.

"Other people since famous came to the Floyd Dells," Anderson later recounted in *My Thirty Years' War,* "Theodore Dreiser, Sherwood Anderson, John Cowper Powys with his manias of interest and his: How extraordinary! for topics that failed to interest him... also Jerome Blum, George Cram Cook, Susan Glaspell, Edna Kenton, Llewellyn Jones and Arthur Davidson Ficke..." Margaret Anderson, beautiful and lively, was often the focus of these salons held at the Dells'.

In 1913 Margaret began to imagine her own literary magazine, to bring her what she wanted most in life — to be surrounded always by interesting conversation. Thus was born the idea for *The Little Review,* the magazine that would bring voice to Chicago's bohemian literary crowd, as well as new and known writers beyond Chicago.

"Often in the night I wake with the sensation that something is wrong, that something must be done to give life form," Anderson wrote. "Sometimes it is merely a matter of changing the furniture in a room. I imagine the whole operation, decide each change with precision, feel suddenly healthy and fall into a deep sleep. In the morning I arrange the furniture accordingly, and it's always a great success."

"So it was for *The Little Review*. I had been curiously depressed all day. In the night I wakened. First precise thoughts: I know why I'm depressed — nothing inspired is going on. Second: I demand that life be inspired every moment. Third: the only way to guarantee this is to have inspired conversation every moment. Fourth: most people never get so far as conversation; they haven't the stamina, and there is no time. Fifth: if I had a magazine I could spend my time filling it up with the best conversation the world has to offer. Sixth: marvelous idea — salvation. Seventh: decision to do it. Deep sleep.

"In the morning I thought no more about it. I didn't need to think. To me it was already an accomplished fact. I began to announce to everyone that I was about to publish the most interesting magazine that had ever been launched. They found me vague as to why it was going to be so interesting, nebulous as to how it was going to be published, unconcerned about the necessary money and optimistic about manuscripts. Where any sane person would have explained that, sensing the

modern literary movement , which was about to declare itself, a review to sponsor it was a logical necessity, I only accused people of being unimaginative because they couldn't follow my elan."

Bitter cold and snow have always been a big part of Chicago's winters. *Chicago Historical Society*

From Room 917 of the Fine Arts Building, Anderson began to publish *The Little Review*. The first issue featured an article by Chicago writer Sherwood Anderson, who had not been published before. Early issues included the works of Carl Sandburg, Edgar Lee Masters, Djuna Barnes, Ben Hecht and Max Bodenheim.

From the beginning, *The Little Review* struggled financially. It could not pay for contributions and often relied on the charity of benefactors to stay afloat. By the third issue, Anderson was being drawn increasingly to the anarchist statements of activists such as Emma Goldman. Financial backing was even harder to find as well as sympathetic landlords who would welcome Anderson and the straggling band of family and staff she sometimes brought with her. But the excitement of the new writers whom they were introducing kept Anderson going.

At one point in 1915, Anderson and her sister were evicted from their rented home in Lake Bluff north of Chicago. Anderson cast her eye on a stretch of beach in nearby Highland Park and decided the outcasts would live there. And they did. For seven months, they lived in tents on the beach, washing and swimming in the lake and cooking over fires. They attracted a great deal of attention for their bohemian life.

"Practically everything the *Little Review* published during its first years was material that would have been accepted by no other magazine in the world at the moment. Later all the art magazines wanted to print our contributors and, besides, pay them," Anderson wrote.

Construction of old Tribune Building in 1901 at Madison and Dearborn streets *Chicago Historical Society*

149

Stereograph of a
suburban railroad
platform

923—Suburban R. R. Train at Platform, Chicago.

Over the next few years, Anderson met Jane Heap, a young woman who would become a friend and co-editor of *The Little Review.* Although she loved Chicago,

Randolph Street in
the heart of the Loop

Anderson loved adventure even more. Heap and Anderson moved the little magazine to California and then New York. Behind in Chicago, bereft would-be lovers and admirers pined for Anderson. Hard-boiled journalist Ben Hecht is said to have thought of hanging a sign over the front of the Fine Arts Building that would read: "Where is Athens now?" And Sherwood Anderson pined: "Did you know, Margaret, that I loved you, that a thousand men, a thousand women loved you... You were not like the rest of us struggling down there in the Chicago mud... You were unreal... were a character in a play. You were a movie or painting come to life."

In New York, Heap and Anderson were charged with distributing obscene material for publishing James Joyce's *Ulysses.* Their obscenity trial was major news, and the beginning of the end for *The Little Review,* although it continued to be published in some form until 1929. Although she fought that charge to the end, Anderson tired of editing *The*

Little Review, handed over the publication to Heap, and headed off to Paris, where she lived for the next 20 years.

Chicago's population continued to boom during the first two decades of the 20th century, increasing from 1.7 million in 1900 to almost 2.2 million in 1910 and 2.7 million in 1920. The major ethnic group was still composed of first- and second-generation Germans, who increased in population to about 500,000 in 1910.

The city's most remarkable achievement during the 20th century occurred just two days into the century when water from the Chicago River flowed through the Drainage Canal toward the Illinois River for the first time. The river was reversed to keep wastes from seeping into the lake and fouling drinking water. It had taken about a decade to build a 28-mile canal, now known as the Sanitary and Ship Canal, connecting the river and the town of Lockport. But the results were almost immediate.

"Water in the Chicago River Now Resembles Liquid," *The New York Times* headlined: "The impossible has now happened! The Chicago River is becoming clear!" it reported. Chicago stank much less; stockyards waste flowed out of town instead of into the river and the lake. Deaths from cholera, dysentery and typhoid fever were greatly reduced.

Several towns along the river system southwest of Chicago filed suit saying they didn't want Chicago's wastes, but their legal efforts failed. Later in January, a dam at downstate Lockport was opened that allowed water from the lake to flow through the Des Plaines and Illinois rivers to the Mississippi River and the Gulf of Mexico.

The new water system greatly improved the health situation, but Chicago was still a dangerous place. Muckraking journalist Jacob A. Riis, who visited the city around the turn of the century, declared that Chicago's slums were worse than New York's. Colleague Lincoln Steffens, in *The Shame of the Cities,* declared Chicago "First in violence, deepest in dirt; loud, lawless, unlovely, ill-smelling, irreverent, new; an overgrown gawk of a village, the 'tough' among cities, a spectacle to the nation."

Traffic comes to a halt on Dearborn Street in 1909. The congestion was caused by a Loop traffic study.

And first in vice.

Just one month into the new century, Minna and Ada Lester, two cultured young women from the South, opened the Everleigh Club on South Dearborn Street and called themselves the Everleigh sisters. The club was an expensive bordello that featured gold-plated spittoons and a gourmet chef. Champagne was the only alcoholic beverage offered. Nights were long and the pace was relaxed at the Everleigh. "You have the whole night before you, and one $50 client is more desirable than five $10 ones," Minna told her girls. "Less wear and tear."

The club flourished until city fathers, incensed that the Everleighs had printed a brochure advertising the glories of the club, ordered it closed. The club was

Selling newspapers was one of the ways boys could support themselves and their families. *Chicago Historical Society*

151

Student artists pose with live model at School of the Art Institute

Height	1m 64.0	Head Length	19.0	L. Foot	25.1	Color of Left Eye.	Circle Lt Haz	Age 16	Born in 18
Eng. Height	5.4½	Head Width	15.9	L. Mid. F.	10.7		Periph. Z	Apparent Age	
Outside A	1m 64.0	Cheek Width	13.0	L. Lit. F.	8.8		sl Bl	Nativity Ill	
Trunk	84.0	R. Ear	6.3	L. Fore A.	43.0		Pecul.	Occupation messenger boy	

Remarks Incident to Measurement

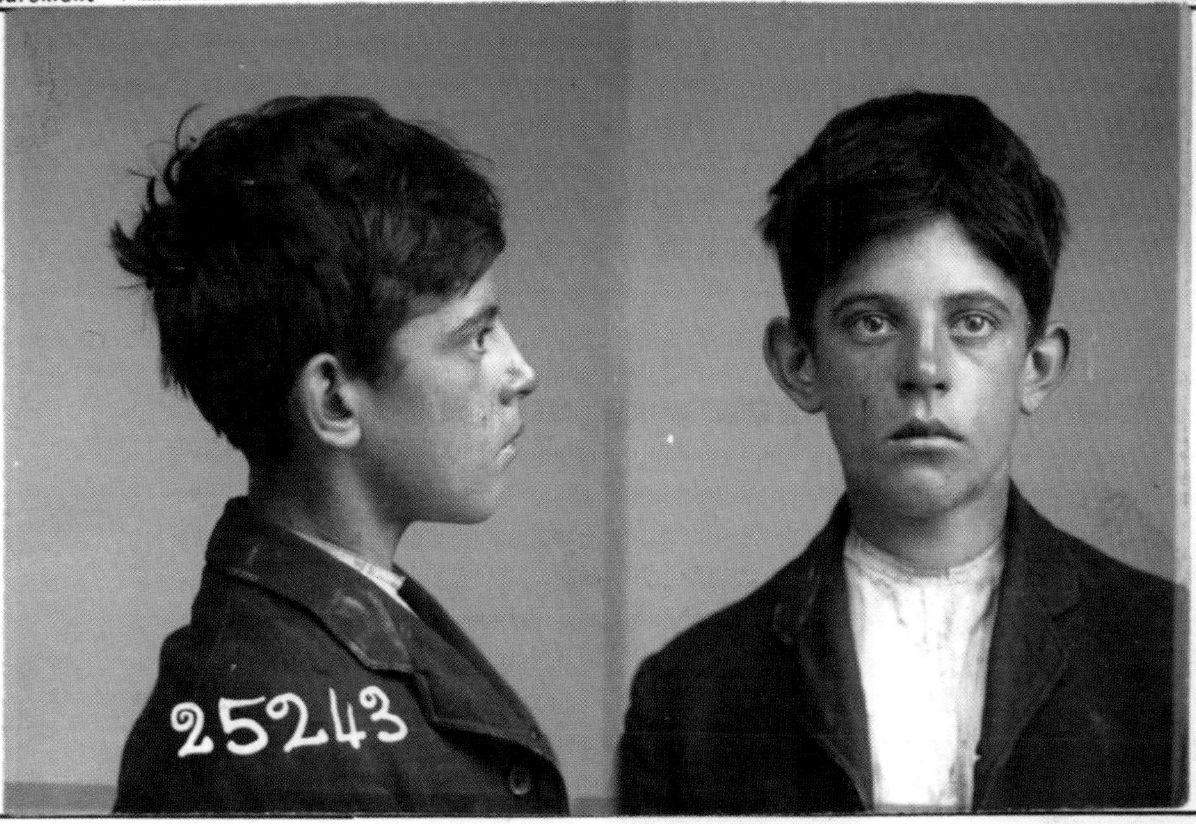

DESCRIPTIVE.

Forehead: Inclin. Rec	Nose: Profile: Ridge Und	R Ear	Beard none
Height M	Base El sl Root M		Hair M D Chest
Width M	DIMENSIONS: Length M, Projection M, Breadth M	Teeth Full	Complexion Fair
Pecul.	Pecul.		Weight 104
		Chin reg	Build med

BUREAU OF IDENTIFICATION,
DEPARTMENT OF POLICE,
HARRISON STREET AND PACIFIC AVENUE.

Description taken July 23 1902

Chicago Police mug shots of suspects from the Bureau of Identification taken between 1895 and 1916
Kenneth C. Burkhart Collection

(Both photos this page) Chicago Police mug shots of suspects from the Bureau of Identification taken between 1895 and 1916 *Kenneth C. Burkhart Collection*

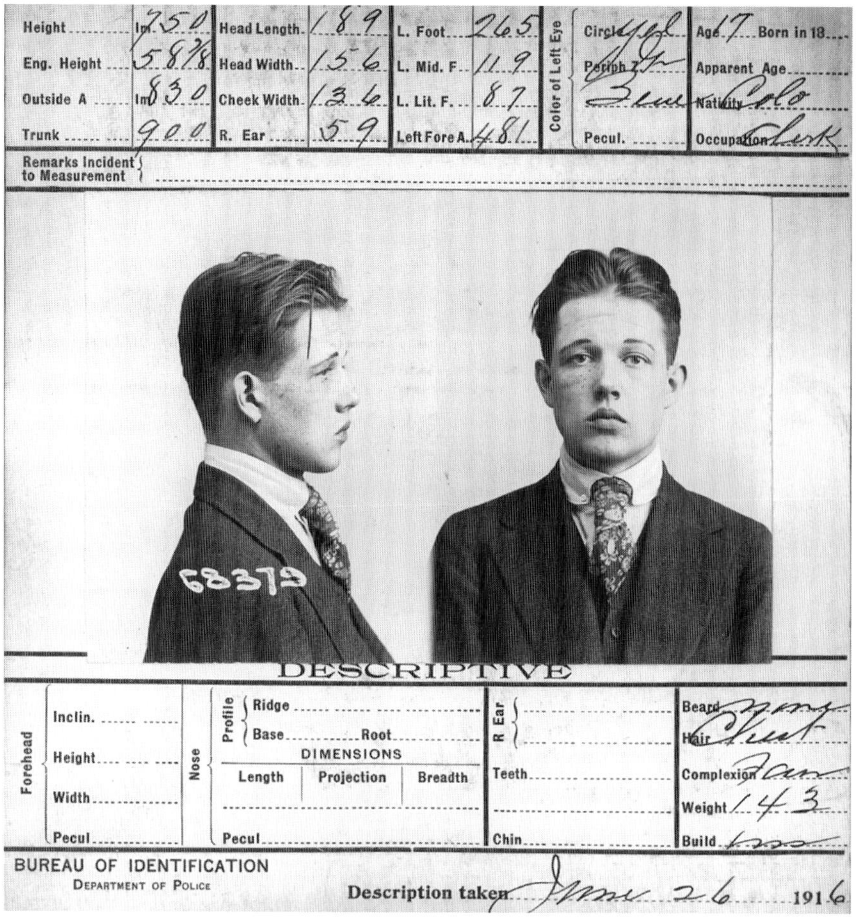

padlocked early on October 25, 1911, after one final great party. All of her *filles de joie* soon found work at other clubs. The Everleighs took a trip to Europe, considered reopening in Chicago and decided to take their money to New York, relocating on Riverside Drive. The club was demolished in 1933. Minna died at age 70 in 1948 and Ada, who moved to Virginia, died in 1970 at age 94.

The Everleighs were the most famous madams, but by far not the only ones. The South Side's Levee district, which ran from Wabash and Clark and from 18th to 22nd streets, was one of the nation's largest Tenderloin districts.

"The Levee's working population consisted of thousands of gamblers, bums, thugs, jackrollers, pimps (called 'cadets'), madams, harlots and thieves," wrote Richard Lindberg in *Chicago Ragtime: Another Look at Chicago 1880-1920*.

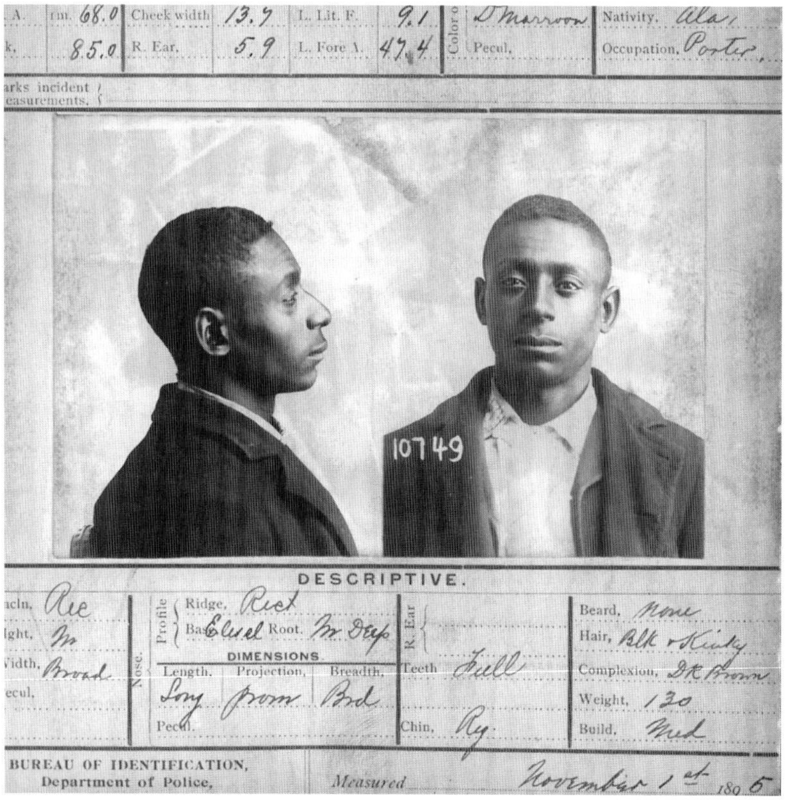

"In the Levee could be found debauchery to satisfy every man's heart's desire: faro joints, dice joints, policy stations, gyp auctions, arcades, hock shops, opium dens, peep shows, dance halls, plain and concert saloons, burlesque houses, and brothels to cater to every taste at rates scaled to every bill clip and coin purse. The Everleigh Club was at the luxury end of the scale, the cribs of Bed Bug Row (a dime or two bits a slommock) at the lowest, with houses such as Saratoga, Victoria, Sappho, Black May's Silver Dollar, Houses of All Nations, the Library, Why Not? and dozens more in between... "

In 1910 a commission determined that more than 27 million "acts of assignation" were taking place annually in Chicago — quite something for a town with fewer than 2.2 million people. Some 5,000 prostitutes were estimated to be working in the city. Half their annual proceeds of $30 million went to cops and politicians. But still, a woman would make $6 a week working six days in a store or factory job and could make $25 a night on a weekend.

One middle-age, overweight prostitute told the commission that she took 30 men a night to her third-floor room. "Why that's terrible!" a commissioner replied in shock. "Yes," said the prostitute, "those stairs are killing me."

So where were the authorities? On the take. High on the list were the lords of the Levee, "Bathhouse" John Coughlin and "Hinky Dink" Kenna, first ward aldermen who set a new standard for public corruption.

Their First Ward Ball was an enormous rowdy party that celebrated vice and depravity. At the 1907 ball, held at the Coliseum on South Wabash, a reporter counted two bands, 200 waiters, 100 policemen, 35,000 quarts of beer and 10,000 quarts of champagne. Even at that, the reporter said, they had to "send for reinforcements" late in the night. Waiters paid $5 apiece for the privilege of working the event, since the tips were so good. Lots of prostitutes and underworld figures took part. After the solid citizenry got incensed and tried to ban the 1908 ball, Bathhouse John quipped: "All right, we'll compromise: We won't let parents bring their children. There!"

The next ball went on as scheduled. "It's a lollapalooza," said Hinky. "All the business houses are here, all the big people. Chicago ain't no sissy town."

Bathhouse John and Hinky Dink chartered a special train to the Democratic Convention in Denver, stocked with 1,000 quarts of champagne, 200 quarts of whiskey, 80 quarts of gin and 12 crates of lemons in 1908. The train ride was a last hurrah, because public complaint helped end the First Ward ball after 1908. It was called the "the crowning disgrace of Chicago."

Carter H. Harrison Jr. was the mayor during the first part of the century. Harrison, whose father Carter H. Harrison Sr. had served as mayor until his 1894 assassination, was quite different from his father. He believed in an open city, with few rules and little interference. He was criticized for not reforming the civil service system and for allowing vice to flourish for years — but he, too, was elected mayor five times. It was not a

First Ward Ball, depicted by John T. McCutcheon in 1908

machine that kept him in power, but his own personality and charm.

The city took liberal strides during the first few years of the century. Free bathing beaches were opened, the Chicago Boys Clubs were organized and the Board of Education decided that young pupils should get free textbooks. Prisoners at Cook County Jail published *The Improvement Journal*. Its motto: "Better late than never."

One dramatic change in Chicago at the turn of the century was the appearance of the car. By 1900 the city was requiring driving tests and charging for driving licenses. The following year, the first official Chicago Automobile Show attracted 20,000 people. About 1,500 drivers were registered in Chicago in 1903. In 1904 the city council set the minimum driving age at 18 and the speed limit at 10 miles per hour. Horses remained the dominant means of transportation through the first two decades of the century, but it was soon clear to many that the future belonged to the car.

In 1900 Susan Winans, the last survivor of Fort Dearborn massacre, died. She was 6 months old during massacre. In 1901 anarchist Emma Goldman was arrested

Police ball at Dvorak Park in 1910
Chicago Park District Special Collections

in Chicago and charged with conspiracy to kill a chief U.S. magistrate.

On March 11, 1902, former Gov. John Peter Altgeld gave a speech in Joliet against British imperialism in South Africa. He spoke for 45 minutes, hesitating, wiping his brow frequently.

"I am not discouraged," Altgeld told the crowd. "Things will right themselves. The pendulum swings one way and then another. But the steady pull of gravitation is toward the center of the earth."

Altgeld concluded the speech and sat for a moment. As he rose to walk off the stage, he fell. He was rushed to a room, but was pronounced dead of a cerebral hemorrhage the next day. Up to 50,000 people came to pay their respects at his coffin in the Chicago Public Library. Altgeld, who died at age 55, was buried in Graceland Cemetery.

The biggest story of 1903 was Chicago's deadliest fire, and the fourth deadliest in world history, at the Iroquois Theater. The blaze erupted backstage during a performance of Eddie Foy's *Mr. Bluebeard* on

December 30. The curtain failed to fall completely, allowing the flames to spread to the seats of the five-week-old theater. The fleeing crowd discovered that the many exits swung inward, and therefore were impossible to open because of the crush of the crowd. The side doors had been locked to prevent people from sneaking in. The blaze raged for 15 minutes, killing about 600 theatergoers. With no hoses, no sprinklers and only two fire extinguishers, little could be done. About one-third of the dead were children. The theater, which reopened as the Colonial, was eventually razed to make way for the Oriental Theater.

Orchestra Hall opened in 1904 for Theodore Thomas' Chicago Orchestra. (Its name would change to the Chicago Symphony Orchestra in 1913.) The hall, designed by Daniel Burnham, continues to be the home of the world-famous orchestra. The early years of the 20th century were the heyday of catalog houses such as Sears Roebuck and Montgomery Ward's. By 1904, 3 million Ward's catalogs weighing 4

Electric locomotive in underground tunnel in 1912

Iroquois Theater before the 1903 fire that killed about 600 people

Elevated trains looped the downtown district around 1905. This is Van Buren Street west from Wabash Avenue. *H.C. White stereograph, Torry Bruno Collection*

Gage Park gardens and water park in 1905
Chicago Park District Special Collections

Mark White Square in 1905 — the South Park Commission introduced the field house.
Chicago Park District Special Collections

Union Stock Yards, Chicago.

pounds each were mailed to customers. Ward was not only a good businessman; he was a bold civic leader. He was a crucial fighter to save the lakefront from development. He won a 13-year court fight against lakefront development that could have forced the Art Institute to move, but Ward never pressed that.

In 1905 two disparate organizations were founded in Chicago: The International Rotary Club civic organization and the Industrial Workers of the World ("The Wobblies"). Jens Jensen, one of the park system's great visionaries, took over as superintendent of West Side parks, and the Field Columbian Museum changed its name to Field Museum of Natural History. It was one of the last relics of the Columbian Exposition.

Reformer Edward F. Dunne was elected mayor in 1905. One of his first acts was to return all theatrical and railroad passes. His stated goal for the public was to take over the privately owned transit system. Dunne was considered a socialist who surrounded himself with "long-haired friends and short-haired women." He appointed attorney

Clarence Darrow as his advisor. Dunne was blamed for increasing liquor license fees — and any attack on liquor was considered an attack on foreigners. He lasted only one term, but later served as governor and as a judge.

The Jungle, Upton Sinclair's expose on the Chicago slaughterhouses, was published in 1906, sparking reforms. Sinclair, who based the book on a diary kept by a Lithuanian stockyards worker, spent only seven weeks in Chicago researching the book. He hoped the book would help improve the conditions of immigrant workers. Instead, it improved the condition of the animals. Within six months, Congress had passed both a Pure Food and Drug Act and a Beef Inspection Act. "I aimed for America's heart, and hit its stomach, instead."

Not all was vice, corruption and filth. Chicagoans searched for amusement in many ways. Many turned to parks. By the turn of the century, Chicago had six major parks — Jackson, Washington, Humboldt, Garfield, Douglas and Lincoln — and a boulevard system that connected them. Small parks, which offered breathing

Opening of Eckhart Park in 1908
Chicago Park District Special Collections

spaces in the crowded city, and field houses — which often included lunchrooms, a public library and sports equipment — were built during this era so that most all Chicagoans had year-round access to park facilities near their neighborhoods.

Private amusement parks, such as White City on the South Side and Riverview on the North Side, also became popular destinations.

One of the most popular pastimes was baseball. The Chicago White Sox was one of the original

American League teams and the winner of the league's first pennant. During this era, the Sox also won pennants in 1906, 1917 and 1919. The team won the World Series in 1906 and 1917 (the only two championships

during the century). The Sox moved from the Chicago Cricket Club grounds, at 39th and Wentworth, to Comiskey Park, at 35th and Shields, in 1910. The National League Cubs won pennants in 1906, 1907, 1908, 1910 and 1918. The team won the series in 1907 and 1908 (its only two championships during the century). The Cubs, a charter team of the National League, moved to Wrigley Field, at Clark and Addison, in 1916. In the 1906 trolley series, the "Hitless Wonders" Sox beat the Cubs, of Tinkers-to-Evers-to-Chance fame.

Seven African-American baseball teams formed the National League of Colored Baseball Clubs in 1910. Chicago was a major city on the Negro League circuit for half a century.

In 1907 the Ravenswood El started running on the North Side, Michael Reese Hospital was opened on the South Side and plans were submitted for the Garfield Park Conservatory on the West Side. In 1908 the city adopted a new street numbering system, still in use today, with the baselines at State and Madison streets. It was implemented during the following two years. In 1909 Frank Lloyd Wright was building his sleek, low Hyde Park house for Frederick C. Robie, changing forever the history of design.

The most ambitious design proposal that year was Daniel Burnham's Chicago Plan. One of its main points —

White City Amusement Park at 63rd and South Park Avenue in 1908

The great Chicago bungalow
Jack Miller Collection

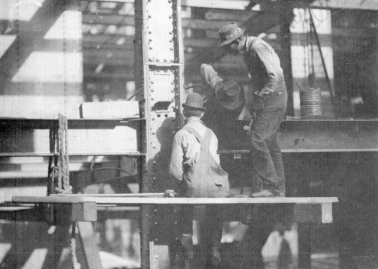

as the University of Illinois at Chicago) and the Civic Center Plaza as results of ideas first proposed by Burnham and Bennett.

In 1910, 10 Chicago meatpackers, including J. Ogden Armour and three Swifts, were charged with conspiracy and monopoly and indicted. Judge Kenesaw Mountain Landis, who later became baseball's first commissioner, instructed a federal grand jury to investigate alleged collusion in Chicago packing companies in restraint of trade. The packers were eventually acquitted by a jury of charges of restraint of trade. But the National Packing Co. "beef trust" was dissolved.

that Chicago's lakefront must be protected — was embraced enthusiastically from the start. Other ideas have been ultimately implemented, such as the widening of Michigan Avenue, the creation of outer forest preserves, the building of piers jutting out into the lake (Navy Pier), and the construction of small peninsulas into the lake (Northerly Island, now the site of Meigs Field airport).

"Make no little plans for they have no magic to stir men's blood and probably themselves will never be realized," Burnham is credited with writing in his City Beautiful vision. "Make big plans. Aim high in hope and work, remembering that a noble logical diagram once recorded will never die but long after we are gone will be a living thing, asserting with growing intensity."

The plan, co-written by Edward H. Bennett, was adopted by the city and served as a behind-the-scenes blueprint for development. The city created a plan commission to carry out the ideas of City Beautiful. City Beautiful was more of an idea around which the city developed. One can even point to the Adler Planetarium, the Eisenhower Expressway built on the Congress Street alignment, the straightened South Branch of Chicago River, Soldier Field, the Chicago Circle campus (now known

In 1911 Carter H. Harrison Jr. ran once again for mayor — and won his fifth and final term. That was also the era that Chicagoan Harriet Monroe began publishing the influential magazine *Poetry*.

"It was on the eleventh of January, 1911, that I finished circling the

Souvenir from Swift & Company, Chicago

Seeing Armour's

Jules Guerin view of Chicago looking west and showing the proposed Civic Center
The 1909 Plan of Chicago

Construction of LaSalle Hotel in 1909
Chicago Historical Society

Souvenirs from the Swift and Armour companies, two giants of the city's meatpacking industry

Eckhart Park wading pool in 1910
Chicago Park District Special Collections

world at the Santa Fe station in Chicago," Monroe wrote in *A Poet's Life.* "I found the city surging with activities and aspirations beneath its commercial surface. The 'Chicago Plan' was being matured under the enthusiastic leadership of Daniel Burnham — the first of the now numerous 'city plans;' and the 20-year litigation to put through its first important feature — the two-story Michigan Avenue Bridge, with Wacker Drive to replace the old produce market along the river — was going on quietly to a triumph. The small park movement — another Chicago idea — was progressing, and the Illinois Central Railroad was being disciplined along the shining shore of beautiful Lake Michigan. The Orchestra was firmly established. The Art Institute was increasing its prestige and its collections."

W.B. Yeats was her "European editor" and Ezra Pound was her "foreign correspondent." *Poetry* was the first magazine to publish T.S. Eliot's classic "Love Song of J. Alfred Prufrock."

Monroe, Margaret Anderson and Floyd Dell, who had become the editor of the avant-garde *Friday Literary*

Twentieth Century Limited leaves Chicago. This was the fastest long-distance train in the world. It could travel to New York in 18 hours.

Review, helped make Chicago the epicenter of early 20th-century literature. In 1900 *Chicago Evening Post* reporter L. Frank Baum published *The Wonderful World of Oz.* Carl Sandburg's poem, "Chicago," with its lines "City of the Big Shoulders," and "hog butcher for the world," became symbolic of the city. Edgar Lee Masters published *Spoon River Anthology,* the best-selling poetry book of its time.

The city, once called 'Porkopolis' by the literary East, attracted poet Vachel Lindsay, novelists Sherwood Anderson and Edna Ferber and Ben Hecht. "It's a fine thing to be a reporter, and young and working in Chicago," wrote Hecht.

Proclaimed actress Sarah Bernhardt: "I adore Chicago. It is the pulse of America."

By 1917 the often-acerbic H.L. Mencken called it "The Literary Capital of the United States." He wrote:

"With two exceptions there is not a single novelist of the younger generation — that is a serious novelist deserving a civilized reader's notice — who has not sprung from the Chicago palatinate; Dreiser, Anderson, Miss Cather, Mrs. (Wyatt) Watts, Tarkington, Wilson,

Sunday afternoon on Lake Shore Drive in Lincoln Park

165

Herrick, Patterson, even Churchill. It was Chicago that produced Henry B. Fuller, the packer of the modern American novel. It was Chicago that produced Frank Norris, its first practitioner of genius."

Meanwhile, the University of Chicago was creating an education center. It was there that educator John

Dewey developed his theories that children could learn by doing and could learn responsibility if they were given freedom at school. It was also there that economist Thorstein Veblen developed his theory of conspicuous consumption. Veblen observed women shopping at Marshall Field's and found that they often bought expensive, needless items to show off. His epic *Theory of the Leisure Class* postulated that their wasteful habits served as a model for people in all financial classes.

During those years, the Field Museum of Natural History was built along the lakefront, becoming the first institution to locate in an area that would later become the "Museum Campus," with the Shedd Aquarium and Adler Planetarium.

In 1912 Republican William Lorimer — who was Carter H. Harrison's arch rival — became the first U.S. senator to be kicked out for bribery and corruption. He returned to Chicago and was a Republican political boss for another decade. Chicago's Chinatown branched out from downtown to the South Side. The cornerstone of the new Fourth Presbyterian Church on Pine Street (later renamed North Michigan Avenue) was laid as well as the cornerstone of the Wabash YMCA at 38th and Wabash. The YMCA became the first home of many African-American immigrants from the South, and the home of important black writers such as Richard Wright.

It was also the year that Chicago police started enforcing rules regarding public bathing. Everyone over 12 had to wear a two-piece suit. Flesh-colored suits and lounging on the beach in vulgar positions were prohibited.

Garfield Park Conservatory in 1913
Chicago Park District Special Collections

By 1914 the underground tunnel system beneath the Loop was virtually complete, transporting coal, ashes, garbage and other materials to and from downtown buildings. Construction on the 62 miles of freight tunnels, 40 feet beneath the surface, had started in 1901. The system worked efficiently until 1959, when its operating companies were liquidated. (This was the system that was later virtually forgotten and was a key factor in Chicago's downtown underground flood in 1992.)

More than 150,000 women registered to vote in Chicago in 1914 for the first time. In Carter H. Harrison's last year as mayor, he finally ordered a close of the Levee's gambling and prostitution houses. Harrison ran for a sixth term in 1915, but lost in the Democratic primary to William Hale "Big Bill" Thompson, who would later set the scene for Chicago's Roaring 20s. The 1915 city election was a watershed event for Chicago because the first black alderman, Oscar DePriest, and the first Latino alderman, William E. Rodriguez, were elected.

In 1913 the first cross-town train ran from Wilmette in the north suburbs to Stony Island on the South Side. Jack Vilas made the first flight across Lake Michigan, and the Shriners built the Medinah Temple on North Wabash Avenue.

That was also the year of the city's worst disaster, the capsizing of the Eastland. Some 844 people drowned in 20 feet of water when the Eastland boat tipped over on the Chicago River just north of the Loop. Most of the casualties were Western Electric Co. employees on an outing. Twenty-two entire families were wiped out.

No exact cause was ever determined for the capsizing, but several theories have been advanced as contributing to the tragedy. One person who almost made the casualty list was George Halas, who went on to start the Chicago Bears. Halas had planned to take the trip to Michigan City on the Eastland that day and had bought a ticket. His name was on the list of the missing. After the incident, two of Halas' college fraternity brothers came to his house to pay respects.

Humboldt Park Refectory in 1916 where speed skating took place on the frozen lagoon
Chicago Park District Special Collections

Troops gather downtown as they ready for World War I.

"I'll never forget the shocked look on their face[s] when I answered the door," Halas said.

Chicago got poised for World War I in 1916, as 130,000 men marched in a preparedness parade through the city. Many Chicagoans did not want to get involved with the European conflict until war was declared in 1917.

Mayor Thompson, who had support from German-American voters, remained an isolationist. He worked hard against America's entry into the Great War and later against Woodrow Wilson's League of Nations and Versailles Peace Treaty. He was known by some during the conflict as "Kaiser Bill."

Stereograph of troops returning on August 4, 1917, and participating in the national Army parade down Michigan Avenue

After a winter fire on West Madison near Union Park
Chicago Historical Society

Sgt. John Edmonson of the Eighth Regiment and his family — this regiment was the pride of Chicago's African-American community. *Chicago Historical Society*

The city celebrated Armistice Day on November 11, 1918. What should have been a joyous end of the decade was particularly gloomy in Chicago. During eight weeks starting in September 1918, more than 8,500 people died from influenza and pneumonia in Chicago. The "Spanish flu" epidemic was worldwide, killing more people than did World War I. It struck Chicago particularly hard. On one day, October 17, some 381 people died because of the influenza. Many public meeting places, such as theaters and dance halls, were closed. Even public funerals were prohibited. Spitting, thought to transmit the disease, was prohibited and spitters were arrested.

Chicago was an early aviation center. Here an airplane flies above Grant Park. *Chicago Historical Society*

In 1918 a traffic planner proposed tearing down the historic Water Tower, which had survived the Great Chicago Fire, to ease the bottleneck on Michigan Avenue. Chicago was never keen about saving landmark buildings. The original Fort Dearborn had been torn down almost a century before. The second Fort Dearborn was demolished during the early 1870s, but the building had long before become rundown. Little thought was given to saving historic buildings until 1960.

Chicago was a rough town trying to become cultured. Wrote Kenan Heise, in *The Chicagoization of America 1893-1917,* "Chicago, on the other hand, was common. It had few pretensions. The town stank of stockyards that were the largest in the world and was covered with soot as befitted the railroad capital of the nation."

By the end of the war, the city had become a powerful magnet. Heise wrote: "Chicago had become the most famous place in the world to go: if you had hope; if you wanted to reform other people or corrupt them; if you wished to make money or spend it; if you just desired to survive or chose to live recklessly; if you couldn't even write or if you hoped to be writer; if you wanted to see America's streets paved with gold or were willing to trudge through dust or mud to go to working the stockyards; of if you were running away, whether from the Tsar, conscription or the neo-slavery of the South."

In 1919 Chicago's power to attract so many people, became its liability when the city erupted in its worst race riot. At least 20 blacks and 14 whites were killed in several days of violence that injured hundreds. Here's how Carl Sandburg described it in his book *The Chicago Race Riots:*

"The so-called race riots in Chicago during the last week of July, 1919, started on a Sunday at a bathing beach. A colored boy swam across an imaginary segregation line. White boys threw rocks at him and knocked him off a raft. He was drowned. Colored people rushed to a policeman and asked for the arrest of the boys throwing stones. The policeman refused. As the dead body of the drowned boy was being handled, more rocks were thrown, on both sides. The policeman held on to his refusal to make arrests. Fighting then began that spread to all the borders of the Black Belt."

A Cook County Coroner's Office report found that the boy, Eugene Williams, died of exhaustion, trying to come ashore safely. He had grabbed a hold of a railroad tie but slipped off and drowned. (Decades later, historian William Tuttle found that Williams had been struck in the forehead by a rock as he floated on a raft near 26th Street.)

An argument soon ensued on the all-white 29th Street Beach, between blacks and whites. A black man pulled a revolver and fired into a group of policemen. The police shot back, fatally wounding the man.

"Once ignited, on July 27, the rioting raged virtually uncontrolled for the greater part of five days," wrote Tuttle. "Day and night white toughs assaulted isolated blacks, and teenage black mobsters beat white peddlers and merchants in the black belt. As rumors of atrocities circulated throughout the city, members of both races craved vengeance. White gunmen in automobiles sped through the black belt shooting indiscriminately as they passed, and black snipers fired back. Roaming mobs shot, beat, and stabbed to death their victims. The undermanned police force was an ineffectual deterrent to the waves of violence which soon overflowed the environs of the black belt and flooded the North and West Sides and the Loop, Chicago's downtown business district. Only several regiments of state militiamen and a cooling rain finally quenched the passions of the rioters, and even then sporadic outbursts punctuated the atmosphere for another week."

Chicago's shame was consummated later that year by the Black Sox scandal. In October 1919 members of the Chicago White Sox, paid off by gamblers, purposely lost the World Series to the Cincinnati Reds. The scandal did not surface for

Inspecting damage of the 1919 race riot
Chicago Historical Society

close to a year, but when the hearings and investigations were concluded, eight ballplayers were banned from the game, including "Shoeless Joe" Jackson, one of baseball's greatest. No gambler was ever punished, nor was Sox owner Charles Comiskey, who learned about the thrown series afterward and attempted to cover it up. The Black Sox Scandal was unimaginable. "Say it ain't so, Joe" became a phrase that became associated with Chicago's underworld reputation. It was a black mark that took decades to overcome.

Construction of Michigan Avenue Bridge in 1920
Chicago Historical Society

Robert S. Abbott

"*With drops of ink, we make millions think!*"

— *Robert S. Abbott*, **Chicago Defender**, *1916*

Chapter Five
1918–1945

5

Nobody was more responsible for the events of 1919 than Robert S. Abbott.

Abbott, the son of ex-slaves, had come to Chicago from rural Georgia in 1897 to study at the Kent College of Law. Unable to find a law job, he turned to printing. With 25 cents in his pocket and a promise to pay his printer following the publication of his first edition, Abbott started a four-page newspaper that sold for 2 cents. He ran off 300 issues of his first paper, published May 5, 1905. He called it the *Chicago Defender*, because he saw the paper as a defender of his race.

The *Defender* was nothing more than a small local paper during its first years, one of several reporting on the happenings and gossip in the tightly knit black community on the South Side. By 1910 the *Defender* started taking on a sensationalistic look. Like the metropolitan broadsheets and tabloids published downtown, the *Defender* started using banner headlines (sometimes in red ink) and departmentalizing the news (such as theater, sports, etc.). Abbott understood the changes he was making, and justified them because it increased his audience.

By 1915 when the paper nicknamed itself the "World's Greatest Weekly," the *Defender* was the major African-American paper in Chicago. And soon it was the major African-American paper in the nation. Abbott was strident; he pushed for equal rights and racial justice. He believed that race prejudice must be destroyed and sought an end of segregation. He fought against lynchings and questioned whether African-Americans should take part in the military.

And he encouraged African-Americans in the rural South to move to the urban North, particularly to his hometown of Chicago. "Come North, where there is more humanity, some justice and fairness!" Abbott wrote. He carefully noted Southern lynchings in his paper and talked about job opportunities in the North.

"Every black man for the sake of his wife and daughter should leave even at a financial sacrifice every spot in the south where his worth is not appreciated enough to give him the standing of a man and a citizen in the community," Abbott wrote in 1916. "We know full well that this would almost mean a depopulation of that section and if it were possible we would glory in its accomplishment."

The *Defender* reached a circulation of 50,000 that year, expanded to 125,000 in 1918 and reached a peak of more than 200,000 after World War I, becoming the first African-American mass-circulation paper in the nation. By then the *Defender* produced two papers, one for Chicago and one for the nation. Railroad porters and waiters were hired to sell the paper throughout the rural

Union Park Pool about 1920
Chicago Park District Special Collections

South. They made a small profit and saw their work as valuable in advancing the cause. Abbott, in turn, supported their work and their unions. The *Defender* became a staple in Southern towns where the Illinois Central stopped. Eventually, the newspaper had more than 2,000 agent-correspondents, circulating the paper as well as sending back news.

News from the North was so valued by African-Americans that some Southern towns passed laws against the distribution and sale of the paper. The Ku Klux Klan threatened agents. One race riot, in Longview, Texas, was sparked by the *Defender's* report of a gruesome lynching in the South.

"A colored man caught with a copy in his possession was suspected of 'Northern fever' and other so-called disloyalties," wrote Carl Sandburg in the *Chicago Daily News*. At least two agents were killed for distributing the paper.

Abbott's Chicago became the Promised Land, and the exodus from the South became the flight out of Egypt. The *Defender* kept hammering away. "I beg of you, my brothers, to leave that benighted land," Abbott wrote. "You are free men. Show the world that you will not let false leaders lead you. Your neck has been in the yoke... Leave to all quarters of the globe. Get out of the South. Your being there in the numbers you are gives the Southern politician too strong a hold on your progress."

The *Defender* was not the only reason for the migration. After World War I, the Klan boasted about 5 million members in the South. Poor schools, daily humiliation, low-paying jobs and a skewed criminal justice system made life for African-Americans in the South almost intolerable.

One million African-Americans came North during World War I to fill jobs in packinghouses, steel mills and foundries.

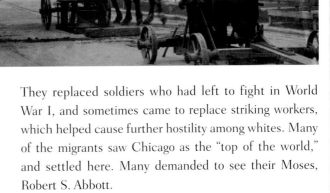

A brownstone house is moved by horse. *Jack Miller Collection*

They replaced soldiers who had left to fight in World War I, and sometimes came to replace striking workers, which helped cause further hostility among whites. Many of the migrants saw Chicago as the "top of the world," and settled here. Many demanded to see their Moses, Robert S. Abbott.

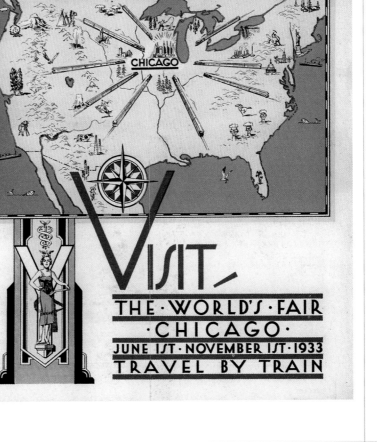

New York Central Lines advertisement

MAKE CHICAGO THE HUB OF YOUR 1933 TRAVELS

CHICAGO

VISIT
THE·WORLD'S·FAIR
·CHICAGO·
JUNE 1ST·NOVEMBER 1ST·1933
TRAVEL BY TRAIN

Poster promotes 1940
African-American
convention held in
Chicago.

African-American
relay team running
track at Douglas Park
around 1936
*Chicago Park District
Special Collections*

Abbott helped expand the Black Belt, the African-American South Side neighborhood that stretched from 31st to about 70th streets and along State Street, Michigan Boulevard, South Parkway (now known as Martin Luther King Drive) and Cottage Grove Avenue. Called Black Metropolis in the 1920s, it was a unique African-American community. Self-sufficient, it became a mecca to Southern African-Americans who arrived at the Illinois Central Station and were directed a few miles south.

This new community, now known as "Bronzeville," reveled with a new attitude. Chicago's early African-American communities were subservient. Decades of humiliation, the short end of opportunities and dozens of bombs against African-Americans created discontent.

By 1915 some 50,000 blacks had recently moved to Chicago. The *Tribune* wrote in 1917: "A new problem, demanding early solution is facing Chicago. It pertains to the sudden and unprecedented influx of southern Negro laborers."

The new problem exploded on the streets in the 1919 race riots.

"America is known the world over as the land of the lynchers and the mobocrats," Abbott wrote. "For years she has been sowing the wind and now she is reaping the whirlwind. The Black worm has turned. A Race that has furnished hundreds of the best soldiers that the world has ever seen is no longer content to turn the left cheek when smitten upon the right."

The *Defender* fed the flames during the first days of the 1919 riot. The paper ran a scoreboard of killed and injured whites and blacks, and helped perpetuate rumors that incensed both communities. But then, Abbott reversed course and published 30,000 handbills with the Defender logo advising the African-American community to be orderly, obey police and stay off the streets. The

Children make sand castles in 1936.
Chicago Park District Special Collections

handbills, signed "Yours for Peace, Robert S. Abbott,"
greatly helped calm the city.

The 1920s was a golden era for Black Metropolis. It
was a "city within a city," where residents could live without
racial restrictions and limitations. The seven-story
Knights of Pythias Building anchored the neighborhood
along with the fancy Binga Arcade Building. At night,
Black Metropolis became a jazz center, the terminus for
jazz and blues musicians from the South. King Oliver,
Louis Armstrong and Jelly Roll Morton played the clubs,
and black businesses, such as the Overton-Hygenic

"BOUL MICH"
by the ELEVATED LINES

Company and Abbott's *Defender*, became national
corporations.

Black Metropolis became a model for African-
Americans all over the nation. It reached its zenith in
the mid-1920s.

"There was prosperity, and money seemed to flow
from everyone's pockets as easily as laughter from their
lips," wrote Roi Ottley, Abbott's biographer. "The
South Side had entered an era of noisy vitality, and the
intersection of 35th and State Streets was the center of
this triumphant existence. The section had indeed
become the capital of clowns, cults and cabarets, and
brought a bumper crop of Negroes to the city, both
migrants and celebrities."

Robert Abbott's *Defender* and the need for factory
workers in World War I spurred the first great migration
of African-Americans to Chicago. The first African-
American church, Quinn Chapel, had been founded in
Chicago in 1847. By 1860, 1,000 African-Americans
lived in Chicago. In 1874 the school system was officially desegregated and by 1890, 15,000 African-
Americans lived in the city. The boll weevil destroyed
cotton in the South and started the migration North.

In the coming decades, the city's African-American
population increased from 44,000 in 1910 to 110,000
in 1920. That comprised about 4 percent of the city's
population of 2.7 million. By 1930 Chicago had nearly
3.4 million residents, and about 7 percent were black.
The city population remained the same through 1945,
but the number of African-Americans grew to about
12 percent.

"Here were colored policemen, firemen, aldermen
and precinct captains, State Representatives, doctors,
lawyers, and teachers," wrote anthropologist St. Clair
Drake. "Colored children were attending the public

The junior gardening club at Stanford Park in 1937 — the park was demolished in 1961 to make way for the Dan Ryan Expressway.
Chicago Park District Special Collections

schools and the city's junior colleges. There were fine churches in the Negro areas, and beautiful boulevards. It seemed reasonable to assume that this development would continue with more and more Negroes getting ahead and becoming educated. There were prophets of doom in the 20s, but a general air of optimism pervaded the Black Belt, as it did the whole city."

Prohibition, which went into effect in January 1920 and lasted until 1933, put its mark on the city, defining a tarnished reputation that still has not been erased. The 18th Amendment made it illegal to manufacture, sell or transport anything containing more than 1.5 percent alcohol anywhere in the country. The law did not strictly prohibit the purchase of alcohol and specified that any liquor purchased before January 16, 1920, could not be confiscated, so nightclubs stockpiled huge amounts of liquor.

"As early as 1920 it was seen that Chicago 'beer-hustling' was getting organized, with at least tacit consent by the City Hall," wrote Henry Justin Smith. "Breweries were known to be open and booming; Chicago's immense thirst was being quenched, law or no law, and public sentiment inclined toward approval of this fact."

Surprisingly, Mayor Thompson did attempt to enforce Prohibition laws at first. Uncharacteristically, he felt that it was his duty to uphold the laws of the nation.

Anna Walker and the Union Park Orchestra in 1936
Chicago Park District Special Collections

A model from the Haymarket Theatre

Acrobatic performers at Garfield Park around 1936
Chicago Park District Special Collections

But, as pressure mounted from ethnic groups — who often saw attempts to curb their drinking habits as an invitation to fight — Thompson reversed himself and virtually declared that Chicago would be an open city for the duration. That created a massive turf war for gangsters, who wanted their share of the underworld business of illegal imbibing.

"The police being indifferent — if not corrupt — and the Federal forces too few, the feudal chiefs of the booze-industry went right on improving their systems and making boundaries based roughly on Chicago's natural divisions," wrote Smith. "Into the ranks of the several armies rushed practically all the clever or athletic young hoodlums 'educated' during the last twenty years. The wages were good, bonuses rich, advancement speedy. Competition was also brisk. When boundaries were crossed, or beer-trucks 'hi-jacked,' there were murders — which the public read about and quickly forgot... Sometimes there would be an outburst of mysterious rage in a crowded street or building; there would be a spurt of fire, a revolver-explosion or two; there would be a body on a tiled foyer, and a dash of a group, "identity unknown," to the street, the roar of a motor."

During the early 1920s a series of gangland assassinations cleared the way for Al Capone's ascendancy as No. 1 mob chief. "Diamond Jim" Colosimo, a top gangster, was murdered

COMPLIMENTS OF
HAYMARKET THEATRE
CHICAGO

by Johnny Torrio and Capone. Seeking to avoid becoming the next hit victim, the "Big Fellow," Capone, rode around in a 7-ton bulletproof car. "Some call it bootlegging. Some call it racketeering. I call it a business," Capone said.

Despite the Prohibition, Chicago had 15 operating breweries and 20,000 saloons. But it was the street murders that made Chicago famous. Colosimo was gunned down in his cafe at 2126 South Wabash in 1920. Capone's younger brother, Frank, was killed in a battle with police. Dion O'Banion, who wanted to control the North Side, was dropped into the chrysanthemums at his flower shop at 738 N. State in 1924. "Little Hymie" Weiss was executed in 1926 right outside Holy Name Cathedral on the Near North Side.

The killings continued through the decade. On February 14, 1929, four gunmen reportedly hired by Capone — two of them dressed as policemen — walked into a brick garage at 2122 North Clark and lined up seven members of rival George "Bugs" Moran's gang. They murdered Bugsy's boys with submachine guns. The event was forever known as the St. Valentine's Day Massacre.

Capone was convicted of tax evasion in 1931 after federal investigators proved that his expenses were far in excess of any legitimate income that he could prove. Even the fact that he had given $58,000 to a police widows and orphans fund was used as evidence of his actual, ill-gotten wealth. He was sentenced to 10 years in prison and $50,000 in fines.

Much of Chicago thrived during the 1920s — because it was an economic good time. The city became an important commercial center for the printing, advertising, metal and clothing industries. It developed a reputation as a no-nonsense business center. "My working day begins when I start to lather my face," said Charles R. Walgreen, founder of the drugstore chain.

The stockyards were expanded and giant movie palaces were built. The forest preserves were opened, the Illinois Central trains were electrified and Grant Park was made into a garden in the city. Golf became the sport of city parks, and horse racing and boxing were legalized in this era when sports first took prominence.

The year 1920 was a landmark time for North Michigan Avenue. The street was widened and the double-level bridge spanning the Chicago River was opened. Nearby, the cornerstone of the Wrigley Building was laid. Down the street, the $10 million Drake Hotel opened. That was also the year that Edith Rockefeller McCormick donated land west of suburban Riverside for a zoological park. The zoo is now called Brookfield.

Double-decker buses, on which one could ride in the wind, were all the rage in 1921. That was the year that the first electric traffic control signals — yellow on top, green in the middle and red at the bottom — were installed. The Field Museum of Natural History opened and the City Council divided the city into its present 50 wards.

The following year, jazz was all the rage as young Louis Armstrong and Ferdinand "Jelly Roll" Morton were helping to turn Chicago into a jazz capital. Jazz wasn't the only new form of entertainment sweeping the city. WMAQ began broadcasting in 1922. Later that year the *Chicago Tribune* started WGN, call letters that stood for World's Greatest Newspaper. In 1925 a radio show called "Sam 'n' Henry," about two hapless African-Americans, began on WGN radio in Chicago. When the lead actors and scriptwriters, white men named Freeman Gosden and Charles Correll, wanted to move the show to WMAQ radio in 1928, WGN claimed ownership of the name, so Gosden and Correll gave the same characters new names: Amos 'n' Andy.

"Big Bill" Thompson was defeated in another bid for mayor by reform candidate Democrat William Dever in 1923. The reform movement was to prove short-lived. Dever, a friend of

(Far left postcard) Maxwell Street Market at Roosevelt Road and 14th Street

A matchbook promotes the Silver Frolics.

The Wrigley Building was built from 1919 to 1924 and is floodlit every night.

185

Ogden Park model boat sailing in 1926
Chicago Park District Special Collections

Sherman Park Fieldhouse and Lagoon around 1920
Chicago Park District Special Collections

Jane Addams, used the slogan "Dever and Decency." He shut down speakeasies — which guaranteed he would have only one term in office.

In 1924 Richard Loeb and Nathan Leopold, rich students at the University of Chicago, were arrested for the thrill killing of 14-year-old Bobby Franks. Attorney Clarence Darrow represented them and, with an emotional argument against capital punishment, averted the death sentence.

By the mid-20s autos were becoming more popular. More than 30,000 new cars a year were added to the streets of Chicago during the decade and by 1930, the city had more than 400,000 cars, or one for every eight residents. Cars were creating ever more congestion downtown and spurring the growth of the suburbs. Said Frank Lloyd Wright: "The automobile is going to ruin this city. Michigan Avenue isn't a boulevard, it's a race track!" The city's suburban population reached 1 million in 1930. Many left Chicago to escape the city's crime and vice, and cars made the escape possible.

Many of the city's architectural jewels were opened or dedicated in 1925. The Tribune Tower, a result of an international architectural contest, was built as was Union Station, the Goodman Theater and Soldier Field, first called Grant Park Stadium.

Chicago connected to the nation and to the world in 1926. Route 66, linking Chicago and Los Angeles by road, was completed that year and Municipal Airport was made accessible for airplanes. (The airport, which would be renamed Midway in 1949, was the world's busiest for years.) The Eucharistic Congress, an international meeting of 500,000 Catholics, was held in Chicago and suburban Mundelein. One paper called it "the greatest religious spectacle witnessed by the western world."

South Michigan Avenue was in the limelight in 1927. The world's largest hotel, the Stevens, opened and the Buckingham Fountain was unveiled. William Hale

gave a $7.5 million donation. Rosenwald was a philanthropist who bettered the lives of countless African-Americans by personally financing the construction of dozens of inner-city community centers and 5,000 schools for African-American children throughout the South.

The last year of the Roaring 20s was also the year when Frank Lloyd Wright's Midway Gardens entertainment facility was torn down to make way for a gas station. The utopian outdoor beer garden had been built on the Midway and flourished until Prohibition. Its demolition was one of the most painful examples of architectural loss in the city's history.

Racial discrimination was far from dead, as Robert Abbott experienced. One cold, snowy night, he arrived in New York late, stopped at a hotel for a room, but was told none were available.

"As I turned away from the desk to go back into the biting cold, a white man came up, followed by another and another, and all were given rooms. One of these white men, seeing what had happened to me, turned back and laughed full in my face — laughed to think that he could get in and I could not.

"I have never forgotten the laugh of vindicative triumph on that white man's face. As I walked into the best establishments in Berlin, Paris, Brussels, and Amsterdam, white hotel attendants rushed forward to greet my wife and myself. I wished that same man could only see me now."

The publisher toured Europe for five months in 1929, being called "M'sieur Abbott" in France. He felt free in much of Europe, but he was refused stays at the top hotels in London and later had problems with his first-class accommodation on his return journey via ship back to the United States. The refusals made front-page news in London dailies, but generally the trip was a success.

Thompson surged back to power that year, re-elected for a third term. By then, his scandals had been forgotten by some, and he was known as "Big Bill the Builder." Construction was a major industry. On North Michigan Avenue, the Medinah Athletic Club and 333 North Michigan Building were completed in 1928 as work on the Carbide and Carbon Building and Palmolive Building continued. On the West Side, the Cook County Children's Hospital was completed and the cornerstone of Chicago Stadium was laid. Work also began that year to straighten the Chicago River between Polk and 18th streets. A bend in the river was removed and a new channel was built, which made it possible to realign railroad tracks and railroad stations. The project, which opened the southwest side of downtown to more development, took more than two years to complete.

The year 1929 saw the rise of landmarks and the demolition of one. The Chicago Civic Opera House and the Museum of Science and Industry were opened. The opera building was the dream of Samuel Insull, who ran public utilities and transportation companies. The museum was the dream of Sears executive Julius Rosenwald, who

The John G. Shedd Aquarium in Grant Park just southeast of downtown
Stadler photo postcard, Torry Bruno Collection

Aquatic tanks in one of six galleries at the aquarium
Stadler photo postcard, Torry Bruno Collection

Matchbook from the Playhouse Cafe

Dr. H. A. Jacobson teaches first aid during lifeguard training in Jackson Park in 1935.
Chicago Park District Special Collections

He wrote: "I have returned with a stronger determination to plunge into the fight and never to rest until our people shall receive the same treatment that I, a foreigner, received in the white man's country — that treatment a white foreigner receives in America, the land of my birth."

The stock market crash and ensuing Depression had a devastating effect in Chicago, the manufacturing center of the nation. At the beginning of 1930, there were 337 banks in Cook County but 18 months later there were only 197. A run on banks in June 1932 meant that five downtown banks paid out more than $50 million in three days. Many factories were forced to shut down. The city, on the verge of bankruptcy, did not pay employees, including teachers, for months. The unemployment rate reached 50 percent. Many men lived in cardboard boxes along Lower Wacker Drive.

The Depression also created an arrested infancy in suburbs such as Skokie. Lots were measured, sewers sunk and roads paved. But then the economy went bad, and hardly any homes were built until the 40s. More than 30,000 lots remained vacant for almost two decades.

Biplanes buzz Chicago. This view was taken from the steps of the Field Museum in Grant Park looking north at the Chicago skyline around 1930. *Keystone View stereograph, Torry Bruno collection*

For the first several years of the Depression, private organizations handled relief programs, but as hard times held on, the federal government established public relief programs. By 1938 about 200,000 Chicago residents were on some sort of government dole and 100,000 people worked for the Works Progress Administration, Franklin Roosevelt's public works program. New Deal projects did provide Chicagoans with jobs and benefits, but it was the start of World War II in Europe that stoked the manufacturing plants of the city and pulled the city from economic chaos.

Wacker Drive and the Chicago River

The Humboldt Park circus in 1936 was held in the park's bicycle bowl, which was demolished in the early 1960s.
Chicago Park District Special Collections

The Municipal Airport, founded as a cinder runway in 1923, is now called Chicago Midway Airport.

City parks, too, fell on hard times during the Depression. In 1934 the South Park Commission, West Park Commission, Lincoln Park Commission and 19 additional commissions consolidated in order to become eligible for more federal money. The new system, renamed the Chicago Park District, was able to secure funds from the Works Progress Administration. More than $100 million was spent to improve parks from 1934 to 1941. The North Avenue Beach House (replaced in 1999), the Zoo Rookery and Promontory Point field house were built during those years. In 1935 the Grant Park concert series started.

The 1930s was a time for heroes and scoundrels. Jane Addams was awarded the Nobel Peace Prize. Alfred "Jake" Lingle, a *Tribune* reporter, was killed by gangsters and buried with full honors in a giant public funeral. A few days later, it was revealed that Lingle was a gangster himself, a double-agent who provided a liaison between city and underworld officials. Samuel Insull, who owned and ran Chicago's electric power company, gasworks and elevated trains, lost his fortune in the stock market crash and had to flee town in front of criminal charges. Insull was later acquitted, but died in disgrace.

Depression or not, 1930 saw the construction of the Merchandise Mart, the world's largest commercial building. At a cost of $32 million, Marshall Field & Co. built it, then sold it in 1945 to the Kennedy family, which held onto it until 1998.

The Adler Planetarium was dedicated in 1930 and the Shedd Aquarium was opened. The Board of Trade

Lake Shore Drive at North Avenue connects the city's parks and beaches.

Building, topped by the statue of
the goddess of agriculture, Ceres,
was opened, too. Most of these
buildings were funded by pre-
Depression money; new development was at an absolute standstill.
Author Anne O'Hare McCormick,
noting the contrast between
Depression and boom times,
wrote: "Chicago is the ideal location for dancing on top of a vol-
cano. Eruptive and exciting, a city
of superlatives. It exaggerates all
the splendor and squalor in
America."

On February 15, 1933, Chicago
Mayor Anton Cermak was fatally
shot in Miami by an assassin appar-
ently aiming for President Roosevelt.
"I'm glad it was me instead of you,"
Cermak was supposed to have said.

It was a most gracious statement
since Cermak and Roosevelt seldom
saw eye to eye. Cermak died weeks
later. His replacement, Mayor
Edward J. Kelly, and his adviser, Pat
Nash, built the Democratic
machine that would dominate
Chicago for decades.

Flush with federal money from
Roosevelt's New Deal, the new
organization doled out jobs for
loyalty. Kelly got 75 percent of the
vote in the 1935 special election and
only five Republicans remained in
the council.

The death of Thomas Dorsey's
wife and child led the blues pianist
to abandon honky-tonk music in
1932. Just a month after his wife
died in childbirth, he penned the
classic gospel song "Take My Hand,

194

Official World's Fair poster designed by George B. Patton

A railroad poster promotes the second year of Chicago's World's Fair.

Precious Lord." Dorsey, a performer, first took the gospel sound to Pilgrim Baptist Church at 33rd and Indiana, then created a national gospel organization and music publishing company. He is considered the father of gospel music.

In the midst of hard times, Chicago held a party. The year 1933 was the city's 100th anniversary and leaders

An envelope illustration welcomes visitors to Chicago in 1933.

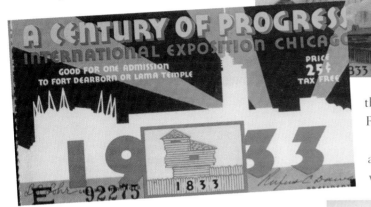

A Century of Progress ticket

the new cars, the new architecture — and Sally Rand, playing peek-a-boo with a pair of ostrich fans.

Sally Rand was never a strip teaser. She never took anything off. She started her six-minute dance wearing nothing... and ended in the same state of

decided to show the world that Chicago was not a cow town or a gangster city of sin, so they created A Century of Progress, a showcase of science and industry. It was a wonderland on the lake to dazzle the eye. General Motors, Westinghouse and Chrysler all signed on. This was to be Chicago's coming out party as a sophisticated grand metropolis. A Century of Progress Exposition, which ran in 1933 and 1934, drew 39 million visitors in its first year to a landfill site along the lakefront that featured a sky ride and other modern attractions. The main point of the fair was to bring attention to progress in business and science, but the center of attention was fan dancer Sally Rand, a failed silent-screen actress who crashed a $100-a-plate opening night benefit party. Born Helen Gould Beck, she took the name Sally because it was short and looked good on a theater marquee and the name Rand from a Rand McNally atlas.

Riding a horse painted white for photographers, she arrived at the main gate of A Century of Progress as Lady Godiva. She was denied entrance because no animals were allowed.

She retreated downtown, bought out a tourist boat at the foot of the Wrigley Building and returned. Looking sure of herself, she was granted admission — and the fair would never be the same.

Sally Rand and her risque fan dance became a major attraction of the fair. People came from Ethiopia to see

Sinclair Oil company advertisement from A Century of Progress

CHICAGO WORLD'S FAIR EDITION

CIRCULATION 2,350,000 **BIG NEWS** SECOND EDITION

Published by Sinclair Refining Company (Inc.), 45 Nassau Street, New York, N.Y.

MILLIONS SEE WEIRD SINCLAIR DINOSAURS

Story on Page 2.

NRA MEMBER
U.S.
WE DO OUR PART

CROWDS NEVER TIRE watching the life-like motions of the roaring dinosaurs that feature Sinclair's exhibit at the World's Fair. In the picture above, an interested group of visitors is looking over three of the strange monsters that roamed the earth millions of years ago. Brontosaurus, who bulked forty tons in life, is recreated seventy feet long. He appears at the top of the photo. Below, cooling himself in a pool, is a Duck-Billed Dinosaur known as a Trachodon, or Rough-Tooth. To the right is a Triceratops or Three-Horned Face. Sinclair has built these life-sized monsters to impress on your mind the vast age of the crude oils used in refining Sinclair Opaline and Sinclair Pennsylvania Motor Oils. It is a generally accepted fact that, by and large, the oldest crude oils make the finest lubricants.

HAVOLINE THERMOMETER *Century of Progress International Exposition* CHICAGO 1933

(Far right)
A brochure for
Sky-Ride Towers and
Ride, one of the
fair's most exciting
attractions

"World's largest
thermometer" at
A Century of Progress

A poster promotes
the racy, popular
A Night in Paris at
the world's fair.

undress. She would use her fans to cover what needed to be covered. "The Rand is faster than the eye," she always maintained.

The Rand was arrested several times for public indecency during A Century of Progress. Fair officials publicly decried the act. But every arrest resulted in more publicity — and, off the record, fair officials realized that the show must go on. Sally Rand, the star of the Streets of Paris and the Italian Village, became the main draw of the fair.

By the end of 1934, when the "Lost City of the Depression" was finally

closed, Rand was making $1,000 a day. She would appear several times at the Chicago Theatre, ferried by water taxi to A Century of Progress. She did a nightclub act and, as she joked, appeared just about every morning at 10 a.m. in court.

Her ostrich feathers became an unofficial symbol of A Century of Progress. She eventually donated the plumes to the Chicago Historical Society. "They can have my fans," she said, "but not my fanny."

In 1934 bank robber John Dillinger, labeled "Public Enemy No. 1," was gunned down by FBI agents outside the Biograph Theater on

North Lincoln Avenue. He was watching the film *Manhattan Melodrama* with two women. One of his molls — the "woman in red" — had told police where he would be. Two years later, Machine Gun Jack McGurn, suspect in the St. Valentine's Day Massacre, was shot in a bowling alley. It was the last of the grand gangland shootings and marked the end of the era.

By the mid-1930s Chicago was showing signs of economic recovery. Jobs returned, and the city regained its title as the nation's manufacturing hub.

"Four years ago I came to a Chicago fighting with its back to the wall," said President Roosevelt in a 1936 speech. "Factories closed, markets silent, banks shaky, ships and trains empty. Today those factories sing the song of industry — markets hum with bustling movement. Banks are secure; ships and trains are running full. Once again it is Chicago as Carl Sandburg saw it. The City of Big Shoulders. The city that smiles and, with Chicago, a whole nation that had not been cheerful for years is full of cheer once more."

Chicago's second-largest minority population in the century, Mexican-Americans, came because jobs in

Mexican folk dancers at a festival in Burnham Park in 1936
Chicago Park District Special Collections

Chicago were plentiful and work in Mexico was scarce. Many worked on the railroads, in steel mills and meatpacking houses, so they settled on the South Side in neighborhoods such as the Back of the Yards and South Chicago. Most of their neighborhoods centered around Roman Catholic churches, which kept alive the language and culture of the homeland. About 1,000 Mexicans lived in the city.

By 1930 Chicago was the fourth most popular destination for Mexicans as the population reached more than

Lake Shore Drive and Chicago in 1936
Chicago Park District Special Collections

Postcard showing the corner of State and Madison streets

Postcard of Lincoln Park Drive and Grant Monument

25,000. That figure dwindled during the Depression. As unemployment soared, many Mexican laborers were forced to return to Mexico.

More work in Chicago meant labor strife. In keeping with its Haymarket tradition, the city continued to be ground zero for labor disputes. By 1937 the CIO had

unionized steelworkers in three of the four largest plants in the area. The Republic Steel plant on the South Side remained open in defiance of a steelworkers union strike in 1937, and a clash between strikers and police outside the plant escalated into tragedy. On May 30, four days after the strike began, strikers marched toward the main gate and began throwing bricks at police officers guarding the plant. The officers charged and shots rang out.

On that Memorial Day 10 strikers were killed and 90 people (including 35 police officers) were injured. The police claimed that the strikers had fired first, but none of the police suffered bullet wounds. A congressional investigation concluded that the police had used excessive force. The strike fizzled, but the union eventually won a new contract.

These were difficult times. In 1929 Robert Abbott branched out to magazines as he published *Abbott's Monthly*, the first major African-American magazine in the nation. The stock market crash and Depression hit him and Black Metropolis hard. The *Defender's* circulation dropped and Abbott folded his magazine. The publisher was forced to sink his fortune into the paper to keep it going.

The Depression also struck Chicago's black community with great impact. African-Americans were restricted to neighborhoods where they could buy or rent and limited in the jobs and political posts they could hold. The stone homes that lined the South Side streets were divided into kitchenettes, two or three rooms each with a tiny cooking facility. By 1935, more than 30 percent of Chicago African-Americans were on relief, and the figure was rising. Cotton crops failed and a new river of migration flowed to Chicago during the 1930s. Abbott, seeing Northern cities crowded with African-Americans, tried to stop the flow — but it was too late. His pleas were ignored. By 1940, 234,000 African-Americans overcrowded Black Metropolis and other similiar communities in Chicago.

Abbott died in his sleep on February 29, 1940, at the age of 72. His death was briefly noted in the major Chicago dailies. His impact on the city was enormous.

Chicago played its role as a hub city during World War II. It was a major production center and a major training center. It was the crossroads of the nation's war effort.

Soon after Japan's attack on Pearl Harbor on December 7, 1941, Chicago transformed itself. Time became compressed; men and women fell in love faster, children grew up quicker, more people took jobs, employees worked longer hours and life seemed sweeter for those able to avoid the tragedy of war.

Chicago was a highly organized Civil Defense District. Air raid wardens arranged blocks and neighborhoods. Gas masks became a domestic staple. By late 1942 companies in Chicago got their first major defense contracts. With men in service, the workweek swelled by 1943 to 48 hours. Many teen-agers quit high school to take jobs. By the end of the year, 130,000 women were part of the labor force. By the end of 1944,

300,000 women were at work. Rosie the Riveter had arrived.

World War II sparked a second great wave of Mexican immigration. Many Mexicans came to work on contracts in the defense industry.

The Chicago Ordinance District — a huge area centered in the city — was a major producer of war goods as companies switched to war production. Electronic companies started making telephones and radios.

The more enduring Chicago companies played large parts: Motorola built the walkie-talkies used by ground troops, and Elgin National Watch Co. manufactured time fuses used in anti-aircraft shells. Dodge-Chicago fabricated airplane engines for the B-29 "Superfortress" and

Decal showing fund-raising effort at Harrison High School

Civil defense poster by artist Samuel Greenburg

Goss Printing constructed anti-air-craft guns. Abbott Laboratories made penicillin, which was used by the military during the war and then came into general use after the war ended, and Kraft Foods prepared military rations, such as American cheddar in a can.

Thousands of Navy recruits trained at the Great Lakes Naval Training Center in nearby North Chicago, the largest facility of its kind in the country. Fort Sheridan, which was established as an army base along the North Shore of Lake Michigan soon after the 1886 Haymarket Riot, was a huge induction center. More than 400,000 soldiers passed through its gates near suburban Highwood.

Chicago became known as "Little Washington" because of the huge bureaucracy set up there. The Stevens Hotel, largest in the world, became the home of a radio school for the U.S. Army Air Forces. All 3,000 rooms were used by soldiers, as were rooms from nearby hotels. The Auditorium Theater was turned into a giant bowling alley for the use of the troops. Lake Michigan steamers were refitted as aircraft carriers with oversize decks so that aviators could practice their skills before being shipped out.

In 1942 flier Edward "Butch" O'Hare became a war hero by shooting down five Japanese planes. He was

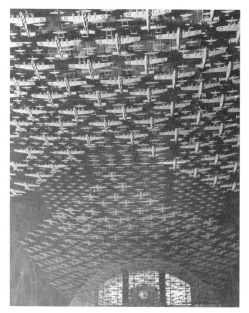

killed the next year, and a Chicago airport was later named in his honor.

At 3:25 p.m. on December 2, 1942, a team of 40 scientists led by Italian physicist Enrico Fermi achieved the first controlled nuclear chain reaction. Fermi had come to Chicago in February of that year. The secret experiment took place under the west grandstand at Stagg Field on the University of Chicago campus. The team did not produce the bomb, but proved Albert Einstein's theory that an atomic reaction is self-sustaining. That proof changed the course of the war, and the course of history.

Life in general focused on the war. Gas and food rationing began and aluminum was collected for recycling at Michigan Avenue and Congress Parkway. Victory Gardens were planted. But not all was war. Pizzeria Uno, the birthplace of deep-dish pizza, opened at Ohio Street and Wabash Avenue on the Near North Side. The city's first subway, under State Street, was completed. Work had begun in late 1938 and proved to be especially difficult and dangerous since the tunnel was built underground in soft clay. Amazingly no cave-ins ever occurred, and the first subway opened on October 17, 1943.

World War II, like World War I, turned the city into a magnet for many ethnic groups, attracting African-Americans up north to fill the ranks of the working class.

About 65,000 African-Americans moved to Chicago during the war years. They were joined in factories by Mexican-Americans, who were recruited to replace white workers in meatpacking, steel and railroad jobs during the war. The war, thus, helped define the postwar city.

On the evening of August 14, 1945, Chicago residents filled the Loop to celebrate the end of the war. About 22,000 soldiers and sailors from Illinois were killed in the war, but this night was for celebration. An estimated 1 million people jammed State, Clark and Dearborn streets to revel after the official word that the war in the Pacific was over. The city would transform again — making the switch from war to peace. But true to its tradition, Chicago was poised for the future.

"Furlough's End"
by Samuel Greenburg, c.1943

Epilogue

Chicago, the city that transformed itself following the 1871 fire, has been re-creating itself throughout the past half-century. The city has softened its rough edges and taken on the luster of a world-class city. In true Chicago tradition, the changes have not happened without determination and defeat and a great deal of hard work.

The 40-story Prudential Building, just east of the Loop, was dedicated in 1955 with an emotional ceremony. The occasion marked, in many ways, the end of the Depression in Chicago. The Prudential was the first skyscraper planned and built after the 1929 stock market crash. Its completion showed a reborn confidence in the center of the city.

The Prudential, once the pride of Chicago, is now dwarfed by a downtown skyline of taller buildings. Dozens of skyscrapers have been built — including the 100-story John Hancock Center in 1969, the 82-story Amoco Building in 1973, and the 110-story Sears Tower in 1974. These and other buildings have created one of the great skylines of the world and an architectural mecca that stretches back to the 1870s.

Much has changed in Chicago since the end of World War II. The world's busiest airport replaced the nation's busiest railroad center. O'Hare Airport, along with Midway Airport and Miegs Field, extend Chicago's tradition as the nation's transportation hub.

Neighborhoods have improved, declined and been improved again. The great migration from the city to the suburbs, so common in many cities, has slowed. Now people are returning to Chicago proper, to be close to work or entertainment. Chicago's population peaked at about 3.7 million during the early 1950s. The next census is expected to put the city's population at less than 3 million, but the metropolitan area grows, both in size and population. The close-in suburbs have been ringed by newer, outlying suburban communities. Chicagoland should top out at nearly 9 million residents in 2000.

Of course, no one single event has defined Chicago in the past 55 years like the Great Fire defined the city. But many events have become seared into the consciousness of Chicagoans. In 1958 fire swept through Our Lady Of Angels School, a Catholic school on the West Side, killing 92 children and three nuns. In 1967, Chicago's great convention center, McCormick Place, burned to the ground. It has since been replaced by much larger facilities.

Perhaps the strangest event was the man-made flood of Chicago's underground freight tunnel system. The system, a series of more than 50 miles of tunnels connecting major buildings in the downtown area, had been largely abandoned since 1959. In April 1992 a construction crew working on the Chicago River drove a piling through the side of one of the tunnels. About 250 million gallons of water poured into the system, flooding the sub-basements in dozens of buildings and causing millions of dollars of damage. It took more than five weeks to pump out the water.

Many of the problems that plagued Chicago for a century persist today. The city still struggles to live down its gangster past — even though Al Capone died in the 1940s. Hoodlums of the gangster era have been replaced by street gangs. Boodling, the term once used for political corruption, has been replaced by clout. Chicago's colorful power brokers, "Bathhouse" John Coughlin and Michael "Hinky Dink" Kenna, are long gone. But politics is still the most competitive, colorful game in town. And it's a game that can — and has — landed some of its players in jail. Aldermen, city and court officials by the dozens have seen the inside of prison as a result of federal investigations such as Operation Greylord, Operation Silver Shovel and several other major investigations.

NEW CHALLENGES FOR THE CITY

In 1987 then-U.S. Education Secretary William Bennett declared Chicago's school system the worst in the nation. The city responded with a bold experiment in decentralized control that put local school councils comprised of parents, school staff and community members in charge at each of the city's more than 500 elementary and high schools. In the mid-1990s, the Illinois legislature took reform one step further by putting responsibility for the schools squarely on the shoulders of Chicago's chief executive. Mayor Richard M. Daley quickly appointed a new school board and executive team that has recentralized much control over school curricula, budgets and standards. Student test scores are improving.

The city's public housing system, hailed during the 1950s as the nation's most beneficent, is in shambles.

Chicago was one of the cities that led the way in the construction of public housing high-rises after World War II. Some said it was an effort to house the city's poor. Others believed it also was a way of isolating African Americans. High-rise housing for the poor proved to be a bust; and the city is now trying to reverse decades of institutional failure. The Chicago Housing Authority is undergoing a transformation that includes the multi-million-dollar demolition of many of its high-rise structures and the renovation of others.

As with schools and housing, Chicago has had its share of controversy over race and ethnic differences. Dr. Martin Luther King Jr. came to Chicago a number of times during the 1960s to lead marches promoting civil rights and fair housing. Following King's assassination in 1968, riots and looting erupted on Chicago's West Side and elsewhere. Later that year, Chicago hosted the 1968 Democratic National Convention that put clashes between anti-war and other demonstrators on nightly newscasts around the country. It has taken decades to recover from those images. In 1996 the city hosted a highly successful — and uneventful — Democratic Convention. All apparently is forgiven, or forgotten.

The years since World War II have been filled with challenges and triumphs.

THE CHANGING CITY

The stockyards and most of the steel mills have been closed and huge manufacturing facilities have shut down, but high-tech jobs have replaced blue-collar jobs. The Chicago metropolitan area is now known as the Silicon Prairie.

Red-brick factories are turning into expensive lofts. New row houses and three flats are changing the look and feel of neighborhoods, attracting suburbanites to move to the city. Navy Pier was razed and built anew, decked out with restaurants, a Shakespeare theater and arcade shops. Showplaces such as the Auditorium, Oriental and

Chicago theaters have been restored in an attempt to re-create the once-thriving downtown theater district. The University of Illinois at Chicago has been growing steadily since first established in 1946.

North Michigan Avenue has evolved into its nickname, The Magnificent Mile, alive with some of the fanciest stores in the nation, glitzy restaurants and movie houses. State Street, which was almost destroyed by a pedestrian mall, is on the rebound as a retail center, and is slowly being re-created with cultural and educational institutions.

Downtown Chicago became something of a 20th-century sculpture capital when a giant untitled Pablo Picasso statue was unveiled in the Civic Center Plaza in 1967. It has been joined by Alexander Calder's "Flamingo," Marc Chagall's "The Four Seasons," Claes Oldenburg's "Batcolumn," Joan Miro's "Chicago" and

Congress Parkway viaduct and plaza reconstruction
Photo by Hedrich-Blessing and DLK Architecture

Jean Dubuffet's "Monument with Standing Beast." City leaders have mandated that public art is an important part of Chicago's fabric. And now the city is building a park of the future, Millennium Park, east of Michigan Avenue, which will be dominated by a giant band shell designed by renowned architect Frank O. Gehry.

Many museums have a new vitality. The Museum of Science and Industry, Adler Planetarium, John G. Shedd Aquarium, and Art Institute of Chicago have all been greatly expanded in recent years. The Museum of Contemporary Art's large new facility resulted from an international design competition. The Peggy Notebaert Nature Museum opened last year in Lincoln Park several miles north of downtown. Smaller, specialty museums add their own charm and expertise to Chicago's cultural vista. They include the Oriental Institute Museum, the DuSable Museum of African American History, Terra Museum of American Art and the Mexican Fine Arts Museum to name a few.

The south end of the Loop has become a center for finance. The city's great trading centers — Chicago Board of Trade and Chicago Mercantile Exchange — keep flourishing, marking the city as the financial hub of the Midwest. They were joined in 1973 by the Chicago Board Options Exchange, where traders exchange stock and other options.

MAKING CONNECTIONS

The Chicago region, always known as a transportation focal point, is now connected by a series of interstate highways that make it easy to travel from the eastern edge of the metropolitan region in Indiana to the northern edge in Wisconsin.

The Congress Expressway, now called the Eisenhower, opened in 1956 and the Northwest Expressway, now called the Kennedy, opened in 1960. The Dan Ryan Expressway opened in 1962 and the Southwest Expressway, renamed the Stevenson, opened in 1964. Along the lakefront, one of America's most beautiful driving roads, Lake Shore Drive, was straightened in parts and streamlined during the 1980s and 1990s in an attempt to achieve better traffic flow and to create a museum campus south of the Loop.

The Chicago Transit Authority, formed soon after the war, coordinates bus and rapid transportation in the city. Subway lines, built during the World War II, are the focal point of the system. A rapid transit line was extended to O'Hare Airport in 1980s and a line was extended to Midway Airport in 1990s.

CHICAGO LEADERS

Jane Byrne was elected the city's first woman mayor in 1979 and Harold Washington was chosen the first African-American mayor in 1983. In 1992, Carol Moseley-Braun became the first woman African-American U.S. Senator.

Mayor Richard J. Daley, elected first in 1955, led Chicago for 21 years. He ran a Democratic machine controlling 30,000 patronage jobs and was a master of obtaining and spending billions of dollars of federal dollars. His son, Richard M. Daley, became mayor in 1989 and was reelected in 1991, 1995 and 1999. He has beautified the city and created a sense of confidence in the business community. He has served during a great economic boom time.

The elder Daley died after a heart attack in December of 1976. His replacement, Michael Bilandic, was defeated by Jane Byrne when Bilandic was unable to keep city streets cleared during a succession of heavy snow storms in the winter of 1978-79. Byrne's leadership, which included years of political turmoil, ended after one term. She was defeated in the 1983 Democratic primary by Harold Washington, who went on to win office. Washington consolidated power during his first term and won re-election in 1987. But late that year, he, too, died of a heart attack.

TRADITION AND PROMISE

Chicago still smarts from its Second City reputation (a name bestowed on it during the 1950s by *New Yorker* writer A.J. Liebling) in part because it boasts such first-rate residents. Writers Gwendolyn Brooks, Studs Terkel and Saul Bellow rack up Pulitzers and Nobel prizes, but few seem to acknowledge Chicago's place in the literary world. Two of the most influential magazines started at mid-century, John H. Johnson's *Ebony* and Hugh Hefner's *Playboy* are still published here. Scientists and economists from the University of Chicago win Nobel prizes at an amazing rate and the city's cultural world is alive. Prominent cultural organizations such as the Chicago Symphony Orchestra, the Lyric Opera of Chicago and Steppenwolf Theatre as well as stars such as Oprah Winfrey and Michael Jordan continue to attract attention and add shine to the city's image. Chicago's Second City, a comedy club established in 1959, has influenced the nation's comedy scene for decades and Chess Records, the early home of rocker Chuck Berry, influenced the music scene.

From the Bulls to the Bears, Chicago is known for its sports teams. Win or lose, they transfix the city. In the spring and summer, Chicago is a Cubs or White Sox town. In the fall it's the Bears and in the winter it's the Black Hawks and Bulls. Ernie Banks ruled Chicago in the 1950s and 60s; Walter Payton in the 70s and Michael Jordan in the 80s and 90s. No team dominated sports during the past decade like the Bulls, who brought home six National Basketball Association championships. And no team has been so dominated as the Cubs, who have not won a pennant since 1945. New stadiums — the United Center and Comiskey Park — have been built during the past generation, but fans still cling to the wonderful, old Wrigley Field. And they cling to Chicago traditions.

Despite all the changes, Chicago retains a reputation for its Midwestern friendliness. It has a rich history and great potential. It's the City that Works.

Buckingham Fountain
Harry Weese Associates

Chicago Today Portfolio

So much has changed since Jean Baptiste Point duSable looked west along this section of the Chicago River. The City in a Garden keeps reaching for the sky while recalling its roots.

Photographs by Churchill & Klehr

Bridges cross the Chicago River.

Gold Coast high-rises cast their shadows on Lake Shore Drive at Oak Street Beach.

Cafe Brauer near the Lincoln Park Lagoon

Chinatown Festival

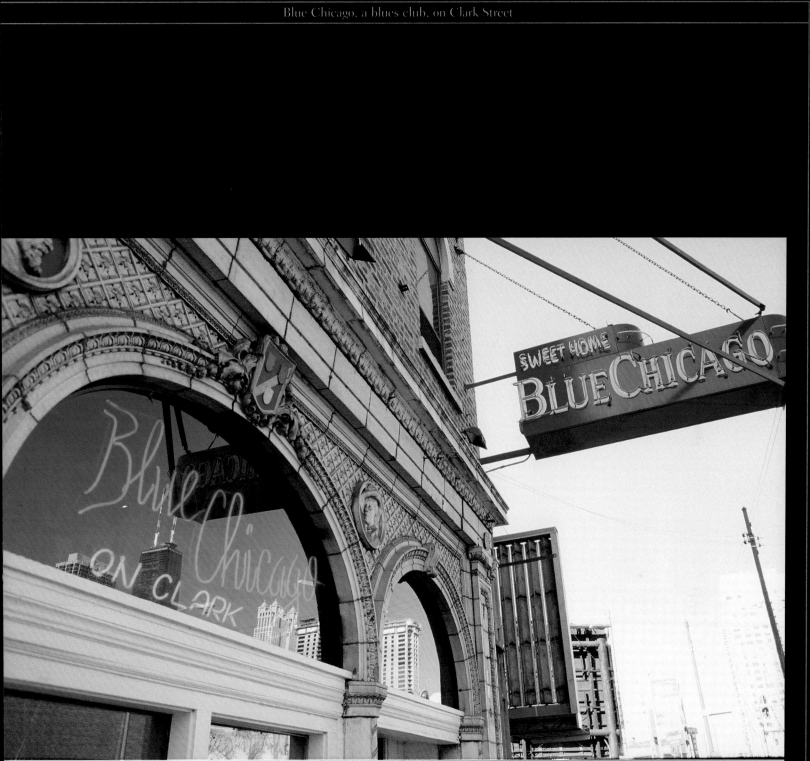

House of Blues Hotel interior

Partners in Chicagoland
Table of Contents

Chicagoland real estate development, management, construction and preservation companies shape tomorrow's skyline, providing and improving working and living space for area residents.

BUILDING A
GREATER CHICAGO

Douglas Elliman-Beitler

J. Paul Beitler serves as chairman of Douglas Elliman-Beitler.

Douglas Elliman-Beitler developed 181 W. Madison in 1989. Today the building serves as the firm's headquarters.

Through its innovative developments and unrivaled property management practices, Douglas Elliman-Beitler Inc. has helped shape the Chicago skyline into one of the city's grandest attributes. The multitude of real estate services offered by the firm has enhanced the city's facade and the performance of existing, integral structures, thus creating properties that allow companies to work in environments that are both efficient and pleasurable.

There is one constant found in the properties developed and managed by Douglas Elliman-Beitler — premier tenant service. In each of its buildings, Douglas Elliman-Beitler infuses the latest technological and design aspects to meet each clients' space and energy needs. In addition, Douglas Elliman-Beitler offers amenities that allow clients to focus on their businesses rather than mundane tasks that can siphon away valuable time. The firm pioneered the inclusion of car-service centers, florists, ATMs and clothing service centers in Chicago's professional buildings.

"We learned that services and human contact were an important part of managing a building," says company president and CEO J. Paul Beitler. "The human exchange that we offer is what has set us apart and has put us in the forefront of real estate management. We help shape people's lives."

The success enjoyed by Douglas Elliman-Beitler is indicative of its business philosophy. Since its inception in 1982, the firm has developed more than 8 million square feet of office space in the United States and has

amassed a management portfolio of more than 25 million square feet of office and retail properties. The world, national and regional headquarters of nearly 50 major corporations are housed in buildings managed by the company.

Anyone who takes a walk through downtown will quickly find Douglas Elliman-Beitler's aesthetic contributions. Among these is the 45-story, 1-million-square-foot tower of dual-pane glass known as Madison Plaza, located on the northwest corner of Madison and Wells streets. Kitty-corner to this building stands the 50-story, 1.1-million-square-foot marvel known as 181 W. Madison, which was developed in 1989 and serves as the firm's corporate headquarters. Other developments include the Chicago Bar Association Building in Chicago's South Loop, Oakbrook Terrace and Triangle Plaza, which were built near O'Hare International Airport in 1990.

Douglas Elliman-Beitler is also responsible for the development of Dearborn Center, a sprawling 35-story, all-glass-exterior building scheduled to house mainstream retailers, along with providing prime office and retail space in the heart of the Loop. As Chicago's first building of the 21st century, Dearborn Center is aimed at providing Chicago companies with state-of-the-art capabilities that will maximize workplace productivity.

Douglas Elliman-Beitler provides building management and leasing services that have allowed for significant renovations to structures located in ideal locations throughout Chicago. Millions of dollars have been put forth by the company to re-energize tired structures and to brighten the workdays of Chicagoans who spend their days inside them. For example, the firm uses works of fine art to visually enhance the interior and exterior of each of its properties. The reasoning behind this is so that these works can be enjoyed by numerous workers on a daily basis rather than the limited number of people who would visit an art museum to view the pieces.

Renowned sculptures and paintings have been placed outside of buildings and in lobbies and halls. Featured outside Madison Plaza is artist Louise Nevelson's "Dawn Shadows," a commanding black steel sculpture representative of the building. At the Oakbrook Terrace Tower, Nancy Graves' "Peripetela '88" set the modern tone for the building and Jerry Peart's soaring "Blue Geisha" stands at Triangle Plaza.

"We want to create buildings that are not just places to work, but also that serve as cultural meeting grounds," says Beitler. "We want to make the city not just a working environment, but also a livable one."

Additional services provided by Douglas Elliman-Beitler include construction management, realty advisory and consulting, leasing, property acquisition and disposition, and parking garage, data center and health club management. This breadth of services, combined with the company's satellite offices in 16 states, positions Douglas Elliman-Beitler as an industry leader in the East Coast and Midwestern real estate markets.

A Shared Vision

Douglas Elliman-Beitler is one of the largest property management firms in Illinois and the largest firm in Wisconsin, with regional offices in New York City and Milwaukee. However, this network of services is rooted in modest beginnings. Beitler began his career in real estate as an office leasing broker for Helmsley-Spear in 1974. At that time, Helmsley-Spear was the nation's largest real estate firm. Within his first year at the company, Beitler became the highest-producing broker in the firm's Chicago office.

By 1977 Beitler had joined Arthur Rubloff & Co. as a leasing agent. Given his successful track record at Helmsley-Spear, Beitler was commissioned by Rubloff & Co. to resolve leasing issues for its oldest and least-profitable buildings. Beitler responded to this challenge by completely filling these buildings with profitable tenants in a short period of time. Beitler would go on to become the youngest corporate officer to be elected to Rubloff & Co.'s board of directors in the 50-year history of the company.

It was at Rubloff & Co. that Beitler met Lee Miglin, who was also serving on the board of directors. Miglin had started his real estate career at Rubloff & Co. in the 1950s, and had worked as an industrial broker and developer. Miglin then shifted his focus to office development,

and excelled in this field. Miglin and Beitler shared many ideas as far as architecture and design, and worked cohesively on projects together. The duo's first development project, the Sperry-Univac Plaza, was promptly filled by several large companies and proved to be a success.

As the working relationship between Miglin and Beitler began to meld, Rubloff & Co. underwent dramatic

Douglas Elliman-Beitler utilizes works of art to visually enhance each of its properties. "Blue Geisha" is featured at Triangle Plaza. "Dawn Shadows" is featured at Madison Plaza.

changes. The company shifted its focus from being an entrepreneurial developer to being more of a corporate services company. Rather than follow suit, Beitler and Miglin left the firm in 1982 to start their own company — Miglin-Beitler, Inc.

Miglin and Beitler shared a common goal in their endeavor — to create the highest-quality and highest-profile office buildings possible in Chicago. The first Miglin-Beitler development was Madison Plaza — a sawtooth-shaped skyscraper that features a pearl granite exterior complemented by reflective glass. According to Beitler, the building was a success architecturally and opened well ahead of competing developers' projects. Unfortunately, upon its completion in 1982, the building

The first Miglin-Beitler development was Madison Plaza in 1982.

opened in an economic environment characterized by 20 percent interest rates and a recession. Beitler recalls that for one year, not one company came to look at the building, as none were looking to expand.

As the national economy improved during the Reagan era, companies looking to expand were in need of additional office space. Madison Plaza met that need head on. The Hyatt Corporation was one of the first tenants in the building, and took up a substantial amount of space. Beitler recalls that once Hyatt broke the building's dry spell, other companies soon poured in. Eventually, other large companies such as Hartford Insurance and National Futures Association would become housed in

> "We want to create buildings that are not just places to work, but also that serve as cultural meeting grounds," says Beitler. "We want to make the city not just a working environment, but also a livable one."

Madison Plaza, making it one of the most vibrant buildings in the area.

The success of Madison Plaza gave Miglin-Beitler the incentive to continue its plan of developing high-quality, high-profile buildings in the area. The company's follow-up project was Triangle Plaza, a sprawling twin tower development — each 14 stories — located near O'Hare International Airport. In 1987 the company contributed to suburban expansion with the development of the Oakbrook Terrace Tower. Upon completion, the 31-story, 700,000-square-foot structure served as the tallest building between Chicago and the Mississippi River. These projects pioneered the development of much-needed office space outside the city and assisted in bringing other developments to the area.

BIGGER AND BETTER

During its inaugural years, Miglin-Beitler expanded its services by acquiring management responsibilities in prominent buildings throughout the city, including the Florsheim Tower on LaSalle Street. Upon assuming these responsibilities, the company put to work its team of management professionals to evaluate and upgrade each building's operations, and garnered feedback from clients as to how to improve management services. This attention to detail allowed the firm to continually expand its management portfolio, and the company has earned several industry awards for its services.

The development of 181 W. Madison proved to be Miglin-Beitler's biggest development project yet, and maintains a lasting impression on the cityscape. Both

Miglin and Beitler wanted to create a building with a stone exterior that had a majestic vertical appearance. The building would have to be light in appearance, so not to appear too gothic, and would exude an ethereal quality amongst some of its dank surroundings.

In 1989, construction of 181 W. Madison was completed, and the building opened to great success. Law firms, stock brokerage firms and several other companies, including the neighboring Northern Trust Company, sought space in the building. For the first time in Miglin-Beitler's history, 40 percent of the building was leased prior to opening, and the majority of that space was not being occupied by the building's owner.

On the heels of 181 W. Madison came the development of the Chicago Bar Association Building in 1990. This 16-story, 105,000-square-foot building was a welcome addition to Chicago's South Loop area, which was lagging in development at that time. With each of Miglin-Beitler's new developments came a greater standing in the industry. The company's reputation for its high level of service became well known, and this attributed to a number of new management responsibilities.

In 1990 the company responded to this growth by launching its greatest endeavor yet. The proposed Miglin-Beitler Tower was to be erected at the southwest corner of Madison and Wells, allowing the company's developments to dominate the intersection. Three of the four corners at the intersection of Madison and Wells streets were set to be occupied by Miglin-Beitler structures — Madison Plaza, 181 W. Madison and the Miglin-Beitler Tower. The tower, at an estimated cost of $400 million, would have weighed in at 125 stories and 1,999 feet tall. Miglin-Beitler had an architect, designer and contractors ready to proceed on the project, along with foundation and zoning permits from the city. However, ground was never broken at the site.

A SERIES OF SETBACKS

When the United States launched Operation Desert Storm and entered the Persian Gulf War with Iraq, the U.S. real estate market crashed. Property values dropped at an alarming rate and international investors turned their backs on the Miglin-Beitler Tower project, killing it completely.

This was the first of several changes for Miglin-Beitler in the 1990s. Subsequently, numerous properties developed and managed by Miglin-Beitler were strategically sold to real estate investment trust companies in the mid-1990s. These properties were actively sought by trust companies because they offered the greatest opportunity for investment appreciation.

A devastating loss for Beitler and the company occurred in May 1997, when Lee Miglin fell victim to the high-profile killing spree of a serial murderer. The absence of Miglin put a strain on the company that was compounded by the announcement by the Miglin estate that Miglin's share would be put on the auction block and sold to the highest bidder. Adding to this turmoil, Beitler's mother passed away unexpectedly a month later.

With the firm's financial stability — and ultimately, its future — in question, a mass exodus occurred within the company. Forty percent of the staff departed within a three-month period. Despite his personal and professional losses, Beitler set out to salvage his company.

THE COMEBACK COMPANY

One of the first steps Beitler took in revitalizing the real estate firm was identifying and securing a new partner. In 1998, Howard Milstein, a prominent New York City investor and businessman, became Beitler's partner after he purchased the Miglin estate stock. Milstein serves as the chairman of the New York-based real estate firm Douglas Elliman-Commercial, and has substantial interests in banking, insurance, real estate and sports franchises. The partnership led to the formation of Douglas Elliman-Beitler, and allowed for the company to be present in eight states.

The joining of these two parties brought the firm back to life, with Beitler serving as chairman. Upon this new foundation, Beitler began to rebuild the firm's

Triangle Plaza, a twin-tower development, is located near O'Hare International Airport.

management and leasing team. He used this opportunity to set into action a new work strategy that would recapture and exceed the successes enjoyed by Miglin-Beitler. First, Beitler set out to acquire commercial office properties ripe for redevelopment and repositioning. Second, he set out to acquire high-profile vacant land sites in the city and suburbs.

One of Douglas Elliman-Beitler's first orders of business in 1998 was the acquisition of five buildings — 360 N. Michigan Ave., 1 N. LaSalle St., 1 N. Dearborn St., 6 N. Michigan Ave. and 59 E. Van Buren St. — from Beitler's former employer, Helmsley-Spear. While seeking to acquire these properties, the collapse of the Russian ruble weakened capital and financial markets and hampered the securing of investor funds for real estate purchases. In spite of this dilemma, Beitler relied on his financial and entrepreneurial skills to close on the single largest portfolio of assets ever acquired in Chicago — at a cost in excess of $200 million.

A $60 million renovation plan has been initiated by Douglas Elliman-Beitler to ensure quality office and retail space at these sites. The work is expected to be completed by mid-2000. Other recent acquisitions include the property at Monroe Street and Wacker Drive on the city's West Side, and the last large development opportunity remaining in Northbrook, known as Techny Property. A 40-acre office campus is planned for this site.

Today, Douglas Elliman-Beitler also provides property management services for Firstar Corporate Real Estate. When first commissioned by Firstar to provide facility management and leasing/disposition services, Firstar's portfolio consisted of some 110 locations. Douglas Elliman-Beitler's innovative management approach has earned it the right to manage Firstar's current banking and real estate portfolio of approximately 1,200 locations. In addition, the firm has been awarded the contract to provide property management services for the entire Firstar real estate portfolio.

Douglas Elliman-Beitler offers its services to Firstar through a property management network throughout the Midwest. This network consists of 25 property management offices, each staffed with a real estate manager and property administrator. This, combined with a standardized computer system, allows Douglas Elliman-Beitler to work cohesively with Firstar to offer complete accounting and facility management services.

The tireless efforts put forth by Beitler since the formation of Douglas Elliman-Beitler have paid off

Upon completion, Oakbrook Terrace Tower was the tallest building between Chicago and the Mississippi River.

considerably. The company's asset and management portfolio has grown from under 9 million square feet to more than 25 million square feet. In addition, the company has nearly doubled in personnel — from April 1998 to present, the staff has grown from 165 people to more than 300.

The work accomplished by Douglas Elliman-Beitler has also left a lasting impression on Chicago and the businesses that call this city home. As a testimony to the firm's achievements, the firm has received numerous industry awards. Within the last 10 years alone, the *Chicago Sun-Times* has heralded the company as Property Management Company of the Year, Developer of the Year and Building Representative of the Year. The company has also earned two Real Estate Achiever of the Year awards from Metro Chicago Real Estate, and an award of excellence for 181 W. Madison by the National Association of Industrial and Office Parks.

The clientele serviced by Douglas Elliman-Beitler and housed in its buildings is just as impressive as its accolades. The firm has managed more than $30 million at capital improvements at the Richard J. Daley Center, the 31-story public use office facility that serves as the city's main courthouse. Other clients include the Chicago Bar Association, CIGNA, IBM, John Marshall Law School and the Wisconsin Department of Transportation.

Further contributing to Douglas Elliman-Beitler's networking capabilities and clientele list is Beitler's and the firm's involvement with several prominent civic, cultural and business institutions. Beitler serves on the board of directors for the Chicago Development Council and the State Street Council, and as an advisory board member for Northwestern University's J.L. Kellogg Graduate School of Management for Real Estate Research and the Chicago Urban League's Affirmative Action Division Advisory Committee. Other organization affiliations maintained by Douglas Elliman-Beitler personnel include the Commercial Real Estate Organization, the Building Owner's and Manager's Association and the Christian Businessmen of Chicago.

FUTURE GROWTH

The goal of Douglas Elliman-Beitler is to become a national, full-service real estate service company specializing in commercial leasing, management, development and corporate services. The steps taken by Beitler within the past few years have ensured the company will meet

Douglas Elliman-Beitler's attention to detail has allowed the firm to continually expand its management portfolio. The lobby of Oakbrook Terrace Tower (pictured).

and surpass that goal. The company's regional offices and properties have already secured the firm's position as one of the most prominent in the Midwest.

As Douglas Elliman-Beitler heads into the future, it will continue to make strategic acquisitions of existing properties and move forward with new development opportunities. To ensure the success of each future undertaking, Beitler has instilled a set of seven principles for the company to follow. This simple yet profound set of tenets urges the firm to strive for: quality of product; quality of service; constant innovation; participation by everyone involved; attracting and motivating the best; being the best; and winning.

Beitler says his company will continue to grow in its market and put its development skills to work in markets across the United States. In addition, Douglas Elliman-Beitler will be utilizing the Internet to allow people throughout the world the ability to view the exterior and interior of its structures and read about its unique approach to property management.

"Management is more than just paying bills," says Beitler. "We want to make life convenient and special for the people in each of our buildings."

TrizecHahn
Office Properties

When TrizecHahn purchased the Sears Tower in 1997, it gave notice to the world of commercial office property that it would carry on the tradition of investing in great buildings made famous nowhere more than in Chicago. But TrizecHahn's involvement in this most architecturally historic city only begins with the Sears Tower; there is much more to the company and to the people behind it than this single monument can attest. The people of TrizecHahn have chosen Chicago as the center of their commercial office property enterprise, locating their corporate headquarters in the Sears Tower. From there, TrizecHahn — one of the largest publicly

traded owners of real estate in the Northern Hemisphere — fulfills its promise of cultivating great properties in significant locales the world over.

The rebuilding of Chicago after the Great Fire of 1871 set in motion an architectural rally that spread across the country, with an influence that has continued to this day. At TrizecHahn, this tradition was molded out of the merger of the Horsham Corporation, a capital-rich Canadian public holding company and the Trizec Corporation, a leading North American real estate company with more than 35 years of development and operating experience. It was a relationship that would epitomize the building of relationships, which has become the hallmark of TrizecHahn's operations. The new company quickly forged an aggressive acquisition strategy, seeking extraordinary, well-positioned properties known for their quality, innovation and outstanding personnel. With over $7 billion in assets, the organization has become one of the largest publicly traded real estate companies in North America. Today TrizecHahn remains a growth-oriented company with an extensive, diverse and high-quality portfolio of landmark office properties in prime locations across the United States and Canada.

That portfolio begins with TrizecHahn's flagship property, Chicago's Sears Tower. Designed by Falzur Kahn of the pioneering firm of Skidmore, Owings & Merrill, it was intended from the start to set precedents in size, height and functionality. In its prominent location as a cornerstone to Chicago's downtown and rooted upon a full city block, the Sears Tower would harbor the 10,000 employees of Sears Roebuck and Company as well as 6,000 other tenants within its 76,000-ton, 1,454-foot-tall steel walls.

In designing the Sears Tower, Kahn envisioned a building that would remain the world's pre-eminent office property for years to come. Even in his initial design, the building's operating, communications and security systems were engineered to such superb, exacting standards that they are still considered to be among the best anywhere. Certainly the celebrated renovation completed in 1992 has helped to maintain the Sears Tower's position as the premier corporate address in America. The 1.5 million people who visit the building's Skydeck annually are a

10 & 120 South Riverside Plaza

testament to all that the Sears Tower is and all it represents — to architecture, to Chicago and to America.

The extraordinary quality epitomized by the Sears Tower is emblematic of TrizecHahn's focus on quality throughout its portfolio. This is a priority evident in TrizecHahn's other Chicago properties as well: Two North LaSalle — a modern fixture at the center of Chicago's connection to world finance and politics — and 10 & 120 South Riverside Plaza — another Skidmore, Owings & Merrill-designed property possessing a distinctively handsome atmosphere both inside and out. It is one of Chicago's foremost riverside properties and one of the most elegant corporate locales in the city. At the time of purchase, however, the buildings were well below the market's occupancy average. Within a year, TrizecHahn brought them to a 96-percent occupancy rate. And TrizecHahn's companywide emphasis on quality has enabled all these buildings to maintain an average occupancy rate over time of more than 90 percent. In fact, four different TrizecHahn properties nationwide have earned the BOMA Building of the Year Award — twice. The company is the landlord of choice in its markets and is known for sparing no effort to increase the value and prestige of its properties.

Led by Casey Wold, president of TrizecHahn Office Properties, TrizecHahn's portfolio has grown by more than 50 million square feet and includes these extraordinary class-A office properties: CN Tower in Toronto, the Grace Building in New York,

Two North LaSalle

Allen Center in Houston, Citicorp Center in Los Angeles, Metropolitan Square in St. Louis, Renaissance Tower and the Galleria Office Towers in Dallas, and the Watergate Building in Washington, D.C. In addition, TrizecHahn is currently constructing the prestigious 800,000-square-foot Bankers Hall II office tower in Calgary, Alberta, Canada.

TrizecHahn has also been a leading innovator in the retail industry for nearly four decades, developing more than 90 high-quality shopping centers such as the award-winning Park Meadows in Denver. Some of TrizecHahn's innovations have included elements now considered retail necessities, such as an oversupply of parking, large anchor tenants and controlled environments. Later projects like Horton Plaza in San Diego have included such features as a farmer's market, a performing arts theater and movie cinemas. By the late 1990s, however, growth in retail sales and

increasing competition among retailers made it difficult to generate above-average returns. After careful analysis and despite success in this niche of the industry,

Chicago at night
from the top of the
Sears Tower

TrizecHahn management decided to divest its retail center portfolio. The proceeds from this sale were invested into the office properties sector, and the company was thus able to augment its purchase of office buildings, further enhancing its growth potential.

More recently, TrizecHahn has set its sights on the considerable potential for expansion to be found in the European real estate market. In the last few years, overseas economic factors have combined to create an environment in which significant wealth and increased disposable income is possible for the working population. There is a corresponding move from the traditional "High Street" type of shopping to more of a U.S. model of the integrated mall shopping experience — complete with parking, restaurants, movies and other entertainment — such as that being developed at TrizecHahn's West End City Center in Budapest, Hungary. TrizecHahn is embarking on projects that will capitalize on this trend. Notable new North American developments of this type that are currently underway for TrizecHahn include Desert Passage at Aladdin in Las Vegas and Hollywood & Highland in Los Angeles — soon to be the new home of the Academy Awards.

Many of TrizecHahn's properties, like Bankers Hall or the Sears Tower, present the image of economic success identified with skyscrapers since the 1960s. TrizecHahn's Chicago properties epitomize this image. The company's commitment to Chicago symbolizes its commitment to developing and investing in architecturally significant and progressive properties all over the globe. Along with great names like Daniel Burnham, Marshall Field and Skidmore, Owings & Merrill, TrizecHahn is forging its own place in the architecture of Chicago history.

Golub & Company

From its headquarters on Chicago's famed North Michigan Avenue, Golub & Company is a leader in commercial and residential real estate operations.

Founder and Chairman Eugene Golub remains deeply involved in many facets of the company's business activities at home and abroad. Michael Newman, President and CEO, sets corporate direction and is at the helm of all operations. Golub & Company's consistent growth and broad-based real estate activities have led to the recruitment of a number of high-level, well-respected executives and middle managers with diverse and specialized skills.

A hands-on, principal orientation continues at the core of all Golub operations, ensuring clients that a senior, decision-making Golub executive will be overseeing their interests.

With roots dating back to the early 1960s, Golub & Company was a leader among a new crop of developers that helped shape Chicago's renowned skyline as it appears today. In addition, Golub was at the forefront of a wave of condominium conversions that stabilized and changed forever the makeup of the city's thriving residential community.

Today Golub is very active in multi-market real estate development, acquisitions, condominium development and conversions, build-to-suit programs, asset and property management, and corporate services. Overall,

(Left to right)
Michael Newman,
Eugene Golub,
Paula Harris
and Lee Golub

Lake Shore Place, a 2-million-square-foot, mixed-use commercial and residential building, is located at 680 N. Lake Shore Drive in Chicago, Illinois.

the company has developed, leased or managed some 20 million square feet of office and mixed-use properties, and has developed or converted more than 6,000 condominium units in Chicago alone. Golub & Company's domestic activities are overseen by Executive Vice President Lee Golub.

Office buildings historically have been a major part of Golub & Company's total business. Highly visible buildings developed by the company include Xerox Centre and 180 North LaSalle in Chicago's Loop and the 625 and 444 North Michigan Avenue buildings. Downtown acquisitions include the 2-million-square-foot, mixed-use Lake Shore Place at 680 North Lake Shore Drive, as well as the 33 North LaSalle and 19 South LaSalle office buildings. In the suburbs, Golub & Company acquired 1603 Orrington in Evanston in 1999.

In other Midwest markets, the company has developed, owns and manages buildings in Kansas City, St. Louis, Indianapolis and Minneapolis.

One of Golub & Company's residential achievements is The Bristol, a 189-unit, award-winning luxury condominium building on Chicago's Gold Coast. Other condominium projects include the Residences of Arlington Town Square, Mallard Cove Condominiums in suburban Arlington Heights, and 40 East Delaware, located in downtown Chicago's Gold Coast. Paula Harris, Senior Vice president, spearheads Golub's highly successful condominium development and conversion programs.

Even before Central and Eastern European countries began opening their borders to foreign development and investment, Golub was quick to foresee the great potential of that region. In 1989 Golub became the first major U.S. real estate firm to initiate development projects in the former Soviet bloc. Golub-Europe, L.L.C. is active today in Warsaw, Poland; Budapest, Hungary; Prague, Czech Republic; and St. Petersburg, Russia. Golub-Europe has offices in each of these cities and also in London and Berlin.

Office buildings completed by Golub-Europe include Warsaw Financial Center, the 750,000-square-foot office tower that set a high new standard of quality for future office buildings across Central and Eastern Europe. Also in Warsaw is Golub's first project abroad: Warsaw Corporate Center, completed and fully leased since 1994. In St. Petersburg, Russia, a private-public partnership led by Golub undertook one of the firm's most challenging endeavors to date, the historic renovation of a 180-year-old residential building to a multi-use retail and office building on the city's most prominent thoroughfare.

Thanks to its many successes in both private- and public-sector projects, Golub-Europe in its relatively short lifetime has become Central and Eastern Europe's most active and well-regarded real estate operation. The reality of private real estate development in the newly emerging, market-based economies can be credited largely to Golub's determination to introduce and deliver western-quality commercial infrastructure into the region. Golub has successfully blended its Chicago-based operating style with the local cultures and customs of these emerging markets. The company has made a significant, long-term commitment of human and financial resources to Central and Eastern Europe.

In the United States and abroad, Golub has vast experience in all phases of real estate development and

operations. As a result, numerous property owners and prominent tenants turn to Golub for real estate expertise, counsel and a full array of real estate services. And throughout its history Golub has joined forces with some of the world's leading institutional real estate investors and financial institutions.

In each relationship and on every assignment, Golub seeks to add value and maximize profitability by increasing revenues and reducing operating costs.

Among the numerous community organizations and charities in which Golub & Company principals play active roles are the Greater North Michigan Avenue Association, The Family Institute and the Y-Me National Breast Cancer Organization. In the fall of 1999 Gene Golub was inducted into the Chicago Association of Realtors' Hall of Fame, an honor reserved for a very few well-respected real estate industry leaders.

The Bristol Condominium, a 41-story, 189-unit luxury condominium high-rise completed in January 2000, is located in the heart of Chicago's Gold Coast.

Warsaw Financial Center, a 32-story, 750,000-square-foot Class A office building, was completed in January 1999 and is located in central Warsaw, Poland.

Cambridge Homes

Over the past four decades Cambridge Homes has been a leader in the greater Chicago housing industry, providing quality housing for more families than any other homebuilder in the region.

In addition to being the largest homebuilder in Illinois for the fourth consecutive year, Cambridge Homes is the area's top award recipient for excellence in housing. The company was recently named the Midwest's Builder of the Decade, has received builder of the year awards from several different publications, including the *Chicago Sun-Times*, and is one of only a handful of builders in the nation to have received the National Award for Construction Excellence. This unparalleled success is the result of what has become known as the "Cambridge difference."

The foundation of the Cambridge difference was conceived in the 1950s when Richard J. Brown, Cambridge's founder and CEO, was introduced to the homebuilding business. As national marketing director of U.S. Plywood, he worked closely with homebuilders all over the country, absorbing the best techniques applied by the most successful builders. Most important, however,

he began to formulate his own unique concepts. Chief among them is his philosophy that there is more to homebuilding than delivering quality homes; it also means creating appealing, cohesive neighborhood settings that maintain their appearance for decades.

From the beginning Cambridge Homes has set high standards that other builders have often followed. Cambridge was the first major homebuilder to offer buyers a wide variety of exterior designs from which to choose, the first to introduce varying neighborhoods with different series of homes in a single residential development and the first to provide completely landscaped parks and recreational facilities for residents to enjoy.

A common thread that runs through the fabric of each successful organization is the integrity and quality of its leadership. Richard Brown is truly a founding father who has set the standard for residential development in suburban Chicago. His son, Doug Brown, who oversees the day-to-day operations of Cambridge Homes as its president, is also a distinguished leader in Chicago-area housing. Under the guidance of this father-and-son team, coupled with a qualified management team with more than 100 years of combined experience with the company and composed of experts in virtually every homebuilding discipline, Cambridge Homes is second to none in leadership. This quality leadership has enabled the Cambridge difference to flourish.

The leadership qualities of Richard and Doug Brown extend well beyond the enduring success of Cambridge Homes. Each is a dedicated leader in the housing industry. Richard Brown has served as president of the Home Builders Association of Greater Chicago and as president of the Home Builders Association of Illinois. He also served as president of the Greater Chicagoland Housing Foundation, chairman of the Production Builders Committee of the National Home Builders Association, as well as a member of the Governors Housing Foundation. He is an inductee of the prestigious Home Builders Court of Honor, a Lifetime Director of the National Home Builders Association and the only major Chicago suburban builder to have received a Lifetime Achievement Award from the Urban Land Institute.

Doug Brown is a member of the Home Builders Association of Illinois as well as the Home Builders Association of Greater Chicago, where for three terms he served as chairman of the Sustaining Builders Council;

The leadership qualities of (left to right) Richard Brown and his son, Doug Brown, extend well beyond the enduring success of Cambridge Homes, the top homebuilding company in the Chicago area. Each is also a distinguished leader in the Chicago-area housing industry.
Photo by Cynthia Howe

and has been an active member of its executive committee and board of directors.

Cambridge's emphasis on customer satisfaction is another cornerstone of the Cambridge difference. The company's goal has never been to be the largest home-builder, but rather to be the best. Regardless of its size Cambridge Homes continues treating each customer as one individual, as one family at a time. Every customer is viewed as being a part of the Cambridge Family. Understanding that buying a new home is one of the biggest decisions people make in their lifetimes, Cambridge goes out of its way to make sure the entire home-buying process is as pleasant as possible for every customer.

Cambridge's commitment to its customers starts with its Total Quality Attitude approach, in which every employee is focused on working together as a team to delight each customer. Cambridge also believes in giving customers what they want, not merely what the company thinks they may want. Determining what buyers want is accomplished through a series of buyer preference studies and focus groups.

Such emphasis on customer satisfaction has borne fruit: Cambridge Homes has one of the highest customer-satisfaction ratings in the nation as determined by an independent research firm that directly compares Cambridge Homes to 175 production builders throughout the country. In fact, the national average is a 78 percent customer satisfaction rating, while Cambridge's rating has averaged in the mid-90 percent range.

Throughout its first three decades, Cambridge Homes experienced steady growth in sales and revenue. From the late 1980s to the mid-1990s the company was consistently one of the top five homebuilders in Illinois. Through the major acquisition of Lexington Homes in 1995, Cambridge vaulted to the top, where it has remained ever since.

Although the Lexington acquisition was the largest of its kind to occur in the history of Chicago homebuilding, it was not the only major purchase by Cambridge Homes in 1995. That same year Cambridge acquired Carillon from Bank of America, which had taken it over from the original developer. Cambridge jump-started the stalled development for active adults by completing the existing neighborhoods, introducing five new home series and building a 32,000-square-foot recreation center. From its inception as the first large-scale, active-adult community in the Chicago area, Cambridge at Carillon quickly

The "Cambridge difference" is exemplified by customer satisfaction, creating appealing, cohesive neighborhood settings and delivering quality-built homes such as this one shown at Prairie View Estates in Geneva.
Photo by Jan Ingve

emerged as the best-selling new home community in the region, and is the only active-adult community in Illinois to make *New Choices* magazine's top 20 listing of the best adult communities in the United States.

Today, Cambridge Homes is the premier builder of regional, active-adult communities, including the development of a smaller, more intimate version of Cambridge at Carillon in Grayslake called Carillon North. It is launching two more active-adult communities in the Chicago area with plans for more in the future.

The next major step in Cambridge's quality growth occurred in January 1999, when it became an even larger and stronger company as part of D.R. Horton, Inc. Cambridge assumed the management responsibilities for the Chicagoland D.R. Horton operation and communities, and it continues operating as it has in the past, only now with the financial backing of a leading national home-builder. Richard Brown continues serving as the company's CEO, and Doug Brown as its president.

Cambridge Homes now offers more than 150 different home styles among 30 series of homes, including single-family, town homes and condominiums, with pricing for the first-time and luxury-home buyer and everyone in between. In addition to providing one of the widest selections of homes, Cambridge communities are spread throughout the entire Chicago region, accommodating the geographic and living needs of virtually every type of home buyer.

In essence, the Cambridge difference is a basic philosophy in which every aspect of the company's business is geared to improving the lives of its customers and fulfilling the American dream of home ownership.

Central Building & Preservation L.P.

Maurice Rivkin founded Central Building Cleaning Company in 1924, promptly earning a reputation for quality work and honesty that attracted a loyal clientele that remain today.

(Right) Little Sisters of the Poor, tuck pointed by Central in 1927, was typical of low-rise institutional projects completed in the pre-Depression era.

Chicago's abusive weather conditions can cause building facades to weaken and decay.

(Far right) More than 60 years of soot and grime were steamed off the old McKesson-Robbins building, revealing an attractive brick and terra-cotta exterior.

Central Building & Preservation L.P. has played a vital role in safeguarding historically significant structures throughout the Chicago area for over 75 years. By providing quality tuck pointing (the replacement of loose, missing or weathered mortar), masonry reconstruction and facade restoration services, this family-owned company has conserved the enduring character of numerous architectural landmarks in the Chicago skyline.

Maurice Rivkin, who arrived in Chicago as a young immigrant in 1907, envisioned his "American Dream" when he founded Central Building Cleaning Company in 1924. Impressed by the innovative, portable sand-blasting process, he deferred completion of law school to start a small business that tuck pointed, cleaned and restored grimy exteriors of buildings darkened by sooty air emitted from coal-burning furnaces throughout Chicago and nearby Gary.

Coincidentally, the 1920s brought a building boom to Chicago, already enjoying international renown for the innovative "skyscraper" architecture of William Le Baron

Jenny, Dankmar Adler, Daniel Burnham and Louis Sullivan a generation earlier. Their novel structural designs substituted the use of concrete and steel skeletons for massive load bearing walls, permitting higher and lighter facades with large windows surrounded by ornate terra cotta, stone and brick masonry. Less able to withstand the ravages of Chicago-type weather — wind-driven rain, sleet and snow — these early high-rise buildings and their successors required frequent maintenance, a service the growing Central Building Cleaning Company was able to perform.

When the Great Depression of the 1930s brought construction and Central's growth to a standstill, the enterprising Rivkin supplemented his income by promoting dances and, later, prize fights that featured future champions Joe Louis and Tony Zale, among others.

Since World War II, Chicago's vigor has again been reflected in its architecture — bigger, bolder and higher. The new generation of buildings also employed new designs — clean architectural lines incorporating concrete, steel and glass replaced decorative facades found in older structures. The prefabricated metal window-wall systems that replaced custom-fit wood-frame windows and masonry walls proved even more vulnerable than their predecessors to Chicago's penetrating, wind-blown rains. Water and air leaks became endemic.

With technological change pervading the industry, Maury's son, Charles, joined Central Building & Cleaning Co. in 1960 as its president, continuing to head the company to the present day. The company broadened its building restoration and masonry repair services, implemented new materials and scaffolding technologies and initiated professional consulting and inspectional services. These enlarged capabilities proved key in the

1970s and 1980s as the tuck pointing industry again changed directions to address the rash of falling concrete and masonry, a consequence of stress from decades of rust expansion of steel framing, supports and anchors. Central specialized in the sophisticated knowledge and repair techniques required to restore the city's aging structures.

In 1992 Tom Rivkin, Maurice Rivkin's grandson, and key employee Tom Powers, became partners in the company, which was renamed Central Building & Preservation L.P. to better represent its restoration and preservation services.

Today after more than 75 years, Central Building & Preservation continues to innovate building preservation techniques. Its success can be credited to the characteristic work ethic of the company's staff, which provides focused and detailed planning to each restoration project. This strategy is integral to the company's unsurpassed reputation in its industry and its decades-long retention of core clients who keep the business thriving.

As Central Building & Preservation has evolved to meet the changing needs of Chicago and its great architecture, the principles that were fundamental to Maurice Rivkin — craftsmanship, dedication to quality work and commitment to the needs of building owners and managers — remain rock-solid after three generations.

(Far left)
To supplement his income during The Great Depression, the enterprising Maurice Rivkin promoted dances and, later, prize fights that featured future champions Joe Louis and Tony Zale, among others.

(Left)
Maintenance problems inherent in the detailing and construction of 1920s structures spurred the growth of the tuck pointing industry in Chicago. Central Building & Preservation L.P. has helped maintain the exteriors of numerous prominent buildings, including the old Carbon & Carbide Building and the stainless steel-clad Executive House.

Modern techniques and materials applied to the old 1920s American Furniture Mart (far left) and to the contemporary Lake Point Towers are typical of Central's daily challenges in preserving the contrasting architectural styles and sizes of buildings that make up Chicago's renowned skyline.

Concord Homes

Concord Homes is a familiar name to everyone involved in the Chicago-area real estate market, a name that has become synonymous with quality and value in contemporary residential development. Since its founding in 1992, the company has been among the region's most successful builders, completing over 4,000 homes throughout the suburbs and, to an increasing degree in recent years, in the city as well.

That latter point makes Concord unique in a metropolitan market where historically, major urban and suburban developers seldom ventured onto each other's turf. It may seem surprising, as well, in light of the dominant role Chairman Ron Benach and the rest of Concord's principals have played in building Chicago's suburbs for some four decades.

In the 1960s Benach co-founded 3-H Building Corporation and began building homes in the northern suburbs. By the early 70s he had built 3-H Corp. into the largest homebuilding company in the Chicagoland area, at which point the firm was sold to national development giant U.S. Home. He promptly started another company, Lexington Homes, where he was joined in the mid-80s by future Concord principals Wayne Moretti, Glenn Rutledge, Roger Mankedick and Jeff Benach. Within a

few years the group had guided the new company to the top of the market, and by the late 80s Lexington was building homes in virtually every corner of the suburban landscape, with annual sales reaching an astounding 1,400 homes. Then in 1989 Lexington was sold, and three years later, Benach and his partners started Concord Homes, which they quickly built into another suburban development powerhouse.

So why would an organization with such an extraordinary track record in the suburbs choose to take on the very different, and very formidable, challenges posed by city development? The answer lies in one of the basic tenets of Concord's company philosophy: the understanding that developers don't create markets, buyers do.

When Chicago's building boom began in earnest during the 1990s, and sales of city lofts, townhomes and mid-rise condominiums started outpacing new home sales in many suburban areas, Concord management knew it was time to act.

The company's first in-town project got underway in 1997 when the company teamed up with Kenard Development to purchase The Sexton, a landmark building in Chicago's booming River North neighborhood. If the timing and location were perfect, so was the building itself. Built in 1906 by a commercial food-processing company, The Sexton was ideally suited for the kind of loft renovation that was revitalizing the area — and that is precisely what Concord did, transforming the former industrial facility into one of the hottest properties in the neighborhood, with over 200 stylish lofts and 17 spacious, upscale townhomes.

By the time the first residents moved into The Sexton in 1999, Concord had already started work on four more city developments. First up was Renaissance Place, a 7-acre conversion plan for the hospital and clinic facilities of the former Chicago Osteopathic Medical Center in Hyde Park. In addition to 204 loft-style condominiums and 28 luxury townhomes, the development also includes 16 traditional, Chicago-style, single-family homes designed to blend architecturally with the classic older homes that characterize the historic neighborhood. That's one reason Renaissance Place has been so well-received by the community since opening in 1998. Another reason is the

1000 Adams, in Chicago's trendy West Loop Gate area

Perhaps the most distinctive of all of Concord's city efforts is the company's Concord City Centre. As the name implies, it is right downtown, in the former Morton Building in the heart of Chicago's Loop. In 1999 Concord began a "gut rehab" of the vintage 23-story office structure, creating over 200 condominium residences, a parking garage and some 7,000 square feet of ground-floor retail space. A number of the residences are unusually spacious, with up to three bedrooms and 3 1/2 baths.

Concord's aggressive push into city development hasn't come at the expense of the company's suburban business; quite the contrary, in fact. Nearly a dozen Concord communities are thriving throughout the northern and western suburbs, from Lombard to Libertyville, Westchester to Hoffman Estates, offering buyers a wide range of choices, from starter-home duplexes to luxurious, semi-custom estate homes. What's more, a similar number of new developments — including Concord at The Glen, the company's much-anticipated contribution to the master plan for the former Glenview Naval Air Station property in the heart of Chicago's northern suburbs — keep Concord's name in the forefront of suburban development.

But company officials acknowledge that their overall proportion of urban developments is likely to grow in the next few years, as more and more buyers of all ages and lifestyles — from first-time buyers and empty-nesters to traditional families with children — seek out the convenience and character of a home in the city. Those, after all, are the buyers Ron Benach and the rest of Concord's management team have been serving so successfully for the past 40 years. And today Concord Homes remains committed to serving them for many years to come — wherever their dreams may lead.

Concord City Center in the heart of the Loop

moderate pricing, especially of the condominiums, which offer middle-class buyers an ownership opportunity previously unavailable in a neighborhood long characterized by walk-up apartments, larger upscale homes, and very little in between.

Two other Concord efforts that have been warmly welcomed by the surrounding community are 1000 Adams and 933 Van Buren, a pair of unique, new-construction, mid-rise condominiums in the West Loop Gate neighborhood. Throughout the planning process of both communities, Concord representatives worked closely with the West Loop Gate community organization and the West Central Association to develop a design that would reflect the neighborhood's character and vision for the future. And the resulting buildings do just that. 1000 Adams (shown on the prior page) has a handsome redbrick exterior with a curved, set-back facade. Its 150 residences combine the space and style of loft living with the structural soundness of brand-new construction. The concept is mirrored at 933 Van Buren, with 180 "new lofts."

Concord at the Glen, the redevelopment of Glenview Naval Air Station

H. B. Barnard Company

While helping to build Chicago since 1892 as a contractor for residential, institutional and commercial projects, H. B. Barnard Company has established a reputation for pride in craftsmanship.

The H. B. Barnard Company is perhaps the only continuing contracting company in Chicago to pass from father to son for four generations. William E. Barnard founded the company under the name W. E. Barnard & Son to work as a general building contractor on a variety of construction projects. His son, Harrison B. Barnard, took over in 1900 and worked as a sole proprietor until 1937, when the company incorporated as H. B. Barnard Company. He ran the company until his death in 1952 and was then succeeded by his son, William B. Barnard, who retired in 1994 but continued to be active in the

company. His son, James B. Barnard, joined the company in 1974 and has been in charge since his father's retirement.

The company was only 16 years old when the famous architect, Frank Lloyd Wright, selected H. B. Barnard to build the now-famous Frederick C. Robie House on Woodlawn Avenue in Hyde Park. Revolutionary in design and construction at that time, the house remains an outstanding piece of workmanship and a testament to the Prairie School of architectural design. Robie, a 27-year-old businessman working for his father's sewing machine and bicycle-manufacturing business, purchased the 60-by-180-foot lot in 1908. Construction began in March 1909 and the Robie family moved in after completion in June 1910.

In 1957 a panel of leading architects and art historians selected Robie House as one of the two outstanding houses built in the United States during the 20th century. The house today is one of Chicago's official architectural landmarks.

H. B. Barnard continued building custom homes for affluent and prominent families in various locations in the cities and suburbs such as Hyde Park, Woodlawn, Beverly and Winnetka. The company also worked on

(Far right) 819 South Wabash Loft Building

Victor Lawson Tower of the Chicago Theological Seminary

commercial and industrial projects. In the early 1930s gangsters shot a superintendent on one of the company's construction projects during a union confrontation. Harrison B. Barnard was so incensed that he formed a committee with other prominent businessmen called the Secret Six. It gathered evidence that was later turned over to federal authorities and used in the conviction of Al Capone.

During his more than 50 years with the company, Harrison B. Barnard also served as building contractor on a wide range of institutional projects. The Chicago Theological Seminary, Chicago Lying-In Hospital and Children's Memorial Hospital were among his clients.

William B. Barnard began working with the family business as a timekeeper and water boy at age 15 in 1937. The company was then building a residence in Winnetka that today is valued at more than $3 million. William B. Barnard worked as an apprentice carpenter before World War II and then as a carpenter and foreman after the war. After becoming CEO he followed the pattern established by his father of maintaining a contracting company based on long-term relationships with architects and with key figures in the business community of Chicago.

The construction business in Chicago has changed since World War II, and H. B. Barnard Company has evolved. The company works on many different building types, including corporate headquarters/office build-outs, retail space, building renovations, industrial buildings and additions, schools and institutions, and medical facilities. While corporations have become more cost conscious in recent years, the company has been able to meet the challenge of building and maintaining strong permanent relationships with clients.

H. B. Barnard Company has built its reputation on customer satisfaction and is able to provide prospective

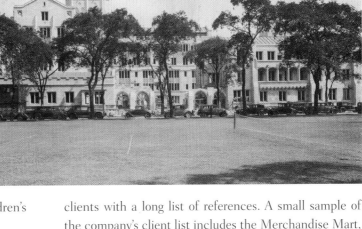

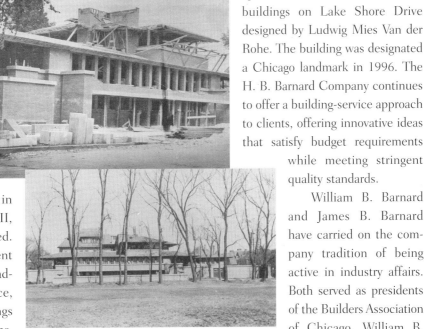

clients with a long list of references. A small sample of the company's client list includes the Merchandise Mart, Harris Trust and Savings Bank, Morgan Stanley and Co., The Art Institute of Chicago, DePaul University, Loyola Medical Center, St. Joseph Hospital, University of Chicago, Hallmark Shops and the Palmer House.

In 1994 H. B. Barnard Company was employed as general contractor to convert two apartments into one at one of the buildings on Lake Shore Drive designed by Ludwig Mies Van der Rohe. The building was designated a Chicago landmark in 1996. The H. B. Barnard Company continues to offer a building-service approach to clients, offering innovative ideas that satisfy budget requirements while meeting stringent quality standards.

William B. Barnard and James B. Barnard have carried on the company tradition of being active in industry affairs. Both served as presidents of the Builders Association of Chicago. William B. Barnard also founded the Chicagoland Construction Safety Council in 1989. In addition to owing their clients first-class quality construction, the Barnards believe they owe something to the construction industry that has provided a livelihood for the family through four generations.

Chicago Lying-In Hospital under construction

Robie House under construction

View of the Robie House after completion

Jones Lang LaSalle

With a rich Chicago history and a global reach spanning more than 100 major markets, Jones Lang LaSalle represents the city in many respects. A leader in real estate services and investment management — boasting more than 7,000 employees worldwide — this dynamic firm works to shape the real estate landscape in Chicago, the United States and across the world for its major corporate, property owner and investor clients. Through its long-term strategic alliance relationship approach, Jones Lang LaSalle has earned a reputation for delivering best-in-class real estate products and services that have redefined the real estate services industry.

The company's history, similar to Chicago's own, is a blend of American and European elements. In March 1999 Jones Lang LaSalle Inc. was born through the merger of Chicago-based LaSalle Partners Inc. and London-based Jones Lang Wootton, creating the industry's largest global real estate services and investment management firm. Its legacy, however, dates back much further.

LaSalle was founded as IDC Real Estate by a group of real estate entrepreneurs in El Paso, Texas, in 1967. From the start, the founders believed they could outperform competitors by taking a long-term, relationship-based approach to real estate vs. providing one-off transactions. This strategy remained the key factor behind its success as well as its expansion and relocation in 1972 to Chicago. Five years later, it was renamed LaSalle Partners Ltd. after its first downtown business address on S. LaSalle Street. During the next 25 years, LaSalle would develop into a publicly traded, fully integrated, global real estate services firm.

The Aon Center, formerly the Amoco Building, is home to Jones Lang LaSalle's American headquarters. It is also the second-tallest building in Chicago.

The 200-year history of LaSalle's merger partner, Jones Lang Wootton, began in 1783, when the company was established as an auction house in London. In 1840 the practice entered into a partnership with James Jones. Subsequently James Jones' son, Frederick, established an estate agency business, which he later combined with his father's auction house and renamed Frederick Jones and Co. upon his father's death. When Frederick Jones retired in 1872, the firm became Jones Lang and Co., with C.A. Lang as the sole partner. In 1939 this firm merged with Wootton and Son (founded in 1892) to become Jones Lang Wootton and Sons.

In 1945 London remained devastated by the bombings of World War II. By assisting the city with postwar reconstruction efforts, the company gained responsibility for a number of speculative development and leasing projects, all the while solidifying its business in this prominent market. In 1958 it branched out, opening offices in Australia in Sydney and Melbourne, with further expansion into Scotland, Ireland and continental Europe in the early 1960s. Quick to recognize the potential opportunities provided by political changes in central and eastern Europe, Jones Lang Wootton and Sons opened offices in Budapest, Prague and Warsaw. By 1969 the firm had shortened its name to Jones Lang Wootton (JLW) and in 1984 moved to its present home in Hanover Square.

Meanwhile, in America, LaSalle Partners was experiencing rapid growth of its own. During the 1970s and 1980s, LaSalle dramatically expanded its real estate businesses by identifying a client need, tackling it more professionally than others and then expanding an initial assignment into an ongoing business. For example, LaSalle's Investment Banking specialty was created in response to market needs for more sophisticated financial expertise than was offered by real estate firms and investment banks of the day. This resulted in LaSalle expanding its expertise to include real estate investment bankers that represented buyers and sellers in some of the most significant real estate transactions of the 1970s and 1980s.

Another leading-edge real estate service concept pioneered by LaSalle and still widely copied today is its Tenant Representation specialty, which was established in 1978. Rather than seeking small individual transactions, the business sought to establish national relationships with major users of office facilities. This ensured its long-term viability by providing long-term occupancy solutions for several of the nation's largest accounting firms, as well as clients in insurance, banking and financial services.

By the early 1970s LaSalle had entered the real estate development business in the Chicago suburbs with projects characterized by high-quality construction and premium amenities, but withdrew from development in the mid-1980s. LaSalle did continue to serve corporate and investment clients as fee manager of development projects; this continues today and can be seen in major public projects such as the renovations of Grand Central Terminal in New York and the recently completed Symphony Center in Chicago.

In the 1970s LaSalle also entered the property management and leasing business, recognizing that the property-manager role went beyond custodial and brokerage responsibilities and extended to creating value for the property owner. The same basic strategy enabled LaSalle to expand into corporate facilities management in the early 1990s. Ultimately the company was awarded national contracts involving millions of square feet of property, making it the largest provider of this service in the United States today.

During the 1970s and 1980s, Jones Lang Wootton continued its own expansion by tapping into the enormous potential of North America, where it opened a New York office in 1975. The increasing flow of British, Middle Eastern and Asian money into the United

States opened up opportunities for JLW to meet the needs of many foreign investors in coming to terms with different market practices, valuation techniques and professional standards.

A strong client-service foundation, common culture, synergistic operating philosophy and rich real estate service success enabled both LaSalle Partners and Jones Lang Wootton to withstand change, provide new opportunities for their clients and continue to grow during the 1990s. As the real estate service industry consolidated and worked to globalize for the advantage of multinational companies in the late 1990s, it was a natural evolution for LaSalle Partners and Jones Lang Wootton to merge in 1999, creating Jones Lang LaSalle. The two companies' common service approach, growth platform, culture and experience provide a unique opportunity to deliver cross-border real estate services and investment management expertise to multinational companies, property owners and investors worldwide. Today Jones Lang LaSalle has offices around the globe, including its American headquarters in Chicago's towering Aon Center, formerly the Amoco Building, located on E. Randolph Drive — a property it leased, occupied, sold and subleased to Aon Corporation, all representative of the full scope of its real estate expertise.

Jones Lang LaSalle is the leasing and management agent for many historic properties in Chicago. Shown here is an interior from the LaSalle Bank Building (c. 1930, when it was known as the Field Building), one of the premier Art Deco structures in the city.

The LaSalle Bank Building (left, c. 1930), formerly known as the Field Building, on S. LaSalle Street in downtown Chicago. Jones Lang LaSalle is the leasing and management agent for this Art Deco structure.

Leopardo Construction

Celebrating its 20th anniversary, Leopardo Construction continues to flourish in the competitive Chicago market. The company has earned its reputation as a premier provider of preconstruction and construction services by satisfying a diverse spectrum of clients while simultaneously building long-term relationships. Many of the prominent sites built by Leopardo Construction can be seen throughout Chicagoland, including major hospitals, schools, loop office suites, corporate headquarters, industrial buildings and retail complexes.

Leopardo Construction's reputation can be traced back to its first major account. In 1984 the company was commissioned by G.D. Searle to construct the first pilot centrifuge for the manufacture of NutraSweet® at Searle's research and development facility in Skokie. Numerous projects quickly followed including a 112,000-square-foot distribution center.

The company's continual success is attributed to the enterprising efforts and drive put forth by company president and founder James Leopardo and his group of devoted professionals. Their dedication to client satisfaction has propelled Leopardo Construction into the "elite" lists numerous times, including *Crain's Chicago Business'* "Top Chicago Contractors" and *Inc.'s* "500 Fastest Growing Private Companies".

In addition to the company's achievements, Leopardo himself has been named "Entrepreneur of the Year" by *Inc.* magazine and has been invited by such esteemed institutions as Harvard Business School to share the innovative business and management strategies he has employed to attain his company's remarkable growth.

To serve a broader market base, Leopardo Construction strategically expanded its operations into several markets — interiors, healthcare, industrial, retail, institutional and office — and developed a specialized staff to meet its clients' unique requirements. Spearheaded by a principal and project team specializing in the nuances of each market, client goals are consistently achieved from the start of preconstruction through project completion. Leopardo Construction also added a downtown Chicago office in addition to its suburban headquarters.

Leopardo Construction orchestrates smooth and timely project delivery by exercising team leadership and structuring the appropriate project strategy. Whether it be design/build, fast-track construction management or traditional competitive bidding, Leopardo's progressive style utilizes the latest technologies and state-of-the-art systems to effectively manage its projects. By partnering with qualified professionals of every discipline, even the most complex projects are consistently brought to fruition. "We want to provide a seamless business approach that creates value beyond the level of our clients' expectations," says Executive Vice President Richard Mattioda.

From retrofitting to fast-track buildouts, Leopardo's interiors market has met the challenge by coordinating a team of professionals, obtaining custom materials and accommodating the clients' needs to maintain a "business as usual" approach, all in extremely tight time frames. Marquee interior projects include office suites at the 333 W. Wacker, 401 N. Michigan and 2 N. LaSalle buildings. High-profile projects have also been completed at the Chicago Hilton & Towers, Palmer House Hotel, Standard

James Leopardo, founder and president of Leopardo Construction
©*Fred Fox Studios*

Development of the Century Mall in Chicago
©*Mark A. Samuels*

Club and Union League. In addition to interior renovations at historically significant structures, Leopardo has constructed high-tech, contemporary interiors for Platinum Technology, divine interVentures, Rockwell International, Associated Press' Chicago bureau, and the law firms of Kirkland & Ellis and Blatt, Hamesfahr & Eaton.

Working closely with Chicago Public Schools and the Public Building Commission, Leopardo's institutional market has constructed enhanced educational facilities for Hearst, Ravenswood, Medill, Sherwood and Shakespeare Schools as well as the new Chicago Public Library Edgebrook and Archer branches and the City of Des Plaines Public Library. In addition, this market spearheaded the Gallery 37 and Steppenwolf Theatre renovations.

Through its healthcare market, Leopardo Construction has enjoyed ongoing relationships with several Chicago-area hospitals, including The University of Chicago Hospitals, Illinois Masonic Medical Center, Northwestern Memorial Hospital, Northwest Community Hospital, Rush-Copley Medical Center and Advocate Healthcare. The company has been commissioned by these healthcare facilities on a continual basis to provide preconstruction and construction services for a wide range of projects, including on-campus surgery and dialysis centers, patient care units, cath labs and MRI units, as well as off-campus medical office buildings.

Leopardo Construction's industrial market has partnered with such industrial giants as Candle Corporation of America, a manufacturer/distributor of candles and home fragrance products, to build the first totally automated candle factory in the world. In addition, Juno Lighting, the leader in design/manufacturing of architectural-grade lighting products, sought Leopardo's design/build experience for the construction of its 525,000-square-foot manufacturing facility. "It wasn't a difficult decision when we were choosing the contractor to construct our new headquarters," says George Bilek, vice president of financing for Juno Lighting. "With an extensive history of success in our past projects, we knew that Leopardo Construction would provide an excellent design/build team."

The company is also experienced in the construction of corporate headquarters, including Yaskawa Electric America North American Headquarters and a state-of-the-art facility for Deublin Company, a manufacturer of flexible unions, both located in Waukegan.

The Des Plaines Library

Whether it constructs new Chicago-area stores for such retail giants as Dominick's, Eagle, Fresh Fields, Walgreens, Home Depot and Best Buy, conducts renovation projects for Century Mall, Louis Joliet Mall and Fado Irish Pub, or constructs theaters for Loews/Cineplex and Landmark Theaters, Leopardo Construction's retail market understands the particular needs of its clients and responds with proven expertise. The recent Century Mall renovation encompassed extensive roof removal, addition of the 5th, 6th and 7th floors to house a new state-of-the-art theater complex with stadium seating, and interior upgrades within the mall including new escalators and elevators, all completed while the mall remained open for business.

The entrepreneurial spirit held by Leopardo when he started Leopardo Construction remains today, and is shared by all employed with the company. As Leopardo Construction continues to strategically expand its operations, it will maintain and build upon its reputation for integrating the highest quality, detail and craftsmanship into each project.

Juno Lighting's 30-acre site in Des Plaines
© 1997 *Aerial Images Photography* Co.

MCL Companies

Daniel E. McLean left banking in 1976 to rehabilitate and sell older buildings, but he began to recognize a market for luxury housing in Chicago that wasn't being served. With his vision, MCL Companies has since gained prominence as a major urban developer by building neighborhoods and communities for professionals who want to live, shop and be entertained in the city.

In order to meet the demand for urban housing with style, McLean has had to survive three recessions, high interest rates in the early 1980s, several rounds of investment partners and the collapse of savings and loan companies. Because he overcame all of these obstacles along the way, Chicagoans have been able to buy town-homes, single-family homes and condominiums that weren't generally available before.

MCL has residential developments on Chicago's North Side in Lincoln Park, DePaul, Old Town and the Gold Coast. South Side residential developments are

Embassy Club, Lincoln Park

located in Hyde Park, the South Loop and Central Station at the foot of Grant Park. These urban neighbor-hoods and communities have attracted young, professional buyers without children; families with children; and empty nesters who have moved back to the city after their children were grown.

River East is an ongoing $750 million development by the north bank of the Chicago River between North

Michigan Avenue and Lake Michigan. Planned as a community for 3,000 residents, the 13-acre site features the 424 CityView condominiums plus two RiverView condominium towers and 19 four-story waterfront town-homes. River East Center has a 21-screen AMC movie theatre, a Bally's Total Fitness health club, restaurants and over 135,000 square feet of retail space. River East Plaza, formally known as North Pier, will eventually include high-profile retailers, specialty shops, restaurants, a riverfront café and five floors of office space. Another $750 million of property is projected for development in River East.

MCL also has developed other commercial property. Piper's Alley Shopping Center in Old Town is a new retail arts-and-entertainment complex anchored by Second City Theater and Sony Theaters. The Old Town Square Shopping Center is part of the "Clybourn Corridor" that serves Lincoln Park and Lakeview and includes a 64,000-square-foot Dominick's Fresh Store and Blockbuster. Clybourn Square has 116,800 square feet of retail space.

McLean entered banking in 1970 in Chicago and helped developers obtain construction and rehabilitation loans for the Lincoln Park and Lakeview neighborhoods. Some of his customers were pioneer developers in those neighborhoods, and he liked what they were doing. While still working as a banker in 1974, he started buying buildings on the side and rehabbing them. When McLean found that he liked doing that more than being a banker, he went into business with some partners the next year and then split off on his own in 1976.

Starting with $5,000 that he borrowed, McLean bought a six-flat in Wrigleyville that cost $50,000. The bank gave him a first mortgage, and the seller gave him a second mortgage. He expanded by joining with a couple of small investors to buy more buildings for rehabilitation and renovation, including one building in the late 1970s with 200 apartments. McLean and his investor partners began buying some condominiums in 1979, but the market crashed in 1980. For the next three years, they had to give up much of what they had built the previous four years. They couldn't sell the condos, so they sold other buildings to stay in business.

After nine years of mostly rehabilitating older build-ings, McLean had formed a vision of building a quality environment that people would want to live in. This was triggered in 1983 when he put 32 units on sale for investors and found himself swamped over a weekend

with people who actually wanted to live in the units as owners. Realizing that people were ready to move from high-rise condos into smaller buildings with yards and garages, McLean bought a lot for development in the West DePaul area. He subsequently bought three more blocks in the same area and built a shopping center plus 108 townhomes over a two-year period.

Other buildings started going up in the same area as MCL's development, and McLean saw that the entire neighborhood was being transformed. From there, he started looking at neighborhoods on the edge of Lincoln Park and Lakeview where he could go in, make an impact and create a neighborhood for larger development. To further his vision, he bought seven acres at Southport and Wrightwood and built the Embassy Club in 1988. It proved that a larger development could make an entire neighborhood take off and that people would pay for good architecture and good quality.

All of the neighborhoods and communities that McLean developed in Chicago have been successful, although he readily admits that he had his share of problems and sleepless nights. He attributes much of the success to having talked to his customers. He spent a lot of time in his sales offices asking customers what they wanted and liked. From these discussions, he created a design center where people can design the interiors of the

houses they buy. MCL was one of the first builders in Chicago and the country to build a design center with a staff that helps buyers customize their interiors.

By the end of 1999 MCL developments stretched from 50th Street on the South Side of Chicago to Belmont Avenue on the North Side and then west to Ashland Avenue. The developments include Cornell Square, Lakewood Commons, Townhomes of Sweeterville, Melrose Townhomes, Montana Homes, The Embassy Club, Dearborn Park (including the Chicago Homes and Prairie Homes), The Residences at Central Station, The Pointe at Lincoln Park, The Oak Club, Old Town Square, The Homes of Mohawk North, RiverView and CityView in River East, Altgeld Club and Near West Side Homes. MCL also bought Fisher Island in Florida for residential development and built the Manor Homes at Cherry Creek in Denver.

McLean sees his business as having grown up with his own baby-boom generation. He began working with baby boomers in the 1970s when they were renters looking for semi-luxury apartments. He was there when they made their first purchases of condominiums and townhomes and then when they traded up to single-family homes or larger townhomes for family use. Finally, he was there for them when they had raised their children and were ready to buy luxury housing in the vicinity of downtown Chicago.

Proud of having built luxury housing that has attracted a mixed group of residents, McLean also has a sense of satisfaction from having built in neighborhoods of Chicago that hadn't seen any new housing in 40 years. He is a man who truly found his destiny.

The Pointe at Lincoln Park, a signature MCL development

Phase I of RiverView's east tower with 99 luxury condos under construction. Phase II (west tower) to break ground in the 3rd quarter of 2000 with 134 condos plus 19 townhomes that will surround the base of the building

TVO Realty Partners

TVO Realty Partners has quietly but rapidly become one of the country's foremost leaders in the ownership and management of apartment communities. Founded in 1983 by Wayne A. Vandenburg, TVO and its affiliate, EPT Management Company, specialize in the acquisition, redevelopment and management of garden, mid-rise and high-rise rental housing.

Located in Arlington Heights, a northwest suburb of Chicago, Tanglewood Apartments was a neglected property when purchased in Late 1999. TVO recognized an opportunity to reposition this 838-unit asset through a $6.8 million renovation program.

The company grew out of Vandenburg's experience as a real estate broker in El Paso, Texas. Vandenburg points to a specific day in 1983 as the turning point of his real estate career. Instead of selling a property, he placed it under contract to his own company. When he sought financing for his new investment, an officer from a bank in the Chicago area suggested that the bank and Vandenburg become partners in the purchase. Vandenburg agreed and with that first purchase, embarked upon a new entrepreneurial endeavor. He soon began to add other properties to his portfolio.

In 1983 Vandenburg formed TVO Realty Partners and was joined in the business by his younger brother, Russell A. Vandenburg. The brothers have always been close. Their childhood and formative years took place against the backdrop of Cicero, a Chicago suburb. At an early age, their parents instilled in them a strong work ethic, which was evidenced by a six-day workweek. Each day their father rose at 4:30 a.m., the aroma of his bacon-and-eggs breakfast stirring the boys as it wafted beneath their bedroom door. As a result, they too would always be early risers.

Both brothers were students and athletes at J. Sterling Morton East High School. Wayne played football and competed in track and field. Russell also played football, in addition to basketball and baseball. Wayne graduated from high school in 1960 and attended the University of New Mexico on an athletic scholarship. As a student, he studied architecture and education. Following his graduation in 1964, he remained at the university as an assistant track and field coach. During this time, he studied for a graduate degree in education and in the spring of 1966 he was appointed the head track and field coach at Texas Western College (soon to be known as the University of Texas at El Paso — UTEP). He continued coaching until 1972 and later became involved in professional sports administration until he entered the real estate industry in 1978.

Russell Vandenburg graduated from UTEP in 1970. Following a similar career path, Russell became a secondary school teacher and a football coach in El Paso, Texas. In 1983 Russell joined TVO where he founded and became the head of EPT Management Company. He assumed responsibility for all administrative aspects of property management, including long-range planning, budgeting, personnel and operations.

TVO initially acquired properties only in Texas, but soon thereafter began to acquire properties across the country. Later, TVO began to focus its interests on assets in the Midwest, a market for which the two brothers foresaw stable, long-term growth. In 1986 Wayne and TVO moved to Chicago. Russell remained in El Paso, where he successfully positioned EPT with the implementation of on-site property-management systems specifically designed to control the financial accountability and operational performance of each of the company's properties.

As TVO grew, Wayne and Russell developed a two-part company philosophy:

- To acquire, redevelop and manage real estate assets that provide residents with a rental home that is professionally managed, well maintained and well respected within the community.
- To present investors with the opportunity to participate in the creation of long-term value while receiving an attractive current rate of return on their investments.

These principles are reflected in TVO's day-to-day operations as well as its ever-increasing investment portfolio.

Even though TVO occasionally acquires properties completely for its own account, a majority of its growth comes from the creation of joint-venture relationships with major institutions, such as pension funds, insurance companies, public corporations and financial institutions. TVO's value-added process begins when an asset is first identified as a potential acquisition. Potential acquisitions are selected from over 3,000 investment opportunities that are submitted annually. TVO's due diligence team, which is comprised of construction management, market research and financial analysis professionals, thoroughly examines the underlying potential of each asset. This team is accordingly in charge of developing and implementing a plan to create increased value for TVO's investors.

TVO seeks to acquire apartment communities that are well located, well constructed and priced significantly below replacement cost. For these reasons, TVO concentrates its acquisition efforts upon properties that are 10 or more years old and are well located in established neighborhoods. When these properties were constructed, they were considered "A" quality assets, but due to neglect and the passage of time they have become "B/C" quality properties. Through renovation programs and proactive management, these properties become market leaders in their respective asset classes and take a step up in style and value. Excellent curb appeal attracts new residents and provides existing residents with a respectable home.

Over the years, TVO has acquired properties in the most desirable areas of greater Chicago. Although many of these acquisitions have been ideal assets to the company's portfolio, some have required substantial renovation in order to successfully reposition the asset for long-term growth. TVO's subsidiary, EPT Construction Management Group, oversees all capital improvements and physical enhancements to each of the properties. With touches such as new or upgraded interiors, new rooflines and landscaping, TVO and EPT transform tired, dated structures into appealing, contemporary environments. Grounds and interiors are continually maintained to high standards by a staff trained and supervised by EPT.

Clover Creek Apartments, a 504-unit apartment community, is well located in the western Chicago suburb of Lombard. Aside from being situated in a submarket where significant rent growth is projected, the return on this investment is enhanced with low-interest bond financing and a property improvement program designed to increase rental income.

Once a property has been repositioned and operations have been stabilized, TVO prepares an analysis to determine the asset's value. Assets that have achieved their business objective are positioned to be sold. TVO makes sound decisions about property sales, which are based upon both the economics of the investment and the business objectives of its partners.

TVO owes its success to the Vandenburgs' ability to be nimble on their feet. The brothers' proactive approach has enabled them to foresee and react quickly to trends in the marketplace. For instance, in 1999 they recognized an opportunity to expand TVO's interests to the rapidly growing European real estate market. As a major investor in and principal of Triomphe Partners, TVO participates in the growth, management and development of the franchise operations for **Coldwell Banker**® residential and **Coldwell Banker** Commercial®. These operations extend throughout Western and Central Europe as well as Scandinavia.

In addition to its overseas ventures, TVO continues to focus on the domestic multifamily housing market. TVO and its subsidiary, EPT, offer residents quality rental homes in apartment communities that are physically sound, professionally managed and committed to excellence through the pride and teamwork of their employees. Through their continuing commitment to the fundamentals of property ownership, property management and the integration of state-of-the-art, technology-based support systems, TVO and EPT will continue to create long-term value for their investors well into the future.

The Prime Group, Inc.

The R.R. Donnelley
Building on
W. Wacker Drive

A small circle of young, ambitious and talented entrepreneurs formed The Prime Group, Inc. in 1981 to develop investment-grade real estate properties. At the helm was Michael W. Reschke who, not yet 30 at the time, was an attorney and CPA who already grasped the complexities of succeeding in the real estate industry. Reschke determined that The Prime Group would commit to quality and excellence while maintaining a "value-add" philosophy that would create unparalleled returns for its owners and investors.

Reschke and his associates stayed focused on their vision and worked diligently until the rest of the industry began to take the new company seriously. In 1986, institutional investors began to recognize The Prime Group's potential and rewarded it with the capital that would propel the company into a period of intense growth. As it expanded and matured, The Prime Group never lost sight of its "value-add" approach, which emphasized floorplate and building efficiencies, the use of high-end materials, world-class architecture, innovative design concepts, the anticipation of rapidly shifting market trends and conditions and, finally, accessing the lowest cost of capital while attracting the best and brightest "human capital" as well. Today, the diversified, full-service real estate company comprises three operating divisions and serves as a holding company for its interests in four publicly traded real estate companies, altogether owning assets of more than $5 billion, employing nearly 4,000 people and offering services that range from design and construction to marketing, leasing and property management.

It was not until the real estate recession of the early 90s that Reschke and his team identified an emerging opportunity in the public equity markets and took several of their successful operating divisions public. These

publicly traded companies are: Prime Retail, Inc. (NYSE:PRT), a real estate investment trust (REIT) headquartered in Baltimore and the largest owner of factory outlets in the United States with 53 centers from coast to coast; locally based Brookdale Living Communities, Inc. (NASD:BLCI), which operates 23 upscale senior living communities in 14 states; Prime Group Realty Trust (NYSE:PGE), a REIT that is the largest owner of office and industrial properties in metropolitan Chicago; and Horizon Group Properties, Inc. (NASD:HGPI), a REIT with a portfolio of 14 factory outlet centers in 11 states. Prime Retail's malls were the first factory outlet centers to be built on the "village-style" concept and include such amenities as food courts and playground areas, and many of Prime Group Realty Trust's office buildings feature state-of-the-art construction, technology and world-class architectural design. Similarly demonstrating Prime's forward-thinking philosophy, Brookdale's senior housing communities emphasize healthy, active lifestyles while providing excellent personal care services.

The Prime Group's Land Development Division owns and develops land in various metropolitan areas and has transformed Huntley, once a sleepy village northwest of Chicago, into the largest master-planned community in the Midwest. When it is completed, Huntley will boast more than 5,600 single- and multi-family homes for senior citizens, a senior independent living facility, a corporate office and industrial park, retail centers, recreational facilities and the grand Huntley Automall. A second division, Prime Outdoor Group, LLC., is setting the standard for outdoor advertising as it acquires and develops outdoor signs in underserved markets across the United States. The company's third division is Prime Residential, LLC, an affiliate that develops upscale multi-family rental and condominium communities across the United States.

As it continues to grow, The Prime Group is always identifying new markets. In both new and current venues, the company's ideology remains as it has always been: to add value, nurture innovation and settle for nothing less than the best.

Chicago Historical Society

Investment banking, insurance and financial service companies, as well as banks, credit unions and other business-related firms provide support for a host of Chicagoland organizations.

BUSINESS & FINANCE

William Blair & Company

Just steps from the world-renowned Sears Tower in Chicago's financial district sits the headquarters of William Blair & Company, a full-service investment banking firm. The mission of the independent, employee-owned firm — a rarity in today's rush of consolidation — is to provide quality investment products and services in order to achieve exemplary, long-term results. Today William Blair & Company provides comprehensive financing, brokerage, research and investment advisory services to companies, institutions and individual investors around the world.

The firm got its start on January 8, 1935, when William McCormick Blair and partner Francis Bonner opened an investment banking firm on South LaSalle Street during the heart of the Depression. At the time, Chicago was viewed as a debtor rather than a creditor, and therefore turned to more financially sound sources outside of the city for help in constructing its buildings, bridges and railroads and growing the economy. Blair and Bonner's plan was to finance the expansion of midwestern growth-oriented companies with the financial backing of a

number of prominent local families including the Swift, Armour and Ryerson families and Blair's McCormick relatives of International Harvester fame. Blair and his partner felt that they could operate a conservatively financed investment firm based on the principles of honest dealings with clients, sound corporate financial advice, unbiased investment recommendations and civic responsibility — standards even stricter than those imposed by the newly formed Securities and Exchange Commission.

William Blair demanded that the firm only recommend investments it had fully researched. This marked the beginning of the firm's research department — a department that to this day maintains a sterling reputation for its quality, in-depth work. Today analysts conduct extensive research into a company's business practices before the firm issues a recommendation on the company's securities.

In most cases, after securing capital for a corporate client, the firm makes a long-term commitment to the relationship, which often includes a partner joining a client's board of directors. In William Blair's view, this approach inspired confidence in investors that their investment was being closely monitored. Today the firm enjoys numerous long-term relationships with local and national institutions.

In 1944 Blair's two sons, Edward McCormick Blair and Bowen Blair, joined the firm, bringing the number of partners to nine. Edward eventually succeeded his father

E. David Coolidge III, chief executive officer, William Blair & Company

Edgar D. Jannotta, senior director, William Blair & Company

as managing partner in 1961, even though William Blair remained active in the firm as senior partner until his death in 1982 at the age of 97.

Under the leadership of Edward Blair and Edgar D. Jannotta, managing partner from 1977 through 1994, William Blair & Company prospered, with the exception of two challenging periods. The first of these was the late 1960s when the inability to process trades resulted in a paper crunch that threatened the industry with a shutdown. Then in the 1970s, the market value of securities and underwriting activity took a serious plunge, and many firms were forced out of business. William Blair & Company survived these crises by maintaining a conservative approach and by helping to finance numerous growth companies including Molex, Oil-Dri Corporation and Safety Kleen, all of which were introduced to the public during the 1970s.

The 1980s were boom years for both the stock market and its investors as junk bonds, hostile takeovers and arbitrage investing gained prominence. William Blair & Company avoided these trends, maintaining its traditional focus on financing small to medium-sized growth-oriented companies and establishing long-term relationships with them. Instead of becoming involved in risk arbitrage and other non-client-focused trading operations, the company continued to adhere to its core belief that the best way to make money for the firm was to make money for its clients.

During the 1980s William Blair & Company opened offices in Atlanta (closed in 1985), London, Vaduz, Liechtenstein and Denver (closed in 1998). The firm opened an office in Zurich, Switzerland in 1995; a San Francisco branch in 1996; and offices in Hartford, New York and Tokyo in 1999. The opening of these additional offices has been fueled by both the slowing of the midwestern economy — the original focus of William Blair & Company — and by the growing global economy. In 1994 the firm moved its corporate headquarters from S. LaSalle Street to the USG (United States Gypsum Corp.) building at Franklin and Adams Streets in Chicago to accommodate future growth.

William Blair & Company expanded its corporate client base to include many companies throughout the United States, and broadened its client list to include healthcare, technology, banks and other financial institutions. (Prior to this time, the firm had primarily concentrated on manufacturing, retailing, distribution and unique service businesses.) Corporate relationships were

William McCormick Blair, founder of William Blair & Company

formed with numerous companies including Jones Lang LaSalle of Chicago; Concord EFS of Memphis; Henry Schein of Melville, New York; Allied Capital of Washington, D.C.; Cheap Tickets of Honolulu, Hawaii; Pro Business of Pleasanton, California; and Viking Office Products of Los Angeles. The company became active in debt, venture, leverage and mezzanine capital financing, and began playing an important role in mergers and acquisitions.

William Blair & Company has continued to expand on its original mission of providing quality investment products and services to individuals and institutional clients. Adhering to a basic philosophy of fiscal conservatism, it maintains an international reputation as one of the nation's most successful underwriters of high-quality, growth-oriented companies, and continues to deliver outstanding results.

The firm's Equity Research analysts continue to identify companies that will provide superior long-term results for the firm's national and international clients. These companies include a wide range of growth firms, ranging from small, newly public niche firms to large corporations that have an extensive track record of growth and success. William Blair & Company's Equity

William Blair's national prominence can be attributed to underwriting highly successful companies and giving excellent investment advice.

Research department specializes in uncovering growth companies in business services, commercial/industrial products and services, consumer products and services, financial services, healthcare and technology. The department publishes detailed reports on over 300 companies located within and outside of the United States.

Through its Investment Banking services department, William Blair & Company provides access to capital for its clients through debt and equity offerings. The Corporate Finance department provides a full range of services for its corporate clients. This includes initial public offerings (IPOs), secondary offerings, merger and acquisition advice, private equity placements, valuations and fairness opinions. The firm investigates a company's business, operations, products, customers and market position to determine the most constructive course of action. It also works closely with company management to prepare necessary registration materials and to identify key investment issues that are essential in generating institutional and individual investor interest.

The Debt Capital Markets department raises capital for clients through senior, medium-term and subordinate note programs, industrial revenue bonds, lease and installment transactions and bank debt. Debt issuers include federal, state and local governments, midsize

publicly and privately held companies, as well as cultural and educational institutions and transportation authorities. The firm has served as lead underwriter for such local institutions as Rush-Presbyterian St. Luke's Medical Center, DePaul University and the Regional Transit Authority (RTA). William Blair & Company has also

earned an excellent national reputation for floating bonds for cultural institutions including the Art Institute of Chicago, The Shedd Aquarium Society, Steppenwolf Theatre Company, Lyric Opera of Chicago, the Museum of Contemporary Art, and the Museum of Science and Industry.

The firm's Institutional Equity Sales departments are focused on helping institutional investors in North America, Europe and the Far East make money for their clients by recommending superior investment products. To reach this goal, they establish relationships with portfolio managers and analysts at mutual funds, pension funds, investment advisory firms, banks and other money management organizations.

The goal of the Private Investor department is to offer clients solid and reliable investment advice in the areas of equities, corporate and municipal bonds, mutual funds and other quality investment products. These recommendations are generated by the firm's Equity Research department as well as the Corporate Finance department. Because the principals of the employee-owned firm assume all financial and legal risks of the business and are the sole source of capital, there is a strong motivation to make wise investment decisions.

The Investment Management Services department offers fee-based asset management for pension plans, endowments, foundations, family estates, and trusts and individuals. The department's broadly diversified customer base represents an approximately equal mix of tax-exempt and taxable portfolios. Five separate investment disciplines and a complete family of mutual funds are available to clients worldwide.

The firm's venture capital and merchant banking expertise is consolidated into William Blair Capital Partners, L.L.C., continuing a long tradition of financing and acquiring emerging growth companies. The group invests in venture capital financings, leveraged buyouts and recapitalizations of well-managed growth companies. All allocations are made with a simple and clear objective: to generate superior long-term capital gains by building successful companies in partnerships with outstanding management teams. Since 1982 the formula has proven successful for both the funds' portfolio companies and limited partners.

William Blair Mezzanine Capital Partners, L.L.C., provides a vehicle for private debt investments. Mezzanine capital — usually in the form of a subordinated loan with a considerable equity interest — is provided in order to facilitate recapitalizations, management buyouts, leveraged acquisitions and internal expansion.

Because William Blair & Company is an independent, employee-owned firm, it attracts top-quality employees and makes a long-term commitment to their professional careers. Rather than acquiring other firms, William Blair & Company has grown by adding services and recruiting highly qualified professionals. In addition, the executive committee encourages an entrepreneurial environment and asks employees to contribute their ideas and assume an active role in decision making. Furthermore, the firm offers a stable work environment for its employees; in fact, the company has never had a layoff, and the rate of turnover remains one of the lowest in the industry. Over 90 percent of the staff is based in the firm's Chicago headquarters, and many of the company's principals have spent their entire careers with William Blair & Company.

Throughout its long history, William Blair & Company has adhered to one of the central tenets of its founder: maintain close ties to the Chicago community. Senior Director Edgar D. Jannotta has served as chairman of the Lyric Opera of Chicago and currently serves as chairman of the board of trustees of the University of Chicago. Both Mr. Jannotta and Senior Director Edward McCormick Blair are past chairmen of the board of Chicago's Rush-Presbyterian St. Luke's Medical Center. In addition, current CEO E. David Coolidge III is a past president of the Better Government Association.

The firm has also carried on the tradition of financing local (as well as national) growth-oriented companies, and makes substantial contributions each year to hundreds of charitable, civic, cultural, educational and medical organizations in the Chicago area through the William

Blair & Company Foundation. In addition, the firm conducts an annual fund-raising drive for United Way, and most employees contribute on a regular basis.

William Blair & Company's strategic planning committee has developed a comprehensive business plan for the future that will enable the firm to continue to be a leading resource for investors, growth companies and institutions with long-term capital needs. By adhering to a basic philosophy of traditional values, integrity and honesty in all dealings, and by offering quality products and services, William Blair & Company will, no doubt, remain one of the country's leading full-service investment banking firms.

Arthur J. Gallagher & Co.

Arthur J. Gallagher (1892-1985), founder, Arthur J. Gallagher & Co.

(Far right) Sterling Bassett was recruited by the Gallaghers to lead the newly created self-insurance division of AJGCo., Gallagher Bassett Services, Inc., on November 1, 1962.

"Big enough to do the job, small enough to care." That's the motto of Arthur J. Gallagher & Co. — an Itasca, Illinois-based firm that plans and administers cost-effective property/casualty and employee-benefit and risk-management programs for clients worldwide. The company is the world's fourth-largest commercial insurance brokerage and risk management services firm, and one of the country's leading third-party claims man-agers and employee-benefit service providers. Client service is provided through a network of over 200 offices in the United States and in six countries abroad.

The company was the brainchild of Arthur James Gallagher, who was born in 1892 on the West Side of Chicago. An excellent ballplayer, Gallagher had hopes of becoming a professional, but in lieu of a baseball career, he attended DePaul High School and completed a three-year accounting course. Upon graduation he was hired by the Prussian National Insurance Company as a bookkeeper.

In 1917 he enlisted in the U.S. Army's Illinois 33rd Division, 108th Engineers, and soon found himself under fire in the trenches in France. After serving his country in many major engagements, he returned to Chicago as an officer at the war's end.

Gallagher obtained employment with Chicago's largest insurance broker, Moore Case Lyman & Hubbard. He started work for the firm in an accounting role, though he realized that the people making the real money in insurance were those in sales. Gallagher pursued a sales position and was finally given a chance to sell. He developed an expertise at cold calling, and soon became the top producer of the firm. Despite his success, he found out that he was not being fairly compensated, so he quit the firm in 1927 to establish his own company — Arthur J. Gallagher & Co.

Gallagher decided to concentrate on commercial insurance, which was his area of expertise. From the beginning, he believed in putting power in his clients' hands by identifying areas of risk and developing and implementing ways to reduce that risk. By doing so, Gallagher could help his clients realize significant savings in terms of money, time, productivity and, most importantly, lives. Risk management was an innovative concept and Arthur J. Gallagher was one of its pioneers.

The New York Stock Exchange crashed on October 29, 1929, and business failures were epidemic. It was difficult selling commercial insurance; nonetheless, Gallagher persuaded business owners that it was important to protect what they had. By persistently knocking on doors, Gallagher increased his business, and by the mid-1930s, he had hired one of his neighbors, Dan Wachs, and later, Ed Keating, to help out with the business. At first, Wachs and Keating provided technical support for Gallagher's sales. Later, they took over the servicing of some accounts and evolved into important producers in their own right.

During the World War II years, Gallagher's young sons, Jim, Bob and John, began learning about the business. They worked for their dad running errands, doing odd jobs and generally acting as "go-fers." Decades later, as chairman of Arthur J. Gallagher & Co., Bob Gallagher remembers the fun of those summers — when he started on the switchboard for $5 a week and moved up to messenger. "We got to watch my dad and Dan and Ed, and I loved it!" he says.

AJGCo. took another major step toward the world of self-insurance when it wrote the first large-deductible fire policy for Bowman Dairy Co. in Chicago. Large deductibles and experience rating are common now, but in the late 1930s they became the first rumblings of a revolution that would sweep the insurance industry. And AJGCo. would be positioned on the front lines of that revolution.

In 1938 the firm also helped create the Retrospective Rating Program of the Hartford Accident and Indemnity Insurance Company, an innovative program that gave customers financial incentives for holding down their losses. This was a step toward self-insurance and the alternative market, a radical concept in the insurance industry.

After serving their country in World War II, all three of Gallagher's sons joined AJGCo.

Significant milestones of the 50s included Arthur J. Gallagher's decision to incorporate the business, giving each of his three sons a 20 percent stake common stock in the company, while he held 40 percent preferred stock. In 1957 Arthur J. Gallagher & Co. landed its largest client to date: Chicago-based Beatrice Foods Company. This relationship with Beatrice led Arthur J. Gallagher & Co. to become a pioneer in self-insurance. In 1958 Our Lady of Angels Catholic School in Chicago was the scene of a horrific fire that claimed the lives of 95 people, most of them children. The tragedy revealed that the Chicago Archdiocese was woefully underinsured. Eventually a request for help reached the Gallaghers. AJGCo. responded by putting together an umbrella policy with much broader terms and coverage that cost half of what the diocese had been paying. This led to a proposal for a self-insurance plan for the entire archdiocese — the Bishop's Plan for Self-insurance was created. Dioceses in other states signed on to the plan and gradually AJGCo. and Gallagher Bassett became nationally known.

"The entire industry was fighting what we were doing and saying it wouldn't work," says J. Patrick Gallagher Jr., current CEO of Arthur J. Gallagher & Co. and grandson of the company's founder. "We played a major role in shifting the industry to self-insurance; in fact, today some estimates place 45 percent of the commercial property/casualty insurance business in programs that are self-insured in some fashion."

Though the agency had put together a state-of-the-art insurance plan for Beatrice Foods in the late 50s, several years later Beatrice CEO Bill Karnes decided he wanted more control over his costs and turned to the Gallaghers for help. Since AJGCo. excelled in placing insurance coverage, not handling claims, it sought out Sterling Bassett, a well-respected claim adjuster for Chicago-based General Adjustment Bureau, who was also Jim Gallagher's neighbor. Sterling resigned his job at GAB, and on November 10, 1962, Gallagher Bassett was formed.

In 1963 Bob Gallagher began his leadership role as president and chief executive officer of the company. In 1965 John Gallagher launched the Summer Internship Program, a program that continues to thrive today. The

program provides college students valuable hands-on experience and a broad perspective on the insurance industry. The program targets students who are in their sophomore and junior years of college, and interns are frequently offered full-time employment with the company after they graduate. Many top managers, including CEO Patrick Gallagher, began their careers in the Summer Internship Program.

The company experienced significant growth in the 1970s. The firm moved into larger quarters on East Wacker Drive in Chicago, and the first shares of stock were sold to Gallagher employees. Revenues topped $10 million, and AJGCo.'s dominance in the self-insurance market took the company to London — an important part of the alternative market — in 1974 for the formation of Lloyd's broker Gallagher, Hinton & Vereker Ltd. This was Gallagher's first step in establishing an international presence. International expansion, including the development of joint ventures and correspondent-broker relationships, is part of the company's ongoing strategy to grow its global capabilities.

In 1975 Gallagher's employee-benefits division, Gallagher Benefit Services, wrote the company's first

The lineup of producers at AJGCo. after World War II was (left to right) John Gallagher, Ed Keating, Jim Gallagher, Dan Wachs and Bob Gallagher. Wachs and Keating started out providing technical support for Arthur J. Gallagher's sales, but evolved into important producers. John Gallagher, Jim Gallagher and Bob Gallagher all joined the firm after serving their country in World War II.

Robert E. Gallagher (center) accepts congratulations from Jay Mahoney (right) of A.C. Partners, AJGCo.'s market maker, and John K. Lyden (left) of the New York Stock Exchange board as the stock of Arthur J. Gallagher & Co. is first traded on the New York Stock Exchange December 1, 1987.

The creativity of John P. Gallagher (1927-1996), son of Arthur J. Gallagher and former executive vice president and vice chairman of the board, took flight in the many facets of AJGCo. He helped in the establishment of Gallagher Bassett Services, Inc.; the development and proposal of the Bishop's Plan; the launch of the Summer Intern Program; introduced the concept of the Annual Marketing Meeting; encouraged the growth of corporate training; and ignited AJGCo.'s international expansion.

(Top far right) President and Chief Executive Officer J. Patrick Gallagher, Jr. (left) began working for his grandfather's company in the summer of 1966 as a second-generation "go-fer." He joined the firm after graduating from college in 1974. Chairman Robert E. Gallagher (right) is the son of Arthur J. Gallagher. Bob began his leadership role as president and chief executive officer of the company in 1963 and celebrated his 50th anniversary with the company in 1997.

(Right) Arthur J. Gallagher & Co.'s international headquarters is located in the Gallagher Centre in Itasca, Ill.

self-funded employee-benefits plan. Since that time, this has become a major source of business for the company. Today Gallagher Benefit Services continues its focus on corporate customers, assisting clients with their employee retirement plans, health and welfare plans and human resource-related services, including design, funding and administration.

The 1980s was another decade of remarkable growth and innovation. In 1982 *Business Insurance* magazine ranked AJGCo. the 10th largest broker in the United States. In 1983 company revenues hit the $50 million mark. In 1984 the firm went public with an initial common stock offering, company revenues topped the $100 million mark in 1986 and the company joined the New York Stock Exchange in 1987. And also that year, *Forbes* magazine named Arthur J. Gallagher & Co. "One of the 200 Best Small Companies in America."

The 1990s brought continued change. Pat Gallagher was named president of the company in 1990 (and CEO in 1995), and in 1991 the company headquarters moved to Itasca, where it occupies over half of a 25-story-building appropriately called the Gallagher Centre.

Mergers and acquisitions continue to be a key catalyst to compounding the company's growth. Through mergers, AJGCo. increases market share, broadens its business mix, and adds new people, locations and areas of expertise. The company's merger and acquisition strategy is based on a philosophy that favors long-term growth over short-term gain. Merger partners are given the opportunity to grow and develop as AJGCo. provides the support system needed to compound their operational growth, business expertise and investment.

The company's Brokerage Services Division, the largest division, has continued to provide a steady source of revenue. This division specializes in the structuring of property/casualty insurance and risk-management programs for commercial, industrial, institutional and governmental organizations through a network of offices in the United States, the United Kingdom and Bermuda, and through correspondent brokers in more than 100 countries.

Gallagher Bassett Services, Inc. (GB), Gallagher's principle subsidiary, ranks among the top three property/casualty contracted claims-management providers in the world, and has more than 130 offices in the United States and overseas. The unbundling of risk management services is a trend impacting the worldwide market and GB is capitalizing on opportunities overseas with offices and joint ventures in England, Scotland, Australia, Papua New Guinea and Canada.

GB offers a broad range of risk management services, including claims and information management, risk-control consulting, appraisals, security consulting and surveillance. The company is linked through a system called RISX-FACS® — a centralized database that provides detailed claims reporting tailored to meet each client's specifications. Accessible through the Internet, the RISX-FACS® system has been a key to Gallagher Bassett's growth, providing clients with information that is timely and accurate. It should continue to be key in acquiring new business.

Gallagher Benefit Services division is a full-service benefits-consulting firm. The division, which posted annual double digit revenue growth throughout the 90s, assists clients in all areas of their employee retirement plans, health and welfare plans and human resource-related services including design, funding and administration. The increasing complexity of government regulatory and reporting requirements is causing employers to continue to outsource the management of their employee-benefits and human-resource functions — creating a robust, long-term growth outlook for this division.

In 1997 Arthur J. Gallagher & Co. formed AJG Financial Services, a subsidiary that specializes in alternative investment strategies and tax-advantaged investments. It manages Gallagher's own investment portfolio and is expanding the availability of some of those strategies and investments to others in conjunction with the insurance services for which Gallagher is known.

Although the company has evolved into a multinational, multimillion-dollar business with thousands of employees, Arthur J. Gallagher & Co. maintains — as it always has — a warm, family-oriented corporate culture. In 1984 Bob Gallagher wrote down a list — that is prominently displayed and respected throughout the company — that describes the company's shared values: honesty, integrity, a competitive spirit, a concern for people, team spirit and professional excellence. This document is called "The Gallagher Way."

Top management — as well as other company employees — participate in numerous civic endeavors. CEO Patrick Gallagher, along with his wife, Anne, is active in Catholic Charities — an organization with a mission to provide compassionate, competent professional services to improve the quality of personal and family life of any person regardless of faith, color or creed. Chairman Bob Gallagher and his wife, Isabel, are co-founders of the Gallagher Scholars Program — a program that was started in 1993 with the encouragement of the late Chicago Cardinal Joseph Bernadin. This program provides mentoring and financial assistance to send inner-city grade and high school students to private Catholic schools. These scholars, in turn, are asked to adhere to a strict code of conduct and are exposed to numerous activities — including a visit to AJGCo. headquarters. The program is funded by Bob and Isabel Gallagher.

AJGCo.'s opportunities for growth are limitless, says Patrick Gallagher. "We're just getting started, and our ability to expand is unbelievable. What we have accomplished so far is truly just the beginning. Our future has never been brighter."

The Summer Internship Program, launched in 1965, continues to thrive today. The program offers college students exposure to all aspects of the insurance and risk-management business and helps them determine if working in that business and working for Arthur J. Gallagher & Co. is a career path with appeal.

Driehaus Capital Management Inc.

The investment services provided by Driehaus Capital Management Inc. are as grand as the Romanesque-style mansion that houses this Chicago-based money management firm. For more than 20 years, Richard H. Driehaus and his team of portfolio managers have helped clients maximize their investment returns by selecting rapidly growing companies with high market potential. As a result Driehaus Capital Management has garnered a renowned reputation throughout the investment industry, and more importantly, among its clients.

In addition Chicago and its residents have greatly benefited from the numerous philanthropic and civic contributions put forth by Richard H. Driehaus, the firm's founder and chairman. The Richard H. Driehaus Foundation provides funding for landmark preservation, architectural design, education, off-Loop performing arts and self-help programs. "It is important for me to give back to the community," says Driehaus. "Chicago's educational institutions provided me with the tools for success."

The innovative investment services provided by Driehaus Capital Management are housed within the Romanesque-style Cable house, located near the city's Water Tower.

Driehaus Capital Management provides investment-management services to institutional clients, high-net-worth individuals and mutual fund investors, specializing in domestic and international aggressive-growth investing. The company currently manages about $7 billion in assets spread between institutional portfolios and mutual funds. "Our commitment to implementing our philosophy over a full market cycle is what sets us apart from other investment firms," says Driehaus. "We rank high in style purity."

Through a systematic approach to analyzing stocks, sectors and market trends, Driehaus Capital Management is able to synthesize corporate and market information and react more quickly than other investment firms. The firm's investment strategies focus on companies that it believes have strong growth prospects, and the firm seeks to take maximum advantage of opportunities that arise in an ever-changing market environment. "Rather than avoid risk, we embrace change," says Robert Moyer, company president. "We accommodate risk and harness it to the advantage of our clients. We are always invested in a very aggressive group of stocks and we employ a high-maintenance style of investing — one that uses an intense philosophy but offers superior performance."

The primary focus of Driehaus Capital Management's portfolio managers is on the revenue and earnings growth, the quality of the earnings and the market time-liness of the stocks they invest in for each portfolio. One of the firm's major strengths is its sell discipline. If an investment fails to meet fundamental or technical criteria, it will be replaced by one that does. Managers are continually monitoring the market for new ideas to include in the portfolios. This dedication to their investment philosophy, style of management and excellence was established by Richard Driehaus more than two decades ago. These are the reasons Driehaus Capital Management has achieved a superior long-term performance record.

BACKED BY EXPERIENCE

Richard H. Driehaus began his career in the investment field in 1965 at Rothchild & Co. and in 1968 joined the firm of A.G. Becker, developing research ideas for the Institutional Trading department. Two years later Driehaus became the youngest portfolio manager for that firm's pension and profit-sharing program and was ranked among the top 1 percent of portfolio managers measured by A.G. Becker's Fund Evaluation Service.

In 1973 Driehaus became a shareholder and director of research for the brokerage firm Mullaney, Wells and Co. and by 1976 had become a money manager of the Chicago and New York offices of Jesup & Lamont. Driehaus set out on his own in 1980 in order to better implement his philosophy and improve the services he offered to his clients, and formed Driehaus Securities Corporation, a registered broker/dealer that concentrated on providing growth-investment research to large institutional clients.

In addition to providing research services, Driehaus managed a limited number of small-cap, growth-style accounts that had been his clients prior to forming the firm. In 1982 Driehaus Capital Management was formed to consolidate the management of these separate accounts. Driehaus Capital Management initially managed pooled accounts of small-cap stocks for investors and then introduced a mid-cap, growth-style product in 1986 and an international growth-style product in 1989. "The goal was to have the investment firm provide superior returns for each of our clients," says Driehaus. "Understanding and exceeding our clients' performance goals is the primary factor in the firm's success. Our best employees are those who place our clients' interests ahead of their own."

In the early 1990s the Driehaus operation shifted its focus from being a research-driven brokerage firm to an investment-management business. Driehaus Capital Management began to market its small-cap growth products to institutional clients and in 1992 began to market its mid-cap growth products. Driehaus Mutual Funds was launched in 1996 with the Driehaus International Growth Fund, and the following year the firm began offering its international growth-style products to institutional clients. Today the Driehaus mutual fund family includes the Emerging Markets Growth Fund, the Asia Pacific Growth Fund, the International Discovery Fund, the European Opportunity Fund and the International Growth Fund.

William R. Andersen heads the firm's international team of portfolio managers, analysts and support staff, who collectively have more than 45 years of investment experience. Andersen joined Driehaus Securities Corporation in 1985 as an analyst for the firm's domestic portfolios. In 1989 he employed the Driehaus growth philosophy to the international markets and this led to the success of the Driehaus International Large Cap Fund L.P. Later this fund would become the Driehaus International Growth Fund. Today the international team specializes in markets in Asia, Eastern and Western Europe and emerging markets. The firm strives to create an environment that acknowledges and encourages individual achievement, while recognizing that the success of the firm is best achieved through a team approach.

A Commitment to Earnings

Driehaus Capital Management considers revenue and earnings growth to be the principal factors in determining common stock prices over the long term, using accelerating sales and earnings growth rates and positive-earnings surprises as fundamental criteria for selecting stocks. Only through sustained earnings growth can cash flows be expanded, dividends raised and book values increased. Driehaus himself has been named to the *Barron's* All-Century Team of All-Stars as one of the mutual fund world's heaviest hitters.

Richard H. Driehaus, chief investment officer, CEO and chairman of Driehaus Capital Management

Tiffany turtleback chandeliers illuminate the traders' desks and provide a historical, artistic touch to this technologically savvy workplace within the Cable house.

Driehaus Capital Management follows a "bottom-up" philosophy when investing, evaluating the fundamental elements of a company's financial condition — such as revenue and earnings growth rates — in determining whether to buy or sell its stock. Portfolio managers work closely with in-house research analysts and information technology support. They continually monitor the investment environment for economic, political and social developments. This allows the firm to try to identify attractive stocks before other firms have fully evaluated their earnings and stock-price potential.

Each day portfolio managers and research analysts access multiple sources of information, such as research reports, market analyses and trade journals, and continually monitor major industry trends. The goal is to know each individual stock within the firm's portfolios — how that stock fits into its peer group and how it relates to the market as a whole. "Success must be re-achieved each day," says Driehaus. "It results from our anticipation of the new needs of our clients and our understanding of the changing nature of the domestic and international security markets."

With its domestic portfolios, the firm purchases the majority of its positions in the capitalization range appropriate to each portfolio. Portfolio managers may, on occasion, purchase shares of larger or smaller companies with capitalizations outside that range to enhance the

overall portfolio. In addition, the firm is not restricted by a sell discipline based on market capitalization — it can hold a position even if a stock has appreciated beyond the initial estimated parameters.

The international portfolios of Driehaus Capital Management focus on companies in both developed and emerging markets and do not instill an upper limit on the capitalization range. The firm places additional research emphasis on country-by-country market trends and market liquidity, currency expectations, accounting and reporting variations and political climates, among other variables. "We plan to increase our international product line as the market continues to expand," says Driehaus.

There are several company-specific factors the firm evaluates when selecting domestic or international stock purchases, including increasing order backlogs, positive same-store sales trends, new-product introductions and broadened marketing capabilities. Driehaus Capital Management also assesses the level of competition within an industry, pricing environment, relevant industry changes and legislative and economic developments.

Any changes in these factors can affect a stock's performance. Driehaus Capital Management continually monitors each holding in each portfolio for changes that could impact current or future earnings. The firm is quick to sell if a stock is not performing well, and would rather take a series of small losses to avoid large losses down the road. This ensures that the firm's investments are concentrated in securities with the greatest likelihood of capital appreciation. "Our investment style is geared toward those willing to accept shorter term volatility," says Moyer. "But over time we are able to create exceptional growth for our client portfolios in a controlled fashion."

A WORKPLACE LIKE NO OTHER

The corporate headquarters of Driehaus Capital Management is located in the Ransom R. Cable house — a sprawling, 20,000-square-foot marvel built in 1886 as the residence and coach house for Ransom R. Cable, president of the Rock Island and Pacific Railway Company. The house, located near the city's Water

William R. Andersen, senior vice president and chief investment officer for the international division of Driehaus Capital Management

The French Room of the Cable house provides an inspiring meeting room for the Driehaus team to strategize its investment options.

Tower, was designed by the prominent Chicago architect, Henry Ives Cobb, and has served as the firm's headquarters since 1994.

Driehaus is dedicated to landmark preservation and today continues to be active in this cause throughout the city. In addition to housing the state-of-the-art trading services offered by Driehaus Capital Management, the Cable house serves as a fitting home for Driehaus' priceless collection of rare and exquisite art.

The Cable house was constructed from northern pink buff dolomitic Minnesota limestone from the Kasota-Mankato district, which gives the structure its distinctive color. Inside, the parlor features polished marbles and woods and is filled with heavily layered velvets, ornate carpets, Louis-Phillipe chairs, a 7-foot Chickering grand piano and *Victory Marchant* by Jean-Leon Gerome (1824-1904).

The reception area's full-length, stained-glass wall is an authentic set of Louis Comfort Tiffany windows that depicts a band of angels and was formerly housed in All Angeles Church in New York City. A breathtaking Tiffany window depicting St. Michael can be found near the mansion's back staircase, and another significant Tiffany production, *Lady With Irises,* is installed in the door that leads to the coach house walkway. In addition, the reception desk features lamps from the workshop of Tiffany or that were inspired by him.

The French Room of the Cable house serves as a meeting room where the Driehaus team makes its investment decisions. The room's table and chairs are reminiscent of those found in the Louis XVI period. Nearby, marble pillars support bronze statuettes that are standing guard over an enameled clock of the 1780s which features moon and sun time, a calendar, and stars and zodiac readings. Below, a white marble Rococo Revival fireplace is protected by a magnificent Tiffany bronze grid of 100 glass squares.

The trading room is located in the upstairs of the mansion and serves as one of the busy areas for Driehaus Capital Management. The room is saturated with works of art, and Tiffany turtleback chandeliers illuminate the traders' desks and provide a historical, artistic touch to this technologically savvy workplace. In fact Driehaus Capital Management is one of the most technologically advanced firms in the investment industry. The firm staffs 12 computer professionals in its information technology department, which is supplemented by outside consultants. State-of-the-art information-delivery systems allow the firm to identify relationships between market data, stock prices, company fundamentals and industry technical patterns. "What we can do through our electronic-trading capabilities and information-gathering positions in Chicago makes us a successful competitor in the world trading market," says Moyer.

The office of Richard Driehaus is anchored by a Renaissance-inspired desk that is complemented by a dark marble fireplace. On the mantle sits a fine neoclassical French clock and two related candelabra. The gilt-bronze Amor Caritas angel, sculpted by renowned American sculptor Augustus Saint-Gaudens in 1898, stands between the two entrances to the office. Tiffany glass is also a prominent feature in this room, from the Tiffany chandelier above Driehaus' desk to the gold favrile glass placed throughout the office. Delicate Tiffany tulip glasses, each serving as its own bouquet, add a warm texture to this regal, professional setting.

The thriving combination of dedication to excellence and success found at Driehaus Capital Management not only allows the firm to continually achieve substantial returns for its clients, but also for the company to serve as a fitting tribute to the past and future treasures of Chicago. As Driehaus says, "We would rather be the best than the biggest. Our goal is to only undertake that in which we can excel. We are always uncompromising in our dedication to excellence."

The office of Richard Driehaus is anchored by a Renaissance-inspired desk that is complemented by a dark marble fireplace, a neoclassical French clock and two candelabra.

Robert W. Baird & Co.

Robert W. Baird's wisdom, experience and integrity helped guide the firm's growth for 41 years.

(Top far right) Baird has been prominent in serving Wisconsin industries and investors since 1919.

Baird has grown into one of Chicago's top 10 investment banking firms.

In the vast sea of financial firms that mark Chicago's business landscape, it is easy for smaller firms to become lost. Robert W. Baird & Co., however, has grown its Chicago operations from a small branch office serving individual investors into one of the city's top 10 investment banking firms, based on its number of banking professionals.

Nationally, Baird is one of the largest investment banking and brokerage firms headquartered outside of New York, achieving an enviable balance among its main businesses. Baird's more than 720 Financial Advisors serve investors through more than 75 offices. Its Capital Markets Group provides a full range of investment banking services to middle-market growth companies in selected industries and to municipalities, schools and government agencies. In addition, Baird offers institutional equity sales and trading, merchant banking services and asset management. Baird also has extensive international capabilities through the 1999 acquisition of a London investment banking firm, now operating as Granville Baird Group Limited. In fact, Baird's cross-border expertise distinguishes it among its peers serving middle-market companies.

BUILDING ON A RICH HERITAGE

As it becomes a key player, Baird follows a road map marked with the integrity of its namesake and the

Midwestern values of its Wisconsin birthplace. The company's roots can be traced to 1919 when the First Wisconsin National Bank of Milwaukee created a securities subsidiary and hired Robert W. Baird to oversee the new unit. Within three years Mr. Baird was named president of the securities firm, a position he held until he became chairman in 1948. Known as a man of high integrity, Mr. Baird insisted that the company's dealings be honest and fair, believing that clients' interests came before those of the firm. That philosophy — which remains the central tenet of how the company conducts business to this day — proved to be so successful that the firm survived the Great Depression when others were forced to merge or close. When the bank was required to divest its securities operations in 1934 in response to the Glass-Steagall Act, the securities firm became an independent entity.

In 1948 the company became the first Wisconsin-based securities firm to join the New York Stock Exchange. As did most companies joining the NYSE in those days, the firm took the name of its lead partner, officially becoming Robert W. Baird & Co.

Throughout his 41-year career at the investment firm, Mr. Baird set a standard for the highest principles in dealing with investors and investment banking clients. His influence and reputation for integrity went far beyond the walls of his own firm. He played an active role in the formation of the National Association of Securities Dealers (NASD) and served as its third national chairman in 1941, beginning a tradition of senior Baird executives serving in leadership roles in the securities industry.

AN ENVIABLE GROWTH RECORD

When Mr. Baird retired in 1960 the company had 65 associates and revenues of a few million dollars. As the company continued to expand its investment services and open branch offices under strong leadership, it remained true to its values and its focus on putting clients' interests first. By 1979 the company had grown to 17 offices throughout the Midwest with revenues of $20 million. It was then that G. Frederick Kasten Jr., the current chairman, became Baird's sixth president.

Baird has produced an enviable record of growth and profitability since 1980. In a volatile industry noted for losses and layoffs following sharp market swings, Baird can proudly say that it has had only one month with a loss since 1980, in the crash of October 1987, and has never ended a year with fewer associates than the previous year. In fact, from January 1, 1980, through 1999, Baird's revenues grew at a compound annual rate of 16 percent to $560.7 million and the return on Baird stock increased at a 19 percent annual growth rate.

In 1982 The Northwestern Mutual Life Insurance Company acquired a majority interest in Baird. This affiliation with a company long recognized for excellence underscores Baird's own commitment to the highest standards of performance for its clients. More than 500 Baird associates also are shareholders in the

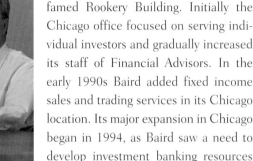

company, giving them a vested interest in Baird's long-term success.

CREATING A MEANINGFUL PRESENCE IN CHICAGO

Baird entered the Chicago market in 1960 by acquiring Wm. A. Fuller & Co., which housed a staff of two in the famed Rookery Building. Initially the Chicago office focused on serving individual investors and gradually increased its staff of Financial Advisors. In the early 1990s Baird added fixed income sales and trading services in its Chicago location. Its major expansion in Chicago began in 1994, as Baird saw a need to develop investment banking resources here. With Chicago holding its own with New York and San Francisco as key financial markets, the opportunities here for Baird were hard to resist.

To lead its Chicago investment banking services, Baird selected three well-known Chicago investment bankers who shared the company's Midwestern values and could also give the company the energetic leadership it needed to build its reputation and services in the highly competitive Chicago market. Paul E. Purcell, Paul J. Carbone and Steven G. Booth joined Baird with a combined 40 years of investment banking experience at a national firm and eventually were joined at Baird by 10 of their

Paul E. Purcell (standing), president and chief executive officer, and G. Frederick Kasten, chairman

Baird's Institutional Equity Sales and Trading Department delivers timely investment and trading ideas to leading institutional investors in North America and Europe.

Judy Scott was named to the first team of *Institutional Investor* magazine's 1999 All-America Research Team.

colleagues. Purcell has been president of Baird since 1998 and became chief executive officer in 2000, succeeding Kasten. Carbone is director of Advisory and Merchant Banking Services. Booth is co-director of Merger and Acquisition Advisory Services.

Baird's entry into the Chicago investment banking market in 1994 began with little fanfare. Known as a successful regional investment banking firm, Baird faced stiff competition from the national firms among Chicago's heavy hitters. Fortunately, Purcell and Carbone were known among their peers and Baird's name was paired with its well-regarded parent, Northwestern Mutual. From its small base, Baird has built the Chicago office into its second largest, hosting more than 100 of the company's total 2,300 associates worldwide, including professionals in the private client, investment banking, merchant banking and fixed income sales trading groups. Baird now ranks among the city's top 10 investment banking firms based on its number of banking professionals.

INDIVIDUALIZED ATTENTION FOR INVESTORS

Baird's Financial Advisors focus on their clients' specialized needs to provide one-on-one advice to help clients achieve their near-term and long-range financial goals. They help clients build and manage their wealth, professionally guiding them through ever-changing markets. Through services such as financial planning, asset allocation and estate planning, Baird Financial Advisors help provide direction and meaning to clients' investment decisions. A team of specialists in various investment products and services support the Financial Advisors, and a variety of fee-based asset management programs also are available. The Financial Advisors work to develop long-term relationships based on integrity and trust.

In the past three years, the number of branch offices has grown by nearly a third to more than 75 locations. Client assets under custody totaled $42 billion at the end of 1999.

A HIGHLY FOCUSED CAPITAL MARKETS TEAM

Baird has significantly expanded its Capital Markets Group throughout the 90s so that it can successfully

deliver high-quality service on every front — equity and debt financing, merger and acquisition advisory services, research, trading and institutional and individual sales. The breadth of investment banking skills and the coordinated team approach enable Baird to provide comprehensive, quality service to middle-market companies in selected industries. Baird combines knowledge of specific industries and market dynamics with investment banking expertise to deliver straightforward advice — advice to help clients achieve their strategic objectives.

Quality research is the foundation of Baird's investment banking efforts. Baird focuses on serving clients in specific industries where its research expertise gives it a thorough understanding of clients' needs and their competitive environment. Areas of specialization include Technology, Industrial and Consumer, Health Care, and Financial Services and Utilities.

With more than 40 analysts, the Equity Research Department is one of the largest among regional firms and has been recognized for its quality and depth of coverage:

• In the 1998 and 1999 Reuters surveys on U.S. small to mid-cap companies, Baird research was ranked higher than any other regional firm by the mutual fund and corporate management participating in the survey. In addition, fund managers ranked Baird's Institutional Services and Research team first in the country in terms of the level of service provided to institutional clients.

• Analyst Judith G. Scott was named to *Institutional Investor* magazine's prestigious 1999 All-America Research Team, earning a place on the first team for staffing industry coverage. While it is unusual for any regional firm analysts to earn All-America recognition, Scott has been honored for two consecutive years.

• Seven Baird analysts have been recognized as All-Star Analysts by *The Wall Street Journal* in recent years in the following industry sectors: Auto and Auto Parts; Health Care; Oil Services; Paper and Forest Products; Pollution Control; Telecommunications; and Utilities.

• Baird ranks as the 16th most active research department in the world, based on the number of published reports in 1999, according to *Nelson's Catalog of Institutional Research Reports*.

A RECORD OF ACHIEVEMENT

Baird's industry expertise translates into action on behalf of its corporate clients, many of whom have been involved in multiple transactions with Baird.

• Since 1995 Baird has raised $11 billion as a manager or co-manager in more than 110 equity transactions.

• A leading participant in the merger and acquisition arena, Baird has advised on more than 125 transactions in the past five years with a total value exceeding $26 billion.

• Baird has raised more than $32 billion in debt capital in the past five years for its corporate and municipal clients.

• Baird also makes private equity investments in growing middle-market companies through Baird Capital Partners, which closed its third investment fund, of approximately $175 million, in early 2000. Completion of this third fund brings assets under management to over $225 million.

Baird also strives to provide continuous client support through its sales and trading professionals. The Institutional Equity Services team provides timely investment and trading ideas to more than 725 institutional clients in North America and Europe and hosts major investor conferences annually featuring presentations by more than 200 companies. Baird also consistently ranks among the most active market makers in its clients' shares. Its Fixed Income Sales and Trading Department works with more than 2,000 institutions and its Preferred Stock Department is one of the most active dealers nationally.

INTERNATIONAL EXPERTISE

The merger of Baird and Granville Baird, London, in late 1999 created a powerful team with international resources to meet clients' needs. Granville has forged an impressive reputation in Europe in some of the same industry sectors in which Baird specializes, including Information Technology, Consumer Products, Marketing Services, Staffing and Outsourcing. Granville's private equity division, Granville Private Equity Managers Limited, has managed funds totaling $1.2 billion since inception more than 25 years ago and currently has funds of approximately $375 million available for investment. A strategic fit both in business lines and corporate cultures, the merger enhances Baird's capabilities with its U.S. clients and enables Granville Baird to expand in the dynamic European market. Granville has approximately 200 employees and nine offices, including offices in London, Paris, Hamburg and Barcelona.

Working with Granville Baird, London, Baird provides transatlantic capabilities to meet client needs.

CLEAR DIRECTION

As Baird has grown in Chicago and across all its markets, it has strived to remain true to its client-focused principles and culture known among its associates as "The Baird Way." With a stated mission of providing the best financial advice, Baird underscores the value of teamwork and reinforces integrity every step of the way, reminding associates, "how we succeed is as important as if we succeed." Following its own road map, Robert W. Baird & Co. knows which way it's heading.

You're in Good Hands with Allstate

The Allstate Corporation

The Allstate Corporation. Allstate Insurance Company, headquartered in Northbrook, Illinois, is the nation's second largest personal property and casualty firm and the largest nonstandard auto provider, insuring one of every eight autos and homes.

The first auto insured. On May 17, 1931, William Lehnertz, a tool-and-dye maker from Aurora, becomes policyholder No. 1 after he returns a coupon in the mail, receives a rate quotation and mails his premium for his Studebaker.

The remarkable story of The Allstate Corporation began on a commuter train. The year was 1930, and it was over a bridge game on the 7:28 a.m. train from Highland Park to Chicago that Carl L. Odell suggested to his friend and neighbor, General Robert E. Wood, that he start an auto insurance company. As the president of Sears, Roebuck and Co., General Wood was certainly in a position to influence decisions. Given the economic devastation of the Great Depression, the potential for the automobile to become primary transportation and the fact that Sears already sold automotive parts, he quickly recognized the idea's merit.

After convincing the board of directors of Sears to grant $700,000 to the venture, Wood immediately got to work. The first Allstate advertisement and coupon appeared in the 1931 Sears catalog, accompanied by a direct mail campaign. About 40,000 applicants responded to the promise of affordable insurance backed by the trusted Sears name, and on May 17, 1931, the first policy was sold to cover a burgundy Studebaker. By year-end, Allstate had a premium volume of $118,323 with 4,217 insureds.

Innovation characterized Allstate from the start. Richard Roskam, the first Allstate agent, worked a card table in a booth at the 1933 World's Fair in Chicago and enjoyed an enthusiastic response. By 1934 customers had to go no farther than

their nearest Sears store. The company began offering rates tailored to factors such as the driver's age, annual mileage and use of the car. This unprecedented customization proved so successful that competitors quickly followed suit.

How did Allstate achieve its success? Allstate's sixth Chairman, Archie R. Boe (1972-1982), noted four factors: the Sears name and in-store accessibility, the innovative management style, the passage of financial-responsibility laws and postwar decentralization.

Allstate began to demonstrate that it could benefit not only from national trends such as new laws that required drivers to have proof of liability insurance, but it could also shape events to the ultimate good of the country. Allstate helped pioneer manufacturing standards and federal safety laws for seat belts, bumpers, air bags and child safety seats, offering customer discounts for advanced devices such as air bags (and later, anti-lock brakes). Each innovation has since become standard and has saved lives.

Starting in 1952 Allstate looked to additional opportunities, such as commercial and health insurance. But it was the subsidiary called Allstate Life Insurance Company, created in 1957, that broke historic sales records in its category. Insurance in force reached $1 billion in 1963. Other key ventures included entering the Japanese market in 1975 and launching Tech-Cor to conduct in-house auto and home repair research and training for claims adjusters. And in the prosperous 1980s, Allstate agents opened stand-alone, entrepreneurial offices outside Sears stores, which now number 10,000 countrywide.

In 1993 Allstate became the largest publicly held insurance company when Sears sold 19.8 percent of its ownership in the company. With its new independence, Allstate took a serious look at its business interests and decided to focus on what it had always done best — provide Allstate insurance through the Allstate agent. The spin-off from Sears was completed in 1995. Today, with annual revenues of $27 billion and assets increasing to $98 billion, Allstate Insurance Company serves over 20 million customers through more than 15,000 agents and approximately 800 life specialists.

One target area for future growth is marketing multiple products to individual customers at every stage of life, including auto, home, life and savings insurance. In 1999, as part of its strategy to expand into additional channels with additional products and brands, The Allstate Corporation initiated several key transactions — the acquisition of American Heritage Life Investment Corp., the acquisition of CNA Personal Lines and a strategic alliance with Putnam Investments to market variable annuities. These actions will further broaden and strengthen Allstate's multichannel, multiproduct, multibrand strategy.

When it comes to sharing success, few companies do it better than Allstate. The spirit of giving dates back to 1952 when The Allstate Foundation was formed to support nonprofit organizations. The Allstate Foundation's focus is on auto and highway safety, personal safety and security and neighborhood revitalization. Today the foundation allocates millions of dollars in grants each year to national and local nonprofit organizations. Allstate employees and agents also commit their personal time and talents. Launched in 1976, the Helping Hands Program continues to rally fully 50 percent of Allstate employees toward volunteer efforts nationwide. Additionally, during times of natural disaster, Allstate employees are often there lending a helping hand on a voluntary basis. In 1997 retired U.S. General Colin Powell recognized the Allstate volunteer spirit and its commitment to America's Promise: The Alliance for Youth.

This expansive volunteer spirit reflects Allstate's corporate culture as a place where people truly enjoy their work and the opportunities offered throughout their careers. In a 1998 survey of 48 leading U.S. companies, Allstate employees reported the highest job satisfaction rating. Leading magazines such as *Fortune, Latina Style, Minority MBA, Working Mother* and *Computerworld* recognize Allstate for the strength of its workforce diversity and other notable achievements. *Forbes* listed Allstate as one of the world's top 50 companies and *Fortune* ranked it among America's most admired. The U.S. Department of Labor honored Allstate as a recipient of its EVE (Exemplary Voluntary Effort) Award.

Corporate responsibility, innovation, financial strength and a customer focus continue to drive the success of The Allstate Corporation. As the company evolves and expands, reaching more people through new products and distribution channels, one thing remains the same: Allstate's complete dedication to meeting the diverse and changing needs of its customers.

Keeping America's promise. Michele Montgomery, an Allstate marketing manager, spends two hours a week tutoring third-grader Kenitra Ruffin near Ruffin's home in Chicago's Cabrini Green housing complex.

Allstate's employee and agent family. At Allstate, employees and agents are its most important assets. A talented, dedicated and diverse workforce is one important reason why Allstate ranks high in corporate America, as well as in the insurance marketplace.

American Invsco

The premier, innovative residences developed by American Invsco Corporation have graced the Chicago skyline for more than 30 years. From immaculate lakefront properties along the pristine Gold Coast to spirited townhomes and condominiums in the South and West Loop, American Invsco provides quality city dwellings that are befitting of Chicago's grand facade.

Headquartered in Chicago, American Invsco has served as a pioneer in the national real estate market, transforming viable, existing properties in desirable locations into refined living spaces. Today, in addition to these offerings, the company serves as a developer of new, prime residential structures in emerging markets throughout the country. American Invsco has navigated the development of more than 30,000 condominiums in more than 40 cities throughout the United States with total property values in excess of $3 billion.

Nicholas S. Gouletas (center), chairman of American Invsco; Steven E. Gouletas, president of new construction and building development; and Nicholas V. Gouletas, president of sales and field operations

The success enjoyed by American Invsco is the result of the entrepreneurial drive put forth by the Gouletas family, which, in 1969, founded the company and spearheaded the concept of converting rental properties into first-class condominiums. As a result American Invsco has changed the face of the real estate market across the country. "Many people believe American Invsco invented the concept of converting rental properties into condominiums," says Nick Gouletas Sr. "Although we appreciate the compliment, condominiums originated over 3,000 years ago in Greece and Italy. American Invsco simply embraced the concept, organized the process and perfected it. Our commitment, belief and hard work is what has made American Invsco the nation's leading condominium developer."

Today that same enterprising drive can be found in Gouletas' sons — Steven E. Gouletas, president of new construction and building development and Nicholas V. Gouletas, president of sales and field operations. Collectively these two possess a successful mix of business and sales savvy that allows American Invsco developments to flourish throughout the country. From Steve's keen analytical approach to mapping areas ripe for new development to Nick's masterful management of condominium marketing, the Gouletas brothers are poised to carry American Invsco to an even higher level of stature within the real estate industry.

Past Chicago projects have included the conversion of Lake Point Tower private residences, which is the world's tallest purely residential building. American Invsco had maintained this property for 12 years prior to converting the rental properties to condominiums in 1988. During the conversion American Invsco conducted record-breaking closings at the site, generating more than $100 million within the first year of sales and more than $150 million in 18 months. The outstanding sales, and more importantly, closing pace achieved with this project remain unmatched within the real estate industry today, and are definitive of American Invsco's capabilities. Today Lake Point Tower houses some of the most sought-after condominiums in the city, offering an astounding view of all aspects of "the city by the lake."

To date American Invsco has converted more than 11,000 homes throughout Chicagoland and is currently responding to the public's overwhelming demand for quality lofts. In February 2000 American Invsco launched Loftominium World. This development encompasses eight loft buildings in Chicago's South and West Loop. The success of this venture showcases American Invsco as a developer in tune with the real estate needs of a variety of markets.

The work performed by American Invsco and the Gouletas family greatly benefits Chicago and numerous other cities. The conversion of rental properties into condominiums promotes home ownership — turning renters into owners — and has allowed city living to thrive despite rampant construction occurring in suburban areas. "Thirty years ago, very few people who lived in Chicago had the opportunity to own their own home — 90 percent of the buildings were rental properties," says Nick Gouletas Jr. "Now 90 percent of Chicago's buildings are privately owned condominiums. American Invsco assisted in giving Chicago back to the people."

Through a dedicated and professional staff that offers comprehensive and specialized services in nearly every facet of the real estate industry, American Invsco is able to meet and exceed the real estate needs of people throughout the country.

The numerous achievements of the Gouletas family have earned American Invsco a renowned reputation in the real estate industry. In 1996 Nicholas Gouletas Sr. was inducted into Chicago's Real Estate Hall of Fame, where he was recognized for his contributions to local, state, national and international real estate and his commitment to growth and development. Chicago Board of Realtors President Annetta Gray has said of Gouletas, "When I look at Chicago's skyline, I see Mr. Gouletas' imprint across the city."

"We are very proud of our father and all of American Invsco's accomplishments," says Steve Gouletas. "For the new century, my brother, Nick, and I look forward to building a new imprint across the city's skyline by constructing new buildings and making development a major part of American Invsco. We are equally excited about the opportunities we have identified internationally."

While the Gouletas family's professional contributions to Chicago and its residents are plentiful, over the past 30 years they have also been active in numerous charitable and civic organizations, including the Center for Excellence in Education, the Chicago affiliate of St. Jude's Children's Research Hospital, Muscular Dystrophy Association (MDA), Jane Addams Hull

Steve on-site as he directs the development of a new luxury skyscraper

House Association and an array of local and national philanthropic campaigns.

As American Invsco continues to thrive in the real estate industry, it will expand its offerings to include new construction and management services in new markets, both nationally and internationally. The end goal is to provide quality homes and exceptional neighborhoods that allow people to realize their dreams of owning property and to make the home-buying experience as pleasurable as it is rewarding. "Real estate is in our blood," says Nick Gouletas Sr. "It dates back to my great grandfather in Athens, Greece, whose passion was to help people achieve their dream of home ownership. I have carried on that legacy and I am now proud to pass it on to the next generation."

Nick emphasizes strategic planning with his team members to capitalize on today's market.

Brinson Partners

For generations, Chicago has been recognized for its leading role in fields ranging from finance and investments to architecture and the arts. It is a city known for its world-class academic institutions, leadership role in financial markets and high concentration of independent

Brinson Partners' main lobby in the Rookery Building shows the work of renowned architects, accentuated with marble and gold accoutrements and ornate woodwork. Throughout its offices, the firm displays its artifact collection featuring various architects' work involved in developing Chicago's LaSalle Street as a major financial center.

thinkers and innovators. Brinson Partners embodies those characteristics, bringing together its expertise in investment management within a national landmark building ("The Rookery") built by one of the early Chicago architectural giants.

Beginning from a trust department within The First National Bank of Chicago in the early 1980s, a group of these innovators, led by Gary Brinson, put their academic discipline and practical experience to work by forming an asset management firm that quickly became a recognized leader in the investment management field. The firm's founders were focused on delivering the benefits of asset allocation — spreading risk around the globe using different weightings to stocks, bonds and other asset classes — based on fundamental investment principles and practices. Using asset allocation theory as a foundation, they offered clients fully integrated global investment portfolios, an investment capability that was relatively unknown at the time. By 1986 its founders' work in translating asset allocation theory into real-world practice was widely recognized in the industry and has since become a key tenet of modern asset management.

Global Capability, Local Delivery

The firm went on to become Brinson Partners, Inc. Based in Chicago since its inception, Brinson Partners has continued to be a leader not only in global investing, but also in performance attribution and risk management.

Today Brinson Partners is a member of UBS Asset Management, the business group responsible for the asset management activities of UBS AG. UBS AG is one of the world's leading financial services groups.

Brinson Partners is one of the largest investment management organizations in the United States, with more than $159 billion of institutional assets under management. The firm's clients include defined benefit and defined contribution retirement plans of corporations, public entities and Taft Hartley organizations, as well as endowments, foundations and family offices. The firm has a significant presence in its own backyard, managing assets for prominent state and local governments, unions and corporations in the central region of the United States.

Rising from Chicago

Within its Chicago headquarters, Brinson Partners has assembled an artifact collection to feature various architects' work involved in developing Chicago's LaSalle Street as a major global financial center. These historical works, including the work of Daniel Burnham (the architect of The Rookery), Louis Sullivan, William Jenny and Frank Lloyd Wright capture the spirit of progress so important to Chicago's emergence as a world-class city.

The office is located on LaSalle Street in the heart of Chicago's financial district. Often referred to as the "commerce canyon" of Chicago, LaSalle Street established its roots as a world-renowned financial epicenter when the Chicago Board of Trade built its home on the corner of LaSalle and Jackson in 1885 — now just a stone's throw from Brinson Partners' headquarters.

Brinson Partners is actively involved in the Chicago Metropolitan-area community, contributing both time and money to a variety of causes primarily aimed at helping Chicago's underprivileged. Each year, Brinson Partners makes allocations to assist numerous community organizations. In addition, Brinson Partners is an active supporter of significant Chicago-based cultural, educational and social service organizations, and many Brinson Partners employees are members of boards of directors for these organizations.

Structured to Succeed

Brinson Partners' commitment to the community is a result of a business culture that emphasizes the importance of strategic partnering. In its dealings with the community,

its clients and its business partners, the organization applies a team-based approach and focuses on the long term.

The structure of the firm is designed to allow professionals to focus on specific areas of knowledge and expertise. This model, which separates investment and client-service functions, has been used by Brinson Partners since the firm was founded. Combined, the investment and client-service functions form one integrated global platform that drives the firm's mission: to deliver long-term, value-added investment performance, and to deliver excellence in client service.

The strength of this platform is represented not just by the international diversity of its clients' locations, but also by the diversity of the investment assets it manages, which are broadly split between balanced funds, equities, fixed income and private markets. The firm believes that in order to deliver superior investment performance in this millennium, this broad, global knowledge is absolutely critical.

Looking Ahead

A fundamental element of Brinson Partners' investment philosophy is the notion that "risk pays for return." A comprehensive understanding of global markets and their interactions allows portfolios of assets to be combined in ways that maximize the return per unit of risk taken. While this idea is not a new one, delivering portfolios that apply this principle to the needs of institutional clients will be a challenge for asset managers in the coming years. The Brinson Partners team is focusing on this challenge today.

This process is based on the same disciplined academic philosophy upon which Brinson Partners was founded. The challenge lies in accelerating globalization, which requires that investment areas (asset classes) are structured to accommodate such a broad scope. The firm is organized globally by asset classes, and in order to increase thought leadership, each area has its own process and organization — applied within the context of the firm's philosophy. Its risk analysis and investment-planning groups serve all asset classes, and help to deliver value-added, risk-adjusted returns across the spectrum of global investments.

Delivering solutions to clients in an increasingly global arena means anticipating shifts in the global investment landscape, and discerning trend from noise. From its roots in Chicago, Brinson Partners is poised to remain a leader in global investing.

Chicago Patrolmen's Federal Credit Union

Chicago Patrolmen's has been serving the financial needs of Chicago police officers and their families since 1938. The credit union was formed when members of the Chicago Patrolmen's Association decided to pool their financial resources for the betterment of all.

Chicago Patrolmen's is one of approximately 7,000 federal credit unions serving over 44 million people in the United States today. Federal credit unions have been serving the nation's consumers for 66 years. Each federal credit union serves a distinct membership that shares a common bond of occupation, community or association.

A federal credit union is a cooperative, nonprofit financial institution organized to promote thrift and provide credit to its members. Federal credit union members are provided with safe, convenient places to save and borrow at reasonable rates, with savings insured up to $100,000 by the National Credit Union Share Insurance Fund.

When Herbert Dalton was appointed as Chicago Patrolmen's first Treasurer in 1938, it was very much a "blue shirts" organization, with membership open only to police officers "on the beat" and their immediate family members. By 1949 Chicago Patrolmen's had grown to

over $1 million in assets. During this period, the credit union's board of directors implemented free life insurance policies on members' savings accounts and a "once a member, always a member" policy. This membership policy permits members to maintain their Chicago

> Despite its growth, Chicago Patrolmen's mission remains the same as it was in 1938: "To serve the financial needs of all Chicago Police Officers and their families in order to help them realize their life's goals."

Patrolmen's accounts when they move up in the ranks of, or retire from, the Chicago Police Department. Both of these policies continue to be critical to the growth and success of the credit union.

In 1974 Daniel Mahoney was appointed as the fifth treasurer of Chicago Patrolmen's Federal Credit Union. Mahoney joined the credit union in 1953, when he was hired as a patrolman by the Chicago Police Department. He rose to the rank of detective before retiring from the Chicago Police Department to dedicate his time to serving the members of Chicago Patrolmen's.

In his 22 years of service, Dan Mahoney grew Chicago Patrolmen's from a $5 million institution occupying three

Chicago Patrolmen's new West Loop home

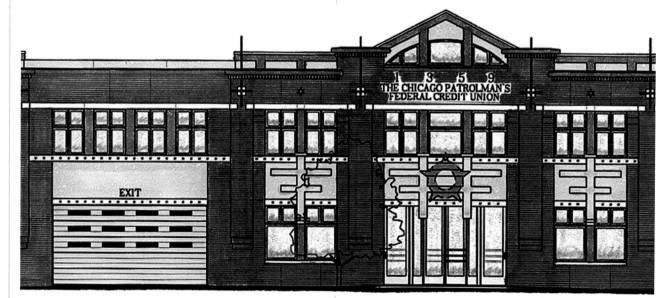

offices on the 17th floor of a building on north Wabash, to a $60 million institution occupying the building's entire second floor. Under his leadership, the credit union implemented several new services including payroll deduction, auto loans, home equity loans and credit cards.

> Including police officers' families, Chicago Patrolmen's serves over 16,000 members. In recent years the institution has grown rapidly, and by 1999 had assets of $100 million.

Mark Mahoney, Dan's son and Chicago Patrolmen's sixth Treasurer, began working at the credit union when he was 8 years old, stuffing envelopes for his father. After receiving an MBA from Loyola University, Mark Mahoney created the credit union's collections department and eventually succeeded his father as Chicago Patrolmen's treasurer in 1996.

Today, Chicago Patrolmen's serves police officers of all ranks, from the newest recruits to the Superintendent of police. Including police officers' families, Chicago Patrolmen's serves over 16,000 members. In recent years the institution has grown rapidly, and by 1999 had assets of $100 million.

Under Mark Mahoney, Chicago Patrolmen's is becoming a full-service financial institution. Over the past three years, automated teller machines, direct deposit, checking accounts and debit cards have been added to its services. Individual retirement accounts, first mortgages and Internet banking are slated to be added in the near future. Despite its growth, Chicago Patrolmen's mission remains the same as it was in 1938: "To serve the financial needs of all Chicago Police Officers and their families in order to help them realize their life's goals." Every day Chicago Patrolmen's strives to fulfill its mission by providing members with competitive financial products and services that facilitate borrowing, promote thrift, and encourage wise money management.

In addition to all its traditional financial services, Chicago Patrolmen's offers personalized service to each of its 16,000 members. The board, management and staff of the credit union strive to help members in any way they can. They make every effort to listen to their concerns, save them money, and assist them in working through financial problems. Whether or not they need a loan, members can sit down with Mark Mahoney and others to talk dollars and cents.

Recently, a member called Mahoney at 9 a.m. He sounded anxious and said that "something really bad had happened." Could he see Mark any time soon? The man was given an appointment for 11 a.m. that same day. And members don't always need appointments. Mahoney was pleased to see another man who simply dropped by his office to say thank you — Chicago Patrolmen's had helped him halt foreclosure proceedings on his house.

At least once a month, credit union representatives visit police districts where they attend roll calls. They listen attentively as police officers talk about Chicago Patrolmen's, accept compliments and complaints with equanimity, then work hard to improve the institution so that it best meets the needs of its members.

Visits to Chicago Patrolmen's offices are pleasant social events for the credit union's members. Tellers know members by name and offer lollypops to their children. To better serve its members, in 2000 Chicago Patrolmen's moved from its crowded headquarters in Chicago's "Loop," to a larger space in a building it has purchased on west Washington Street. The new site features drive-through banking lanes, an outside automatic teller machine, and free off-street parking.

With the move, Chicago Patrolmen's future is brighter than ever. Mahoney has an ambitious goal for the institution. He would like to see every Chicago police officer, and every one of their family members, signed up as a member.

Freeborn & Peters

Described by the *Chicago Tribune* as a "litigation powerhouse," Freeborn & Peters is one of Chicago's top law firms to the city's thriving business community. While its clientele is national in scope, it represents such Chicago-area business icons as Commonwealth Edison,

The Wacker Drive headquarters of Freeborn & Peters

BP Amoco, 3Com Corporation (formerly U.S. Robotics), Acxiom Corporation, the Illinois Central Railroad and Information Resources, Inc. In addition to representing the city of Chicago, Cook County, the Chicago Transportation Authority and the Chicago Public Schools, it is also the same 100-plus-lawyer firm that won the landmark $9.2 billion settlement for the state of Illinois against the tobacco industry. This, along with many other precedent-setting cases, has made Freeborn & Peters one of the country's most sought-after law firms.

While the firm represents many of the most prominent companies in the Chicago business community, it also serves a wide range of national and international clients, including Microsoft, McDonald's, the Burlington Northern/ Santa Fe Railroad, US West and AIG. Additionally, as the "entrepreneur's law firm," Freeborn & Peters is one of the pre-eminent firms in the Midwest to emerging-technology companies, representing such businesses as Quotesmith.com and Tunes.com.

Understandably, Freeborn & Peters is proud of the role it has played in the development of Chicago's rich cultural and business heritage. For example, it represented Chicago-based modem manufacturer U.S. Robotics (now 3Com) literally from its infancy through its initial public offering. Similarly, the firm came up with the original idea, and represented Illinois Central in implementation of a plan for the development of Chicago's Millennium Park, which will be located on the site of the former railroad yards near Michigan Avenue and Randolph Street. The genesis for this idea took place during negotiations between Illinois Central and the city of Chicago regarding use of the property and will serve as a cornerstone of Chicago's world-class public parks system.

Of course, it wasn't always this way. Michael Freeborn remembers when the firm started in 1983 with just six lawyers who broke away from an old-line

Chicago law firm to start their own. "I was one of the six founding partners," Freeborn explains. "For my part, I wanted to join a smaller, less-structured firm." Originally, the six founding partners were evenly split between corporate and trial lawyers. As the firm's reputation grew, so did the number of its attorneys. This growth, which was fueled without the benefit of merging with another firm, eventually forced it to move from its modest surroundings in the heart of the city's financial district to its current location as the largest tenant in the world's tallest reinforced-concrete building, which rises from the prairie on South Wacker Drive.

As the firm grew, it was able to attract the best legal talent both locally and across the nation. Among its partners are Fred Foreman, former U.S. Attorney for the Northern District of Illinois under former President Bush, and William Holmes, formerly with the Federal Trade Commission and author of the widely used and cited treatise *Intellectual Property and Antitrust Law*. Additionally, the firm's partners serve as faculty and board members of a variety of Chicago universities and institutions, including the John Marshall School of Law and the Kellogg Graduate School of Business at Northwestern University.

Keeping this new firm busy and growing was an expanding team of trial lawyers handling multimillion-dollar cases — literally from New York to Hawaii and from Anchorage to Tampa — as well as corporate lawyers representing entrepreneurs and emerging-technology companies through various stages of financing and development. This combination of trial skills and business acumen earned Freeborn & Peters, one of the city's youngest firms, honors from *Crain's Chicago Business* as one of the top law firms in Chicago.

As a trial lawyer, Michael Freeborn has represented companies in complex cases involving antitrust, employment, environmental, product liability and securities issues. During those years he has witnessed many changes in the legal profession. "Throughout my career as a lawyer, I've seen an increase in competition and the commercialization of the practice of law," says Freeborn. "When I first started practicing, there wasn't as much focus on the economics of the practice of law. Back then, it wasn't so crucial to apply business methods to the delivery of legal services. But the competition was good for our firm. We grew. Firms that didn't respond to that trend have dissolved or gotten smaller."

This competition stimulated Freeborn & Peters to seek innovative ways to serve its expanding client base,

and by the close of the 20th century this 17-year-old law firm led the industry in the use of technology as a means to be continually responsive in a rapidly evolving marketplace. It installed sophisticated document management systems before many other firms even knew such systems existed, and it continues to deploy creative technical solutions to the most difficult knowledge management problems. This cutting-edge, entrepreneurial culture allows it to attract "the best and the brightest" legal talent who want to join this young, aggressive firm that knows how to win.

This innovative approach was present from the firm's inception. As the lead lawyer for the Manville Trust asbestos litigation from 1988 to 1991, Michael Freeborn's team handled 10,000 asbestos claims against Manville in nine Midwestern states. Before the Manville Trust became insolvent, the firm's lawyers tried the cases of 28 Midwestern plaintiffs. "Out of that 28, we obtained 25 verdicts in favor of the Trust," said Freeborn. "In these cases, the Trust never had to pay more than it had offered in settlement prior to trial. We're proud of that." Manville also turned to Freeborn & Peters to coordinate 100,000 pretrial discovery proceedings. In order to accomplish this task, the firm created a national discovery-coordinating center comprised of a database of standardized answers and objections. It was a job only an aggressive, technically agile law firm could accomplish.

Though Freeborn & Peters continues to devote its considerable resources to such high-profile cases, it is also known for devoting these same resources to charitable and public-interest causes. The firm encourages its attorneys to participate in pro bono matters through such organizations as the Legal Assistance Foundation of Chicago as well as The Pillars, a social service organization that assists over 3,500 children, families and individuals each year. Similarly, the firm takes seriously its civic responsibility. It annually donates dozens of computers to local schools and social organizations, and its employees and partners volunteer at a variety of local homeless shelters and other community organizations.

Through its sophisticated legal work and community involvement, Freeborn & Peters continues to embody Chicago's "big shoulders" spirit. "We are proud of our association with the city of Chicago," says Freeborn. "And we look forward to continuing in our role as one of the premier firms to Chicago's business and civic communities."

Heller Financial, Inc.

The story behind Heller Financial, Inc. is similar to the story behind the city in which this commercial lender is housed. For just as Chicago started from meager beginnings and grew into a sprawling metropolis, Heller Financial started as one man's vision and grew into one of the nation's premier commercial finance companies. And just as Chicago was destroyed by fire, only to be rebuilt into an even greater city, Heller Financial was severely challenged by the economic woes of the late 1970s and was sold in the 1980s, only to resurface with a renewed strength and its most successful earnings to date.

Today Heller Financial is one of the leading commercial lenders in the United States, with more than $18 billion in assets. The company offers a wide range of financing solutions to middle-market and small business clients. These solutions include equipment financing and leasing, sales finance programs, financing based on collateral and cash flow, as well as health care and commercial real estate financing. In 1999 the company's small

Heller Financial, Inc. is one of the leading commercial lenders in the U.S., offering a wide range of financing solutions for more than 80 years.

business subsidiary became the nation's No. 1 Small Business Administration lender by total volume, according to U.S. government lending figures.

For more than 80 years, the services offered by Heller Financial have allowed companies to secure financing for ventures that allow for growth. However, the Heller Financial of today is a leaner and more focused operation than it has been in 25 years, which has allowed for record revenues and greater client services. This success has invigorated employees and the company's stock, which, after an extended absence, triumphantly returned to the New York Stock Exchange in 1998 and raised more than $1 billion for Heller Financial's majority stockholder.

Heller Financial was founded in 1919 by Walter E. Heller, a South Side entrepreneur. At the time, Heller had teamed with mortgage banker Seymour Marks to form Heller-Marks, a finance company designed to fund the automobile industry. Marks left the company a year later, and it was renamed Walter E. Heller & Co.

With the new company came new direction. Heller & Co. began financing taxicabs, home improvement-related companies, installment notes for businesses and commercial accounts receivable. Heller also developed relationships with local banks to increase the amount of funding the company could provide. Selden Swope, a former employee with Continental Bank, dealt with Heller in the 1920s. "It was simple in those days," he is quoted as saying. "Mr. Heller would sit at my desk and tell me how much money he needed — $1 million, $2 million — and tell me a brief story about why he wanted the money and how his company was getting along."

Heller & Co. became a premier asset-based lending company early on. Heller & Co. also initiated another lending practice — factoring — in which Heller & Co. would purchase a manufacturer's accounts receivables and then extend a line of credit for that amount.

Heller & Co.'s lending practices allowed for tremendous success from the 1940s through the 1960s. The company acquired several other lending companies in the United States, and also began to finance Hollywood movie and television productions. The postwar business boom inundated Heller & Co. and brought additional revenues, as the company extended lines of credit to hundreds of new businesses. In addition, the company started a real estate financing program to provide construction loans to commercial real estate developers who were immersed in the 1950s housing boom.

In 1956 the company's stock went public on the New York Stock Exchange and subsequent years allowed for U.S. and overseas expansion for Heller & Co. Offices were opened in New York, Massachusetts, Texas and Florida, and business ventures were launched in Puerto Rico, Germany, England, Mexico, France, Italy and the Philippines, which led to the formation of Walter E. Heller Overseas Corp. This expansion into international ventures was Heller's last major accomplishment before he died in 1969.

The 1970s and early 1980s brought increased interest rates and decreased business for the company. Banks stepped up their services as providers of low-interest business loans and caused increased competition for finance companies. Heller & Co. suffered as a result, and the company was forced to absorb the losses of several companies it had financed that were now bankrupt.

In 1983 the company was purchased by Tokyo-based The Fuji Bank Limited, one of the world's largest banks. The acquisition strengthened Fuji Bank's position in America's middle business market.

To provide the company with a new identity but still capitalize on Heller's early successes, Heller & Co. was renamed Walter E. Heller International Corp. Fuji Bank also injected new management into the company while maintaining a core of pre-acquisition employees. After the acquisition, more than 40 managers from Heller's operations were flown to Japan to interact with their Japanese counterparts and to begin building a relationship.

Both companies were able to learn from each other — the Japanese taught the Americans how to gain more market share through growth and the Americans taught the Japanese how to be more aggressive in the U.S. market. Heller diversified its services to meet the low-risk needs of a small and middle-market companies, while at the same time eyeing high-risk opportunities that would advance the company's portfolio. In doing so, Heller returned to many of the same lending practices that Walter Heller had instilled in the company during in the early days — asset-based lending and factoring for small and mid-size companies.

In 1998 Heller successfully completed one of the largest initial public offerings of the year, returning once again to the New York Stock Exchange as a public company. Today Heller Financial provides its clients with a number of financing services through its five core business units — Heller Corporate Finance; Heller Real

Heller Financial, Inc. was founded in 1919 by Walter E. Heller, a South Side entrepreneur.

Estate Finance; Heller Leasing Services; Heller Healthcare Finance; and Heller Small Business Finance. Additionally, Heller International provides financing in select countries around the world. The company structure has paid off — several acquisitions reminiscent of the company's early days have occurred, and the company has achieved record net income. The company also has expanded its presence in North America with the formation of Heller Financial Canada, Ltd.

As Heller Financial continues to grow, so do the charitable donations the company generously gives to Chicago. The company's charitable contributions committee donates funds to innovative educational programs for inner-city and underprivileged youth. By helping fund these alternative programs, the donations provided by Heller Financial have a significant impact on the city.

Through its numerous financial and community services, Heller Financial nurtures many of Chicago's young minds and future entrepreneurs. Walter E. Heller would have been proud of Heller's success as a company and community leader.

Kemper Insurance Companies

The Kemper Insurance Companies have provided businesses and families with innovative coverage and peace of mind for more than 88 years. What started as an insurance operation in Chicago offering workers' compensation policies to the city's lumber companies has evolved into an industry leader that today provides comprehensive insurance policies to clients throughout the United States and in many foreign markets.

Kemper's personalized service and prompt response to claims has earned the company a renowned reputation throughout the insurance industry and in each of the markets it services. From large businesses to individual

Chicago became an important lumber city in the early 1900s because of its access to the Chicago River. It was then that the late James S. Kemper helped lumbermen form what became the first Kemper company, Lumbermens Mutual Casualty Company.

accounts, Kemper is able to meet all of its clients' needs through an array of quality property-casualty insurance products and risk-management services.

Four separate yet equally dynamic business groups exist within the Kemper operation. The Business Customer Group serves as Kemper's flagship enterprise, offering insurance products and services to domestic businesses. This group is complemented by Kemper International, which primarily services U.S. companies with overseas operations. Kemper Casualty Company addresses the specialty and large-risk property-casualty needs of businesses, and the Individual and Family Group offers a full line of personal products. Collectively

these business groups allow Kemper to serve as a premier and profitable world-class insurance company in the commercial and personal markets.

The Kemper Insurance Companies was founded in 1912 as the Lumbermens Mutual Casualty Company. It was formed out of Illinois' passage of the workers' compensation law that same year, which required lumberyard owners to provide insurance to protect their workers in case of injury.

James S. Kemper, a 26-year-old agent with the Central Mutual Insurance Agency in Van Wert, Ohio, had been sent to Chicago in 1911 to investigate a number of lumberyard fires. Kemper's entrepreneurial spirit led him to open his own agency later that year, selling insurance to the lumber industry during the day and writing out the policies in longhand at night.

Kemper's drive and keen business skills impressed several Chicago lumberyard owners, who asked Kemper to serve as vice president and general manager of an upstart company — Lumbermens Mutual Casualty Company. Kemper accepted and in November 1912 Lumbermens Mutual Casualty Company issued its first workers' compensation policy to the Rittenhouse & Embree Lumberyard.

As a mutual insurer (managed for the benefit of its policyholders), Lumbermens Mutual was able to help lumber companies save money and attracted a large clientele. This spurred growth for Lumbermens Mutual and allowed the company to expand its offerings to auto, fire and liability insurance. In 1913 Lumbermens Mutual was one of the first companies to sell auto insurance. Early policyholders included New York Yankee Babe Ruth, who was in need of coverage for his Packard sedan.

By 1923 Kemper's business began to boom. A receptionist fed up with answering the ever-ringing phone "Lumbermens Mutual Casualty Company, Lumbermens Insurance Agency and National Underwriters," changed her opening line to "Kemper Insurance." This simple address reassured clients of the integrity that Kemper brought to the industry, and became the familiar corporate identity for the company that today continues to offer quality insurance products, top-notch service and competitive prices.

Headquartered in the northwest suburb of Long Grove, Kemper employs more than 8,000 people worldwide, with operations nationwide and overseas in Sydney, Australia; Brussels, Belgium; Toronto, Canada;

Frankfurt/Main, Germany; Paris, France; Singapore; and Tokyo, Kobe, Nagoya, Osaka and Yokohama, Japan. Kemper products are sold through more than 1,900 independent commercial agents and brokers, and through more than 1,400 independent personal lines agents.

Kemper provides an extensive line of insurance products that cover all business and personal needs. The Business Customer Group provides an array of valuable business products, including workers' compensation, small business, commercial auto, package and executive-protection insurance policies, along with services such as loss control, claims-management expertise and audits of workers' compensation medical bills. This group also offers a package policy that addresses the specialized property and liability insurance needs of small businesses in a variety of professions, including law firms, medical and dental offices, architecture and engineering firms and manufacturers.

Kemper Casualty has an expansive property-casualty portfolio designed for large-risk and specialty businesses. This group offers a variety of policies, including excess casualty, environmental, professional liability, property and financial lines. Kemper Casualty also continuously introduces new product lines that meet specific client needs. For example, Kemper's Guaranteed Receivable Insurance Protection guarantees hospitals and health care providers collections from insurance companies and government agencies.

The Individual and Family Group offers quality coverage of cars, homes, personal belongings and other items at competitive prices. In addition, this group offers a comprehensive package that covers property, belongings and personal liability all in one policy.

Kemper International features branch offices in key international locations, and through strategic alliances with some of the world's largest insurers, participates in the globalization of businesses around the world. This group offers insurance solutions not only to clients based in the United States that operate businesses overseas, but also to foreign-based clients with businesses in the United States.

Kemper's professional offerings are complemented by its equally thoughtful approach to community service. In 1999 alone Kemper contributed nearly $2 million to education, youth programs, the arts, and health and welfare services. Kemper is also an avid supporter of its employees' community-service efforts, matching dollar

for dollar the gifts they contribute. This has allowed for significant contributions to organizations such as the Rehabilitation Institute of Chicago, the United Negro College Fund, City of Hope National Medical Center, Boys and Girls Clubs of America, and the Museum of Science and Industry.

Since 1968 Kemper has served as sponsor of the Kemper Insurance Open, a PGA Tour event that raises funds for local charities. Since its formation, the Kemper Insurance Open has raised more than $5 million for 220 charitable organizations.

Kemper remains committed to growth and quality coverage as it continues to expand to meet the ever-changing needs of its clients and the markets it serves. Driven by empowered, knowledgeable and ethical employees, Kemper is positioned to build on the trustworthy foundation established by James S. Kemper nearly a century ago.

Kemper's renowned reputation as an insurance provider is rooted in its long history of excellent customer service in situations ranging from the routine to the catastrophic. Today Kemper remains a trusted and stable company committed to quality and is also a focused, innovative, creative and flexible provider of contemporary solutions — like rapid catastrophe response.

Chairman and CEO David B. Mathis (right) and President and Chief Operating Officer William D. Smith lead Kemper today. Under their direction Kemper has acquired or started 20 new operations in order to expand its line of products and services to meet the needs of its customers.

Marketing Innovators International, Inc.

Marketing Innovators can provide customized programming as well as turnkey information systems for the strategic management and tracking of incentive programs.

Just minutes from O'Hare International Airport sits the corporate headquarters of Marketing Innovators International, Inc., a full-service, performance-improvement company that has been recognized by *Crain's Chicago Business* as one of the largest woman-owned businesses in metropolitan Chicago, and by *Working Woman* magazine as one of the largest woman-owned businesses in the United States. The Rosemont, Illinois, firm helps companies throughout the United States retain, motivate and recognize their employees through a variety of innovative incentive programs. "Our goal is to inspire employees to improve their performance, which results in increased productivity and profitability for companies," says Chairman and CEO Lois M. LeMenager. Under the leadership of LeMenager, Marketing Innovators has experienced tremendous growth, dramatically increasing its size and scope over the past 20 years.

The company was founded in 1978 and initially focused its efforts on incentive travel awards to be given to deserving employees. A few years later, LeMenager originated the concept of companies awarding retail gift certificates for exemplary job performance. Marketing

Marketing Innovators provides clients with a variety of incentive and recognition awards, including customized debit cards and gift certificates from hundreds of national merchants.

Innovators now designs and implements incentive programs whereby employees can choose from a variety of gift certificates from more than 200 local and national merchants. Marketed as the Freedom to Choose® program, it was considered to be the first new award concept in the incentive industry since its inception and has been influential in the development of electronic gift cards.

In its early years the firm worked largely with companies in the agricultural and pharmaceutical industries,

then focused on other business sectors. Today it creates customized incentive programs for numerous Fortune 100 companies, including clients in the communications and public utilities arenas, and Marketing Innovators prides itself on the long-term relationships formed with its clients. Three- and four-year contracts are common, and Marketing Innovators has worked with some of its clients for as long as 15 years.

1980 was a pivotal year for Marketing Innovators, as it signed an exclusive contract with JCPenney to promote and sell JCPenney gift certificates to corporations — another way companies' top performers could be rewarded. In 1999 the company launched a new JCPenney Gift Card. Especially popular during the December gift-giving season, employees can choose from over 300,000 JCPenney products and services by visiting one of 1,800 stores nationwide or by ordering merchandise from the retailer's numerous catalogs. In addition, the JCPenney Incentive Sales division markets the gift cards to nonprofit organizations for their fund-raising efforts.

JCPenney Incentive Sales operates as a full-service division of Marketing Innovators at the company headquarters in Rosemont. In 1998 the JCPenney Supplier Diversity Development Awards program honored JCPenney Incentive Sales with its Supplier of the Year Award for the Stores Division.

The firm's award-winning Creative Services department works with companies to design a wide array of impressive collateral materials that promote employee incentive and recognition programs: everything from promotional brochures and posters to imprinted specialty items. In addition, Marketing Innovators offers program management and results-tracking that provide full-service administration and evaluation of clients' incentive programs.

The MIPERC® Performance Tracking System allows incentive program participants to compare results against established objectives, while the MIBANC® Personal Account System manages the tracking and fulfillment of earned award credits by establishing personal accounts for employees. All of the data regarding an employee's account can be transmitted to a secure Web site that can be easily accessed by program participants.

LeMenager has established a staff of highly skilled professionals to develop solutions that recognize and motivate the employees of companies throughout the United States.

The company practices what it preaches by rewarding employees for their ongoing work efforts. Appreciation is shown on a regular basis, and a climate of concern about the welfare of employees and their families exists, which is often a rarity in today's corporate environment.

In recognition of her significant achievements in business and in the incentive industry, CEO Lois LeMenager has received numerous awards. Among her many honors, she was awarded the 1999 Entrepreneurial Success Award from the U.S. Small Business Administration. In October 1999 she was inducted into the Junior Achievement Business Hall of Fame, reflecting her ongoing work mentoring young people. As an active member of the Chicagoland Chamber of Commerce, LeMenager has served on its board of directors since 1998, and has been a vital member of the National Association of Women Business Owners, which honored her as one of Chicago's most influential women business owners. She also belongs to a number of other professional organizations including the American Management Association; the American Marketing Association; the National Association of Female Executives; the Society of Incentive and Travel Executives; and is a charter member of the Rosemont Chamber of Commerce.

As Marketing Innovators International, Inc. keeps on growing and prospering, Lois LeMenager and her staff of dedicated professionals will continue to provide outstanding customer-driven solutions to clients throughout the country. In the years to come, Marketing Innovators will continue to play an important role in the incentive program industry and therefore positively impact the lives of thousands of employees throughout the country.

For the past 20 years, Marketing Innovators has been an important partner to JCPenney as the exclusive representative of JCPenney Incentive Sales.

Chairman and CEO Lois LeMenager has led the company through tremendous growth, dramatically increasing its size and scope over the past 20 years.

1972 the NYSE allowed member firms to offer life insurance, Mesirow Financial created its Insurance Services Division and now is an insurance leader. Recognizing Chicagoans' growing wealth and evolving business community in the mid-1970s, the company began its Investment Management business, providing specialized investment advisory services to institutions and high-networth individuals. It strengthened its capabilities in the 1980s, adding Private Equity services for emerging public companies as well as small to midsized privately held companies seeking growth capital. Mesirow Financial now is one of the leading private equity firms in the Midwest, having financed successful ventures such as U.S. Robotics and Fender Musical Instruments. Also in the 1980s and 1990s, the company expanded with Advanced Strategies, or nontraditional asset management, as well as the Real Estate and Investment Banking Divisions.

COMMITMENT TO CHICAGO

Despite several national services, Mesirow Financial is firmly rooted in Chicago. It has been a key player in the growth of the metropolitan area, economically and structurally, through growing and insuring businesses, financing municipalities and overseeing many high-profile real estate projects, as well as in effecting a steady economic base in the wealth of individuals.

Mesirow Financial's strategic partnerships have helped increase Chicago's attractiveness for business and economic development. In the 1980s the company assisted city government in developing and managing a Chicago Capital Fund, a fund pool for growth capital to neighborhood businesses. Most recently, it is assisting the municipality in attracting technology companies by setting up a Technology Fund with the city of Chicago. It can also provide funding and consulting services to these new companies.

Its acquisition of Stein & Company in 1997 allowed the firm to further bolster its role in the city by expanding to full-scale developer. In many cases Mesirow Financial becomes the insurance provider and financing partner in its real estate deals — a prime example of its multidisciplinary approach.

The company has successfully pursued and completed such prominent design/build deals as the $175 million Chicago Board of Trade expansion, the $44 million University of Chicago Graduate School facility, the $675

million McCormick Place expansion and the $153 million Metcalfe Federal building. It is also active in military base developments with its suburban Glenview Naval Air Station and Fort Sheridan projects. Plus, as in all of Mesirow Financial's services, a team of experts — a combination of real estate development, finance and marketing expertise — drives the process.

Mesirow Financial is also proud to be a strong contributor to the growth and vitality of society through its significant financial and volunteer contributions to hundreds of local charitable, cultural and civic organizations.

WORKING AS A TEAM FOR CLIENTS

As financial services companies face off, Mesirow Financial's relationship strategy is pitted against other firms boasting high technology and promises of high returns for chancy investments. Since not many companies have the depth and breadth of experts and associations across the board, the firm banks on its important relationships. The firm recruits the most talented professionals in each business and compensates them well for developing and building their relationships. The professionals work to earn their clients' trust by demonstrating a solid

The McCormick Place Expansion is a prime example of a design/build project of Mesirow Financial's Real Estate Division.

understanding of their needs and objectives. With this understanding, they are also able to develop innovative solutions to a range of needs.

Mesirow Financial's clients listen to their advisers, like their individualized creative approach, and more often than not grow their relationship with the company by taking advantage of their range of high-quality services.

And because it works, Mesirow Financial sees no reason to change. The strategy remains the same — it'll get by with a little help from its friends.

The Northern Trust Company

Northern Trust's headquarters building on the northwest corner of LaSalle and Monroe streets

Occupying one room on the second floor of the Rookery Building on the southeast corner of LaSalle and Adams streets, The Northern Trust Company opened its doors on August 12, 1889. The founder and president, Byron Laflin Smith, was assisted by a cashier who doubled as a secretary; an assistant cashier who also served as assistant secretary and the only teller; two bookkeepers; and a general man. In 1893 the bank operated a branch at the World's Columbian Exposition in Jackson Park.

Outgrowing its quarters, the bank leased space in the Chamber of Commerce Building and again in the Rookery Building before purchasing property at LaSalle and Monroe streets — the center of Chicago's business and financial district. The bank moved into its present headquarters, a Corinthian-columned granite-and-marble home on South LaSalle Street, in 1906.

Since the beginning, The Northern Trust Company has distinguished itself by maintaining a reputation for providing highly attentive, quality service. Amidst mergers and acquisitions, Northern remains the sole Chicago-based independent bank in Chicago. While other banks are generating a profit primarily through layoffs and branch closures, this venerable institution is opening offices, adding staff and generating stellar financial returns.

Byron Laflin Smith died in 1914 and his eldest son, Solomon A. Smith, took over the helm at age 37, becoming the youngest bank president in Chicago and one of the youngest in the nation. During World War I the bank became the headquarters for bond sales and was instrumental in helping Chicago surpass the goals of four Liberty Bond Drives and a postwar Victory Bond campaign.

During the stock market crash of 1929, Northern received increasing deposits, its clients attracted to the bank's stable record. While many banks were folding, Northern Trust experienced unparalleled growth, a remarkable feat during such difficult times.

Northern played an important role in World War II bond drives, and its reputation grew. Its corporate trust business prospered, and the bank assumed management of numerous corporate pension plans. Correspondent bank accounts and corporate and individual accounts outside the Chicago area represented close to half of the bank's commercial deposits.

In the 1950s Northern Trust developed new products and services, including the mechanization of many bank functions, because of technological advances. Solomon A. Smith was named chairman of the board in 1957; his son, Edward Byron Smith, became president and Solomon B. Smith was named vice chairman. Solomon A. Smith retired from active service in 1963 and died soon after. Edward Byron Smith then became chairman of the board.

The following decade saw the construction of a 14-story addition to the main bank building that was completed in 1965. Northern became the first Illinois-chartered bank to establish a branch outside of the United States with the opening of a London branch in 1969. A 31-story building at Wacker and Adams streets was completed in 1974 to house the bank's growing computer and operations staff. In 1990 Northern Trust centralized its operations activities in a state-of-the-art, 500,000-square-foot building on South Canal Street, and recently it expanded its technology activities in another facility across the street.

The passage of the Employees Retirement and Income Security Act in 1974 was a watershed in Northern's evolving trust business. The Act mandated that assets held in corporate benefit funds be overseen by an independent master trustee or custodian. Northern capitalized on its expertise in the trust business and with technology to become a leading provider of master trust and custody services, with assets under administration currently totaling more than $1 trillion.

Edward Byron Smith retired in 1979 after serving as chairman since 1963, becoming chairman of the executive committee in 1979 and honorary chairman in 1981. The succeeding chairmen and chief executive officers — E. Norman Staub, Philip W.K. Sweet Jr., Weston R. Christopherson and David W. Fox — witnessed the growth of the bank's trust business from $25 billion in assets in 1980 to $614 billion in 1995. William A. Osborn assumed leadership of Northern Trust Corporation in 1995. By 1999 Northern Trust had $1.5 trillion in trust assets under administration, including $300 billion for which Northern has investment discretion.

Northern has earned distinction as a leading provider of personal fiduciary, asset management, personal and private banking, master trust and retirement services, trading and investment services, global custody and treasury management services. A century-long tradition of combining high-touch service and expertise with industry-leading technology distinguishes Northern in its two primary businesses — Personal Financial Services and Corporate and Institutional Services. Supported by Worldwide Operations and Technology and Northern Trust Global Investments, these two businesses provide revenues evenly and create a unique profile for Northern Trust in the financial services industry.

Northern is well-positioned to offer private banking, trust and investment management services through a network of 74 offices in 10 states — Illinois, Florida, Arizona, Texas, California, Colorado, Michigan, Missouri, Ohio and Washington. In distinctive, well-appointed facilities, experienced staff work in a client-service culture that is unparalleled in the industry.

A nationwide marketing strategy tailored to suit the interests and needs of clients at each location includes hosting events featuring prominent speakers from a wide range of fields. Through strategic philanthropy, Northern contributes substantially and provides use of its facilities to many cultural, civic and charitable organizations.

Corporate and Institutional Services provides trust, custody, investment, retirement and treasury management services to corporations, governments, financial institutions, public retirement and Taft Hartley funds and nonprofit organizations in 35 countries. Northern continues to expand its global business, both for U.S. clients investing in foreign markets and for international clients. To compete successfully in this arena, Northern has made a commitment to investing substantial resources to develop technology such as Northern Trust Passport®, Northern's proprietary, state-of-the-art desktop information system that gives clients instant access to their accounts.

The Northern Trust Company has stood as a symbol of stability, innovation and growth amidst a changing environment for more than a century. Its commitment to providing superior service in an increasingly competitive marketplace positions Northern well for future success.

A high-tech, high-touch approach drives Northern Trust's leading position in the corporate and institutional business worldwide.

Northern has built an outstanding reputation for delivering highly personalized financial services.

Safeway Insurance Group

When Safeway opened its doors with an initial investment of $25,000 in 1962, founder William J. Parrillo was told that he couldn't survive selling nonstandard automobile insurance. He didn't accept that theory and today presides over one of the largest privately held companies in the Chicago area.

Bill Parrillo, chairman and president of Safeway, began his career selling life insurance in the 1950s but moved into nonstandard automobile insurance because he liked the business and foresaw how he could operate a profitable company. He formed Safeway Mutual Insurance Company in 1959 and converted it into Safeway Insurance Company three years later. He attributes his success to putting money back into his company for growth and to the loyal team of business associates he has nurtured.

William J. Parrillo, Safeway founder

Nonstandard automobile insurance is for drivers who have difficulty getting or cannot obtain standard coverage. Until recent years, large insurance companies tended to ignore this business; high-risk drivers with tickets or accidents on their records often were forced into assigned-risk pools with costly premiums. Meanwhile, Safeway carved a niche in this market by focusing almost entirely on servicing drivers with special needs.

> Based on insurance industry research, Safeway has grown into the largest privately held automobile insurance group in the country.

From the beginning, Safeway competed with smaller insurance companies started by agents writing nonstandard automobile insurance. Since starting his company, Bill Parrillo has seen at least 70 of his competitors enter and leave this business. Many of these companies failed because they didn't reinvest their profits back into the company or were unsuccessful in managing the business.

In the 1960s and early 1970s, Safeway wrote nonstandard automobile insurance only in the Chicago metropolitan area. This changed in the late 1970s when the company began expanding into other states. Today the company also has offices in Alabama, Arizona, California, Florida, Georgia, Louisiana, Mississippi and Texas. In expanding, Safeway has usually concentrated its insurance operations in large metropolitan areas such as Atlanta, Dallas, Houston and Phoenix, maintaining a statewide presence in smaller states such as Alabama, Louisiana and Mississippi.

General agents in Alabama and Georgia solicit business and underwrite policies, while Safeway works directly with independent agents in the other states. However, each of these states has a company executive in charge of operations. The home office in Westmont, Illinois, centralizes all corporate activities, with underwriting and claims decentralized to the different states. Employees of Safeway handle all claims.

Safeway now consists of seven property/casualty companies, and the majority of premiums come from liability insurance coverage for high-risk drivers. A.M. Best Company, the leading independent rating authority, gives Safeway an "Excellent" rating, based on the consolidated financial condition and operating performance of the company and its insurance subsidiaries. Best also notes that the company has a management team of experienced insurance personnel. This includes Bill Parrillo's son, William G. Parrillo, and Robert M. Bordeman. In addition, the company maintains a very experienced employee base with low turnover.

Safeway management built the company by putting together a network of more than 2,000 insurance agents in nine states who solicit business for the company; more than 100 of those agents are in Chicago. All of these agents are independent and can place nonstandard automobile insurance for customers with other companies, but most have established a long-term relationship with Safeway. Some of them have been placing business with the company since the very beginning. Safeway has never had an in-house agency force.

Insurance agents keep doing business with Safeway because the company stresses loyalty. The company policy is that it has chosen to work with these particular insurance agents; they are loyal to the company, and the company is loyal to them. One example of this policy is that the company purposely avoids saturating the market with insurance agents. As a result, agents who place business with Safeway can develop a sales territory for the company without fearing that it eventually will be carved up into smaller and smaller pieces by other agents selling the same product.

In areas where Safeway has an established network of insurance agents, the company doesn't undercut them on call-in business. People frequently call Safeway seeking to buy auto insurance directly from the company, but these potential customers are turned over to a head underwriter and given the names of insurance agents to call in their area. By accepting this direct business over the telephone, Safeway could avoid paying commissions to an insurance broker. Instead, the company values the strong relationship based on loyalty that it has with its insurance agents and gives the call-in leads to them.

In Chicago, Safeway also produces or writes nonstandard automobile insurance customers from six large insurance brokerage firms. These firms, in turn, get their own business from small insurance agency subproducers. These subproducers sometimes want to work directly with Safeway in order to avoid sharing the commission with a large insurance brokerage firm. However, Safeway is loyal to these larger firms and will not contract with subproducers already writing business through one of the brokers.

Selling auto insurance directly to customers and the ability to sell insurance over the Internet have brought new competitive pressures into the insurance business. In recognition of this, Safeway has been offering preferred auto insurance directly to customers in California because the company does not have an established network of insurance agents in that state. Independent insurance agents will continue to be the company's main distribution system in the states where a network has been established.

Since 50 to 60 cents of every premium dollar goes to handling claims, managing claims has been another key factor in the success story of Safeway. Fraudulent claims and misrepresentations can adversely affect an insurance company's financial performance. Safeway has succeeded over the years in putting together an honest team of business associates to work with in the claims end of the business, which includes insurance adjusters, appraisers, auto body shops and attorneys.

Based on insurance industry research, Safeway has grown into the largest privately held automobile insurance group in the country. Yet the company still has unused licenses to operate in eight states. After four decades of success, Safeway continues to look forward to the opportunities ahead.

Corporate home office, Westmont, Illinois

Van Kampen Funds Inc.

The investment services provided by Van Kampen Funds Inc. have helped support the financial well-being of four generations of investors throughout Chicago and the United States. Through its array of mutual funds, unit-investment trusts and retirement-plan vehicles, Van Kampen strategically partners with financial advisors to help investors build and preserve wealth.

Headquartered in Oakbrook Terrace, Van Kampen employs more than 1,400 professionals and is assisted by a network of 32 offices worldwide, with major offices in Houston and Kansas City. With roots in money management dating back to 1926, the firm has consistently taken a sound, research-based approach to investing backed by superior customer service. This has earned Van Kampen a renowned reputation among financial advisors and throughout the investment industry.

For 10 consecutive years, Van Kampen Funds has received the DALBAR Mutual Fund Service Award recognizing outstanding shareholder service among investment firms nationwide. It is the only firm to receive this award every year since the award's inception in 1990. The firm has also received accolades from highly respected financial publications including *Money* magazine and *The Wall Street Journal* for its strong investment performance, and many of its equity funds have received Standard & Poor's select performance rating.

> ## For 10 consecutive years, Van Kampen Funds has received the DALBAR Mutual Fund Service Award recognizing outstanding shareholder service among investment firms nationwide.

Today, with more than $90 billion in assets under management or supervision, Van Kampen Funds is one of the largest wholesale mutual fund companies in the country. It has achieved this status through a successful investment strategy that utilizes patience, discipline and a long-term approach to money management. In addition, the firm is widely respected for its commitment to financial advisors and their business needs.

Van Kampen's investment expertise dates back to 1926, when a small investment advisory firm was formed that would later become part of the American General Capital Company. This firm, which would eventually be called American Capital, became a mutual fund pioneer in the 1950s and later was recognized as a premier manager of equity products. The same kind of entrepreneurial spirit was exhibited by Robert D. Van Kampen, who quickly became recognized as a leader in financial services. Eventually the two parties would merge to form the money-management powerhouse today known as Van Kampen Funds.

At only 21 years of age, Chicago native Van Kampen went to work selling bonds at a local investment firm in 1960. By the age of 28, his superior sales skills had earned him the nickname "The Charger," and his salary surpassed

From its headquarters in Oakbrook Terrace, Van Kampen Funds offers premier investment services throughout Chicago and the United States.
Photo by Brad Baskin

(Far left)
Van Kampen is committed to providing the highest level of customer service to support financial advisors and help investors achieve their goals.

Van Kampen portfolio managers and research analysts are dedicated to the core values upon which the firm was founded years ago — excellence, teamwork, leadership and integrity.
Photo by Brad Baskin

that of the firm's chairman. This prompted the firm to modify its pay system from commission to straight salary, propelling Van Kampen to venture out on his own.

Van Kampen's plan to form his own money-management firm was both ambitious and simple. He wanted to enlist the most expert talent and structure the firm around a philosophy of aggressiveness and flexibility. The company grew rapidly and eventually became known as Van Kampen Merritt.

Van Kampen Merritt quickly established itself as a leader in unit-investment trusts and municipal bonds. Subsequent company growth during the 1980s was propelled by Van Kampen's foray into mutual funds. This laid the groundwork for a merger with American Capital in 1994. American Capital's equity product line was a perfect fit with Van Kampen's fixed-income strength, and the union improved both firms' distribution capabilities and national presence.

Today, as part of Morgan Stanley Dean Witter, Van Kampen Funds offers more than 50 open-end and 39 closed-end mutual funds and has sponsored more than 4,000 series of fixed-income and equity unit-investment trusts. The company also provides service, administration and management for retirement plans and institutional accounts.

Included in Van Kampen's portfolio are investment choices that fit a wide array of financial goals. From aggressive growth funds that invest in the emerging-technology sector to more conservative fixed-income

funds, Van Kampen offers a range of investment options to help meet the varying needs of investors.

In addition to the firm's comprehensive offerings, Van Kampen provides advisors and investors with a team of investment professionals dedicated to creating and distributing superior investment products and services. Each employee practices the core values upon which Van Kampen Funds was founded years ago — excellence, teamwork, leadership and integrity. These attributes are fueled by training, development and growth opportunities within the firm.

> Backed by four generations of money-management experience, Van Kampen Funds continues to provide quality investment products to investors throughout the nation.

Backed by four generations of money-management experience, Van Kampen Funds continues to provide quality investment products to investors throughout the nation. In the years to come, Van Kampen will remain committed to providing a wide variety of superior investment products, along with the highest level of customer service to support financial advisors and help investors achieve their goals.

Wheels, Inc.

It was 1939 and a young man named Zollie Frank had been in the automobile dealership business for three years on Chicago's North Western Avenue. When two executives from Petrolagar, a local pharmaceutical company, stopped in to purchase a couple of cars, they mentioned they often helped their new salesmen buy personal cars to get them started in their jobs. However, the salesmen, equipped with sales training and automobiles they could keep, were often hired by other companies, taking their new cars with them. Did Zollie Frank have any solutions, the executives wondered?

The ingenious Mr. Frank certainly did. He suggested that he lease cars to their salesmen, instead of selling them. That way the company would have control of the automobiles and not lose a major cash outlay. A deal was made with Petrolagar — Frank's first leasing client — and a new industry, fleet management, was born. Over 60 years later, Petrolagar is now American Home Products and still a client of Frank's fleet business, which has grown into Wheels, Inc.

Headquartered since 1984 in Des Plaines, Wheels has grown to 200,000 vehicles on lease and over $1 billion in annual revenue, but the company still abides by Zollie Frank's original values. Integrity, reliability, loyalty to clients, employers and suppliers, and "the belief that every client should feel as though they're our only client" were the convictions of founder Zollie Frank, and are the beliefs by which Wheels continues to operate.

Jim Frank, Zollie's son, now leads Wheels, Inc. — a role he assumed in 1975. Today Jim heads an organization that does business across North America and in Europe and whose client list reads like a Who's Who of commerce. Among Wheels' clients are such well-known names as Abbott, Baxter, Keebler, SC Johnson, Pfizer, the state of Michigan, Nationwide Insurance, ServiceMaster, Bristol-Myers and Sony. With its state-of-the-art information

technology, skilled employees and a culture focused on customer service, Wheels, Inc. remains at the forefront of the fleet management industry.

And exactly what is fleet management? Today, with fleets numbering thousands of vehicles, fleet management has become much more than car leasing. Through many specialized services, Wheels minimizes driver downtime and hassles, controls fleet costs and reduces fleet administration. Wheels assists its clients in selecting and obtaining the right vehicles for their applications, whether a basic sales sedan or a complex work truck. Also, Wheels uses its buying power and expertise to manage a wide network of service providers; supports driver needs 24 hours a day, seven days a week; sells used vehicles for its clients at the best-possible prices; processes millions of individual transactions related to fleet vehicle expenses; and provides sophisticated information tools and support to manage it all.

Wheels' computer systems make managing fleet information and transacting business with Wheels easy and fast. Its Internet-based FleetView™ provides complete access to fleet information and lets fleet managers

order new vehicles; DriverView™ lets drivers order vehicles and check information such as company policy or the status of an order. New information technologies, led by the Internet, are revolutionizing the fleet management industry. In 2000 Wheels will transact over $500 million of e-business with its clients via the Internet.

Vehicle acquisition and delivery near the driver are important parts of Wheels' service. Wheels purchases nearly 60,000 vehicles a year, making it a major player with the vehicle manufacturers and an effective advocate for its clients. The company also manages relationships with over 5,000 car and truck dealers across the United States and Canada who receive the vehicles and prep them for drivers. Through its highly sophisticated ordering system, Wheels is able to order directly from the factory virtually any fleet vehicle, for any driver, equipped exactly as specified. In addition to factory ordering, vehicles needed immediately can be purchased from retail dealer stock.

After getting the driver into a new vehicle, selling the used vehicle becomes a key service. Vehicle depreciation

accounts for over 50 percent of total fleet cost, and selling used vehicles at the best-possible prices is critical to managing depreciation expense. Wheels Remarketing Service personnel are experts in used-vehicle pricing and outlets. They use sophisticated pricing information systems and a national network of wholesale auctions, resale dealers and Internet-based retailers to sell used vehicles for their clients quickly and at prices that are often well above national wholesale averages.

Wheels client vehicles are typically driven by sales and service personnel whose time is precious and whose work directly affects revenue and customer satisfaction. To keep them on the road, Wheels provides a range of services that save drivers time, minimize vehicle down-time and control fleet operating costs. These services assist drivers with such typical vehicle-operating needs as license renewals, maintenance, fuel and accident repairs.

Wheels Registration Management Program handles all vehicle title and registration needs for drivers. New registrations, license renewals and payment of various vehicle taxes are all handled by Wheels service representatives through an advanced computer system and direct links to state agencies.

The Wheels Maintenance Assistance Program (MAP) simplifies vehicle maintenance and minimizes maintenance costs. Drivers can phone service representatives 24 hours a day, seven days a week for emergency assistance or routine questions. Wheels' ASE-certified advisors direct drivers to nearby approved service facilities and

ensure proper repairs are done. Wheels arranges a replacement vehicle if needed; negotiates the best rates on maintenance repairs; handles all of the paperwork and payments; and makes available to clients a complete maintenance history through its FleetView™ system.

To simplify fuel purchases and manage fuel costs, the Wheels Fuel Management Program uses a single, universal credit card that allows drivers to pull into nearly any gas station, swipe the card, enter their pin ID and odometer reading, fill the tank and drive away. Transactions are electronically paid, recorded and downloaded to the Wheels billing system. Clients receive complete online reporting of fuel purchases.

When accidents occur, drivers receive prompt phone and emergency roadside assistance. The Wheels Collision Management Program handles the details related to collision-related administration, including the filing of accident reports and insurance claims; directing drivers to an approved repair facility; negotiating repair costs; and paying invoices. Like Wheels' other services, clients have full online reporting capability.

Servicing the needs of its clients — that was what Zollie Frank believed and it remains the credo by which Wheels, Inc. operates as a leader in the fleet management industry. Just as it did 60 years ago, Wheels continues to help its clients meet their transportation needs and achieve their business goals.

Wheels, Inc.
founder
Zollie Frank

Wheels, Inc.
President
James Frank

Daniel J. Edelman, Inc.

Chairman and Founder Daniel J. Edelman was recognized in 2000 with an honorary street in his name for his contributions to the PR field and to civic and charitable organizations.

Daniel J. Edelman, Inc. and its two operating companies, Edelman Public Relations Worldwide and PR 21, have deep roots in Chicago's business and cultural community. In October 1952 Chairman and Founder Daniel J. Edelman opened a small office in the Merchandise Mart. The company's office is in the Aon Center.

Today Edelman Worldwide is the world's largest independent public relations firm and employs more than 1,700 people in 38 offices in North and South America, Europe and Asia-Pacific. PR 21 was formed in 1998 as a second agency with a strong focus on branding and marketing. It has a staff of 75.

More than 350 employees work at Edelman Chicago, which is co-headquarters along with its New York office. PR 21 employs 40 people in Chicago and has three other offices in the United States.

Delivering superior client service and instilling a working environment where smart people can thrive have driven Edelman's growth and success. For the past two years, the Chicago office of Edelman Worldwide has earned the distinction as "Office of the Year" in recognition

of its growth, energizing work environment and distinguished service to clients.

Edelman Chicago's clients include Fortune 500 corporations, health and pharmaceutical firms, professional services providers and technology leaders. Among its clients are companies such as Microsoft and AT&T, as well as leading Midwest-based corporations including Sears, Kraft, ConAgra and Manpower.

Dedication to client service has built enduring relationships that have extended in some instances for more than 25 years. Edelman Excellence represents the firm's commitment to service quality on behalf of each client and involves open and ongoing communications between Edelman's people and their clients.

Chicago also is the nerve center for nationwide and global Internet initiatives on behalf of clients. Edelman was the first public relations firm to embrace the Web. Today the Edelman Interactive Solutions group, based in Chicago, helps clients gain a competitive communications advantage in an increasingly connected world. Its award-winning teams have developed more than 200 Web sites. Employees can access extensive internal resources on its intranet and proprietary research tools that are essential for developing new creative strategies and solutions for clients.

In addition to award-winning client programs, Edelman Worldwide for nearly 50 years has been a leader and innovator in the development of public relations practices, standards and ethics in the United States and internationally. Its Edelman University offers continuous learning opportunities that enhance employees' professional skills and helps them build more meaningful careers.

Edelman also encourages its employees to become involved in their communities. Chicago employees have reached out to help the elderly, inner-city youth and others in need through volunteerism and charitable days. Edelman also provides pro bono public relations counsel for numerous nonprofit organizations, including groups supporting breast cancer awareness and organizations that locate missing children.

The "Search for North America's Best Singing Pet" contest on behalf of Bayer Advantage flea control products is among many award-winning Edelman programs.

Photo by Jack Delano of the Farm Security Administration, Courtesy Library of Congress

MANUFACTURING & DISTRIBUTION

In addition to producing exceptional goods for individuals and industry, Chicagoland manufacturing and distribution companies provide employment for area residents.

AAR

David Storch, CEO

Founded in 1951, AAR has been profitable every year since and has grown into a billion-dollar public company by supplying value-added products and services to the aviation/aerospace industry.

Combining an aggressive marketing strategy with conservative financial management, AAR has established a reputation in the aviation industry for delivering what it promises. The company serves commercial, military and general aviation customers worldwide in a variety of ways, including supply, repair and manufacture of aircraft parts and systems.

The AAR philosophy today under David P. Storch, CEO, continues to focus on strong customer relationships, performance guarantees, low costs, high availability of parts and services, short turnaround times and personalized customer service.

The company was started by Ira Eichner, AAR chairman, to sell war surplus equipment to the general aviation industry. The military at that time was putting out a lot of surplus electronic equipment, and he became involved in selling surplus radios to aviation companies. Operating initially out of an office in downtown Chicago, Eichner put surplus items in the back of his Studebaker and drove from city to city to call on customers and other surplus businesses. He often bought equipment at one place and then sold it on subsequent sales calls. Right from the beginning, Eichner built a reputation of being reliable by delivering what he said he would.

The company was named Allen Aircraft Radio in 1956 and moved to a larger facility in Elk Grove Village in 1961. The company also began repairing radios before selling them and then progressed into overhauling electronic equipment. Used equipment was bought and then stored in a warehouse. When a customer called with a specific need, the equipment was reconditioned and brought up to manufacturing specifications before being sold with a warrantee.

Allen Aircraft Radio was incorporated in 1966, and company stock was first made available to the public a year later. The parent company name was officially changed to AAR in 1969. A turning point for the company at this time was signing a contract to handle all of Boeing's surplus material. This put AAR in the airframe business.

While sales continued to grow during the 1960s and 1970s, AAR also began to pursue a business strategy of expansion through acquisition. The company acquired two aircraft-and-radio supply companies in 1967, followed by six more acquisitions between 1968 and 1980. In 1972 AAR stock was listed on the American Stock Exchange. Reflecting growth of the company, AAR common stock was listed on the New York Stock Exchange in 1980.

After nearly 30 years in business, AAR had developed into a large supplier of parts and services for general aviation aircraft. In 1981 AAR purchased Brooks & Perkins, which proved to be another

Engine Component Services

turning point. The general aviation business slumped in the early 1980s, and AAR's purchase of Brooks & Perkins manufacturing in Cadillac, Michigan, enabled AAR to continue its profits during the downturn in this sector of the aviation industry.

During the 1980s AAR entered the F-16 component overhaul business through a contract with the Dutch Air Force. The success of this program enabled the company to design F-16 accessory programs that meet the needs of the defense industry worldwide. Today, AAR services high-technology fighter aircraft such as the F-16 and C-130 for numerous military/government customers, including the U.S. Air Force.

AAR continued its aggressive move into the commercial airline business, making four more aircraft company acquisitions during the 1980s. A change in organization also gave impetus to increasing the company's commercial airline business. AAR had been organized by function, with separate departments for purchasing, sales and research. Each product line now became a self-supporting and self-sustaining business unit with a general manager and controller at each location. After each unit was put in charge of its own purchasing, sales and research, sales to commercial airlines increased.

Storch joined AAR in 1979 and began development of the company's engine business. After achieving dramatic growth, he started the AAR Aircraft Turbine Center. Following three decades of servicing the aviation industry with radio equipment and aircraft accessories, the company now added engine products and services to its capabilities. AAR's Turbine Center under Storch was so successful that sales grew from $1 million to $100 million within 5 years, paving the way for the company to expand into engine sales and leasing and aircraft sales and leasing for commercial and transport aircraft. Storch was named president and chief operating officer of the corporation in 1989, and he became AAR's CEO in 1996.

While many companies in the aviation industry have been consolidating, AAR's business strategy has been to position itself uniquely in the marketplace by offering a variety of products and services. Through diversification the company has become a specialist for businesses wanting to outsource their aircraft needs for spare parts and maintenance. In the process, AAR has expanded into a diversified group of

businesses with 40 facilities and more than 2,900 employees in 12 countries throughout North America, Europe and Asia.

A key trend in the aviation/aerospace industry is for companies and organizations to look for more cost-efficient ways to supply and maintain their aircraft fleets. They are doing this by reducing the number of suppliers they deal with, entering into long-term supply agreements and outsourcing their inventory management. AAR has

Comprehensive
Aircraft Services

Engine Sales
and Leasing

been able to take advantage of these market changes by providing on a more economical basis what aircraft companies have previously done in-house.

The company also has become a leading independent supplier to the aviation/aerospace industry due to the quality of its broad range of products and services, as well as to speed of delivery and price. AAR primarily supplies parts and equipment, performs technical services and manufactures proprietary products for the global aviation industry.

AAR's principal customers today are domestic and foreign commercial airlines, regional/commuter airlines,

Composites

Landing Gear
Services

AAR has expanded into a diversified group of businesses with 40 facilities and more than 2,900 employees in 12 countries throughout North America, Europe and Asia.

business aircraft operators, aviation OEMs, aircraft leasing companies, domestic and foreign military organizations, and independent aviation support companies.

AAR invested heavily in technology during the 1990s, as a means of providing better service to customers and as a way to reach new customers. The company under Storch has become an Internet-based systems company, migrating from mainframe computers to open systems to the Web. The company also has created individual Web sites for commercial airlines, general aviation, and military/government customers. The commercial site gives visibility to every product and service that AAR has for commercial airlines, as do the other two sites in their respective areas.

In December 1999 Storch announced formation of a new business unit, AAR e-Business, with responsibility for bringing E-commerce initiatives to market. One E-commerce initiative, AAR Online Parts Warehouse, gives customers 24-hour access to stock quantities, pricing and order processing. AAR Online Partner Services provides customized Internet-based inventory systems, and AAR SuperSpares is a site where flight-critical parts can be ordered and delivered in as little as one hour.

For example, AAR's inventory management program enables its customers to do all planning and provisioning via the Internet using a Web-based system. Once into the AAR system, customers look at their inventory, what inventory is staged for them on consignment, what they have under repair and what they want to purchase from inventory.

One of AAR's primary goals in establishing Web sites for E-commerce business is to enhance customer service. Customers can access one of the Web sites and look at their order status or order history. If previous paperwork for an order has been lost, they can come into the system, look over a part they bought a year ago, find the images that relate to that part and print it. When an aircraft part has problems, AAR can provide online digital documentation. The customer has a picture and explanation within minutes, saving time and money.

AAR is also developing its general aviation Web site to give customers the option of buying through the site with a credit card. This is a forerunner of expanding into a broader retail market. There are hundreds of thousands of private airplane owners in the United States and many more internationally. AAR is creating a very sophisticated search engine to get customers to the right parts.

At the beginning of 2000 AAR and SITA (an integrated telecommunications and information organization for the air transport industry) formed a joint venture, Aerospan.com, to establish an innovative electronic marketplace for supplying the $80 to $100 billion air transport industry. Through Aerospan.com, 15,000 airlines, aviation/aerospace companies and other industry customers are able to buy and sell products instantly. One of Storch's goals is to have Aerospan.com steadily expand into the $500 billion aerospace market.

These E-commerce initiatives are just the latest example of AAR's history of adjusting and adapting quickly to changes in the aviation/aerospace market. The company's investment in technology and internal systems has enhanced its ability to deliver quality products and services at a fair price on time. The Internet is a business and communications tool that allows AAR to be even more successful at serving the aviation/aerospace industry.

Over the past 50 years, AAR 's hallmark has been to combine marketing skill, financial strength, technical knowledge, distribution expertise and IT capability to support its

Cargo Systems

customers with creative solutions that meet their needs. With its breadth and diversity, AAR will continue to move forward by developing innovative products and programs that enhance the profitability of its customers.

Aircraft Components Services

Boise Cascade Office Products

Boise Cascade Office Products provides businesses throughout Chicago and the world with an innovative, one-stop resource for office supplies. Boise's vast network of products and services — from paper clips and computers using next-day worldwide distribution capabilities — meets the needs of both small and large businesses and assists offices in running efficiently and profitably.

Headquartered in Itasca, Boise has served as a leader in the office supplies industry for more than 25 years.

Headquartered in Itasca, Boise has been an industry leader for more than 24 years. The company started as the office supplies division of the Boise Cascade Corporation — a Boise, Idaho-based producer of pulp, paper and building products. In 1995, to assist in the explosive growth of its office supplies division, Boise Cascade Corporation created Boise as a separate, publicly traded company.

Boise's vast supply of office products and services provides a one-stop resource for businesses throughout Chicago.

The formation of Boise has allowed for an increased market share beyond corporate expectations — all the while meeting the company's goal of premier customer service. Since 1995 Boise has successfully expanded its operation throughout Australia, Canada, France, the United Kingdom and the United States, acquiring 45 office-supply businesses along the way. Today the company employs 12,000 people and has sales in excess of $3 billion per year.

What has allowed Boise to flourish is the personal approach the company takes to each client. Through its Internet, mail-order and customer-service outlets, Boise strives to provide clients with pre-eminent customer service and office products that increase productivity and improve the work environment. Rather than serve as a bulk provider of paper and staples, the company goes beyond basic office supplies to offer technological hardware and services, office-management programs, promotional products and furniture to numerous *Fortune* 500 companies.

In addition Boise provides offices with an efficient and effective way to purchase office supplies by incorporating cutting-edge technology into its operation. The company's OrderPoint Internet purchasing system, for example, allows end-users in the office the access to purchase their own office supplies, thus cutting administrative costs for such duties. The company was a pioneer in Internet service as the first contract stationer to have a World Wide Web presence, and has been cited as one of the top 10 business-to-business Internet operations by *PC Computing Magazine.*

Boise also strategically teams with suppliers to develop programs and services that are beneficial to clients and the community as a whole. Management training programs that exude total quality principles are available to assist office managers in improving office processes. Boise's Supplier Diversity program

mentors minority-owned office-supply businesses. Boise works with these minority- and women-owned business enterprises to help them become suppliers to large corporations. The goal with this innovative program is to support diversity and to help these businesses grow and compete on a larger level.

Through a variety of product lines, including Boise Technology, Boise Marketing Services Inc. and Boise Office Furniture, Boise offers one of the broadest selections of office products and services in the industry.

BOISE IS BORN

The Boise Cascade Corporation was established in 1957 as the result of a merger between the Boise Payette Lumber Company of Boise, Idaho, and the Cascade Lumber Company of Yakima, Washington. Today the Boise Cascade Corporation is one of the nation's largest integrated paper-and-forest-products companies. It features manufacturing, distribution and converting operations throughout the United States, and owns or controls approximately 2.4 million acres of timberland to support these operations.

In 1964 Boise first entered the office products industry as a way to distribute its paper products. It acquired the Honolulu Paper Company, a distributor and retailer of office products and stationery on the Hawaiian Islands. Today this operation continues to thrive as part of the Boise company.

A second, key acquisition occurred in 1964 as Boise took over the Chicago-based Horders office supplies operation and the Associated Stationers Supply Company, which was established in 1917 as Horder's wholesale department. Horder's had become established in Chicago with a seven-story building serving as its headquarters, and by 1958, Associated Stationers had 11 branch warehouse operations in the Midwest and Southeast. Boise's acquisition of Horders allowed it to move into these facilities, and additional growth allowed for the company headquarters and distribution center to be moved to a more modern, two-story facility in Itasca in 1976.

To focus on the changing needs of its growing corporate customer base, Boise sold its wholesale distribution operation in 1992. This allowed the company to pursue the contract-stationer market throughout the United States. It was during this period that Boise focused on its nationwide-distribution capability. Some markets were opened with a series of startup center stores, while others

Boise's presence throughout Australia, Canada, France, the United Kingdom and the United States allows prompt delivery service to each of its clients.

The Reliable Corporation provides personalized customer service combined with a full-featured Internet presence.

were established by acquiring a local operation. By the end of 1994 Boise had grown from 18 distribution centers to 30.

A RELIABLE MOVE

To assist in the nationwide expansion of its direct-mail office products division, Boise acquired The Reliable Corporation in 1994. The Reliable Corporation, based in Schaumburg, had already made a name for itself as one of the nation's leading direct marketers of office products. Today the company operates as a wholly owned subsidiary and serves the needs of medium to small companies as well as home office users.

The Reliable Corporation was founded in 1917 as The Reliable Stationery Company. The company was purchased and renamed in 1936 by Sol Zenner, who also added a strong sales force to the company to service contract accounts. In 1953 Zenner began to experiment with the mail-order business in an effort to expand Reliable's presence and profitability. The company published its first catalog in that year and watched its sales increase dramatically. In 1960 the company acquired the Commercial Stationery Co. in Chicago and its sales exceeded $1 million.

It was at this time that Zenner's son, Merrill, joined the company as a salesman. Merrill worked with Reliable over the next two decades, becoming involved with most areas of operation within the company. This experience would prove valuable in 1978, when his father passed away unexpectedly, leaving Merrill to run the company.

The groundwork performed by Sol Zenner in forming The Reliable Corporation had proved successful — in 1979 the company exceeded $10 million in sales. When Merrill Zenner took over, he noticed that the company was being pulled in two different directions. Zenner's father had built a strong sales force to service the company's clients; however, the establishment of the mail-order catalog had flourished. Zenner felt it was difficult for the company to maintain focus and direction due to its two different businesses.

In 1983 Zenner made the decision to concentrate on the company's direct-mail business. He sold Reliable's list

Boise offers its clients pre-eminent customer service and office products that increase productivity and improve the work environment.

of 8,000 contract accounts to Publix Office Supplies, a Chicago competitor, and also worked out a deal that provided each Reliable salesperson with an equivalent job at Publix.

A leaner operation, The Reliable Corporation went about expanding its direct-mail catalog business — sending out catalogs to up to 10 million businesses. Throughout the 1980s the company experienced double-digit growth each year. In 1989 at the peak of its game, The Reliable Corporation mailed more than 30 million catalogs to small and midsized businesses, and offered 6,500 different products from 350 suppliers to its more than 400,000 customers.

The company also opened large distribution sites in Georgia, Delaware and Nevada to ship to customers more efficiently and guarantee delivery within eight hours of placing an order. The company's success was reflected in its growth to more than $150 million in sales. However, Zenner continued to run the business as a family operation, often walking through the halls and taking time to speak with employees.

A real paradigm shift in the office supplies industry occurred in the late 1980s and early 1990s. The advent of the office products superstore offered office supplies at greatly reduced prices in a supermarket environment. This flattened the wonderful business streak that Reliable had enjoyed in past years. Although The Reliable Corporation still turned annual profits, growth slowed as many clients shopped these new discount stores.

Throughout this period of change in the office supplies industry, Reliable maintained invaluable relationships with a core group of customers to whom it continued to provide office supplies. As Boise Cascade Office Products looked to expand in 1994, it took note of Reliable's position.

The subsequent acquisition proved beneficial for both companies. Boise became involved in the direct-mail business while Reliable enjoyed the backing of Boise's vast resources and worldwide presence. Today Reliable's direct-mail sales have returned to double-digit sales and profit growth. The company has rededicated itself to personalized marketing and services, and has expanded its offerings via the Internet.

A FULL-SERVICE COMPANY

Since its formation in 1995 Boise has established various product lines through which it is able to meet the

complete office supply needs of companies. Each of these divisions is tailored to offer the best products and company services and to provide a premier customer-service experience.

Boise Technology, for example, provides companies with technological hardware and software, including CPUs, servers, hard drives and printers. This division also offers sales-and-support teams that provide leading information technology solutions with world-class service and support. In fact the Boise Technology sales force has become one of the largest technology-solutions providers in the country.

Boise's promotional products subsidiary, Boise Marketing Services Inc., was formed to respond to the growing use of promotional products in the corporate world. These products can be used as advertising specialties, incentives and premiums to enhance a corporate image, increase loyalty, build brand awareness or drive sales.

Boise Marketing Services is composed of marketing professionals who offer an array of marketing programs tailored to each specific business. These programs include corporate-merchandising programs; employee-recognition programs; sales-promotion programs; incentive-based promotions; direct-marketing programs; sweepstakes programs; online stores for company merchandise; and sports-marketing programs.

Boise Office Furniture offers companies a large selection of office furniture and services, including delivery, assembly and setup. The specialists in this division use state-of-the-art CAD systems to design offices and coordinate furnishings. This division also conducts an ergonomic evaluation to ensure a healthier, more user-friendly work environment.

A fourth Boise division is its integrated supply business, in which Boise teams with other companies to offer services and other types of products to clients. For example, Boise teams with Wallace to offer Boise-Wallace Single Source, which offers not only office supplies but printing solutions to joint customers. From office supplies, furniture, computers, customized letterhead, business forms and collateral pieces, Boise-Wallace Single Source offers a broad product selection to corporate America.

Boise-Wallace Single Source is designed to reduce the costs of ordering, tracking, receiving and paying for office supplies through a streamlined purchasing process that includes one paper or electronic catalog; one order-entry vehicle; one source for customer service; and one set of usage trends and reports. This single-source agreement, which is sought after by many businesses, provides the value associated when dealing with a sole supplier while at the same time offering the expertise of two industry specialists.

Boise will continue to expand its operation and increase services in the future as it looks to enter additional markets throughout the world. Boise's continuing focus on customer satisfaction, increasing office productivity and infusing technology into the workplace will allow its clients to focus on the more important task of running a successful business.

Through its Internet, mail-order and customer-service outlets, Boise provides offices with an efficient and effective way to purchase office supplies.

Boise will continue to expand its operation and services to meet the changing needs of the office supplies industry.

Hollister Incorporated

From the beginning, John Dickinson Schneider worked hard to be responsive to real-life needs of people and delivering products and services to meet those needs.

As an employee-owned, independent manufacturer of quality healthcare products, Hollister Incorporated has deep roots in Chicago. The founder, John Dickinson Schneider, established the company in Chicago in 1921. He was 23 years old.

The 1920s were times of industrial expansion and rapid change. The automobile was changing the face of America. It was the beginning of the Jazz Age. John Schneider's company began as a printing company that bore his initials, JDS Printer Craftsman, Inc. Through the Roaring 20s and even through the Great Depression of the 1930s, JDS Printer Craftsman, Inc. built a solid reputation for quality and service. John Schneider always equated

John Dickinson Schneider's company began as a printing company that bore his initials, JDS Printer Craftsman. Through the Roaring 20s and even the Great Depression of the 1930s, JDS Printer Craftsman, Inc. built a solid reputation for quality and service.

quality products with quality service; for him, they were one. From the very beginning, his company's underlying principle was "Only First Class Is Good Enough."

From the company's earliest days, there was a palpable sense of community — a connection to people. For many employees and customers, that connection was best symbolized by Minnie R. Schneider. Kate — as she was sometimes known — had married John Schneider in 1933. Together, John and Minnie built their company on the principles of Quality Products, Quality Service, and Quality Employees. Those principles formed the basis of their philosophy, and ultimately, the promise of their company.

The company's first healthcare-related products were birth certificates — painstakingly printed with the utmost concern for quality and detail. John Schneider's company printed these heirloom-quality birth certificates for the Franklin C. Hollister Company.

In 1948, after the death of Franklin Hollister, John Schneider purchased the Hollister Company and entered what was for him, a new industry. His new hospital-products company — now a subsidiary of his printing company — began to develop new and innovative healthcare products. The Ident-A-Band® patient identification bracelet — manufactured on converted printing presses — revolutionized and helped set the standard for patient identification in this country. The Dry Plate Footprinter enabled delivery room nurses to make clear, reliable prints of newborn babies' feet. Other products followed throughout the 1950s: a hospital signage system, a circumcision device and an umbilical cord clamp.

The company's success allowed for continued growth and expansion. Hollister Limited was established in Canada in 1958. In 1965 the company moved its major production center to a new plant in Kirksville, Missouri. The corporate headquarters remained in Chicago.

John Schneider listened to his employees. He was genuinely interested in them, their careers, their futures and their families — and he recognized their contributions. He knew — perhaps instinctively — that his employees were a direct link to his customers and to his company's success. Early in the 1960s an employee who had a family member with an ostomy came to John Schneider with an idea to develop ostomy products. John Schneider decided to manufacture those products, and in so doing, he revolutionized ostomy care. With dynamic innovations and quality products, Hollister began to provide much-needed solutions for thousands of people who had undergone ostomy surgery.

Through the late 1960s and into the 70s, other products followed. The name Hollister became synonymous with quality healthcare products, not only in ostomy, but also in wound care, continence care, identification, obstetrics and healthcare information management. By 1972 John Schneider's company was out of the printing industry and was 100 percent into the medical products industry. Two new manufacturing plants were built in the 1970s — one in Stuarts Draft, Virginia, and another in Ballina, Ireland. The company's world headquarters remained in Chicago on East Chicago Avenue. Two blocks away stood the Water Tower on Michigan Avenue — one of the few Chicago landmarks that survived the great fire of 1871.

With the growth of Hollister Incorporated, John Schneider continued to look toward the future. In 1977 he established a trust, which effectively made a gift of his company — his life's work — to his employees. John Schneider wanted to ensure that Hollister would continue

Together, John and Minnie Schneider built their company on the principles of Quality Products, Quality Service and Quality Employees. Those principles formed the basis of their philosophy, and ultimately, the promise of their company.

as an independent, employee-owned manufacturer of quality healthcare products. He established the trust to secure the future of the company that he and Minnie Schneider had built together. In 1981 the corporate headquarters of the company was moved to its current location in Libertyville, Illinois — 40 miles north of downtown Chicago.

As an independent, employee-owned company, Hollister has made a dynamic commitment — a commitment to provide the highest standards of quality in its

With its corporate headquarters located near Chicago, Hollister products are currently available in more than 90 countries on six continents through its network of direct sales and distribution, as well as a combination of branch offices, joint ventures and wholly owned subsidiaries.

Hollister wound care and therapy products are designed to help healthcare professionals provide quality patient care while increasing patient comfort.

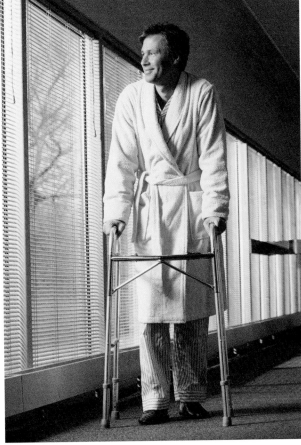

Hollister is dedicated to life from the moment it begins with obstetric products and the Ameda line of breastfeeding pumps and accessories.

In addition to quality ostomy products, Hollister has developed an extensive line of quality wound care products: dressings, collectors, tube attachment devices and other products that allow healthcare professionals to effectively treat, manage or prevent wounds.

In the development of continence care products, Hollister — again — leads the way in technological innovation. From the world's first vented leg bag, to advanced diagnostic and treatment equipment for pelvic floor therapy, Hollister offers comprehensive systems for diagnosis, treatment, and management of incontinence. For people who suffer from incontinence, Hollister products help provide a higher quality of life — and dignity.

For mothers who are breastfeeding, Hollister has a comprehensive system of products that allows new mothers to provide the best nutrition possible for their babies while continuing an active, modern lifestyle. The highly acclaimed line of Ameda breast pumps and accessories provides nursing mothers with the most natural, effective and comfortable breastfeeding products available.

As the company enters the 21st century, its Mission is unchanged: to help healthcare professionals deliver

healthcare products and services — a commitment to world-class performance. In every line of the company's products — including Ostomy, Wound Care, Continence Care, Breastfeeding, Obstetric and Newborn products, as well as Identification and Risk Management products — Hollister continues its tradition of innovation and its relentless pursuit of quality.

As always, the foundation for new product development is research. Hollister scientists, using advanced materials, equipment and processes, continue to push the technological envelope. In order to help ensure the highest-quality products, Hollister engineers design and build almost all of the company's manufacturing equipment. Patented designs and exclusive processes help provide assurance that customers receive the finest-quality products available.

Nowhere is the commitment to world-class performance better illustrated than in ostomy product technology. Worldwide, Hollister continues its leadership role in ostomy, and continues to provide increasingly higher-quality products. The overriding goal is to improve the quality of life for people who have had ostomy surgery.

better products and services, and to make life more rewarding and dignified for those who use our products.

As Hollister continues to expand its product line, it is also expanding its presence around the world. The company's European headquarters is located in Wokingham, England — 50 miles outside of London. Divisional headquarters for Asia, Latin America, the Middle East and Africa is at the corporate headquarters in Libertyville. Hollister has four major manufacturing centers. In the United States there are manufacturing facilities in Kirksville, Missouri, and Stuarts Draft, Virginia. In Europe the company has manufacturing facilities in Ballina, Ireland, and Fredensborg, Denmark.

Today, Hollister has a significant worldwide presence. The company provides healthcare products and services in over 90 countries on six continents. Hollister is committed to establishing a leadership position as a manufacturer of quality health-care products internationally, just as it has done in the United States. The rededication of people and resources to this important goal is an example of how Hollister is keeping the promise to improve the quality of human lives and foster a spirit of worldwide community. With its continued expansion into international markets, Hollister is serving the global community. In many ways, however, the spirit of Hollister remains the same — the same as the original entrepreneurial venture that began in Chicago in 1921. John and Minnie Schneider's fundamental values and principles still form the foundation. The enduring legacy of the Schneiders has provided a substrate for continued success and achievement.

Hollister Incorporated is in the health-care industry, but the business of the company is in serving — serving customers and the community as a whole. The promise of Hollister — and its greatest strength — is in its commitment to people, a commitment embedded in the very fabric of the company. At Hollister, "fulfilling the promise" means

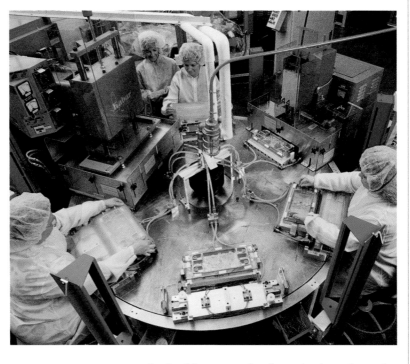

meeting the healthcare needs of people throughout the global community. That is the purpose of the company and the vision of its leaders. With deep Chicago roots, Hollister Incorporated is striving to fulfill that promise.

Teamwork between all areas has led to a commitment to establishing a leadership position as a manufacturer of quality healthcare products internationally.

Hollister Ostomy and Continence Care products restore physical and emotional well-being.

Rose Packing Company

When William Richard Rose joined his family's business, Rose Packing Company, in late 1949, the company was losing $1,000 to $2,000 each week. Since then the company has grown to more than $100 million in sales and is among the small percentage of family-owned businesses that survive into the fourth generation.

Rose Packing specializes in fresh, smoked and processed pork products such as pork back ribs, Canadian-style bacon, pork sausage and hams. As each generation of the Rose family has built on the one before it, the guiding principle has been to keep the business strong for successive generations. The family attributes its success to faithfully following four business goals: survive by not gambling, be profitable, present a good image and assist sister companies in their endeavors.

With four members of the Rose family guiding the company during the first 75 years, Rose Packing has survived depressions in the food industry, limited space, scarcity of funds, inadequate machinery, financial problems and shifts in national food tastes. Hiring from within the family and company, institutional accounts and diversification of products and services have all been key factors in the business surviving.

It all started when 51-year-old Louis Rose leased a three-story building on Fulton Street in 1924 and opened Rose Packing. He left North Dakota at age 16 in 1889 by riding a cattle car to Chicago, where he found a job as a drover for Armour and Company. His job involved transporting cattle between pens or to the slaughterhouse. Louis Rose's great, great, great-grandfather left Scotland in the 1740s and emigrated to Canada. Family members subsequently moved to Delaware, Iowa, and North Dakota.

After taking night classes at the Armour Institute of Technology, Louis Rose became an accountant and worked as a traveling auditor for Armour. No one in the family is quite sure why, but he left Armour in the 1920s and founded Rose Packing with his 27-year old son, Gregory Rose, and his 26-year old son, William Arthur Rose. Both would become successor presidents of the company. Since his two sons were antagonistic to each other, Louis Rose sent his younger son to open a sales office in Buffalo, New York, sometime between 1924 and 1926.

Rose Packing began as a processor of beef, with bull meat as a specialty, and the company continued to expand during the 1920s and early 1930s. At some point between 1927 and 1934, the company began selling Canadian bacon under its own label. Envisioning more growth, Gregory Rose leased office space near the Chicago stockyards plus 20,000 square feet of storage space a block away. However, the distance of 40 blocks between the office and Fulton Street plant resulted in an inefficient operation.

In the early 1930s Louis Rose had to cope with three other problems. First, he had to make sure his company survived the Depression, which hit meat packers as hard as it did almost everyone else. He also struggled to control his diabetes and rein in the speculative tendencies of his son, Gregory. In late 1934 Louis Rose died of diabetic gangrene. He was 61 and had spent 40 years in the meat business.

Louis Arthur Rose, William Arthur Rose, William Richard Rose

Rose Packing Company executives (L to R, standing): Peter Rose, Norman Wetherton, Henry J. Vandenbergh, Michael Sheridan, Dwight Stiehl, president, and Gary Scherer. (L to R, seated): William R. Rose and Margaret Cosgrove

851 Fulton Street housed the 1924 beginning of Rose Packing Company

Gregory Rose became president of Rose Packing upon his father's death and served in that capacity from 1935 to 1947. Unfortunately for the company, he liked to gamble on the commodity market and on horses. William Arthur Rose had moved from Buffalo to open a sales office in New York City in early 1934, but he now returned to Chicago. Both Gregory Rose and William Arthur Rose were strong in buying and selling and in developing relationships with suppliers and customers, but neither had experience in meat production. As a result, Gregory Rose hired a plant superintendent to handle production.

In the early 1940s Gregory Rose leased a six-story, 100,000-square-foot sausage factory on N. Green Street, just around the corner from the Fulton Street plant. Prior to this, Rose Packing was a boning house that took apart slaughtered animals and sent the parts to other companies for processing. The company was now able to process its own meat and began manufacturing its own Canadian bacon in 1942. This resulted in a tremendous increase in pork boning and nearly a total reduction in beef boning. Gregory Rose also won a government contract for C-rations during this period.

During World War II the government required all meat processors to own and operate their own slaughterhouses. Since packinghouses could no longer buy previously slaughtered meat for processing, Gregory Rose purchased the Davies Meat Packing Company and its slaughtering facilities in Danville, Illinois. After the war, however, the slaughterhouse became less and less efficient. Instead of getting hog carcasses shipped from Danville, William Arthur Rose wanted to buy the same meat for less money on the open market. This led to more confrontations between the two brothers.

In 1947 the two brothers split the business. Gregory Rose took the Danville facility, while William Arthur Rose kept the leased facilities in Chicago and the name of Rose Packing Company. Two years later Gregory Rose filed for bankruptcy in Danville. He next purchased a thousand-acre farm in Arkansas in order to raise hogs.

This, too, ended in bankruptcy. His mother, Daisy Rose, sold her stock in Rose Packing in 1951 in order to bail him out. This left William Arthur Rose as sole stockholder. When Gregory Rose died at age 66 in 1963, he was almost penniless after having spent what was left of the money he had inherited from his mother when she died in 1960.

When William Arthur Rose took over total control of Rose Packing, the meat packing industry was in a postwar depression. The company consisted of a leased factory at one location, leased office space at another, and half of a cold-storage facility at a third location. There was insufficient revenue to keep them all viable, as rent and salaries were consuming income. William Arthur Rose's strength was sales, so he added to his sales staff and also hired a salesman, Carl E. Wetherton, in 1948 to sell Canadian bacon to chain store accounts.

Despite the additional sales staff, Rose Packing continued to lose money during 1949 and 1950 and relied on borrowing on accounts receivable. William Arthur Rose then announced his intention to sell the company for $150,000, but his son, William Richard Rose, was now working full-time in the family business and convinced his father not to sell for at least one year. Using his engineering background, William Richard Rose then began to restructure the production facilities. Working in unison with the plant superintendent, Walter Gleason, William Richard Rose obtained, invented and hand-built air-operated, electrically timed equipment to replace some of the labor-intensive practices in the plant. He also weeded out people who fought change and consolidated operations at the Green Street location. By 1952 William Arthur Rose had given up his idea to sell the business.

William Richard Rose prepared plans during 1956 for a one-story facility that would allow for efficient movement of meat with fewer workers. The new 67,900-square-foot plant in Stickney was ready for operation in 1957. At the end of the first fiscal year in the new building, Rose Packing cleared $100,000 after taxes. It was the first time the company had made any significant amount of money since World War II. Expansion began within two years, and the original building has since tripled in size.

William Arthur Rose served as president and William Richard Rose as vice president from 1958 to 1977. Although often opposed at least initially by his father, William Richard Rose continued to create new machinery and new operating methods to improve Rose Packing. There were 120 employees in the plant in 1958, and there are more than 450 today out of the 600 people working for the company. Although automated machinery moved meat through the plant, it took William Richard Rose until 1965 before he was able to overcome his father's objections and begin computerizing office functions.

The 1970s were a period of excitement and expansion for Rose Packing. The Chicago Union Stock Yard closed in 1971, but Rose Packing was flexible and began to grow by supplying fast-food restaurants. This included Canadian-style bacon for McDonald's, and Rose Packing today has about half of the McDonald's business around the world. In 1973 William Richard Rose bought 17 acres of property and converted a farmhouse on it into the company's new corporate headquarters on S. Barrington Road in South Barrington. William Richard Rose subsequently began flying to the Stickney plant, which only takes 15 to 20 minutes.

William Arthur Rose stepped down in 1977 at age 79 after 30 years as president, but he continued as chairman of the board and treasurer. William Richard Rose, grandson of the founder and third generation in the business, succeeded as president. Three months later he purchased Ashland Cold Storage on W. 43rd Street — an investment his father had opposed. With 22,000 pallet spaces and 220,000 square feet, the facility holds more than 25 million pounds of product for over 300 customers. Rose Packing is less than 15 percent of Ashland's business.

William Richard Rose has faced three major crossroads in his life since World War II. When he enlisted in the U.S. Marine Corps in 1945, he had an opportunity to go to Officer Candidate School. If he had pursued OCS, he would not have been in a position at Rose Packing to talk

Rose Packing Company
Headquarters,
Barrington, Illinois

his father out of selling the company. The second cross-road occurred in 1949 when his wife became pregnant. If he had returned to college to pursue his engineering studies, he also would not have been at Rose Packing when his father wanted to sell the company. The final and biggest crossroad was when William Richard Rose bought a 20-acre farm in Barrington in 1957. As the landowners around him began selling their land in order to retire, he bought more than 1,000 acres with other partners and 500 acres on his own. As a result, he was able to gain half of his wealth by benefiting from upswings in real estate values.

In the late 1970s William Richard Rose began turning over more responsibility to fourth-generation family members and to employees from other families that had been loyal to Rose Packing for many years. His son, Peter Rose, became vice president in charge of plant operations. Dwight Stiehl, who started working at the plant in the late 1960s, became president of the company in August 1999 when William Richard Rose moved to chairman of the board. Stiehl is the son-in-law of Walter Gleason, who started at Rose Packing in 1936, served as plant superintendent and then vice president, until his death in 1979. William Richard Rose's son-in-law, Henry J. Vandenbergh, joined the company in 1979 and was subsequently promoted to vice president, secretary and treasurer. Norman C. Wetherton joined the company in 1962 and also rose to the position of vice president. He is the son of Carl Wetherton, who was hired as a salesman in 1948 and eventually headed Rose Packing's sales department until his death in 1975. Gary E. Scherer, a cousin to the Rose family, was hired in 1979 as manager of Ashland Cold Storage and became vice president of operations.

While guiding the tremendous growth of Rose Packing for 50 years, William Richard Rose found time to expand into other areas. He formed what became the Barrington Construction Company in the early 1970s and built 150 houses in three South Barrington subdivisions. Although he phased out of the home construction business in 1987, the construction company is still a Rose sister company. Mill Rose Farm Nursery, which provided plantings for the subdivisions, also continues as a sister company. He also started Countrywood Realty in the 1970s but sold it to the employees in 1983.

Since moving the Rose Packing headquarters to South Barrington in 1973, William Richard Rose has

Current Rose Packing Company facility in Stickney, Illinois

Millrose Restaurant & Brewing Company, Millrose Country Store, and Rose Packing Company Headquarters (upper right corner) in Barrington, Illinois

opened the Millrose Country Store in 1974 and the Millrose Brewing Company Restaurant in 1991. The store offers Millrose hand-crafted beers, gourmet potables, unique gift items and a variety of meat products. In 1998 *Restaurants and Institutions* magazine ranked the restaurant the 67th largest in the country in sales volume. Six 125-year-old barns were moved to create the restaurant, banquet rooms and country store. The company also owns the Marco River Marina in Marco Island, Florida.

William Richard Rose's philosophy is that he allows himself to be wrong 25 percent of the time, but he hasn't been wrong very often since joining Rose Packing when it was losing money. He instilled new life into the company by streamlining production, entering the computer age, making changes when necessary and nurturing a fourth generation of family members and key employees to gradually take over responsibility of running the company.

333

Ryerson Tull, Inc.

Joseph T. Ryerson, founder, owner and active head of the Ryerson company from 1842 to 1883

Joseph T. Ryerson, 29, arrived in Chicago as an agent for a Pennsylvania iron manufacturer in 1842 — just five years after the Illinois town became a city. He leased a building on the banks of the Chicago River with $1,500 of inventory; two years later he bought property on nearby Lake Street and built his own iron store there. During his first four years in Chicago, Ryerson slept above his store.

A decade later Ryerson moved his growing metals business out onto the prairie — across the river from where the Merchandise Mart now stands. The Great Chicago Fire of 1871 completely destroyed the business and Ryerson's home as well, but he immediately issued a statement promising continued service and rebuilt on the same site. By 1882 the company moved to new, larger quarters three blocks west. Primary customers throughout the 19th century were boilermakers who required firebox and flange iron plates and heads, sheet steel, corrugated furnaces, tools and hundreds of other items that ultimately helped fuel the railroad industry. Joseph Ryerson died in 1883 and his son took over leadership of the business.

By the next century the customer base was expanding and changing as new markets developed, including those for farm implements and buildings constructed with load-carrying steel skeletons. Unprecedented industrialization and mechanization demanded more steel. In 1903 the new Ford Motor Company sought to purchase Ryerson products; sent to check its credit, one of the founder's grandsons reported, "in my opinion, it would be perfectly safe to extend regular credit."

The Chicago offices and warehouse completed a move to its present location at 16th and Rockwell streets in 1908. The next year a New York plant, the first outside Chicago, opened to better serve East Coast customers. By 1929 there were 10 service centers strategically located across the country. Early photos show teams of horses pulling wagons to transport Ryerson metals, but that picture quickly changed with the advent of trucks.

Innovation and responsiveness to customers' requirements continued to characterize the company. In 1911 it began to offer alloy stocks for new railroad, automotive and machinery needs. Stainless steel first became commercially available in 1924; two years later Ryerson was the first to offer stocks of this superb product.

In 1933 the company introduced mechanical tubing and Ryertex thermosetting plastic laminates. Ryerson's Certified Steel Plan, implemented in 1937, set new standards for the service center industry. But employees were also a high priority — a 1927 photo shows Chicago plant workers staging a symbolic burial of the unfortunate "I.M. Carelessness" as part of an early safety campaign. Even tuba and snare drum players were present to enliven the event.

Edward L. Ryerson Jr., a grandson of the founder, entered the family business in 1909 at age 23 and became president in 1929. The year 1935 was pivotal for the

(Far right) Hard at work — the industrious, properly attired office work force c. 1914 or 1915

Earliest-known photo of a Ryerson iron store, the fourth location in Chicago. Note the transportation methods of the day — horses on Wells Street and masts of sailing ships on the Chicago River behind the building.

The gradual switch from horse and wagon began about 1908. By 1920 this impressive fleet of trucks was serving Chicago-area customers. Note hard tires and acetylene head lamps.

company due to its merger with Inland Steel Company of Chicago. Ryerson continued operations as a wholly owned subsidiary with Edward Ryerson serving as its president until 1937. He was chairman of Inland from 1940 to 1953.

Throughout his career and into his retirement, Edward L. Ryerson received prestigious awards and was a leader in civic affairs, including serving as founding chairman and president of the Chicago Educational Television Association from 1953 to 1967. He was a trustee of the University of Chicago from 1923 to 1956 and instrumental in founding The Community Fund of Chicago, which preceded the United Way movement. Twice he served as a delegate to the Republican National Convention. He was chief of an American steel and iron ore mining delegation to the Soviet Union. In 1966 he began donating woods and farmland to what has become the 550-acre Ryerson Conservation area of the Lake County Forest Preserve District in Deerfield.

Soon after the end of World War II, Ryerson added two service centers on the West Coast. As customer use of continuous feed equipment continued to increase, Ryerson responded by offering coil inventories and installed slitting equipment for the first time. The Industrial Plastics Division added fiberglass structural shapes, pipe, tubing, bars and sheets to its product line.

Since its inception Ryerson functioned as more than a supplier of metals. Processing in a variety of forms was always an important aspect of the business, and by 1966 a majority of all orders required sawing, shearing, slitting, burning or another form of processing to specification. Today these exacting operations include computer-controlled laser, plasma and flame cutting equipment, precision saws, centerless grinders and close tolerance coil processing lines.

By 1967, at its 125th anniversary, Ryerson was the nation's leading supplier of steel from stock, the largest aluminum distributor and a major distributor of industrial plastics. Photos of the day showed massive steel coils covering entire facility floors and various lengths and widths of tubes and bars stacked to the ceiling. But the company never forgot its roots. Juxtaposed with photos of the gleaming modern images are sepia-toned photos of a past that included horse-drawn wagons and bun-haired ladies seated before manual typewriters.

Growth and exceptional service continued to drive the operation forward throughout the 1970s and 1980s. Milestones included the establishment of a stainless plate center in Chicago in 1977 and a new Chicago plate processing facility in 1979. By 1983 the Grinding Division operations were consolidated in Chicago. During the next year the company achieved its first billion-dollar sales year.

Inland Steel continued as the manufacturing arm of the company while Ryerson focused on distribution and processing. In 1986 Inland acquired Atlanta-based J.M.

Tull Metals, founded by Joseph Tull in 1914. This well-established and highly regarded distributor greatly expanded the company's geographic presence in the southern United States.

Four regional headquarters were created in 1990 — Atlanta; Chicago; Seattle; and West Chester, Pennsylvania — to be closer to customers and respond more quickly to

changing business conditions. Ryerson Tull Coil Processing, also based in Chicago, became a separate business unit to focus on the needs of customers requiring processed flat rolled steel. The next year stocks of copper, brass and bronze were added to better serve machine shops, screw machine shops and original equipment manufacturers. And 1992 marked 150 years for Ryerson.

Renamed Ryerson Tull, the company made history in 1996, beginning an era which would give it a solid, new foundation for the 21st century. That was the year Ryerson Tull made an IPO of 13 percent of its shares on the NYSE. This milestone event led to full independence in 1999 after the steel manufacturing business was sold. A distinctive new logo executed in burgundy and navy symbolizes the strength and depth of the new company.

The company's strengths include size for increased buying power, a nationwide network of facilities, a broad product line and extensive value-added services such as early-stage fabrication. With profitable growth as a strategic initiative, Ryerson Tull gains additional market share through internal expansion and selective acquisitions. In 1997 the company acquired Thypin Steel Company, a distributor and processor of carbon and stainless steel products. The move resulted in an expanded presence in the eastern United States, worldwide buying relationships and additional product expertise. A second acquisition the same year gave Ryerson Tull a new presence in Virginia. Omni Metals Inc., the third acquisition of 1997,

(Far right) The Ryerson Tull Metallurgical Services Group provides customers with high-level technical assistance and design support. Here two members of the group analyze customer material to verify its suitability for specific applications.
Photo by Richard Mack

High-speed slitters at Ryerson Tull Coil Processing hold extremely tight tolerances to exceed commercial standards and customer requirements.
Photo by Tony Kelly

enabled Ryerson Tull Coil Processing to better serve the appliance industry in Tennessee. In 1999 the company acquired Washington Specialty Metals to solidify its position as a leader in the high-growth stainless steel market and to gain a presence in Canada.

The Washington acquisition represented the basis for the formation of the Specialty Metals Group. This

unit positions Ryerson Tull as the premier processor and distributor of specialty metals. Another commercial unit, the Flat Rolled Products Group, services large-volume users of processed carbon steel with quality products and creative solutions. For large customers with multiple locations, the National Accounts Group provides customized service that is unique in the marketplace. Benefits include centralized purchasing with nationwide coverage, as well as cost reduction and value-added services. The consultative Metallurgical Services Group provides material science expertise and design support to help customers make the optimal material choices for given applications. Through early involvement in a project and state-of-the-art tools such as finite element analysis, the group helps customers shorten product development time.

Although growth was traditionally focused on the domestic market, today Ryerson Tull is an international leader with joint venture distribution centers in Mexico, India and China. Six locations in Mexico enable the company to capitalize on economic growth in that country and to serve U.S. customers with operations there. The 50 percent-owned joint venture with The MacSteel Group, a leading international steel trading operation, provides access to markets in over 25 countries worldwide.

As an immense company that offers an array of materials and value-added services, Ryerson Tull applies its vast resources to partner with customers and provide solutions specific to their needs. Ryerson Tull's geographic presence across North America, deep product line and diverse end-market experience create a "one-stop shopping" experience for its customers. The company's historic ability to respond to external market factors continues to set it apart.

Through its expertise in just-in-time inventory management, material specification, part design and metallurgical services, Ryerson Tull helps customers realize product, process and cost improvements. The company's broad range of value-added capabilities also enables customers to outsource many first-stage processing services as well as the fabrication of semifinished parts and subassemblies. By outsourcing noncore functions, customers can improve asset utilization, increase efficiency and reduce costs.

Much has changed since 1842 and the statistics speak for themselves. Today Ryerson Tull is North America's leading distributor and processor of metals with approximately $3 billion in sales and over 5,000 employees worldwide. It carries over 100,000 inventory items at over 70 service centers in North America and serves over 50,000 customers. The customer base is well diversified among industries such as machinery, fabricated

metal, transportation, construction, mills, electrical equipment and others. The product mix is approximately evenly divided among carbon flat rolled, stainless/aluminum, bars/tubing/structurals and fabrication/plate.

E-commerce solutions are an integral part of Ryerson Tull operations and a point of differentiation in the marketplace. RyTEC (Ryerson Tull Electronic Commerce) is a proprietary order system that streamlines customer interaction and supply-chain management with 24-hour access. The company has an equity interest in MetalSite, the premier Internet marketplace for the metals industry. MetalSite provides neutral purchasing and sales opportunities at a level available nowhere else.

Ryerson Tull is large and established, yet well positioned and innovative. The company was already 25 years old in 1867 — four years before the Great Chicago Fire burned down the city and the entire business. It turned 50 before the turn of the last century. It was already 75 by the time World War I was raging in 1917. And in 1942, halfway through World War II, Ryerson was a solid 100 years into its successful history of serving not only customers but the community as well. In 2042 the small Chicago iron store, above which the resourceful Joseph T. Ryerson slept for four years, will celebrate 200 years of being the industry leader.

(Far left) Superior fabrication capabilities benefit Ryerson Tull customers. These assembly-ready parts were laser cut, formed, painted and delivered on a just-in-time basis to an equipment manufacturer.
Photo by Richard Mack

Uniformity and exact duplication of parts is assured by Ryerson Tull plasma/punch fabricating systems that cut, punch, drill, tap and scribe in one CNC setup.
Photo by Richard Mack

IMC Global Inc.

IMC Global Inc. plays a prominent role in the production of the world's food supply. As the world's largest and lowest-cost producer and seller of concentrated phosphates and potash, and one of the world's largest producers of animal feed ingredients, the company provides the international agricultural community with nutrients to nourish the land and animals that feed an ever-increasing global population. IMC Global also serves as the world's third-largest producer of salt, which is used for food processing and deicing applications.

IMC Global's name is representative of its presence in world agriculture. From its corporate headquarters in north suburban Chicago, IMC Global oversees several dozen phosphate, potash and salt mining operations in the United States, Canada and the United Kingdom. The company also maintains offices in Beijing; Hong Kong; Singapore; Tokyo; and São Paulo, Brazil, and employs approximately 7,500 people.

What has allowed IMC Global to expand into a worldwide operation — with annual revenues of more than $2 billion — is its ongoing commitment to producing innovative, environmentally friendly and cost-efficient solutions to feeding the earth's rapidly growing population. Through the company's agronomic research and the use of its crop nutrients, growers are able to produce

higher crop yields and ultimately a greater amount of food on the same amount of land.

IMC Global also is recognized as an international leader in promoting advances in food production. Through its ongoing series of World Food Production Conferences, the company provides a unique forum for the world's leading agronomists, economists, trade experts and government policy leaders. These conferences have occurred throughout the world for more than 45 years and allow leaders to openly discuss and debate agricultural trends, conditions and advances. The collective goal of conference participants is to find solutions for achieving global food security and forever end the human misery of hunger and malnutrition. The 1998 conference, held in Melbourne, Australia, attracted more than 200 leaders from the global agricultural community. They came from 35 countries and represented the highest levels of industry, academia, research and government. IMC Global is the only company in the world to sponsor this type of event.

IMC Global's massive worldwide network is rooted in humble beginnings. In the early 1900s Thomas C. Meadows, an entrepreneur in Tennessee's phosphate mining business, formed the United States Agricultural Corporation. The company was established to provide basic fertilizer nutrients to U.S. growers. However, the company did not have access to a sufficient supply of potash, a potassium compound which, in addition to phosphate, is an essential plant nutrient.

In 1909 Meadows and his brother-in-law, Oscar L. Dortch, teamed with Waldemar A. Schmidtmann, the foster son of a highly successful Austrian industrialist whose holdings included Kaliwerke Sollstedt — a thriving potash mine in Germany. The three acquired the Schmidtmann holdings in the potash mine and formed the International Agricultural Corporation in New York. Two core businesses were now in place for what would later become IMC Global.

Phosphate mining operations proved lucrative in Tennessee and Florida and opened doors for other business ventures. In 1927 IMC Global built its first phosphate chemical plant in Wales, Tennessee. Here the company manufactured concentrated phosphates that were used in detergents and other cleaners. By 1940 IMC Global had opened a potash mining operation in Carlsbad, New Mexico.

IMC Global's New Wales facility in Florida is the largest plant of its kind in the world, producing concentrated phosphates for commercial use in domestic and foreign markets.

Advancing technology in the mining of phosphates and potash ores — and the acquisition of smaller mining companies — helped IMC Global expand its operations. Draglines and other new pieces of automated equipment were eventually introduced and allowed for large-scale mining of phosphate and potash. In the first year of operation at Carlsbad, for example, 50,000 tons of potash was produced. Today, the Carlsbad operation yields more than 1.5 million tons of product in the same time period.

In the 1960s IMC Global significantly expanded its involvement in potash production by becoming the first company to mine the nutrient from beneath the prairies of Saskatchewan, Canada. This potash deposit had been discovered by an oil exploration crew at the 7,400-foot level, beneath a diverse series of the earth's geological layers. One of these layers was known as the Blairmore — a 200-foot-deep mass of semifluid quicksand under explosive pressures (up to 475 pounds per square inch). Using a method called "tubbing," IMC Global froze the liquid quicksand and lined a downward shaft into the earth with cast iron panels, each weighing four tons. All together, seven million pounds of cast iron tubbing and 17,000 giant bolts were used in creating a permanent hole in the Blairmore strata. This allowed for two mines to be opened — one in 1962 and the other in 1967.

At the Canadian mines 200-ton machines known as "continuous miners" are used to remove up to 1,000 tons of potash per hour. The potash is then taken to aboveground refineries for processing, storage and shipment to agricultural markets throughout the world.

In 1975 the company expanded its manufacturing capabilities by opening the New Wales facility in Mulberry, Florida. This modern complex continues to be the world's largest plant of its kind, producing concentrated phosphates for commercial use in domestic and foreign markets.

As IMC Global entered the 1990s, the company made strategic moves to solidify its leadership position in phosphate and potash. In 1993 IMC Global entered into a joint venture that launched IMC-Agrico, a phosphate mining and fertilizer production company. The joint venture greatly increased IMC Global's phosphate production capabilities and created the world's largest and today the lowest-cost producer of phosphate crop nutrients.

In 1996 IMC Global merged with The Vigoro Corporation. This merger increased the company's revenues by 40 percent and doubled its potash capabilities.

Giant mining machines, called draglines, give IMC the capacity to produce more than 18 million short tons of phosphate rock annually from its vast reserve base in central Florida.

Following the Vigoro merger IMC Global began producing more potash than any other company in the world and at the lowest cost. In 1997 the company again increased its specialty potash capabilities and revenues through the acquisition of Western-Ag Minerals in Carlsbad, New Mexico. This acquisition was located adjacent to IMC Global's existing Carlsbad potash mine and processing facility. By mid-1999 the company had combined the two facilities and extended the life of potash mining in the Carlsbad Basin to more than 30 years.

On the heels of the Western-Ag acquisition, IMC Global merged with Freeport-McMoRan. This merger, which gave the company 80 percent ownership of the IMC-Agrico joint venture, put IMC Global in control of the world's largest phosphate operation.

IMC Global has continued to strengthen its low-cost, market-leading positions in crop nutrients and animal feed ingredients while building on its core competencies in mining, chemical processing, international distribution, logistics and marketing. Long recognized in the global agricultural and food industries for a commitment to "feed the land that feeds the world," the IMC brand name has become synonymous with excellent product quality, process and technical innovation, outstanding customer service and a culture of continuous improvement.

IMC Global is the world's largest and lowest-cost producer and marketer of potash, which is an essential plant nutrient. The company sells its potash products in more than 30 countries.

The fruits of the labor put forth by IMC Global's founding members have paid off considerably, and the company's continuing expansion, focus on low-cost production and excellent customer service, and overall willingness to better itself have also reaped considerable benefits. Not one year has gone by in which IMC Global has not tried to expand its product line or market share through acquisition or internal growth. Today the company is composed of three central business units — IMC Phosphates, IMC Potash and IMC Feed Ingredients. Each serves both domestic and international customers.

IMC Phosphates accounts for approximately 31 percent of U.S. phosphate production capacity and 10 percent of the world's production capacity. The business can produce 8.5 million short tons of concentrated phosphates, primarily DAP or diammonium phosphate, from approximately 4 million short tons of phosphoric

IMC Global's crop nutrients allow growers to produce a greater amount of food on the same amount of land.

acid capacity. IMC Phosphates has an annual capacity of more than 18 million short tons of phosphate rock, with total proven reserves of about 500 million tons, or a supply of more than 30 years. With four surface mines and five strategically located finished phosphate manufacturing plants, IMC Phosphates has direct access to multiple deep-water ports for export shipments, as well as the Mississippi River for transporting product by barge to the nation's large farming region. In 1999 IMC Global exported its phosphate products to more than 30 countries through the Phosphate Chemicals Export Association, or PhosChem. Exports represented 60 percent of the company's 1999 phosphate shipments, with North American agriculture accounting for the remaining 40 percent.

IMC Potash is the world's largest and lowest-cost producer of potash. With an annual production capacity of about 10.5 million short tons, the business features several of the lowest-cost mines in the world and the broadest product line in the industry, with some 17 percent of its annual shipments for industrial customers. In 1999 nearly 70 percent of IMC Potash's shipments were for North American customers, with the remainder for international destinations. IMC Potash accounts for about 45 percent of Canadian and U.S. production capacity and 16 percent of the world's production capacity. There are four potash mines in Saskatchewan and two in the United States.

IMC Feed Ingredients is an offshoot of IMC Global's phosphate and potash mining operations and benefits from a secure supply of key product inputs from IMC Phosphates and IMC Potash. With an annual capacity of 800,000 short tons, this business unit is one of the world's largest and lowest-cost producers of phosphate and potassium feed supplements and is backed by strong name recognition, nutritional expertise, product line breadth and innovation, and an extensive distribution network. IMC Feed Ingredients products are used by major producers of livestock and poultry feeds, nutritional supply companies, and direct producers of meat, milk and eggs.

IMC Global moves into the new millennium well positioned to meet the world's growing demand for its products and services. With its award-winning environmental practices, modern facilities, and highly skilled and motivated work force, the company is fully prepared for tomorrow's challenges and opportunities. IMC Global intends to build on its proud past as it secures its place in the future.

Baxter International Inc.

Baxter International Inc., whose corporate headquarters is in Deerfield, Illinois, was founded in 1931 as an innovator in intravenous (IV) therapy. Prior to Baxter's IV technology, only large research and teaching hospitals were able to prepare the solutions and equipment. As a result, solutions were inconsistent in quality, limited in supply and often produced adverse reactions in patients who received them. Physicians turned to the still risky therapy only when the need was urgent and other means of therapy were not available.

Baxter believed the problems that plagued IV therapy could be overcome by manufacturing large, carefully controlled batches of IV solutions, bottled in glass vacuum containers. Baxter revolutionized an industry following through on that belief, introducing the first commercially prepared intravenous solutions in 1931.

In 1933 the company opened its first manufacturing facility in a renovated automobile showroom in Glenview, Illinois. There, six employees turned out the complete line of five IV solutions in glass containers. Today, IV therapy is the preferred method for hospital physicians to treat patients because the solution is given directly into the bloodstream and the effects are immediate and can be accurately controlled over time.

Baxter has a long line of firsts in the IV therapy field. In addition to pioneering the first commercially manufactured IV solutions in 1931, Baxter introduced the first plastic containers for IV solutions in the early 1970s, the first electric portable infusion pump in 1982, the first frozen intravenous drug solutions in the mid-1980s and the first needle-free IV access system in 1991.

In 1939 Baxter introduced the first sterile blood collection and storage unit, the Transfuso-Vac® container. Prior to this technology, blood could normally be stored for only 24 hours; Baxter's system allowed each bottle of blood to be stored safely for up to three weeks and "banked" for future use, making blood banking practical for the first time. Baxter's invention furthered Dr. Bernard Fantus' vision for a hospital blood bank, which he first established at the Cook County Hospital in Chicago in 1932.

In 1956 Baxter introduced the first commercially available artificial kidney machine for hemodialysis, a treatment for end-stage renal disease, a life-threatening condition in which the kidneys fail. Baxter was also a pioneer in home-based dialysis, introducing its first peritoneal dialysis system in 1978. Today Baxter is a leading manufacturer of peritoneal dialysis and hemodialysis products.

Some of Baxter's most significant acquisitions and organizational changes have included its 1985 acquisition of American Hospital Supply, making Baxter a broad-based health-care products distributor, in addition to a developer of medical technologies. In 1987 it acquired Caremark, which it spun off in 1992. In 1996 Baxter renewed its focus on its core technologies of I.V. systems/medical products, blood therapy, renal therapy and cardiovascular medicine with the spin-off of its health-care products and cost-management services businesses as a new, separately

In 1939 Baxter's first sterile blood collection and storage unit, the Transfuso-Vac® container, made blood banking practical for the first time.

traded company called Allegiance Corporation. And, in 2000 Baxter spun-off of its CardioVascular Group as a separate, publicly traded company, Edwards Lifesciences, allowing Baxter to dedicate more resources to its remaining three businesses.

Baxter's technological breakthroughs have paved the way for blood banking, intravenous therapy, open-heart surgery, and have allowed patients suffering from hemophilia, heart or kidney disease to lead nearly normal lives. It continues to focus on developing critical therapies for patients' life-threatening conditions worldwide.

Quill Corporation

Entrepreneurial initiative and a passion to give customers truly outstanding service transformed Quill Corporation from a one-man, local office-supply dealer into a $630 million national dealer in just 43 years. Jack Miller founded the company with an enterprising mindset, a will to succeed and a $2,000 loan from his father-in-law.

Miller was born in Chicago in 1929 and began his working career at age 13. His diverse jobs included delivering dry cleaning on his bicycle, setting pins in a bowling alley, ushering at a movie theatre, creating ice cream treats at a soda fountain and helping in his father's live-poultry store.

Miller worked his way through the University of Illinois. He sold ads for the school newspaper and earned money working as a dishwasher, art-class model and professional acrobat. Summers he dug ditches, loaded freight cars and did whatever difficult, dirty job paid the most.

When Miller finished college — with a degree in advertising, no debts, and no idea what he wanted to do to make a living — he thought about being a lumberjack and even went to Oregon with that in mind. But by the time he got there, he had decided that wouldn't be such a good idea. So he turned around and came home.

For a few months he worked for his dad and his older brother in their poultry stores, scraping chicken droppings from the pans set beneath the birds' cages and mopping floors. Before long he was rescued from the poultry business by an uncle who offered him a sales job in his specialty-food manufacturing company.

For the next five years Miller traveled around the country calling on distributors who sold to restaurants and institutions. Miller enjoyed the job until he married. Within a year he realized that constant travel and a new marriage weren't a good combination, particularly since there was no opportunity to own part of the company.

Miller found another job as a minority owner in a subsidiary of a sample-case manufacturer. He worked as a distributor of briefcases, calling on firms in Chicago and creating a mail order catalog for firms nationwide. After a year the major stockholder sold the company. Because Miller's ownership was to be paid for out of profits and had not yet been paid, he received nothing from the sale.

Miller, 27, decided to start his own business. Because he had been calling on business firms in Chicago, he decided to go into the office-supply business providing products they all bought. He found a wholesaler who would sell him merchandise as he needed it if he put up a $300 deposit.

Miller borrowed $2,000 from his father-in-law, made the deposit, installed a phone in the chicken store so his dad could take calls for him and, with some catalogs from the wholesaler, began cold-canvassing businesses. Each morning Miller called the wholesaler and ordered whatever he had sold the day before. Then he spent the day on the street selling. In mid-afternoon he picked up his orders at the wholesaler, rushed to his dad's store to sort the merchandise, packed it into cartons, and rushed to the United Parcel Service depot before 6 p.m. so it could be delivered the next day.

In spite of competition from 156 other office-supply dealers in the Chicago area, Miller began to build the business, even making a small profit the first year. A year-and-a-half later his younger brother, Harvey, joined him in the business. Harvey — who had left college to join the Navy during the Korean War — was working as a sales clerk in an electrical supply company. He was married with one child, but was willing to take the risk of going into this small, fledgling business. Harvey borrowed $2,500 from his mother-in-law for his share of the business. Each of the brothers drew $90 a week, more than the company was earning at the time.

For office space they emptied two tons of coal from an unused coal bin in Jack's wife's uncle's basement and

By 1998, when Quill Corporation was sold to Staples, Inc., the headquarters occupied over 442,000 square feet on 15 acres in Lincolnshire, Illinois.

connected phones to the phone in the chicken store. They split the city in half; each took half as his territory and both were on the street selling every single day.

In 1960 they moved into a small storefront location on Irving Park — their first "real" warehouse and office — and hired a bookkeeper and inside sales person. They had already begun to receive some good results from mailings that Jack had started his first year in business by mailing a penny postal card with five specials to 150 businesses he called on regularly. Other mailings followed, building toward a 16-page "flyer" with increasing circulation. The brothers soon found themselves having to stay in to take the growing volume of telephone orders. Gradually they found that they had slid into the mail order business.

They had become pioneers in selling office supplies by mail. When their dad closed his retail store to focus on selling only to wholesale accounts, the brothers moved into his building on Sheffield Avenue near Wrigley Field. He now had a desk in their office, and their people answered his phone when he was out. The business prospered and they soon moved to a 27,000-square-foot warehouse on Belmont near Halsted.

By 1970 they had a solid business with over 30 employees. That year they first published their "Customers' Bill of Rights." It has been reprinted in every semi-annual catalog since that date as an expression of their passion for great customer service. In part it reads:

"As a customer, you are entitled to be treated as a real, individual, feeling human being. . . with friendliness, honesty and respect. As a customer, you are entitled to full value for your money. As a customer, you are entitled to a complete guarantee of satisfaction. As a customer, you are entitled to fast delivery. As a customer, you are entitled to speedy, courteous, knowledgeable answers on inquiries. As a customer, you are entitled to the privilege of being treated as an individual and dealing with individuals. As a customer, you are entitled to be treated exactly as we want to be treated when we are someone else's customer."

In 1973 the brothers moved to a 37,000-square-foot distribution center and office designed and built for them in Northbrook, Illinois. They were now doing $3.5 million in volume and growing steadily. They asked their older brother, Arnold, to join the company.

In a successful harmony of talent and skill, Jack Miller (foreground) and his brothers, (left to right) Harvey L. and Arnold, gave Quill a legacy of exemplary customer service and deep concern for its employees.

Arnold had spent the past 20 years in California, mostly in his own CPA firm. He had the business experience and the financial expertise the Millers needed. When Arnold joined them he found a company that was doing well, but using second-hand manual typewriters. He convinced them to buy their first new IBM electric typewriter and made other efforts to get them out of their basement-start-up mentality.

The brothers worked together extraordinarily well, dividing their responsibilities. Jack handled marketing, Harvey handled operations and Arnold handled financial, legal and human resources. Over the years they learned to let each other handle their own areas with little interference, meeting daily over lunch for business updates. From time to time, various Miller children worked in the company.

In October 1980, they moved once again to a new 165,000-square-foot corporate headquarters on 33 acres in Lincolnshire. A few years later it was expanded to 375,000 square feet. By the late 1980s Quill had become the largest privately held direct marketer of office products in the United States, with over 800,000 business and institutional customers nationwide. The company annually mailed over 75,000,000 catalogs and sale flyers, with over 12,000 listings for office supplies, machines and furniture.

To provide next-day delivery to almost every customer in the United States, they opened distribution centers across the country. By the late 1990s they had nine. Having gone aggressively full-bore from their first electric typewriter in 1974 into computer systems soon after,

Quill Customer Bill of Rights

Restated and approved at Lincolnshire, Illinois, on Tuesday the Seventh of December, One Thousand Nine Hundred and Ninety-Nine.

The undersigned officers and the more than 1,200 employees of Quill Corporation express a desire to clearly state the principles and ideals which guide all of us at Quill in our relationship with our customers. We feel this unusual step is necessary at this time because we find ourselves, when we are customers...both as individuals and as a company...frequently dissatisfied with the way we are treated. Lack of interest, discourteousness, bad service, late deliveries and just plain bad manners are too common. We can't tell others how to run their businesses (except by not buying from them). But we can and will run Quill as we feel a business should be run. Therefore, **the following is a list of what we consider to be the inalienable rights of our customers.** *We expect to be held to account whenever we deny any of these rights to any customer.*

1. **As a customer, you are entitled to be treated like a real, individual, feeling human being**...with friendliness, honesty and respect.

2. As a customer, **you are entitled to full value for your money.** When you buy a product, you should feel assured that it was a good buy and that the product is exactly as it was represented to be.

3. As a customer, **you are entitled to a *complete* guarantee of satisfaction.** This is especially true when you buy the product sight unseen through the mail or over the phone.

4. As a customer, **you are entitled to fast delivery.** Unless otherwise indicated, if your stock order is placed by 6 p.m. (local time), the order should be shipped the same day. In the event of a delay, you are entitled to immediate notification, along with an honest estimate of the expected shipping date.

5. As a customer, **you are entitled to speedy, courteous, knowledgeable answers on inquiries.** You are entitled to all the help we can give in finding exactly the product or information you need.

6. As a customer, **you are entitled to the privilege of being an individual and dealing with individuals.** If there is a question on your account, you are entitled to talk with or correspond with another individual so the question can be resolved immediately on the most mutually satisfactory basis possible.

7. **AS A CUSTOMER, YOU ARE ENTITLED TO BE TREATED EXACTLY AS WE WANT TO BE TREATED WHEN WE ARE SOMEONE ELSE'S CUSTOMER.**

Jack Miller
Jack Miller
Founder

Harvey Miller
Harvey Miller
Founder

Arnold Miller
Arnold Miller
Founder

Founded in 1956, Quill has <u>always</u> worked hard to service our customers in <u>every</u> way. In 1970, we published our beliefs about customer service for all to see and to measure our performance against. We still hold these beliefs today and we will continually strive to serve our customers to the best of our abilities.

Larry Morse
Larry Morse
President

early in 1997 they were ready to move directly into the new dot-com world.

By 1998 Arnold, 73, had been through several bouts of cancer and was anxious to retire. Harvey was tired of the daily grind and eager to spend time on charitable and other interests. Jack was not eager to continue on alone. None of the children wanted to step in to lead the company. The Millers decided to sell.

Concerned about keeping the unique, highly service-oriented Quill "brand" in the marketplace and about assuring that their 1,200 employees would be treated well, they sold to Staples, Inc., a company they knew well and whose leaders they respected. They never put the company up for sale publicly, nor did they entertain any other offers.

In May 1998, the sale was completed. Arnold retired a few months later, Harvey a year after that and Jack on January 31, 2000. It was, as the Millers say, a wonderful ride and a great experience.

Over the years Quill had become an integral part of their lives, in many ways defining who they were. The company, and the brothers individually, had been honored with many awards from a great many organizations.

Looking back, Jack says they see themselves as part of a special generation of entrepreneurs — the generation that began so many of the country's businesses following World War II. These entrepreneurs were passionate about their businesses — businesses they spent the better part of their lives building.

In his farewell comments to the Quill people, Jack Miller said, "Each of us in our own lives and in our own business careers can make some very good things happen if we have the passion and the dedication to want to make them happen. It is a passion and dedication Arnold, Harvey and I hope we have passed on to you.

"It will now be up to you to make sure Quill remains Quill . . .with all the great customer service, all the concern for one another, and all the integrity that includes. We will be watching from wherever we are. We have left you a great legacy. Cherish and nourish it."

Diversified Food Group

DFG Foods, L.L.C. (DFG) offers an appetizing array of food products and services to individuals, corporations and retail establishments throughout the United States and the world. More than 500 million high-end appetizers, hors d'oeuvres, canapés and desserts are solicited by DFG's clients each year, allowing a taste of excellence to each that bite into one of the company's products.

DFG has flourished since its inception in 1995 due to the entrepreneurial spirit and drive put forth by Chairman and CEO Andrew J. Zahn. Prior to his affiliation with the company, Zahn had served as president of Mama Tish's International Foods and as president of the Zahn Investment Group. A member of the Young Presidents organization since 1994, Zahn's keen business skills have allowed DFG to thrive and have earned him entrance into the Entrepreneur Hall of Fame. In addition, Zahn, who is married with two children, is active in the Jewish United Fund and the Leukemia Research Foundation.

Every aspect of the DFG operation is tailored to customer service and satisfaction, from immaculate, state-of-the-art food-production sites to renowned chefs and food brands. DFG's ability to package and ship its delectable products overnight anywhere in the United States, Canada, Mexico, United Kingdom and other western European nations allows clients to simply unpack food items and serve. DFG also offers a Web site that allows corporate customers and brokers to log in and access account information, check orders and purchase products online.

The chefs employed by DFG are members of the exclusive 100-member Golden Toque. These chefs oversee the food scientists, researchers and technicians involved in the food-production process at DFG's Chicago and New Jersey facilities and also develop new products and recipes, evaluate current products and prepare customer samples for continuing product evaluation. This allows DFG to keep pace with changing consumer tastes and preferences so its clients can as well.

DFG prides itself on demanding more from its operation than any other regulating body and goes beyond complying with health and safety audits. Supporting DFG's high operational standards are on-site testing laboratories and two full-time, in-house microbiologists who ensure the company's food production process is not tainted in any

way. DFG also recently infused more than $25 million in upgrades in each of its production facilities, providing quality and efficient food production by both hand and machine.

The food products offered by DFG feature some of the most celebrated brands in the food-service industry — Casino Chef, Cohen's, Restaurantic, Barney's and Wilton

Foods. This collection features Casino Chef's Mexican, Asian and Italian Specialties and Restaurantic's fresh, hand-made canapés, along with a complete line of kosher food products, including potato knishes by Cohen's, quiches by Barney's and Wilton Foods' fish almondine, blintzes and desserts. Today DFG serves as the most complete frozen-kosher supplier to retailers and the food-service industry.

As DFG moves forward, it will continue to acquire food brands that complement its existing premier line of products and expand it operations to meet the changing needs of the food service industry. The end goal of the DFG experience is to provide clients with a helping hand in ensuring that parties, meetings and other gatherings feature some of the most exquisite appetizers and desserts available, and that each guest walks away saying, "Everything was just perfect."

DFG Foods, L.L.C. offers more than 500 million high-end appetizers, hors d'oeuvres, canapés and desserts to individuals, corporations and retail establishments throughout the United States and the world.

The enterprising drive of Chairman and CEO Andrew J. Zahn has allowed DFG Foods, L.L.C. to prosper.

Azteca Foods, Inc.

Azteca Foods, Inc. started as a dream in 1969 among 10 Mexican-Americans who were members of the Azteca Lions Club in Pilsen. They took their life savings of $80,000 and turned their dream into a multimillion-dollar, family-owned business. Today that business is owned by the Velasquez family.

This business, located on the southwest side of Chicago, was launched at a time when Mexican restaurants in Chicago were leaving Latino territory and establishing themselves in the mainstream, explains Arthur Velasquez, the founder and president. He built this business with wife and lifelong business partner, Joanne, and many dedicated employees.

Azteca grew by promoting tortillas all across America and beyond, until it manufactured two million tortillas a day or 50 million a month. Sprawled over 110,000 square feet, the Azteca plant is a state-of-the-art, air-conditioned facility with 135 employees and high production level lines.

The humble tortilla has gone through a few incarnations at Azteca, explains Mr. Velasquez. To meet the demand of 30,000 supermarkets and 2,000 restaurants, the Azteca plant must operate 24 hours a day. If anyone has ever wondered how a tortilla is made, Azteca has the process down to a science.

Flour is stored in 200,000-pound silos, from which it is pneumatically pumped, sifted and weighed into 1,000-pound mixers. Water and vegetable shortening are added from 80,000-gallon tanks, as well as baking powder and other ingredients After the dough is mixed, dough balls are dumped into troughs and then automatically loaded into a hopper and extruder. After they are automatically divided, they drop down a funnel feeder and are pressed with up to 900 pounds per square inch of pressure. The Azteca die-cut flour tortillas are produced alongside at even higher outputs. They bake for 35 seconds in a three-pass oven at a temperature of 450 degrees Fahrenheit. They are cooled, then packaged and stored in a huge, air-conditioned warehouse. From there, they are distributed to 35 states, South America, Europe and Canada.

Azteca has come a long way because of several innovations. For the first time in history, the tortillas were refrigerated to extend their shelf life to 90 days. Azteca combined quality ingredients, a patented recipe and a unique package. The packaging was made of a high-density, co-extruded polyethylene film that blocked odors, held in moisture and provided flexibility.

Mr. Velasquez, with an MBA from the University of Chicago, still had more ideas, but had gotten to the point where the company needed an infusion of capital to advance and compete. The Velasquez family sold Azteca to Pillsbury in 1984. In the meantime, Mr. Velasquez, with his strong business background, fit in well with the Pillsbury business culture and continued to keep his hand in shaping the tortilla business. Within five years, the company had doubled in size, and by that time, Pillsbury had invested $30 million in research, development and plant expansion. In 1989 the Velasquez family decided that it was time for Azteca to return to its original owners. They assembled an investor group, acquired venture capital, and purchased their tortilla company back, developing it into the wholly

Joanne and Arthur Velasquez and other family members are involved in the business.

owned family business that it is today.

Although the company founders never forgot their Mexican roots, they surged forward in the tortilla world, steering their business into new cultural territory. They did that through inventive marketing of their tortillas, which involved intensive promotion of nontraditional uses. Their goal was to position the flour tortilla on equal footing with a slice of wheat bread. From there, the tortilla was used in imaginative dishes, including Mexican lasagna, sandwich wraps, pizzas, streudels, and pastry-type desserts. They crossed ethnic boundaries to promote the tortilla as a complement to Italian, Polish and Chinese fillings.

It wasn't long until they sold Azteca tortilla chips to baseball parks. "We couldn't decide between the Sox and the Cubs in Chicago, so we decided to go into both ballparks," laughs Mr. Velasquez.

Although the Velasquez family has national influence, they still are very involved in the Chicago community. Mr. and Mrs. Velasquez and their children belong to at least 25 boards in the city, including grammar schools, high schools, the Chicago Metro Board of Junior Achievement, the Mexican Fine Arts Center Museum, The Children's Museum, the Big Shoulders Fund and the Museum of Science and Industry. As past president of the Tortilla Industry Association and past national director of the Mexican-American Legal Defense and Education Fund, Mr. Velasquez has a strong presence in the Chicago Latino community. In fact, he was the first Latino elected to any statewide office when he became trustee of the University of Illinois from 1974 through 1980.

At Azteca, family is very important, and it is no surprise that many family members play an important role in running the company. Those family members include a brother, three children and three sons-in-law. Altogether, Mr. and Mrs. Velasquez have six children and 10 grandchildren.

They must know the recipe for success because employees relish the close-knit atmosphere. In fact, the average tenure of an employee is 15 years. With that kind of loyalty, it was no accident that tortillas have become as common as apple pie in America. But the tortilla hasn't stopped here. In fact, to meet the burgeoning European demand for Mexican food, Azteca Foods Europe is currently being planned in Spain for the fall of 1999. From there, the future of the tortilla is limitless, and it will be a legacy that the family will carry on for several more generations. Viva Azteca!

Azteca's plant is located in the southwest part of Chicago.

Azteca manufactures corn and flour tortillas, Bake and Fill Salad Shells and tortilla chips.

Seymour of Sycamore, Inc.

A sample of the many products that Seymour offers

When Edward H. Seymour began demonstrating aerosol spray paint to customers in 1949, he helped create a whole new industry that has proven very lucrative for the Chicago metropolitan area. Since that time, Seymour of Sycamore, Inc. has developed into one of the largest independently owned, basic aerosol paint manufacturers in the world by staying on the cutting edge of technology.

Located about 50 miles west of Chicago, Seymour of Sycamore has continued to expand to serve customer needs in the 21st century. The company's combined manufacturing, warehousing and office facilities now occupy approximately 170,000 square feet and have been updated to include state-of-the-art computers and printing presses. The laboratory produces a constant stream of new products to meet consumer and regulatory demand.

Because of Seymour's pioneering efforts, Chicago is considered the birthplace of aerosol spray paint. As with

any innovative product, it took time to catch on, but catch on it did, and many paint companies in this area have since produced aerosol paint. But paint is only a small portion of the whole aerosol industry today, as personal products have grown to be the largest sector.

The paint and coatings industry is a very challenging one because it is heavily regulated at the federal, state and local level, but Seymour of Sycamore has always striven to be in the forefront with new technology to meet

ever-changing regulatory demands. The company works closely with the National Paint & Coatings Association (NPCA), which acts as a guide on regulatory matters. Seymour of Sycamore continually reformulates paints to meet government mandates for the aerosol industry, which is also subject to rules from the Environmental Protection Agency. Laboratory workers use the latest technology, resins, and solvents to reduce volatile organic compounds (VOCs) in aerosol spray paint. VOCs are organic chemicals and petrochemicals that emit vapors when they evaporate.

Nancy Seymour Heatley, owner and CEO

Seymour of Sycamore today is a leading manufacturer of high-quality aerosol and bulk products for the industrial and consumer markets. The product line includes general-use and fast-dry enamels, lacquers and engine paints; specialty aerosol products and original equipment manufacturer's Matchmaker services; Wavemaster marine products; and high-performance paints, lubes and chemicals. The products are manufactured without lead, chromates, chlorofluorocarbons or chlorinated solvents. The company offers a wide variety of paints, including Hi-Tech paint, Spruce paint, Fresh-n-Quick paint, Spray-Glo paint, vinyl paint, farm and industrial enamels, graffiti/paint remover, bumper and trim paint and vinyl paints. Seymour's marking system was the first on the market and now includes traffic paints, utility markers, tree log and lumber markers, as well as upright markers for mines and construction.

Edward Seymour was in the paint industry for many years before he formed Seymour of Sycamore. He worked with Alcoa Aluminum Co. of America, and aluminum was the first pigmented paint he produced and put in a can. Seymour took a spray gun and used it to demonstrate his aluminum paint, which has proven to be one of the most important and innovative technological developments for the paint industry during the 20th century.

When going on sales calls, Seymour used a can of paint with an aerosol propellant and spray head similar to the one used in the marketing of pesticides and deodorizers. He sprayed the paint on various surfaces as part of his sales demonstration and found that customers were very enthused about the spray component to paint. With financial support from a local bank, Seymour then established his company to produce aerosol spray paint. He always gave his wife, Bonnie, credit for suggesting that he demonstrate paint with an aerosol spray. They had bought a spray deodorizer after moving into a new home with an unpleasant odor, and this was the inspiration for her idea to use an aerosol spray for paint.

Because aerosol spray paint was something new to the paint industry and presented some technological challenges, Seymour of Sycamore had some early struggles. Seymour persisted, however, and perfected the aerosol spray can. Paint was formulated specifically for aerosol application and mixed on a mass production line, which used machinery that was custom-built or engineered specifically for the new process. New modifications and improvements were frequently added to meet Seymour's standards of high quality.

The company grew and began to need more space, so Seymour had a new plant built at the edge of Sycamore. The plant was specially designed for the new production and packaging of paint. During the 1950s and 1960s hardware wholesalers and paint distributors were the primary customers for Seymour of Sycamore. The company developed a new division in the 1960s to serve the automotive market and then also entered the private-label business.

An industrial distribution division was added in the 1970s, and the company was soon producing 30 chemicals plus its line of paints. By the end of that decade, Seymour of Sycamore had moved into foreign distribution and was shipping products to more than 35 countries. Foreign markets soon accounted for 15 percent of the company's total sales.

Seymour's daughter, Nancy Seymour Heatley, subsequently inherited the company. As president and CEO she guided Seymour of Sycamore to a near doubling of sales during the 1990s. The number of employees also increased during that period from 50 to 125.

With a Ph.D. in psychology, Heatley's emphasis has been to form a good team and get a lot of energy going to sell paint. She attributes the company's growth in recent years to selecting the right people. While doing a great

Seymour of Sycamore's headquarters in Sycamore, Illinois

deal of promoting from within, Heatley also has brought in executives with a background in the paint business. In addition, she assumed charge of export sales and has expanded Seymour of Sycamore's markets in Europe, Asia, Canada and Mexico. Seymour's philosophy is that people are Seymour of Sycamore's most important asset. Seymour of Sycamore is in the National Registry of Woman-owned Industries.

Stewarts Private Blend Foods, Inc.

Located on the northwest side of Chicago in the Logan Square neighborhood, Stewarts Private Blend Foods, Inc. is a company with a long and distinguished tradition of manufacturing quality coffees and teas. These products are distributed to some of Chicago's finest clubs, restaurants and hotels, and to grocery stores, gourmet shops, offices and institutions throughout the United States. Today Stewarts Private Blend Foods remains Chicago's oldest family-owned coffee company.

Former General Motors executive William A. Stewart, a world traveler and connoisseur of fine coffees and teas, founded the company in Chicago in 1913. At the age of 25, Stewart started producing coffees and teas in a small coffee-roasting plant in Chicago, then moved the company into a larger five-story building on West Washington Boulevard in 1925. The firm then became known as Stewart & Ashby Coffee Company because of the financial assistance of Stewart's good friend, Mr. Ashby. (The company changed its name to Stewarts Private Blend Foods after Ashby's death.)

Stewart traveled throughout the world — particularly to the Orient — to find the best blends that would produce the rarest coffees and teas. Gourmet coffees and teas were a rarity during this time, and many of Chicago's most elite establishments — including the elegant Drake Hotel and retailer Marshall Field & Company — requested that Stewart develop coffees and teas to please their discriminating patrons. Stewarts' specially formulated coffees and teas became known as "The Best of the Best," and trains that traveled from Chicago to cities throughout the country were well-stocked with Stewarts special blend coffees and teas. In fact, in 1927 the Chicago and North Western Railway requested an additional 25 pounds of Stewarts coffee for President Calvin Coolidge's train excursion from Chicago to Black Hills, South Dakota. Yet another honor was bestowed upon Stewart

(Lower left) 1933 Chicago World's Fair coffee can. (Upper left) During World War II, because of a shortage of tin, the company used glass packaging. (Lower right) Metal can packaging c. 1960s. (Upper right) Stewarts Mini Bin®, which won a 1990 packaging award

when his Private Blend coffee was chosen as the "Official World's Fair Coffee" during the 1933-34 Century of Progress World's Fair held in Chicago. The company supplied several thousand mugs with the Stewarts Private Blend logo that were quickly snatched up by fairgoers.

In 1941 William A. Stewart died, and his son, Donald R. Stewart, became president of Stewarts Private Blend Foods, remaining at the head of the firm until 1975. (He died in October, 1998.) After World War II, many large coffee companies in the Chicago area acquired family-owned firms. Stewarts, however, remained independent, refusing to be bought out by the larger companies. In 1957 the company moved its corporate headquarters and manufacturing facility from West Washington Boulevard to its present location on Wrightwood Avenue in the Logan Square neighborhood.

During the late 1950s and 1960s, convenience foods became an important part of the American culinary experience. Revolutionary new freezing, dehydration and packaging methods changed the cooking, eating and drinking patterns of consumers. Americans traveled more frequently and developed an interest in international cuisine and more sophisticated tastes and flavors. And American women moved out of the home into the workplace in increasing numbers.

In response to these societal trends, top management at Stewarts Private Blend Foods changed course and made several important strategic decisions. Recognizing that domestic grocery sales — long a dominant part of the business and constituting about 60 percent of sales — would experience slower growth, the company decided to broaden its base in the faster-growing food-service, institutional and specialty-food arenas.

The company placed a new emphasis upon supplying its coffee and tea products to a rapidly growing segment of the market: fast food chains, restaurants and gourmet specialty shops, and the kitchens of hotels, healthcare facilities, schools, government agencies and the military. Most of these products — including gourmet teas, flavored teas and decaffeinated coffees — are in a dry form that facilitates ease and speed of preparation, shelf-life stability, flavor consistency and cost control. Today Stewarts Private Blend Foods has more than 20 food-service brokers working with the firm's field sales managers to market the company's food-service products.

In addition to being a major supplier for retail grocers and food service operations throughout the United States, the company also formulates and manufactures quality teas and coffees for other food manufacturers and grocery chains that are sold under custom or private labels. Supplying gourmet coffees and teas to the workplace has became yet another priority for the firm.

In 1975 William A. Stewart, Donald R. Stewart Jr. and Robert C. Stewart, grandsons of the company's founder, assumed mutual leadership of the company. Other members of the management team include Dave Griffiths, vice president of special projects; Ed Fabro, vice president of plant operations; Robert Tomkins, director of marketing and Elita Pagan, comptroller. The family-oriented company maintains an open-door policy for its approximately 50-person staff, encouraging employees to contribute their ideas and frequently including them in product taste testings. Unlike many larger coffee companies, Stewarts Private Blend Foods is able to develop new products in a timelier fashion and respond more quickly to the needs of its customers.

The company continues to develop and manufacture the rarest coffees and teas that reflect the changing tastes of the American consumer. Its Private Blend coffees, sold in vacuum-packed metal cans and flexible packaging, utilize a unique roasting and blending of the highest-quality Arabica coffees and produce between 30 percent to 50 percent more cups to the pound than ordinary commercial blends. Stewarts Private Blend Limited Reserve coffees are available ground or in whole bean form and are packed in the company's award-winning Mini-Bins® and in foil vacuum bags. Chocolate raspberry cream, Swiss mocha almond and hazelnut are a few of the delicious flavored coffees sold by the company, and Stewarts' no-fat liquid coffee flavorings — available in caramel, amaretto and Irish creme flavors — just to name a few, contain only 15 calories per serving. Stewarts Private Blend specialty teas complete the company's product line and are produced in a variety of delectable flavors including passion fruit, cinnamon apple, peach mango, orange spice and black currant. Besides being available in many retail establishments, the teas and coffees can be purchased by going online and accessing the company's Web site.

(Back) Founder William A. Stewart and (front) son Donald R. Stewart

Chicago World's Fair coffee cup distributed by Stewarts Private Blend Foods

Roasting and blending the rarest gourmet coffees and teas from around the world will continue to be the top priority for Stewarts Private Blend Foods. The company is continually developing exciting new flavors and products, and plans to begin distribution of its products outside of the United States. With an ongoing commitment to excellence first established in 1913 by its founder, William A. Stewart, there is no doubt Stewarts Private Blend Foods will remain Chicago's own "The Best of the Best."

A Stewarts Private Blend Foods truck

U.S. Can

As one of the world's leading manufacturers of quality metal and plastic containers, U.S. Can provides packaging for an array of commonly used consumer goods and specialty products. From aerosol cans that deliver personal-care and household products to paint cans, cookie tins and industrial containers, U.S. Can meets the complete container needs of product manufacturers throughout the world.

Hundreds of millions of aerosol cans are manufactured annually at U.S. Can's Elgin, Illinois, manufacturing facility outside of Chicago.

From its headquarters in Oak Brook, U.S. Can oversees its immense international operation of 28 manufacturing facilities throughout the United States, Europe and South America. This global presence allows U.S. Can to serve as the No. 1 manufacturer of aerosol cans in the United States and the No. 2 manufacturer in Europe. U.S. Can also produces nearly half of the 1-gallon paint cans sold in the United States each year, and its general line products greatly support the automotive and household markets throughout the United States.

U.S. Can has enjoyed profitable revenues and extensive growth throughout the years due to its continuing drive for product improvement and customer satisfaction. In each of its product divisions, U.S. Can has an ongoing commitment to improving manufacturing, quality and technology processes while at the same time offering premier customer service.

U.S. Can boasts a dynamic heritage. It evolved from the combination of Sherwin-Williams' can-manufacturing facilities; Southern Can Company, a renowned innovator in aerosol-container production; and Continental Can, a well-known packaging-industry leader. That strategic combination enabled U.S. Can to expand rapidly from its original roots in metal container production to related products in plastics, custom, specialty and general line containers to meet the needs of automotive, health and beauty, specialty retail and assorted other industries.

Today, three distinct, progressive product divisions exist within the company — Aerosol Products; Custom & Specialty Products; and Paint, Plastic & General Line Products. Staffed by business leaders and employees that are involved from product inception to delivery, these divisions collectively produce a wide range of round, oblong, square, aerosol and specialty containers. In addition U.S. Can provides specialized services such as lithography and engraving to serve as a one-stop shop for container needs.

U.S. Can's Aerosol Products division offers the widest range of aerosol sizes (diameters and heights) in the industry and numerous manufacturing locations geographically located to maximize customer service. The company applies the most advanced technological and environmentally sound practices into each of its production facilities. The company also offers upscale metal graphics to provide its clients' products with the highest-quality product image. For example, U.S. Can's Slim Look™ line of aerosol cans provides upscale packaging for personal-care products such as body fragrances, hair applications and cosmetics.

The Aerosol Products division also leads its industry in the field of barrier packaging, where a plastic liner is placed inside a can to provide a propellant delivery system for product formulations that were previously incompatible with conventional steel aerosol cans. These products include shave gels, lotions, creams, pastes, caulks and certain kinds of foods such as cheese spreads. U.S. Can's piston and Sepro® lines of packaging separate products from the can and its propellant (a gaseous compound) to ensure product integrity.

U.S. Can has taken great strides to educate the public on the use of aerosol cans and to dispel the myths and misconceptions regarding their use and the environment. A backlash against the use of aerosol cans occurred prior to the U.S. Environmental Protection Agency's 1978 ban on the use of chloroflurocarbon (CFC) propellants, which were commonly used in the aerosol industry. Today, no CFCs are used by aerosol-product manufacturers, allowing the can to serve as a sophisticated package and application method for numerous products that are beneficial to the everyday lives of people throughout the world.

U.S. Can's Custom & Specialty Products division maintains only a small percentage of the company's sales volume, but holds a significant presence in this highly fragmented niche market by providing functional and decorative tins, specialty containers and other products. This division services a number of clients, from retailers and fund raisers to infant-formula manufacturers and the U.S. Government, and provides containers for distinctive promotional, institutional and retail products.

U.S. Can's Paint, Plastic & General Line Products division is a pioneer in the metal-container production industry. It served as the production facility for Sherwin-Williams when the company first started making metal paint containers more than 125 years ago. Today, this division not only produces round cans for paint and coatings, but also produces oblong cans for products such as turpentine and charcoal lighter fluid, and plastic pails and containers for other industrial and consumer products.

The Paint, Plastic & General Line Products division boasts an array of containers and tailors products to meet the specific needs of each client. This division also offers U.S. Can's extensive lithography capability to provide appealing product appearance. U.S. Can innovations such as the Accupor® and EZ-Spout® container spouts allow for user-friendly end products, and all of the company's steel containers are made from at least 25-percent recycled steel and are fully recyclable. In addition, this division's complete line of plastic containers services a number of industries that package chemicals and solids.

U.S. Can maintains a comprehensive approach to customer service to ensure that it remains at the forefront of its industry. The company operates its own training facility at Elgin Technical Center for courses in electrical programmable logic control and electric systems to continually update employees on advances in manufacturing processes. In addition, U.S. Can's corporate operation and manufacturing facilities have received ISO-9001 certification — a distinguished global rating system acknowledging operational excellence.

U.S. Can will continue to expand its operation through acquisitions that allow the company to better

U.S. Can produces a vast array of specialty containers for major retailers throughout the United States.

serve its current customers and establish a wider customer base. The company actively seeks packaging companies throughout the world that complement and expand its existing product base, thus creating an added value for shareholders.

In the mid-1990s U.S. Can expanded its aerosol operations into Europe and in 1998 formed a joint venture with an Argentinean aerosol manufacturer in Buenos Aires. At the close of 1999 the company acquired May Verpackungen, a leading manufacturer of specialty food packaging and aerosol cans in Erftstadt, Germany, which has allowed it to become an international leader in the aerosol industry. Today, additional facilities are located in France, Spain, Italy, Germany, England and Wales. U.S. Can is implementing this acquisition/growth strategy into its other product markets as well.

With an ongoing commitment to meeting customer needs, attracting and refining an empowered work force, and improving its products and processes, U.S. Can will continue to serve as a leading supplier of quality packaging products in years to come.

From its beginnings in the paint can industry, U.S. Can remains a leader in the paint and general line business.

Learning Curve International

John Lee, president, Learning Curve, with Thomas Wooden Railway System Fixtures and Toy Box

Since its inception in 1993 Learning Curve has become the market leader in the design, manufacture and distribution of playtime enrichment brands that stand for a commitment to learning, adventure and imagination. From the very beginning the Learning Curve name has been a hallmark of quality, providing customers with a trusted source for playthings that help release a child's full potential through wholesome, meaningful play. By backing each of its brands with an unconditional lifetime guarantee, Learning Curve pledges its commitment to parents, children and retailers each and every day.

Today Learning Curve brands are featured items in better specialty toy, hobby, gift, department, school supply, book and museum stores, offering playtime enrichment opportunities for kids of all ages and interests along the "learning curve" from birth to age 12. The company of today is a natural outgrowth of the business model that veteran retailer John Lee transplanted to Chicago in 1993.

John Lee's move to Chicago was a strategic one. He came seeking venture capital and the talent required to grow his fledgling start-up into the market leader it had the potential to be. What he found here put Learning Curve on the fast track for future success.

The successful launch in 1993 of the Thomas and Friends™ Wooden Railway System at Toy Fair, the industry's leading international trade show, attracted the attention of Chicago business partners Dick Rothkopf and Barry Gersowsky. The two connected with John Lee and Learning Curve was full steam ahead!

Infant with Lamaze® Infant Development System® Stacking Rings

With over 3,000 retail accounts, Learning Curve's Thomas Wooden Railway System was propelled to best-seller status, paving the way for future brand introductions. Following closely on Thomas' heels was the introduction of the Lamaze® Infant Development System®, a phase-oriented brand of infant playthings carrying the name of the trusted childbirth and early parenting organization. The Lamaze® line was created in conjunction with child development specialists Drs. Dorothy and Jerome Singer of Yale University, who have continued as influential advisers for Learning Curve on product development across all its brands.

Since those early days, Learning Curve, with worldwide distribution, has grown into one of the largest manufacturers of developmental playtime enrichment brands. In addition to the Thomas Wooden Railway System and the Lamaze® Infant Development System®, the Learning Curve family of award-winning brands includes the Kid Classics line of preschool play products, Learning Curve Soft Toys collection; the FELTKids® Play System, the Small Miracles line of dress-up apparel and accessories, Lionel®/Great Railway Adventures and the Robotix® construction system.

The company remains focused on the core principles of quality, exceptional service and consumer-focused branding — something to which the founders attribute its sustained, exponential growth.

As Learning Curve looks to the future, partners John Lee, Dick Rothkopf and Barry Gersowsky are committed to standing by Learning Curve's core philosophy. By providing children with playthings that reward curiosity, open realms of adventure and encourage kids to explore, Learning Curve appeals to a child's sense of fun. And by providing parents with playthings that are safe, nonviolent and heirloom quality, Learning Curve will continue to build its base of loyal customers well into the future.

LoDan Electronics, Inc.

"Interconnecting" describes not only the business of LoDan Electronics, Inc., but the company's philosophy as well. Through the manufacture of cable assemblies, LoDan Electronics has built a 30-year success story around the interconnect technology industry. As a perfect metaphor, LoDan's growth has been tied to the company's ability to stay linked to its customers and to create a strong staff network within its own walls.

Raymond A. Kedzior and a former partner founded LoDan in 1967 as an electronics manufacturers' rep firm that shortly thereafter evolved into a specialized distribution company. Listening to his customers' needs convinced Kedzior to restructure LoDan and move into manufacturing. At the time, both the computer and telecommunications industries were new and growing rapidly in many directions. Rather than manufacture a product, Kedzior's instinct guided him toward providing cable assemblies that original equipment manufacturers (OEMs) could use within their growing and ever-changing markets. The OEMs' fields ranged from avionics and medical equipment to cellular infrastructure, data networking and wireless communications.

As the electronics market mushroomed, so did LoDan Electronics; as the industry became more sophisticated, so did the cable assemblies LoDan produced. The company's output has included coaxial cable assemblies, micro-miniature wire termination products and wire harnesses, attracting business from leading global corporations like Motorola, 3 Com, Hughes Network Systems and Andrew Corporation. By meeting regularly with their client firms' engineers, who ranked among the industry's early visionaries, LoDan executives not only could react promptly to customer requests but soon began to anticipate them. With the electronics industry changing so quickly, projecting its customers' needs gave LoDan a competitive edge. The company's quality control procedures, which call for thorough testing of all systems to make sure they meet government safety regulations, have added to LoDan's reputation for impeccable service.

By the mid-1990s LoDan's growth curve took a sharp upturn. Again with an ear to the industry, Kedzior, who became sole owner in 1991, anticipated the need for quality contract manufacturing and added that capability to what LoDan could do for its customers. In this endeavor, LoDan provides the logistic and assembly effort on electro-mechanical products and ships them back to the customer for application. At this time LoDan also hired executives in professional disciplines crucial for securing global success, including Executive Vice President Lawrence A. DiVito, who continues to oversee the company's finances. As a result of these efforts, LoDan has more than doubled its earnings in the past seven years, with today's revenues exceeding $50 million. In the late 1990s the company moved into a 100,000-square-foot facility in the northwest suburb of Arlington Heights.

Consistent with its proactive policies, LoDan Electronics has been ahead of the trend in staff management. Basing strategies on his belief in a direct relationship between the company's productivity and the continuing education and personal achievements of its staff, Kedzior implemented "ACT," which encourages an Attitude that welcomes new ideas, a Commitment to providing quality products and service and Teamwork in the factory as well as in the office — to make the best use of individual talents while keeping ideas circulating and motivation high. Always an equal opportunity employer that embraced diversity, LoDan reflects Chicago's melting pot of cultures and currently counts up to 30 different nationalities within its workforce of 150 skilled employees in direct manufacturing and 60 in professional positions. The company wants the connections employees make with each other to be as strong as the interconnections created by the cables it produces.

Raymond Kedzior, founder of LoDan Electronics, Inc.

MacLean-Fogg Co.

MacLean-Fogg uses state-of-the-art technologies and manufacturing capabilities to produce innovative locking fastening systems, allowing it to serve as the largest wheel fastener manufacturer in the world.

The MacLean-Fogg Company plays a vital role in the successful day-to-day operation of numerous industries throughout the world by providing a vast line of high-performance fasteners and component systems, and greatly assists the power and telecommunications industries with its innovative connecting and insulating devices.

MacLean-Fogg, based in Mundelein, is the largest wheel fastener manufacturer in the world. The company consists of two business groups, the MacLean Fasteners and Components Company and the MacLean Power Systems Company, which utilize 18 manufacturing facilities. These business groups use state-of-the-art technologies and manufacturing capabilities to produce locking fastening systems, automotive components, precision-machined components and specialty insert-molded components, along with connectors, insulators, line hardware and fiberglass products for the world's power and telecommunications industries.

MacLean-Fogg was founded in 1925 by John MacLean on the North Side of Chicago and is still owned by the third generation of the MacLean family. Initially MacLean-Fogg serviced the booming railroad industry by offering the #1 lock nut — still offered by the company today — which prevented railroad car joints from rattling loose and was widely used throughout the North American rail industry.

MacLean-Fogg is a leading provider of high-quality connectors, insulators, line hardware and fiberglass products to the world's power and telecommunications industries.

Innovative product development, selected acquisitions and joint ventures have allowed MacLean-Fogg to expand into a worldwide enterprise with facilities throughout North America, South America, Asia and Europe. Today the company is a market-share leader in each of its product categories, servicing a number of leading manufacturers, including Ford, General Motors, DaimlerChrysler, Freightliner, PACCAR, John Deere and Caterpillar, along with many of the major suppliers to those companies. MacLean-Fogg's unique proprietary and patented products assist clients in lowering production costs by minimizing time and labor for assembly and installation and improve the overall quality of the final product.

Formed in 1986, MacLean Power Systems offers a comprehensive line of quality electric-utility and telecommunications products, including innovative transmission and distribution conductor-support devices and connectors, silicone rubber insulators, fiberglass products and line hardware. This product line is backed by MacLean Power Systems' dedication to product research, development and manufacturing, which ensures superior products and services are delivered on time to customers worldwide.

MacLean Power Systems' product line includes polymeric insulators and fiberglass brackets and crossarms that serve as viable product alternatives for electric utilities to help speed installation, reduce costs and improve line performance. The group's silicone rubber insulators have shown better performance on high-voltage transmission lines than ceramics and other polymer insulators, especially in areas of high contamination. The Reliable brand automatic line splice for current-carrying applications provides a secure connection regardless of wind, ice loading and other climatic conditions, and allows for fast line repair when storms down power lines.

MacLean-Fogg will continue to grow in both sales and profitability as it expands its operation through acquisitions and the development of new products. This drive and past successes position MacLean-Fogg as a world-recognized force in the manufacturing of fasteners, components and power systems products.

Scala Packing Co. Inc.

The premier meat products produced by Scala Packing Co. have made Chicago the proud home to the renowned Italian beef sandwich and initiated the phenomenon of beef stands that exist throughout the city — and the country — today. Scala has been offering delectable meats and other food products for more than 75 years with an unrivaled approach to customer service — making the Scala name synonymous with quality.

Headquartered in Chicago, Scala Packing Company was founded in the early 1920s by Pasquale Scala, who had immigrated to the United States at the turn of the century. Upon his arrival, Pasquale went to work on the city's West Side, selling an array of goods out of a street cart. Pasquale's enduring entrepreneurial drive, along with his ability to prepare top-quality, flavorful meats, eventually led him to producing meat products out of space in the old Lucca Bakery on south Western Avenue.

From the first day that Pasquale began offering his meat products to the people of Chicago, it was clear what set Scala Packing apart from its competitors. He prepared his meats with a proven recipe of superior taste, patience and great care. The high demand for Pasquale's products prompted the opening of Scala Packing Company on Harrison Street in 1925 on the city's West Side, with sausage produced in the rear of the building and goods sold out of the storefront. Scala Packing soon became revered among its loyal customers for placing quality over quantity — a tradition that continues today.

While the ensuing Great Depression took a toll on all Chicago businesses, it provided an unforeseen business opportunity for Scala Packing. At a time when food and other goods were scarce, Scala Packing helped introduce to Chicago the concept of serving thinly sliced beef on a bun, loaded with gravy. This meal was originally introduced at weddings and banquets where the meat was sliced thinly so there would be enough to feed all the guests. Since the meat was thin, it was served with bread and soaked in gravy so that each guest's appetite would be satisfied.

Pasquale and his sons, Bob and Ralph, ingeniously began to market this sandwich as a delicious alternative to the commonly sold Italian sausage. Many capitalized on this alternative, and beef stands sprouted throughout the city. Their locations now offered menus that included Italian lemonades, Italian sausage and, for diversity, the new Italian beef. The popularity of the sandwich spread quickly and the rest is Chicago history.

Today, Scala Packing's tradition of excellence continues through a third generation in Pasquale's grandson, Pat, who is pioneering Scala Packing into a national operation. Many cities and states tout Scala's renowned reputation and offer its meat products at sporting facilities, pizzerias, grocery stores and other establishments. Scala's products have not only been heralded professionally by the Food Channel Network, but it has been said that a person cannot fully enjoy the Wrigley Field experience until he or she has had a Scala beef sandwich in the ballpark.

"The most indigenous thing that Chicago can call its own — above pizza — is the beef sandwich," says Pat. "The people here understand what a good beef sandwich is. Chicago is our home."

Scala Packing Co. initiated the phenomenon of beef stands that exist throughout Chicago today, and has been offering delectable meats and other food products for more than 75 years.

Scala Packing Co. was founded by Pasquale Scala in 1925 on Harrison Street on Chicago's West Side.

357

Superior Graphite Co.

Superior Graphite Co. was founded in 1917 by Irish immigrant William J. Carney. During World War I Carney recognized a business opportunity due to the demand for graphite. The need for this raw material (used for refractories and in iron and steel) grew as the production of machinery and weaponry increased. In response to this growing market, Carney started a small mining interest in Alabama called the Superior Flake Graphite Co. After the war, business dwindled, causing the mine to close.

Carney moved his operation to the Midwest and opened a new plant in Bedford Park, Illinois. Nephews Marvin and William Joyce helped him run the new business, which began by supplying graphite chiefly to the metal casting (foundry) industry.

Superior experienced another surge in business during World War II. Since local graphite resources were scarce, the company opened several mines in graphite-rich Mexico to satisfy the increasing demand.

Through the late 1940s and early 1950s, the company shifted its product focus and sought to expand its graphite uses. In 1954 the name was changed to Superior Graphite Co., reflecting a broader range of graphite raw materials. In the late 1950s grandson Peter Carney, a geologist, joined the company. Carney became company president in 1960. Currently heading the company as CEO with his son, Edward, acting as president, Peter Carney was and is a driving force in the company's new-product creation.

During the 1960s Peter Carney searched for sources of natural graphite abroad. Finally, he decided to find ways to offer better-quality graphite products that would meet new industry standards. Tougher environmental regulations also played a role in the company's new direction. Since natural graphite is a difficult substance to purify, Carney decided to invent a process to produce high-purity carbon/graphite synthetically. Criteria for development included domestic sources of raw material, environmentally sound technology and a continuous process.

After six years of research the company produced its first material, trademarked "Desulco." Desulco is made in a patented high-temperature continuous furnace that operates at a temperature of nearly 2,500 degrees Celsius. At these temperatures, sulfur and other impurities are vaporized from the starting material. The resulting product is 99.9 percent pure carbon, making it the ideal additive for iron and steel melts. Lightweight, high-strength iron castings and clean steel products require high-purity additives to meet their tight product specifications.

Other uses have been developed for this technology, such as making unique materials for the battery, lubrication, friction products, advanced ceramics and oil well-drilling markets. Quality control at plants in Kentucky and Sweden ensure that every product meets the company's rigid purity standards. Superior also manufactures graphite electrodes for electric arc furnaces used in the making of steel. Superior's Arkansas plant has perfected the continuous graphitization of electrodes in its high-temperature furnace system.

Superior Graphite has transformed itself from a mining company and processor of minerals to a high-technology developer of unique materials. With manufacturing plants in three different continents, worldwide sourcing of raw materials and global sales coverage, the company is looking forward to the challenges that the future will bring to world business. With its creative workforce and adaptive technologies, Superior is well positioned to assist industry in developing new materials for an increasingly complex and interconnected world.

A 1961 photo of Superior Graphite Co.'s original Chicago plant site. The plant is still in operation today.

Warp Bros./ Flex-O-Glass, Inc.

In 1924 a 20-year-old Nebraskan lad with $800 in his pocket cranked up his Ford Model T and chugged his way to Chicago to start a company that produced window coverings.

Harold Warp, whose prior primary business experience had been tending the family's chicken coops, was certain that a material he had concocted to cover the coop windows would be a big hit with farmers. He just needed to get the word out that Flex-O-Glass, a plastic window material for which he held a patent, had proven in test after test to be better for the health and growth of chickens than regular glass panes, which blocked the all-important ultraviolet rays chickens need for sturdy growth.

Warp knew Chicago was the place to settle his company because it was an easily accessible sales center to other parts of the country. With his older brother John at his side, Harold flung open the doors on a storefront factory that sat on the then-unpaved Cicero Avenue on the Windy City's West Side, and declared Warp Brothers open for business.

Wasting no time, Harold Warp spent $160 to advertise Flex-O-Glass in a homestead magazine and then proceeded to toil away in the factory alongside day-laborers he recruited from North Avenue. At night he and brother John slept sprawled on a mattress in the middle of the factory floor. Within two years, the young entrepreneur's business had become so successful that he spent $200,000 on advertising.

As Flex-O-Glass caught on, the business expanded by selling other plastic products, from the first Tape-On Storm Window Kit to Coverall, the first plastic sheeting available to consumers. In 1966 Warp developed the 25-foot Carry-Home roll of polyethylene sheeting, which has been widely copied by other manufacturers. Today there is also Plast-O-Mat ribbed shelf liner that provides an easy-glide, easy-clean surface. And for moving and storage there are the popular Banana Bags available in sizes up to 5 feet by 9 feet to cover large objects such as mattresses and sofas. For the agricultural and industrial markets there is a variety of Greenhouse Films that can endure tough outdoor environments.

Although the bulk of the sales were made through mail order, the late Harold Warp would still travel two weeks each month to personally pitch his products to hardware dealers. He became a popular character throughout Chicago

and other parts of the Midwest. Even Gene Autry, Roy Rogers and Minnie Pearl were among the radio entertainers who hawked Flex-O-Glass on WLS radio during the national Barn Dance program Warp sponsored for 25 years.

His son and namesake, Harold G. Warp, took over the family business. Under the young Warp, who began working at the company in 1971 when he was 24, the business has grown to offer more than 100 varieties of plastic products, primarily plastic sheeting, all of which are made in the United States. The father of two, Harold G. Warp is hoping a third generation of the Warp clan will one day carry on plastic innovations for the company his father so proudly built.

(Far left)
John and Harold Warp, 1924

The first factory, on N. Cicero Avenue, four blocks from the present factory

Harold G. Warp runs the company today.

Harold Warp would fly over county fairs and toss out samples from his Swallow airplane in 1928. He kept this plane at the airfield at Cumberland Avenue and Irving Park Road.

Chicago retail establishments and service industries offer an impressive variety of choices for Chicagoland residents and visitors.

MARKETPLACE

Marshall Field's

In the 1850s Chicago was a city of muddy streets, busy saloons and merchants on the make. It was in this rough-and-tumble atmosphere that one of the world's most renowned and elegant department stores — Marshall Field's — had its humble origins.

A merchant named Potter Palmer began the Field's legend. Palmer opened a dry goods store on Lake Street in 1852, selling everyday items — material for sewing, men's suspenders, ladies' undergarments and the like. What was unusual about his store was his sales strategy, which was unlike that of any other Lake Street merchant. Palmer offered sale prices, displayed his merchandise attractively in the windows and offered a lenient return policy. But his most important innovation was his decision to target a segment of the buying population that had been previously ignored — women.

Chicago was changing and so was the role of women in society. As more women began to gain economic power and social influence, Palmer was determined to gain their trust, respect and patronage.

Because of his remarkable sales intuition, Palmer's dry goods store was highly successful. Soon, though, his operation began to compete with his considerable real estate interests, such as his creation of a hotel that would become Chicago's famous Palmer House.

In 1865 Palmer started a partnership that would resound throughout Chicago for years to come. He recruited an ambitious salesman named Marshall Field to join him in his enterprise. Field's colleague, Levi Leiter,

an accountant, also joined the firm. The store name changed to Field, Palmer, Leiter & Co. Field received top billing, since Palmer had decided that his would be a silent partnership, managed by his brother Milton Palmer.

Marshall Field, born in 1834, was a serious-minded, hard-working man from a Massachusetts farm. He arrived in Chicago in 1856 where he quickly made a name for himself as a skilled salesman. He saw his golden opportunity with Field, Palmer, Leiter & Co., and wasted no time in developing the store according to his vision.

A devoted, creative businessman, Field set several innovative retail policies into motion. For example, he instructed his sales staff that: "the customer is always right." Field's commitment to guest service had its roots in these early days. Field always wanted to be sure that his customers were receiving proper treatment, in one case demanding that a clerk "give the lady what she wants!" Field also instituted a "one-price" policy, eliminating the usual retail practice of bargaining with the customer.

Field agreed with Palmer that targeting female customers would guarantee future success. Although the company was primarily a wholesale establishment, Field saw value in placing more attention on retail goods, such as fashion and fine-quality household items. He was so successful that in 1867 Field & Leiter purchased the interests of Potter and Milton Palmer. The firm was renamed Field, Leiter & Co.

In 1868 the business moved to a six-story, white marble structure at State and Washington streets, the current address of the flagship store. Known as the Marble Palace, the building was distinguished by its elegant architecture and atmosphere. Field used the Marble Palace to its fullest, filling it with the latest fashions, fine materials and beautiful furnishings. The women of Chicago were enchanted.

Field, Leiter & Co. offered a sampling of extremely luxurious items — such as $2,000 sheets — designed to attract the nouveau riche. But Field wanted his store to be the favored shopping place of all women, not just the wealthy. Field sold a distinctive blend of expensive and reasonably priced merchandise. No matter what the cost of his merchandise, however, Field always insisted on quality. "Quality is remembered long after the price is forgotten," was a favorite saying.

Field also desired that the fashions and taste of his store should mirror those of Paris, those considered the

(Far right) Marshall Field in 1860

Marshall Field c.1900

fashion and culture capital of the world. Field was the first merchant west of New York to offer foreign goods. In 1871 he established his first foreign buying office in England, sending his brother Joseph Field abroad to handle operations.

The early success of the company lay in more than just its merchandise. Levi Leiter, Field's partner, devised a 30-day revolving credit policy, a revolutionary concept at the time. The savvy Leiter believed that his plan would result in a better cash flow, allowing Field's to operate in the black and expand more of its sales initiatives.

As Field, Leiter & Co. was establishing itself as Chicago's premiere store, the Great Chicago Fire of 1871 stopped it momentarily in its tracks. The Marble Palace was reduced to rubble and Field's carried a loss of $2.5 million. The store was able to salvage just $200,000 in merchandise. Still, the civic-minded Field paid his staff on time and donated clothing and blankets to the community. Field wasted no time in setting up shop in a temporary location. He ordered merchandise from New York and sold his goods from a horse-barn that had survived the fire. As customers came flocking back to Field's, profits resumed. The partners reopened their store on State Street in 1873.

In 1877 tragedy struck and the store burned to the ground once more. Field opened an "Exhibition Store" on what was then known as Michigan Boulevard. However, State Street still beckoned Field. He decided to rebuild on State Street and to make several attractive improvements, such as wider aisles, a grand staircase and formal greeters. In the spring of 1879 Field was on hand to welcome his customers to the elegant new State Street location.

Field's long-time partner Levi Leiter decided to retire in 1881. The company name changed to Marshall Field & Co. — and a star was born.

Dubbed "the Merchant Prince" by local media, Field continued to build on his vision. He allied himself with two men that would have a powerful effect on Marshall Field & Co. — John Shedd and Harry Selfridge. Shedd, who came to be known as the "world's greatest merchandiser," began his career at Field's as a stock boy.

Legend has it that Shedd was hired after telling Field: "I can sell anything."

By the 1880s Shedd was head of Field's wholesale division. Field made him a partner of the firm in 1892. Shedd was responsible for many changes that contributed to the store's success. He analyzed sales figures and came up with better ways of choosing and offering merchandise. Because of his own elegant taste, he insisted that Field's continue to sell only the finest-quality items.

Harry Selfridge began his career at Marshall Field & Co. in the 1870s, also as a stock boy. Known as "mile-a-minute Harry" because of his constant flow of creative ideas, he was eventually promoted to head of the retail division. Selfridge became a partner in 1889 and orchestrated many retail improvements, including the famous "Bargain Basement," introduced in 1885. He would go on to great fame abroad as the proprietor of the premiere London department store named after him.

During Selfridge's years as a partner, another major innovation took place. In 1890 Marshall Field's opened its first tearoom. Legend has it that Field decided his store needed a restaurant after seeing a group of salesclerks and female customers enjoying chicken pot pies in a back room. Apparently, an enterprising milliner had made a practice of serving homemade lunches to her customers in order not to lose their business during lunchtime.

The first tearoom had only 15 tables and served 56 people the first day. By the end of the year 1,500 meals were being served daily. In 1907 Field's opened the Walnut Room, its most elegant restaurant. The Walnut Room remains a Chicago institution.

In 1892 Marshall Field & Co. gained worldwide fame when the Columbian Exposition came to Chicago. Selfridge draped the store facade in patriotic bunting, and people from around the globe got a taste of Field's magic as they passed through its doors.

Large display windows were installed at State and Washington in 1897. Harry Selfridge hired the talented Arthur Fraser to design window displays, thus beginning another Field's tradition. Fraser's windows not only showed off Field's fine merchandise selection, they were works of art that drew many excited onlookers.

Field's gave birth to yet another longstanding tradition in 1897 with the installation of the "Great Clock." The first of these majestic timepieces was installed at the corner of State and Washington Streets after Field noticed that his customers had designated the corner as a regular meeting spot. A second clock was added at the corner of State and Randolph in 1907 and "meet me under the clock" became a common Chicago phrase. The clock was immortalized by artist Norman Rockwell in his 1945 painting and today both clocks remain Chicago landmarks and symbols of Field's.

Marshall Field announced plans for a renovation of the State Street store in 1901. He commissioned architect Daniel Burnham, founder of the Chicago School of Architecture. Among other changes, Burnham devised a grand entrance flanked by majestic granite columns.

Before he could see his plans come to fruition, Field died from pneumonia in 1906 at the age of 71. At the time of his death, he was one of the wealthiest men in the world. Field left $8 million to the city of Chicago for the construction of the Field Museum of Natural History. He also donated the land on which the University of Chicago was built. Chicago grieved for the fallen retail magnate and civic leader with a capacity-house memorial service at the Auditorium Theater.

His trusted associate, John Shedd, was named store president. Stanley Field, Field's nephew, served as Shedd's vice president as well as on the Marshall Field & Co. board of directors. Stanley Field was a board member for more than 60 years and went on to guide the Field Museum of Natural History.

Shedd unveiled many of the new State Street renovations to the public in 1907. The store was transformed with marble floors, granite columns, a dome-shaped ceiling of Tiffany glass and the famous Walnut Room rotunda. Many of these changes, made from 1892 to 1914, remain in the State Street store to this day.

Like his mentor Marshall Field, Shedd cultivated the store as a center of women's fashion. In 1914 Field's advertising department first published a magazine called *Fashions of the Hour*. The publication featured covers by famous illustrators and discussed fashion trends, home decorating, culture and the arts; it reached a circulation in the tens of thousands. Its effect on Field's was lasting. Field's current marketing vehicles — newspaper advertising, TV spots, fashion collection books and more — have their roots in *Fashions of the Hour*.

While Shedd certainly recognized the importance of the female consumer, he also courted male customers just as aggressively. Shedd's brainchild, The Store for Men, was opened in 1914. There men could buy everything from suits to work boots; personal shopping services were also offered. During World War I the in-store restaurant, "The Men's Grill," was used as a canteen for the soldiers stationed nearby.

One of the hallmarks of Shedd's presidency was his idea that Marshall Field & Co. should promote public service. Under his leadership, the store held several fund-raising drives and charity campaigns. During World War I Field's sold war bonds and assisted returning soldiers.

John Shedd retired in 1923 after 50 years with the company. One of the

An early State Street store window

legacies of his career was the Shedd Aquarium, created as part of a $6 million donation.

James Simpson, Field's former secretary, was named president. Under Simpson's management, Field's thriving retail business was pushed to the next level. Simpson instituted the nation's first in-store book signings in the Field's book department. Visiting authors like Gertrude Stein, Carl Sandburg and Somerset Maugham made it the most celebrated store book department in the country.

Simpson's vision led to an awareness of the growing suburban population, then an untapped market for Field's. To establish Field's suburban presence, Simpson opened stores in Oak Park and Evanston in 1929 and in Lake Forest in 1931.

More expansion took place in 1929 with the acquisition of Frederick & Nelson, a Seattle department store. Frederick & Nelson revealed its secret recipe for a chocolate mint candy it had manufactured, originally called "Franco." Renamed "Frango®," the confection was a hit and continues to be a lasting part of the Field's tradition.

The successful Simpson was featured on the cover of *Time* magazine in the same year. Simpson introduced the Merchandise Mart, the world's largest commercial building, in 1931. This gigantic structure was to house Field's wholesale goods as well as its executive offices. The Mart was also expected to attract other wholesale tenants.

Simpson retired from Marshall Field & Co. in 1932 to become director of Common-wealth Edison. He left during the Great Depression, but nationwide economic hardship did not destroy the fiscally conservative Field's. Marshall Field & Co. continued to look ahead and make improvements.

Under the direction of new President John McKinlay, the company installed store escalators at a cost of nearly half a million dollars. Completed in time for the 1933 Chicago World's Fair, the new escalators emphasized Field's tradition of customer convenience and drew even more shoppers into the store.

Hughston McBain, an innovative Field's leader, opened The 28 Shop in 1941. This in-store designer boutique was modeled

after the fashion salons of Paris. Its name was derived from the address of its private entrance on 28 East Washington Street. Joseph Platt, one of the set designers for *Gone with the Wind*, designed The 28 Shop's luxurious interior, and the grand opening was packed with celebrities and the press.

January 1920 cover of Fashions of the Hour catalog

The Great Clocks

365

The Great Tree in the
Walnut Room

McBain was promoted to company president in 1943. Bright, creative and devoted to the traditions brought forth by his predecessors, McBain set out to revitalize the business. Due to continuing wholesale division disappointments, McBain sold the Merchandise Mart in 1945. Today the Merchandise Mart is a center of commerce and a tourist destination, housing a wide variety of retail stores and business offices.

As the country was swept into World War II, McBain

The 28 Shop

led Field's in demonstrating its support for the war effort. It featured exclusively American designers in The 28 Shop, manufactured army goods in its mills, sold war bonds and launched a patriotic ad campaign.

During the celebratory years following World War II, McBain decided to enliven Field's storewide holiday festivities. The Great Tree was first brought to the Walnut Room in 1907. In 1946 a new holiday theme adorned the Great Tree in the form of holiday sprite Uncle Mistletoe. Aunt Holly joined him a year later. Still an annual Field's tradition, the Great Tree draws hundreds of thousands of visitors.

McBain also focused attention on the Toy Department, filling it with an amazing array of items from all over the world. Animated store windows, still a Field's tradition, drew delighted crowds. The store's interior was completely transformed with elegant holiday decorations throughout. This gala holiday celebration, with modern additions, continues to be a much-anticipated annual event at the State Street flagship store.

For example, in 1994 red-and-green-clad "Jingle Elves" joined the winter holiday celebration. The elves pay subway fares, hold doors for guests at Chicago-area museums and perform other "random acts of kindness." In addition to the winter holiday events, Field's started a springtime holiday celebration in 1993 with its annual flower show. During this two-week celebration, the State Street store interior is adorned with live blooms from around the world, while the store windows are also filled with beautiful flowers, plants and animated characters.

As the store approached its 100-year anniversary in 1952, the company implemented plans for suburban expansion. In 1956 Field's opened what was at the time the world's largest shopping center. Called Old Orchard and located in Skokie, Illinois, this "suburban State Street" featured a 310,000-square-foot Marshall Field's store.

Also in 1956 Field's opened a suburban branch of Frederick & Nelson, and in 1959 a Field's store was introduced in a suburb of Milwaukee. In 1962 a large Field's came to Oakbrook Center, a mall located in a suburb west of Chicago. Throughout the 1960s Marshall Field & Co. emphasized suburban growth and expansion into Midwestern regions such as Wisconsin and Ohio.

In 1975 Field's opened its Water Tower location in the world's first vertical mall. Located on Chicago's Magnificent Mile, Water Tower Place was named for its proximity to Chicago's historic water tower. It features many stores, including a large Marshall Field's store, offices and private condominiums.

Field's continued to see growth opportunities in suburban areas, opening stores in many Illinois locations. In 1978 Field's completed a merger with John Bruener Company, a California-based home furnishings retailer. Field's continued its growth with the purchase of five Lipman's department stores from Dayton-Hudson Corporation in 1979.

In 1982 the company merged with BATUS Inc., a Kentucky-based holding company for B.A.T. Industries. Under BATUS, Field's continued to develop its suburban and out-of-state locations. More stores were opened in Texas and Wisconsin from the early- to mid-1980s. The company then shortened its name to "Marshall Field's."

In a well-publicized merger, Marshall Field's was acquired by the Target Corporation (formerly Dayton Hudson Corporation) in 1990. Along with Dayton's and Hudson's, Field's is one of three distinguished department stores owned by the retail group.

In 1992 the company once again proved its mettle in a time of crisis. Water from the Chicago River rushed through the tunnels that connect many buildings in the Loop and Field's State Street store basement was flooded with 28 million gallons of water. Just one week after the flood, floors one through nine were reopened, followed by the restaurants and lower levels a few weeks later.

Also in 1992, the State Street store finished the five-year, $115-million renovation project begun in 1987 — the largest in retail history. This renovation was followed by improvements to Field's suburban Illinois locations. A massive Water Tower renovation was completed in 1996.

In 1998 Marshall Field's State Street store completed a $10-million renovation of its historic 7th floor that includes a museum-style Archive Exhibit, Walnut Room improvements, an Events Center and new food options like the Frango Café and "7 on State," which boasts the world's first gourmet food bars.

Marshall Field's has a long-standing tradition of supporting the communities in which it does business. Through its community giving initiative, Project Imagine, Marshall Field's places a special emphasis on supporting arts and cultural institutions. In Chicago, Project Imagine programs have included Marshall Field's Free Tuesdays at the Museum of Contemporary Art, Marshall Field's Day of Music at the Chicago Symphony Orchestra and Marshall Field's Pops at Ravinia.

Fashion shows, always a Field's tradition, are another part of the Project Imagine initiative. The 28 Shop Show benefits the Museum of Contemporary Art and has featured designers Donna Karan, Carolina Herrera and Missoni. The annual Marshall Field's Fash Bash brings designers and entertainers together for a dynamic, celebrity-filled evening, with the proceeds benefiting the Art Institute of Chicago.

Through Project Imagine, Marshall Field's gives 5 percent of its federally taxable income back to the communities it serves. So every time a guest shops in its stores, they are sponsoring a concert, underwriting a new play or supporting an art exhibition.

In its evolution from a small dry goods store on Lake Street to a world-renowned department store, Marshall Field's has become not just a Chicago institution but a symbol of quality, fashion and elegance throughout the world. Field's will continue to treat its guests to quality, tradition, guest service and community involvement. As Field's looks to it colorful past for inspiration, it is confident that its future will build on respected traditions and create new ones for future generations to enjoy.

The 28 Shop Show benefiting the Museum of Contemporary Art featuring designer Donna Karan

Hartmarx Corporation

Headquartered in downtown Chicago, Hartmarx is the leading manufacturer of quality men's and women's apparel and an authority for business and casual dressing, offering the finest brands and designer names in the industry. Styles range from the impeccably tailored men's look of Hart Schaffner & Marx and Hickey-Freeman to the classic women's career styles of Barrie Pace and Austin Reed; from the tailored clothing and trousers of youthfully exciting Tommy Hilfiger to the smart golfwear of Bobby Jones and Jack Nicklaus. They also include the modern, tailored look of Kenneth Cole and the nautical, tropical sportswear of Pusser's of the West Indies.

The history of Hartmarx is truly interwoven with that of the country. For years Hartmarx was known as "America's First Name in Men's Clothing" and now markets multiple sportswear lines that in 1998 accounted for over $100 million in sales. On its 50th anniversary in 1937, *Time* called it "a national institution." The firm weathered everything from two world wars and the Depression to the recessions of the early 1970s and 1980s and a wrenching restructuring in the 1990s. Just as remarkably, Hartmarx celebrated its 100th anniversary in 1987. Indeed, few existing American companies can trace their roots to a time when key historical events, such as the surrender of Apache Indian chief Geronimo and the introduction of the Kodak box camera, changed the country forever.

Today Hartmarx is a pure wholesaler that develops working partnerships that make it the supplier of choice for a broader range of retail channels than any other American clothing company. These include fine specialty and leading department stores, value-oriented retailers, direct-mail catalogs and greengrass (pro and resort) shops. All told, there are eight divisions, 26 designer labels and brands, a product mix that ranges from $65 knit shirts and cotton chinos to $1,000 suits and volume of about $725 million. The company continues to diversify its offerings with growing sportswear business and new designer names.

It all began in 1872, six months after the Great Chicago Fire, when Harry Hart, 21, and his 18-year-old brother, Max, opened a retail clothing store on State Street and called it Harry Hart & Brother. In a city where nearly 100,000 citizens had lost so many possessions to

Hart Schaffner & Marx building front, 1888

YOU probably wear a sack suit; very common style; and as usually made, very commonplace. Not as we make them; you can see for yourself; we get distinction of style, even here.

You have a variety to choose from this fall: our famous Varsity, single- and double-breasted; straight-front; three- and four-button; and the "regular sack" in various styles. All our cloths are "exclusive patterns." Sack suits $15 to $35.

Style Book shows them; sent for six cents.
Our label insures your satisfaction; a small thing to look for, a big thing to find.

Hart Schaffner & Marx   Good Clothes Makers
      Chicago   Boston   New York

Harper's magazine advertisement, 1904

Standard pricing was instituted — an industry first that signaled the integrity of the fledgling firm. Nattily dressed company sales representatives would go on the road in their silk toppers, spats and walking sticks, with as many as 20 wardrobe trunks holding their sample garments — impressive but cumbersome. One salesman thought of the then-revolutionary idea of selling from convenient swatches of fabric samples. It was an innovation quickly adopted by competitors. There would be numerous other firsts, including the industry's first national magazine advertisement in 1897. Schaffner and his successors commissioned famous illustrators to create artwork for the ads and suggested they show clothes realistically. One 1904 ad featured three gentlemen and a lady inspecting a Yale vs. Princeton football game placard. They did not stand stiffly, but naturally, with a hand in a pocket or holding a walking stick behind the back; each position was an opportunity to show how well their Hart Schaffner & Marx suits draped and moved with the body, yet held their fine, sophisticated shape.

In 1900 a guaranteed all-wool policy was announced at a time when truth in labeling was not exactly a widespread

the fire, there obviously was a desperate need for clothing. Further, since Chicago had recently become a major transportation center, the wholesale business was a natural development for the time. And consumer acceptance of ready-to-wear clothing was increasing.

Harry and Max were sons of German immigrants who arrived in Chicago in 1858. The brothers, ambitious and hardworking individualists, understood the value of a brand name. In 1875 as business increased, they opened a second store on Clark Street. They also started to have suits made for their stores, which caught the eye of a downstate Illinois merchant who ordered several garments for his own customers. About this time two brothers-in-law, Levi Abt and Marcus Marx, joined the Harts, and the partnership of Hart Abt & Marx was formed in 1879.

By the end of 1887 Abt decided to leave the firm, but Joseph Schaffner, a distant and brilliant cousin of the Harts, joined the company and Hart Schaffner & Marx came to be. That year, 1887, marked the start of what would become a legendary American company. The shy Schaffner, who had been working as a bookkeeper, brought new ideas and creativity to the clothing business.

RAINCOATS that are something more than mere water-shedders; all-wool, stylish overcoats, rain-proof—that's our idea. If it's yours, ask for them.
Send six cents for the Style Book.
Hart Schaffner & Marx Good Clothes Makers
Chicago   Boston   New York

Introduction of water-shedder wool coats, *Munsey's* magazine, 1908

Loving couple, 1915

concept. In 1906 the company introduced proportioned suits with 14 basic body types and would ultimately make more than 250 specialty sizes. In 1912 Max Hart, searching for new style trends abroad, spotted a camel's hair coat in England, and the company quickly launched the original in the United States. Three years later, the company developed and guaranteed color fastness. And it introduced the first tropical-weight wool suit in 1917.

By 1905 immigrants from Italy and Eastern Europe swarmed into Chicago and many went to work for the clothing industry. Companies set up contract shops in unsanitary factory lofts and workers' homes, but Hart Schaffner & Marx operated differently. It consolidated the sewing, basting and buttonholing operations directly under its supervision in a 12-story fireproof building in downtown Chicago.

In 1911 annual sales reached an impressive $15 million.

The company switched to making officers' uniforms during World War I. After the Armistice was declared in 1918, departing American troops at French embarkation centers were greeted with an ingenious advertising campaign. Signs read: "Stylish Clothes Are Ready for You in the Good Old U.S.A. All wool, guaranteed by Hart Schaffner & Marx." In 1919 so many of the soldiers responded that the company's sales were the highest for any single year in its history to date.

Hart Schaffner & Marx quickly picked up on the excitement of the Roaring Twenties as it added new flair to its men's suits, sportcoats and overcoats. Because there were no men's fashion magazines, the company produced seasonal Style Books, sold to consumers through national ads, as well as to retailers to help move product. Begun around 1898, the Style Books reached distribution of several million by 1925. Each Style Book was an original work of art, a suggestion of a lifestyle that might include an afternoon of rowing or an evening masquerade party. It was also in the mid-1920s that the firm decided to return to its retailing roots by acquiring retail stores.

The 1928 annual report stated that the profit for the year was the largest in company history. But the stock market crash of 1929 and the Depression changed that picture. Deficits from 1930 to 1934 totaled over $8 million as sales volume in suits dropped 55 percent. In 1935 the company finally turned itself around, and the following year it introduced another first — pants with zippers. After World War II Hart Schaffner & Marx worked at capacity to accommodate the pent-up demand for business apparel for the returning veterans. The year 1946 was the most profitable in company history.

In the early 1950s the company made its first major manufacturing acquisition, the well-known Society Brand Clothes, which were the first to introduce the raglan shoulder coat and hook-closure trousers. In 1953 after purchasing a downtown building and consolidating several outlying factories into the one location, Hart Schaffner & Marx introduced the first Dacron® polyester and wool suit, which revolutionized the industry. By mid-decade the company was doing more business in the suit and coat industry than its four largest competitors combined.

From the 1960s to the 1980s the company grew tremendously in both the manufacturing and retail segments. Fortune 500 status, frequent stock splits and solid morale fueled the momentum. In 1963, a landmark year for merchandising, sales passed the $100 million mark for the first time in Hart Schaffner & Marx history. In 1964 the company bought Hickey-Freeman, makers of high-quality clothing since 1899. Known for its popular and uniquely comfortable elastic-waistband Sansabelt Slacks, Jaymar-Ruby became another acquisition in 1967. Two years later Hart Schaffner & Marx bought M. Wile & Co., a tailored clothing company that now markets upscale brand names such as Pierre Cardin, Daniel

Hechter and Perry Ellis. An agreement was reached in 1968 with professional golfer Jack Nicklaus to launch a collection under his name and that of Hart Schaffner & Marx. It was the first venture by a sports personality with a top-quality men's clothing line. In 1969 the company introduced Austin Reed of Regent Street, a famous British men's retailer, to this country. In 1970 M. Wile & Co. inaugurated Johnny Carson Apparel Inc., a line of intermediate-priced suits and sportcoats. When Carson wore a garment on his show, 10 million viewers saw it. This period was the dawn of celebrity endorsement, and Hart Schaffner & Marx was a pioneer in this exciting new form of marketing.

In the early 1970s new international enterprises included the purchase of one-half interest in Roberts of Mexico, a licensing agreement with Christian Dior of Paris and the introduction of clothing featuring the award-winning Italian designer Nino Cerruti.

Midway through the decade, automatic equipment was installed in the manufacturing and warehousing operations, including computerized cloth-cutting systems.

Hart Schaffner & Marx introduced Christian Dior tailored clothing. Allyn St. George, an American designer of tailored clothing, was added to the M. Wile & Co. line, and Intercontinental Apparel Inc., the U.S. licensee for Pierre Cardin suits and sportcoats, was incorporated into Hart Schaffner & Marx. Into the 1980s, when Americans were spending almost $100 billion for apparel, the company had the foresight to readily meet the changing needs of consumers by introducing Henry Grethel tailored clothing and Racquet Club clothing, which appealed to the younger, more contemporary customer.

On the retail side Hart Schaffner & Marx for years was the nation's largest menswear retailer. After acquiring its first store, Wallachs, in 1926, the company followed up over the next five decades by obtaining such highly respected institutions as Baskin and Capper & Capper (Chicago), Hastings (San Francisco), Silverwoods (Los Angeles), F.R. Tripler (New York), Raleighs (Washington, D.C.) and Jas. K. Wilson (Dallas). Some stores were obtained in the 1930s during the Depression. In 1949 the company went against conventional wisdom that insisted

Saturday Evening Post advertisement, 1918

on downtown locations by signing a lease in one of the first suburban shopping centers. Twenty years later it made its initial entry into the women's store field by acquiring Chas. A. Stevens (est. 1881) of Chicago. By the late 1960s Hart Schaffner & Marx owned almost 200 stores, and by the late 1980s the number jumped to over 460.

The 1980s represented a milestone decade in the history of the company for at least three reasons. In 1983 the name was changed to Hartmarx Corporation. The name Hart Schaffner & Marx continues as a subsidiary. Two years later sales and earnings rose for the 10th consecutive year. Then in 1987 this consistently strong and innovative leader celebrated its centennial. Over 1,000 notable guests attended the special anniversary event.

But by 1990 several years of declining profits due to changes in the retail environment, expensive leases and poor retail performance plagued the company. According to the Hartmarx annual report, 1991 was the company's worst year since the Depression, just as it was for many other companies during the economic recession of the time. In the fall of 1992 Hartmarx came very close to declaring bankruptcy for the retail stores. And then began one of the great corporate turnaround stories. That same autumn, Hartmarx began a comprehensive operational

Samuel Nelson Abbot advertisement, 1932

and financial restructuring to focus on the profitable core wholesale business, eliminate the underperforming retail operations and restructure the balance sheet. Among the back-on-track measures taken from 1992 through 1995 was selling off the principal retail operation; this contributed to a 26 percent reduction in debt. A $30 million stock sale helped Hartmarx return to profitability. It reported a net profit of $6.2 million in 1993, the first profit in four years after three years of multimillion dollar losses.

The late 1980s and 1990s was a period of active yet highly selective acquisitions that complemented and enhanced the Hartmarx name. The result was an eclectic product portfolio sold through a variety of distribution channels and targeted to meet the needs of specific consumer niches by appealing to them with a wide range of price points and fashion statements. The prestigious British line of Gieves & Hawkes was added in the late 1980s. Early in the next decade Hartmarx acquired licensing rights for Bobby Jones, Jack Nicklaus, Cerruti 1881 and Karl Lagerfeld as well as MM by Krizia and KM by Krizia, one of Italy's premiere fashion houses.

Hartmarx's most successful launch occurred in 1994 with the licensing of a casual pant sporting the Hilfiger label; this continues to be the company's fastest-growing product. Other successes followed. In 1995 Hartmarx licensed Perry Ellis and Daniel Hechter. In 1996 the company acquired Plaid Clothing Group's assets, including such outstanding labels as Burberrys, Claiborne, Evan-Picone, Palm Beach and Brannoch. The next year featured the introduction of Hickey-Freeman sportswear, Kenneth Cole tailored clothing, Pringle of Scotland and Desert Classic golfwear. Hart Schaffner & Marx sportswear was established in 1998.

Hartmarx strengthened its position in Canada with two key acquisitions in 1998. The first was Coppley, Noyes & Randall, which made Hartmarx the largest supplier of quality tailored clothing in Canada. Brands include Coppley, Cambridge, Alar Flusser, Mateo Mass and Keithmoor. The second key acquisition was that of the Royal Shirt Company of Canada. Another global acquisition in 1998 was the business and trademarks of Pusser's of the West Indies, with its carefree yet stylish nautical collection. Hartmarx continues to solidify its presence in the international market. The company operates production facilities in cost-efficient Mexico and Costa Rica; sources its sportswear and part of its tailored clothing in Italy, Scotland and the Far East; and has over 30 licensing agreements in 16 countries.

Although the early 1990s was a difficult period for Hartmarx, the company successfully redesigned and repositioned itself with a strategic change of direction. E.O. Hand, chairman and chief executive officer, noted Hartmarx is no longer just "your father's suit company" but a major marketer of multiple sportswear lines. Men's suits continue to command about 40 percent of the business, but diversity and balance are proving to be highly successful growth strategies within a broadening array of markets. Womenswear, including the Barrie Pace catalog and other brands such as Hawksley & Wight, accounts for about 8 percent of the business, with the biggest label being Austin Reed for investment-quality career wear. For menswear, the successful strategy of brand extension incorporates even the traditional, premium Hickey-Freeman and Hart Schaffner & Marx lines, which have segued into sportswear, shirts, neckwear and belts in better specialty stores and are currently producing outstanding profits.

The game of golf is a decidedly fast-growing sport. According to the National Golf Foundation, there are an estimated 26.5 million golfers in the United States and over $2 billion is spent on golf apparel each year. For many players, looking good on the fairway is just as much a part of the game as trying to break 80. But the same look is exceedingly popular off the course as well. For comfort that is casual yet respectable, golfwear is often the attire of choice for all manner of occasions, both business and social.

Hartmarx offers three strategically distributed lines of golfwear at various price points that range from luxury to value. In 1998 combined sales of $75 million represented about 7 percent of the business. The average price point for shirts of the premium Bobby Jones line is $160 at retail, with 50 percent distribution to better specialty stores and the balance to pro and resort shops. Launched in 1998, the Player's Collection in the Bobby Jones line appeals to seriously active golfers, with shirts retailing for under $100. The Nicklaus Silver line is primarily sold in upper-moderate pro and resort shops. And the Desert Classic line is a value-oriented product that is manufactured exclusively for Sears Roebuck & Co.

As fashion evolved from the constricting and formal styles of the Victorian Age to today's increasingly casual mode, Hartmarx witnessed and helped influence it all.

Train depot, 1937

Today's diverse fashion conventions mean Hartmarx labels may be anything from classic to contemporary, depending on the individual who wears them and the image they seek to project. Whatever the style, consumers can always count on beautiful clothing and sportswear to enhance their personal and professional lives.

From the 1800s, throughout the past 100 years and now into the 21st century, the history of Hartmarx Corporation spans three exciting centuries of timeless style. It has come a long way since the first days of one store and two well-dressed brothers.

Urban Attitudes

CHRISTIAN DIOR MONSIEUR

The look of elegance comes as naturally as

Christian Dior evening wear advertisement, 1986

RTC:
The In-Store Agency

Although some enjoy the experience of shopping, many cringe at the thought of entering a retail store. If the Chicago firm, RTC Industries, has anything to do with it, those in the latter group will start to change their minds about shopping.

One's satisfaction with, and enjoyment of, the shopping experience holds the key to the success of many of the world's retailers and brand marketers. As consumers, people have more shopping choices and more ways to spend their money than ever before. And with the advent of the Internet, consumers now have the choice to buy without the time or hassle of traditional store shopping.

Retailers and brand marketers know this. And they know they must work harder to earn the consumer's time, interest and shopping dollar. That's why they are collec-

tively turning their attention, and their marketing dollars, to the medium of the retail environment. Beyond TV, magazine or billboard advertising, a company's marketing efforts inside the store are aimed at attracting, engaging and motivating consumers to buy.

To whom do retailers and brand marketers turn for help with in-store marketing? There are less than a dozen firms in the world with the talent and muscle to serve and advise the international giants of the retail and brand world. Chicago happens to be home to one of the largest and most successful firms in this specialized field.

Here is the story of how RTC started 50 years ago, and today remains a family-run growth business as a result of vision and the willingness to embrace change.

When black-and-white TVs took the 1950s by storm, who would have noticed the small, spiral-wound packing tubes that Round Tubes and Cores Company of Chicago supplied as fast as the sets flew off store shelves? Half a century later, the company now known as RTC Industries has grown to become the world's largest corporation exclusively dedicated to creating or enhancing retail environments. According to Walter Nathan, company founder, some tubes are still made, but the business purpose has become much broader, focused on providing solutions in the form of in-store marketing programs. The company's expertise encompasses the design as well as the manufacture of store fixtures, displays, store-within-a-store feature shops and interactive kiosks. Facilities in 18 countries allow RTC to provide its services to global brand marketers such as Procter & Gamble, Coca-Cola and Nike and to leading retailers such as Toys "R" Us, Walgreens, Kmart and Sephora, the fast growing cosmetics chain.

It was in the mid-1980s that Richard Nathan, son of company founder Walter, and a colleague, Howard Topping, began to rethink the way RTC would do business. The focus throughout the first 20 years in the merchandising sector of RTC's business had been on designing and manufacturing standard display products, a collection of proven, but basic display units that

Sephora: The famous "fragrance testing organ" in a new Sephora Cosmetic Store, built and installed by RTC

were produced in different sizes and colors. It was a highly successful approach that kept the company growing and allowed for international expansion, but the exciting world of customized merchandising, with virtually unlimited possibilities for creativity, also beckoned. It was more about building relationships than taking orders, and RTC was gearing up to embrace it.

RTC's business plan from that point was slowly, but consistently, focused on the development of global relationships with clients who shared RTC's strategic vision for the importance of the in-store environment. The success of this approach led to one more change in the company. Today, the company is known as RTC: The In-Store Agency.

Functioning as an in-store agency means that RTC manages the entire retail merchandising process. Creativity is still the key driver behind all of this and is represented in the visual aspects of the in-store program. Creating a motivating shopping experience for the consumer also requires sound program planning and implementation. RTC's ability to successfully bundle these skills, together with the creative component, is the broader offering behind the growth of the company.

It all begins with strategic consulting. At this stage, RTC consultants work with clients to establish a plan for translating their marketing goals inside the store. The unique characteristics of the client's brand, insights on consumer buying behaviors and "fit" within a retailer's store operation are all considered.

The service program continues with the generation of design ideas. Teams of specialists with the unique expertise of designing for the in-store environment develop creative ideas that will connect the goals of the consumer, the product brand and the retailer brand.

When Toys "R" Us needed a Star Wars Feature Shop to showcase movie merchandise, RTC delivered with dimensional images of beloved characters, a You-Are-There spaceship control panel and a magnificent Millennium Falcon suspended from cables overhead. RTC made 850 of these spaceships, which required

Nike: Nike Store Interior — executed and built by RTC

collaboration with, and final approval by, Lucasfilm. They were so effective that thousands of customers lit up store switchboards with requests to buy them. The toy-store giant reported that this feature shop was its most successful ever.

RTC designers work in collaboration with Nike's own design team to create the latest innovations at retail. The Nike brand is recognized worldwide for creativity and innovation, and that reputation is supported, in-store, with programs that stand apart from any other experience at retail.

For the upscale Sephora cosmetics stores, RTC literally merchandises every square foot of retail space. The result is a clean, futuristic presentation of unlimited choices for beauty products.

RTC's partnerships with some of the finest global brands — Coca-Cola, FedEx, Kraft, Timberland and others — result in merchandising solutions that change the shopping experience and, ultimately, build brand equity and sales.

But RTC is not finished at this stage. End-to-end service includes helping the client sell their new merchandising program to the retailer. This vital step helps ensure practical success. RTC also handles the logistics of warehousing, distribution and installation — functions that competitors often dismiss. For Nike the company maintains a database on every Nike store-within-a-store, which includes the original store layout, changes that have been made and repair/replacement records. Communication with the client is efficiently managed through a mutual Web site. Leveraging technology is a cornerstone of RTC's operation.

It is uncommon for a company in this field to supply superiority across the continuum of strategic research,

Oil of Olay: Oil of Olay wall unit with its latest lit-up configuration — designed and built by RTC

creative design, manufacturing excellence, technical support and deployment. But that is RTC's strength as a total in-store program manager rather than a display builder. Clients benefit from the continuity of total merchandising solutions with messages that hit hard and tell a consistent story.

Highly successful global brands need a global in-store agency. With offices and plants in North, South and Central America, Europe, Asia and Africa, RTC is one of the few with the power to launch multinational programs to deliver the all-important brand image around the world, in a manner that is coordinated and cost effective.

The RTC Industries story began in 1950, with Walter Nathan as founding partner. When Round Tubes

and Cores began making the paper tubes for TVs, it was one of three such manufacturers in the United States. Other RTC tube products were used in electronics, as cores for rolls of plastic, paper or cloth, as well as mailing tubes. Orders rolled in, yet the tubes were merely components, not marketable products, and so business volume was largely beyond the manufacturer's control.

The solution was in candy canes, which the company essentially viewed as decorative tubes. They began manufacturing the festive holiday decorations to brighten streetscapes and homes. For the first time, people could experience an emotional reaction to the company's products. It represented the first step toward RTC's ultimate creative destiny.

The wheels kept turning. During a fishing trip up to International Falls, Minnesota, Walter Nathan toted his poles inside — what else — a tube rigged up with endcaps and a handle. Other fishermen took such an interest in the nifty case that it soon became the Rod Caddy, and anyone flipping through Sears Catalogs in the late 1950s could purchase it.

Next up was a request from a customer for small, transparent candy canes that could be filled with candies and sold at retail. The first order, in 1957, was for 10,000 units. In 1958 the customer bought 50,000 canes, and in 1999, RTC was making 30 million each year when it decided to spin off that portion of the business.

The evolution from tubes to merchandising displays happened in the early 1960s. In the same decade, the company sold its TV electronic component business. Someone in the company noticed that many store Christmas displays featured signs held aloft by round poles. Round Tubes and Cores decided that this could be the next product in its developing line. The addition of plastic connectors to the poles created inexpensive, easy-to-assemble, knockdown etageres for use in trade shows. They then replaced the plastic connectors with molded shelves. These became the company's first in-store displays. Once again business boomed; in 1970, the company adopted its new name, RTC Industries, and later that decade, achieved annual sales of approximately $10 million. Today that annual total has grown to $150 million.

RTC's ability to maintain an excellent reputation globally is directly related to its human resources. Associates' enthusiasm, performance and loyalty allows the company to preserve its leadership role in the industry. In 18 countries around the world, RTC seeks to build a strong and dedicated team of talented individuals, working in unison to advance the clients' business in the in-store environment. RTC believes its work is both challenging and rewarding for individuals at all levels.

It is the commitment of the Human Resources Team to maintain RTC's reputation as a great company to work for, where people build their careers. They take pride in designing the many benefits offered that care for Associates and their families. RTC also continually evaluates its compensation program in order to stay competitive in the market.

RTC Industries values and respects diversity among its Associates. As a global industry leader, Associates from all over the world take pride in the company's reputation and their contributions to its success. They frequently have the opportunity to apply their talents in overseas branch offices, where they can learn different cultures and gain new perspectives. It is a competitive industry, so staying on top provides a challenge for everyone. Associates continually have to think "out of the box," as there is a creative component to everyone's job.

RTC Industries takes an active interest in civic responsibility. In its hometown of Chicago, RTC participates in, project manages, and corporately sponsors Chicago Cares Serve-A-Thon, a citywide initiative that gets done what needs doing — everything from painting school buildings to landscaping and creating murals. Each holiday season, RTC Associates ring the Salvation Army kettle bells, and the company matches whatever contributions they collect. Through Schaumburg Township's Adopt-A-Family and Toys for Tots initiatives, the company supplies less-fortunate families and children with holiday gifts. Each quarter the company selects a different service project. Recently in Chicago, Associates helped the Chicago Park District clean, rebuild, and landscape neighborhood parks. RTC's own associates also benefit by attending free English as a Second Language (ESL) and computer classes with half of their class time paid at their regular wage.

RTC Industries literally creates worlds around products, worlds that people want to spend some time in — having fun, learning and buying. The moments that they choose to spend in those worlds represent the client's last opportunity to market their product, and the consumer's first chance to take that in-store experience home and make it their own. That is the power of understanding,

Coca-Cola:
A Coca-Cola end cap — for large supermarkets, by RTC

and it happens every day in countless stores around the world as a result of RTC's creative contributions.

In 2000 RTC Industries celebrates its 50th anniversary. Those first decades represent half a century of not only building a company, but of helping to redefine an industry that is one of the world's most dynamic. What RTC Industries achieves in the next 50 years promises to be even more exciting for clients, consumers and RTC Associates worldwide.

RTC's world headquarters, with managers from 15 countries, March 2000

Lettuce Entertain You Enterprises

Big Bowl on Cedar
Photo by
Mark Ballogg
©STEINKAMP/
BALLOGG
CHICAGO

Thirty years ago there were no salad bars. If customers wanted a salad, a waiter would bring them a little bowl of lettuce, shredded carrots and a tomato wedge. Nobody gave salad much thought at all — until Richard Melman opened his first restaurant in 1971. This 29 year old thought lettuce should be — well, more entertaining. It should be torn into pieces, carefully laid into a big bowl and set upon a counter filled with ice. It should be near other bowls of chopped and sliced vegetables — all kinds of healthy, colorful ones. There should be more bowls filled with cheese, chicken, breads, grains, olives, dressings and fruit, too. People should walk up to this brimming counter with a big, clean plate and load up — anyway they wish — without any supervision

from a waiter. In fact they should be encouraged to pile their plates high — and come back for more.

That was the concept for the first Lettuce Entertain You restaurant, which is still open three decades later. It was in Lincoln Park, and it was called R. J. Grunts. It meant something: R was for Richard; J was for Jerry Orzoff, his best friend and mentor; and Grunts was for the sound customers would make "pigging out" on the food. It was an inside joke and everybody in Chicago got it.

Richard Melman

Since then Lettuce Entertain You has mushroomed into a $200-plus million enterprise of 5,000 employees working in 75 restaurants. Most are in Chicago, but some are in other cities, such as Tokyo and London. They have funky names. Café-Ba-Ba-Reeba! was Chicago's first tapas ("little dishes") bar. Or they have catchy names. Ben Pao means firecracker, and it exploded with robust offerings of Northern-style Chinese cuisine. Lettuce restaurants also have romantic names. Ambria offered the city's finest French cuisine in an elegant atmosphere.

What was the secret to Melman's success?

"It seemed that every job I had when I was younger was restaurant related," says Melman. "It was natural for me. I wasn't a good student. I flunked out of college. But I loved the restaurant business."

He grew up working for a restaurant named after him on Broadway and Belmont Avenue. Ricky's Restaurant was owned by his father, Morrie Melman, who had big plans for his son. Richard's fantasy, however, was to play

When he travels, he's sure to carry something that belonged to his mentor. Melman doesn't hesitate to say he attributes all of his success to Orzoff.

Richard Melman continued to move forward. He met his wife, Martha, at R. J. Grunts. Soon they were a family with three children — two boys and a girl.

Lettuce grew too, one creatively concocted restaurant at a time. After R. J. Grunts, Lettuce opened four more restaurants in the next five years. Melman had also entered the world of fine cuisine. In 1976 he reopened the famous Pump Room on Chicago's Gold Coast. In 1980 he visited France to learn more about fine dining. He returned to Chicago to open Ambria, which is still going strong 20 years later.

for the Cubs. He stoked his dream by playing ball in his Logan Square neighborhood and by going to Wrigley Field to see his favorite team play. The turning point came when he was 20 years old. One busy Sunday he skipped work to play a championship softball game in Grant Park. When he came back, his father was boiling mad. Morrie told Richard he had no more confidence in him, didn't think he could develop a sense of responsibility and didn't want to see him in the family business ever again.

Profoundly shaken, Richard asked for one more chance. This time he would be really serious about the restaurant business. He meant to prove himself. He pushed himself hard for several years. And then when he asked to become his father's partner, Morrie refused.

Enter Jerry A. Orzoff, a local real estate agent who immediately and unconditionally believed in Richard Melman's ability to create and run restaurants. Richard thrived in this partnership and relied on Orzoff for support and advice. When Orzoff died in 1981 of diabetes-related complications, Melman grieved deeply. To this day he prominently displays Orzoff's pictures in his home and office.

When questioned about why he kept building restaurants, he said, "Success is an aphrodisiac. The more success I had, the more excited I became to do more. We really had a good foundation, which was based on two things — having the right financial foundation and the right people to move the concept forward. It's a very conservative approach."

Inspired by success, Melman kept looking for more opportunities. He took additional trips to Europe to study food and style. He honed his skill in discovering

Mon Ami Gabi,
Las Vegas
Photo by
Mark Ballogg
©*STEINKAMP/*
BALLOGG
CHICAGO

the right location and trendy cuisine. He developed a knack for handcrafting restaurants with unique ambiences.

In all he has opened more than 75 one-of-a kind concept restaurants in the last 30 years. Although Melman is seen as creative and artistic, he attributes

Steve Ottmann

his success to doing the basics very well. This involves good food, good people and good value. He trusts his instincts, as does his team of 38 partners.

"I always have a vision when I open a restaurant," Melman says. "I'll usually have an idea for years before I turn it into a restaurant. Then if I find the right location, the right space, the right deal, I'll take the idea and do it. It's worked nicely."

To create a restaurant, Melman usually works with about 10 people, including chefs, general managers, operating partners, architects and marketers. The team creates a blueprint, or script, of the restaurant and carefully maps out each detail. Each restaurant is a creation unto itself. They brainstorm the restaurant's menu, layout and design. Then they hire staff. Here too, Melman uses his magic touch, by hiring the right people and training them well.

Melman always planned to create one-of-a-kind restaurants, but his partners wanted Lettuce to grow faster. The fastest way to grow is through replication. While Lettuce continued to build one-of-a-kind restaurants, it also started to focus on duplicating existing restaurants.

Scoozi!
*Photo by
Mark Ballogg
©STEINKAMP/
BALLOGG
CHICAGO*

"Duplicating isn't what drives Rich," says CEO Steven Ottmann. "But the economy of business has changed in the last 30 years. To attract the right people, we needed to speed up our growth. We needed to open more than two or three new restaurants a year — which was all we could do if we concentrated only on new ones. If we know restaurants work, we can hand them off to people who want to grow."

In the year 2000 Lettuce opened its sixth Big Bowl, a casual Asian café specializing in noodles and stir-fry. It also opened its third Wildfire, featuring classic, American cuisine prepared over a natural wood fire.

Five years earlier, Lettuce sold two very successful restaurant concepts to Brinker International, which now has 50 Corner Bakeries and 12 Maggiano's Little Italies. Even though Melman sold these restaurants, he still stays involved in them as a stockholder and through consulting. "I take pride in the concepts and admire what Brinker has done with them," says Melman.

Lettuce has consulted with other businesses too. In addition to McDonald's, Lettuce has consulted with Krispy Kreme Doughnuts, Campbell Soup Co., Chart House and Popeye's Chicken. They all wanted to stay ahead of the restaurant game, and they listened carefully to what Melman's people had to say about the future of eating.

"People are going toward a higher flavor profile," says Ottmann. "That means tastier. They want food with a very clear taste, that's spicier, more distinct. That's why Asian and Latin foods have become so popular. People have become experimental, more interested in different cuisines. They want to know they're eating something exciting."

They also want to know they're being listened to, which is a point that a Lettuce restaurant tries to make every night. Right after opening day at a new restaurant, Lettuce employees ask customers what they want.

"Part of our culture is to have a high regard for the customer," says Ottmann. "Customers will always tell you what they like, if you listen. We're very tuned into listening and setting aside our egos. As a result we try to make one little change every week. If we make 52 changes in one restaurant in a year, we're on top of things."

It is a credo that gave Chicago and the rest of the world at least 75 great places to eat. It is also how Lettuce became this town's top-rated restaurant maker.

McDonald's

All over the world people recognize McDonald's Golden Arches. At the same time, the company's heart and soul are firmly fixed in Chicago. Entrepreneur Ray Kroc's first McDonald's restaurant opened on April 15, 1955, in the nearby suburb of Des Plaines. Legendary Chicago Bulls basketball star Michael Jordan has served as company spokesperson. People from dozens and dozens of nations come to Chicago for training at Hamburger University.

Number One
Store/Museum in
Des Plaines, Illinois

Kroc's far-reaching vision made McDonald's a food service industry giant. At age 52 he dedicated his life to building the company. Based on strong Midwestern values, his success story serves as an inspiration to anyone who has ever dreamed of making it big.

The history of McDonald's is rich with lore and legend, much of it surrounding Kroc himself. Kroc was born just outside Chicago in Oak Park, Illinois. He left high school at age 15 and trained as a World War I Red Cross ambulance driver.

After the war Kroc returned to the Chicago area where he pursued two careers. At night he played the piano for a local radio station. Beginning in 1922, during the day, he sold paper cups for the Lily Cup Company. By 1926 he had set music aside and had found his niche in sales.

But selling paper cups was not necessarily how Kroc wanted to spend his life. While working at Lily, he pursued his salesman's quest for the ultimate product, keeping his eyes open for the right opportunity. What he found was the "Multimixer," a machine that made five milkshakes at one time. By 1953 he was earning a good living as the product's exclusive distributor.

Selling Multimixers drew Kroc to the original McDonald brothers' hamburger stand in San Bernardino, California. The stand sold 20,000 milkshakes each month, making it a prime user of the Multimixer. At first Kroc's interest in the stand resided only in his desire to sell mixers.

But Multimixers were soon a small part of the picture. One day in 1954, Kroc paid a visit to McDonald's during lunchtime. When he saw the rapidly moving line of customers buying bags of burgers and fries, his first thought was: "This will go anyplace. Anyplace!" In that moment, his focus changed from selling mixers for hamburger stands to selling the stands themselves. A great salesman had discovered his ultimate product.

Kroc convinced the McDonald brothers to name him as their exclusive franchising agent. On March 2, 1955 he formed a new franchising company, McDonald's System, Inc.

As he moved forward with his plan, Kroc retained the McDonald's formula of a limited menu, quality food, an assembly-line production system, and fast, friendly service. The menu included just nine items: hamburgers, cheeseburgers, three soft-drink flavors, milk, coffee, potato chips, pie, French fries and milkshakes. Prices were low and the drive-in, take-out stands appealed to young suburban families on tight budgets.

To the basic food services at each new franchise, Kroc brought his own demanding standards and Midwestern values, which he abbreviated as "Quality, Service, Cleanliness, and Value," or QSC & V. This elbow-grease approach to food service has remained an essential part of the business.

In 1961 Kroc bought out the McDonald brothers. This gave him complete control to develop the potential of the McDonald's system according to his vision.

Kroc set out to create 1,000 restaurants. Along the way, he served the company's one billionth hamburger in 1963 on the Art Linkletter Show. That year, he approved the Filet-O-Fish sandwich, created by McDonald's franchisee Lou Groen, as the first new item added to the original menu. In 1967 the first international McDonald's restaurants opened in Canada and Puerto Rico. That year McDonald's organized its All-American High School Band.

Ronald McDonald was created by two Washington, D.C., owner-operators, John Gibson and Oscar Goldstein. The clown's original 1963 costume consisted of a tray-shaped hat loaded with a Styrofoam burger, a bag of fries, and a milk shake cup; shoes shaped like buns; a nose fashioned out of a McDonald's soda cup; and a simulated hamburger belt buckle. In 1965 Ronald McDonald appeared for the first time in network television commercials, thereafter quickly becoming the company's official spokesperson to kids across America.

In 1968 Kroc reached his goal of 1,000 restaurants. Meanwhile, Fred Turner, a vital member of Kroc's team, was working his way up the McDonald's ladder. He had joined the organization as a franchisee applicant in 1956, but that same year Kroc encouraged him to come to work for McDonald's System Inc. His assignment was to develop the McDonald's operations department.

Two years later, Turner was appointed company vice president. He took Kroc's original vision and built on it to improve consistency and conformity among the various franchises. His goal was to make certain that customers would find the principles of QSC & V in operation no matter where in the country they stopped to buy McDonald's hamburgers. To guarantee that every franchisee would carry out company standards, he created the "Operations and Training Manual" that became the definitive company handbook. Thirty years later franchisees continue to rely on its clear, concise descriptions.

Turner expanded on Kroc's concept of the owner/operator. McDonald's franchisees were required to spend their time in their restaurants working hands-on with their employees. That meant a single owner/operator would not oversee hundreds of units, nor could anyone already focused on running another type of franchise buy a McDonald's franchise. Owning McDonald's franchises — the average number is currently about three per owner/operator — had to be a full-time, best effort commitment.

"Don't worry about making money," Kroc told franchisees. "Love what you're doing and always put the customer first — and success will be yours!"

To further ensure uniformity in every aspect of the McDonald's operation, in 1961 Turner created Hamburger University. The school started in the basement of a Chicago-area franchise. Owner/operators were instructed in subjects such as the type of potatoes required and the formula to be used for hamburger meat. The two-week curriculum included demonstrations of McDonald's equipment.

Today, Hamburger University is housed in a sparkling Oak Brook, Illinois, facility with seven separate auditorium classrooms and a 227-room lodge where students live during training. Courses are taught in 21 languages. Owner/operators, store managers, assistant managers with management potential and corporate executives from all over the world attend the school. They receive essential training in how to manage a local $1.5 million restaurant business that is open every day of the year except Christmas.

Although Hamburger Universities now operate in Germany, Japan, Austrailia, Brazil and the Untied Kingdom, international franchisees and managers vie for the chance to receive training in the United States. They arrive at Hamburger U. eager to visit the 80-acre Oak Brook home-office campus.

Ray Kroc, founder

(Left to right)
Fred Turner,
senior chairman

Mike Quinlan, former
chairman and CEO,
board member
and chairman of
executive committee

Jack Greenberg,
chairman and CEO

No other restaurant company, before or since, has opened anything that compares with this full-time training center. Bringing owner/operators to the company's Midwest "heartbeat" home office encourages their commitment to McDonald's QSC & V principles. Those who attend forge connections with McDonald's that in many cases last a lifetime.

Turner also saw suppliers as playing a major role in the consistency of McDonald's products. He coined the phrase "The Three Legged Stool" to describe the interdependence of company, owner/operators, and suppliers. He saw each as equally supporting the weight of the McDonald's system. For one to prosper, all had to prosper.

At a time when no one inside or outside the industry contemplated the international development of hamburger restaurants, Turner chose Japan as the site for the first McDonald's outside of North America. Although Japan's own cuisine had almost nothing in common with American cuisine, Turner felt that its citizens' affinity for hard work and their natural tendency to strive toward perfection meant Japanese owner/operators would carry out the company's standards to a "T."

In 1971 McDonald's moved its corporate headquarters from downtown Chicago to a new, eight-story office building in Oak Brook, Illinois. Other notable happenings included the introduction of McDonald's Cookies, the Egg McMuffin, the "twoallbeefpattiesspecialsaucelettucecheesepickelsonionsonasesameseedbun" Big Mac promotion and the formation of the first McDonald's All American High School Basketball Team. In 1974 Turner

became CEO and the first Ronald McDonald House opened in Philadelphia, Pennsylvania.

Ronald McDonald House was conceived in Philadelphia in response to the plight of Philadelphia Eagles linebacker Fred Hill, whose daughter Kim had been hospitalized for leukemia. The Philadelphia Children's Hospital and the Eagles recognized the hardships of families with hospitalized children and sought McDonald's support to build them a Philadelphia home-away-from-home. Local McDonald's franchisees helped raise $50,000 for the first house.

Today, in neighborhoods worldwide, Ronald McDonald Houses offer shelter for families of seriously ill children being treated at nearby hospitals. They range from a five-bedroom facility in Youngstown, Ohio, to a walk-up apartment in Vienna, Austria. In September 1999 the 200th Ronald McDonald House opened in Budapest, Hungary. More than two million families have been helped by Ronald McDonald Houses and their more than 20,000 volunteers.

Ronald McDonald's Children's Charities was founded in 1984 in memory of Ray Kroc, who died that year. Now called Ronald McDonald House Charities, it is one of the world's largest children's charities. RMHC issues grants to hundreds of organizations serving children. The funding helps develop and support programs, primarily in the areas of health and wellness.

Like Turner, the next leader of McDonald's worked his way up through the ranks. Mike Quinlan began in 1963 as a part-time mailroom employee, and served as CEO from 1987 to 1998. By the time he took the reins,

McDonald's was establishing itself as a global company. Quinlan ramped up international development and strove to set McDonald's apart, to make it the No. 1 class act of the quick-service restaurant industry in terms of customer satisfaction.

Expansion was also high on Quinlan's agenda. He opened the first Moscow McDonald's, and offered franchises in countries such as Poland, Estonia, South Africa, Honduras and Jamaica. By the end of 1998, McDonald's had 4,421 franchises in Europe, 5,055 in Asia/Pacific, 1,405 in Latin America, and 1,447 in other countries worldwide.

Quinlan launched "McRecycle USA" — an environmental program with a goal of spending at least $100 million annually on the purchase of recycled materials — and was instrumental in United Airlines' decision to offer young passengers McDonald's Friendly Skies Meals.

When Jack Greenberg took over as CEO in 1998, McDonald's had 1.5 million employees throughout the world. With 13,000 locations in the United States and nearly 12,000 in other countries, Greenberg saw the opportunity for McDonald's to further leverage its global strength.

While Oak Brook had always overseen its far-flung restaurants, on-site management had for the most part been handled by self-contained executive "shops" in the various countries. With direction from Oak Brook, each had developed a bit of its own culture and some individual methods for improving business. For instance, in Russia, managers had to make a special effort to teach employees to smile and say, "May I help you?" In India, to reach the vast population that does not eat beef, executives developed the Maharaja Mac, a burger made of lamb.

Greenberg recognized the value inherent in building closer connections among these mini-headquarters. Why not take good ideas from France and apply them in Australia? Sharing management techniques would benefit everyone who was part of the Three Legged Stool.

With leading market shares in the food industry worldwide, Greenberg plans for the company to continue building McDonald's restaurants. At the same time, he will seek opportunities to use the company's infrastructure and resources to promote growth in new directions.

Toward that goal, McDonald's recently acquired interests in several food-related businesses, Donatos Pizza and Chipotle Mexican Grill in the United States and Aroma, a cold sandwich and specialty coffee chain in London. These operations will benefit from McDonald's expertise in restaurant site development, supply chain management and marketing.

Huge as the company has become, today the principles on which it was built remain strong. In Chicago's Bronzeville neighborhood in August 1999, at the opening of the 25,000th McDonald's restaurant, Greenberg echoed Kroc's original statement to his franchisees: "None of us is as good as all of us," when he told new franchisee Eileen Porter, "You're in business for yourself, but you are not in business by yourself."

McDonald's Restaurant — Golani Junction, Israel

900 North Michigan Shops

International style and incomparable fashion are the signatures of 900 North Michigan Shops, which features a world-class mix of retail, cinemas, restaurants and the Four Seasons Hotel. This mixed-use complex also contains an office tower, luxury condominium residences, and valet and self-parking.

900 North Michigan Shops made its debut in September 1988. Designed by Kohn, Pedersen and Fox Associates and Perkins & Will, the 66-story structure consists of a 58-story, limestone-and-glass tower rising

from an eight-story base of limestone, granite and marble. The building — topped by the four signature lanterns — anchors the north end of Chicago's Magnificent Mile.

The fashionable art deco building features a sophisticated and elegant shopping experience. Six levels of retail offer more than 70 unique and distinctive shops,

including the first Midwest Bloomingdale's department store. Many of the retailers are exclusive to 900 in the Midwest and represent an extensive international lineup, including Lalique, Gucci, MaxMara, Pavillon Christofle and rue Royale. 900 North Michigan Shops also features

> The fashionable art deco building features a sophisticated and elegant shopping experience.

recognizable retail names like J. Crew, Club Monaco, Montblanc and Coach. The second level of the center offers live piano music on weekends throughout the year and a stunning sculptured marble fountain. A dramatic, 21-foot circular window on the fifth level overlooks Michigan Avenue and creates an alfresco atmosphere for the restaurants and cafes on levels five and six.

In addition to offering the most fashionable address on Michigan Avenue, 900 North Michigan includes 550,000 square feet of prime office space, 106 luxury condominium residences, a Four Seasons Hotel and an attached parking facility with valet and self-parking for 1,750 cars.

Four Seasons Hotels and Resorts — internationally recognized for the finest service and quality — operates the 343-room luxury hotel. Amenities include a gourmet restaurant, an informal dining room and two cozy lounges; a full-service health club with a skylighted swimming pool; and meeting and function rooms, including an opulent grand ballroom that can accommodate up to 1,000 guests.

The top 19 floors of the building are dedicated to The Residences. Residents enter from a private, street-level lobby on Delaware Street. Each residence is afforded a spectacular view of the city. Amenities include a 24-hour doorman, concierge, use of the Four Seasons Health Club, selected hotel services, valet services and special access to all components of the mixed-use complex.

From Oak Street on the north to the Chicago River on the south, Chicago's "Magnificent Mile" offers a concentration of fabulous shopping, dining and entertainment. The opening of 900 North Michigan Shops solidified the status of North Michigan Avenue as a world-renowned shopping street that can compete with the world's fashion capitals.

Oakbrook Center

Oakbrook Center offers visitors the best in shopping, dining and entertainment, all within a beautifully landscaped setting. Located in DuPage County at the confluence of several expressways, the center annually draws 25 million people from all over the Midwest and around the world. Tourists who come to the open-air regional shopping center spend nearly $2 billion each year at Oakbrook Center and in the surrounding area.

Greenery and eight fountains or pools add interest to the center's white brick and marble buildings. A landscape maintenance crew cares for more than 3,200 trees — 2,500 are evergreens — and keeps the public gardens tidy. The mall draws garden clubs from downstate Illinois, Indiana, Iowa and Wisconsin. Those who arrive in spring are treated to the sight of 125,000 tulips. In summer 130,000 annuals grace the grounds and in autumn they are replaced by 75,000 chrysanthemums.

The gracious setting is a shopper's paradise, with six department stores — Neiman Marcus, Lord & Taylor, Marshall Field & Co., Saks Fifth Avenue, Nordstrom and Sears — 160 specialty stores, 18 restaurants and eight movie screens. The center also includes two general office buildings, one professional office building and a hotel.

Oakbrook Center opened in 1962 with 20 stores. It was developed by Philip Klutznik, founder of a predecessor company of the current owner, Urban Shopping Centers, Inc. (NYSE: URB). At the time, shopping centers were an innovation in retailing. Marshall Field's and Sears anchored the center. A Jewel supermarket was also in place, fitting with the original concept of Oakbrook as a center designed to satisfy the basic shopping needs of area residents.

But Oakbrook Center soon began to grow. In the early 1970s Bonwit Teller arrived, followed in 1973 by Lord & Taylor. In 1981 Neiman Marcus and Saks Fifth Avenue moved in, with Nordstrom completing the department store picture in 1991.

Besides providing shops, restaurants and movie theaters, Oakbrook Center offers three annual entertainment events. The Annual Classic Car Show on Father's Day — a 31-year tradition — attracts families, history buffs and auto enthusiasts from around the world. Each July the center holds its Invitational Craft Exhibition. September brings the two-day Invitational Fine Art Exhibition. Each juried show has been held at Oakbrook for more than 35 years and attracts more than 100,000 visitors.

Holiday shopping is alive at Oakbrook Center, offering a winter wonderland for both children and adults. A spectacular display of over 150 evergreen trees draped in colorful lights, along with large holiday wreaths tied with red bows measuring over 6 feet, welcomes shoppers as they enter Oakbrook Center. The focal point of the holiday decorations, a 30-foot holiday tree dressed in over 7,000 gold stars and red ornaments, has become a holiday attraction for many visitors from neighboring states. White lights twinkle from store to store guiding shoppers through this magical center while children visit with Ol' Saint Nick at one of the many department stores.

The elegance and beauty of Oakbrook Center can also be found in numerous hotels and resorts that surround the center. The hotels — Renaissance Oak Brook, Hyatt Regency, Oak Brook Marriott, Drake and Hilton — offer shuttle service to and from the center. Golf courses are plentiful around Oakbrook Center, with the Oak Brook Hills Resort offering 18 holes of championship golf, and Cog Hill Golf and Country Club offering four courses, including Dubs Dread, where the PGA Western Open is annually held. Other top attractions include The Drury Lane Theater, Morton Arboretum, Oak Brook Polo Club, Cantigny Gardens and the First Division War Museum.

It's easy to find out what's happening at the center. In an up-to-date touch, Oakbrook has its own Internet site, providing a mall directory and information on store hours, directions and special events.

More than a shopping experience, a visit to Oakbrook Center is an adventure.

©1997 Don DuBroff

387

Old Orchard Center

Visitors to Old Orchard Center enjoy a unique and distinct shopping experience unlike any other in the Midwest. Shoppers are surrounded by artistic sculpture, lavish fountains, brick-paved walkways and award-winning landscape designs. Guests come to shop, relax and linger to enjoy the ambiance.

(Right and below)
Photo by
Steinkamp/Ballogg

Even when Old Orchard Center debuted in 1956 it had the distinction of being the prototype for the open shopping mall concept. It was developed in response to post-World War II suburban expansion by Phillip Klutznick, a pioneer in the shopping center world and founder of a predecessor company of the current owner, Urban Shopping Centers, Inc. (NYSE: URB). Klutznick chose a site with easy access to the new Edens Expressway, which had been constructed to serve suburban dwellers.

The architect's original design treated the shopping center as a community that included a series of brick walkways which had storefronts facing each other, instead of lining the parking lot. The center's unusual plan encouraged shoppers to stroll from store to store and promoted the perception of shopping as a social event. Marshall Field's was strategically placed in the center of the site, encompassed by a mix of stores.

The center's innovative approach to environmental planning turned shoppers into friends and quickly defined Old Orchard Center as the shopping center of choice for the North Shore. Beautiful and well constructed to begin with, the center was once again to be a prototype but this time for architectural transformation. Expansion, redevelopment and re-merchandising completely transformed the mall in September 1995. Nordstrom premiered at the newly renovated center, followed by Bloomingdale's, complementing the existing anchor stores Marshall Field's, Saks Fifth Avenue and Lord & Taylor.

European-inspired design accentuates Old Orchard Center's unique outdoor shopping environment, harmonizing with the center's classical, garden-like character. Lush landscaping, original sculptures, flowing fountains, colorful mosaics and interactive play areas for children embellish the center.

The center's award-winning landscaping has always been a point of pride. During the spring and summer months the selection of perennials that bloom in the center is changed several times throughout the season. Over 220,000 fresh flowers, including tulips, roses, annuals and chrysanthemums grace the walkways for shoppers. Additional amenities of Old Orchard Center are a 10-eatery food court, children's play areas, seven full-service restaurants and movie theaters.

Spring 2001 will mark another milestone year in the history of this prestigious center with a theater/restaurant expansion. A 40,000-foot addition will house a six-screen Loews Cineplex Movie Theater and two additional full-service restaurants, enhancing the center's entertainment options.

Old Orchard Center's distinguished shopping experience has attracted customers since 1956. Its dedication to customer satisfaction and to providing a superior product continues to pass the test of time.

Water Tower Place

Water Tower Place offers truly unique shopping, restaurants and entertainment opportunities. This 74-story, mixed-use complex features eight levels of retail, a luxury hotel, cinemas, restaurants, prime office and professional space, condominium residences and an

Water Tower Place is one of the most recognizable landmarks and tourist destinations in the city of Chicago.

underground parking facility. Located on North Michigan Avenue, Chicago's "Magnificent Mile," the center is within walking distance of some of Chicago's most popular museums, attractions and hotels.

Opened in 1975, Water Tower Place derives its name from the historic Water Tower just across the avenue — one of the few structures to survive the 1871 Chicago Fire. The center contains one of the first vertical shopping centers in the country and ranks among the most commercially and economically successful mixed-use properties in the United States. Water Tower Place was the recipient of the Urban Land Institute Award for Excellence for large-scale development in 1986. This international award is regarded as the most prestigious that can be achieved in the development industry.

Water Tower Place introduced many famous retailers to the Midwest market, becoming a catalyst for the retail boom on Michigan Avenue. Retailers making their debut to downtown Chicago at Water Tower Place include names like Abercrombie & Fitch, Crane & Co. Paper Makers, Lord & Taylor department store, The Walking Co., Papyrus, Foodlife and Warner Bros. Studio Store.

Visitors entering Water Tower Place from North Michigan Avenue encounter a lobby highlighted by abundant tropical plants and a cascading waterfall. Upon entering the center atrium they are greeted by a dramatic, eight-story glass elevator. In addition to Marshall Field & Company and Lord & Taylor, Water Tower Place offers more than 100 specialty shops, cinemas, several restaurants and the popular Foodlife eatery.

This unique retail site combines the luxurious Ritz-Carlton Hotel with 100,000 square feet of prime office and professional space, opulent condominium residences and a four-level parking facility to create a dynamic environment.

Water Tower Place brought the first Ritz-Carlton Hotel to the United States in 50 years. The hotel is consistently rated as one of the world's most luxurious. It features 431 rooms, suites and apartments on 22 floors and an elegant 12th-floor lobby, several restaurants, a ballroom, private function rooms and a full-service health club. Water Tower Place is one of the most recognizable landmarks and tourist destinations in the city of Chicago. Each year more than 20 million visitors enjoy the unique shopping, dining and entertainment options at the center. Urban Shopping Centers, Inc. (NYSE: URB), based in Chicago, is an owner of the property.

Ace Hardware

Ace has been "the place with the helpful hardware folks" since 1924. That's when founder Richard Hesse initially joined with other Chicago-area hardware dealers and established Ace Hardware as a buying group to purchase merchandise in bulk at the lowest possible cost and to cooperate in promotional efforts.

The cooperative concept — and Ace's pledge and commitment to be a retail support company providing independent retailers with programs and services — proved attractive and popular to existing and new dealers across the country. By the company's 75th anniversary in 1999, the company had retail sales topping $13 billion and a product selection of more than 60,000 items. Ace has branched from its Chicago roots to see its sign hanging on more than 5,100 stores in all 50 states and in more than 65 countries worldwide.

Ace incorporated in 1928 and the following year opened its first distribution center on West Ontario Street in the heart of Chicago to warehouse all the stores' products. This facility served retailer needs well for many years as Ace maintained a steady growth pace. In 1969 Ace launched an aggressive expansion program and opened its second distribution center (now called "retail support centers," or RSCs) in Benicia, California, soon followed by a third RSC in Atlanta. Today, Ace operates 18 RSCs, including two in Canada. The largest, located in Princeton,

Illinois, measures 1.1 million square feet. Nearly three-quarters of Ace's 5,100 corporate employees are involved with the retail support centers, which operate 362 days a year, 24 hours a day. The centers use the latest technology to hold down the cost of distribution and provide optimum levels of service and order fill accuracy to Ace retailers, allowing them in turn to best serve their customers.

Many of the products warehoused at the RSCs carry the Ace Brand name. Ace Brand products are available in every major hardware category, are tested to ensure quality and offer consumers considerable value. Another significant Ace "brand" is Ace Paint. Ace operates two Chicago-area paint-manufacturing facilities that produce up to 20 million gallons of paint annually.

Upon its 50th anniversary year in 1974, Ace moved its corporate headquarters to the western Chicago suburb of Oak Brook, Illinois. By then, Ace was a well-entrenched household name with entertainer Connie Stevens introducing a national advertising campaign featuring the slogan, "Ace is the place with the helpful hardware man." Since then, Ace has become "the place with the helpful hardware folks," a slogan, along with Ace's current spokesperson John Madden, that continues to be highly recognized by consumers.

Ace started its transition to a dealer-owned cooperative in 1974. The company accelerated its efforts in providing retailers with market research, personalized recommendations in product selection, advice on store layout, and similar leadership in virtually all areas of retail support. Today Ace provides retailers with a number of merchandising programs, such as Ace's Discovery Process, which optimizes the consumer's product choices and purchasing experience within core departments such as paint, electrical, plumbing, and lawn and garden. Ace's dealer-owned cooperative structure gives stores the freedom and flexibility to be independently owned and operated, while enjoying the buying power and market synergies that can be had by being a member of a group of 5,100 stores.

The company's growth and visibility have not been confined to its member stores, retail support centers and promotional campaigns. Ace's interests took a charitable direction in 1991, when it established the Ace Hardware Foundation. The Foundation supports two charities: natural disaster relief through the American Red Cross and Children's Miracle Network (CMN), an organization that annually benefits more than 12 million sick and injured children. Total Ace corporate donations through the Ace Hardware Foundation total more than $3.3 million each year.

One of the keys to Ace's success has been its exceptionally strong leadership. Today 11 dealer-owners and one director-at-large make up the company's board of directors and its management team consists of experienced, knowledgeable industry experts. Ace is consistently included on *Fortune* magazine's list of the 500 largest and most influential companies in the nation.

In the 21st century Ace is expanding its levels of store ownership beyond the dealer-owned cooperative format by operating corporate-owned stores. These outlets give

the company an opportunity to fine-tune retailing best practices for the benefit of all Ace stores.

Ace has never been more focused on providing consumers worldwide with helpful service, quality products and overall value. A new store prototype, called the solutions concept store, has been rolled out that caters to the do-it-yourselfer. It features a shopping environment unlike any other home improvement outlet and emphasizes convenience, selection, information, and, above all, fun. A customer-focused team, committed to effectively and efficiently providing solutions for customers' lifestyle needs, is at the core of the store's operations.

E-commerce is also playing a large role in Ace's future. Ace has partnered with OurHouse.com to give consumers the products and information they need to complete their home projects, and refers them to their nearby participating Ace store for additional services.

The stronger focus on project-oriented and lifestyle merchandising meshes with a heightened recognition of the growing market of female shoppers in the home improvement industry. With building trends in the United States showing no signs of slowing down and the international market continuing to produce newfound opportunities, Ace is well positioned to continue to be "the place" for millions of consumers worldwide throughout the 21st century — just as it has been for the past seven and a half decades.

Chicago Convention and Tourism Bureau

Since the 1800s Chicago has been known as a convention city. Although the city hosted the World Columbian Exposition in 1893, the first recorded Chicago convention took place decades earlier in 1847 when the U.S. River and Harbor Convention met to discuss the St. Lawrence River. By 1907 the city was beginning to establish itself as a world-class visitor destination.

Aware of Chicago's bright future as a convention and trade show capital, a local business committee was formed to attract more conventions and trade shows to the city. In 1943 the Chicago Convention and Visitors Bureau was founded to serve as the city's primary sales agent for meetings of all types and sizes. The Bureau merged with the Tourism Council of Greater Chicago in 1970 to form the Chicago Convention and Tourism Bureau, and in 1980, the Bureau was selected by the Metropolitan Fair and Exposition Authority (owners and managers of McCormick Place) as the principal sales agent for the convention facility.

Today, more than 150 years after the city hosted its first convention, Chicago is the country's premier convention and trade show destination. In 1998 alone, Chicago hosted more than 4.8 million people who attended over 34,000 conventions, trade shows and other group meetings. During that same year over $5.3 billion was spent by convention and trade show delegates while in Chicago.

There are a number of reasons for Chicago's tremendous success within the convention and trade show industry, including its superior facilities: McCormick Place and Navy Pier.

The McCormick Place Complex (which includes the North Building, the South Building and Lakeside Center) is located on Chicago's magnificent lakefront and is currently the largest exhibition and meeting facility in North America. With 2.2 million square feet of exhibit space and 114 meeting rooms, McCormick Place can handle any size convention, trade show or business meeting. The convention center also boasts the largest ballroom in Chicago and houses the 4,249-seat Arie Crown Theater.

Designed for speed and convenience, McCormick Place has a skilled work force that can move a convention or trade show in and out quickly and efficiently. As the convention center selected by more of the top 100 trade shows than any other, McCormick Place has a 24-hour marshalling yard that can handle up to 600 trailers. Other features include three complete business centers providing show managers, exhibitors and guests with all the essential services, including typing, copying, faxing and shipping. Catering experts can deliver meals to meeting rooms or to booths on the trade show floor. A new fiber optic network allows exhibitors to transmit high-speed data and images inside or outside the building, while meeting rooms with electronic key cards offer safety and security. In addition, the facility has more than 10,000 parking spaces.

Chicago's other major convention facility, Navy Pier (also on the shores of Lake Michigan), opened in 1995 to offer versatility to exhibitors and to provide an alternative location for small to midsized events. Navy Pier, which also is the state's most popular tourist destination, offers spectacular views of the skyline and has more than 170,000 square feet of exhibit space and 44,000 square feet of surrounding breakout rooms. Other features of the Pier include an array of full-service restaurants, exciting retail stores, a children's museum and parking for more than 1,800 cars. Trolley buses operate along the Pier, providing convention and trade show delegates with easy access to any location.

Getting to and from Chicago is another major factor contributing to the city's appeal as a convention and trade show destination. Chicago's two major airports, O'Hare International and Midway, welcome more than 80 million passengers each year, and domestic airfares to Chicago are

The South Building of the McCormick Place Complex, which opened in January 1997, offers 840,000 square feet of divisible exhibition space, which brings the entire facility's exhibit space to 2.2 million square feet — the largest convention center in North America.
Chicago Convention and Tourism Bureau

among the lowest to and from any city. O'Hare International also greets passengers in 17 languages, as the city is a center for international commerce.

In addition, Chicago is centrally located for group attendees driving on the nation's interstate highway system. Exhibitors come to Chicago knowing that nearly 14 million people live within a two-hour drive of Chicago and that 16 percent of the population of the United States is located within a 300-mile radius of the city. When meeting here, groups average greater attendance than they do in any other U.S. city.

Chicago has been hosting conventions for more than 150 years, but its thriving convention and trade show industry was jeopardized in 1967 when McCormick Place burned to the ground. However, extra effort and personalized attention by the staff of the Chicago Convention and Tourism Bureau helped retain almost every convention until a new McCormick Place was built four years later.

With a staff of sales and marketing specialists, the Chicago Convention and Tourism Bureau continues to offer personalized attention and services to businesses and other organizations that hold meetings in the city. Housing, transportation and preregistration can be arranged with just one telephone call to the bureau's One-Stop Chicago service, while information about restaurants, cultural events and entertainment is readily available. In addition, 1,400 members of the bureau provide products, services and expertise needed to assist groups with their meetings.

As part of One-Stop Chicago, the Chicago Convention and Tourism Bureau helps groups reserve lodging for their meetings. There are more than 78,000 hotel rooms in the city. Of these, about 28,000 rooms are located in Chicago's central business district. Another 5,500 rooms will be added during the next few years. Average room rates also are lower in Chicago than in other major cities such as New York, Boston, Los Angeles and Washington, D.C.

The Chicago Convention and Tourism Bureau offers additional special services to groups meeting in Chicago. MarketChicago provides promotional services that groups can use to sell and market their events, while public relations services can help build higher attendance. Through TeleChicago, telemarketers average an increase of 13.5 percent in attendance for conventions and other meetings. DataChicago gives group planners detailed demographics about current and potential clients and customers, while Client Request Forms can be used to forward all a group's needs to the appropriate vendors.

The Chicago Convention and Tourism Bureau also has an Ambassador Task Force with 40 members from the city's hospitality community who personally greet delegates attending conventions and trade shows. The Ambassadors take part in welcome receptions as part of their effort to combine small-town friendliness with big-city services. The task force augments Mayor Richard M. Daley's initiative, "Chicago: We're Glad You're Here," which is designed to welcome convention and trade show delegates to Chicago.

For more than 100 years, Chicago has maintained its position as the country's premier convention and trade show destination. Thanks to its state-of-the-art meeting facilities, its centralized location and the services provided by the Chicago Convention and Tourism Bureau, its future will continue to shine.

Located on Lake Michigan just east of Chicago's downtown, Navy Pier has been a Chicago landmark since it first opened in 1916. Since its renovation in 1995, Navy Pier has become one of the most frequently visited tourist attractions in Chicago and the home to hundreds of conventions and trade shows. *Chicago Convention and Tourism Bureau*

Located on the shore of Lake Michigan, Lakeside Center is a truly distinct meeting facility for midsized events. Outdoor seating next to a spectacular fountain and a walking path along the lake are located just outside the building's doors. *Chicago Convention and Tourism Bureau*

Cragin Industrial Supply

John and Sophie
Szafraniec, founders
of Cragin Hardware

In the early part of the 20th century, Chicago's northwest-side Cragin neighborhood grew as European immigrants searched for better economic opportunities in the States. In a migrant community that developed in Cragin, families worked together, worshipped together and tried to realize their dreams of prosperity. In this atmosphere of community and neighborhood pride, Polish immigrants Sophie and John Szafraniec arrived in the United States in 1916 and began to lay a foundation for their new life in America.

In 1927 the Szafraniecs had saved enough money to buy a small hardware store located on Chicago's Grand Avenue. The original name, "Cragin Hardware," remained because the Szafraniecs wanted to emphasize their store's strong neighborhood ties.

Now a fourth-generation family business, the Szafraniec's dream is thriving today as Cragin Industrial Supply, one of the most prominent Chicago-area businesses of its kind, with vendors and clients stretching up into Wisconsin and Canada.

From 1927 until the early 1940s, Cragin Hardware operated strictly as a hardware store. Its shelves were stocked with the usual fare — light bulbs, hammers and housewares. Because automobiles were sparse and public transportation not considered practical for everyday shopping, Cragin residents stayed in the neighborhood

and patronized local businesses. Because of this trend, the Szafraniecs' small business prospered. Residents indeed came to view Cragin Hardware as "your neighborhood hardware store," the store's original slogan.

Even the devastation of the Depression era did little to dampen the thriving business. People still needed the basics, and they frequented the store to acquire their necessary household goods, repair tools and other items.

As the region's only retailer of its kind, the Szafraniec family was able to keep afloat with a minimum of financial loss.

By this time, Sophie and John's son, Chester, was beginning the tradition of working in the family business. He was on hand to help his parents run the store as the neighborhood grew — and Cragin's customer demand grew along with it. To accommodate the growing business, a second storefront was opened on Armitage Avenue in the early 1940s, a few blocks away from the original Grand Avenue location. However, this new expansion proved to be a short-lived development. World War II draft notices arrived for son Chester Szafraniec and the other young men of the Cragin neighborhood, cutting short the future of the new storefront. In 1943 the Armitage Avenue Cragin Hardware location was shut down, never to reopen.

Tremendous growth and change characterized the Cragin business in the 1960s. In 1960 Chester Szafraniec and his wife, Florence, took over business operations for Chester's retired parents. Shortly thereafter, the area became less residential as an influx of industrial businesses sprung up in Cragin and the surrounding areas. Local machinists, tool and die operators and other of the area's industrial employees began patronizing Cragin Hardware in search of various

Original storefront on
Grand Avenue

supplies. Cragin Hardware saw an opportunity to enhance its profits by shifting its product line. In 1961 Cragin Hardware became Cragin Industrial Supply.

This change in product line proved to be a momentous decision for the Szafraniecs. Soon the business found itself attracting a clientele with a large demand for the industrial supplies it began to offer — cutting tools, specialty fasteners and hydraulic equipment, to name a few. Cragin Industrial Supply strove to serve its new industrial customers using the same personable approach that had served it so well with its neighborhood hardware customers.

With the new product focus and a desire to stock supplies so that they would be readily available to customers, more storage space became a necessity. In the early 1960s the company built a warehouse on Laramie Avenue, where it remains today. At this time, the retail store continued to be operated from the Grand Avenue location. (Today, the Laramie warehouse and retail store are attached.)

Then, during a booming business period in 1976, tragedy struck. A fire engulfed the Laramie Avenue warehouse, wiping out the merchandise. The Szafraniec family wasted no time in their efforts to rebuild. The Grand Avenue store stayed open while the difficult process of replacing stock and reconstructing the warehouse began. Within months, the warehouse was back in operation and Cragin Industrial Supply was meeting its ever-increasing customer command.

Just as Cragin Hardware was known as "your neighborhood hardware store," Cragin Industrial Supply quickly became an invaluable resource to its clients and vendors. As the Cragin Industrial Supply slogan proclaims: "If we don't have it, you don't need it."

The Szafraniecs believe that the key to their continued success is the firm belief in selling not only products, but relationships. As in the early days, Cragin Industrial Supply maintains its "small-business" attitude. Bob and John Szafraniec, sons of Chester and Florence, and Bob's wife Christine currently handle the daily business operations. Their goal is to stay committed to building customer loyalty and providing personal attention for each customer's needs. For example, many vendors and customers who call to place orders are known by name.

Bob and Christine's sons, Robert Jr. and Christopher John (CJ), continue the family tradition by working with their parents and grandparents to make Cragin Industrial Supply thrive for a fourth generation.

Cragin Industrial Supply stays competitive with an aggressive marketing campaign. In addition to a successful product catalog, a company Web site gives this "small neighborhood store" an edge in the ever-widening marketplace. Radio and television advertising, considered years ago to be unnecessary due to the nearly constant stream of local customers, is now a regular part of Cragin's marketing efforts.

Cragin Industrial Supply today has come a long way from "your neighborhood hardware store" of the 1920s-1940s, or even the Cragin Industrial Supply of the 1960s. Today Cragin has necessarily acquired some of the trappings of corporate life in order to compete with the larger retailers — holding regular business meetings, hiring outside salespeople and working with advertising firms. But the company never loses sight of the small-business strategy that has served it so well for so many decades.

It's a formula that has kept this family business successful for more than 70 years, and one that should guarantee Cragin Industrial Supply's future success. The Cragin conviction that "people like to do business with people" has proved to be not only a throwback to the company's small-business origins, but a belief that propels them forward today. In a world dominated by voice mail, e-mail and computer-generated phone calls, offering personal attention will always make a business stand apart from the competition.

Chester, Florence, Jack, Bob, Christine and Christopher Szafraniec in front of Cragin Industrial Supply, 1999

Hilton Chicago

During the 1920s Chicago experienced a time of growth and change. Movies, jazz and dancing were popular, and the Loop was a hub for business and entertainment. In step with the spirit of the city, the world's largest hotel at that time was built along hotel row on south Michigan Avenue. The Stevens Hotel was designed to last, and so it has as the Hilton Chicago.

The Stevens Hotel opened its doors in May 1927, occupying an entire block across from Grant Park. The dream of the founder, James W. Stevens, was to have a hotel that would offer the world's most extensive convention facilities for at least 50 years. The hotel has done better than that. Renamed the Conrad Hilton Hotel in 1951, the hotel underwent a $185 million remodeling project in 1984 before reopening as the Hilton Chicago. The Hilton has been an integral part of the history of Chicago during the past eight decades, serving presidents, royalty, diplomats, politicians, athletes, movie stars, business leaders, members of society and the general public.

Built at a cost of $30 million, the 28-story Stevens Hotel had 3,000 rooms and was done in French classical and rococo styles. The hotel also featured five sub-basements, a miniature 18-hole rooftop golf course, a hospital, a 1,200-seat theater with talking motion picture equipment, a five-lane bowling alley and a 27-seat barber shop. Modeled after the Palace of Versailles in France,

Exterior of the Hilton Chicago on S. Michigan

the spacious Grand Ballroom was given four steel trusses by architects to keep the room free of structural pillars. The Stevens Lounge was done in French architecture and furnishings, while the Grand Stair Hall contained frescos, bronze and crystal chandeliers and steps of imported Belgian Marble. The hotel was large in scope, grand in design and elegant in appearance.

America was at war in the early 1940s, and the U.S. Army took over the Stevens Hotel in 1942 for use as a barracks. Candidates for the Army Air Force's technical training command school were housed in the hotel for one year. The Grand Ballroom was turned into a mess hall during that time, and hotel rooms were used as offices. After the Army left, the hotel was purchased by the Avenue Hotel Corporation and reopened for guests in November 1943.

The 1940s were exciting years at the Stevens Hotel. The legendary African-American actor, singer and political activist, Paul Robeson, attended a banquet in his honor at the hotel in 1940, and he spoke and sang at a testimonial dinner in 1946. It was the era of big bands, and the Frankie Masters Orchestra played many engagements in the Boulevard Room at the Stevens. Numerous organizations held conventions and business meetings at the hotel. The 100th Anniversary of the Chicago Board of Trade was celebrated in the hotel in 1948, and WMAQ-TV introduced what was to become big-screen television theater at the hotel in 1949.

The Stevens Hotel was purchased in 1945 for $7.5 million by Conrad Hilton and became part of the country's first coast-to-coast hotel chain. While Hilton revitalized the Stevens through many structural renovations and additions, customer service remained the No. 1 priority. The Conrad Hilton continued the hotel's tradition of being a center for political, social and business activity. Ice skating shows were held in the Boulevard Room. More than 700 of Chicago's business, civic and social leaders were guests in the Grand Ballroom in 1954 for the first Consular Ball, a diplomatic event that continues today. Famous entertainers such as Nat King Cole, Ella Fitzgerald and Dean Martin sang for private parties at the hotel.

By 1944 when it hosted both the Democratic and Republican conventions, the Stevens Hotel was well established as the hub of political activity in Chicago. This tradition also continued at the Hilton. Thousands of members of the Cook County Democratic Party attended political functions and parties at the hotel in the post-World

War II years. As mayor from 1955 to 1976, Richard J. Daley was always prominent at these events, walking from ballroom to ballroom greeting fellow Democrats.

In early 1968 before 2,200 people in the Hilton's International Ballroom, Lyndon B. Johnson announced he would not be a candidate for a second term as president. The Democratic National Convention was held in Chicago in late August of that year, and delegates at the Hilton had a ringside view as antiwar protestors clashed with police and national guardsmen on Michigan Avenue outside the hotel. The Democratic National Convention returned to Chicago in 1996, and visiting delegates also stayed at the Hilton.

The Hilton has always been part of the sports and entertainment scene in Chicago. During a draft-day party at the hotel in 1984, the Chicago Bulls announced that they had acquired Michael Jordan. World Soccer Cup festivities were held at the hotel in 1995. The Chicago Bears held their first convention for fans at the Hilton in 1998, featuring players from the past and present. The Chicago Cubs and Chicago Blackhawks also have held annual functions at the hotel.

Offering a unique architectural location, the Hilton has been the filming site for a number of movies. The hotel appeared in *U.S. Marshals, The Fugitive, My Best Friend's Wedding, Home Alone II, Primal Fear* and *The Package.* In addition, television shows such as "Early Edition," and "ER" have been filmed at the Hilton.

Anticipating changes in Chicago's hotel industry has been a major factor in the Hilton's longevity. The first intensive rehabilitation program occurred in 1956 when

The Great Hall of the Hilton Chicago

two imperial suites were added to the 26th floor. These suites have served Queen Elizabeth II of England and every U.S president from Harry Truman to Bill Clinton. The number of rooms in the hotel was then reduced from 3,000 to 2,400 in 1960, which allowed for larger and more elaborate facilities.

The Hilton completed construction of its $2.5 million convention exhibition and banquet complex, Hilton Center, in 1962. This gave the hotel the world's largest ballroom — the International Ballroom — as well as the world's largest hotel and display area. The lobby of the hotel was restyled in 1968. To protect its interest in the nation's competitive convention market, the Hilton closed in 1984 and underwent the largest single hotel restoration-and-renovation project up to that time.

The Hilton today offers 1,544 guest rooms (including 55 suites), a full-service business center, fitness facilities and more than 234,000 square feet of meeting, banquet and exhibit space. The elegant Conrad Hilton suite is one of the specialty suites that have enabled the Hilton to continue its tradition as Chicago's premier meeting and convention hotel. With a 1,400-square-foot parlor, two king bedrooms and one twin bedroom, the suite can entertain 100 guests for stand-up receptions and sit-down dinners. Known for its beauty and history, the suite features tapestry, lush custom-made carpets, chandeliers, a library with a bar and billiard table, hardwood floors and three balconies overlooking the lake and city.

The Hilton combines historic luxury with modern conveniences and remains committed to servicing every guest who walks in the door.

Queen Elizabeth II arrives at the Conrad Hilton for an official visit to Chicago in 1959. She is accompanied by Mayor Richard Daley (*left*) and Conrad Hilton (*right*).

The Martin-Brower Company, LLC

In 1955, when The Martin-Brower Company received its first paper-products order from a new and unproven restaurant in Des Plaines, a Northwest Chicago suburb, Martin-Brower treated it like it was a valued, long-term customer.

Others were not too sure about the new restaurant and its basic concept. After all, who wants to buy hamburgers by the bag? History showed that billions and billions of hamburgers could be sold that way, especially from unique stores featuring Golden Arches.

Today, Martin-Brower, with headquarters in suburban Lombard, supplies paper products and much more to more than 5,700 McDonald's restaurants. North of the border, Martin-Brower of Canada, Ltd., offers coast-to-coast service to another 1,000 or so McDonald's units. To serve McDonald's outside of the United States and Canada, Martin-Brower and a partner formed a joint venture that supplies McDonald's restaurants in Brazil, Puerto Rico and Mexico. That business, combined with Martin-Brower's previously established Caribbean-Central America office at Pompano Beach, Florida, gives Martin-Brower claim to being McDonald's largest distributor in the world.

Clearly what has been good for McDonald's has been good for Martin-Brower. These days the company's 2,500 employees generate sales of more than $3.4 billion a year. The company sends home a message to those employees: You and the Martin-Brower Company are partners in service, quality and value.

Throughout its history the company has undergone numerous changes, including mergers and being acquired, but it was serving one big customer — McDonald's — and doing it very well, that shaped the company of the 21st century. Fully conscious of that fact, Martin-Brower management formulated a vision statement that should win an award for brevity: Martin-Brower will be the leader in providing value in

Martin-Brower truck, Brazil

supply chain logistics to the McDonald's family worldwide.

To that end, the company has developed a program called Good Management Principles (GMP) to equip and train all employees in ways to exceed customer needs and expectations. The program instills a commitment to teamwork, pride in workmanship and leadership development, combined with an in-depth understanding of McDonald's goals and needs, to empower Martin-Brower to go beyond the usual meaning of quality and valuable service to customers.

And as McDonald's expands into new markets at home and abroad and adds new restaurants, Martin-Brower will expand its GMP concepts to meet new needs.

In concrete terms, Martin-Brower is the exclusive distributor of frozen, refrigerated, dairy and dry foods, as well as paper products, to about 45 percent of all U.S. McDonald's restaurants. In addition, the company furnishes most operating and cleaning supplies, as well as promotional and premium items and toys from 15 full-service distribution centers, four Hubs scattered strategically around the country and 30 throughout the Americas.

That's quite a few giant steps from the business formed in 1934 by J.J. and E.M. Brower. They provided services to paper jobbers, whose main customers were grocery and department store chains. That partnership was dissolved in 1945 and the company began doing business as A.J. Brower, and a year later, as Brower Paper Company. The business grew, especially as a supplier to restaurants, retail stores and industrial accounts. Over the years several strategic mergers and acquisitions fueled company growth until 1964 when Martin-Brower Corporation was formed.

By this time the company was mostly a paper-products supplier to McDonald's and several other fast-food restaurant chains. Martin-Brower in 1967 became a publicly traded company in the over-the-counter marketplace.

The company operated independently until 1972, when the Clorox Company purchased it. During this period McDonald's was becoming more and more committed to the "total supply" concept, in which a single distributor supplied McDonald stores with frozen and dry foods as well as paper products. McDonald's awarded the first such program to Martin-Brower in the Baltimore area.

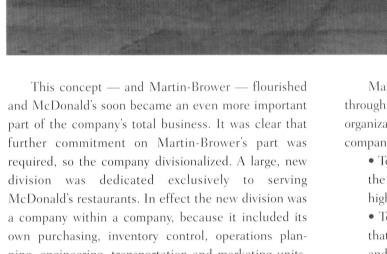

This concept — and Martin-Brower — flourished and McDonald's soon became an even more important part of the company's total business. It was clear that further commitment on Martin-Brower's part was required, so the company divisionalized. A large, new division was dedicated exclusively to serving McDonald's restaurants. In effect the new division was a company within a company, because it included its own purchasing, inventory control, operations planning, engineering, transportation and marketing units, all serving McDonald's. Another division served other fast-food restaurant chains, including Long John Silver's, Burger Chef, Red Barn, Baskin-Robbins, Brown's Chicken and others.

Then in 1979, Dalgety Limited of London, England, purchased Martin-Brower from Clorox Company. Martin-Brower maintained its autonomy as part of Dalgety, a large agribusiness company.

And then in 1998, Reyes Holdings, a group of six independently managed companies, purchased Martin-Brower from Dalgety Limited. Reyes Holdings is the major beer distributor in North America, with operations in Los Angeles; Washington, D.C.; Chicago; and Virginia. Beer distribution is Reyes Holdings' major business now, but the company is venturing into the food industry to diversify its businesses. Reyes Holdings found Martin-Brower's vast experience in supply-chain management a major attraction, of course, and those synergies are realized every day now as the organization makes further inroads into the food and food-distribution areas.

Martin-Brower has undergone a great deal of change through the years but has emerged from each a stronger organization. While the concepts are hardly new to the company, it has codified these guiding principles:

- To meet and exceed the needs and expectations of the McDonald's family, thereby being recognized as a high-quality distributor.
- To believe in people, to work to eliminate barriers that prevent people from taking pride in their work and to involve everyone.
- To fully develop each individual's potential through leadership, training, recognition and teamwork.
- To recognize that often problems are in the processes and not due to actions of particular individuals or unique circumstances.
- To continually improve all processes, with a focus on defect prevention rather than detection, recognizing incremental improvements are as welcome as innovative breakthroughs.
- To improve our business strategically through benchmarking and the incorporation of innovative ideas and technology.
- To make decisions combining the experience with accurate and timely data, using objective decision-making processes.

Few companies could hope to succeed with just one customer, but Martin-Brower has flourished in that situation. But of course it helps if that one customer is McDonald's, arguably the most recognized trademark in the world.

Nordstrom, Inc.

John W. Nordstrom standing in front of Wallin & Nordstrom shoe store on 2nd Avenue in Seattle

"On our opening day, our total sales amounted to twelve dollars and fifty cents. I will never forget that first day. I had never fitted a pair of shoes or sold anything in my life, but I was depending on Mr. Wallin's meager knowledge of shoe salesmanship to help me out. Well, this opening day, we had not had a customer by noon, so my partner went out for lunch. He had not been gone but a few minutes when our first customer, a woman, came in for a pair of shoes she had seen in the window. I was nervous and could not find the style she had picked out in our stock. I was just about ready to give up when I decided to try on the pair from the window, the only pair we had of that style. I'll never know if it was the right size, but the customer bought them anyway."

—John W. Nordstrom
The Immigrant in 1887

Nordstrom's founder, John W. Nordstrom, was not a natural-born shoe salesman. Yet he was insightful enough to realize the importance of giving the customer what she wanted. Little did he know that his unorthodox approach of appeasing that first customer would serve as an example for all future generations of Nordstrom employees — simply put, listen to the customer, and then do everything within your power to ensure they're satisfied when they leave your store.

Women being fitted for shoes in the Nordstrom store on 5th and Pike in Seattle

At the age of 16 John W. decided to leave his home in Sweden and journey to America. Barely able to speak a word of English, John W. moved across the United States holding various jobs until he read a newspaper headline that would change his life — "A Ton of Gold" had been found in Alaska, and the very next day he booked a passage from Seattle on a coal freighter bound for the Klondike. Within two years, he had accumulated $13,000 and returned to Washington State in search of a business to invest in. In 1901 Nordstrom teamed up with friend and shoe repair shop owner, Carl Wallin, to open Wallin & Nordstrom, a shoe store.

It was a real family business, with John W.'s children involved at early ages, operating throughout the Depression, world wars and the economic prosperity in the 50s; Nordstrom eventually grew to be the largest independent shoe retailer on the West Coast.

In 1963 Nordstrom purchased Best Apparel, a Seattle-based retailer, and became what Nordstrom is today: a fashion specialty retailer. About this time, the third generation of Nordstroms was becoming an important part of the management team. Like their fathers and grandfather before them, they had learned the business literally from the ground up, spending their childhood days stocking shoes and sweeping floors.

The second-generation brothers had all previously agreed to retire when each reached the age of 65. Beginning in 1968, the company was turned over to the family's third generation. These men continued to run the company with the same philosophy their grandfather and fathers had used before them.

In August 1971 Nordstrom made its first public offering and began trading on the Nasdaq, setting the

Nordstroms Shoes

is executive vice president, East Coast general manager; Blake Nordstrom is president of the Nordstrom Rack Group; Dan Nordstrom is CEO and president of Nordstrom.com; Erik Nordstrom is executive vice president, Northwest general manager; and Pete Nordstrom is executive vice president, director of full-line store merchandising strategy for children's, cosmetics, junior, lingerie, men's and women's active sportswear.

Nordstrom continues to expand its operations across the country. In 2000 the company will open new stores in Atlanta, Georgia; Frisco, Texas; Broomfield, Colorado; Boca Raton, Florida; Roseville, California; and on Michigan Avenue in downtown Chicago.

On September 22, 2000, Nordstrom Michigan Avenue will welcome its first customers through a dramatic, two-story lobby from Grand Avenue at Wabash Avenue and through the Michigan Avenue entrance of the North Bridge Project. The steel-framed building features a limestone-hued, pre-cast exterior accented with golden-granite trim and bronze store-front framing. Inside, custom floor and wall coverings and state-of-the-art lighting systems create unique merchandise environments throughout the store. Custom casework and fixtures support the focus of merchandise vignettes and boutiques that explain seasonal trends and fashion statements.

As the company nears its 100th anniversary, Nordstrom remains committed to its founding principles of providing customers with the best service, selection, quality and value.

Wallin & Nordstrom

stage for greater growth and expansion. In 1975 new stores were added in Alaska and the first Nordstrom Rack store was opened in Seattle as a clearance center for full-line store merchandise. Today there are Nordstrom Rack stores across the country offering clothing, shoes and accessories at 30 to 75 percent off regular retail prices.

In 1978 Nordstrom entered the highly competitive California market with the opening of its South Coast Plaza store in Orange County. And in 1988 Nordstrom opened its first East Coast store at Tysons Corner in McLean, Virginia. Other stores followed in the Northeast and were soon followed by the first store in the Chicago area in 1991 at Oakbrook Center. Thereafter, Nordstrom Old Orchard followed in 1994 and Nordstrom opened at Woodfield Shopping Center in 1995.

Also in 1995 the third generation of Nordstrom family members retired as co-chairmen after guiding the company through nearly three decades of successful expansion. Today the company is led by Chairman and CEO John Whitacre with group presidents leading the company's five business units: Nordstrom Full Line Stores, Nordstrom Rack, Nordstrom.com, Nordstrom Product Group, and Nordstrom fsb (credit division).

The tradition of family participation remains strong today with five members of the fourth generation assigned to key leadership positions in the company. Bill Nordstrom

Nordstrom Michigan Avenue — opening September 22, 2000

Salerno

"We have built an organization to produce not all the biscuits in the world, but the best. Only the finest products are good enough for you, our consumers."

These are the profound words of Salerno founder Fred G. Salerno and the philosophy of the company today.

Salerno has been producing fine-quality cookies and crackers since 1933. The Salerno Butter Cookie has become a Chicago legend. Over the years the cookies have retained their old-fashioned, melt-in-your-mouth flavor. Today's adults who, as children, slipped the cookies over their index fingers are likely to remember the advertising jingle:

"Mommy! What is it dear? I want a Salerno Butter Cookie.... You can lookie, lookie, lookie but you'll never find a cookie with a better butter batter than Salerno!"

A native of Italy, Mr. Salerno came to this country as a young boy of 12 in 1889. He secured a job as a pan greaser with the Sawyer Biscuit Company at age 17. He

Group Photo: Fred Salerno (seated front), George Salerno (back) and Alyce Salerno (far right) with family friend Jimmy Durante and (far left) his associate

Classic Salerno In-Store Display

passed through the various stages of apprenticeship to the position of baker and, in the classic American tradition, he worked his way up through all departments to become president of that company.

Fred Salerno was no ordinary man. He was a mechanical genius and at one point held 87 patents on bakery equipment. In 1913 the Salerno Machinery Company was founded to manufacture and sell bakery equipment worldwide. Among his major inventions was the first marshmallow-depositing machine. Marshmallow cookies were introduced in England and Ireland under the name "Salerno-Creams." Another Salerno invention — the sandwich-creme filling machine — was used by biscuit manufacturers nationwide.

In 1925 Fred Salerno and R. Lee Megowen (then Sawyer's Secretary-Treasurer) were instrumental in forming the United Biscuit Company (today the Keebler Company) and served as vice president and secretary-treasurer respectively of that company while maintaining their positions with Sawyer.

In 1933, in the midst of the darkest years of the Great Depression, Mr. Salerno and Mr. Megowen resigned from their positions with Sawyer and United and founded the Salerno-Megowen Biscuit Company. The venture was given little chance of succeeding and close friends tried to dissuade Mr. Salerno from risking his savings in such a poor economic climate. However, he persisted, and from the beginning the company was a success.

Fred Salerno, well known for his baking and production skills, quickly became recognized for his sales and marketing techniques as well. He never lost the "common touch." Turning his creative genius to packaging, he replaced the simple designs then in vogue with cartons

decorated in four or five colors. He introduced cellophane over-wraps for staple items — a first in the industry. He created a successful advertising schedule using radio, billboards and newspapers.

Under the guidance of Mr. Salerno, the Salerno salesmen became known as merchandising men. Mr. Salerno continually drove home the point that "The sale was never complete until the product was consumed in the home, to the satisfaction of the customer." Quality in-store service was stressed on the part of their merchandising men. Consequently a strong, dedicated and loyal sales team was developed and is still growing today.

While remaining a partner in the company, Mr. Megowen moved East in 1936, when he purchased another biscuit company. He spent most of his time in the East until his death in 1954.

Fred Salerno's son, George F. Salerno, joined his father's business as a young man. Following the same American tradition as his father, he worked his way through company ranks to become president in 1952. Fred Salerno remained involved in the company until his death in 1968.

Carrying on his father's philosophy of "Only the finest quality will do," George Salerno also had his father's mechanical talents and held patents in his own name. He was a perfectionist in production methods and at the same time extremely "people-oriented." His reputation in the food industry surpassed that of his greatly respected father. Sadly, George Salerno died suddenly in 1970 at the age of 61.

Fred Salerno's daughter, Alyce F. Salerno, was also active in the company throughout her life. She gained intimate knowledge of the baking business first hand and for several years served as Salerno's chairman of the board. Her keen intelligence and good judgement were invaluable in continuing and improving the company.

Throughout the 1970s Salerno maintained the home-made flavor of its products while introducing new items to its line. Each new Salerno product had to pass rigorous tests before being added to the line. Not only were the mixing and baking formulas very strict, but each and every ingredient was laboratory tested against rigid standards.

In the 1980s Salerno acquired the Mama's label from a family-owned South Side Chicago company. Mama's Oyster Crackers are among the best-selling oyster crackers in the country. The Mama's line of inexpensive, good-tasting products has become a nice complement to the Salerno line and has a fine following of its own.

In the late 1990s Salerno expanded its services to become a snack-distribution service as well as a producer of baked goods, distributing such items as Snyder's Pretzels and Chi Chi's Tortilla Chips.

Salerno baked goods are available in 29 states. The Butter Cookie is Salerno's hallmark and remains a Chicago favorite to this day. When consumers are asked what Salerno means to them, they typically answer, "home," "comfort," and "memories." Salerno still produces such classics as Ginger Snaps, Royal Grahams, Royal Stripes, Iced Oatmeal, Bonnie Shortbread, Almond Windmill, Coconut Bars, Graham Crackers, Saltines and Dainty Oysters. Salerno's holiday cookies, Santa's Favorites, in three flavors — Almond Crescent, Gingerbread and Anise Flavored — have become a family tradition in many households. Available for only three months each year, the Anise Flavored Santa's Favorites (previously known as Salerno Jingles), rank as the company's third-best selling cookie.

In 2000 Salerno was acquired by Parmalat, a baking and dairy company based in Colechio, Italy (a city near Parma). The new owner's plan is to grow the company and expand the Butter Cookie to other regions of the country.

Classic Salerno Butter Cookie advertisement

The connection with an Italian company takes Salerno back to its roots, when Fred Salerno — an Italian immigrant — created what would become Chicago's Original Butter Cookie. And in the great tradition of Fred G. Salerno, Parmalat is committed to the philosophy that "Only the finest quality will do."

From pan greaser to president, an American dream realized gave life to a Chicago legend and a family tradition. For this, much gratitude is offered to the Salerno and Megowen families.

Sara Lee Corporation

Most people know and love Sara Lee Corporation for its cheesecake and pound cake, but many don't know that the company's presence extends far beyond the dessert aisle of the local grocery store. Today, Sara Lee Corporation's broad array of high-quality, brand-name food, apparel and household products generates annual sales of more than $20 billion, with 40 percent of that revenue earned outside the United States. The company markets to consumers in more than 140 nations, and its 138,000 employees work in 40 different countries.

Chairman John H. Bryan (right) and President and CEO C. Steven McMillan (left)

Sara Lee's continuing goal is to build leadership brands in consumer packaged goods and, in the process, create long-term stockholder value. Currently, real growth in earnings per share averages 8 percent to 10 percent annually.

In addition to its well-known baked goods, the company's food brands include, among many others, *Hillshire Farm, Jimmy Dean* and *Ball Park* in the United States, *Aoste* in Europe and *Zwang* in Mexico.

The Branded Apparel business includes the *Hanes* and *Hanes Her Way* megabrand, *L'eggs* and *Champion*. *Coach* purses and other accessories also are part of the Sara Lee family, as are *Playtex, Bali, Wonderbra* and, in Europe, *Dim* intimate apparel.

Sara Lee Corporation has a rich heritage of philanthropy and sets aside at least 2 percent of pretax income annually for cash and product contributions to nonprofit organizations. The Greater Chicago Food Depository is one of many local organizations that benefit from the company's grants and food donations.

The company's coffee and tea products are highly ranked in Europe and include the *Douwe Egberts, Pickwick* and *Superior* brands. Also strong overseas are the company's household and body care products, which include the *Kiwi* and *Sanex* brands. Sara Lee's foodservice business includes PYA/Monarch, the fourth-largest full-line foodservice company in the United States.

Today, Sara Lee is the world's leading manufacturer and marketer of hosiery and shoe care products, the leading North American intimate apparel maker, the second-largest retail coffee company in Europe and the U.S. leader in retail frozen baked goods and retail packaged meats. This diverse range of goods all grew from a small company founded in 1939 by Canadian Nathan Cummings. The C.D. Kenny Company was a small, Baltimore-based distributor of wholesale sugar, coffee and tea, but expansion began almost immediately. The Kenny Company acquired Sprague, Warner & Company in 1942 and became Sprague Warner-Kenny Corporation, the largest grocery wholesaler in the United States. That same year, Cummings moved the company's headquarters to Chicago. By 1945 further acquisitions had created a diverse collection of products, and the company changed its name to Consolidated Grocers Corporation and later, in 1953, to Consolidated Foods. It wasn't until 1956 that Consolidated Foods acquired the Sara Lee Bakery.

In the 1960s the company focused on foreign investments and non-food enterprises. This period marked entries into the apparel and personal care industries, and the acquisition of Electrolux (no longer a Sara Lee brand) and the Fuller Brush Company brought Consolidated Foods into the direct sales business. By the time the chairman, John H. Bryan, was elected president and a director in 1974, Consolidated Foods was earning nearly two-thirds of its profits from non-food businesses. The board of directors renamed the company "Sara Lee Corporation" in 1985 to communicate the firm's consumer marketing orientation, as well as its commitment to high-quality, brand-name products.

Sara Lee is committed to building its brands. For example, the *Coach* brand had revenues of

$18 million, mostly in sales of fine handbags, in the early 1980s. After joining the Sara Lee family, *Coach* has grown to become a global business with revenues of $500 million, offering business cases, travel collections, watches and furniture, in addition to its prestigious handbags.

Developing new products that both anticipate and respond to consumer needs has always been a core strength of the corporation. Recent examples include the popular *Sara Lee Cheesecake Bites*; individually packaged *Ball Park Singles* hot dogs; *Hillshire Farm Lean & Hearty* lower-fat sausages; seamless, microfiber *Bali Barelythere* underwear; and sheerest-leg hosiery from *DKNY Skin* and *Hanes Silk Reflections Beyond Bare*.

Sara Lee Corporation's broad array of high-quality, brand-name food, apparel, household and body care products generates annual sales of more than $20 billion. Its leading brands include *Sara Lee, Kiwi, Jimmy Dean, Hanes* and *Douwe Egberts*.

Sara Lee's story also includes a rich heritage of philanthropy, commitment to the arts and involvement in the Chicago community. In 1981 the company established the Sara Lee Foundation to oversee all philanthropic activities. The company's policy is to set aside at least 2 percent of pretax income annually for cash and product contributions to nonprofit organizations. In addition to these tangible donations, the corporation strongly encourages staff volunteerism.

The arts receive 40 percent of Sara Lee's cash grant funds, and Chicago's museums, theaters, parks and music centers are frequent beneficiaries. Hunger is another major corporate concern. Sara Lee regularly funds more than 25 organizations working to wipe out hunger and maintains a longstanding relationship with Second Harvest, a charity that distributes grocery products to 200 food banks across the country, including the Greater Chicago Food Depository.

As the world's largest company named after a woman and with a customer base that is 85 percent female,

Sara Lee is committed to improving women's lives. The company earmarks 20 percent of Foundation donations for programs focused on women. Sara Lee's Women's Roundtable brings female leaders from a variety of disciplines together to discuss contemporary issues and the Sara Lee Classic, held annually in Nashville, Tennessee, showcases professional women golfers and has raised more than $500,000 for charity over the years.

The company has been recognized many times for its spirit of giving, and in 1998 U.S. President Bill Clinton awarded the National Medal of Arts to the company. This exceptional honor has been bestowed upon only six other corporations in the award's 25-year history. President Clinton cited, among other reasons, the company's "Millennium Gift" of 52 major art works from the renowned Sara Lee Collection to museums around the world. In presenting the medal to John Bryan, Clinton praised the corporation's tradition of funding the arts, proclaiming, "From the cakes they bake to the paintings they share, Sara Lee does, indeed, nourish the world."

Sheraton Chicago Hotel & Towers

If the three basics of real estate are location, location and location, the Sheraton Chicago Hotel & Towers has met them all. The hotel's position at the confluence of the Chicago River and Lake Michigan offers guests spectacular skyline views, sunset visions of elegant river bridges, starlit sights of the deep blue lake and relaxing moments on outdoor decks and walkways. And the hotel is also within walking distance of great shopping along Michigan Avenue's Magnificent Mile.

The Sheraton opened its doors in March 1992 with the goal of providing the finest convention and business accommodations in Chicago. The hotel may have been designed with that in mind, but lobby and guestroom decor project a relaxing, friendly atmosphere that contrasts delightfully with the hustle-bustle world of business. Imported marble, rich inlaid woods, palms and leather club chairs warm the interior. Carpets contribute to a soothing quiet.

At the reception desk guests are greeted by staff members trained specifically to assist the discriminating businessperson and conventioneer. A 24-hour guest-relations service and 24-hour room service add to the hotel's comfort.

A warm, inviting lobby welcomes guests at the Sheraton Chicago.

Guests occupy 1,204 elegant rooms equipped with in-room safes, coffee makers, mini-bars, voice mail, irons and ironing boards, complimentary newspapers, two-line phones and cable TV, Lodgenet movies and Nintendo video games. Forty-four "Corporate Club" rooms provide business travelers with oversized desks, Hewlett-Packard printers, fax machines and copiers.

The Towers — a hotel within a hotel — occupies the Sheraton's top three floors. Besides all the amenities available in the hotel's basic rooms, guests in Towers rooms enjoy plush bathrobes, and receive complimentary pressing and turn-down service. Three presidential suites offer the ultimate in luxury. All Towers guests are free to spend time in a bi-level lounge overlooking the Chicago skyline. The luxurious space provides complimentary continental breakfasts and late-afternoon hors d'oeuvres, as well as nightly cocktail service.

Business people and convention-goers are welcome to use the hotel's business center, which is equipped with fax machines, copiers, Internet access, computers and printers. Portable telephone rental and secretarial services are also available.

All meetings at the Sheraton Chicago benefit from the layout and design of the 34 breakout rooms. The two wood-paneled executive boardrooms provide the perfect setting for the exclusive meeting. All function space is situated above ground level, allowing generous amounts of natural light. Two sets of escalators eliminate unnecessary congestion. The River Exhibition hall — at 35,000 square feet — can be divided into two smaller exhibition halls. Each half is permanently equipped with electrical outlets, compressed air, gas and telephone connections. Seven loading docks with direct access to the exhibition hall ensure safe delivery of equipment. Separate convention registration areas provide efficient check-in.

The culinary staff includes world-renowned chefs who will coordinate anything from a deluxe banquet for 4,000 to an intimate breakfast for the members of a company board. Ice sculptures, gourmet sit-down dinners, cocktails and hors d'oeuvres — the excellent cuisine matches the perfect setting and ensures successful business entertaining.

For smaller business parties and general dining pleasure, five distinctly different restaurants and lounges offer a variety of food and atmosphere. Shula's Steak House — named after former Miami Dolphins Coach Don Shula — is "America's Steak House." Spectators — a riverfront sports bar with a club-like setting — features beverages, imported cigars, Chicago-style sandwiches and snacks. Waves, The Lobby Bar, is suitable for evening cocktails and networking.

For casual dining Riverside Café offers bistro-style cuisine for breakfast, lunch and dinner. The Esplanade Express — a seasonal light-dining outdoor café located

along the Chicago River — serves sandwiches, salads and desserts. For people attending shows in the exhibit hall it's the perfect place to stop for a snack.

The hotel ballroom is the building's focal point and — at 40,000 square feet — the largest hotel ballroom in the Midwest. Designed for both business and social events, it can be divided into five or 10 separate sections. The latest sound equipment, 22-foot ceilings, audio-taping capabilities and an adjacent kitchen support the ballroom.

A 13,000-square-foot Ballroom Promenade — designed for registration, morning and afternoon breaks and cocktail parties or receptions — complements the ballroom with windows overlooking the Chicago River. Enormous crystal chandeliers create an elegant atmosphere.

When the workweek ends, the hotel welcomes couples and families looking for relaxation and a base for exploring Chicago. Bed-and-breakfast and special occasion packages draw guests from around the Midwest. In summer they watch Fourth of July fireworks from the hotel's outdoor spaces. New Year's Eve packages include festivities for couples and families. A boat dock allows convenient boarding for water excursions on yachts such as Chicago's Odyssey.

The hotel's health club — frequented during the week by business people using free weights, fitness machines, treadmills, a dry sauna and the services of a masseuse to work away the tensions of busy days — turns into a family establishment on weekends. Kids swim in the indoor pool while parents take advantage of the sun deck. Those fond of outdoor fitness can enjoy nearby lakeside jogging and biking paths.

Business people and families alike benefit from the Sheraton's proximity to downtown Chicago. The hotel is within walking distance of the Magnificent Mile shopping area, the Art Institute, the Loop business district, restaurants, clubs, the Theatre District, the John Hancock Center and Symphony Center. Entertainment on the nearby and newly renovated Navy Pier includes a giant Ferris wheel, cruise boats, the Chicago Children's Museum, fine dining, ice skating, the Shakespeare Theatre and more.

The Sheraton is a winner in the hotel industry. Since it opened it has received 18 awards, including the "Pinnacle Award" from *Successful Meetings* magazine, the "Gold Key Award" from *Meetings & Conventions Magazine*, the "Award of Excellence" from *Corporate & Incentive Travel* and the "Four Diamond Award" from AAA Motor Club. The latter is based on reports from AAA's 60 full-time professional field inspectors. Only upscale establishments that provide their customers the utmost in service, atmosphere and quality — like the Sheraton Chicago Hotel & Towers — receive that rating.

Lake Michigan makes a glorious nighttime backdrop.

Windows in the Ballroom Promenade overlook the Chicago River.

Stanley Stawski Distributing Company

On Chicago's near northwest side, on a residential street, a four-story structure stands at the end of the block. "St. Stanislaus College" is carved into the third story's façade. On any given day, a number of semi trucks are lined up here, waiting for something. The truckers who have been here before know what they're picking up from this busy building with its single dock door. The newcomers will soon find out why they're waiting so long and what for. Some of the world's finest beers come in and out of this unassuming location, in and out by the container load.

In Chicago, the name "Stawski" is synonymous with excellent imported beers, wines and spirits from Central Europe. Stawski Distributing Company has been in business since 1959. At the time, Poland was still under Communist rule, so making connections and acquiring product was not as easy as picking up a phone. Distributing to 30 states, not a day goes by without the company receiving phone calls and e-mails requesting information on where to purchase its fine imported goods. Many people across the country who are of Polish descent have grown up with things like **Krupnik** Honey Liqueur or **Wisniowka** Cherry Cordial and they will call looking for these wonderful things they remember their parents and even their grandparents drinking. Many requests come from people who have traveled — to Poland for instance — and have tried **Okocim** or **Zywiec** beers or **Zubrowka** vodka (vodka flavored with Bison grass), and upon their return they want to know where to find these products in their own home state. Stawski's business extends beyond the obvious, handling products from Austria, Brazil, Bulgaria, Croatia, The Czech Republic, Germany, Hungary, India, Latvia, Lithuania, Romania, Russia, Slovakia, Slovenia, Turkey, Ukraine and Thailand.

Stawski's importing-and-distributing company is in the second-best place in the world, given that Chicago's Polish population is second only to Warsaw's. Like any other culture, the Poles enjoy having a part of their homeland with them always, and it's not only in their hearts but on their dinner tables. This perhaps explains the long lines at Polish delis all around the city: good breads, meats, cheeses and prepared meals, along with excellent beers, wines and spirits, are all here in Chicago for a population that demands them. Polish people like to eat, drink, dance, and dream big dreams, and thanks to Stanley Stawski's big dream, many ethnic wants in Chicago have been fulfilled.

Barfly, a local publication in Chicago, featured an article about Chicago distributors entitled "Where Have all the Distributors Gone?" The article speaks of "distributors only focus(ing) on the brands that have marketing dollars," how distributors today are "not in the business of building brands" and how many are leery of holding on to brands that can't sell 1,000 cases per month. As the article states, there's only a handful of distributors around today "that still have the vision of trying new brands and giving them a chance." Stawski Distributing is named as one of

Photo by Kerry Hilger

these companies. It is considered a "mom-and-pop" distributing company and that seems just fine with them. In product line, it's the difference between having four children or 400! All its products get special attention. Everyone within the company, from the sales team to the ultra-hardworking men in the warehouse, knows the beers, wines, and spirits inside and out, delivering quality products and service to their customers.

At a time of Federal Express and fax machines, Mr. Stawski still takes it upon himself to meet with his suppliers abroad, face to face. He's been doing it this way for 40 years and jet lag hasn't stopped him yet. It's thanks to his palate and his desire to handle only quality products that the company has the following: **Zywiec Beer** (the world's best-selling Polish beer) and the whole line of craft-brewed **Okocim Beer**(s) from Poland; **Golden Pheasant Beer** from Slovakia; **Radenska Mineral Water** from Slovenia; **Utenos Beer** from Lithuania; **Radegast** from the Czech Republic; **Obolon** from the Ukraine; and two fine lines of Polish spirits and liqueurs.

Seeking out products is only the half of it, for many wonderful products have come Stawski's way simply by word of mouth. Friends and acquaintances, and even the occasional traveler, will find a product from another country not currently available in the United States and approach Stawski with it, wanting eventually to be able to find it at their local neighborhood liquor store. Representatives from breweries and distilleries come to the warehouse with products they want the company to import, promote or handle. They come, having been told by associates in the industry that Stawski is *the* company to do business with. Suppliers and other importers want their goods to go to a company that understands and

appreciates them, and they need to know that special attention will be given to their quality products.

Started like many family businesses, with a good idea, borrowed money and not much space, Stanley Stawski Distributing Company was born. Mr. Stawski had had prior experience working as a liquor salesman for two other companies and had learned about import/export as well. The business was run out of the family garage on Kolmar Avenue. Friends were recruited to unload shipments and deliver product. Outgrowing the varied spaces the company occupied, it finally found room enough at the current location on Haddon. The space it currently resides in is its biggest one yet, but still the business grows and soon it may find itself moving yet again.

Stawski's building is still equipped with the original lockers, chalkboards and a full basketball court on the top floor (only sometimes visible when beer inventory is low). And visitors shouldn't be surprised upon visiting, for on any given day they may come across the wafting aroma of "Jajecznica" (scrambled eggs with bacon) coming from the kitchen upstairs where the warehouse men sometimes cook their "Drugie Danie" (second breakfast). Overall, clients are made to feel welcome at Stawski Distributing, with family and warm hearts, good humor and camaraderie, and above all, first-quality products and personal service.

Photo by Kerry Hilger

System Parking

With urban development altering the city landscape, parking is an essential commodity for the busy Chicago city-dweller.

Since 1920, System Parking has specialized in providing customers with tailored parking solutions. From expansive surface lots to modern, high-rise office buildings, System Parking has assisted its clients in profitably managing parking operations while keeping costs at a minimum. The company attributes its success to the talented individuals who tirelessly work to find new and innovative ways to meet customer expectations. System Parking has moved to the forefront of the parking industry by concentrating on increasing the bottom line without compromising service levels. For example, System Parking offers its customers a comprehensive amenities package that includes complimentary jump starts, lockout service, window cleaning and tire changing — just to name a few of the added extras.

Hotels are an essential part of System Parking's overall operations. As a result System Parking management strives to exceed hotel expectations by emphasizing the importance of making a favorable impression on all hotel guests. From the moment someone arrives at the hotel entrance, a friendly, courteous System attendant is there to assist with baggage and valet park the car. Some of System Parking's most notable hotel clients include the Drake, the Hyatt Regency, the Fairmont and the Swissotel.

Besides hotels, System Parking also extends its service philosophy to include valet operations for area hospitals as well. While the hospital experience is not often regarded as a fond memory, System valet attendants are ready to assist patients and families in whatever way they can. Major medical clients include Chicago's Rush Presbyterian-St. Luke's and suburban Arlington Heights Northwest Community Hospital.

In 1920 the concept of parking as a lucrative business was such a novel idea that Jack Hazard, the initial founder of System Parking, was able to expand his operations rapidly with virtually no competition to contend with. The new Louisville, Kentucky, company hired young Thomas P. Phillips as a parking attendant in 1953 and because of his exceptional efforts he was rewarded by being promoted to a supervisory position in Chicago. Over the years Phillips was promoted to division manager, regional manager, vice president and president of the company. During his tenure the company grew to 800 locations.

Phillips came out of retirement in 1994 to purchase controlling interest in System Parking's Illinois operations. He established the corporate headquarters in Chicago. Since then, this division of the company has experienced continued growth, expanding to 160 locations in 10 cities and some 900 employees.

These days System Parking promotes family values, both figuratively and literally. Others in the figurative "family" include Dennis P. Quinn, president, and an employee since 1968; Thomas J. Cullen, vice president and in-house counsel and minority shareholder, an employee since 1954; and Shevket Dardovski, division manager and director of operations-Chicago, an employee since 1975.

Most of these and other System Parking managers are Certified Parking Facility Managers, and many others are engaged in the rigorous home-study course sponsored by the National Parking Association. System Parking Inc. was one of the first parking operators in the country to participate in this accreditation program.

One of the first System Parking garages, c. 1930s

What accreditation means to clients is that services they contract for will be executed professionally and courteously. System Parking has developed and adheres to stringent employment practices, including screening and background checks on candidates and employees, reference checks, and both formal and on-the-job training.

Each client is a unique situation for System Parking, and is treated accordingly. For example, hospitals, office buildings and hotels are major customers for the company, but experience has proved that they must be treated differently. Office and residential buildings tend to have the same parkers over and over, while hospitals and hotels accommodate an ever-changing stream of parkers. The latter groups cannot be expected to know details posted weeks ago. Staffers are instructed and trained to use their parking expertise when catering to customer needs. In addition, hospitals and hotels might have large numbers of employees who work irregular hours at times, and this can create unusual demands on parking facilities, but System Parking employees are trained to cope with such problems.

Hotels have extraordinary short-term parking needs, too, such as during conventions and conferences. System Parking

arranges for such overflow needs and even runs shuttle services when appropriate.

Even in the most carefully operated facilities there is occasionally a claim for vehicle damage. System Parking has developed plans and policies for resolving such claims promptly and fairly with a high degree of motorist satisfaction.

Cleaning and maintenance responsibilities, which are scrupulously followed, are spelled out in detail in the company's arrangements with clients.

In the end, of course, it is how clients regard System Parking's services that leads to long-term, mutually satisfying relationships. In many instances, System Parking's staff in effect become the client's staff — going to work at the client's location daily, serving as the client's doormen and attending client staff meetings. Swissotel Chicago has been a long-term client of System Parking, and its general manager had this to say about the company:

"The relationship between the Swissotel Chicago and System Parking has always been very strong, and the employees of System Parking have always exhibited the utmost courtesy and professionalism with a strong dedication to our guests and our 'Swiss' standards of hospitality and service."

The impressive Rush-Presbyterian-St. Luke's Medical Center parking garage is System Parking's largest operation in Chicago.

One of the many surface lots operated by System Parking throughout the greater Chicagoland area

411

The Terlato Wine Group

For more than 40 years, the Terlato Wine Group (TWG) has dedicated itself to a simple philosophy — "place quality first." Adhering to this principle has helped TWG achieve a scope unmatched in the wine industry.

The Terlato Wine Group is a wholly owned family business: (seated) Anthony Terlato, CEO; son William (right), president, Paterno Imports; and son John (left), president, Pacific Wine & Spirits

TWG is involved in almost every aspect of the premium-wine business. Its ventures range from producing and importing wine to marketing, sales and distribution. Flagship companies include Paterno Imports, a full-service wine importer and marketing firm headquartered in Chicago; Rutherford Hill Winery, a world-class Napa Valley wine producer; and Pacific Wine & Spirits, a Chicago-based distributor. It is one of the few remaining family-owned wine businesses in an industry characterized by mergers, acquisitions and increasing globalization.

Guiding the company's growth is the Terlato family. At the helm, Anthony (Tony) Terlato, chairman and chief executive officer of the Terlato Wine Group, first discovered his passion for fine food and wine working in his father's retail wine store. In 1956 he joined his father-in-law, Anthony Paterno, at wine distributor Pacific Wine Company, where he quickly rose to the position of president. With his keen insight into the wine trade, Tony helped create Paterno Imports and positioned it along with Pacific as leading forces in the emerging premium wine market. Recognized as an industry leader "at the forefront of wine's evolution and revolution," by *Wine Spectator* magazine, Tony's unwavering commitment to quality and innovation guides all of the group's initiatives.

Directing the day-to-day activities of TWG's two primary firms are Tony's sons, William (Bill) and John. As president and chief operating officer of Paterno Imports, Bill oversees marketing activities for more than 30 elite brands and seeks out the wine world's rising stars to add to Paterno's portfolio. Pacific Wine & Spirits president John Terlato commands Chicago's leading distributor of premium wines.

Paterno Imports is responsible for more than 25 percent of premium imported wine sold in America, including: Santa Margherita, Frescobaldi, Mastroberardino and Lungarotti from Italy; M. Chapoutier, Ruinart and Domaine Laroche of France; Torres from Spain; and Boutari from Greece. Paterno also markets top California wines such as Rutherford Hill, Markham, Cuvaison, Rochioli, Freemark Abbey and Glass Mountain Quarry.

The international headquarters of the Terlato Wine Group is housed in Tangley Oaks, a 60-room, 26,000-square-foot estate that has earned a place on the National Register of Historic Places.

Santa Margherita is a prime example of Paterno's powerful brand-building and marketing organization. Some 20 years ago, Tony Terlato discovered Santa Margherita and introduced the Pinot Grigio varietal in the United States. Today this wine consistently ranks as America's most-requested imported wine and the most popular Italian wine in the *Wine & Spirits* "Annual Restaurant Poll."

Pacific Wine & Spirits has been the leading supplier of wine to restaurants in Illinois, a position the company has held for three decades. Pacific also dominates the retail market, supplying both independent retailers and chain stores with the market's top-selling Californian Cabernet Sauvignon and Sauvignon Blanc, as well as the No. 1 Australian and Italian wines. Pacific's quality proposition — shaped by its extensive portfolio, advanced training programs, high-level account service and disciplined account management — distinguish it as an industry model.

TWG's association with Rutherford Hill Winery, a pioneer in California Merlot, began through Pacific Wine & Spirits in the 1980s and grew to include Paterno Imports in the early 1990s. When the partnership that owned Rutherford Hill decided to sell in 1996, the Terlatos saw the opportunity to apply their love of wine, commitment to quality and best-practices knowledge of the industry to a wine of their own.

The Terlatos' mark on the winery was immediate. Working closely with their winemakers, Tony, Bill and John decided to eliminate 14,000 cases of wine from their first blend. This was done to ensure that the 1995 vintage of Rutherford Hill Napa Valley Merlot reflected the core quality philosophy of the family. The Terlatos also improved the sourcing of Rutherford Hill's grapes, adding to the blend more than 810 tons of reserve quality grapes harvested from some of the finest

vineyards in Napa Valley. With these innovations, and more than $10 million in capital improvements, the Terlatos have realized continuous quality enhancements with each new vintage.

The acquisition of the Rutherford Hill Winery strengthened TWG's position as a wine producer, adding to the wine production joint ventures they had already entered. These included Glass Mountain Quarry Wines with Markham Vineyards/Mercian Inc. in California and Entre Nous with the renowned French winemaker Michel Chapoutier in France. TWG continues to pioneer these innovative alliances, most recently forming an Australia-based partnership uniting Michel Chapoutier and Trevor Mast of Mount Langi Ghiran in Australia.

The Terlato family's sense of quality and attention to detail is also evident at Tangley Oaks, the corporate headquarters of both the Terlato Wine Group and Paterno Imports. Purchased in 1995, the Group launched a two-year preservation and restoration project of the 60-room, 26,000-square-foot estate and its interiors. Originally commissioned by meatpacking heir Philip D. Armour III in 1916, the Terlato family restoration earned the manor a place on the U.S. Department of the Interior's National Register of Historic Places. The restoration included furniture from the Armours' private collection which is now used in the corporate offices. Tangley Oaks is said to be one of the finest reproductions of Tudor Gothic manor homes in America.

The Terlato Wine Group's growth has been shaped by its commitment to quality and innovative spirit. With the third generation of leadership firmly in place, the industry's only vertically integrated, family-owned wine company is in a unique position to define and lead this dramatically changing market.

Santa Margherita is a prime example of Paterno Imports' disciplined brand management — and America's most requested imported wine.

A passion for wine and a commitment to quality inspired the Terlato family to purchase Rutherford Hill Winery.

The Signature Room at the 95th

It is not just the view of four states and beautiful blue water that distinguish The Signature Room, a 180-seat restaurant perched 1,000 lofty feet above Chicago's glittering Magnificent Mile. It is also the contemporary American fare, a stylish offering that satisfies with natural ingredients harvested from the surrounding heartland.

This is The Signature Room, a casual, upscale restaurant that graces the 95th floor of the John Hancock Center. This legendary Chicago skyscraper, affectionately called Big John, is noted as much for its innovative architecture as for its record-setting height.

It was in 1993 that The Infusion Management Group reinvented The Signature Room. The Infusion Management Group is a team of Chicago restaurateurs that includes co-owners Rick Roman and Nick Pyknis, along with Luigi Millacardi, vice president of operations, and other professionals. The partnership's name is a culinary nod to the art of imparting natural flavors from herbs and spices into sauces.

The lunch buffet, available Monday through Saturday, features a fine selection of seasonal salads, poultry and fish specialties, chef's soups and carving selections. The lunchtime à la carte menu includes appetizers, salads, sandwiches, main course specialties and desserts. Lunch is frequently available for extended hours during the holiday shopping season and major city events.

Each evening as the sun sets and the city redirects its pace, locals and visitors from around the world look to The Signature Room for an unforgettable dining experience. They begin with creative appetizers such as roasted portobello and plum tomato tart or asparagus and crabmeat strudel. Entrée choices include seared salmon filet with pineapple; cilantro and green onions in a red curry sauce; vanilla-scented duck breast with mushrooms and potato pancakes in an herb broth; vegetarian penne pasta with asparagus and sun-dried tomatoes; applewood smoked pork chop with bourbon-and-molasses barbecue sauce; roasted rack of lamb with Dijon mustard and herbs; sautéed chicken breast with wild mushrooms and black forbidden rice; grilled New York strip steak with roasted garlic; and other contemporary interpretations of classics. Dessert may be blueberry tart with crème anglaise or white chocolate and raspberry mousse bombe. The award-winning wine list offers global vintages with an accent on the wines of California vintners. In addition to providing a world-class dining experience, The Signature Room gives back to the community through its monthly four-course dinners. In its first seven years of running

this special program, The Infusion Management Group donated over $350,000 to local not-for-profit organizations.

Sunday brunch, with nearly 60 selections and live jazz, is a destination event at The Signature Room. The buffet feast offers health gourmet salads, fresh vegetables, smoked salmon and trout, lox and domestic caviars, alongside tempting omelet, pasta and carving stations. An array of pastries and freshly baked breads round out the choices. Young diners enjoy their own repast of pizza, macaroni and cheese, and other child-approved choices.

And then there is that signature view. To the east is Lake Michigan with its intriguing shipwrecks beneath the blue, and historic Navy Pier with its 150-foot Ferris wheel and musical carousel. Breathtaking cityscapes unfold to the north, west and south, treating diners to majestic views of Chicago's past, present and future landmarks. No wonder hardly an evening passes at The Signature Room without another gentlemen asking his love for her hand in marriage.

On May 6, 2000, The Infusion Management Group redefined the concept of banquet dining and entertaining with the grand opening of The Signature Room at Seven Bridges in west suburban Woodridge. The largest facility of its type in the area, this stunning, 35,000-square-foot venue features contemporary American cuisine, banquet halls, conference rooms and an outdoor garden terrace. It is set within the Seven Bridges complex, which offers a championship 18-hole golf course, IMAX theater, fitness center, ice arena, restaurants and a gracious landscape for civilized living, all within the I-88 corridor where an estimated 25 percent of Fortune 500 companies have offices.

The Signature Room adds the celebratory touch to Seven Bridges, and has quickly become the area's premier choice for weddings, private parties, corporate events and charity affairs. With the flexibility to accommodate parties from 50 to 1,100, it welcomes everyone and frees groups from having to travel downtown to accommodate their large-scale gala events.

Thoughtful amenities abound. Brides appreciate the private studios available for changing and relaxing during their weddings as well as the immaculate landscaping for photography and the miniature crystal lanterns that grace their guests' tables. Professionals who use the conference rooms value the advanced computer, audio and visual technologies. Groups that book the larger banquet halls — Sonoma, Columbia and Monterey — enjoy the way the acoustically superior, barrel-curved ceiling and customizable lighting enhance their occasions, whether they are business meetings or fashion shows.

Designed by award-winning architects Aumiller Youngquist, The Signature Room at Seven Bridges features distinctive blue-glass skywindows and a gently curved exterior that complements the site's winding roads. The interior is a rich stage set of neutral colors and natural materials such as mahogany woods, textured wall coverings and marble flooring.

The Signature Room at Seven Bridges serves restaurant-quality food in a banquet environment. Foods are ordered fresh for each occasion. The kitchen staff utilizes state-of-the-art equipment, such as a griddle that tilts sideways for effortless cleaning and a combination steam, convection and conventional oven that doubles as a plate warmer.

Event planners of all types enjoy creative menu options. Starters may include paté on brioche with grainy mustard or poached sea scallops with citron caviar. Entrées may include grilled beef tenderloin with a white truffle demi-glace, sautéed Atlantic salmon with ginger butter sauce or roasted lobster tail with butter sauce. Desserts range from poached pear in spiced Zinfandel syrup to Amaretto cheesecake with crème anglaise. A variety of bar packages are available to suit every taste and budget.

The Signature Room atop the John Hancock Building and The Signature Room at Seven Bridges are

already changing the way Chicago dines and celebrates. These are homegrown places, built on years of hometown experience. These are places where the wishes of patrons are surpassed, and the events are nothing short of grand.

Abt Electronics & Appliances

Original Abt store on Milwaukee Avenue, 1970

Since Jewel Abt gave $800 to her husband Dave to start a business in 1936, Abt Electronics & Appliances has become the place to shop for many Chicago-area residents.

Starting with three employees at a store in the Logan Square area of Chicago, Abt Electronics & Appliances has grown to more than 650 employees and now occupies 9 acres on Waukegan Road in Morton Grove. Third-generation family members work in the store, which has almost every brand-name, high-end electronics product and appliance on display in its showroom.

The original Chicago store was called Abt Radio and sold many smaller electronic products such as radios, vacuums, toasters, washers and ovens. Jewel Abt did all the bookkeeping. The family garage was used as a warehouse, and the store had a small service shop. After World War II Abt was one of the first stores in the area to sell televisions. By 1955 the family had a van for deliveries and a warehouse about one-half of a mile from the store. There were two vans by 1968, and the average delivery run was eight stops per day.

The Abt family opened a second store on a 1-acre site on Dempster Road in Niles in 1971. The new store had parking, a warehouse, an elevator and a lot more space. The original Chicago store closed permanently in 1977. The Niles store doubled to 24,000 square feet in 1986 but was bursting at the seams only four years later. The current Morton Grove store opened in December 1990, but a 43,000-square-foot addition had to be added in 1996 to keep up with business. By recent count, 46 trucks, 38 custom-install step vans and 46 service vans are making about 5,000 service calls and deliveries each week. Business is booming, and Abt is again in need of a larger facility.

With a history of continuous growth in what is a very competitive business in Chicago, Abt Electronics & Appliances gets 92 percent of its business from repeat and referred customers. Less than 1 percent of sales is budgeted for advertising. The company has never reduced its workforce, and employee turnover is minimal. The company philosophy of providing each customer with exceptional service has resulted in a large customer base of third- and fourth-generation shoppers.

Abt has withstood intense competition from large chain stores and survived the test of time by giving personal service, doing installations and repair work, maintaining competitive prices and meeting changing customer needs.

In 1998 the store opened a new mobile electronics division that has brought in younger customers. Also in 1998 Abt launched its Web site, which currently reaches out to 10,000 customers daily. It is one of three original Sony- and Panasonic-authorized e-commerce retailers.

A *Chicago Tribune* article from November 1996 states, "Abt's keys to success are the family's almost fanatical devotion to quality service and competitive pricing, its development of a higher-end niche, its in-the-trenches mode of management and its down-to-earth, low-key approach to selling and showroom décor." From Abt Electronics & Appliances' humble beginning, the business has grown over time into one of the largest single-store operations in the country.

Abt's current location, Morton Grove

Crate and Barrel

Just north of Chicago in Northbrook, Illinois, sits the headquarters of home furnishings giant Crate and Barrel, which has come a long way from its humble beginnings — a 1,700-square-foot store located in a converted elevator factory in the Old Town neighborhood. From a one-store, three-person operation, this Chicago-based retailer has become a leader in the retail home furnishings industry.

The company got its start when husband and wife Gordon and Carole Segal, both 23, were in their Chicago kitchen washing some classic Arzberg dishes they had purchased in Europe. Wondering why they couldn't find this kind of dinnerware in the city, they decided to open a store featuring unique and affordable contemporary housewares that were imported directly from small European workshops and factories. With $17,000 of capital, they opened their first store on Wells Street. It featured lumber on the walls and crates and barrels for displaying merchandise — hence the name Crate and Barrel. It was a success from the start, with sales of $90,00 the first year and twice that volume the following year. Today the company posts sales of more than $600 million and employs more than 4,000 people.

Much of Crate and Barrel's seasonal merchandise cannot be found in other stores, and its buying team travels throughout the world seeking merchandise that is distinctive, functional and affordable — everything from gourmet cookware and accessories to colorful linens, pillows, rugs and furniture. Items change with each season and are displayed in artistic arrangements using natural light and spotlighting to highlight each assortment of merchandise. A user-friendly gift registry enables brides and grooms-to-be to select merchandise that gift givers can then purchase at a store, by phone or on the Internet. Its distinctive catalog, first mailed out in 1967, continues to be sent to customers seasonally, eight times a year.

The sales staff at each Crate and Barrel store is an integral part of the retailer's success. They have expert product knowledge and are well-trained to handle customer needs in a professional manner. The company believes in developing its associates as merchants so they feel challenged in their jobs.

The best associates are chosen to head specific departments in the store — the kitchenware or glassware areas, for example — and are typically responsible not only for maintaining displays and keeping inventories, but for training fellow staff members in the nuances of their products.

In 1977 Crate and Barrel began selling and developing its furniture collection. Included in the stylish collection is a variety of fashionable sofas and upholstered chairs; dining room tables and chairs; bed frames, dressers, armoires, nightstands and entertainment centers; lamps and sconces; office furniture; and casual accessories. Most of Crate and Barrel's furniture is crafted in the United States, and a great deal of the product mix is developed by Crate and Barrel's design team.

The company continues to grow by adding stores throughout the United States — about four to six a year. Its flagship Michigan Avenue store opened in Chicago in 1990, and Crate and Barrel entered the New York market in 1995. CB2, a store with a younger attitude, opened in early 2000, selling housewares and some furniture and catering to a young, urban clientele.

Crate and Barrel has always made a strong charitable commitment to the communities in which it has stores by supporting AIDS-related causes, breast cancer research and educational institutions within the inner city. In addition, non-saleable merchandise is given to various establishments including SROs (single resident occupancies), shelters, preschools and Headstart programs.

Taking risks and anticipating trends enables Crate and Barrel to stay a step ahead in the marketplace. With its motto — stay humble and stay nervous — firmly in place, this stylish and contemporary retailer will continue to remain a leader in the retail housewares and furniture industry.

EthnicGrocer.com

Thanks to EthnicGrocer.com, ethnic communities and home cooks all over the United States can now shop for more than 10,000 high-quality imported foods and consumer products from around the world by logging on to the Internet.

This creative new company, headquartered in downtown Chicago, makes sure authentic groceries are delivered the next day for an international meal of, perhaps,

The colors.
The aromas.
The tastes.

tandoori chicken and puri (bread) from India; rice and pork dumplings from China; or albóndigas con chipotle from Latin America. And for the cook who wants to learn, EthnicGrocer.com features easy-to-follow recipes and fascinating information about culinary customs and products from many countries.

This cyber-entry into the $64 billion-a-year ethnic food and consumer product market was started while the

co-founders were still in business school. With solid business experience behind them, Subhash Bedi and Parry Singh were enrolled in Northwestern University's Kellogg School of Management. In a class on entrepreneurship, they presented the idea of Internet shopping centers for international foods, music, movies, housewares and other consumer products and received their first round of venture capital funding. By the time they graduated in June of 1999, they had nine employees, revenues from their first e-commerce site, and more than $1 million in the bank — proving that they had passed their course in entrepreneurship!

By October 1999 the company had launched four separate Web sites targeting the Indian, Hispanic and Chinese living in the United States, as well as "foodies." The company has its corporate eye on sales well over $2 billion in a couple years, from home cooks and large and emerging ethnic communities, and also restaurants and other foodservice operations. The company employs more than 200 — a cultural and ethnic microcosm of Chicago's diverse mix.

The four sites cater to different audiences. Designed for the cooking enthusiast, EthnicGrocer.com specializes in authentic foods imported from China, Italy, Mexico, France and other countries, plus recipes and cooking advice. The site also features foods and recipes from emerging cuisines, such as Korea and Vietnam.

The Indian Web site is a one-stop shop for authentic Indian foods and products. The site serves authentic Indian groceries, movies, crafts, and even bindis, and helps Indians living here celebrate their heritage and cultural traditions.

Another Web site offers one-stop shopping for all Latin American products. The selection comes from Mexico, the Caribbean, South and Central Americas, and includes everything from chiles to CDs. The product mix includes hundreds of music titles, books by Latin writers and a wide selection of traditional sweets, spices and food ingredients for authentic Hispanic cooking.

A fourth Web site offers a cultural "quick fix" for overseas Chinese — a place to buy foods, tea, books and music from their homeland. The site, the first e-commerce site in both English and Chinese, sources products directly from Greater China, tying its consumers to the rich customs and cultures of the country.

The variety of food products available on the four Web sites is staggering, which it must be for the company to attain its goal of being the premier global marketplace.

Harlan J. Berk, Ltd.

In business since 1964, located on North Clark Street in the heart of the financial and governmental district of the Loop in Chicago, Harlan J. Berk, Ltd. is the most unusual store in the city, possibly even the country. While the company primarily handles coins from 600 B.C. to the present, it also has an impressive antiquities department with primary emphasis on objects from ancient Europe and the Middle East. The cultures involved date from 6500 B.C. to 1300 A.D. and include Vinca, Sumeria, Assyria, Egypt, Greece, Rome, Byzantium and even the Vikings.

Harlan J. Berk, Ltd. also has an impressive inventory of historical autographs and documents, in addition to a book department that specializes in reference material related to the areas it deals in. The ancient coin department, one of the largest in existence, stocks over 5,000 fine Greek, Roman and Byzantine coins, plus over 25,000 lesser coins. A fully illustrated color catalog is issued six times a year, covering the areas of ancient coins and antiquities.

The U.S. coin department deals in everything from Colonial and early U.S. coins to the 50 state quarters. It also stocks all types of bullion coins, silver, gold and platinum from every major issuing country and the United States. In paper money it carries U.S. paper money from its inception in 1861 to the present, Confederate and Colonial currency as well as fractional currency that was issued by the Union during the Civil War. The world department not only handles paper money from the Ming Dynasty to the present, but also coins from 1500 to date from every country in the world that has issued them.

The extensive inventory is handled by a staff of 16 that includes seven senior experts — each with more than 25 years experience — who have at their disposal a 13,500-volume library that is available for public use in special research situations. The staff has won 16 literary awards, written five books and contributed to 35 more. They very actively write in periodicals and have produced over 400 articles since 1965. The store has a complete Web site that includes buy or bid sales, fixed-price items, regular auctions and articles written by the staff.

Though all of this is impressive, the experts and staff at Harlan J. Berk, Ltd. are friendly and always happy to see and speak with anyone interested in collecting. When you walk through the door of this establishment, you move with ease through the centuries, even the millennia. You can hold history in your hand and even take it home.

MVP.com

MVP.com is the premier source for outdoor and sporting goods merchandise, combining the insight of a specialty store with the breadth and depth of selection provided by a category killer. The Internet site offers consumers 50,000 unique stock keeping units plus advice from top athletes and product specialists who help customers select the best products and learn how to use them.

MVP.com was founded in October 1999, announced in December 1999 and launched in January 2000. John Elway, former Denver Broncos quarterback and 1999 Super Bowl MVP, serves as chairman of the company. John Costello — with more than 25 years of successful consumer marketing, information services and retailing experience — is president and CEO.

With financial backing from leading Silicon Valley firm Benchmark Capital and Los Angeles-based Freeman Spogli , MVP.com formed strategic partnerships that enabled the site to go to market quickly. Galyan's Trading Co., the Indianapolis-based athletic apparel and equipment retailer — had been searching for a dominant retail partner to build its online presence and became a partner in October 1999, providing fulfillment and land-based marketing and merchandising opportunities. In December MVP.com announced a four-year advertising alliance with CBS Corporation worth $85

million. In March 2000 MVP.com completed its acquisition of SportsLine.com's online domestic retail business, which features more than 90,000 items for sale. MVP.com now operates the Sportsline.com retail site.

Former Chicago Bulls basketball star Michael Jordan and hockey great Wayne Gretzky serve on MVP.com's board of directors and along with Elway form the nucleus of MVP.com's Athlete Advisory Board. Consumers can access a wealth of information from these elite athletes by using links to special "MVP Edge" pages on the site. MVP Edge is organized into four key areas:

"Buyer's Guides" provide consumers with detailed information on key features to consider when selecting gear and apparel. A glossary is also available to help with unfamiliar sports and outdoors terms.

"Checklists" identify required gear and apparel for specific activities to help MVP.com shoppers be prepared and properly equipped.

"Shopping Assistants" collect responses to specific questions from individual consumers, analyze the input and provide customized product recommendations that meet the consumer's needs.

"Instructional Videos" provide expert information on training and technique in a broad range of sports, for both beginners and advanced participants.

After navigating the site, consumers can make their purchase online or call MVP.com to speak with customer service representatives 24 hours a day, seven days a week. Product specialists also are available to provide advice on buying the right gear and getting the most out of it. Among those offering their expertise through this unique service are collegiate soccer players and marathon runners.

The site's unique combination of merchandise, insight and exceptional service enables MVP.com to provide an unparalleled consumer experience. Consumers find products that fit their needs and information to refine their training, enhance their performance and achieve their personal best in sports and outdoor activities. With this successful formula, MVP.com is poised to become the dominant online retailer of sporting goods and outdoor equipment and apparel.

MVP.com views Chicago — with its strong community of technical experts, its pro-tech civic environment and its great quality of life — as a uniquely attractive place to launch and run an Internet company.

Since 1873

Phillips Bros.
Insurance Agency Inc.

Phillips Bros. Insurance Agency Inc. is a landmark among Chicago businesses, having thrived for more than 127 years in the Loop as a trustworthy provider of commercial and personal insurance. Throughout four generations, this family-owned company has earned a renowned reputation and enjoyed numerous long-standing client relationships — many of which have lasted 100 years.

Today Phillips Bros. Insurance Agency Inc. represents the largest and most-distinguished insurance companies in the United States, including CNA, Travelers, CHUBB, the Fireman's Fund and Safeco. In addition, the agency continuously explores and meets the ever-changing insurance needs of its multitude of personal and business accounts. As a result, Phillips Bros. Agency offers a comprehensive line of innovative policies that satisfies both the personal and professional coverage needs of its clients.

Phillips Bros. Insurance Agency Inc. was founded in 1873 by Joseph Phillips, who was joined in 1890 by two of his sons, Sam and Abe. After the deaths of Joseph in 1900 and Sam in 1910, the agency continued to expand through the efforts of Abe and his brother Louis, who gave the agency its current name. Louis' expertise in administration and Abe's superior sales and marketing skills account for the phenomenon of Phillips Bros. Insurance Agency Inc. today. In fact many of Abe's original accounts continue to be serviced by the agency.

In 1946 Louis' son, Edward, joined the company. A graduate of the Wharton School of Finance at the University of Pennsylvania and an officer in the U.S. Army, Edward catapulted the agency to its current prominent status, expanded the scope of all insurance operations and incorporated the agency. By 1962 Phillips Bros. Insurance Agency Inc. was offering direct contractual agency/company arrangements. It was under Edward's leadership that the agency's premium volume escalated as many clients appreciated the integrity and expertise of the agency and its competitive pricing. The personal attention Edward dedicated to each client secured the agency's loyal clientele, and attracted many new clients. Rather than insuring merely a business or a building, Edward sought to provide peace of mind by insuring each client's life, family and commercial enterprises.

In 1975 Edward's son, Kevin, joined the family operation and worked closely with his father, observing his integrity and sincerity in helping his clients. Together the two solidified Phillips Bros. Insurance Agency Inc. as a modern, full-coverage provider that gives clients sophisticated, current coverage and promptly pays claims.

"When you get a handshake from a Phillips, then you've got a deal," says Kevin. "That's when insurance is at its best." As current president of the company, Kevin practices the high-quality service standards established by his father, who passed away in 1998. "My father is a legend in this industry," he says.

The integrity and competence put forth by the Phillips family have allowed Phillips Bros. Insurance Agency Inc. to excel and evolve into one of Chicago's leading insurance providers. The high degree of integrity established by Joseph Phillips more than a century ago has continued under Kevin's sophisticated leadership, as he guides the agency into the technological age of the 21st century.

Kevin E. Phillips, president of Phillips Bros. Insurance Agency Inc., provides Chicago residents and businesses with comprehensive insurance coverage using the high-quality service standards established by his great grandfather, Joseph, more than 127 years ago.
Photo by Brad Baskin

R.H. Love Galleries

The collections of historic American art found at R.H. Love Galleries Inc. are as refined and spirited as the man responsible for putting them there. Richard H. Love has been involved with art since the age of 9, when he won his first "Best of the Show" award in grade school. Today, Love, an avid painter himself, serves as an art historian, writer, curator and media personality.

R.H. Love Galleries Inc., housed in Chicago's Nickerson Mansion, contains fine artwork from America's Colonial to early modern periods.

R.H. Love Galleries is housed in the city's Nickerson Mansion, which has been called "The Marble Palace." This architectural landmark, built in 1883, provides a proper setting for the works displayed in the gallery, which range from Colonial to contemporary pieces.

Love's foray into the art world was fueled by an enriching education. He studied art through high school and took part in an independent studies program in Europe from 1961 to 1964 during a tour of duty with the U.S. Army. In 1966 Love opened his first art gallery in a former barber shop in Steger, Illinois. He received a bachelor of arts degree from the University of Illinois in 1968 with majors in studio art and art history. In 1972,

after receiving his master's degree from Northwestern University, Love resumed independent art studies in Europe, where he also exhibited his own art.

Love has conducted extensive historical research in the field of 19th century American painting. He is a renowned author of numerous scholarly publications, including *William Chadwick* (1978); *Cassatt: The Independent* (1980); *John Barber: The Artist, The Man* (1981); *Theodore Earl Butler: Emergence from Monet's Shadow* (1985); *Kenneth Noland: Major Works* (1986); and *Louis Ritman: From Chicago to Giverny* (1989).

Most recently, Love published a monumental scholarly monograph on Carl W. Peters (1897 - 1980) — the American Scene and regionalist painter from Rochester New York. *Carl W. Peters: American Scene Painter from Rochester to Rockport* is the most elaborate book ever published by the University of Rochester Press.

Love's profound interest in the arts has kept him active outside of the gallery. In the mid-1970s Love provided Chicago radio listeners with his "Comments on Fine Art" segments, broadcast on WEFM and WBBM. In 1976 Love developed the television program "R.H. Love on American Art" for Channel 26 in Chicago. This show would later become "American Art Forum," which brought together artists, critics and art scholars for discussion, and was nominated for three local Emmy awards.

Love's prominent role in the art community has allowed him several honors, including appointments by former Illinois Governor James Thompson. Several pieces of Love's work were also included in Governor Thompson's private collection at the State of Illinois Center in Chicago. Love's paintings were recently featured at the Mid-America Science Museum in Hot Springs, Arkansas. In addition, six of his paintings were purchased for the Bio-Medical Building on the Medical Science campus of the University of Arkansas at Little Rock.

Today R.H. Love Galleries serves as a vital asset to Chicago's art community. Through its exhibits and Love's continuing research in the field, R.H. Love Galleries showcases an aspect of American art that has been undiscovered by many.

Ragold

Ragold Inc. has roots in Germany but has grown well in the fertile soil of Chicago, the candy capital of the nation.

Velamints, the popular, low-calorie, peppermint breath mints, were welcomed by American consumers when they were offered in 1977. They had been a best seller in Germany, where they had been produced by Ragolds Susswaren Gmbh for many years. Initial U. S. supplies were produced in Germany, but in short order Ragold Inc. became a real Chicago company, with local production, promotion and consulting, says Rainer Schindler, chief operating officer.

"We considered a number of cities for our U. S. headquarters, but Chicago easily won out because of its good business climate, central location and long history as a candy producing center," he says. "All the resources we need for our business are here, and Chicago has always been a great transportation hub. This is the right place for us."

He is the son of Joerg Schindler, president of the German parent. The original company was established in 1887 at Karlsruhe, Germany. Karl Schindler, Joerg Schindler's father, took over active management of the German company in 1924. Joerg assumed the leadership position upon the death of his father in 1952. Another of Joerg's sons, Oliver Schindler, is managing director of sales and marketing for the German operation.

Even though it is a relatively young U. S. company, Ragold Inc. has long-term connections with Chicago support businesses. Almost from the start, it has relied on Cramer-Krasselt, a prominent Chicago ad agency, for marketing insight and leadership. Local custom manufacturing is done by the venerable F & F Foods on Chicago's West Side. Legal counsel is provided by Ross & Hardies, an old Chicago law firm. Ragold is also an active member in two American confectionery trade associations.

During the 1980s Ragold launched an innovative line that continues to grow in popularity. The Juicefuls line is unique — hard candies filled with real fruit juice and fortified with vitamins. Flavors include green apple, mandarin orange, peach, raspberry and cherry.

The company also fleshes out its product lines by forging alliances with other world candy makers when profitable opportunities present themselves. In 1998 Ragold teamed up with Chocolates Garoto S. A., a large Brazilian chocolate producer. Ragold has fashioned an elaborate broker network, and many of Garoto's 45 products go through that network into U. S. markets. Likewise, another arrangement with Pernigotti S. p. A. of Italy offers American chocoholics another source of high-quality goodies. Right at home, a licensing agreement with United Feature Syndicate Inc. gives Ragold the right to sell Dilbert

Joerg Schindler, president of Ragold's German parent company

Improve-mints and other candies bearing the likeness of America's most beloved comic strip computer geek.

Ragold Inc., while legally the U. S. subsidiary of a German parent, is free to independently pursue novel partnerships and arrangements to continually expand its offerings. Father and son Schindlers confer often, manage by consensus and crisscross the Atlantic as though they were commuting from Chicago's North Shore.

The senior Schindler, Joerg, is in fact a prominent figure in the U. S. candy industry, even though he lives and works in Germany. In 1998 he was inducted by the National Confectionery Sales Association into the Candy Hall of Fame — an honor rarely bestowed on non-Americans.

Chicagoland transportation, media and energy companies keep people, information and power circulating throughout the region.

NETWORKS

ComEd — A Unicom Company

The history of electric energy in northern Illinois since the late 1800s follows the priorities of Commonwealth Edison's top leaders, each of whom responded to the social and economic trends of their time.

John W. Rowe was named chairman, president and CEO of Unicom, parent company of ComEd, in 1998. Under his administration, Unicom Corporation and PECO Energy Company, the two largest nuclear utilities in the country, agreed to merge in 1999 with the goal of creating a merged new entity. Rowe said the merger provides the

John W. Rowe, chairman, president and CEO of Unicom Corporation

scale, scope, resources and base to build the leading energy delivery business and establish the company as a significant competitor in the newly emerging retail energy marketplace. The new holding company, Exelon, will create the nation's largest electric utility based on its 5 million customers.

Rowe's long-term vision is that the larger holding company will be able to provide a wide spectrum of energy-related services across the country and, in the process, gain the respect and admiration of consumers, competitors, regulators and investors. The goal is to create the most recognized and admired utility services company in the world. His priorities include improving service reliability and power quality. In addition to producing a stronger company with better service, the merger will hasten retail competition and attract investors.

Just as Rowe is directing Unicom into the more competitive energy marketplace of the 21st century, his predecessors after World War II helped guide ComEd into the age of nuclear energy. Willis Gale was elected chairman of ComEd in 1953, and his vision was to guide the company toward nuclear-generated electricity. In December of that year President Dwight Eisenhower announced his Atoms for Peace Plan, which encouraged peacetime use of atomic energy. Congress followed up with the Atomic Energy Act of 1954, allowing private industry to own and operate nuclear energy plants in cooperation with the federal government.

Under Gale's direction, ComEd submitted a proposal in 1955 to the Atomic Energy Commission for construction of a nuclear energy plant, and a permit was issued the following year for construction of the Dresden nuclear generating station. Dresden first produced nuclear-generated electricity in October 1959 and was recognized as the country's first large-reactor generating plant paid for by private industry. ComEd's nuclear program revolutionized energy production. The company had been using coal almost exclusively, and Gale recognized the benefits of diversifying into another fuel.

In the summer of 1955 ComEd became the first public utility to use a computer for computing and printing electricity bills. Demand for electricity grew at twice the rate of the economy between 1945 and 1965. Gale stepped down in 1961 and was replaced as chairman by Harris Ward, who furthered the company's development of nuclear energy. ComEd celebrated its 75th anniversary in 1962, and Ward noted that the average cost of residential electricity had dropped from 19.5 cents per kWh in the early days of the company to less than three cents.

Ward retired in 1973 and was succeeded by Thomas Ayers. Ayers made ComEd the country's foremost nuclear utility, but he also initiated a period of social activism in civil rights, equal opportunity employment and housing and social progress for the city. James J. O'Connor became chairman in 1980, continuing development of the nuclear program and maintaining the company's leadership in social issues. During his tenure ComEd celebrated its 100th anniversary in 1987 and subsequently became part of Unicom Corporation in Chicago. O'Connor also helped position the company for changing conditions in the electric utilities industry, which has been restructured in Illinois to promote more competition. In 1998 O'Connor retired after 34 years with ComEd.

"Just imagine what would happen to a community like Chicago if our service stopped." That's what Samuel L. Insull said in 1912 during Commonwealth Edison's 25th-anniversary celebration, and it still holds true today. He was the first of the ComEd chief executives who have had a vision of what electricity could do for northern Illinois. From the electric light to computers, electricity has changed everyone's living habits.

Thomas Edison developed the first practical incandescent light bulb in 1879 and introduced his system of better lighting through electricity to Chicago during the 1880s. The forerunner of ComEd, the Chicago Edison Company, was founded in 1887.

In 1892 Chicago Edison's board of directors elected Insull as president. Only 32, he had immigrated to America to work as Thomas Edison's business manager and personal secretary. Chicago Edison was merely one of more than 20 small electric lighting companies in the city, so Insull began an aggressive marketing plan to acquire the smaller electric lighting companies. He also

Samuel L. Insull, the first chairman of Commonwealth Edison

guided a merger in 1907 to form Commonwealth Edison, giving Chicago a unified energy supply for the first time.

Insull, who was a technical, financial and marketing genius, had a vision that electricity at that time could only be provided efficiently by a single supplier with large-scale, central-station service. He also saw the importance of mass consumption of energy for everyday living. The availability of electricity led to the invention of a number of labor-saving appliances, and in 1909 Insull opened the first store in Chicago devoted to selling electrical appliances. This helped achieve his goals of increasing the use of electricity and maintaining low average rates for customers. He simultaneously stressed the need to maintain an efficient company with adequate capacity to serve the growing number of customers for electricity.

Insull also developed the Lake County Experiment, which proved it was technically and economically possible to provide electric light and energy to rural and suburban areas. The wider use of electricity allowed more members of the middle class to move to the suburbs. The number of ComEd customers grew from 415,000 to 950,000 between 1919 and 1929. More than one-third of Chicago homes had electricity by World War I, but 10 years later almost 95 percent of the city's families were being supplied with central-station electric service.

During his 40 years as head of ComEd, Insull built the company from virtually nothing to one of the largest electrical utilities in the company. He promoted the idea of alternating current transmission grids so electricity could be transmitted over long distances. He also pioneered the financial structure for an electric business. The state of Illinois gradually came to accept Insull's idea of granting exclusive territorial rights to utility companies in exchange for the state's right to regulate service and establish price. Providing quality service at the lowest possible price has been the guiding philosophy of ComEd from Insull until today.

When the stock market crashed, Insull's companies served more than 4 million customers, stretched over 35 states and produced about one-eighth of all electricity and gas consumed in the United States. But utility stocks dropped steeply after the stock market crash, and Insull resigned from ComEd in 1932.

Although he had built his career in retail at Marshall Field & Company, James Simpson was chosen to succeed Insull as chairman of ComEd in 1932. The company was in a state of financial collapse at that point, and he stepped in to pick up the pieces from the complicated structure put together by Insull. During the next seven years, Simpson reduced the number of ComEd companies from 77 to 12.

Simpson initiated this corporate streamlining policy so that management could focus on the company's primary business of supplying electricity. He foresaw the need to substantially reduce ComEd's holdings and investment in non-utility companies. In addition, he achieved operating economies by reducing wages and stock dividends. Simpson's strategy of corporate streamlining in a period of tight budgets between 1933 and 1939 improved the financial condition of the company and enhanced its credit standing.

In 1934 electricity sales began to increase again. During the Depression of the 1930s, the average household in Chicago increased its consumption of electricity by 45 percent. In 1933 appliances consumed more than half of all electricity used in homes, surpassing energy demands for lighting for the first time.

Charles Freeman, an attorney, worked with Simpson on the legal and financial reform at ComEd, and he was chosen to run the company in 1939. He launched a three-year construction program in 1941 to meet the additional demand for energy from defense contractors during World War II. He also started a new $400 million construction program between 1948 and 1951 to meet the increased demand for energy after the war. During this period, ComEd began investigating the potential for generating electricity with atomic energy.

Because each of its chief executives had a vision of where to take the company, ComEd today provides electricity to 3.4 million customers in the northern one-fifth of Illinois. The company has 10 nuclear units in operation, and improving nuclear performance remains a priority. However, ongoing restructuring presents challenging times for electric utilities. The changing rules will continue to require a new vision.

The Old Edison Building, December 1937

Donlen Corporation

For more than 35 years Donlen Corporation has been in the business of supplying dependable and comprehensive fleet management services to companies nationwide. Today it remains one of the nation's largest fleet leasing and management companies, with subsidiaries in Canada and strategic alliances overseas.

This privately held company was founded in 1965 by Donald Rappeport and Leonard Vine and today remains a family-owned business. Since 1965 the company has grown to more than 170 employees with more than 70,000 vehicles under lease and management. Headquartered in Northbrook, Donlen offers a vast array of vehicle services that provides corporations a "one-stop" shop for all of their vehicle needs. Donlen's continued success over the past 3 1/2 decades can be attributed to an ongoing commitment to provide highly personalized customer service with award-winning technology.

The fleet management industry began to exhibit changes during the 1970s and early 1980s as lessors began offering several value-added services to attract new business. Companies not only wanted to provide vehicles for their drivers, they also needed a way to maintain these vehicles and manage operating costs. Donlen met this challenge by creating Donlen Fleet Management Services, a subsidiary that quickly became one of the fastest growing areas within the company, providing numerous services ranging from maintenance consultation to fuel management.

In 1986 Don's son, Gary, joined Donlen as vice president of sales after a successful career at Hewlett Packard. Combining his previous experience in both sales and technology, Gary Rappeport sought to bring Donlen to the forefront of the technological revolution. In 1997 Donlen became the first company in the fleet management industry to offer customers an Internet e-commerce site. The following year Microsoft awarded that application first-place honors in its "best e-commerce solution" category.

Today Donlen remains under the leadership of Gary Rappeport, who is the company's president and CEO. It is his conviction that the single most valuable benefit that his company can furnish customers is highly personalized and responsive customer service. "Though continually striving to move forward in technology, personal service and quality still remain our highest priorities," says Rappeport.

The same effort put forth by Donlen Corporation toward personalized customer service can also be witnessed by the company's community-service endeavors. Frequent blood drives are held at the company's headquarters along with collections for food and clothing drives. Donlen is also a longtime financial supporter of youth-oriented programs such as The Boys and Girls Clubs of America and Children's Oncology Services of Illinois, a nonprofit organization that supports One Step At A Time camps for children with cancer and leukemia. Says Rappeport, "The city of Chicago has been good to Donlen and we feel it is important to give back to Chicago whenever possible."

Gary Rappeport, CEO of Donlen Corporation

Donlen Corporation, based in Northbrook, is one of the nation's largest fleet leasing and management companies, offering highly personalized customer service with award-winning technology.

Tribune Company

Tribune Company has been an integral part of Chicago since 1847, with the founding of the *Chicago Tribune*. The newspaper's first issue consisted of 400 copies cranked off a hand press in a single rented room at LaSalle and Lake Streets. Today, Tribune is one of the nation's leading media companies, with operations in television and radio broadcasting, publishing and interactive ventures. Tribune has businesses in 23 major U.S. markets and reaches nearly 80 percent of U.S. households every day.

In its infancy, Tribune grew as the city developed. When the Great Chicago Fire raged through the city in October 1871, the wooden building housing the company was destroyed, as was most of the city. When all seemed lost, the *Chicago Tribune* printed a historic editorial, declaring: "Chicago Shall Rise Again." Its editor and part owner, Joseph Medill, was elected mayor for one term and led the city's reconstruction. He acquired full control of the newspaper in 1874 and directed the company until his death in 1899. Medill's two grandsons, Robert R. McCormick and Joseph Medill Patterson, took over leadership of the company in 1912.

A century of family leadership, starting with Medill, ended in 1955 with the death of Robert McCormick, president of Tribune and publisher of the *Chicago Tribune*. In 1983, Tribune went public.

Since its founding, Tribune has been an industry leader and driver of change. Tribune expanded into radio in 1924, with the launch of WGN Radio — the call letters reflecting the *Chicago Tribune's* slogan, "World's Greatest Newspaper." At the time, people believed radio would mean the death of newspapers; however, the *Chicago Tribune* and WGN Radio thrived individually. In 1925 a new headquarters, Tribune Tower, was built for the growing company. Its neo-Gothic design was chosen from 263 entries in a $100,000 international competition, and today, the Tower is designated a Chicago landmark.

Tribune moved into the infant television industry in 1948 when it established WGN-TV in Chicago, followed by WPIX-TV in New York. Tribune formally established its broadcasting company in 1981, and in the same year, acquired the Chicago Cubs major-league baseball team. Today, Tribune owns and operates 22 major-market television stations across the country, including national superstation WGN, and is the largest station group not owned by a network. WGN-TV and many Tribune stations are affiliates of the growing WB Television Network, in which Tribune holds a 25 percent equity stake. The company has been at the forefront of digital television.

Tribune also expanded its newspaper business dramatically, most recently through a merger with The Times Mirror Company in 2000. In addition to the

Completed in 1925, Tribune Tower is a Chicago landmark standing at the gateway to North Michigan Avenue, the Magnificent Mile.
Photo by Bob Fila

Chicago Tribune, the company publishes 10 market-leading newspapers, including the *Los Angeles Times*, *Newsday*, *The Baltimore Sun*, *The Orlando Sentinel* and the *Sun-Sentinel* of South Florida. In total, the papers have won 90 Pulitzer Prizes. Tribune is now the third-largest U.S. newspaper publisher in circulation. Tribune's syndication service, Tribune Media Services (TMS), was founded in 1933 and has grown into a major distributor of news and entertainment information that millions of people receive through newspapers and computers, including movie and television listings and cartoon strips. Many classic comic strips were created at TMS, including Annie, Dick Tracy and Brenda Starr.

Tribune has been a technological leader in the evolution of news and information. The company's innovations include the first remote radio broadcast, the first live television sporting event, and the use of instant replay and live aerial news coverage. The *Chicago Tribune* was a pioneer among newspapers in the use of color.

Tribune was the first media company to foresee the impact of information technology and the Internet on the daily lives of Americans. The *Chicago Tribune* became the first successful newspaper online when it debuted in 1992 on America Online. The substantial growth in Tribune's electronic businesses culminated in the creation of Tribune Interactive in 1999, bringing together the interactive functions of Tribune's newspapers, television stations and other Internet products and services. Tribune has a dynamic online presence locally and nationally, with a stake in national-brand classified advertising services. Over the years, Tribune has invested

aggressively to build a strong position in new media. Through Tribune Interactive, the company is accelerating efforts to develop online products and services that consumers value, 24 hours a day.

Tribune works hard, not only to bring the news, information and entertainment that people want, but to ensure the vitality of the communities where it does business. Employees generously donate their time, talent and money to help improve people's lives, ranging from volunteering in family shelters to tutoring youngsters to organizing recovery efforts after natural disasters.

Most Tribune business units participate in the communities program of the Robert R. McCormick Tribune Foundation. Money raised through community activities is combined with matching dollars from the foundation, enabling Tribune's businesses to significantly increase their local giving. In 1999 charitable funds sponsored by Tribune businesses and supported by the foundation awarded grants totaling more than $41 million. Monies typically go to nonprofit organizations dedicated to such causes as children, homelessness, hunger and health care. The company also is a strong supporter of the United Way/Crusade of Mercy.

With its strong position in major U.S. markets and talented employees committed to serving customers, Tribune is well positioned to grow and continue as a leader of innovation and change. And as a world-class city for business and a growing center for technology, Chicago is a great home base for Tribune, just as it has been for more than 150 years.

Chicago Tribune columnists and writers often lend their expertise to CLTV News, WGN-TV and Radio and Tribune's online products. Photo by Glenn Kaupert

Tribune's print and online products are the leading source of news and information in Chicago and other major markets.

Lawyers, architects, doctors, engineers, photographers, advertising and other professionals provide essential services to the Chicago area.

PROFESSIONAL SERVICES

Bartlit Beck Herman Palenchar & Scott

It is fitting that the law offices of Bartlit Beck Herman Palenchar & Scott are housed in Courthouse Place, the historic, Romanesque-style landmark that served as the Cook County Criminal Courts building for 35 years. The firm, which has been ranked one of the top 10 firms in the United States by *International Commercial Litigation* after only six years in business, is poised to become a part of Chicago law history itself.

Within the same building in which Clarence Darrow defended Leopold and Loeb and the Black Sox scandal unfolded, the partners of Bartlit Beck Herman Palenchar & Scott have established a law firm that operates unlike most others. From the firm's billing methods, use of technology in the courtroom and structure of the business to the office's regulation-height basketball hoop and playing floor (complete with 3-point line), there is nothing conventional about Bartlit Beck Herman Palenchar & Scott, and that is intentional.

The firm's founding partners — Fred H. Bartlit Jr., Philip S. Beck, Sidney (Skip) N. Herman, James L. Palenchar, Donald E. Scott and Mark E. Ferguson — and 12 other attorneys left the 400-lawyer firm of Kirkland & Ellis in 1993 to create an intimate and energetic work setting that was free from the slow-moving and committee-laden practices of larger firms. They wanted to practice law in a way they felt was more efficient and cost-effective for their clients, and which would contribute to more courtroom victories. "I felt the practice of law should be one of the most satisfying ways to spend your life — chances to work with very small groups of very talented people," says Bartlit. "But for many, it was turning into a miserable existence. Most lawyers are simply high-paid serfs; cogs in timekeeping machines with no training, leadership, mentoring or feedback."

The decision to start Bartlit Beck Herman Palenchar & Scott with a clean slate and fresh approach was not motivated by the desire for money or prestige. The founding partners had enjoyed lengthy and prosperous careers with Kirkland & Ellis. Bartlit, for example, had spent 33 years there, and was 61 when he left. Instead, the new firm was an opportunity to put into place the disciplines, practices and work conditions under which the partners felt they performed at their best. "Working together in small teams… we usually set up tables in a big room, and all worked in that one open space, amidst the din of other conversations and debates, copiers and printers whirring and other distractions," says Ferguson, who practiced at Kirkland & Ellis for 10 years. "We fed off one another and did things that we never would have been able to do from the solitude of our individual quiet offices."

To create an energetic and creative work environment, the partners of Bartlit Beck Herman Palenchar & Scott designed their offices to include a "Forum" — an open work area with movable desks where the lawyers can shoot baskets under 19-foot ceilings and brainstorm on clients' cases. "I'm not the kind of person who gets ideas sitting by myself," says Bartlit.

In addition to creating a functional workplace, the partners instilled a set of practices that would ensure Bartlit Beck Herman Palenchar & Scott would not fall into the pattern of the large firms that previously held them back. These practices would also allow for greater success with clients.

First, the partners agreed that the firm's roster would never grow into hundreds of lawyers; today, the firm employs 38. By keeping the firm small, the partners turn away a large number of potential clients. However, Bartlit says, by staying small, the firm is able to assemble a crack team of lawyers that puts forth 100 percent for its clients on each case. Bartlit says managing partner Skip Herman is able to assemble a team of lawyers with varied skills

Bartlit Beck partners (Back, left to right) Philip S. Beck, Sidney (Skip) N. Herman, Donald E. Scott. (Front) Fred H. Bartlit Jr.

The office's "Forum" allows lawyers to shoot baskets under 19-foot ceilings and brainstorm on clients' cases.

that mesh and complement each other. "Skip knows the strengths and weaknesses of everybody," says Bartlit. "Everybody does what they're best at. As our basketball court reminds us, forwards play forward; guards play guard. Skip is our Phil Jackson who puts it all together."

Another vital practice for the firm is its billing method — one that is based on expertise, experience and results rather than traditional hourly billing. Clients pay a flat fee to the firm for its services, and a bonus is paid for a courtroom victory. Bartlit says this result-based billing ensures that the legwork and research for each case is done by experienced lawyers, not inexperienced associates. The founding partners of Bartlit Beck Herman Palenchar & Scott are not ones to rest on their laurels. They participate in their cases at every level, from reviewing documents and interviewing witnesses to writing closing arguments. As Herman puts it, if he is unable to assemble a team of lawyers he believes can get a job done, the founders will do the job themselves.

This non-competitive hierarchy allows for a unique work environment that motivates all employees to work together and creates mutual respect. "There is a desire and a motivation to work together," says one employee. "From the mailroom up to the top, this place operates as a team."

A third practice of the firm is the extensive use of technology in the courtroom. Bartlit, who has only become computer savvy in the past 10 years, says the firm's non-hourly billing structure creates incentives for extensive use of technology, which provides experienced

lawyers with an efficient tool to research and prepare for cases. Larger firms, however, he says, have no incentive to embrace technology since it cuts down on the number of hours spent on a case. "Seventy percent of what hourly lawyers spend their billing time for, computers can do faster and better," says Bartlit. Co-founder Beck agrees. "Not only do computers help us work faster, they also help us work better. We have seen tremendous improvements in the quality of work as we have become more computer proficient."

Through specially tailored computer programs and digital presentations, Bartlit and his fellow partners provide jurors a clear view into their courtroom argument. Past jurors have cited the computer presentations as effective, stimulating and helpful in understanding a case. In addition, the Fred Bartlit Center for Trial Strategy has been established at Northwestern University School of Law to provide a consistent, national focus on increasing both quality and efficiency in litigation.

The strides taken by Bartlit Beck Herman Palenchar & Scott to excel in the law profession have paid off considerably. *The National Law Journal* has labeled the firm "the nation's hottest defense boutique, with a roster of litigation stars; the attorneys at Bartlit Beck try cases all over the country, often of the bet-your-company variety, with an unparalleled record of success."

Through mid-1999, the six founding partners have a combined trial record of 85-8-1 and try cases throughout the United States in diverse areas such as antitrust, securities, product liability and patent infringement, among others. In their short history they have racked up more top defense verdicts (as selected by *The National Law Journal*) than any firm of any size in the country. Receiving nationwide recognition and being in such high demand is something usually enjoyed by firms that have been established for more than 100 years. But Bartlit Beck Herman Palenchar & Scott has reached that level in under 10.

Bartlit points out that his firm is unique in that most of its litigation is outside Chicago. Clients located all over the world are selecting his firm for trials outside Chicago solely on merit, quality and experience. "They are not selecting us because we are the home firm or know the judges, but solely because they are convinced we are the best firm in the U.S."

Leo Burnett Worldwide

Leo Burnett Worldwide is responsible for some of the world's most memorable and influential merchandising icons.

From a headquarters building that bears its name in Chicago's North Loop, Leo Burnett Worldwide pursues the business of building some of the world's most valuable brands, including McDonald's, Coca-Cola, Walt Disney, Marlboro, Kellogg, Tampax and Nintendo.

The landmark campaigns created here have made Chicago home to some of the world's most memorable and influential advertising icons. Among the more historical are The Pillsbury Doughboy, Tony the Tiger, the Jolly Green Giant and the Marlboro Cowboy. And more recently it has produced brand-building campaigns for Altoids Curiously Strong Mints, Heinz Ketchup, Hallmark, Coca-Cola, Kraft, Procter & Gamble, Toys "R" Us and art.com, to name a few. It accomplishes its trade by adhering to a simple philosophy: turn consumers into

passionate brand believers by creating meaningful connections between people and the products and services they buy.

Leo Burnett Worldwide is a subsidiary of B|Com3 Group, Inc., a marketing communications holding company formed with the merger of The Leo Group and The MacManus Group, based in New York. Tokyo-based Dentsu Inc., the largest single agency brand in the world, holds a significant minority interest in the combined entity. Today, the combined organization, which is headquartered in Chicago, generates more than $2 billion in annual revenues from more than 500 operating units in 90 countries. It employs 17,500 people, with more than 2,500 of those employed in Chicago.

In spite of its global successes and presence, Leo Burnett Worldwide remains rooted in the city in which it was founded. While the hub of the advertising industry is located on New York's Madison Avenue, Leo Burnett Worldwide is housed in the Leo Burnett Building, which was erected along the Chicago River in 1989. Today the building also serves as a fitting monument to the man who helped shape the advertising industry.

A BOWL FULL OF APPLES

Leo Burnett was a man of many words, well chosen. His words first inspired his clients, then his agency, then generations of professionals. In perhaps his most famous speech, 1967's "When to Take My Name Off the Door," Burnett outlined to his employees a series of conditions under which he would demand that his name be taken off the company doors. That time was "When you lose your passion for thoroughness...your hatred of loose ends...When you stop rededicating yourselves every day to the idea that better advertising is what the Leo Burnett Company is all about...When you start believing that, in the interest of efficiency, a creative spirit and the urge to create can be delegated and administered and forget they can only be nurtured, stimulated and inspired." The speech was captured on video and is frequently replayed to remind Burnett employees what they have to do and what they have to avoid.

Today, Burnett's words ring true throughout the halls of Leo Burnett Worldwide. The agency embraces each new client as though it were its only account. "Leo Burnett has never been about size for the sake of being big," says Walter Petersen, senior vice president of corporate affairs worldwide. "It is about building leadership brands by creating emotional connections that turn buyers into brand believers."

Leo Burnett first set out to make that connection in July 1935. In the midst of the Great Depression, Burnett drew eight other seasoned industry professionals from their jobs to start the Leo Burnett Company. The company set up temporary shop in a suite at Chicago's Palmer House Hotel. The makeshift office was composed of four desks, two typewriters and a drawing board, along with three clients — Real Silk Hosiery, Hoover and the Minnesota Valley Canning Company (today known as Green Giant, and still a client).

On Aug. 5, 1935, the Leo Burnett Company officially opened for business in the London Guarantee Building on Michigan Avenue. One of the company's early trademarks was introduced that day when a bowl of apples was set out on the receptionist's desk. The apples were meant as a welcoming gesture to visitors and potential clients. When word of the agency's opening got around, one newspaper columnist wrote that it wouldn't be long before Burnett was selling the apples instead of giving them away.

But that cynicism only propelled Burnett and his associates to work harder. For its logo, the company decided on a hand reaching for the stars. This fitting symbol remains a prominent feature throughout the company today. "When you reach for the stars you may not quite get one," Burnett was fond of saying, "but you won't come up with a handful of mud either."

Within its first three years of business, the Leo Burnett Company acquired six additional clients, including the Pure Oil Company and the Brown Shoe Company, which led to ads centering on the Buster Brown character. In 1940 the company beat out 27 other ad agencies nationwide to acquire the American Meat Institute account, its first account to bill $1 million. To service this

growth, the company expanded its operation to include the 15th floor of the London Guarantee Building. In 1941 the company opened an office in New York's Rockefeller Center to meet the growing needs of its East Coast clients.

With each new office came a bowl full of apples, which today can be found on the reception desks in every Burnett agency. In fact, more than two million apples have been given away within the past 10 years, and each day thousands are given away throughout the world, providing food for thought to many Burnett visitors.

A NEW WAY OF SELLING

With a solid financial foundation and a revered reputation, the Leo Burnett Company was prepared for the droves of new household and consumer products that were being introduced to American consumers via television. The company helped sell these products by creating icons that tapped into the "inherent drama" of a given brand. Several of Burnett's characters remain as effective today as they were more than 50 years ago.

The Leo Burnett Building was completed in 1989 to house the company's worldwide operations.

Leo Burnett, pictured here with his ubiquitous black portfolio, continues to be one of the advertising industry's most-celebrated legends.

Leo Burnett creates advertising based on insights that turn consumers into brand believers.

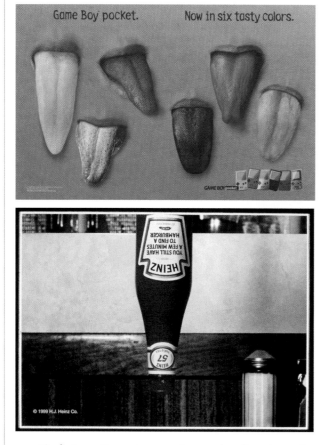

Each Leo Burnett campaign spoke directly to its intended consumer. Tony the Tiger and Toucan Sam proved trusted allies for children eating their Kellogg's breakfast cereals. The Pillsbury Doughboy offered homemakers fresh dough from the refrigerator, while the Lonely Maytag Repairman offered a reliable washer and dryer.

By 1969 the Leo Burnett Company had expanded into a global operation. Through acquiring the London Press Exchange, Burnett grew overnight to a company with 32 offices in 23 markets. Subsequent acquisitions have provided the company with its current global ranking as one of the largest agency networks in the world. With each new venture, the characters, campaigns and Midwestern sentiments launched by Burnett became recognized internationally.

On June 7, 1971, Leo spent his typical day at the office and returned to his Lake Zurich farm. That night, he passed away at the age of 79.

In reverence of the man who started it all, Leo Burnett Worldwide has closely followed the tenets of Burnett's "When to Take My Name Off the Door" as it moves forward. One caution in particular has stood out as an example of something the agency will not do: "When

you lose respect for the Lonely Man — at his typewriter or his drawing board or behind his camera or just scribbling notes with one of our big black pencils — or working all night on a media plan... When you forget he's the man who, because he is reaching harder, sometimes actually gets hold of — for a moment — one of those hot, unreachable stars."

A COMPANY LIKE NO OTHER

Today, Leo Burnett Worldwide is poised to meet the growing media and technological needs of clients through

the specialized family of B|Com3 companies. Starcom Worldwide, its media services partner company, provides its clients with innovative media planning, investing, research and tools.

After launching in 1997, Starcom Worldwide went on to win nearly $3 billion in new business in its first two years. The subsidiary continues to be a leading purchaser of all U.S. media for its list of blue-chip clients.

Starcom Worldwide's global billings for 1999 totaled $8.5 billion. In addition, Starcom was named *Advertising Age's* first "Media Agency of the Year" in 1999 and received *Adweek* magazine's "President's Award" the same year.

In 2000 *Advertising Age* named it "Media Machine of the Year." This success has also led to the formation of two new Starcom divisions, Starcom IP and StarLink. Starcom IP is a global unit designated to meet IP (Internet Protocol)-based media needs. StarLink provides media planning and buying services for small to mid-sized advertising agencies and operates independently of Starcom Worldwide.

In May 2000 B|Com3 merged Starcom Worldwide with MediaVest Worldwide, the media services company owned by The MacManus Group, to form Starcom MediaVest Group. Starcom and MediaVest continue to operate as separate companies in North America and the United Kingdom.

Several other U.S.-based subsidiaries provide an array of advertising and support services to Leo Burnett clients. Vigilante is an agency that targets urban consumers and offers its services to such clients as Major League Baseball, Nintendo and Sprint. Lápiz, which means "pencil" in Spanish (a reference to the big, black pencils Leo loved to write copy with), ranks as the third-largest Hispanic agency in the country. Williams-Labadie Advertising develops strategic healthcare communications for medical professionals. Giant Step provides agencies with strategic digital solutions, including e-commerce development and online media services. TFA/Leo Burnett Technology, a business-to-business technology agency with offices in Chicago, Boston, Austin and San Francisco, has been ranked as the second-largest business-to-business agency in the United States. The Lab: Unexpected Solutions provides creative business consulting to a host of blue-chip clients. And Capps Digital provides graphic arts and imaging solutions.

Leo Burnett Worldwide has received numerous accolades from the advertising industry, including being named "Agency of the Year" by both Advertising Age and Adweek in the same year, and Advertising Age's "Global Agency Network of the Year" in 2000. In addition, the company has been named one of "The 100 Best Companies to Work For in America." The work environment and benefits provided through Leo Burnett are unprecedented. On August 5 of every year — the company's birthday — each Leo Burnett employee receives a dollar for every year the company has been in business. In addition, the company also gives special gifts to employees who reach their fifth, 10th, 15th, 20th and additional milestone anniversaries with the company.

Starcom Worldwide, The B|Com3 Group's media services subsidiary, provides its clients innovative media planning, investing, research and tools ahead of the marketplace.

A continuous drive to meet the high standards set by its founder years ago is the reason Leo Burnett Worldwide is at the forefront of the global industry today. "A real sense of creative mission, sincerely felt through the agency and expressed in many big and little ways, obviously is the only thing that can carry us forward from here," Burnett wrote in 1967. "This is indeed the true secret of growth and stability in an advertising agency."

Forging the B|Com3 alliance: (Clockwise from left) Roy Bostock, Rick Fizdale, Roger Haupt, and Yutaka Narita

APAC
Customer Services, Inc.

It took Ted Schwartz just two and a half decades to build APAC, a customer service company approaching $500 million that is today a premier provider of large-volume outsourced programs for customer-relationship management. APAC currently serves major clients such as UPS, MCI WorldCom, Merck Medco and Citibank along with numerous other Fortune 100 companies.

The year was 1973 and Schwartz, a 19-year-old Rogers Park native and graduate of Lane Tech High School, already knew what he wanted to do with his life — to control his own destiny. For all the newspapers he sold, the cars he washed, the carpets he cleaned and the gas he pumped throughout high school, Schwartz knew something else — that customer interaction fascinated him.

Ted Schwartz (standing) took his own capital in 1985 and the entire operation of APAC Customer Services to a fully computerized, 150-workstation customer-contact service center in west suburban Schiller Park.

But it was the radio-advertising sales job, where Schwartz quickly moved into management, that focused his interest and led to his launch of Allstate Promotional Advertising Corporation, or APAC. The first radio station that responded to his direct-mail campaign was in Delta, Colorado, so Schwartz headed west with $200 and a colleague who had some business experience, a running Volkswagen and a credit card. Fifteen months later, headquarters was back in Schwartz's hometown, Chicago.

By 1976 APAC outgrew its Peterson Avenue facility and moved to north suburban Skokie where, throughout the next 10 years, it achieved a dominant position in the industry. In 1982 at the suggestion of a friend and former competitor, Schwartz put APAC's telephones to work in the evenings by entering the emerging teleservices industry. Three years later he took the biggest gamble of his life, boot strapping with his own capital a state-of-the-art, 150-workstation, fully computerized center in west suburban Schiller Park, where the entire operation then moved.

By 1990 sales reached $4 million, and the company relocated to Deerfield, a north suburban community that it continues to call home. Schwartz made the difficult decision to sell off the radio-advertising aspect in order to capture the singular focus APAC needed to advance. And grow it did, to $13 million in sales by 1992. That was the year the concept of customer care, in addition to customer acquisition, became a major cornerstone of APAC's service end and the name was changed to APAC Teleservices, Inc. At the time it was almost unheard of for clients to truly outsource their customer service function, but APAC made it work. Yet APAC did much more. It renewed customer service, put it back on center stage. With the focus shift, the APAC name came to signify "All People Are Customers".

For APAC, taking care of other companies' customers means developing a strategic plan that provides the optimal customer experience. The objective becomes not to minimize the cost but to maximize the lifetime value of customer interaction — and to make it a priority. It is a model of relationships rather than transactions. Supporting the key human element is APAC's powerful technology platform, which offers tools such as quality monitoring (a concept pioneered by APAC), interactive voice response, smart-selection systems and advanced customer-interaction systems.

The pace of APAC's growth accelerated in the 1990s. In 1995 it earned the UPS account, which represented the nation's largest outsourcing contract in the industry. APAC launched its IPO the same year. Accolades and awards poured in as quickly as did new clients. *Business Week* recognized APAC as the nation's fourth-fastest-growing company in 1996. Also in 1996 J.D. Power and Associates named APAC No. 1 in customer satisfaction for Sprint/PCS in California and for Ameritech in Michigan. Gallup surveys conducted on behalf of Blue Cross Blue Shield Association yielded near-perfect scores for APAC. Trade journals such as *Card Marketing* and *TeleProfessional* consistently bestowed top honors upon

APAC, the company that achieved 1,371 percent growth in net revenues from 1994 to 1998, and increased share-owners' equity by 633 percent during the same period. In 1999 the name became APAC Customers Services, Inc., to more accurately reflect the company's main focus.

In the late 1990s APAC formed Customer Assistance.com, Inc., a wholly owned subsidiary designed to introduce a full suite of electronic customer-relationship management solutions. Never before had such exciting possibilities been available to clients. The technology core of CustomerAssistance.com is e.PAC, a scaleable, channel-neutral platform that supports a broad range of integrated, Internet-based functions. It facilitates interaction between customers and service agents both electronically and personally. The element of human intervention is key and certainly hearkens back to APAC's origins and evolution.

In practical terms, e.PAC enables online customers or shoppers to select their preferred method of interaction. Options include online chat, e-mail or an immediate or scheduled call back from a service agent. The customer chooses how often they wish to interact, at what level and

with what form of technology. With real-time synchronization of customer and agent screens, agents can share forms, share browser control, provide split screen comparisons and even push Web pages to customers for their review. Sharing forms, for example, allows the agent to assist a customer who is unfamiliar with the proper completion of a form, thereby eliminating frustration and missing data. Agents are also trained in cross-selling to alert shoppers to other offers at a given site. The experience of mutually navigating around a site effectively replicates the immediacy and individual attention of traditional retailing but with a 21st century edge. And yet APAC maintains it is the customer's experience, and how they feel about it, that makes the difference no matter what the technology.

APAC Customer Services today has about 18,000 employees and more than 60 customer interaction centers in 15 states. It serves clients in a variety of fields including automotive, energy, financial services, government, healthcare, hospitality, insurance, parcel delivery, pharmaceutical, retail, telecommunications and travel. APAC frees its clients to concentrate on what they do best, while providing the ultimate in measurable service to their customers.

Schwartz' vision of delivering excellent customer service tomorrow is a blending of the traditional with the technological. He anticipates great e-commerce potential within the business-to-business and consumer markets. Toward this end the company recently formed a strategic alliance with a leading provider of e-business solutions.

The acronym APAC, "All People Are Customers," as Schwartz proudly exclaims, is the culture, vision and mission of APAC.

Key for APAC Customer Services is providing clients with sophisticated technology to help optimize the total customer service experience while simultaneously giving employees training and the right tools to improve their quality performance and increase job satisfaction.

Chairman Ted Schwartz (pictured) led the creation of CustomerAssistance.com in the late 1990s. This wholly owned subsidiary offers a full suite of electronic customer-relationship management solutions. At the core is e.PAC, a scaleable, channel-neutral platform that supports a broad range of integrated, Internet-based functions.

Understanding Clients'
Technology for Over 80 Years

Brinks Hofer Gilson & Lione

MEET THE NAME PARTNERS: (Left to right) Henry Brinks, a graduate of George Washington University Law School, has handled numerous patent trials and been active in a dozen of the leading intellectual property law and bar associations.

Roy Hofer, known in the firm as "The Coach," graduated first in his class from Georgetown University Law School. He served as president of the Chicago Bar Association (1988-89).

Jerome Gilson, a graduate of Northwestern University School of Law, specializes in trademark and unfair competition law. He has been admitted to and has practiced before seven Courts of Appeals.

Richard Lione, a George Washington University Law School graduate, has been counsel to a wide spectrum of clients in numerous jury and non-jury cases involving all aspects of intellectual property law.

Brinks Hofer Gilson & Lione has successfully served intellectual property clients for four generations. Founded in 1917 as Wilkinson & Huxley, today the firm has over 100 attorneys as well as numerous scientific advisors, patent agents and paralegals who understand, protect and defend clients' technology. With headquarters atop Chicago's NBC Tower, Brinks Hofer Gilson & Lione also has offices in San Jose, Indianapolis, Ann Arbor and Arlington, Virginia.

Brinks Hofer is a modern, highly diverse intellectual property law firm — the largest in the Midwest — and one of the largest in the country. Attorneys litigate, counsel and practice in patent, trademark, copyright, trade secret, Internet and related areas of law, and routinely handle a myriad of assignments in fields as diverse as electrical, chemical, mechanical, biotech, pharmaceutical and computer/Internet technology.

Brinks Hofer represents clients throughout the world. In 1999, after a worldwide survey, Euromoney's Managing Intellectual Property once again named Brinks Hofer the top intellectual property litigation firm in the central United States in two categories: patent law, and trademark and copyright law. Locally, in 1998 Brinks Hofer was ranked the "No. 1" firm in intellectual property in Chicago.

These distinctions reflect only the most recent chapter in the firm's illustrious tradition. In 1930, while handling an active law practice, Henry Huxley, in response to a request by Dean Wigmore, began teaching a course in patent law at Northwestern University Law School. George Wilkinson argued several landmark trademark cases before the United States Supreme Court. Both Wilkinson and Huxley, and later James Hume, rose to the top ranks of the American Bar Association's Section of Patent, Trademark and Copyright Law.

James Hume, a prominent partner in the firm from 1947 to 1983, was a giant in the field of patent law. Many of his trials during the early days of commercial litigation involved travel to other cities, and at one point he flew with Charles Lindbergh, then a Postal Service pilot. In 1943 Hume was cleared by the FBI to assist the Manhattan Project atomic bomb research scientists, offering counsel on the status of patent rights owned by a group of scientists that included Drs. Leo Szilard and Enrico Fermi. The inventions were used in making the first atomic bomb and later in peacetime uses of nuclear power.

Howard Clement, a name partner from 1956 to 1983, also enjoyed great distinction. Like his predecessors, he successfully tried numerous patent cases for major businesses. In addition, Clement was a trustee of the University of Illinois for several terms, and he was appointed by President Lyndon Johnson to the President's commission to make recommendations for the revision of the United States patent system.

Roy Hofer, a name partner since 1983, is an experienced patent litigator with a national reputation who has written, lectured and instructed widely on trial techniques and intellectual property law.

In addition to holding leadership positions in several local and national bar associations, he was appointed by the Chief Judge of the District Court of the Northern District of Illinois to its Advisory Group on the Civil Justice Reform Act of 1990 (serving 1991-94) and to the Merit Selection Panel for Magistrate Judges (serving 1996-98).

Jerome Gilson, also a name partner since 1983, is one of the country's most distinguished trademark lawyers. Head of the firm's Trademark Practice Group, he has specialized in trademark and unfair competition law since joining Brinks Hofer in 1963. Since then, he has written and edited, and continues to supplement, the leading treatise, Trademark Protection & Practice (Matthew Bender); has tried and argued numerous trademark cases; has actively helped to modernize the Lanham Act; has assisted in drafting the Restatement of the Law (Third) of Unfair Competition; was counsel to and a board member of the International (formerly United States) Trademark Association; and was named by his peers as "Top Trademark Practitioner in the World" in a Managing Intellectual Property survey (1998).

During the 1980s the firm's practice grew to accommodate the needs of major new clients, including Fortune 500 firms and medium-size businesses, nonprofits, universities, small businesses and individual inventors. Brinks Hofer is a pioneer in the computer age — among the first to equip

PROTECTING THE POWER OF IDEAS.

> ## Brinks Hofer Gilson & Lione has successfully served intellectual property clients for four generations.

lawyers with computers — and quickly adapts to changes in the field of intellectual property litigation.

By this time, patent owners had begun to demand jury trials in infringement actions, and Brinks Hofer developed jury trial expertise at a time when few intellectual property law firms had done so. Firm lawyers have continued to achieve substantial awards for clients. Roy Hofer led a patent infringement trial team that obtained a final judgment of $165 million, and partner Jerold Jacover led another team of firm lawyers through a jury trial resulting in a judgment of $40 million.

Many talented lawyers have contributed to the growth and success of the firm. They have tried cases, argued appeals, written books, headed associations, taught law school courses and served their communities. Above all, Brinks Hofer Gilson & Lione continues to serve clients, the legal profession and the community with distinction.

Frankel

The wealth of creative ideas and solutions offered by Frankel has helped build some of America's best-known brand names. For more than 38 years, the agency has developed promotional programs designed to accelerate both brand acceptance and sales. As a result, Frankel today is one of the nation's leading full-service marketing agencies.

Headquartered in Chicago, Frankel is part of the global network of advertising and marketing agencies owned by the Paris-based Publicis SA, which is one of the world's largest communications groups. Frankel itself is the largest and most well-known promotional marketing agency in the United States.

With its origins rooted in sales promotion, Frankel has expertise in direct and database marketing, sports marketing, sweepstakes and games, entertainment marketing, retail design, merchandising and sales promotion. Frankel also integrates interactive and electronic communication media and technology with other marketing media to deliver complete, integrated leading-edge programs.

Since its inception, Frankel has been committed to immersing itself in its clients' business and creating ideas and solutions built around market intelligence, knowledge of trends, retail expertise and above all — consumer insight. This has resulted in numerous agency-of-record assignments and long-standing relationships with many of its clients.

This tradition continues today as the agency is sought by blue-chip clients such as McDonald's, Visa, United Airlines, Frito-Lay, Nestlé and the U. S. Postal Service. Many of these clients have utilized Frankel's unique marketing services for numerous years, including McDonald's, which has partnered with the agency for more than 25 years. Today Frankel represents five of the top 10 nationally promoted brands.

The overwhelming success that Frankel has enjoyed is the result of the vision of its founder, Bud Frankel. In 1962 Frankel set out to form a marketing agency that utilized sales promotions to launch brand names and sales. Frankel's detailed approach to sales promotion shifted the focus of the marketing industry from "selling something" to the client to serving as a marketing partner with the client — working collectively to attain brand-name recognition and sales.

Frankel's efforts elevated client contact in the marketing industry from the print shop to the boardroom. Each product serviced by the agency was done so with the belief that promotion is the action dimension of marketing. It was through these efforts that Frankel spearheaded promotion marketing and demonstrated that it is an integral part of an overall marketing plan, not an isolated discipline.

From its origins in sales promotion, Frankel has evolved into a comprehensive marketing agency with expertise in everything from direct and database marketing to retail design and online promotion. Frankel is also the leader in promotional marketing technology initiatives. It offers patent-allowed digital marketing products through its Siren Technologies and BrandGuard divisions.

Renowned campaigns launched by Frankel include McDonald's tie-ins with Disney films and the chain's Teeny Beanie Babies promotions. Frankel is also responsible for the global promotional marketing program by Frito-Lay in conjunction with the release of *Star Wars: The Phantom Menace*. Other landmark campaigns include Visa's Magic Moments, a holiday sweepstakes in which the credit card company chooses one second as its "Magic Moment," and all purchases recorded at that second are free.

Frankel has been recognized as an industry leader by its peers and trade publications. The agency received *Advertising Age's* Agency of the Year award in 1989, followed by *PROMO* magazine's Agency of the Year honor in 1997. The agency has won numerous industry awards including the Super Reggie — one of the most prestigious and recognized marketing awards.

In addition, Bud Frankel was the recipient of the 1999 Silver Medal Award from the American Advertising

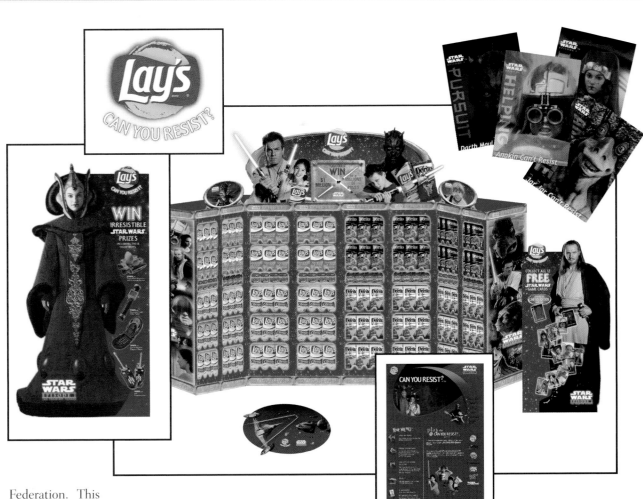

Frankel launched Frito-Lay's innovative global promotional marketing program for the theatrical release of *Star Wars: The Phantom Menace.*

Federation. This prestigious award honors individuals who have had a significant impact on the field of advertising and marketing. Frankel is also co-author of *Your Advertising's Great...How's Business?*, which showcases the unique marketing philosophies he established years ago.

Today, as part of Publicis SA, Frankel stands poised to offer its unrivaled marketing services to clients throughout the world by enabling them to transform the way people experience and buy their products and services.

Frankel's Siren Technologies division has introduced Dynamic Digital Signage, which provides digitally updated information for leading consumer-marketing clients such as United Airlines and McDonald's.

445

Harza Engineering Company

As engineering consultant for the $279-million project to rebuild 13 kilometers of Chicago's shoreline, Harza has performed a number of consulting services including inspection, condition assessment, review and design of alternative treatments and evaluation of hazardous, toxic or radioactive waste issues.

Radial gates on the main spillway at the 3,200-MW Yacyretá Multipurpose Project on the Rio Parana along the border between Argentina and Paraguay. Harza led an international consortium of firms in the planning, design and construction management of the project, which provides irrigation, fish passages and a navigation lock, as well as recreational and hydropower facilities.

Harza Engineering Company is one of the modern reasons Chicago still carries its reputation as the city of broad shoulders. Chicago, as a center of global commerce and transportation, provides Harza with the global reach necessary to pursue its business interests worldwide. Close to home, the company's massive land reclamation efforts along the lakefront and Chicago River have preserved and enlivened some of the city's greatest attributes. "Chicago is not only a hub of commerce, but also a first-class city," says Harza President and CEO Refaat Abdel-Malek. "We work all over the world and have offices in more than 30 locations. We have found, through the years, that Chicago serves as an excellent location for our headquarters."

From its headquarters, Harza Engineering Company maintains its scope of consulting engineering services to local, national and international operations. For 80 years, the company has served as a worldwide leader in the development of dams and hydroelectric plants, generating power and developing water resources in 90 countries on five continents. In addition to these markets, Harza develops vital infrastructure such as airports, roadways and hospitals, and engineers wastewater and stormwater management projects. Harza offers nearly every aspect of project development — from planning to project startup.

Ten separate yet cohesive business units exist within Harza — Hydropower; Power Systems; Infrastructure; Water & Environment; Program & Construction Management; Fossil Power; Privatization & Project Development; Trade Finance & Procurement; Harza-Hidrobrasileira; and Hydro-South America. Each unit complements the company's core competency of providing clean water, reliable power and innovative engineering in Chicago and throughout the world.

Harza Engineering Company was founded in 1920 by Leroy F. Harza, a mechanical and civil engineer who opened a small Chicago office with the hopes of putting his engineering skills to work designing dams and power plants. The company's formation coincided with the growing needs of U.S. utility companies looking for ways to meet the country's increasing electricity needs. Some of Harza's early clients included the Chicago-based Insull Utilities Group and the Great Lakes Power Company of Canada, for which he designed several plants on the Montreal and Michipicotan rivers.

The company enjoyed success and recognition in the United States early on due to Leroy Harza's pioneering designs. In 1924 he designed the 275-foot-tall Dix River Dam in Kentucky, which, at the time, was the tallest rock-filled dam with a concrete face in the world. Today this type of design is used for dams throughout the world. Additional projects in Texas, Nebraska and Oklahoma led the way for establishing offices throughout the United States. Currently, offices are located in California, Colorado, New York, Oregon, Washington and Wisconsin, as well as throughout the world.

In 1938 Harza attained one of the largest engineering contracts ever given to a private civil engineer at that time. The Santee-Cooper Project in South Carolina was a $57 million endeavor launched by the state and federal government. The project consisted of a channel connecting the Santee and Cooper Rivers, with 37 miles of dams, two spillways, a navigation lock and a hydroelectric powerhouse. The success of the Santee-Cooper Project opened the door for additional opportunities overseas and in the United States. In 1942 Harza was hired by the government of Uruguay to redesign its Rio Negro dam development. The success of this project launched the company's international business with electric power, irrigation, and land reclamation and flood control projects in El Salvador, Honduras, India and the Philippines.

Today Harza Engineering is responsible for some of the world's largest engineering efforts and has consulted on projects in more than 90 countries. The company provided planning, design and construction management services for the Guri Hydroelectric Project in Venezuela — one of the largest hydroelectric plants in the world — and is responsible for the design of the two tallest rock-filled dams in the world — Derbendi Khan Dam in Iraq and Ambuklao Dam in the Philippines. To serve the company's growing South American clientele, Harza has established offices in São Paulo, Brazil; Lima, Peru; and Kito, Ecuador.

Harza has also built strong relationships in China through a 20-year, distinguished history working on projects that provide flood control and power generation as well as improve irrigation and water supply. Harza has been involved in the conceptual study, review, and construction management of the Ertan Project beginning in 1979. Harza has provided services for the Baise Multi-purpose Dam; the Tongbai, Guangdong and Tianhuangping Pumped-Storage Projects; and the Tianshengqiao, Gonzui, Longtan and Lingjintan Hydroelectric Projects. Harza is also assisting with Three Gorges, the largest hydroelectric project in China.

In addition to engineering services, Harza assists overseas clients with privatization and development of hydroelectric power and other water resources projects. In 1998, for example, the company submitted proposals for more than $125 million in financing for clients in the Dominican Republic, Egypt, Honduras, Israel, Jordan, Mexico, Oman, Uganda, Uruguay and Venezuela. "Our international clients look to the United States for the latest advances and technology to meet their engineering challenges," says

Managing Partner Edward F. Carter. "In water, power and infrastructure development, they look to Harza."

Harza Engineering has also developed world-class projects in the United States, including the Bath County Pumped-Storage Project in northwestern Virginia, the largest project of its kind in the world, and the Eastside Reservoir Project in southern California, the region's largest surface water storage reservoir. In Chicago the company served as engineer of the $4 billion Tunnel and

Reservoir Plan (TARP), also known as the Deep Tunnel project. Working with the Metropolitan Water Reclamation District of Greater Chicago, Harza designed a system of deep tunnels and surface reservoirs to prevent detrimental combined sewer overflow from entering Lake Michigan and outlying streams.

The Deep Tunnel project earned several industry awards and accolades for the company, including being named "One of the Outstanding Engineering Achievements in the United States" by the National Society of Professional Engineers. The Deep Tunnel concept is being used throughout the United States and internationally.

In addition to its professional contributions, Harza plays an active role within the Chicago community. The company both sponsors and participates in programs such as mentoring, science fairs, Illinois Engineers' Week and Principal for a Day in the public schools. For its own employees, the company offers the L.F. Harza award, which highlights technical excellence in individual and team accomplishments.

Harza has participated in much of Chicago's infrastructure development and, more recently, rehabilitation. While the company will continue to offer its engineering services to developing countries throughout the world, it will remain dedicated to a better Chicago. "Our success is due, in no small part, to the vitality and spirit of Chicago and its people," says Carter. "We're from Chicago and we're proud of it."

Working with city of Chicago staff, Harza provided all technical and administrative control, public information and final design during the construction of the 79th Street Tunnel. The project involved excavation of approximately 5.8 kilometers of a 4.9-meter-diameter, machine-bored tunnel with live connections to the existing potable water supply system.

447

Legat Architects

For over 35 years Legat Architects has been providing responsive architectural design based on the firm's ability to listen and respond to client needs. With studios in Chicago, Oak Brook, Schaumburg, Waukegan, Palatine and Crystal Lake, and with a staff of over 140, Legat ranks as the third-largest architectural firm in Illinois. Joseph J. Legat, chairman of the board, started the firm in Waukegan in 1964 and was joined by Wayne Machnich in 1968.

Deciding to compete for larger commissions, Legat Architects made major changes in company philosophy and focus. Until these changes occurred, Joseph Legat had been involved in all decisions and in every project. For the firm to grow, it needed more architects in day-to-day client involvement so that the founder could focus his efforts on the design and quality of projects.

Machnich assumed the role of president, an initial step to implement the firm's new focus and philosophy. The leadership was shared with five other key architects and the firm committed to developing separate studios in the Chicagoland area. These decisions were the key factors in causing the company to sustain controlled growth. Each of the studios has access to the resources of the firm's design, management and construction administration departments and each studio is responsible for the successful development of its individual projects. With the

change in management philosophy, the firm began to grow at a rate of 20 percent annually, which has continued to date.

Exceptional project management accounts for the fact that 75 percent of Legat's business is repeat work from satisfied clients.

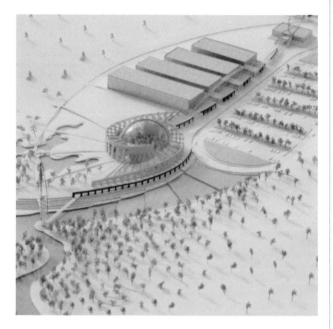

The project types in which Legat Architects specializes include:

• Corporate Architecture — The Corporate Division is headed by a corporate facility design specialist who has designed more than 30 high-rise office and multi-use facilities worldwide.

• Interior Design — The company's newest division was formed to meet the increasing special interior design requirements of existing and new clients.

• Health Care Planning — Building upon 20 years of design experience in acute care, skilled care, continuing care retirement communities and senior living facilities, Legat Architects continues to design comfortable and stimulating health care environments.

• Governmental Facilities — A growing part of the practice is the design of buildings for state, county and city clients. Building types include municipal centers, public works facilities, recreational developments, public safety projects and correctional facilities.

• College and University — In Illinois alone, the firm has worked with more than a dozen colleges and universities, providing master planning, facility assessments, science and technology facilities, performing arts centers and student services projects.

• Roofing Analysis and Design — Headed by an internationally recognized expert on roofing systems design, the firm's roofing specialists use cutting-edge technologies and appliances for roofing system repair, replacement, and design.

• K-12 Education Projects — New schools, renovations and additions account for completed projects by the firm at approximately 250 schools. Serving over 75 school districts, Legat Architects is the largest educational design firm in Illinois.

• International Projects — For more than 10 years Legat Architects has been expanding into the international market. Its international group has integrated American architectural abilities with a global understanding. From the Pacific Rim to Eastern Europe, the firm has completed over 40 projects in 35 countries

(in every continent except Antarctica) for manufacturing, laboratory, education, hospitality, health care, office and employee use.

Since establishing his practice, Joseph J. Legat has contributed his time and expertise to public service and architectural enlightenment. His diversified architectural experience has been widely recognized for innovations in the design and planning of interior spaces and significant buildings. His knowledge of financing methods, cost control and building efficiency has resulted in cost-effective programs.

Legat Architects is committed to using technology to its utmost potential for producing the highest-quality product, service and ease of communications. It sees knowledge, skills and creativity as the tools on which the architect relies when shaping the environment, and prides itself on a continuing program of acquiring and developing these traits.

Design, service, competence and attention to detail — these are the elements that bring success to Legat Architects' projects.

McClier

The Rookery

Why is McClier Chicago's premier design-build firm? Because the city and the company share a common value: beauty, applied for practical purpose. This kindred spirit was evident in one of the firm's earliest projects — the restoration of the Rookery Building in the early 1990s. As described by Robert Bruegmann (*Inland Architect,* July/August 1992), the Rookery is an "immense and complex structure overflowing with energy and teeming with unexpected detail ... both a witness and key player in the rise of LaSalle Street as Chicago's premier business street, the development of the office building type, [and] the role of Chicago in American history ... Luckily, [those involved] with the Rookery renovation included individuals who were not just competent, but who approached their tasks with passion." This passion resulted in McClier's designation as Firm of the Year for 1999 by the Landmarks Preservation Council of Illinois.

Among the many awards won for this renovation, a few in particular bear witness to its importance to Chicago — the National Honors Award from the American Institute of Architects (AIA), the National

Preservation Award from The National Trust for Historic Preservation, the above-mentioned Preservation Project of the Year from the Landmarks Preservation Council of Illinois (LPCI), and the Readers' Poll for Best Renovation from the *Chicago Tribune.*

So many of McClier's projects reflect this same passion for the places and things of importance to Chicago — to its history, its neighborhoods, and its commerce.

Like the Rookery, the Reliance Building has a proud and significant past. Among the first skyscrapers to feature thin stone and terra cotta hung off a steel frame and the liberal use of glass in its facade, the 102-year-old structure was crumbling away by the mid-1990s. In the project to restore the building, timing was everything. Because the city didn't think "Old Reliable" could withstand another winter, all the work — repairing or replacing damaged terra cotta; replacing all the windows; replicating a terra cotta cornice; and reinstating a pair of bays — had to be finished between the Christmas seasons of 1994 and 1995. One reason McClier was able to adhere to this strenuous schedule is its unique ability to deliver a complete and integrated solution, from planning through execution. The restored Reliance Building won the 25th Anniversary Award from the LPCI, as well as the Special Recognition Award from the AIA Chicago.

Reliance Building

Given its affinity with the city, McClier was a natural choice for Mayor Daley's "Neighborhoods Alive" program in 1998, which focused on helping local communities improve their infrastructure. McClier served as the contractor to renovate key sites in three ethnic areas: Humboldt Park, where the company restored the historically significant Receptory and Stable to its original splendor; Pilsen, called by August Chidichimo, Chicago Department of Transportation, "a port-of-entry community for people from Mexico" (Paula J. Drieci, *CEG*); and Chinatown, where "a drab and wasted area was turned into a lively and attractive town center and gathering place" (Lee Bey, *Chicago Sun-Times*, August 17, 1998). The result in each case was a renewed excitement about city living, a reborn enthusiasm for the diversity that makes Chicago the all-American town

McClier's impact on Chicago's commercial interests is just as powerful. In fact, McClier has been the design-build force behind the brick and mortar of some of Chicago's quintessential enterprises.

The *Chicago Sun-Times* turned to McClier to provide a complete range of services — from planning and site selection to design, engineering, and construction — for a new $100 million production facility located on the city's southwest side. The 300,000-square-foot facility merges printing, inserting, distribution, and fleet maintenance to increase operating flexibility and productivity in an ultramodern plant. Just as important was the project's impact on the city's economy. At a press conference kicking off construction, Mayor Daley praised the *Sun-Times* for "laying the groundwork for future development along the river" rather than moving important jobs to the suburbs (*Chicago Sun-Times*, March 28, 1998). Daley also captured the importance of the newspaper's role in Chicago life: "The very fact that there are two major dailies in Chicago [shows] the 'I-will' spirit of the city."

And what says "Chicago" more than its bustling airport? In 1999 McClier was named the prime consultant to lead a team managing the $1 billion capital improvement program at Chicago O'Hare International Airport. As the program manager, McClier facilitates communications between the Department of Aviation (DOA), the regulatory agencies, the airlines and all other airport stakeholders. McClier also coordinates the efforts of the DOA staff and all consultants and manages the implementation of the program from the inception of each individual project through construction completion.

Other McClier projects for key Chicago companies show the design-build firm's impact across many industries: for Abbott Laboratories, a "greenfield" plant designed to complement mature trees in the area; for Trans Union Credit, a 300,000-square-foot corporate headquarters including a 50,000-square-foot, state-of-the-art data processing center; for Sara Lee, a research and development center that consolidates the operations of three facilities in one location; and for Amoco Corporation, an employee development center, the first of its kind, combining both technical and nontechnical training in a single program.

If the reach of McClier bridges the historic to the high-tech, nowhere is that more obvious than in the rehabilitation of Lakeside Press. The old printing plant, where R.R. Donnelley published millions of magazines, catalogs, telephone directories and books, is being literally transformed into a cyberspace center called "the largest planned Internet and telecommunications facility in America," (Mayor Daley) and "the building that will make Chicago competitive with California's Silicon Valley and North Carolina's Research Triangle" (Gary Washburn, *Chicago Tribune*, July 9, 1999). The site will allow tenants — companies such as Frontier Communications, with customers like Yahoo! and E-Toys whose combined sites receive 72 billion hits a month — to share resources such as power, fiber-optics access and security that would be prohibitively expensive if purchased by each user. The "fortress-like" structure will include 85 watts of electrical power per square foot, compared to the five watts in a typical office building.

"We like to think that our projects bring together the best of all worlds — the old and the new; the aesthetic and the technical, the city, its people, and its businesses," says Grant McCullagh, chairman and CEO. Vice Chairman Frank Cavalier and President Tom Rossiter agree. "We're a Chicago firm all the way."

Paige Personnel Services

Phones were answered through a switchboard. Words were deleted by pink erasers with plastic brush ends. Notes were taken in shorthand, and figures still computed on comptometers, as adding machines were just arriving on the scene. Letters, memos and reports were produced on typewriters, copied on "ditto" machines and delivered not via fax or e-mail but by messenger or

Paige President
Karen Rae Horwitz

through the U.S. Mail. Keypunch was a cutting-edge skill. The women who took secretarial and clerical office jobs — and it was only women who did this work — were concerned with the hourly wage the position paid, not its benefits or opportunities for advancement. It was the mid-1960s, and no one quite realized that all of that was about to change.

The 35-year journey of Paige Personnel Services from its inception as Miss Paige Placement Service to prominence as the Chicago metropolitan area's largest locally owned office-staffing service company is just as much about the environment it inhabited as it is about a company's growth. The progress of technology, America's transformation from a manufacturing economy to an information economy and the changing roles of men and women all shaped Paige's evolution.

Paige founder Sidney Horwitz had a vision. After learning the staffing business by working for a downtown employment agency, he foresaw an agency that would operate throughout the suburbs and market only to women. Horwitz would name the company after Miss Paige, a fictional, ideal office worker of his own creation.

Horwitz realized his dream in 1964 when he opened Miss Paige Placement Service in the Six Corners area of Chicago's North Side. The Miss Paige image — a professionally dressed, efficient-looking woman who wore cat's-eye glasses and held a telephone receiver with a curly black cord — became the company's logo and a fixture during the 1960s and 1970s in the Yellow Pages, brochures and related advertising.

Aside from a failed attempt to add a temporary services division, the company prospered and seemed unshakable until the nationwide white-collar recession that unfolded in the early 1980s. It was time for personnel agencies to give up or redefine. The people at Paige chose the latter course.

Patricia Whitney and Karen Rae Horwitz had been with the company since the 1970s and had watched it dwindle from six offices and 32 staffing consultants to four offices with a total of only nine consultants. They managed Paige for absentee-owner Horwitz, who, seven years earlier, had moved to the West Coast to open another staffing company. The turning point for Paige came when Horwitz returned home to Chicago and asked Patricia and Karen Rae to become partners and help him rebuild the company. A few years later he married Karen Rae.

Change began with the very concept upon which Paige was founded. The company's new name, Paige Personnel, was central to its revamped image as Paige no longer would place only women. Additionally, this time the launch of a temporary division was going to succeed. Karen Rae Horwitz took the helm of the temp division and incorporated it as a separate company; Whitney guided activities in the perm unit.

As the company changed, so did its clients and their needs. Firms welcomed an agency that helped them both fill permanent positions and prepare for temporary vacancies in the office due to illness or vacation. These new, mostly service-company clients were more interested in whether the employee — temporary or permanent — had up-to-date computer skills than whether it was a male or female. But just as Paige was feeling secure in its recovery, another recession struck. It was 1991 and high costs forced companies to restructure. They were laying off staffers, not hiring them. Budgets had no room for either the expense of temporaries or permanent-agency fees.

So Paige weathered the economic storm by remaining close to its clients and faithful to its commitment to providing highly qualified candidates. As the recession lifted and gave way to a period of steady growth, the agency began to flourish, but client needs shifted once more. The concept of flexible staffing became a mainstay of corporate America, and Paige responded to this new paradigm. In addition to supplying qualified temporary employees to cover for illnesses and vacations, Paige developed the ability to staff a special project or an entire department.

By the mid-1990s the temporary business grew so substantially that it began to compete against the permanent division. At about this time, Sidney Horwitz decided to retire. So as many of its client companies had done several years earlier, Paige found it necessary to restructure in order to thrive.

Karen Rae Horwitz became president of both firms and immediately merged the temp and perm companies into a single entity doing business as Paige Personnel Services. She retained Whitney as vice president of the perm, or direct-hire, division, promoted Nancy Nesti to vice president of the temporary division and hired Richard Schuster as executive vice president to oversee daily administrative operations and assist in charting a course for additional growth. Now Paige would resume building.

(Clockwise from top) Karen Rae Horwitz, president; Richard L. Schuster, executive vice president; Nancy A. Nesti, vice president; and Patricia A. Whitney, vice president

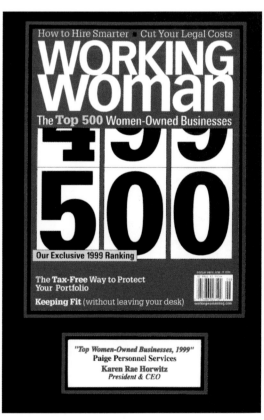

Working Woman's top 500 issue

Today Paige counts 11 local offices with over 100 employees, including more than 50 permanent placement consultants, 35 temp specialists and 15 accounting and administrative staffers. Revenues exceed $47 million; placements are 35 percent male. Annually, Paige employs over 8,000 temporaries. Clients range from small firms to Fortune 500 companies and include nonprofit and professional associations. Paige is annually named by Crain's Chicago Business as one of Chicago's "Top Staffing Services" and for two consecutive years has been listed among Working Woman magazine's "Top 500 Woman-Owned Businesses in America."

Immediate plans call for an increased presence on the Internet and expansion into new locations with an added focus on placing higher-level managerial and professional candidates. Paige Personnel Services remains a truly home-grown firm whose history mirrors both the disappointments and the vast potential that molded the late 20th century Chicago business scene.

Seyfarth Shaw

The law firm of Seyfarth Shaw was founded amid the plethora of labor relations problems that Chicago industries faced in the 1940s and 1950s. At a time when strikes, collective bargaining and arbitrators were commonplace — and relations between labor and management were strained — Seyfarth Shaw helped Chicago companies negotiate labor agreements that kept the city working.

Prior to the firm's founding, Henry Seyfarth, Lee Shaw and Owen Fairweather had established themselves as pre-eminent labor lawyers with the firm of Pope and Ballard. In 1945 these three set out on their own to represent companies against the myriad of labor problems that arose from the administration of the Fair Labor Standards Act and the National Labor Relations Act. Each of the founders brought a distinctive personality and array of talents to the firm and shared the goal of creating a leading labor law, corporate and commercial litigation practice with a national presence.

The comprehensive scope of the firm was strengthened by the addition of corporate attorney Ray Geraldson (who was made a partner in 1950) and attorneys in several other fields, including commercial litigators and workers' compensation lawyers. This ability to fully represent the labor and management needs of companies — coupled with a renowned reputation for being fair and competitive — spurred the early success and growth of Seyfarth Shaw.

In its early years the firm anticipated and stayed abreast of key changes in labor laws, allowing it to expand its experience and presence throughout the United States. The U.S. Supreme Court's 1949 decision that a pension was a deferred wage and thus a mandatory subject for collective bargaining allowed the firm to expand its offerings by drafting and negotiating pension agreements.

In 1956 the firm's services were solicited by Chicago restaurants that did not want to be forced into illegal arrangements with culinary unions. The firm's handling of these matters brought it to the attention of the Nevada Resort Association, which hired the firm in 1967 to handle similar disputes. This venture, along with the firm's representation of California growers in labor law problems stemming from the California Agricultural Labor Relations Act, led to the firm opening its Los Angeles office.

Additional achievements in a number of legal arenas accelerated the firm's expansion throughout the United States. With this growth, the firm tailored its legal services to meet the complete needs of its business and public-sector clients, offering experience in the areas of business law, contracts, employee benefits, environmental issues, safety and health, litigation, and regulatory and legislative practices.

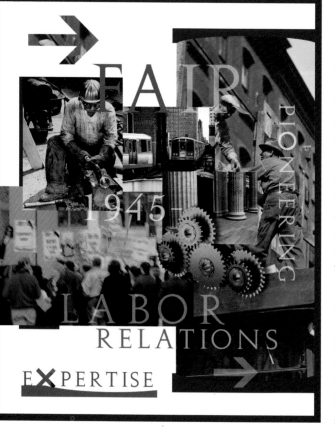

FAIR PIONEERING
1945-
LABOR RELATIONS
EXPERTISE

Today more than 200 Fortune 500 companies are represented by the firm — along with industrial and manufacturing companies, financial institutions, newspapers, hotels, healthcare organizations, airlines, railroads, and federal, state, local government and educational entities. Firm offices are located in Atlanta; Boston; Chicago; Houston; Los Angeles; New York; Sacramento; San Francisco; Washington, D.C.; and Brussels, Belgium.

For more than 55 years Seyfarth Shaw has excelled in labor and employment law, serving as one of the largest practitioners in this specialty area nationwide. It

offers unparalleled experience, unequaled resources and efficient services in all aspects of federal and state labor and employment law. The firm also acts as national labor counsel for several large corporations that require complete and prompt response to labor crises. *The Wall Street Journal* hails Seyfarth Shaw as "the nation's pre-eminent law firm in representing management in labor matters."

Other areas in which the firm excels include its business and finance practice, which covers business law matters for large, publicly held corporations, insurance companies and investment and commercial banks, along with small private corporations, entrepreneurs and individuals. The firm is also well versed in contract law and has litigation and arbitration experience in such diverse fields as antitrust, securities, shareholder rights, and construction and insurance defense, among others. Additional services provided by the firm include estate planning, probate and trust administration, tax planning and structuring, and real estate services.

The environmental practice within the firm provides comprehensive coverage of air, water, land, health and safety concerns. This practice caters to public and private entities that have potential environmental liability, including manufacturers, school districts, banks, real estate developers and engineering firms. The firm's environmental attorneys practice in virtually every state in the nation at federal, state and local levels.

Seyfarth Shaw also offers its labor and employment law experience to the public sector and healthcare market. The firm has one of the largest public-sector practices in the country, representing federal, state and county agencies, city governments, public schools, colleges and universities. The firm also represents more than 200 hospitals and healthcare organizations throughout the country.

At the core of the firm's operation is a dedication to client service. The philosophy that the firm was founded upon — a client's problem is the firm's problem — still holds true today. Seyfarth Shaw stands 450 attorneys strong and remains committed to growth.

Every employee of Seyfarth Shaw takes a hands-on approach to developing lasting relationships with clients. The firm scouts top law school graduates, and through its Lawyer Development Committee, operates an in-house continuing-education program to help attorneys hone their professional skills and become more productive more quickly.

In addition the firm creates publications, reference tools and training programs designed to help clients change their employees' behavior and reduce future litigation. Seyfarth Shaw at Work, the firm's training and consulting entity, provides legal training and consulting services to managers, human resource professionals and employees on numerous topics including discrimination law, hiring and promoting, sexual harassment, diversity, performance management and positive employee relations.

Seyfarth Shaw also plays an active philanthropic role in Chicago, providing numerous hours of pro bono work for charitable organizations. The firm also works closely with the NAACP to pioneer civic causes throughout the city, such as the open-housing movement.

The integrity of Seyfarth Shaw is underscored by numerous accolades from its peers in the legal industry. The firm has been rated the No. 1 labor and employee benefits firm in the country by a *Global Research* survey, and an *International Corporate Law* survey ranked the firm No. 1 in Illinois and among the top 10 firms in its category nationwide.

A. Eicoff & Co.

The growth of A. Eicoff & Company parallels the growth of Chicago in one striking way. When Alvin Eicoff founded the agency in 1965, Chicago was a meat-and-potatoes town. Similarly, the Eicoff ad agency offered clients "no-frills" television direct response advertising. Over the years, Chicago has become a much more sophisticated and diverse city. During this time, Eicoff has diversified its broadcast advertising services and become a highly innovative and successful advertising agency.

Both the city and the agency recognized that their market's needs were changing and responded accordingly. Ron Bliwas, who has been the president and CEO of Eicoff since 1981, recalls that a few significant events changed the agency's direction. In the 80s Fortune 500 companies became increasingly interested in television direct response because of its ability to deliver fast, measurable results. Around that time Eicoff was purchased by Ogilvy & Mather, providing the agency with exposure to additional corporate clients. And third, trade-support advertising became increasingly attractive to advertisers. This promotion-oriented strategy involves television commercials that include the names of store chains in targeted markets, producing increased retailer support for the advertised product.

In a relatively short period of time, Eicoff's clients came to include many of the country's leading advertisers. They were attracted to the agency because it was skilled not only at producing results but for doing so with cost-effective, image-conscious commercials.

While Ron headed the agency during this initial growth period, chairman emeritus Al Eicoff was on hand to remind the agency of what it did best and what made it unique. A television advertising pioneer, Al has always had the knack of knowing "how to make the cash register ring." His media buying and creative innovations have become standard practices throughout the industry. His vision, combined with Ron's aggressive growth strategy, helped Eicoff become the world's leading television direct response agency.

In the 90s, as the Magnificent Mile effectively balanced its traditional landmark buildings with new construction, Eicoff too maintained its tradition of results-oriented television advertising while embarking on exciting new projects. With the proliferation of cable stations, there were many more opportunities for direct response advertisers to reach their markets. Eicoff capitalized on this trend by creating "niche" divisions that became agencies-within-the-agency. HitVision, for instance, uses direct response techniques in commercials that increase visits and sales at "dot.com" sites. Eicoff Direct Health offers direct-to-consumer advertising for healthcare-related companies.

Today Eicoff consistently ranks in the top 15 agencies in Chicago. Its executives are asked to speak at conferences and association meetings around the world and write articles for trade publications. Al Eicoff is in the Direct Marketing Hall of Fame. Ron is on the board of the Direct Marketing Association, has been named as one of the most influential people in the industry by *Response* magazine, and appears frequently on *Crain's Chicago Business's* prestigious "Who's Who in Chicago Business" list.

While the agency will no doubt continue to grow and change like Chicago itself, it will remain as unique as the city's miles of lakefront and architectural landmarks. Just as there is no other Second City, there is also no other ad agency that specializes in television advertising for immediate, measurable results.

President and CEO Ron Bliwas

Banner Personnel Service, Inc.

If it hadn't been for one man's vision and dynamism, Banner Personnel Service, Inc. never would have made it onto the landscape of Chicago's job placement industry. And if it weren't for the continued commitment of the man's wife, Banner wouldn't be leading that industry into the 21st century.

James M. Singer, fresh out of college and newly married, got into the personnel field when he went looking for a job himself. Living in Kentucky with his wife, Emel, Jim happened to pick up a *Chicago Tribune*. Job opportunities seemed endless in the Windy City, so he made appointments with some personnel agencies there. After meeting with the charismatic, success-driven candidate, the vice president of the very first agency hired Jim Singer himself.

As quickly as he took to the business, the business took to him, and after two years Jim was managing four branch offices. The absentee owners asked if he was interested in buying them out but the books revealed a troubled company. Jim took a pass on that offer but found it had whetted his entrepreneurial appetite. Even though the country was in the grip of a recession, he took over the lease of an insolvent downtown employment agency, purchasing its contents lock, stock and barrel. With a staff of three, Banner Personnel opened its doors for business in September 1970.

Just before the winter holidays, having lost her job because of the recession and expecting the couple's first child, Emel Singer joined Banner's office staff. As the years went on, she worked alongside her husband, answering phones, keeping the books, calculating the payroll — whatever was needed — while the Singers' two children slept through their infancies amid the steady buzz of Banner's office.

The early years were a great struggle as Banner focused its efforts in placing direct-hire, professional-level employees. When the firm added office-staffing services in the mid-1970s, the company began to take off and grew again in 1982 when Jim launched Banner Temporary Service, Inc. They were heading for a "banner" year in 1986 when Jim Singer was diagnosed with stomach cancer. He died less than a year later in December 1987. Emel was left with two adolescent children, 152 employees and a multilocation business. No one thought the new chairwoman and CEO could handle it all — no one except her loyal and dedicated

staff, whose unwavering support encouraged Emel to continue building Banner.

A drop in revenues during the 1990 "white collar" recession, however, sent Emel looking for advice. She hired old friend Robbie Brown, a management consultant,

(Left to right)
Emel Singer,
Patty Oliver
Photo by Brad Baskin

who today serves as Banner's president. Robbie directed Emel toward the tough decision of closing the company's original heart and soul: the professional division. Banner continued to flourish throughout the 90s, expanding into more than a dozen additional branch offices, and once again, a professional accounting & finance division specializing in permanent and contract placement services.

The company provides an average of 40,000 hours of temporary staffing services per week, as well as placing hundreds of individuals in permanent jobs with Chicagoland clients. Born of Jim Singer's dream and fueled by the Banner team's determination, today Banner is a $30 million company anchored on prestigious, lakefront Michigan Avenue, dedicated to providing professional, ethical staffing services.

Bostrom

Ken Monroe, president and CEO of Bostrom Corporation

French political commentator Alexis de Tocqueville, in his lasting *Democracy in America* (1835), noted that when two or three Americans discover they have a common interest, they often form an association. It's quite possible that at their second meeting, they see that they need help running their new association.

In Chicago, Bostrom Corporation has been helping international, national and smaller associations do just that since the Great Depression.

In those early days, the company was known as Storms and Wescott. Situated in the heart of the Heartland, Chicago was a natural choice for launching a consulting and management business for associations. Glenn Bostrom saw more potential and purchased the business in 1965, bringing with him innovative management systems and techniques. Under his leadership, Bostrom Corporation grew from four employees to more than 60 working at offices in Chicago; Washington, D. C.; Monterey, California; and Scottsdale, Arizona. Robert Becker assumed the presidency in 1996 and served until his death in 1999. Bruce Becker, Robert's son, succeeded him.

Robert Becker brought to Bostrom a rallying cry of "real-world, innovative and exciting" to describe association management. He persuaded his son Bruce to give up his sales and marketing career in Japan to join Bostrom in 1994.

"I was lured here by my father and found that a career at Bostrom allowed greater learning and growth potential," Bruce says. Bruce kept the firm's senior leadership talent and clientele intact through the troubled times following Robert's death, and continued pursuing top talent. Under Bruce's stewardship, Kenneth Monroe, formerly chief operating officer with the American Medical Association,

was retained as executive vice president. Monroe became president and CEO in 2000. Marta Hayden, formerly with the Monterey Convention Center, joined Bostrom as vice president of sales and marketing. Randy Lindner, CAE, was promoted to executive vice president and oversees the various offices. John Dee, CPA, became general manager and chief financial officer of the Chicago office. Charles McGrath, CAE, became vice president and general manager of the Washington, D.C. office.

Bostrom's success stems from concentrating on things it can do better for associations than they can do for themselves. Bostrom's offices become the associations' offices — handling everything of concern, including accounting, filing, member services and retention, marketing, event management, communications and consulting.

Members of any association possess a common interest and often great expertise in that common area. That does not mean they are experts at running their association. Bostrom's consultants stand ready to help with such typical trouble areas as board political problems, inability to make good — or any — decisions and overall efficiency. Specifically, the aid may involve leadership training or revising bylaws to make them a useful management tool instead of a dust-gathering document.

Bostrom's role with association clients has become more critical as people become busier and busier. Some years ago, Bostrom management saw that association managers, like their counterparts in the for-profit sector, were confronted with doing more with fewer people and resources. Another related problem was that association managers were seeing dwindling membership rolls, and perhaps more troubling, a decline in volunteerism. Busy professionals are loath to take on one more thing.

"Bostrom Corporation is run by people with professionalism and integrity and has a culture based on excellence, quality service and adding value to our clients' and people's lives," says Ken Monroe. "We want to assist our clients by helping to determine their vision and growth strategies for the future."

Brad Baskin Photography

Photographer Brad Baskin started out in high-end, ready-to-wear fashion advertising, shooting models that represented 1980s images of professional men in suspenders and women in camel blazers. The photos promoted the clothing, but what fascinated Baskin were the faces. After apprenticing with some of the top Chicago photographers, Baskin moved into his own studio in the River West area and began pursuing portrait photography.

His work became popular among local performers needing photos for their actors' comps, and soon Baskin was shooting workers in all occupations. In addition to studio portraits, Baskin would go on location to the workplace to capture executives at the office, factory workers at the assembly line and service providers in the process of performing their duties. Today, Brad Baskin continues to work for ad agencies, graphic design firms and individuals. His focus remains on applying photography as an exploration and expression of the human spirit.

FCB Worldwide

The Great Chicago Fire no longer smoldered in 1873, but in that year Daniel M. Lord ignited a spark that still blazes with all the creative fire of a company destined to impact virtually every household in the United States. What became Lord & Thomas is today FCB Worldwide, a global advertising agency that is the largest in the United States, with billings in the billions.

Early campaigns that came out of the Chicago office literally launched national brands. Palmolive Soap became the product of choice "to keep that schoolgirl complexion." Sales of Kleenex tissues practically doubled with radio show sponsorship in the 1930s. These successes joined those of the East and West Coast offices, which produced legendary results for Clairol, Sunkist and Levi Strauss.

By 1912 Lord & Thomas was the country's largest advertising agency, and Albert Lasker, generally referred to as "The Father of Modern Advertising," owned it all. It was Lasker who persuaded William Wrigley, a client, to rename Cubs Park as Wrigley Field in 1926, in order to raise awareness of the chewing gum. Copywriter John E. Kennedy defined advertising as "salesmanship in print," and his "reason why" copy helped drive the business, and indeed the industry, forward.

In 1942 Lasker handed over the entire agency, except for its name, to the managers of its primary offices: Emerson Foote in New York, Fairfax Cone in Chicago and Don Belding in Los Angeles. Thus Foote, Cone & Belding opened with $22 million in billings and went on to flourish throughout the second half of the 20th century with powerful new campaigns and solid client partnerships

that frequently broke records for longevity. The "Hallmark Hall of Fame" television concept first aired in 1951. In 1954 FCB Chicago won assignments for several Kraft brands, including Kraft Caramels. The sweets were packaged with recipes and sticks for making caramel apples; this promotion was so successful it moved not only Kraft Caramels, but apples as well. And then there were the animated bugs that came to life in the 1960s and spent the rest of their days scuttling away from cans of Raid and becoming oddly beloved in households across America. The S.C. Johnson animated Raid television campaign continues to build that brand around the world with the longest-running campaign in that medium's history.

In 1963 FCB was the first major agency to make an IPO; in the next 30 years the company would grow by 4,000 percent. And 1970 was marked by the retirement of Fairfax Cone, who will always be remembered as a leader with uncompromising ethical principles and a quirky sense of humor.

In 1987 FCB Chicago moved into the gleaming, 20-story building that is its present prestigious address. That same year FCB Worldwide was named Agency of the Year (*Advertising Age*), an honor that was repeated in 1990 (*Adweek*). True North Communications became the holding company of FCB in 1994, with an emphasis on expanding in new technologies, global media buying and marketing services. FCB Worldwide entered the 21st century much as it did the 20th — in grand style, with innovation and client focus. Today it is the largest U.S. advertising agency and fifth-largest global communications company, with offices in 92 countries and billings of $8.8 billion.

Emerging campaigns will undoubtedly become tomorrow's legends. In creating ideas that sell, FCB Worldwide has somehow become more than a force that moves products. Its own products, from Smokey Bear to Raid's Y2KBug, move us.

Grant Thornton

When Alexander Richardson Grant, a talented 26-year-old accountant, opened his own business in Chicago in 1924, he probably had little idea that he was sowing the seeds for a worldwide accounting and management consulting firm.

Today Grant Thornton has offices in major U. S. cities and 100 countries overseas, employing nearly 20,000 people. Annual U.S. revenues are $380 million

> **Grant Thornton's clients are focused on growth. They embrace technology. And they are global in their perspective.**

and the client list reads like a "who's who" of international business. But the firm doesn't limit its help to big, worldwide companies; quite the contrary.

When Dom Esposito, a former managing partner in the New York office, assumed the CEO post in 1999, he launched special programs to help the owners and senior management of middle-market, entrepreneurial companies achieve their business and financial goals. Grant Thornton has developed an operating model to facilitate the transition from a more-traditional accounting firm to a market-driven, wealth-creation, professional-services firm in tune with the still-developing Internet marketplace.

Esposito outlined his vision for the new business era as Grant Thornton observed its 75th anniversary in 1999, on the threshold of the new millennium.

"During our 75 years," he said, "we have staked a claim on the middle market, which recognizes us as a leading service provider in that space. Our work ethic distinguishes Grant Thornton from our largest competitors and has enabled us to create very close, trusted business-adviser relationships with our clients. To do this, we search for the best people in the business who are focused on providing value-added, customer-oriented service in an innovative, flexible and rewarding work environment."

Grant Thornton finds the new century an exciting time in which to work with so many middle-market companies and their people. The companies are focusing on — and experiencing — dramatic growth through rapidly developing technology. And whether they are small start-ups or multibillion-dollar organizations, they are not afraid to expand and even explode traditional business models in pursuit of radically different results. Obviously, Grant Thornton offers a great deal more than accounting services, the original offering of Alexander Grant. The two main areas are:

- Business advisory services to help clients create wealth through profitable business growth. Included are traditional professional services such as accounting, audit, tax consulting, corporate finance/risk management and enterprise solutions.
- Financial advisory services help Grant Thornton clients enhance, preserve and distribute wealth by addressing individual, family, business and ownership issues.

Thanks in large part to the dramatic growth of the Internet, smaller and younger companies are finding they want to — indeed must — plunge into international business at a relatively early stage. Grant Thornton recognized that need and established International Business Centers in California, Chicago, Miami, New York and Texas. These centers assist clients in exploring international markets and then developing the business plans to profit from them.

Grant Thornton's clients are focused on growth. They embrace technology. And they are global in their perspective. Grant Thornton's mission in the 21st century is to help these leaders of our new entrepreneurial economy achieve both their business and personal goals.

Susan E. Loggans & Associates, P.C.

Susan E. Loggans
©1997 *John Reilly Photography*

When attorneys at Susan E. Loggans & Associates, P.C., enter the courtroom, they take their seats on the plaintiff's side. Their physical location exemplifies a total dedication to representing people who have been injured or killed as a result of negligence or other improper conduct. The firm's promise — "We will fight for you!" — manifests a deep devotion to no-nonsense litigation.

A strong desire to work as a trial lawyer led Illinois native Susan E. Loggans to an interest in personal-injury law. During the early 1970s, when she was a student at DePaul University College of Law in Chicago, few women worked in the field, but Loggans did not let that stand in her way. She connected with a prominent Chicago-area personal injury lawyer who served as her mentor and — after receiving her JD in 1974 — spent three years working as an associate in his firm.

In 1977 — having developed a reputation as an aggressive young trial lawyer — Loggans headed out on her own. Because of her high visibility as a woman in what was still a largely all-male field, clients sought her out. Connections she had made while participating in the Association of Trial Lawyers and chairing its 60,000-member Tort Law Section brought her referrals. Soon she was deluged with cases, all involving people who had been victimized in some way.

From the beginning Loggans made a special commitment to defending children who were brain damaged as a result of events surrounding the birth process. She has represented hundreds of these children — most of whom have cerebral palsy — in medical malpractice cases. Typically the children need full-time attendants and require computers to help them communicate. Their families have enormous medical bills, but most have been offered no monetary compensation until Loggans takes on their cases. Without the compensation she wins for them, many of these children would die.

Loggans' numerous multimillion-dollar recoveries in medical malpractice cases have given her unique standing among personal injury lawyers. A forerunner in establishing the liability of health maintenance organizations, she won a $16 million cash settlement against an HMO — one of the largest settlements of its kind in the nation.

Chicago — a city known for its hard-working, down-to-earth citizens — appreciates these same traits in Loggans. Over the years her firm has grown. She directs a cadre of six attorneys — among them experienced trial lawyers in demand as authors and lecturers — in the many aspects of tort law. She also personally supervises a 20-member support staff.

Named as one of the countries "Top 15 Trial Attorneys" by the *National Law Journal* in 1985, Loggans has had a remarkable career. She has published numerous articles in professional journals and popular publications, donated her time to universities and law schools and led innumerable bar association sections, committees and programs. Inspired by her interest in helping disabled children, she has served as a member of the board of directors of United Cerebral Palsy in Chicago for 15 years.

Hard work and achievement have brought Loggans both local and national recognition. She has appeared on "Oprah," NBC's "Today" and "Montel Williams." For several years she hosted her own nationally syndicated radio talk show and more recently, she has appeared on FOX news and on a weekly Chicago television show.

As her practice continues to grow, Loggans remains committed to helping people. She considers her talent a God-given resource and — by training other lawyers to handle the kinds of cases that mean the most to her — she plans to pass her legacy on to others.

Tetra Tech EM, Inc.

Consultants, scientists and engineers at Tetra Tech EM, Inc. (Tetra Tech) are working hard to clean up the environment, ensure clean water and air, safely manage industrial and municipal wastes and help protect and support the sustainable development of the world's natural resources. From its beginning in Chicago as a provider of environmental consulting services, Tetra Tech has continued to grow and diversify its areas of expertise into the fields of management consulting, information technology, infrastructure engineering and training.

The company prides itself on looking at its clients' problems using a creative, "out-of-the-box" mentality, making its engineers true consultants, not contractors. Tetra Tech can assess the scope of a problem and design and implement practical solutions that make use of innovative technologies and tools. Over the years Tetra Tech has provided consulting services to many federal government clients as well as numerous state agencies, municipalities and private clients in a wide range of industrial sectors.

Tetra Tech was founded in Chicago in 1982 by Tom Brisbin, who at the time was working at a large, traditional civil engineering firm. He recognized the growing opportunities for contracts supporting the federal government as it implemented new and emerging environmental regulations. With an initial focus on hazardous waste issues, Tetra Tech succeeded in obtaining a number of small contracts. Then in 1984 the company won its first large EPA contract, supporting projects nationwide. This contract allowed Tetra Tech to grow and diversify its staff, open new offices around the country and expand its areas of technical expertise.

From the outset Tetra Tech has operated in a manner radically different from other, more-traditional engineering firms. The company set aside all hierarchical systems of employee advancement and created an atmosphere where every employee had the chance to make a difference. Leveling the playing field meant that any employee could advance simply by taking on more responsibility and doing good work.

Unlike most large consulting firms, Tetra Tech operates its offices under one cost center. This organizational structure allows the company to share work and resources among its offices. The best available person from anywhere in the company can be assigned to support a project anywhere in the world. Clients benefit from Tetra Tech's local responsiveness and the ability to tap into the resources and expertise of the entire firm without having to overcome any bureaucratic obstacles.

Since 1996 the company has been the largest subsidiary of Tetra Tech, Inc., a Pasadena, California-based engineering and consulting firm. Tetra Tech, Inc. is one of the nation's largest engineering and consulting firms. Publicly traded on NASDAQ, the firm operates in resource management, infrastructure engineering and communications systems.

Tetra Tech EM, Inc. is part of the Tetra Tech Resource Management Group. Still headquartered in Chicago, the company continues to grow and diversify its client base and service areas. A particular source of pride is the work that Tetra Tech has been doing for the city of Chicago over the past two years. The firm has been hired

In the office or in the field, Tetra Tech works with its clients to provide sound solutions to a vast array of environmental and infrastructure issues.

to investigate and clean up some of the largest and high-profile "brownfield" sites in the city. This type of innovative technical approach and service to clients and the community is turning Tetra Tech into one of the most-successful consulting firms in Chicago, throughout the United States and around the world.

Town & Country Pediatrics

Dr. Howard Rice

Town & Country Pediatrics was launched on the North Side of Chicago in 1972, at a time when patients trickled in slowly, one by one. The lethargic pace almost caused the owner, Dr. Howard Rice, to rethink his priorities of owning a pediatric practice.

"My problem was that all I knew was how to be a doctor," Dr. Rice recalls. "I didn't know what I needed to run a business. But I stuck it out and waited for patients."

His perseverance paid off because by the turn of the millennium, his practice was booming with 16,000 patients, three offices, 10 doctors, two nurse practitioners and an administrator. "It's all held together by a computer," Dr. Rice laughs. In truth, it's all held together by Dr. Rice, whose life's journey brought him this successful practice.

A graduate of the Indiana University School of Medicine, Dr. Rice has been practicing pediatrics for almost 40 years. He finished his residency in pediatrics in 1962 at Riley Children's Hospital in Indianapolis. Shortly thereafter, he was drafted and spent two years at Laughlin Air Force Base in Del Rio, Texas, as the head of their pediatric department.

In 1964 he and his wife, Jean, came to Chicago, where he joined a pediatric practice on the North Side of Chicago. During the next eight years, he learned the "ins and outs" of running a pediatric practice while he honed his pediatric skills as a practitioner. By 1972 he was ready to take the next step in his lifelong dream, which was to be the owner of his own pediatric practice.

That's when he opened an office on Lincoln and Webster. He had already joined the staffs of Children's Memorial Hospital in Chicago, Evanston Hospital and Prentice Women's Hospital. While waiting for his practice to grow, he took a job in the mornings at the Augustana Home, a home for retarded children.

Soon the neighborhood changed over with older people moving out and younger families moving in. It wasn't long before the children's parents found his practice. Within six years, Dr. Rice had a partner. Within eight years, he opened another office in Woodale, Illinois, which eventually moved to Northbrook, Illinois. With one office in the city and the other in the country, he called his practice "Town & Country Pediatrics." By 1990 the Lincoln & Webster practice was bursting at the seams, and Dr. Rice moved to his present location on Clybourn Avenue. Soon he'll be expanding into an even bigger office, moving from 3,200 square feet to 7,500 square feet.

"I like children," says Dr. Rice, who has four of his own children and four grandchildren. "If you take good care of them, you can have a long relationship with them." His waiting room is often filled with parents who grew up as his patients and who are bringing in their children for treatment. Dr. Rice listened to the parents' stories of going to an emergency room at night when his office was closed and their wishes of being with their own doctor. That was all he needed to hear to set a new goal: To keep his pediatric practice open 24 hours a day, seven days a week. But he'll need to wait until his practice has 25,000 patients. If history is any indication, Dr. Rice is destined to raise the bar in the pediatric field by keeping a doctor's office open 24 hours a day.

(Back row, left to right) Drs. Diane C. Holmes, Howard M. Rice, Irene J. Freeman, Dori S. Kazdin, Barbara N. Johnston, Diane DiMaggio, (Front row, left to right) Drs. Anne L. Wyman, Ellen M. Papacek, Brian R. Hirsch, Kenneth S. Polin

Chicago Historical Society

465

Educational, health care, cultural and service organizations contribute to the quality of life enjoyed by Chicagoland residents and visitors.

QUALITY OF LIFE

The University of Chicago Hospitals

The University of Chicago Hospitals represents the achievement of the remarkable. Physicians here are united by the desire to practice medicine, advance research and educate the physicians of tomorrow, enabling them to play a leading role at the forefront of medicine. Bringing all of these elements together gives the University of Chicago Hospitals the opportunity to provide unparalleled care to its patients.

The Duchossois Center for Advanced Medicine opened in 1996. A state-of-the-art resource, the facility brings the knowledge and resources of the University of Chicago to the outpatient setting.

Physicians, researchers and scientists at the University of Chicago Hospitals have always been leaders in medical research and teaching. What makes the University of Chicago Hospitals unique is its ability to deliver innovations from the laboratory to the patient's bedside, bringing advanced care to patients more quickly and effectively than at other institutions. Backed with the resources of an academic medical center, physicians treat patients with a multidisciplinary approach. For example, radiologists, medical and surgical oncologists, pathologists and radiation oncologists all work closely together to treat a lung cancer patient. This approach to treating patients is part of the reason that, for the past several years, *U.S.News & World Report* has ranked the University of Chicago Hospitals among the top 14 hospitals in the nation. Additionally, *Good Housekeeping* cited seven of its physicians as being among the nation's best for treating cancer in women. Eleven Nobel Prize winners in medicine or physiology are affiliated with the University of Chicago Hospitals.

The University of Chicago campus is a tree-shaded and ivy-covered collection of Gothic and modern buildings in historic Hyde Park. The community is famous for its diversity and urban sophistication. To the east is the beautiful lakefront. Museums, ethnic restaurants and blues clubs complement the academic and medical environment on campus.

Planning for the University of Chicago Hospitals dates back to 1898, and the dream of William Rainey Harper, the university's first president. Harper envisioned the integration of medical research, education and patient care on the University of Chicago campus. In 1927 that dream came true with the opening of Billings Hospital.

During the five years following 1927, physical expansion accelerated with the opening of hospitals for both children and women. The emerging network largely served patients from Chicago and the Midwest, but their advancements included nuclear medicine, nitrogen mustard to treat lymphomas and leukemia, chloroquine to suppress malaria, and fluoridated water to help prevent tooth decay. In 1943 Leon Jacobson, MD, administered the first successful cancer chemotherapy.

After World War II the medical center continued to expand under the direction of Lowell T. Coggeshall, MD, with the addition of eight modern hospitals and laboratories from 1950 to 1969. Funding sources were composed of government grants and private gifts, including $12 million from the Pritzker family, which gave the medical school its identity as the Pritzker School of Medicine.

In subsequent decades, physicians forged break-through methods for transplants, as well as treatments of diseases such as cancer and diabetes. In 1972 Janet Rowley, MD, demonstrated that cancer is a genetic disorder. In 1988 Christoph Broelsch, MD, performed the first split-liver transplant, an operation that allows two patients to share an organ. A year later, physicians at the University of Chicago Hospitals successfully transplanted a portion of a liver from a living donor. And in 1992 Graeme Bell, PhD, discovered a genetic link to type-2 diabetes.

The tradition of new discoveries and groundbreaking research translates into an outstanding reputation as one of the nation's premiere medical centers. *U.S.News & World Report* consistently ranks the cancer program at the University of Chicago Hospitals among the top 10 in the nation. The endocrinology and gastroenterology programs have also been consistently ranked among the top 10 nationwide. Cardiology, geriatric medicine, gynecology, neurology, orthopaedic surgery, pulmonary medicine, rheumatology and urology have also been named among the best in the country.

Medical advancement at the University of Chicago Hospitals continues to drive change. Physicians and researchers here developed three-dimensional, noninvasive imaging techniques that integrate MRI, CT and PET data, enabling scientists and physicians to view the brain and any abnormalities with pinpoint accuracy. University of Chicago Hospitals electrophysiologists implant smart defibrillators on an outpatient basis without the need for an open-chest procedure. Patients with severe coronary artery disease benefit from newly developed interventional techniques, such as percutaneous revascularization. Neurologists here contributed to the development of

beta interferon, the first drug ever to show significant results in lessening the severity and number of multiple sclerosis attacks.

Such advancements drive change in the hospital buildings as well. The current network features Bernard A. Mitchell Hospital for primary adult inpatient care, the University of Chicago Children's Hospital for pediatric inpatients, Chicago Lying-in Hospital for inpatient obstetrical and gynecological care for women, Duchossois Center for Advanced Medicine for outpatients, and Louis A. Weiss Memorial Hospital, which delivers adult inpatient and outpatient care on Chicago's North Side. The combined facilities admit over 30,000 patients each year.

The 525,000-square-foot Duchossois Center for Advanced Medicine welcomes outpatients and visitors with a soaring atrium under glass, a lobby waterfall, convenient valet parking and a 10,000-square-foot food court. The center has helped physicians and other healthcare professionals redefine the concept of excellent, efficient outpatient care. *Modern Healthcare* and the American Institute of Architects' Academy of Architecture for Health cited its sleek design for cost-efficiency that does not sacrifice quality.

The idea to build the Center for Advanced Medicine began in 1988 with the recognition of a new direction in the healthcare industry toward outpatient care. By 1990 the planning committee had drafted its master plan, then

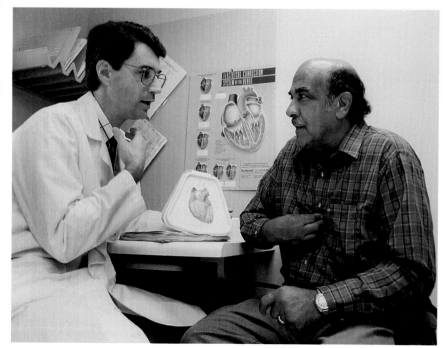

Breakthroughs made in research directly influence the superior care given to patients here.

traveled to key facilities across the country to harvest the best ideas from each. Back on campus, they asked those who would use the building what they desired, and implemented recommendations along the way. In 1994 the Richard Duchossois family donated $21 million to build the center, making it the largest dollar amount ever received by the university from a family in a single gift.

The Center enables physicians to provide the most innovative care on an outpatient basis. Physician offices are located adjacent to related diagnostic and treatment services for convenience and efficiency. The examination rooms, numbering more than 200, can accommodate family members and medical students, along with the physician and patient. Adult and pediatric specialties in the six-story facility include ambulatory surgery, the Breast Center, the Cancer Resource Center, cardiology, gastroenterology, neurology, orthopaedic surgery, plastic and reconstructive surgery, pulmonary medicine, transplant surgery and urology.

Helping to facilitate the transport of critically ill or injured neonatal, pediatric and adult patients from the scene of an emergency or during interhospital transfer to the University of Chicago Hospitals, is the University of Chicago Aeromedical Network (UCAN), a medically-equipped helicopter. UCAN is staffed 24 hours a day, seven days a week by a pilot, dispatchers, flight nurses and emergency medicine physicians.

In 1967 the University of Chicago Hospitals opened Wyler Children's Hospital, which consolidated pediatric care under one roof. In 1996 the name was changed to the University of Chicago Children's Hospital. A pediatric level-1 trauma center, the University of Chicago Children's Hospital provides comprehensive care to infants, children and teenagers. It features one of the largest pediatric intensive care units in Chicago, along with a neonatal intensive care unit for premature and critically ill infants. Physicians here performed more pediatric liver transplants in the past decade than any other facility in the world. Clinical specialties include allergy, arthritis, asthma, cancer, cardiology, child development, diabetes, ear/nose/throat, emergency medicine, gastroenterology, genetics, gynecology, infectious disease, neonatology, neurology, orthopaedics, psychiatry and several surgical specialties. Community physicians often refer their patients — especially high-risk cases — to the hospital for advanced treatment that draws on the finest expertise, experience and diagnostic technology available.

Research and teaching join together for patient care that benefits young people around the world. Children and families have access to the newest therapies available. Experts here have shown that investigational treatments, proven safe and effective on adults, can benefit children diagnosed with certain conditions. Studying and understanding rare forms of childhood disease is a top priority here.

The softer side of the University of Chicago Children's Hospital puts a friendly face on technology. Child Life Specialists, the Clown Care Unit, the Daily Snack Program, the Kids' Advisory Board and moveable aquariums are just a few unique programs available here. City skyline murals, bedside computers with kids-only Internet access, colorful art boxes, pizza in the playroom and a courtyard basketball hoop are just some of the amenities available to children.

The University of Chicago Hospitals is dedicated to its surrounding neighborhood. There are several programs of community outreach. Asthma is on the rise, and the local need is especially urgent — 15 percent of Chicago school children have asthma, three times the

One of the first to be designated as a comprehensive cancer center by the National Cancer Institute, the U of C tests the latest therapies for patients with all types and stages of cancer.

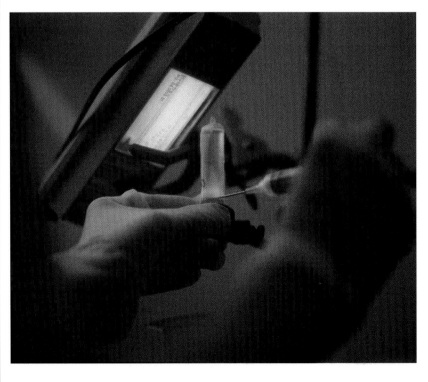

national average. The Asthma Center's outreach project is a massive, aggressive effort that involves visiting area schools to educate teachers and school nurses about early warning signs.

Although the University of Chicago campus remains the hub of medical activity, the University of Chicago Hospitals offers a growing network of sites for convenient accessibility to world-class care. On Chicago's North Side, patients visit Louis A. Weiss Memorial Hospital for primary and specialty care. In Hyde Park, the Windermere Senior Health Center and Dental Associates serve the needs of older adults who reside in the community. A new Senior Center will provide care for older adults on the city's South Side. Those who live or work in downtown Chicago can see a physician at the University of Chicago Physicians Group and Dental Associates for primary, specialty and dental care. The University of Chicago Hospitals and Health System also includes several sites throughout the city, suburbs and Northwest Indiana.

The University of Chicago Program for Executive Health, located at the Center for Advanced Medicine, focuses on the special needs of busy professionals who are highly valuable to their companies and families, yet often are at higher risk for problems such as heart and lung disease. Consultations with physicians who are ranked among the best in the state, along with comprehensive diagnostic testing, are performed all in one day. Results are often available that day so that physicians may explain results in great detail.

Until 1999 it was not possible to quantify the effects of healthy lifestyle habits. Since the cause-and-effect linkage was unclear, it was difficult to find motivation to discard poor habits. University of Chicago physician Michael Roizen, MD, helped change this perspective with the publication of *RealAge: Are You as Young as You Can Be?* Chairman of Anesthesia and Critical Care and an internist, Dr. Roizen offers a thorough and straightforward explanation of how healthy lifestyle habits can impact one's actual, or physical "RealAge", if not one's chronological age. For example, Dr. Roizen and his team determined that having a total cholesterol count of

greater than 280 makes a 50-year-old's RealAge 53, but when that number dips below 170, they effectively have a RealAge of 49. Dr. Roizen describes the benefits of healthy lifestyle habits and preventive health care in measurable terms so that readers can make immediate changes to lower their RealAge, demonstrating that they can have more control over the aging process.

For healthcare professionals, the University of Chicago Hospitals continues to represent the opportunity to advance the entire field of healthcare in a supportive, collegial atmosphere. At most other hospitals, physicians consult with experts from across the country to diagnose or treat a difficult medical condition. However, at the University of Chicago Hospitals, while physicians certainly seek opinions from around the nation, most of the advice and counsel they seek comes from their distinguished colleagues across the campus.

Advancements in medicine and technology allow today's physicians at the University of Chicago Hospitals to practice medicine quite differently than their colleagues from long ago. What has not changed, however, is William Rainey Harper's vision of the University of Chicago Hospitals as a place for the integration of medical research, education and patient care. Harper's vision endures today with the University of Chicago Hospitals' commitment to conduct groundbreaking research, to educate the next generation of physicians and to provide superlative patient care. Today's goal is the same as it was in 1898 — to remain at the forefront of medicine.

Gothic architecture alongside modern buildings gives the U of C campus its character — acknowledging the past and looking to the future.

471

The University of Chicago

For more than a century, the University of Chicago has reigned at the top of academia, unsurpassed in its reputation for devotion to teaching and research. Private, nondenominational and coeducational, the university offers the distinctive combination of one of the very best liberal arts colleges within one of the world's leading research universities.

Training minds to think independently and creatively always has taken precedence. First University of Chicago President William Rainey Harper noted, "The question before us is how to become one in spirit, not necessarily in opinion." Chicago has a reputation for challenging traditions and blazing trails while at the same time upholding long-established standards of the highest scholastic merit.

Founded in 1891 by Standard Oil tycoon and philanthropist John D. Rockefeller, the University of Chicago is situated on a 200-acre campus in historic Hyde Park. The campus, which appears on the National Register of Historic Places, retains the original old-world ambience created by architect Henry Ives Cobb. The cloistered quadrangles and gothic architecture trimmed in ivy and bedecked in gargoyles affirm the classic dignity of the institution, yet share the campus with buildings by modernist architects Ludwig Mies van der Rohe, Eero Saarinen, Frank Lloyd Wright, Cesar Pelli and Ricardo

Legorreta. Wright's Robie House, considered the most recognized building on campus, has been voted one of the most important pieces of architecture of the 20th century.

Since its inception, Chicago has attracted stellar students as well as faculty. More than 70 Nobel laureates have been University of Chicago alumni, faculty or researchers, and 113 alumni currently serve as presidents or provosts of other universities. Three of 12 National Medal of Science winners for the year 2000 are University of Chicago faculty members. A recent year's graduates earned three Rhodes Scholarships, an achievement unsurpassed by any university in the nation. Of the more than 12,000 students at Chicago, about one-third are undergraduates. Employees total 12,000, including about 2,000 faculty members and 5,200 medical center personnel.

The university operates on an annual budget of approximately $800 million, with about $250 million devoted to research. Chicago's endowment exceeds $3.5 billion. Programs around the world, including graduate business programs in Barcelona and Singapore, and undergraduate programs in Europe and Africa, supplement courses at the Hyde Park campus.

In addition to the undergraduate college and graduate divisions, the University of Chicago comprises six professional schools, an extensive library system, laboratories, museums, clinics, a lower school, a dedicated continuing studies program and the nation's leading academic press. These ancillary units have garnered notable reputations of their own. The Oriental Institute, which has supported research and archaeological excavation in the Near East since 1919, includes a museum that houses major exhibits of art and antiquities, holds adult education classes and conducts special events for children. The largest university press in the country, the University of Chicago Press has more than 4,000 titles in print and each year adds up to 300 more. The University of Chicago Hospitals have on staff more nationally ranked specialists than any other hospital in the state. The highly regarded Laboratory School educates 1,600 students from preschool through 12th grade, half of whom are children of faculty. For the other end of the age spectrum, the Graham School of General Studies offers liberal arts and professional continuing-study programs.

The most recent addition to the University's educational facilities is the first charter school in the country sponsored by a university. Chicago-area institutions affiliated with the university include Argonne National

Listed on the National Register of Historic Places, the 200-acre campus of the University of Chicago blends classic architecture with buildings designed by prominent modernists.

Laboratory, Chapin Hall Center for Children, National Opinion Research Center and Yerkes Observatory.

The university has achieved tremendous milestones in diverse fields. The "Chicago School of Economics," which refers to the modern economic theories developed by such Chicago scholars as Milton Friedman and George Stigler, focuses on reduced government spending, deregulation, stable monetary policy and lower marginal tax rates. In physics, it was the Chicago team led by Enrico Fermi that achieved the first controlled, self-sustaining nuclear reaction, paving the way for development of the atom bomb. In 1989 the University of Chicago Medical Center performed the nation's first liver transplant from a living donor. The Alpha Proton X-Ray Spectrometer, designed and built at the university, conducted chemical analysis on the surface of Mars during the 1997 Mars Pathfinder mission.

Some of the university's most wide-reaching influence has been in the area of urban sociology. With the city of Chicago as their backyard to serve as an urban laboratory, university researchers could study how neighborhoods were formed; it was the first time that researchers seriously examined a city as a political and social entity. Early University of Chicago social scientists provided the framework for future sociologists to study metropolitan areas, and Chicago scholars throughout the 20th century have helped to shape national policies on education,

housing, poverty, race relations, census taking and other inner-city concerns. During Franklin Roosevelt's presidency, Chicago's School of Social Service Administration was called upon to lay the groundwork for Social Security and the New Deal.

As land owner, large employer, resident and intellectual center, the university continues to play a significant role in the character of Hyde Park. Its contributions to the neighborhood range from outreach medical programs to legal aid, literacy programs and youth theater.

The university also has contributed much to the evolution of higher education itself. From the beginning, the school admitted women and minorities. Chicago

created the four-quarter system of study as well as the "core" undergraduate curriculum that remains a model among many colleges today. The university developed the first liberal arts continuing education programs for adults; the business school was the first to offer a Ph.D. and to institute a mid-career program for working executives. Recently, Chicago joined a consortium to offer non-credit courses over the Internet.

It surprises many people that in the early days, the University of Chicago was known not only for its research and academic rigor, but for football. The Chicago Maroons team was a founding member of the Big 10, and the "Monsters of the Midway" won five conference titles between 1899 and 1924. In 1935 Chicago became the first school to boast a Heisman Trophy winner, Jay Berwanger. Chicago continues to encourage talented student athletes to achieve competitive success as well as academic distinction, and today the university fields 19 varsity teams in the Division III University Athletic Association. Chicago athletes and teams had an outstanding record of success during the 1990s, winning 12 Academic All-American awards, nine NCAA postgraduate scholarships and team championships in men's basketball, women's cross-country, women's soccer, softball and wrestling.

Its wealthy founder once called the University of Chicago "the best investment I ever made." To its city, the eponymous university serves as an enduring ambassador, equating Chicago with excellence, passion and innovation.

The University of Chicago is located in the tree-lined neighborhood of Hyde Park, nine miles south of the Loop.

Graduates from the University of Chicago go on to have distinguished careers in business as well as academia.

Career Education Corporation

Founded in 1994 by Chairman, President and CEO John M. Larson, Career Education Corporation is one of North America's largest providers of private, postsecondary education. The company, which is headquartered in Hoffman Estates, owns and operates 17 schools at 28 campuses in 15 states and two Canadian provinces.

Chairman, President and CEO John M. Larson

These schools offer a variety of bachelor's and associate degrees and nondegree programs in four career-oriented disciplines, including information technology; visual communication and design technologies; business studies; and the culinary arts — fields of study that have strong entry-level employment opportunities and ongoing career- and salary-advancement potential. All areas of study emphasize hands-on training and enable students to be exposed to current technologies and to the instruction of expert faculty members. In addition, all CEC schools have a low teacher-student ratio, with one instructor for an average class size of 18-20 students.

Brooks Photography Institute

Career Education Corporation's mission statement emphasizes an ongoing commitment to quality education

and career-focused learning and to the hiring of dedicated professionals "who inspire individual worth and lifelong achievement." The company continually strives to provide its students — who average 26 years of age — with a purposeful education that will prepare them for a workplace where highly skilled employees are increasingly in demand.

The implementation of a solid strategic plan has enabled CEC to pinpoint, then acquire and improve schools that can be made more profitable. These include academic institutions that are undermanaged both financially and from a marketing standpoint, yet maintain strong curricula, excellent reputations and broad marketability. With a strong management team in place, CEC adds its own expertise as well as the needed resources to expand each school's curriculum, while at the same time investing in needed capital improvements and enhanced marketing programs. Over 3,500 individuals are employed with Career Education Corporation throughout the United States and Canada, and more than 22,000 students are enrolled at CEC academic institutions. In 1999 *Crain's Chicago Business* ranked Career Education Corporation No. 7 on its list of "Chicago's Fastest-Growing Public Firms."

In 1998 Career Education Corporation made its initial public offering and is traded on NASDAQ under the symbol CECO. A well-thought-out acquisition plan enables CEC to acquire schools and expand programs, while at the same time granting each school a significant amount of operational autonomy. The investment in these policies fosters a sense of personal responsibility and gives Career Education Corporation an important advantage in recruiting and retaining highly motivated, entrepreneurial-type individuals at all of its campuses.

"Unlike a lot of other people in private, proprietary education, we are a decentralized company and each of our schools retains its own identity and culture," says Dr. Jon Coover, CEC's vice president of marketing. "As a decentralized company, we function as a support pin for each and every one of our independent, profit-oriented schools. As we acquire new colleges, we put into place fundamental and basic procedures and processes in order to have clear and accurate reporting for the markets and for our customer base, made up of employers, students and stockholders. When we go into a new marketplace, we seek out and look at schools that are either No. 1 in their market or close to No. 1. And all of the schools that we acquire are regionally or nationally accredited."

After acquiring a school, Career Education Corporation brings in its own divisional training directors as well as its own (six) regional management teams that are each responsible for four to seven CEC colleges. The regional teams help with the hiring, training and motivation of CEC employees. In order to determine if a particular school should introduce a new area of study, CEC surveys community residents, surrounding businesses and students to find out if the establishment of a new curriculum is warranted.

Career Education Corporation currently owns and operates the following educational institutions in the United States and Canada:
- Al Collins Graphic Design School, Tempe, Arizona
- Scottsdale Culinary Institute, Scottsdale, Arizona

- Brooks College, Long Beach, California
- Books Institute of Photography, Santa Barbara, California
- California Culinary Academy, San Francisco, California
- California School of Culinary Arts, South Pasadena, California
- Gibbs College, Norwalk, Connecticut
- International Academy of Design, Tampa, Florida
- Cooking & Hospitality Institute of Chicago, Chicago, Illinois
- Harrington Institute of Interior Design, Chicago, Illinois
- International Academy of Merchandising and Design, Chicago, Illinois
- Katharine Gibbs School, Boston, Massachusetts
- Brown Institute, Minneapolis, Minnesota
- McIntosh College, Dover, New Hampshire
- Gibbs College, Montclair, New Jersey
- Katharine Gibbs School, Piscataway, New Jersey
- Briarcliffe College, Bethpage, New York
- Briarcliffe College, Patchogue, New York
- Katharine Gibbs School, Melville, New York
- Katharine Gibbs School, New York, New York
- Western Culinary Institute, Portland, Oregon
- Allentown Business School, Allentown, Pennsylvania
- School of Computer Technology, Pittsburgh, Pennsylvania
- Katharine Gibbs School, Providence, Rhode Island
- Washington Business School, Vienna, Virginia
- School of Computer Technology, Fairmont, West Virginia
- International Academy of Design, Toronto, Ontario
- International Academy of Design, Montreal, Quebec

Many educational institutions have experienced significant growth after being acquired by Career Educational Corporation. Numerous students flock to two CEC schools — Al Collins Graphic Design School in Tempe, Arizona, and the International Academy of Design in Toronto, Canada, where they learn about the burgeoning career field of computer animation, among other areas of study. Al Collins Graphic Design School — Career Education Corporation's first acquisition — was purchased by CEC in 1994;

Katharine Gibbs School, Piscataway, New Jersey

Katharine Gibbs School, Boston

since that time, its student population has nearly doubled and revenues have almost tripled. The school graduated its first computer animators in 1998 and offers a program that combines newer computer-animation techniques with traditional animation methods. At the International Academy of Design, students are taught both animation techniques and are awarded associate degrees in occupational studies and animation at U.S. campuses. Graduates of both schools — as well as at other CEC schools in the United States and Canada that offer visual communication programs — obtain jobs in television and film, advertising, industrial and corporate communications, architecture, design and engineering, and in the scientific, medical and legal fields.

Brown Institute in Mendota Heights, Minnesota, was acquired by CEC in 1995; since then, the student population has grown by more than 60 percent and revenues have almost doubled. This growth was fueled in part by the upgrading of the school's information technology and visual communication curricula and by marketing outside of the Minneapolis area. Brown Institute opened a new culinary arts school in 1999 that includes a modern, 120,000-square-foot culinary facility. Currently about 60 percent of the student population is recruited from the Minneapolis/St. Paul area, and the rest are reached through the school's aggressive out-of-state marketing campaign.

In October 1998 CEC entered into an agreement with the world-renowned Le Cordon Bleu cooking school to establish Le Cordon Bleu culinary programs in North America. The Cordon Bleu curriculum — which offers expert instruction in American and French cuisine — will be gradually added to CEC's culinary arts programs as well as to culinary schools CEC acquires in the future, and will prepare students for careers in upscale restaurants as opposed to institutional settings.

The Katharine Gibbs schools — long recognized as a leader in the field of business studies — were acquired by Career Education Corporation in 1997. CEC expanded the curriculum from its original focus on business studies to include information technology and visual communication studies and introduced new advertising and marketing programs. As a result of these changes, enrollment has increased nearly 50 percent and the student population, formerly predominantly female, now has a large male contingent.

Numerous Career Education Corporation alumni have gone on to achieve distinction in their fields. These individuals include International Academy of Design graduates Daniel Giles, director of men's fashion, Holt Renfrew, and Mariko Nakagawa, interior designer at Yabo Pushelberg; California School of Culinary Arts graduates Cliff Karimi, executive chef at Interlude restaurant, and Janet McCracken, food writer at the *Los Angeles Times*; Brooks College graduate Byron Lars, an internationally acclaimed fashion designer; and Brown Institute graduates Rod Grams, U.S. senator from Minnesota, Chuck Hagel,

Brown Institute

U.S. senator from Nebraska and NBC San Diego anchorwoman Bree Walker.

Since the company's founding, Career Education Corporation has achieved record revenues and strong earnings. Student enrollment has continued to increase — with many schools having doubled their enrollment — and close to 93 percent of the schools' graduates obtain employment within six months of graduation. These impressive statistics are the result of intensive local, regional and national marketing efforts by Career Education Corporation that are specifically designed to highlight each school's strengths. Three sectors of the marketplace — current high school seniors and recent high school graduates, the nontraditional local adult market and out-of-state individuals — are targeted in a variety of ways including direct mail, high school recruiting, infomercials and television commercials, print advertising and CEC's Web site, which was implemented in 1997. High school students participate in career and financial aid seminars, and adults who reside in state are typically targeted by television, direct mail and newspaper advertisements. CEC's out-of-state division relies heavily on 30-second television spots and infomercials. Career Education Corporation's marketing efforts are continually monitored by the company's local and regional directors of admissions. A fourth leg of CEC's intensive marketing campaign — the international leg — was implemented in the fourth quarter of 1999; its goal is to recruit students from countries outside of the United States, including China, France and Japan.

The Internet is one of the most important ways in which Career Education Corporation reaches and interacts with students. In addition to the company's Web site, which provides information about each school for prospective students, CEC provides "distance learning" opportunities to working adults who possess a bachelor's degree, and offers them educational products and services through video, Internet and other distribution channels. Career Education Corporation's 10-month CPA Track

Scottsdale Culinary Institute, Scottsdale, Arizona

program offers adults the opportunity to enroll in accounting courses in preparation for the CPA exam.

Keeping abreast of various economic, demographic and societal changes has enabled Career Education Corporation to experience substantial growth since the company's inception in 1994. The rapid growth in recent years of information technology services has increased demands on new workers and required that they have training beyond the high school level; in fact, the number of high school graduates as well as the number of students enrolled in postsecondary education is expected to dramatically increase within the next decade. The spectacular rise in the demand for skilled workers has attracted increasing numbers of students to CEC's four core areas of study — computer technologies, visual communication

Scottsdale graduation

Pastry class

a student loan program; a further financing option for students is CEC's Professional Education Loan program that supplements federal, state and private financial aid for students. Prospective students can obtain information about various financial aid programs and fill out applications online by visiting the company's Web site, and they have the opportunity to meet with financial aid counselors at each school to obtain further information.

Since some CEC schools attract 40 percent or more of their student population from out-of-state, CEC advisors also help students locate suitable housing accommodations. CEC advisors help the many students who attend classes while working find appropriate part-time positions; trained CEC professionals also provide resumé-writing assistance and offer sound advice regarding networking, effective interviewing techniques and finding rewarding jobs once students complete their course work.

and design technologies, business studies and culinary arts. According to government statistics, there is a particular need for employees in the areas of Web design, accounting, business administration, marketing, office management and in the restaurant industry — and CEC will continue to focus its resources in the areas where there is the greatest need for skilled workers.

In addition to offering academic programs with strong career-advancement potential, CEC assists students in many other ways. To meet increased educational costs, Career Education Corporation, in partnership with the Student Loan Marketing Association (Sallie Mae), created

Career Education is well positioned for superior long-term growth. It will continue to acquire reputable and marketable schools in the United States and Canada, and may acquire or establish academic institutions outside of North America. In addition, CEC is increasing its efforts to recruit international students, specifically in the Pacific Rim, Latin America and Scandinavia. Its ultimate

(Far right) Classroom

Tech classroom

(Far left)
Art class

Cameramen

goal is to become the largest quality provider of post-secondary education.

The company is also planning on implementing new services and products that have strong long-term growth potential. In addition to the establishment of distance learning for working adults, CEC looks forward to producing and marketing educational publications and expanding its contract training operations — a program that provides customized training for businesses and governmental entities. Furthermore, Career Education Corporation plans on setting up "mega-campuses" in the Chicago, Los Angeles and New York markets — markets that are leading business and cultural centers. CEC will identify further acquisition opportunities in these top markets and strive to make the schools leaders in delivering the four types of career training the company provides.

Career Education Corporation's management team continues to identify and acquire choice schools throughout the United States and Canada and carry out aggressive marketing and recruitment programs to attract top-performing students. Company founder, President, CEO and Chairman of the Board John M. Larson is ably assisted by: Patrick K. Pesch, senior vice president and chief financial officer; Jacob P. Gruver, senior vice president of operations; Nick Fluge, senior vice president of operations; Robert W. Nachtshiem, vice president and controller; J. Patrick Andrews, vice president of advertising; Dr. Jon R. Coover, vice president of marketing and admissions; Patricia Kapper, vice president of education and placement; Mark J. Tobin, vice president of student finance and

regulatory affairs; James R. McEllhiney, vice president of regulatory compliance; Todd H. Steele, vice president of strategic planning and development; Mari-Ann Deering, vice president of human resources; and managing directors Steve Sotraidis, Carol Menck, Arlin K. Schmidt, Stephen Bartolini, David I. Schuchman, Julia A. Slick and Brian R. Williams. The company's six-member board of directors meets regularly to discuss company performance and to formulate future goals.

These goals for the future include the acquisition of two or three schools a year, the expansion of eight or nine educational programs per year, the opening of new CEC branch campuses, advanced degree offerings and an internal yearly growth projection of about 20 percent. CEC will carry on its intense marketing campaign of recruiting new students from the United States and abroad and will continue to place great importance on the retention of students once they begin their studies at a CEC academic institution. All CEC schools will continue to adapt to the changing needs of the marketplace and maintain the mission of offering a curriculum that focuses on areas where employer demand is strong.

Also crucial to the continued success of Career Education Corporation and to the students that CEC serves is what Jack Larson, CEC's chairman and president, calls "our moral report card." "Having a moral report card means ensuring that when our students complete their education that they are in a competitive posture for job interviews and find placement in their careers. That is our ultimate goal."

Northwestern Memorial Hospital

Since 1992, the people of Chicago have named Northwestern Memorial their most-preferred hospital. According to the National Research Corporation *Healthcare Market Guide 1999,* Chicagoans who make healthcare decisions cite Northwestern Memorial as their first choice for best quality, best physicians, best nurses and most-personalized care. When asked which hospital has the best reputation, they name Northwestern

Wesley Hospital, c. 1901. Wesley's first permanent facility stood at 25th and South Dearborn streets from 1891 to 1941.

WESLEY HOSPITAL

Memorial. In the late 1980s, the leaders of Northwestern Memorial crafted a vision that would create the most-advanced hospital of the 21st century — one where people who deliver the most compassionate care could access the highest level of technology available anywhere.

Occupying an entire city block in Chicago's downtown Streeterville neighborhood, Northwestern Memorial Hospital is the embodiment of a vision for healthcare in the 21st century. It unites breakthrough design, state-of-the-art technology and world-class, patient-focused care in a structure that stands as a landmark addition to Chicago's history of famed architecture. Dedicated in 1999, the building anticipates and accommodates future advancements in patient care and medical science. It is the newest addition to a medical center that, in partnership with Northwestern University Medical School, has pioneered medical developments and community partnerships, making Northwestern Memorial a national leader in patient care, education and research.

To understand the real achievement of this innovative hospital, though, is to know its past. As the second-oldest hospital in Chicago, the story of Northwestern Memorial is an evolution of the finest thought and research in healthcare, the most-dedicated caregivers and the greatest spirit of philanthropy — extending back more than 135 years. Today's extraordinary medical center is built upon the history of two major Chicago healthcare institutions: Passavant Memorial and Chicago Wesley Memorial hospitals. It is an amazing story of "heart and soul" that parallels the growth of Chicago itself.

The roots of Northwestern Memorial's values, traditions and successes can be traced back to the time of the Civil War. Traveling from Pennsylvania, Lutheran minister William Passavant Sr. arrived in Chicago to establish Deaconess

Hospital, a 15-bed mission hospital in a small house at Dearborn and Ontario streets in 1865. During that summer Rev. Passavant was both fascinated by a city of "rush and enterprise unequalled in the West" and alarmed by the impact of such rapid growth. Inadequate medical care, substandard housing and sanitation, an infected water supply and outbreaks of cholera, smallpox and typhoid fever made life particularly grim for thousands of newly arrived immigrants.

From the start, difficulties beset Deaconess Hospital. In 1866, an outbreak of cholera caused the small facility to be overwhelmed with the sick and dying. Despite these early challenges, the Board of Health endorsed the hospital for its cleanliness and order. The hospital also gained the backing of a number of influential citizens. Chicago's first mayor, William B. Ogden; newspaper publisher and former lieutenant governor William Deacon Bross; and prominent lawyer Ezra B. McCagg were members of the first Board of Visitors in 1867.

With newfound friends and financial support, Deaconess Hospital's success seemed assured. But on October 8, 1871, the Great Fire that ravaged so much of the fledgling city also engulfed the wood-framed hospital. "The flames came around the buildings so suddenly," Rev. Passavant wrote, "that the sick were saved only by the providence of God — the sisters even losing their own clothes. With the exception of a few movables, the expense book, and the door key, everything was consumed."

It would take Rev. Passavant 14 daunting years to rebuild. Finally the Emergency Hospital opened in December 1885 on West Superior Street, where it would remain for four decades. Reflecting the city's own burgeoning growth in industry, the hospital primarily treated accident and emergency cases from nearby rail depots, docks and factories. A number of eminent physicians and surgeons joined the staff, including Ralph Isham MD; Frank Billings MD; and its first chief surgeon, Christian Fenger MD. Following Rev. Passavant's death, the hospital was renamed in his honor, and its scope, size and service to the community expanded significantly. By the turn of

Passavant Memorial Hospital, c. 1930

the 20th century, a Woman's Aid Society had been formed and a school of nursing established, ensuring Passavant Memorial Hospital's vital leadership in providing healthcare to Chicagoans.

In much the same way that Passavant Memorial Hospital was founded in connection with the Lutheran deaconess movement, Isaac Newton Danforth MD established Wesley Hospital in partnership with the city's Methodist deaconesses. A well-known physician and strong supporter of the Methodist Episcopal Church, Dr. Danforth ardently rallied the support of clergy, business and civic leaders, as well as Northwestern University trustees. Dr. Danforth proposed a new hospital in conjunction with the Chicago Training School for City, Home and Foreign Missions and the Chicago Deaconess Home. "The advantages of this plan are obvious," Dr. Danforth affirmed. "It furnishes a refuge for the sick poor; it offers clinical facilities to our students..."

And so on Christmas Day 1888, the first patient was received in several rented rooms of the Chicago Training School located at Dearborn and Ohio streets. Named in honor of John Wesley, the religious leader who started free dispensaries in England a century earlier, the hospital soon moved and expanded to accommodate more patients. In 1891, hospital trustees agreed to strengthen ties to Northwestern University by securing property along

Opened in May 1999, the new, 2-million-square-foot medical center features two pavilions connected by a covered driveway.

South Dearborn Street between 24th and 25th streets as a joint location for a larger hospital, Northwestern University Medical School and several other university departments.

By the early 1900s, Wesley Hospital was prospering in its new home and was well-known for its excellent medical staff and nurses, patient amenities and its Lake Bluff convalescent home. Like Passavant Memorial, Wesley benefited from the generous support and vision of a long line of prominent trustees including: William Deering, co-founder of International Harvester; Gustavus Swift, founder of Swift and Company; Norman Harris, founder of Harris Bank; and Arthur Dixon, founder of the Arthur Dixon Transfer Company. In 1914, Wesley was renamed Wesley Memorial Hospital, following a $1 million gift from James Deering in memory of his father, William, and his sister, Abby Deering Howe.

Weathering the storm of World War I and Chicago's immigrant boom, both Wesley Memorial and Passavant Memorial continued to expand in the early decades of the 20th century as leaders in scientific discovery, clinical research and the development of medical education. It was during this period that leaders at Passavant warned of complacency and stressed that the hospital could never remain the same, but must move forward to survive. Passavant Memorial was offered an affiliation with Northwestern University Medical School and a loan of land and funds to build a new hospital on the Streeterville campus. In 1929, Passavant Memorial opened as a new, 325-bed facility on East Superior Street. The wood-paneled walls of its main lobby and other areas were noted for creating an inspiring sense of well-being for patients.

Reflecting the turmoil felt in Chicago and across the nation, the Depression years of the 1930s were difficult for both hospitals. Wesley Memorial emerged from

On May 1, 1999, the new $580 million Northwestern Memorial Hospital opened its doors to patients on time and on budget.

this period with a new orientation and agreed to move north to Northwestern's medical school campus. In December 1941, on the eve of World War II, a new, 525-bed Wesley Memorial Hospital was dedicated. Made possible by a $3 million gift from Inland Steel founder George Herbert Jones, the impressive new facility, with its soaring Gothic archways, quickly became known as the "Cathedral of Healing" for its patient-focused environment. It was renamed Chicago Wesley Memorial Hospital following a 1954 merger with Chicago Memorial Hospital.

Matching the accelerated tempo of Chicago's growth into a metropolis after World War II, both hospitals embarked on a path of expansion that enhanced the city's reputation as a center of medicine and research. Passavant and Wesley were nationally recognized for their world-class medical staff, quality of care, clinical

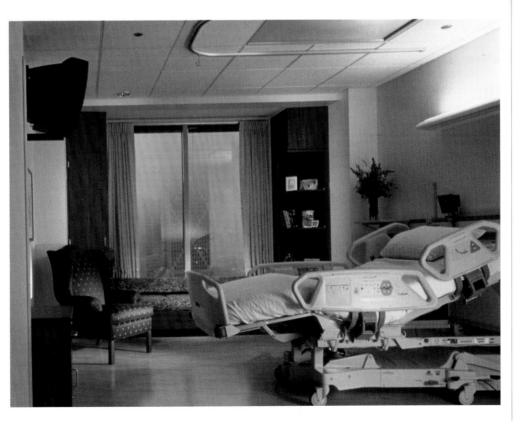

All patient rooms in the new facility are private and feature large windows and home-like furnishings.

Doctors use the latest in digital "filmless" images and picture archiving to speed diagnosis and treatment of patients.

Memorial's hard-earned reputation for delivering the best in science and service to patients.

By the late 1980s, healthcare was in a period of rapid transition. In a bold move, the hospital's board of directors began planning for a model of 21st century healthcare. In 1991 one square block (bordered by Fairbanks Court, St. Clair, Huron and Erie Streets) was selected as the site for a 2-million-square-foot facility combining both inpatient and outpatient care. Ground was broken in October 1994, and over the next five years, the largest privately funded construction project in Illinois took shape. As part of its commitment to the community, the hospital awarded more than $100 million in construction projects to businesses operated by women and minorities.

On May 1, 1999, the new $580 million Northwestern Memorial Hospital opened its doors to

As part of its commitment to the community, the hospital awarded more than $100 million in construction projects to businesses operated by women and minorities.

advances and educational programs for physicians and health professionals. They also cultivated and extended their thriving, local community outreach efforts, which were a mainstay from their earliest years. A network of auxiliaries, board members and numerous volunteers raised much-needed funds for care and improvements and also provided countless hours of assistance to patients and families.

The neighboring hospitals drew closer in the 1960s when they began cooperative planning with the creation of the McGaw Medical Center of Northwestern University. As a final acknowledgement of their long-shared vision, Passavant Memorial Hospital and Chicago Wesley Memorial Hospital consolidated in September 1972 to become Northwestern Memorial Hospital, the largest private hospital in the Midwest and one of the nation's premier academic medical centers.

The union of two of Chicago's oldest and most prestigious hospitals underscored a commitment to meeting the future challenges of healthcare, while upholding a shared legacy of compassionate care, innovative medical education and pioneering research. The addition of Prentice Women's Hospital and Maternity Center and the Stone Institute of Psychiatry in 1975 further strengthened Northwestern

patients on time and on budget. Of that amount, $126 million came from philanthropic sources. The new hospital was built from the "inside out" with input from patients, families, physicians, staff, Northwestern University Medical School, donors and the community to provide convenient access to a wide range of healthcare services.

Eight shared floors form a base connecting two towers: the Feinberg Pavilion for inpatient care and the Galter

Pavilion for outpatient care. The Feinberg Inpatient Pavilion includes a 24,000-square-foot emergency department, 32 operating rooms, and nearly 500 private patient rooms, including more than 90 intensive-care beds. Each room has a large window that patients can see out of even when lying in bed; a window seat that converts to a bed, allowing a family member to stay overnight; and artwork that has been selected to promote a healing environment.

A unique feature of the facility is the Health Learning Center. Supporting a variety of learning styles, from introductory books and advanced medical journals to interactive and Internet-based education, the center offers patients, visitors and the public a way to find answers to their healthcare questions in a welcoming library environment. This gift to the community, as well as the Florence and Ike Sewell Museum, are free and open to the public.

As the primary teaching hospital for Northwestern University Medical School, the quality of medical care is enhanced through the integration of education and research in an environment that encourages excellence of practice, critical inquiry and learning. The medical staff includes more than 1,200 physicians, with faculty appointments in virtually every medical and surgical specialty. More than 500 physicians are members of the Northwestern Memorial Faculty Foundation and another 500 have independent practices. In addition, the Northwestern Memorial Physicians Group brings medical treatment to people in local communities.

In total the hospital has approximately 4,500 employees and 800 volunteers. Through their special

> Northwestern Memorial supports area clinics that serve low-income patients as part of its commitment to the community.

attention to putting the needs of patients and families first, the hospital staff reflects Northwestern Memorial's devotion to its mission of providing the best-possible patient experience.

Being part of Chicago means being active in the community. Northwestern Memorial supports area clinics that serve low-income patients, including Erie Family Health Center and Winfield Moody Health Center. The hospital has also "adopted" the Bryd Academy elementary school and partners with the Medical Explorers' branch of the Boy Scouts, United Way, American Heart Association and other organizations. In addition, it supports a number of internships for young people interested in healthcare careers.

Another connection with the community is Northwestern Memorial's Stone Institute of Psychiatry. It has a long-standing partnership with Lawson House YMCA to provide the homeless population with mental health care. The hospital also offers a wide range of community health classes and screenings, including the Healthy Transitions program for seniors.

With some 7,000 newborns delivered a year, Prentice Women's Hospital and Maternity Center provides care for more births than any other hospital in the state. However, the hospital has outgrown its current space. Hospital leaders continue to look to the future and plans are underway to build a new women's hospital on the site of the Wesley Pavilion on East Superior Street. Expanded campus research facilities are also in development to accommodate an additional 165 investigators.

From humble beginnings as a 15-bed mission hospital to a state-of-the-art medical campus serving a dynamic American city, Northwestern Memorial's evolution is fully interwoven with Chicago's history. Their shared future is bright and their partnership to better the lives of Chicago's citizens continues.

The Health Learning Center is a staffed, full-service medical and wellness library that offers up-to-date information to the community.

Museums In the Park

Museums In the Park is an association of nine museums located on Park District land throughout the city of Chicago. The relationship between the Chicago Park District and Museums In the Park has existed since 1893 and is a nationally recognized, model public-private relationship. Local real estate tax dollars flow through the Chicago Park District to Museums In the Park to support the maintenance of the structures occupied by its member museums and to assist its member museums in meeting their responsibility to educate the children, and all citizens, of the city of Chicago and the state of Illinois.

The nine museums have a significant role in education, tourism and the economy of Chicago and Illinois. 1.2 million children in school groups enrich their educational experience by visiting these institutions annually. Many more children benefit through technology and other educational programs, including collaborative educational programs, some of which are described herein. Together these museums provide thousands of jobs and have an economic impact of more than $354 million annually. Tourism has been a significant industry in Illinois and these museums have been very instrumental to the tourism growth that has been experienced in Illinois.

Adler Planetarium

Chicago Historical Society

CHICAGO HISTORICAL SOCIETY

Founded in 1856 by Chicago's leading entrepreneurs, the Chicago Historical Society (CHS) is Chicago's first cultural institution and functions as the communal memory of the city. This memory is encoded in a collection of more than 20 million objects and documents that compose one of the nation's most unique and important resources for understanding the evolution of America into an urban society and nation. Functioning both as a museum and a research center, CHS also offers a broad variety of engaging educational programs for the public and schoolchildren, including traveling exhibitions; dance, music and other performing arts; lectures; symposia; classes; field trips; and tours.

CHS offers visitors unique opportunities to learn local history from multiple perspectives and to appreciate the interplay of national, regional and local trends and events. Long-term exhibitions on American history from 1765 to 1865 help to explain Chicago's early development and rise as a city. The Chicago History Galleries likewise illustrate the city's steel-skeleton-frame architecture, its mail-order business, its contributions to popular culture, and its myriad of inventions and innovations that have shaped Chicago's identity as a unique, world-class city.

In the 21st century, CHS will continue its efforts to collect, interpret and present post-World War II Chicago (especially the city's rich and diverse neighborhoods and ethnic populations) in the context of national events and trends.

ADLER PLANETARIUM & ASTRONOMY MUSEUM

State of the art in 1930 when it opened as the first planetarium in the Western Hemisphere, the Adler Planetarium & Astronomy Museum remains on the cutting edge of technology at the dawn of the 21st century.

The Adler's 60,000-square-foot Sky Pavilion has as its centerpiece, StarRider™, the world's first interactive digital theater. The new Sky Pavilion also showcases four exhibition galleries where visitors can uncover the marvels of the dynamic universe.

The landmark 1930s building was recently renovated and effectively combined innovative and interactive exhibits with a respect for its history. The project included the refurbishment of the Zeiss Sky Theater, installation of the Gateway to the Universe gallery and the creation of a new History of Astronomy Gallery, which houses one of the pre-eminent collections of scientific instruments, rare books, photographs, early maps, charts and star atlases in the world.

THE ART INSTITUTE OF CHICAGO

One of the world's leading art museums, The Art Institute of Chicago reveals 40 centuries of human creativity. From ancient Chinese bronzes to the latest works by contemporary artists, from Rembrandt's paintings to African wood carvings, the collections include some of the finest art ever produced.

Paintings, sculptures, prints and drawings, photographs, art of Africa and the Americas, textiles, decorative arts, and architectural fragments and drawings — all are displayed in this eclectic museum. Especially noteworthy is the internationally acclaimed collection of Impressionist and Post-Impressionist pictures, with many outstanding examples by Monet, Renoir, Degas, van Gogh and other painters of the period. Additional highlights include the 68 enthralling Thorne Miniature Rooms,

which are fascinating to all ages, and the Chicago Stock Exchange Trading Room, designed by Adler and Sullivan and reconstructed from the original building.

The Department of Museum Education provides free public programs to encourage people of all ages to explore the world of art, and its Kraft Education Center offers fun-filled family programs throughout the year. The Restaurant on the Park serves elegant, leisurely lunches, and the Court Cafeteria serves quick family meals. The Museum Shop sells unique gifts and paper products, many based on the collections, plus a large inventory of art books. Visitors can enjoy exhibitions from worldwide collections, included in general admission unless otherwise noted.

THE MUSEUM OF SCIENCE AND INDUSTRY

For most of this century the Museum of Science and Industry (MSI) has been helping visitors explore scientific and technological advances that have changed the way people live and work. The building was born during one of history's most spectacular moments, the 1893 World's Columbian Exposition, and with such auspicious beginnings, it was clear that great things lay ahead.

The institution beloved by millions began as one man's inspiration. In 1926 the museum's founder, Julius Rosenwald, imagined a place that would stimulate America's "inventive genius" by enabling visitors to learn through hands-on discovery. When the museum opened its doors in 1933, Rosenwald's dream came to life. Countless individuals have since dedicated themselves to advancing Rosenwald's vision by updating MSI's exhibits, cementing relationships within the community and preserving the museum's grand infrastructure.

The museum's first leaders had big plans. They set the standard by building a coal mine within the museum. Since then MSI has brought a World War II submarine across Lake Michigan, driven a 727 jet down Lake Shore Drive and become the final splashdown site for the Apollo 8 space capsule.

Now, a technological revolution is catapulting society forward at blinding speed. The museum's role in inviting guests to experience these innovations, making science and technology accessible and interesting, has never been more important.

The Michigan Avenue entrance of the Art Institute of Chicago, 1983

The Museum of Science and Industry has inspired more than 160 million visitors and encouraged their creativity in making sense of the 20th century. The museum invites the public to join it for the adventures that await in the 21st.

The Peggy Notebaert Nature Museum, sheltered by towering trees *Photo by Ron Schramm*

THE PEGGY NOTEBAERT NATURE MUSEUM

Dedicated to scientific literacy for all, the Chicago Academy of Sciences was founded in 1857 by a small group of scientists headed by Robert Kennicott, a dynamic young explorer with a zeal for collecting plant and animal species.

Fascinated by the biodiversity of the great prairies, Kennicott combed Illinois collecting and naming species never before scientifically documented. His collections made up the Academy, which became renowned for its educational programming and conservation initiatives.

Today, Kennicott's dream lives on in the Peggy Notebaert Nature Museum, a stunning new facility that brings the outdoors in. Dedicated to exploring and nurturing one's relationship with the environment, the new museum combines the beauty of nature with cutting-edge scientific discovery.

The Nature Museum is home to six permanent exhibits, including the spectacular 2,300-square-foot Judy Istock Butterfly Haven, a glass-enclosed atrium aflutter with over 400 native Midwest butterflies. Wilderness Walk, which houses specimens from the Academy's early collections, pays homage to Illinois' woodland, dunal and prairie landscapes and stands as a valuable anthology of the plants, animals, birds and insects that existed in great numbers in Illinois over 100 years ago.

The Academy, which was the first museum to rise from and honor the Illinois prairie, encourages all its visitors to embrace and protect that glorious, yet endangered, expanse

of land. Through educational programming, special family activities, lecture series, group tours and many other unique events, the Nature Museum offers its visitors a rich experience.

THE MEXICAN FINE ARTS CENTER MUSEUM

The Mexican Fine Arts Center Museum (MFACM) was founded in 1982 and opened its doors in 1987 because local activists sought to fill a gap in the presentation of their culture in Chicago. The foundation of this important institution was more than a political coming together of educators. It was an emotional response by Mexicans, educators and community activists concerned about the lack of historical or artistic representation in the educational system and local art institutions. The founder was Carlos Tortolero, the executive director.

In 1997, only 10 years after opening its doors in the Pilsen/Little Village Community of Chicago, MFACM became the first and only Latino museum in the nation to be accredited by the American Association of Museums. MFACM's programming includes visual arts exhibitions, performing arts presentations, educational programs, the Yollocalli Youth Museum and Radio Arte, a youth-operated public radio station.

In marking the MFACM's 10th anniversary, groundbreaking for the museum's expansion took place on October 23, 1997. The grand opening is scheduled for April 2001. The expansion will enable the museum to serve a larger audience. The expansion will create the *Mexicanidad* permanent exhibition gallery, which will display the works of Mexicans and Mexican-Americans from ancient times to the present, making it the first-ever international compilation of Mexican culture in one exhibit.

THE FIELD MUSEUM

Chicago's Field Museum is one of the world's great museums of science, environment and culture, a focus of public learning and scholarly research. It's a treasury of more than 20 million objects, from ancient mummies, to endangered plants and animals, to Sue, the biggest and most complete *T. rex* ever found.

Throughout the museum, scores of exhibitions engage visitors in the excitement and adventure of learning. One can explore an Egyptian tomb; watch real fossils being uncovered by skilled preparators; shrink to the size of a bug and discover the world beneath one's feet; be immersed in the cultures and environments of Africa, China, the Americas and much more.

A center for research, The Field Museum was founded to provide a permanent home for the natural science and anthropology collections featured in the World's Columbian Exposition of 1893. Today, its cultural, archeological, botanical, zoological and geological collections total more than 20 million objects — and it's adding to them every day.

From the rain forests of southern Chile, to Wyoming's fossil lakes, to the highlands of Madagascar, The Field Museum supports the studies of more than 70 scientists. Its researchers are at the center of issues of global importance — working, quite literally, to save the Earth.

As its scientists learn about the world, so does the public. At The Field Museum, opportunities for lifelong learning abound. Its exhibitions, of course, are a major avenue of self-directed learning. But it also offers a wide range of public programs.

SHEDD AQUARIUM

The year was 1924. John Graves Shedd, one of Chicago's prominent civic and business leaders, bestowed a generous and truly unique gift upon his fellow residents of the city: $2 million earmarked to construct the world's largest aquarium. While John G. Shedd did not live to see his project completed, his name remains synonymous with the institution that has garnered international respect as one of the world's finest museums of aquatic life.

Physical construction for the Aquarium began in 1927, and the building was completed in 1929. On May 30, 1930, Shedd Aquarium debuted with the greatest variety of sea life ever exhibited at one institution and as the first inland aquarium to maintain permanent exhibits of both saltwater and freshwater animals.

In 1991 its first major addition opened, and the Oceanarium, the world's largest indoor marine mammal pavilion, drew 2 million people a year to see Pacific white-sided dolphins, sea otters, beluga whales and more.

Opened in summer 2000, the Amazon Rising exhibit highlights the aquatic inhabitants of the Amazon. Guests see diverse aquatic and terrestrial life including piranhas, catfishes, stingrays and sideneck turtles, as well as marmosets, birds, butterflies, giant spiders and a sloth.

Future plans include highlighting one of the most spectacular ecosystems on Earth, the Indo-Pacific coral reefs, which are severely threatened by overfishing, rapid coastal development and other human activities. The exhibit and new addition, opening in 2002, will feature a half-dozen species of sharks, stingrays, jellyfish and seahorses, along with a number of fragile reef-building corals.

THE DUSABLE MUSEUM OF AFRICAN-AMERICAN HISTORY

Founded in 1961 by teacher and art historian Dr. Margaret Burroughs and other leading Chicago citizens, the DuSable Museum of African-American History is one of the few independent institutions of its kind in the United States. Developed to preserve and interpret the experiences and achievements of people of African descent, it is dedicated to the collection, documentation, preservation and study of the history and culture of Africans and African Americans. The DuSable Museum is proud of its diverse holdings, which number more than 150,000 pieces, and include paintings, sculpture, printworks and historical memorabilia.

Chicago is a city rich in African-American history. The museum is named for Jean Baptiste Point DuSable, an African-Haitian who in 1779 established the trading post and permanent settlement that would become known as Chicago.

Permanent exhibits at the DuSable Museum include: "Harold Washington in Office," "Treasures of DuSable: Selections From the Permanent Collection of Art," "Distorted Images," "Fight to Fly: Blacks in Aviation" and "Africa Speaks."

The DuSable Museum remains a community institution dedicated to serving the cultural and educational needs of its members. Through expanded programming the DuSable Museum is preparing for the new century. In the future, as in the past, it will remain a cultural institution devoted to excellence and to providing cultural enrichment for all.

Shedd Aquarium

Landmarks Preservation Council of Illinois

The Landmarks Preservation Council of Illinois is the state's leading voice for historic preservation. From the rubble of the 1971 demolition of Adler and Sullivan's masterpiece Old Chicago Stock Exchange, LPCI rose to become a 2,000-member, statewide organization. In the almost 30 years since its founding, it has gone on to save countless architectural and historic treasures throughout the state of Illinois. It has established a variety of programs that continue to facilitate, educate and promote historic preservation.

LPCI's founding mission was to stop the demolition of significant buildings in downtown Chicago. Its mission today is the same, only broader — the scope and geography now embrace architecturally and historically significant archeological sites, structures and historic districts in all the cities, towns and rural areas of Illinois. The list of accomplishments is impressive.

Henry Demarest Lloyd House, Winnetka

SAVE BUILDINGS

After leading the charge but failing to save the Old Stock Exchange, the fledgling organization improved its ability to garner popular, political and media support. Through other more successful advocacy efforts, resources such as the Marquette Building, the Chicago Theater, the Reliance Building and St. Mary of the Angels Church in Chicago, as well as the Bloomington Courthouse Square, Oakbrooks' Mayslake and the Zimmerman archeological site are among those that have been saved for future generations.

An untested preservation strategy was used to save the Henry Demarest Lloyd house in Winnetka in 1976. After the property was donated to LPCI, a conservation easement was placed on it and it was then resold to private owners. With a conservation easement, all subsequent owners are bound in perpetuity to preserve and maintain the critical historic features of the property. LPCI monitors their performance to ensure long-term preservation. The donation/easement/resale strategy was repeated at the Fitzpatrick House in Lockport and the David Adler-designed Kuppenheimer House, also in Winnetka. The success of these easements led to LPCI's Easement Program, which today holds easements on 48 historic properties throughout the state. That count doesn't include Fort Sheridan, where an easement program is an integral part of its successful preservation. Fort Sheridan is a former army base whose 96 historic structures are being converted to upscale, single-family homes, town-houses and apartments.

In neighborhoods with limited economic resources and prior history of inappropriate alterations to housing stock, a private owner willing to step up to the plate can be hard to find. In such cases, LPCI has taken on the role of owner and developer. Pulling together skilled professionals and volunteers, the organization rehabilitated three houses in the Tri-Taylor Historic District as well as two of the Frank Lloyd Wright-designed Waller Apartments. The finished residences were resold to moderate-income owners.

FACILITATE PRESERVATION

With the complex legislative and financial system that makes up the economy, buildings can be lost because existing regulations and tax implications encourage demolition and new construction rather than preservation.

Throughout its history, LPCI has been active in sponsoring legislation that removes obstacles and establishes incentives for preservation. The first five-year effort led to the establishment of the Illinois Historic Preservation Agency in 1976. Charged with administering statewide preservation planning, landmark designations, historic resource surveys and review of the rehabilitation of historic buildings to ensure that they meet preservation standards, the agency has become a vital force for preservation in the state. LPCI supports and cooperates with the state without losing sight of the need to push and prod it to even greater action at critical times.

The panoply of tax incentives for the rehabilitation of historic buildings has grown over the years, and LPCI has been the initiator and/or ardent supporter of much of the enabling legislation. The statewide property tax freeze for single-family homes, later expanded to include up to six-unit owner-occupied residences, and the Cook County Class L incentive, which extends property tax relief to commercial properties, were major achievements of LPCI. Hundreds of homeowners throughout the state have benefited from the property tax assessment freeze, while early results of the Class L program successes can be found in eight approved projects, including the completed Crown Plaza Hotel (formerly Allerton) and the Burnham Hotel (Reliance Building).

Tax benefits may not provide enough dollars to make a preservation project economically feasible. Recognizing the crucial need for real "bricks-and-mortar" money, LPCI established its revolving Preservation Fund in 1976 after the sale of the Lloyd property. Over the years the fund has awarded low-interest loans for needy projects throughout the state. In addition to being the catalyst for the already-mentioned Tri-Taylor and Waller projects, another loan program was the Neighborhood Initiative. Loans of up to $10,000 were made available for homes on Chicago's boulevards. One of the buildings to benefit was the Ida B. Wells House, residence of the late 19th/early 20th century black social reformer.

Unfortunately, even with favorable-interest loans, the economics of some projects just don't pencil out. Though small, LPCI's Endangered Grants Program can offer up to $5,000 on a quick turnaround basis to fund some critical step towards saving an important property for a community. The need for grant money continues to be so important that the organization was successful in the 1999 legislative session in seeing a statewide Heritage Trust Fund established. Adequate and regular funding for this grant-making arm of state government is a top priority.

EDUCATE

Citizens of Chicago and Illinois are vastly more aware today than they were in 1971 of the wealth of architectural and historic resources throughout the state, thanks in no small measure to LPCI. Beginning with the first publication of the "Loop Inventory" in 1975, through technical

(Far left)
Marquette Building, Chicago
Photo by Chicago Architectural Photographing Company

Chicago Theatre
Photo by Don Dubroff

Fort Sheridan Officer's House, Chicago

(Far right)
Waller Apartments,
Chicago

Henry Demarest Lloyd
House, Winnetka

publications on historic building materials and design guidelines for rehabilitation of historic buildings, LPCI seeks to educate. Tours such as the Sacred Places Tour have been delighting participants to the wonders of ecclesiastical architecture since 1978. For almost 20 years, the organization-sponsored statewide preservation conference has brought together preservation experts with those seeking preservation advice. Held in historic communities throughout the state, it has increased awareness of important but too frequently overlooked historic resources in the smaller cities and towns of Illinois.

PROMOTE

Sometimes educational efforts need a boost through more aggressive marketing and promotion. The Ten Most Endangered Historic Places Program, begun by LPCA in 1995, draws attention to the most critical preservation problems faced by the state each year. The public announcement in Springfield and the accompanying media excitement have contributed to saving an array of historic resources that reflect the richness of the state: the Grand Valley of the Kickapoo archeological site, the Skokie North Shore train station, the Wagner farm in Glenview and the Frank Lloyd Wright-designed Glasner House in Glencoe, among many others.

Everyone likes attention for the good things they do and preservationists are no exception.

Tri-Taylor House,
Chicago

The Preservation Awards program, begun in 1991, honors projects that promote preservation in a variety of ways — model rehabilitation projects, media coverage, educational efforts, advocacy, community leadership and the Preservation Project of the Year. Now sponsored by and called the Richard H. Driehaus Foundation Preservation Awards, recent winners have included Holy Family Church in Chicago, the Baha'i Temple in Wilmette and the Normal Theater.

THE FUTURE

The Landmarks Preservation Council of Illinois has grown over the last 30 years into a mature, stable, not-for-profit organization. Although it has never lost sight of its vision, it is no longer the scrappy organization it started out as. Protests, picket lines and lawsuits are still used as effective tools, but so are ordinary diplomacy and compromise. Today, government officials, developers and property owners recognize its expertise and listen to what it says. LPCI operates with a broad-based statewide membership, a strong board of community leaders, loyal donors, a professional staff and a sound endowment fund. Preservation in Illinois has come a long way since 1971, but the job is never over. LPCI intends to be around for the next 30 years and for years after that. Its goal is to ensure that the architectural and historic resources of Illinois endure so that future generations may enjoy the physical presence of their cultural heritage.

CINN

The Chicago Institute of Neurosurgery and Neuroresearch (CINN) has revolutionized the treatment of neurological disorders by combining state-of-the-art medical technology with a holistic approach to quality patient care. By placing the physical and emotional needs of patients above its bottom line, CINN has pioneered subspecialized healthcare and the development and use of non-invasive neurological treatments.

Working in partnership with many prominent hospitals throughout the Chicagoland and Northwest Indiana area, CINN draws patients from throughout the country who are suffering from neurological disorders. This renowned institute offers subspecialty neurosurgery with expertise in benign and malignant tumors, skull base tumors, vascular neurosurgery, stereotactic radiosurgery, back and neck surgery, epilepsy, pediatric neurosurgery and spinal instrumentation surgery.

The formation of CINN is the result of the efforts put forth by Dr. Leonard J. Cerullo, CINN founder and chair of the department of neurosurgery at Rush-Presbyterian-St. Luke's Medical Center. His goal was to create a traditional "family doctor" setting with sophisticated medical resources that would provide patient-friendly methods of treatment. Cerullo's creed when forming the institute was parallel to that of architect Daniel Burnham when designing Chicago's layout — "Make no small plans."

"The goal of CINN was to offer premier personalized care with a minimum of red tape," says Cerullo. "By acquiring optimum equipment and treatments and by recruiting neurosurgeons and clinical professionals committed to quality care, we have exceeded this goal and set the bar for service in the healthcare industry."

CINN became a reality in 1987 through a collaboration with Columbus Hospital. The institute went about obtaining innovative technology that allowed for alternatives to surgical practices commonly used when dealing with neurological disorders. One such alternative is the Leksell Gamma Knife®, which allows for non-invasive treatment of brain tumors and other abnormalities. The Gamma Knife uses high intensity gamma rays — with no physical invasion of the brain — to control brain tumors. CINN was one of the first centers in the United States to use this technology.

"Our physicians choose the least-invasive approach to treating patients," says Sharon DeRosa, chief operating officer for CINN. "Humanism is at the core of our operation."

The institute's recruitment process ensures that each doctor, nurse and employee shares the high level of consideration for patient care held by CINN. In addition CINN has set up a treatment program that offers a detailed explanation of disorders and counseling for patients. "We seek the participation of our patients and their families in the care process to ensure the best outcomes achievable," says DeRosa.

Jerome McBride of Westchester was referred to CINN after he was diagnosed with a brain tumor in 1996. McBride says in addition to successfully removing the tumor, Dr. Cerullo and the CINN staff provided comfort and education during a difficult time. "It was an unbelievably good experience — given the conditions," says McBride. "All of the staff were attentive to detail and exceptionally compassionate."

While CINN's continuing medical research is poised to provide dramatic breakthroughs in the healthcare industry, providing compassionate, pre-eminent patient care remains at the forefront of the institute's agenda.

The Chicago Institute of Neurosurgery and Neuroresearch (CINN), founded by Dr. Leonard J. Cerullo in 1987, serves as a pioneer in the treatment of neurological disorders and quality patient care.

Advocate Health Care

Advocate Health Care, a "new" company with roots 100-years deep, became a great organization to serve Greater Chicago while the Windy City was becoming the pride of the prairies. Now, it is the market share leader in the area and noted for its commitment to excellent service through listening and responding to the health care needs of a diverse community.

Trinity Hospital's renovated labor and delivery suites provide new mothers with a single room for the entire birthing process.

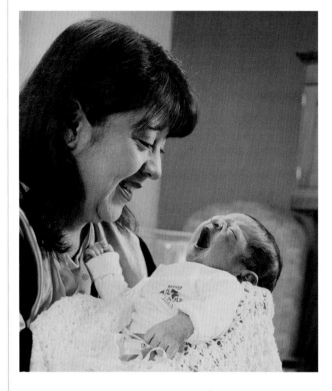

Advocate Medical Group operates the Midwest's first outpatient PET (positron emission tomography) Center, which offers the most powerful diagnostic imaging tool available.

Advocate Health Care is doctors, nurses, hospitals and more. Offering a continuum of health care services, Advocate brings together more than 4,200 physicians, eight respected local hospitals, many outpatient health care facilities, home health and long-term care and dozens of Advocate Health Centers and physician practices across the six-county Chicago area. Advocate also offers a toll-free customer service center, HealthAdvisor[SM], that can help consumers quickly obtain the medical information they need on doctors, health-related topics or seminars. Advocate's Web site offers additional health information.

Many of these services are made possible through partnerships with other community members such as libraries, churches, schools, social service organizations, government agencies and other health care providers. Generous support from individuals, foundations and corporations helps Advocate, a not-for-profit organization, provide an extra measure of excellence and compassion.

Today's robust Advocate Health Care was born in 1995 when EHS Health Care and Lutheran General HealthSystem joined forces to better serve their communities. EHS Health Care traced its beginnings to 1906 and grew out of the Evangelical Synod of North America. Lutheran General HealthSystem goes back to 1897, when Norwegians from Chicago's Northwest Side formed it as Norwegian Lutheran Deaconess Home and Hospital.

These church affiliations evolved into Advocate's present-day sponsorship by the Evangelical Lutheran Church in America and the United Church of Christ. From their beginnings, both organizations concentrated not only on physical healing, but broad beneficial programs of social work and education that extended well into their communities, ever mindful of their faith-based mission to heal and to help.

Today's Advocate Health Care ranks as the leading integrated health care delivery system in both Chicago and the nation. The March 1999 issue of *Modern*

Healthcare, an authoritative industry magazine, reported on a study by the SMG Marketing Group, noting in a headline that "Chicago's Advocate tops on analysis of performance, integration, physician participation." Included was a list of the top 100 integrated health care networks in the country — with Advocate in the No. 1 position. SMG's study analyzed each system's performance in seven key areas: hospital utilization, financial performance, services and access, outpatient utilization, contractual capabilities, physician participation and integration.

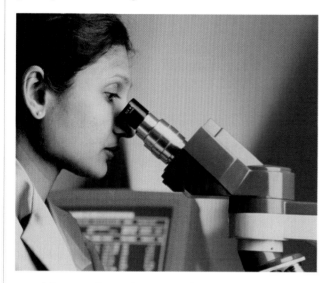

Advocate also ranks as one of the metropolitan area's largest employers, with 21,500 associates working throughout the system. They help to treat more than 1.2 million people at Advocate's hospitals and other health care facilities each year.

Ever-increasing numbers are not the goal at Advocate; however, meeting patient and community needs better is. Advocate's vision is "to be a nationally recognized faith-based system with the best people, service and health outcomes in Chicagoland." To achieve that vision, Advocate has identified five core strategies:

- Service breakthrough: providing patients and their families with service that exceeds their expectations and distinguishes Advocate customer service from others.
- Work life quality: creating a work environment, culture and systems that result in high levels of employee commitment.
- Clinical excellence: guiding patients to the most appropriate level of care in a timely fashion and managing care seamlessly across the continuum in a consistent, high-quality and cost-effective manner.

- Technology leadership: Using state-of-the-art clinical and information technology to support service breakthrough, clinical excellence and other strategies.
- Innovative growth: serving more people by expanding current services, designing new programs and developing the network of services through strategic alliances and partnerships.

Richard Risk, Advocate's president and CEO, believes Advocate's vision and strategies are meaningful tools to empower associates.

"If we all understand Advocate's priorities, then we have a framework for prioritizing our own activities, " Risk notes. "At the same time, a strategic plan is a tool that unifies Advocate so that our collective resources are harnessed for a common purpose — achieving and fully implementing our mission, values and philosophy, or MVP, as we call it."

Advocate defines its mission as serving "the health needs of individuals, families and communities through a wholistic philosophy rooted in our fundamental understanding of human beings as created in the image of God." Serving as an internal compass guiding Advocate's relationships and actions are five values: compassion, equality, excellence, partnership and stewardship.

Ultimately, the yardstick for measuring the success of any organization is best wielded not by the people who work for that institution, but rather by those who are served by it. That must be in the back of Richard Risk's mind when he says, "We'll know we've achieved our MVP when our patients can say 'I've been to Advocate and I've been to other places, and Advocate is different and better than anything I've ever experienced.'"

Advocate's systemwide, centrally managed laboratory service provides high-quality, state-of-the-art test results to all sites of care.

More than 400 residents are trained in Advocate's graduate medical education program each year.

Alexian Brothers Health System

A small frame house in Chicago served as the Alexian Brothers' first hospital in the United States.

The history of the Alexian Brothers Health System is rooted in a value system that emphasizes compassion and a tradition of reaching out to the poor, the sick and the dying, and maintaining a commitment to the disenfranchised members of society. Serving individuals of all socioeconomic levels and promoting healing of the whole person — body, mind and spirit — through physical, psychosocial and spiritual care remains the mission of the Alexian Brothers, whose corporate head-quarters is located in the Chicago suburb of Elk Grove Village, Illinois. Under the skillful leadership of Alexian Brothers Health System President and CEO Brother Thomas Keusenkothen and Chairman of the Board Brother Larry Krueger — who oversees the nationwide system of Alexian Brothers health care facilities — Alexian Brothers offers superb medical care to individuals in Illinois, as well as in Wisconsin, Missouri, Tennessee and New Jersey. The Alexian Brothers also maintain health care ministries in Belgium, England, Ireland, Germany, India and the Philippines.

The Alexian Brothers' tradition of promoting healing of the whole person — body, mind and spirit — continues today.

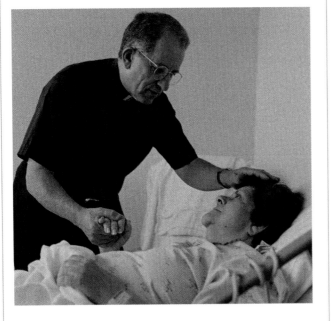

The Alexian Brothers trace their roots to the Beghards — men who served the sick, poor and homeless in Germany and other countries 700 years ago. The Beghards evolved into religious communities and some chose as their patron, Saint Alexius, the son of a wealthy Roman senator, who devoted his life to serving the poor. In 1481 these communities were designated as the Congregation of Alexian Brothers.

1866 marked the Alexian Brothers' entry into the United States. Brother Bonaventure Thelen arrived in New York from Germany and that same year, opened a hospital — the Alexian Brothers' first — in a small frame house at Dearborn and Schiller Streets in Chicago. Land for a new hospital on Franklin Street was purchased in the 1860s. This facility, which opened a year later, provided housing for the Alexian Brothers as well as accommo-dations for 70 patients.

The hospital was completely destroyed in the Great Chicago Fire of 1871, and patients and the Alexian Brothers had to be housed in temporary wooden barracks until a new facility could be built. A 170-bed hospital was completed in 1873, then enlarged several times. Once again, though, fate intervened. This facility — which had admitted 338 patients at year's end, half of them charity cases — had to be torn down to make way for the Chicago Elevated Railway, which was being planned to provide public transportation for a rapidly growing metropolis. The hospital property was sold to the railway for $200,000, and with this money, the Alexian Brothers bought a tract of land at Belden and Racine avenues in Chicago and opened a new, modern hospital. This hospi-tal provided exemplary medical care to people of all social classes until 1968, when a larger hospital was built in Elk Grove Village, Illinois.

Today, Alexian Brothers Medical Center in Elk Grove Village serves the health care needs of the community by providing the highest-quality care in the following areas: acute, skilled nursing and trauma care; cardiac, cancer, obstetrical and pediatric care; outpatient treatment and day surgery; physical rehabilitation, speech and occu-pational therapy; and ophthalmology, pharmacy and pastoral care. Other services include a women's center (including mammography suites); a stroke unit; and infertility programs.

St. Alexius Medical Center in Hoffman Estates, Illinois, is also an essential part of the Alexian Brothers Health System. Purchased in 1999, the 344-bed community hospital and trauma center — like all Alexian Brothers facilities — reflects the Alexian Brothers' holistic perspective and respect for the advantaged and disadvantaged alike. Acute, skilled nursing and emergency care is provided in a wide range of areas including cardiology, oncology, pediatrics, obstetrics and gastroenterology. Other services include speech therapy, occupational therapy and physical rehabilitation, diagnostic imaging, pulmonary diagnostics, breast care and outpatient treatment are also delivered to those in need.

Adjacent to St. Alexius Medical Center and reflecting the Alexian Brother's longstanding commitment to mental health is a 100-bed psychiatric facility — Alexian Brothers Behavioral Health Hospital — that offers outstanding care to those persons requiring intensive inpatient treatment as well as a comprehensive offering of outpatient programs.

Community-based programs are also a vital part of Alexian Brothers Health System. Both Alexian Brothers Medical Center and St. Alexius Medical Center offer numerous outreach programs to serve the needs of area residents. In partnership with Arlington Heights-based Northwest Community Health Care, Alexian Brothers Medical Center provides funding for the Community Family Health Center in Mount Prospect — a health clinic that is staffed by bilingual professionals and largely serves an Hispanic clientele. Also offered, in conjunction with Catholic Charities, is the Catholic Charities Physician Referral Service. Other community-based programs include the Parish Nurse Program, the Community Health Alliance and the Community Outreach Health Services. St. Alexius Medical Center offers classes, preventive education programs, health screenings and a speakers bureau for community organizations; educational and social activities for senior citizens; and a diabetes education program that provides classes and instruction for individuals with diabetes and their immediate families.

The Alexian Brothers have, throughout their long history, provided health care to all individuals no matter what their ailment. In the late 1980s, a time when treating individuals with the AIDS virus was unpopular, Alexian Brothers took a leadership role and opened Bonaventure House/Center for Assisted Living in Chicago. Today, the facility provides housing, medical care and social services to persons impacted by HIV and AIDS. Salus Place in

Brother Thomas Keusenkothen, C.F.A., is the president and CEO of Alexian Brothers Health System, headquartered in Elk Grove Village, Illinois.

St. Louis and The Harbor in Waukegan, Illinois, also provide compassionate care to those afflicted with HIV and AIDS.

In recent years Alexian Brothers Health System has expanded its range of services for the elderly to reflect the rapid aging of the U.S. population. Continuing care retirement communities (CCRCs), which provide a homelike environment and a wide array of activities for seniors, feature independent-living apartments, assisted-living units and nursing home care. Other services for seniors include low-income housing, free-standing nursing homes, adult day-care programs, hospice care and transportation for seniors' visits to the hospital or doctor. Alexian Brothers is currently developing programs that will enable seniors to remain in their homes as long as possible with the aid of skilled nursing services, social services, meals, physical, occupational and recreational therapies and other programs.

The Alexian Brothers have a long and distinguished history of delivering excellent care to all persons, no matter what their station in life. In the years ahead, they will, no doubt, continue to adapt to the needs of a changing society by continuing to provide skilled and compassionate care to individuals in need.

Chicagoland Chamber of Commerce

The Chicagoland Chamber of Commerce plays a vital role in the wealth of economic and commercial success enjoyed by Chicago and Northeastern Illinois. For more than 100 years, the Chamber has provided invaluable networking and legislative services that continually propel growth and prosperity for the region and thousands of businesses within it. Today, as a result of the Chamber's efforts, the Chicago area is positioned as one of the most business-friendly regions in the country.

Headquartered in downtown Chicago, the Chicagoland Chamber of Commerce represents the collective interests of 2,500 member businesses that employ more than 1 million people in six counties. Through an active network of committees and task forces, this voluntary association of professional men and women makes vital contributions to the civic and economic development of the Chicago area.

Landmark accomplishments of the Chamber include the establishment of Daylight Savings Time — in conjunction with the U.S. Chamber of Commerce — and the formation of the National Citizen's League for the Promotion of a Sound Banking System, which brought about the passage of the Federal Reserve Banking Act in 1911. Additional achievements include the creation of the Chicago Crime Commission and the Chicago Convention and Tourism Bureau, both of which evolved into independent associations; the introduction of Fire Prevention Day, which became the nationwide

Fire Prevention Week; and the formation of the master parking plan for Chicago, which mapped out central-area garages and lots in the city.

Today, the Chamber continues to produce and market aggressive programs and services that benefit area businesses and generate economic success. The Chamber also maintains a political presence at the city, county and state levels to ensure that the legislative and regulatory climate in Illinois remains conducive to business. As a result, Chicago has been rated one of the 10 best cities in which to do business by *Fortune* magazine.

Founded in 1904, the Chamber is a direct lineal descendant of the Chicago Board of Trade (founded in 1848) and operates under a charter dated 1897. Upon its formation, the Chamber was the first regional chamber of commerce in the United States, creating a strong and unified forum for Chicago-area business owners to promote their operations and voice needs and concerns. Five separate, issue-based councils exist within the Chicagoland Chamber of Commerce: Economic Development; Membership and Revenue; Communications; Government Affairs; and Small Business.

Chicago's reputation as a commercial leader is fueled by the Chamber's aggressive marketing of the region as a premier destination for business and travel. The Chamber continually campaigns for high-quality transportation and infrastructure throughout that area, working with both local and state officials. The Chamber created the Midwest Asia Aviation Coalition in 1997 and pushed for a new air service agreement between the U.S. and Japan. In early 1998 U.S. and Japanese officials signed the agreement, which resulted in additional non-stop flights between Japan and O'Hare that are predicted to bring as much as $1 billion in new investment to the Midwest.

In 1998 the Chamber formed the Midwest Aviation Coalition to promote freight and passenger capabilities throughout the region. MAC, as the group is known, was instrumental in lobbying at the federal level and having the high-density rule at O'Hare removed. The Chamber and the Metropolitan Planning Council created Business Leaders for Transportation, a 70-company coalition addressing both infrastructure and public transportation concerns in Northeastern Illinois. The Chamber promotes international trade through Chicago's Sister Cities program and in- and out-bound trade missions.

The Chamber also strategically partners with city, county and state agencies in the area of economic

Aerial view
of Chicago
City of Chicago
©Peter J. Schulz

development. The Chamber is actively involved with the city of Chicago in the Chicago Partnership for Economic Development, which recruits and assists U.S.-based companies interested in relocating to the city. The Chamber works with the Cook County Economic Development agency to provide the same service at the

county and regional level. The Chamber also participates with the Civic Committee of the Commercial Club in co-funding World Business Chicago, which attracts international investors and corporations to the area. Since its inception in 1997, World Business Chicago has brought 20 international firms to the region, most of which are dot.com and information technology companies.

The innovative programs offered by the Chamber allow both area businesses and residents to be productive. The Education to Careers program works with the Chicago Public Schools and City Colleges of Chicago to equip and prepare students for the workplace environment. The Chamber has also established the Youth Motivation Program, which is the oldest business-based role-model effort in the Chicago Public Schools, and the Illinois Business Education Coalition, which leads the effort for uniform, statewide funding levels for schools and standardized testing and competency to provide a well-educated work force for the 21st century.

The legislative efforts put forth by the Chamber allow Chicago-area businesses to expand and prosper in a safe environment. The Chamber has consistently championed handgun-control legislation that seeks to deter violence and combat the negative effects that gangs can have on businesses and neighborhoods.

Over the years, the Chamber has successfully facilitated the growth of electronic business throughout the Chicago area, allowing the city to be home to more Internet service providers than any other city in the country. The Chamber's goal is to position Chicago as an e-commerce leader comparable to Silicon Valley. The Chamber's Internet home page currently receives more than 69,000 hits per month, with 16 percent of those being business-to-business queries that benefit Chamber members.

The Chamber's Chicagoland Entrepreneurial Center offers services to all small and emerging businesses in the region, regardless of affiliation with the Chamber. In the past two years, the Center has served more than 15,000 companies with its comprehensive programs and services.

The benefits that businesses receive as members of the Chamber are numerous. In addition to workshops and seminars, businesses have access to discounted health and dental insurance, consulting, computer, phone and shipping services, among others. The Chamber also provides exclusive member-to-member discounts, which allow members to save on products and services when dealing with other members.

As a pioneer among chambers of commerce throughout the United States, the Chicagoland Chamber of Commerce serves as a role model for other major metropolitan areas to follow. Through a dedication to actively participating in civic growth and development, the Chamber has made Chicago and Northeastern Illinois a better place in which to live and work.

Aerial view of Chicago's lakefront
City of Chicago
©Peter J. Schulz

Sears Tower
City of Chicago
©Peter J. Schulz

Corporate Travel Management Group

More than 24 years ago, Corporate Travel Management Group founder and CEO Bonnie Lorefice was one of the first entrepreneurs in the country to recognize the need for a service focused exclusively on business travel.

Today CTMG is one of the largest woman-owned travel management firms in the United States. The company offers its clients the opportunity to work with a travel management partner of the ideal size. CTMG is sophisticated — providing leading-edge technology and an international service framework. And it is involved — providing strong customer service and client access to its executive staff.

Corporate Travel Management Group has been under the able leadership of CEO Bonnie Lorefice since she founded the company in 1976. With help from a loyal staff of key managers, she has led the company from a small, three-person office to a national company employing more than 150 people.

The global economy makes travel a given for people in almost any kind of business. Rather than handling the time-consuming tasks of booking airline, rental car and hotel reservations themselves, companies hire CTMG to do their travel planning for them.

CTMG's 24 years of growth has occurred through Lorefice's conscious plan to develop a large and loyal client base, rather than through mergers and acquisitions.

Having started with three employees, CTMG has grown to include more than 150 today. The company maintains its worldwide headquarters in the Chicago suburb of Lombard, with regional offices in Chicago, Dallas and New York. Client firms throughout the United States host satellite offices, and international partners are located in Europe, South America, the Middle East and the Pacific Rim.

CTMG also has two subsidiaries — Oakbrook Travel/Emerald Cruises and Corporate Motivations. Oakbrook Travel/Emerald Cruises is the company's leisure division, offering exceptional vacation planning for client employees and the general public. Corporate Motivations specializes in organizing meetings, conferences and incentive travel.

The growth and success of CTMG has not gone unnoticed. Bonnie Lorefice has consistently been named as one of the Top 100 women in travel by *Travel Agent* magazine. She was also inducted into the Chicago Entrepreneurship Hall of Fame in 1998, and CTMG has been named to the Top 500 list of women-owned companies by *Working Woman* magazine. The company is also registered as a woman-owned business enterprise (WBE), which makes it an ideal partner for government and businesses working on public projects.

Because CTMG delivers a large volume of business to travel vendors like airlines and car rental companies, it can negotiate significant discounts for its clients. CTMG handles every aspect of corporate travel. Its agents make travel easy by processing the vast majority of airline tickets electronically. The company also manages frequent-flier programs, tracks clients' travel expenses, arranges group travel for business conferences and meetings, handles incentive travel contests and plans personal travel for employees.

More than simply booking business travel, CTMG is committed to understanding its clients' business goals and building a travel program that will contribute to those goals. In this way, CTMG acts as a consultant and partner for each client. CTMG business partners vary in size and style but share common expectations. Each is looking for a top travel program managed by a team of experienced, involved travel consultants. Each wants a

program driven by providers who understand that strong service and performance have a direct, positive effect on financial issues.

CTMG has always been focused on customer-centered corporate travel management. This means focusing on consultation, account management, steady client-base growth, technological development and long-term partnerships. Clients represent a wide diversity of industries, size and travel requirements, and many have honored CTMG for its excellent service. One longtime client, GTE Directories, has repeatedly recognized CTMG as a Quality Service Vendor in its own successful bid for the Malcolm Baldridge Award.

The key to offering this level of service is a strong commitment to customers and employees. CTMG is one of the few travel management firms in the nation to maintain a wholly owned-and-operated 24-hour reservations center staffed by its own experienced agents — who have an average tenure of seven years. This is one of the highest levels in the travel industry.

International knowledge and partnerships are another way that CTMG stands out from other travel management companies. The company has built strong relationships with airlines, hotels and car companies around the world. Also, CTMG has a dedicated international staff available to provide faring, ticketing and en-route service 24-hours-a-day.

The staff and leadership of CTMG believe that the future of travel planning is online. As a result, all of the company's units make extensive use of the Internet. Clients can visit the corporate Web site and obtain

detailed information about CTMG; read the bimonthly travel newsletter; and link to travel tools such as weather reports and rail timetables.

CTMG works constantly with travel industry leaders to build and utilize the latest tools in travel planning. In conjunction with the SABRE travel database, CTMG provides clients with innovative ways to track and book travel plans via the Internet. From any Internet connection travelers can tap into the CTMG Web site, click on "Virtually There Trip Review" and access the latest copy of their itinerary. CTMG clients can also opt to plan and book their own travel plans online using the password-protected SabreBTS system. It allows businesses to have the convenience of online booking with the policy enforcement, customer service and support that every CTMG customer receives.

The Internet is not the only area where CTMG is leading the way. More than 10 years ago, Lorefice originated the idea for AutoCOP, a PC-based software program that checks and adjusts travel records at multiple levels. This ensures the lowest available fares and accurate passenger records. CTMG continues to develop new proprietary technologies to help assure clients that their travel dollars are properly spent and reservations are complete and proper.

The managers and staff at CTMG know that being successful in the ever-changing world of travel requires the best people and the best technology. People must always be part of any technical solution, because personal customer service and the expertise that knowledgeable agents offer will never go out of style.

At CTMG people and technology work together to provide the best travel management services for its clients. Its AutoCop quality control system is a key component in delivering exceptional customer service.

The main reservation center at CTMG's world headquarters is staffed by experienced agents 24 hours a day, seven days a week. Assistance is always just a phone call away for CTMG clients.

DePaul University

Since 1898 DePaul University has made access to high-quality, value-driven education a reality in Chicago. For a century DePaul has taught waves of first-generation college students and educated some of the city's most important political and business leaders. Mayors Richard M. Daley and Richard J. Daley and McDonald's Corporation CEO Jack Greenberg are among its alumni.

The nation's largest Catholic university, DePaul has campuses in the Lincoln Park neighborhood, the Loop and four suburbs. The university offers more than 130 undergraduate and graduate degree programs, and its students and faculty reflect a wide range of ethnic, religious and economic backgrounds.

Originally known as St. Vincent's College, DePaul opened its doors on Sept. 5, 1898. It first 70 students were primarily sons of Chicago's Catholic immigrants. Classes were held in a remodeled church on what was to become the school's Lincoln Park Campus.

From the beginning, the university embraced the ideals of its namesake, St. Vincent de Paul. The Vincentian religious order that founded and continues to lead the college values access to education, respect for individual human dignity, community service and a holistic view toward educating the entire person.

In 1907 the Rev. Peter V. Byrne, C.M., the college's first president, led the effort to draft a new charter and create DePaul University. Rejecting the rigid curriculum

of most contemporary Catholic colleges, Father Byrne and his faculty set up a modified elective system modeled after Harvard and other elite schools. DePaul attracted Catholics who previously would have chosen a public university for professional studies or practical sciences.

Byrne declared that "this institution is Catholic and must ever remain Catholic." Yet it also was open to all faiths. The charter stated that "no test or particular religious profession shall ever be held as a prerequisite to

admission...or for election to any professorship." Demonstrating its commitment to diversity, DePaul admitted women students in 1911, becoming the nation's first coeducational Catholic university. Through the years the university also welcomed Jewish students, who were denied admission to some universities.

Adaptive and open to change, DePaul grew in size and stature. The university was ahead of its time in tailoring programs to adult learners. It opened a campus in the Loop in 1917, an era when most colleges shunned the hustle and bustle of urban centers. After World War II it capitalized on the return of GIs and educated tens of thousands of nontraditional-aged students eager to better themselves.

As part of its mission of accessibility, DePaul opened its first suburban campus in 1977 in Des Plaines. Other

campuses followed in Oak Forest, Naperville and, in 1998, Lake County. The university has become the Chicago area's dominant provider of professional education for part-time and adult learners.

Both the Lincoln Park and Loop campuses saw extensive improvements in the 1990s. DePaul purchased the landmark Goldblatt's Building at State Street and Jackson Boulevard and spent $70 million to renovate it. Dedicated in 1993 and renamed the DePaul Center, the facility houses the College of Commerce and student services offices and is regarded as the university's front door.

The changes to the Lincoln Park Campus dramatized DePaul's transformation from the "little school under the el" — primarily serving commuter students — to one of the nation's best urban universities with an attractive campus and a large residential population. A hallmark of the renewal is the John T. Richardson Library, dedicated in 1992 as DePaul's first freestanding library.

A high-tech science building was dedicated in 1998, and the following year marked the opening of the mammoth Ray Meyer Fitness and Recreation Center, named for the famed basketball coach who led the Blue Demons to 724 wins from 1942-84. The center's numerous amenities include a six-lane swimming pool, four basketball courts and weight and fitness training. New to the campus, too, was an athletic training center for DePaul's 15 Division I athletic teams.

The Lincoln Park Campus also saw the addition of several state-of-the-art residence halls. The university's 15 residence halls accommodated 2,500 students in the fall of 2000.

The growth at the Lincoln Park Campus is ongoing. A comprehensive student union — housing a chapel, a cultural center, food service, a bookstore and lounges — is another recent addition.

Through its eight schools and colleges DePaul awards more than 3,900 degrees annually. The schools and colleges are innovative and influential. The College of Commerce's Kellstadt Graduate School of Business is consistently ranked among the top 10 part-time graduate business programs in the nation. The College of Liberal Arts and Sciences features strong interdisciplinary programs. The College of Law created the nation's first health law curriculum. The School for New Learning was

a pioneer in offering credit for life experience and nontraditional education exclusively for adult students.

The School of Computer Science, Telecommunications and Information Systems features the largest and most diverse technology curriculum in the Midwest. The School of Education offers vital outreach programs such as the Center for Urban Education. The School of Music, one of the nation's finest, includes dozens of faculty members who are acclaimed professional musicians. The Theatre School is a standard of excellence in U.S. professional theater training.

DePaul's faculty is committed to teaching. Nearly all classes are taught by faculty members, not graduate assistants. Class sizes are small, and the ratio of students to professors is just 15 to 1, making personalized instruction a reality.

True to the vision of its early leaders, DePaul at the turn of its second century remains both remarkably diverse and strongly value-laden. Its 19,500 students hail from 88 different countries. Nearly 30 percent of full-time freshmen are the first in their families to attend college. DePaul enrolls more minority students than any other private university in Illinois.

Service is the university's trademark, manifested in the service learning completed by students and the public service of faculty members, who have championed an international court, assisted the poor in El Salvador and lent their expertise to low-income neighborhoods in Chicago. St. Vincent evinced a special love for the neglected, and DePaul continues to emulate his noble spirit of action.

DePaul's faculty is committed to teaching; nearly all classes are taught by faculty members, not graduate assistants.

Opened in 1999, the Ray Meyer Fitness and Recreation Center includes a running track, a six-lane pool and four basketball courts.

Lexington Health Care and Rehabilitation Centers

The success that George Samatas has made for himself, his family and his fellow countrymen is a prime illustration of the American Dream come true. A native of Albania, Samatas came to the United States more than 50 years ago with the shirt on his back and an overwhelming ambition to succeed. Today, assisted by three generations of his family, Samatas sits at the helm of a thriving enterprise dedicated to serving and caring for people throughout the Chicago area.

The numerous successes achieved by Samatas are the direct result of his unfaltering work ethic and desire to serve others, which is reflected in his business portfolio. Throughout the course of his career, Samatas has established a number of service-oriented businesses, from first-class restaurants and hotels to premier senior-care residences. With each venture, Samatas has made a conscious effort to earn a living and be productive to the community at the same time. "The focus has always been on the service, not the money," says Samatas. "By addressing the needs of the community and our residents, we have been able to prosper. Here, in America, everybody has the opportunity to succeed."

When Samatas first came to Chicago in 1946, he vowed to pursue a dream of providing a prosperous life for his family and to allow his children personal and professional opportunities that he was without during his life. Samatas worked diligently toward his goal with each business venture, driven by the continual hardships he endured in providing for his family. Eventually Samatas found an ideal business climate in which to put his skills to work — providing superior senior-care service for residents in the area. "My father's entire life has been focused on service," says son Jim. "His goal has always been to help others."

Samatas has earned a renowned reputation in each of the fields he services through his enduring commitment to first-class customer service. Firmly rooted in the mindset that "the fish stinks from the head," Samatas conducts every aspect of his businesses in a superior manner, and expects the same high level of service from the more than 3,000 people he employs. If management fails to offer a high standard of service within a business, Samatas says, employees and other staff will follow suit. "If the head is no good, every other aspect of the business is destined to fail," he says. "You need to take care of your customers before you take care of your bottom line."

To ensure the success of each of his businesses and to fulfill his goal of providing new opportunities for his family, Samatas strategically surrounds himself with immediate and extended family members in management positions. In addition to equipping his businesses with trustworthy leaders, Samatas is able to foster the personal and professional development of his family and reap the rewards of their individual talents. "There is nothing more rewarding than working together as a family while providing a service to others," says Samatas.

The professional mentoring that Samatas provides to his family fulfills his goal of providing new and challenging opportunities that he went without while growing up. Today, children, grandchildren, nieces and nephews have all embraced the opportunity to work with Samatas and to learn from his drive and motivation. "He saw his

George Samatas first came to Chicago in 1946 with an unfaltering work ethic and a goal to succeed. Today he is at the helm of numerous thriving enterprises throughout the Chicago area.

dream and he went after it — that is inspiring to me," says grandson Jeremy. "I have learned a lot from him as a grandfather and from a business standpoint. I hope to carry on his passion for life to the next generation."

The work environment created by the Samatas family is ideal, utilizing open communication and an ongoing commitment to growth and expansion through new and enhanced services. "As a close family there is a bond that you cannot emulate with other people," says his son Jim. "That was attractive to me — to put that bond in a work environment and to challenge ourselves to be the best. When it works, there is nothing sweeter."

That bond is successfully put to work every day at the numerous Lexington senior-care residences and other business ventures that Samatas owns and operates throughout the Chicago area. Each facility boasts an unprecedented, personalized approach to care. Steps are taken to ensure that each detail of a residence, from decor, programs and meals, are first-rate, and that a positive demeanor is presented by staff members at all times. "The personal service we give to our residents is what sets us apart," says George Nikias, administrator for the Lexington Square retirement community in Elmhurst. "We're one big family that shares a closeness with each other."

Through an enduring drive to succeed, a devotion to family and a dedication to service, the life and ways of George Samatas will live on for generations to come. The business opportunities that Samatas has provided allow family members to realize their individual talents and potential, and also to learn from Samatas' proven approach to business. Samatas has personally mentored and nurtured numerous people with the realization that there are many ways to prosper, but doing so in an ethical way is the most rewarding. "He has shown us that it's not how much money you make, but what you do with your life,"

The Seneca Restaurant in Chicago was one of Samatas' first business ventures, which he owned and operated from 1949 to 1963.

says Jim. "Each of us have been given the opportunity, guidance and support to share his vision and dream."

Today each enterprise owned and operated by the Samatas family is positioned for growth and expansion, a result of Samatas' lifetime dedication to cultivating the individual strengths of his family. As Samatas' offspring position themselves to manage the businesses that Samatas started nearly half a century ago, they will follow the successful blueprint that he has laid out for them. "It is so fulfilling to see my children and their children putting their talents to use in an worthwhile manner," says Samatas. "The success of my family has made me prosperous beyond all expectations."

Today the Samatas family operates numerous health care facilities and related services dedicated to caring for seniors throughout the Chicago area.

Loyola University Chicago

A great fire was raging in Chicago due west from Mrs. O'Leary's barn on October 8, 1871, threatening everything in its path, including the 1-year-old St. Ignatius College on the near South Side at Roosevelt Road and Racine Avenue.

Fr. Arnold Damen, S.J., who had opened the doors of St. Ignatius in 1870, was not in the city. He was in New York, preaching a mission, when he learned that the fire was roaring toward his beloved school.

Damen spent the night on his knees praying that his new college, the future Loyola University Chicago, would be spared. The object of his prayers was small — one building with just four priest-professors and 37 students in a curriculum designed to offer a six-year classical education in the Jesuit tradition — but it meant the world to him.

Miraculously or not, the wind shifted, turning the fire toward Chicago's downtown business district where it destroyed some 17,000 buildings and caused $200 million in damage — but Fr. Damen's school was spared. Five years later, in 1876, the college awarded its first bachelor of arts degrees.

Loyola University Chicago grew with the city, and its increasingly important role in the Chicago community was seen as early as 1874, when the *Chicago Tribune* noted in an editorial that, "This valuable college is growing in numbers and is now one of the most prominent institutions of learning in the city." Clear evidence that Loyola was meeting a community need is shown by the fact that by 1895, enrollment had grown to 494 students.

A little more than a century later, Loyola University Chicago has approximately 13,350 ethnically and religiously diverse students from across the United States and dozens of countries. They study at five campuses: Lake Shore Campus on Chicago's far North Side; Water Tower Campus on Chicago's Magnificent Mile (North Michigan Avenue); Mallinckrodt Campus in north suburban Wilmette; Medical Center Campus (home of the Loyola Stritch School of Medicine) in west suburban Maywood; and the Rome Center of Liberal Arts in Italy. Students are enrolled in 144 programs that lead to 27 different academic degrees.

Loyola continues to prove itself no less valuable to Chicago today than in 1870 through programs such as Chicago Studies and its Center for Urban Research and Learning. Chicago Studies, which was first offered in fall 1999, is a graduate-level interdisciplinary program that helps students develop a deeper understanding of the city and its people while broadening their knowledge of how other major cities work. The Center for Urban Research and Learning was created in 1996 to bring together academic research and urban-policy issues. Working throughout Chicago, CURL researchers put their academic expertise to work to address real social and economic issues such as welfare reform and fair housing.

Loyola's professional schools have brought it other distinctions for many decades. The School of Law, established in 1908, exemplifies the Jesuit

Aerial view of Loyola University Chicago Lake Shore Campus on Chicago's North Side

Rev. A. DAMEN S.J.

The university also has added to Chicago's reputation for world-famous architecture, most notably through the Madonna della Strada Chapel at the Lake Shore Campus. Construction began in 1938, as the nation was struggling to shake off the Great Depression. A striking blend of modern classicism and Italian Renaissance, this magnificent building is a "must" on any architectural tour of the city. "Loyola's poem in stone," as it is known, came about through the efforts of the Rev. James J. Mertz, S.J., a teacher-priest who organized and carried out fund-raising campaigns to raise the $700,000 needed to build this chapel, located on the shore of Lake Michigan.

In addition, Loyola's Water Tower Campus in the heart of North Michigan Avenue features both old and new in the form of Lewis Towers, the oldest building facing the historic Water Tower, as well as the university's new 15-story building on East Pearson Street that houses Loyola's nationally recognized School of Business Administration and Graduate School of Business.

In the last analysis, universities are for the students, and how they regard their schools is telling. Take this comment, for example: "I think every alumnus of Loyola must feel that he was given more than he was ever able to give or will be able to pay for. In this most material day, the record of the men and women who have made a great college out of a prairie mission is a lasting inspiration."

The quote has a modern ring to it, but it was uttered by Leo McGivena, class of 1916.

Rev. Arnold Damen, S.J., founder of Loyola University Chicago

tradition by its commitment to social justice through programs such as the Institute for Health Law, the ChildLaw Center and the Center for Public Service Law. The Loyola Stritch School of Medicine, whose remarkable reputation spans the world, was created in 1909 and named for the late Chicago Cardinal Samuel Stritch in 1948. It is located at the Loyola University Chicago Medical Center in west suburban Maywood.

Dedicated faculty members are a Loyola tradition. Among the 1,100 current full-time faculty members, 97 percent hold Ph.D. degrees or the highest academic degree available in their fields. Faculty members are called upon often to offer expert opinion and knowledge on current events and public affairs by such news organizations as *The Wall Street Journal*, *Business Week*, "ABC World News Tonight," "NBC Nightly News," "The Today Show," CNN and National Public Radio. Faculty members have received prestigious awards from the National Endowment for the Humanities, the National Institutes of Health, the National Science Foundation and the John Simon Guggenheim Foundation.

Rev. John J. Piderit, S.J., current president of Loyola University Chicago

507

McCormick Place and Navy Pier

McCormick Place and Navy Pier are much-acclaimed and highly recognizable landmarks along Chicago's lakefront. Through the years these two facilities have grown, changed and evolved into the magnificent structures they are today.

Navy Pier

McCormick Place, with 2.2 million square feet of exhibit space, is now the largest and most successful convention center in the nation, and with nearly 8 million visitors annually, Navy Pier remains the No. 1 tourist attraction in Illinois. McCormick Place and Navy Pier are owned and managed by the Metropolitan Pier and Exposition Authority (MPEA). MPEA is a municipal corporation created by the Illinois General Assembly, whose mission is to attract trade shows, conventions and public events to Chicago and, in the process, strengthen the economy of the area.

Scott Fawell, CEO of Metropolitan Pier and Exposition Authority

The McCormick name came from Colonel Robert R. McCormick, the *Chicago Tribune* owner and civic leader who first stumped for a Chicago convention center in the 1940s. Though he didn't live to see his dream realized, the convention center opened its doors in 1960. Fire later leveled the facility in 1967, but thanks to financial support from the state, a new and bigger McCormick Place opened on the same site in 1971.

Connected to the original East Building by a walkway, the North Building was opened in 1986. The South Building was later added in 1996 and in 1998, an 800-room Hyatt Regency McCormick Place Hotel opened, offering conventioneers lodging and an easy walk to and from the exhibition hall.

Navy Pier first opened in 1916 and originally served as a shipping pier, linking world ports with Midwestern markets. From 1946 through 1965, Navy Pier was the home to the University of Illinois, Chicago. However, the Pier was stagnant during the 1970s and 80s until responsibility for it was transferred to the Metropolitan Pier and Exposition Authority. Following a major refurbishment, Navy Pier now bustles every day of the year and has become a "must see" for millions of Chicago visitors and residents as well. Most visible is the 150-foot-tall Ferris wheel, which affords great views of the cityscape. Excursion boats with views of Chicago's fabled skyline offer endless possibilities for sightseeing and dining.

Although the Pier hosts many state and regional conventions in its 170,000 square feet of exhibition space, it is best known for its recreational facilities which include parks, entertainment attractions, gardens, shops, and restaurants. New to the Pier is the Chicago Shakespeare Theater, which celebrated its inaugural season in 1999

and is recognized internationally for its artistic excellence and creative approach.

Chicago has often been called "the city that works" because of places like McCormick Place and Navy Pier, which create enormous economic benefit for Chicago and every corner of the state of Illinois. According to Scott Fawell, Metropolitan Pier and Exposition Authority CEO, "As long as we continue to work together with the mayor, the governor, our state legislature and civic leaders, McCormick Place and Navy Pier will continue to be valuable assets to the city and our state. Cooperation will continue to be a recurring theme for us as we forge ahead in the 21st century."

Over the years, McCormick Place and Navy Pier have given Chicago the resources to open the best restaurants, build the greatest hotels, create a state-of-the-art transportation system, attract the best collections and exhibits to the city's world-renowned museums and cultural attractions and, most importantly, create jobs — more than 44,000 as a direct result of McCormick Place and Navy Pier.

McCormick Place generates more than $250 million in state and local taxes. The economic impact from trade shows and conventions exceeds $5 billion annually. More than 5,200 Illinois companies exhibit at McCormick Place every year, with more than two-thirds of them located outside the Chicagoland area.

McCormick Place and Navy Pier remain No. 1 because they have continued to meet both the challenges of competitors and the demands of customers. The success of both facilities has made the MPEA one of the biggest economic generators for the state of Illinois.

"The challenge for McCormick Place and Navy Pier is to constantly reinvent themselves to maintain a competitive edge in the ever-changing convention and tourism market," Fawell says. "We will continue to pursue innovative opportunities and set new standards in customer service to preserve the economic benefits provided by McCormick Place and Navy Pier."

McCormick Place Grand Concourse and South Building, west entrance

509

The Morton Arboretum

The year was 1922. F. Scott Fitzgerald and Cole Porter were on the charts; Amelia Earhart was in the sky; and women were rejoicing in their newly won right to vote. And 25 miles west of Chicago, a philanthropist with a vision for the future, a heritage of conservation and a familial mandate to "plant trees" dedicated his family estate as a protected habitat for woody plants. The mission of The Morton Arboretum — "to encourage the planting and conservation of trees and other plants for a greener, healthier, and more beautiful world" — is a living tribute to Joy Morton.

From Joy Morton's legacy has grown a remarkable institution, an outdoor museum that is a second home to everyone who loves nature and seeks a greener world. Spanning 1,700 acres, The Morton Arboretum in west suburban Chicago is a destination for families on weekends, schoolchildren on field trips, and owners of ailing plants who find experts and sound horticultural advice. The Arboretum is also a nationally and internationally preeminent research institution in the areas of plant diseases, conservation and the preservation of endangered plant species. Whether helping people to connect with plants in cyberspace, rescuing Asian elms from extinction or beautifying Chicagoland's expressway commute, The Morton Arboretum is an outdoor museum and research institution where ideas have grown — for more than 78 years.

Joy Morton, founder of the Chicago-based Morton Salt Company, was 67 when he established The Morton

Arboretum. His father, J. Sterling Morton, founded the original conservation holiday — Arbor Day — in Nebraska in 1872. With the input of Dr. Charles Sprague Sargent (former director of Harvard University's Arnold Arboretum) and O. C. Simonds (a renowned landscape architect), Morton transformed his Thornhill family estate into a beautiful place to visit, a world-class research center, and a living laboratory to advance the sciences of botany, horticulture, taxonomy and plant ecology.

Visitors to The Morton Arboretum can enjoy its woodlands, wetlands, gardens and restored native prairie by hiking its 12 miles of trails or driving its 11 miles of paved roads. The Arboretum's renowned Sterling Morton Library is open to the public, and in its circulating collection, it houses 28,000 volumes in horticulture, botany, floristics, taxonomy and natural history. The library is also world-renowned for its collections of rare botanical books and prints and the archival papers of noted landscape architects such as Jens Jensen and Marshall Johnson.

Today, Joy Morton's living legacy features more than 40,000 plant specimens that represent 3,600 types of trees, shrubs and other plants selected for their hardiness and adaptability to the extremes of northern Illinois' climate. Among the collections is a glorious Himalayan White Pine that came as a seed from the Berlin Botanic Garden in 1926. And on the shores of Lake Marmo (named for Joy Morton's wife, Margaret Morton), the dark green needles of a graceful Eastern Hemlock are mirrored in the waters.

The trees, shrubs and other plants, abundant on the Arboretum's 1,700 acres, do more than beautify the grounds. The Arboretum is an outdoor laboratory, where researchers gauge how well plants adapt to climate extremes, road conditions and the challenges of urban growth. "The Morton Mile," a cooperative project between

the Arboretum and the city of Chicago's Gateway Green Expressway Partnership, is another living laboratory where the durability of 40 different trees, shrubs and other plants are tested under the harshest urban conditions. Other collaborations that have drawn upon the Arboretum's expertise include the landscaping of Chicago's Lake Shore Drive and Museum Campus, as well as Chicago's current development of the new Millennium Park.

The concept of The Morton Arboretum as a living laboratory transfers well to its Education Program, which annually offers 350 classes, certificate programs, workshops and lectures. Last year, fifth graders from Aurora's Gombert School recorded their annual Arboretum field trip on the Internet. In addition to collecting and analyzing scientific data from six wetland sites at the Arboretum, the work-in-progress Web site also has digital photos of the trip, students' journal entries and poems. All of the Arboretum's Youth and Family Education Programs are based upon science standards and goals from the Illinois State Board of Education — reinforcing the relevance of The Morton Arboretum as a living laboratory.

Beyond its national and international stature as a plant research and education center, The Morton Arboretum remains a destination for families and children and a draw for local and out-of-town visitors. During four seasons of

beauty, visitors and members enjoy weekend activities, nature arts and crafts, special events that celebrate the seasons, and guided walks and tours.

A 1,700-acre outdoor museum is just the beginning of The Morton Arboretum's outreach and its importance to an increasing number of regional, national and international audiences. Arboretum researchers and scientists are breeding new trees and shrubs to enhance the environment and advance its conservation mission. The Arboretum's vast plant collections are displayed not only for people to study and enjoy, but also to encourage the planting and conservation of trees and other plants. The Education Program shares its knowledge and learning with area schools, young people and their families and an increasing number of adults. Even after 78 years, Joy Morton's vision continues to guide the Arboretum's work for a "greener, healthier, and more beautiful world."

National-Louis University

National-Louis University has been a pioneer in education and teacher preparation for more than 100 years. By helping to develop innovations such as kindergarten-teacher training, the Parent Teacher Association (PTA) and bachelor of education degrees, the university has played an active and historic role in establishing America's elementary and early childhood education system.

Today the university continues to promote advanced learning through groundbreaking educational programs, which include establishing national standards for preschool centers and the Best Practice Network, an exemplary learning program used in Chicago public schools. As the nation's expert in teaching and learning, National-Louis has created an environment that accommodates both students who come from a traditional learning background and those who face special challenges in continuing their education.

National-Louis University is headquartered in the South Loop, surrounded by several other universities and colleges as well as the Art Institute and the Chicago

Symphony Orchestra Center. Its location befits the high level of education the university delivers in each of its three colleges — the National College of Education, the College of Arts and Sciences and the College of Management and Business. Altogether, National-Louis University offers more than 30 academic programs and 14 degrees extending to the doctoral level.

In addition to its five Chicago-area campuses, National-Louis University has academic facilities throughout the United States — Washington, D.C.; Missouri; Wisconsin; Florida; and Georgia — and also in Poland and Germany. In addition, the university offers instruction at more than 70 off-campus sites throughout northern Illinois and metropolitan areas surrounding all of its campuses. This immense presence allows the university to educate more than 15,000 students per year.

National-Louis University was founded in Chicago in 1886 as Miss Harrison's Kindergarten Training School. Elizabeth Harrison, one of the pioneers of childhood education, opened the school to fill a void in teacher training at the kindergarten level. By 1926 the school's enrollment had grown to the point where expansion was necessary. The main campus was moved from Chicago to Evanston and the school was renamed the National College of Education.

The National College of Education specialized in education and became one of the first teacher colleges in the United States to offer a four-year education degree. This raised the standards of teacher preparation throughout the country. The college was also instrumental in founding the PTA, and later played a major role in launching the national Head Start program, which remains prominent today. Head Start is a federally funded program designed to meet the comprehensive needs of elementary students — especially those of low-income families — by providing social, health, nutritional and psychological support.

For more than 80 years, the National College of Education served — and continues to serve — as one of the finest education colleges in the country. In the 1970s the college diversified its services and brought its expertise in teaching and learning to other areas. The school began to offer degree courses in allied health, applied behavioral sciences and human services, which led to the formation of the College of Arts and Sciences in 1982. In 1989 the school established its College of Management and Business and offered numerous business programs.

National-Louis University's state-of-the-art urban campus is located in a landmark building on Michigan Avenue directly across from the Art Institute of Chicago. National-Louis has been an innovator in teacher education and adult learning for more than a century.

In 1990 the college received a transformative gift from trustee and benefactor Michael W. Louis that helped to elevate the school from college to university status. The Louis gift remains one of the largest gifts to a private educational institution ever given in the state of Illinois. With the university status came a new name — National-Louis University.

Today National-Louis University educates people throughout the world with sites throughout the United States and a heavy presence in Europe. In 1992 the university helped establish Wyzsza Szkola Biznesu, a private business school in Nowy Sacz, Poland. In recent years, that school has been No. 1 among all private schools in Poland, and the student population has grown from 65 in its first year to more than 3,300 today. In 1999 NLUWSB became the first U.S. university to offer degrees to students in Eastern Europe.

Students enrolled at Wyzsza Szkola Biznesu are able to attend National-Louis University and live in the United States through an exchange program, and vice versa, allowing students a multicultural experience as part of their education. National-Louis University also offers teaching programs through the Department of Defense Dependents Schools in Italy, Spain, England and Germany.

While the university maintains an international scope, perhaps some of its greatest attributes are the groundbreaking educational services offered in the Chicago area. For example, the Baker Demonstration School, which operates out of the university's Evanston campus, is a private laboratory school for prekindergarten through eighth grade. This progressive school serves as a demonstration site for educational practices and as a facility to assist in the education of the university's teachers-in-training.

The Baker Demonstration School was founded in 1918 by Clara Belle Baker as the Children's School with the intent of linking children's learning habits and activities with teacher preparation programs. The school combines children and teachers from diverse communities and integrates a number of classroom disciplines that provide insight for teachers-in-training as to the most effective learning processes.

The Baker school focuses on each child's abilities, and the lessons move at the student's own developmental

National-Louis University is renowned for its individualized programs for both traditional-age college students and working adults who return to undergraduate or graduate studies later in life.

pace and personal style. Teachers work together in teams and children learn collaboratively in an effort to ignite creativity, inquiry, active learning, critical thinking and problem solving. These proven methods allow for results that are shared through the teaching programs of the university's National College of Education.

Another landmark program offered by National-Louis University is its Best Practice Project — a partnership with the city of Chicago in which the university's most effective teaching and learning techniques have been put to use in Chicago public schools to improve student performance and enhance the learning environment. As a result of this project, National-Louis University has also launched the Best Practice High School on Chicago's West Side, which allows university faculty to implement innovative educational strategies that were previously unavailable to public school students. This acclaimed high school serves as a model of urban secondary education for public schools throughout the United States.

As National-Louis University moves forward with its commitment to educational reform, it will also further build on its diverse student body. Students of all ages, colors and backgrounds can be found in the university's classrooms, including adults who are working full time or contemplating career changes; teachers and administrators who want to further their education; and immigrants and other language minorities with limited English skills. The university's goal is to take the progressive learning environment created by this diversity and transfer it to classrooms throughout Chicago and the world.

Northwestern University

The class of 1880 posed under "the old oak tree," a campus landmark of that time. Northwestern was one of the first major private universities in the country to become coeducational, admitting women as early as 1873.

Stretching for a mile on the shore of Lake Michigan 12 miles north of Chicago lies the 240-acre Evanston campus of Northwestern University. The handsome campus features a mix of historic buildings and modern architectural showplaces. The oldest building on campus is University Hall, which was dedicated in 1869 and now houses the English department within handsome limestone walls and Gothic archways

A private school, Northwestern enrolls almost 18,000 students and consistently ranks among the nation's top 10 in many academic areas. It employs almost 6,000 people and operates on a budget of over $955 million. But a century and a half ago, this world-class institution began in a law office above a hardware store.

In 1850 nine Chicagoans, Methodists all, met to lay out a plan for a university that would serve the Northwest Territory — now Ohio, Indiana, Illinois, Michigan, Wisconsin and part of Minnesota. One year later, Northwestern University was established, and classes began in 1855 with one building, two faculty members and 10 students.

Visionary decisions made in the 19th century continue to guide Northwestern. Although the Methodist church

Northwestern's Chicago campus, located just east of North Michigan Avenue, is home to its professional schools, including law, medicine, dentistry and the evening program for the business school.

initially provided resources and support, this was to be an institution for all students regardless of faith. Women were admitted as early as 1873. Locating the university on farmland outside city limits presented a unique opportunity to create and shape a community around it; in fact, Evanston was named after university founder John Evans. Early associations with medical and law schools in Chicago eventually led to world renown in these professional schools.

Early student rivalries may have differed in nature, but not in spirit, from those of today. For instance, dunking

involved sending underclassmen into the cold waters of Lake Michigan. In 1891 a street fight occurred over whether freshmen or sophomores had the right to sport walking canes while strolling about the campus. But the early administration of Northwestern had larger concerns. Financial difficulties, frequent leadership turnover and uneven growth characterized its first decades. But in 1881 John Evans pledged $50,000 of his own money to be payable when the university matched the sum with $150,000. The money was raised, old debts were paid and financial stability was finally possible. The same year, Dr. Joseph Cummings became president and hired Reverend Robert Hatfield to raise revenue instead of continuing to wait for the church to bestow it. Hatfield's efforts yielded a gift of $45,000 to build a science hall and additional funds for a men's dormitory and an observatory.

With 2,000 students enrolled in 1895, Northwestern was the third-largest university in the country after Harvard and the University of Michigan. The early 20th century represented a milestone. The board of trustees recognized the value of appointing savvy business leaders to the presidency, including Walter Dill Scott in 1920.

Under Scott's leadership, the university broadened the scope of its professional schools. The current 25-acre Chicago campus opened in 1926, and the Medill School of Journalism, among the first in the country, opened in 1921 with support from the *Chicago Tribune*.

During the Depression, many organizations faced dire straits. Northwestern and the University of Chicago were no exception, and strong consideration was given to combining the two schools, but they ultimately decided against it. The most significant change to Northwestern's Evanston campus occurred in the 1960s when 85 acres of Lake Michigan were filled in to create additional building space. Today the area, known as the lakefill, features extensive landscaping and modern buildings.

Two major developments propelled Northwestern to world-class status. The School of Commerce, always well respected, became the Kellogg Graduate School of Management in 1976 and is now widely regarded as among the top five in the world. The other was the achievement of exceptional financial stability, with a current endowment of about $3 billion and no deferred maintenance problems — unusual among established academic institutions.

Northwestern's reputation for academic excellence in both teaching and research extends far beyond what was once the Northwest Territory. *U.S.News & World Report* consistently ranks the undergraduate programs among the top 20 nationally. Most undergraduate students come from Illinois, but California is second, followed by Michigan and Florida. For the 1999 freshman class, mean combined test scores were 1364 on the SAT and 30 on the ACT. Prominent alumni include Arthur Andersen, William Jennings Bryan and Saul Bellow. Students excel in community service, with about 3,000 volunteering each year in the areas of hunger and homelessness, literacy, women's issues, senior citizens, health and youth. The presence of Northwestern enhances surrounding communities with exciting athletic competitions, theatrical performances, art exhibits, lectures and conferences.

The diversity of programs offered at Northwestern is extraordinary for a university this size, and the emphasis is on education, not simply training, even in the professional schools. Class sizes are distinctively small, and faculty members teach over 95 percent of all courses. In Evanston, the schools include the Judd A. and Marjorie Weinberg College of Arts and Sciences, the School of Education and Social Policy, Robert R. McCormick

School of Engineering and Applied Science, The Graduate School, Medill School of Journalism, Kellogg Graduate School of Management, School of Music and School of Speech. Northwestern's dynamic Chicago campus is home to its professional and graduate programs. In Chicago, students attend the Dental School, School of Law, Medical School and some Kellogg programs. Northwestern's School of Continuing Studies offers courses for nontraditional students on both campuses.

A charter member of the Big 10 Conference, Northwestern is the only private institution in that competitive league. Its first intercollegiate football game was played in 1882, and the Wildcats went to the Rose Bowl in 1949 and 1996. Northwestern athletes excel in many individual sports such as tennis and swimming, demonstrating the kind of singular drive they possess.

The future is indeed bright for Northwestern University. Today's leaders took a hard look at the university's past and embraced the vision of the first board of trustees, which resolved "to make it a university of the highest order of excellence." Ambitious plans include investing in faculty, intensifying undergraduate education, redesigning graduate education, strengthening professional education and enhancing the infrastructure. Strategies include promoting teaching across academic boundaries and a major building program.

The highest order of excellence — how that enduring mission will be interpreted over the next 150 years promises to make Northwestern University an exciting place to be.

With more than 200 acres on the shore of Lake Michigan, Northwestern's Evanston campus provides a beautifully landscaped setting for a mixture of historic buildings and modern architecture.

Resurrection Health Care

As Chicago's largest Catholic health care system, Resurrection Health Care blends a long faith tradition with cutting-edge health care resources to offer its patients a diverse continuum of care. The health care network's holistic philosophy toward health and its commitment to new medical technologies can be found in each component of Resurrection's network. This attitude is reflected in Resurrection's monarch butterfly logo, which represents life transitions, community and renewal.

Resurrection Health Care began with the Sisters of the Resurrection. The Congregation of the Sisters of the Resurrection was founded in 1891 by a devout Polish widow named Celine Borzecka and her daughter, Hedwig. In 1900 four Sisters left Europe and came to the United States to establish a ministry, eventually settling on Chicago's northwest side. Due to the needs of the booming Polish immigrant community, the Sisters opened a girls' school, Resurrection Academy, in 1915. Known as Resurrection High School today, it was recognized as one of the nation's top schools in a recent *U.S News and World Report*. The Order received another honor in 1999 when Sister Alice Kotowska, C.R., was beatified for her patriotism and leadership in the late 1930s.

After becoming known throughout their northwest-side neighborhood for devoted community involvement, the Sisters of the Resurrection were asked to sponsor a much-needed hospital. Under the direction of Sister Gregory Krzak, C.R., the hospital's first administrator, plans for a modern medical facility were drafted. The resulting facility — Resurrection Medical Center — opened its doors in 1953 after being constructed on a 52-acre farm that the Sisters had purchased in 1920.

Currently, the Resurrection Health Care system includes four hospitals: Resurrection Medical Center, Chicago; Our Lady of the Resurrection Medical Center, Chicago; St. Francis Hospital, Evanston; and the most recent addition, Westlake Hospital, Melrose Park.

Resurrection Health Care also includes one of Illinois' largest home health care companies and numerous neighborhood health care centers and outpatient facilities. Resurrection is also the largest provider of Catholic-sponsored senior services in Chicagoland with 10 nursing homes and three retirement communities. Resurrection provides patients with many areas of expertise: cardiac care, cancer care, orthopedics, rehabilitation, children's services, emergency care and behavioral health.

Resurrection Medical Center and its affiliates were brought together as a corporation in 1981. Under the new name of Resurrection Health Care, the not-for-profit health care system looked at ways to expand its services, offer the latest technology and provide all age groups with the best care. "For all of you, all of your life" is the motto Resurrection uses to explain its approach to a broad continuum of health care services — everything from maternity care to long-term care for senior citizens.

In fact, senior services are a priority for Resurrection, which serves the highest concentration of people over the age of 65 in the state. In addition to its nursing and retirement facilities, Resurrection sponsors a number of

Resurrection Medical Center and adjacent professional office building located near O'Hare International Airport

community-based programs for seniors. For instance, the Adult Day Services program provides health services, personal care and social contact for older adults. Resurrection also offers Alzheimer's care, home health services and a senior outreach program that matches isolated seniors with community volunteers.

Pursuit of state-of-the-art technology is a priority for Resurrection Health Care. The corporation is constantly looking ahead to offer its patients the latest diagnostic advancements. For example, the Heart Scan at St. Francis Hospital provides physicians with computer-enhanced imaging for faster, more accurate diagnosis of heart disease. In addition, Resurrection Medical Center is one of the nation's first hospitals to offer patients the advantages of the R2 Image Checker, a computer-assisted mammogram screening technology that improves breast cancer detection.

Along with the latest technological advancements, Resurrection participates in research involving protocols and clinical trials. By participating in a five-year national Study of Tamoxifen and Raloxifene (STAR) begun in 1999, Resurrection doctors will evaluate the role that the osteoporosis drug Raloxifene plays in the prevention of breast cancer. Each year, Resurrection physicians participate in dozens of other research endeavors.

As a teaching organization, Resurrection Health Care's four hospitals offer patients the benefits of a health care system in which the latest medical knowledge is readily available. For decades, its medical-staff faculty members have been committed to physician training and education. This is where doctors train doctors. Currently, the residency programs at Resurrection cover a wide range of specialty areas — family practice, internal medicine, emergency medicine, OB/GYN, surgery, radiology, psychiatry and anesthesiology — and attract students from major Chicago medical schools. Resurrection hospitals have affiliations with Loyola University, University of Illinois, Northwestern University and the Chicago Medical School.

Resurrection Life Center

In addition to physician training, Resurrection Health Care is actively involved in other related areas of medical education, including nursing, pharmacy and physician assistants as well as continuous medical education for members of its medical staffs.

Through its broad range of services, Resurrection Health Care offers the latest medical technologies while also providing an atmosphere of compassion and care for its patients. The mission of the Sisters of the Resurrection, who celebrated 100 years of U.S. ministry in 2000, continues to guide the hospitals and their many facilities as they strive to provide patients with both the latest technologies and sensitivity to their medical needs. Resurrection's roots in faith offer it inspiration as it strives to serve the community with the best medical care available, while never losing sight of patients as individuals.

Resurrection Health Care at Harlem-Grand

Saint Mary of Nazareth Hospital Center

ANCHORING CHICAGO'S CUTTING-EDGE NEIGHBORHOODS

Saint Mary of Nazareth Hospital Center is located amidst some of Chicago's oldest and most established neighborhoods, which have, in recent years, become some of Chicago's most cutting-edge communities. Located in the heart of Ukrainian and East Villages, Wicker Park and Bucktown, and just a mile from the new River West neighborhood, Saint Mary of Nazareth Hospital Center is an outstanding, ultramodern healthcare center that serves as an anchor to the Victorian mansions, classic Chicago brownstones and unique single-family homes as well as coffeehouses, restaurants, galleries, nightclubs and storefront theaters that make up some of Chicago's most vibrant communities.

Saint Mary of Nazareth Hospital Center is located amidst some of Chicago's most cutting-edge communities.

THE CHALLENGE OF OUR HEALTHCARE MISSION

Founded in 1894 by the Congregation of Sisters of the Holy Family of Nazareth, Saint Mary of Nazareth Hospital Center serves each patient in the spirit of family-centered care that characterizes the Sisters' hospital ministry.

OUR OPTION FOR THE POOR

Saint Mary of Nazareth Hospital Center has a century-old tradition of serving the poor of Chicago's near northwest side. Saint Mary of Nazareth was founded in 1894 by Blessed Mary of Jesus the Good Shepherd (Frances Siedliska). She and 11 of her Sisters of the Holy Family of Nazareth came to Chicago and began to care for Polish immigrants who were needy, sick, economically deprived, without prestige and who literally had "no friends in court" as they came to their new homeland of America.

THE FIRST TWO HOSPITALS

The **first** Saint Mary of Nazareth hospital, a three-story brick building that had previously been a private dwelling, contained 24 beds and was dedicated May 6, 1894. The sisters collected 25 cents for the first day's operations and a total of $126 by the end of the year. Despite all the difficulties, the hospital grew, even if it did not prosper. By 1902 the **second** Saint Mary of Nazareth Hospital was dedicated — a six-story facility constructed on an entire city block and incorporating some of the most advanced features of its day. Launched with a small, inexperienced, but determined band of Sisters, a few dedicated physicians, modest physical facilities, and irregular and discouraging financial prospects, Saint Mary's did not merely survive, it grew and prospered. It became a respected center for the practice and teaching of medicine in Chicago.

GROWTH AND CHANGE

During the next 25 years Saint Mary of Nazareth's people would survive the turbulence of World War I, a terrible Depression and the horror of World War II. By the end of 1944 the medical staff had 126 members, 41 Sisters were registered nurses and patient admissions had risen to an annual peak of 10,500 (including 1,816 newborns). The war years also saw economic and social changes come to Saint Mary's neighborhood. The predominance of Polish patients gave way to many nationalities. By the early 1960s the community was suffering a dramatic economic decline and the hospital structure built in 1902 had become outmoded and overcrowded. The Sisters had to make a critical decision about Saint Mary of Nazareth's future. Should they relocate their hospital to the suburbs as other city hospitals were doing? Or should they stay on the near northwest side and build a new facility to serve the growing, diverse populations of Polish, Ukrainian, Hispanic, African, Filipino and other groups that were moving into the area?

COMMITMENT TO SERVE THE COMMUNITY

With the help of a major government loan and significant cash donations from numerous friends, the Sisters built the **third** Saint Mary of Nazareth Hospital Center, the structure that stands today on Division Street between Oakley Boulevard and Leavitt Street. Dedicated in 1975, the 16-level, 490-bed hospital was and still is one of the most modern-looking hospital facilities in the city.

SAINT MARY OF NAZARETH HOSPITAL CENTER TODAY

In the new millennium, the Sisters, medical staff, employees and volunteers at Saint Mary of Nazareth continue their mission and ministry of service to the poor. Polish immigrants still begin their new lives in the hospital's service area. Ukrainian senior citizens come to Saint Mary's for care. Needy families of Puerto Rican, Mexican and African ancestry, in addition to families of many other nations and ethnic groups, turn to Saint Mary's. Young artists, who make up the third-largest population of working artists outside of Manhattan and

Sister M. Bernadette, CSFN, RN, child life specialist.
Saint Mary of Nazareth Hospital serves each patient in the spirit of family-centered care that characterizes the hospital ministry of its sponsors, the Sisters of the Holy Family of Nazareth.

San Francisco, and who inhabit nearby Bucktown, also turn to Saint Mary's for care. Providing for the healthcare needs of all those in need continues to be a primary goal of Saint Mary of Nazareth's healthcare ministry.

Saint Mary of Nazareth (all private rooms) is accredited by the Joint Commission on Accreditation of Healthcare Organizations (JCAHO). Its medical staff, composed of 345 men and women, represents a wide range of training and talent. Approximately 80 percent of its medical staff are board certified in their specialty or subspecialty fields.

From state-of-the-art Magnetic Resonance Imaging services to cardiac diagnostic equipment usually found only in major university medical centers, Saint Mary of Nazareth brings each patient a number of dramatic avenues for conquering disease and disability.

FACING THE FUTURE

Today Saint Mary's Sisters and leaders again face a future of searching, questioning and risky decision-making as the hospital continues to adjust to the effects of managed care and government budget reform. "In the future we will witness new healthcare configurations and new ways to describe them, like alliances, networks, markets, households and many more," says newly installed hospital President and CEO Sister Sally Marie Kiepura, CSFN. "In the years ahead Saint Mary of Nazareth's Sisters, medical staff, employees and volunteers will meet the challenges of tomorrow and continue to offer the best medical care possible to all those in need of it."

The Talbott Hotel

The Talbott Hotel has been welcoming visitors to Chicago since 1987. Owner Basil Kromelow presides over his European-style, 150-room property with a warm and loving touch.

Kromelow's family business, The Gold Coast Group, is composed of The Talbott Hotel, The Elms and the Delaware Towers. Kromelow serves as president and his son Jason serves as executive vice president. His other son, Eric, is international sales manager at The Talbott, where Kromelow's daughter Audrey serves as transportation manager and handles special projects.

Family hotel history began with Kromelow's father. Jack Kromelow sold hotel insurance during the Depression and in the 1940s began purchasing properties.

In 1959 he bought his first major apartment-hotel, The Elms. In 1963 he acquired the nearby Delaware Towers and in 1965 he bought Twenty East Delaware Apartments.

When Kromelow began investing, the area around his properties was seedy and tough. Saloons, prostitutes and their clients made it less than attractive to tourists.

The Talbott's cozy lobby

But he believed in the neighborhood and was determined to be part of what he viewed as its inevitable revitalization. Over the next 15 years, Kromelow worked with neighborhood associations, city commissioners and local business owners. Gradually — with the birth of Chicago's Water Tower Place shopping mall, the John Hancock Center, and new hotels, condominiums and movie theaters — the neighborhood came alive.

Basil Kromelow aspired to joining his father's business. He spent the summer of 1956 in Europe where he became familiar with boutique-style hotels unlike any he had seen in the United States. He dreamed of transforming one of the Kromelow properties into an owner-operated hotel with a sense of warmth and hospitality to match those he had seen in Paris, Venice and Florence.

Kromelow turned his dream into reality in 1987 when he converted Twenty East Delaware Apartments into The Talbott Hotel. With fantastic shopping a mere block away on Michigan Avenue, transportation in easy reach and 40 restaurants within 300 yards of its door, the small hotel was soon drawing business people and tourists.

Today the Talbott lobby offers a soothing environment for tired sightseers and hassled business travelers. Oriental rugs, antique chests, working fireplaces that once graced one of the city's mansions, deep leather sofas and artwork depicting English hunting scenes invite guests to sit down, relax, chat and enjoy afternoon tea with homemade brownies. In his typical hands-on style, Kromelow collected the antiques and prints himself.

Kromelow's staff members personalize guests' visits to The Talbott. Everyone from the doorman to Kromelow himself greets guests by name. The concierge, at his newly remodeled, completely computerized marble desk, makes dinner reservations, hires limousines and finds tickets to the best shows in town.

At 9:30 each morning Kromelow and general manager Patti Koehn meet with the hotel staff to discuss the day's events. Kromelow describes the meeting as a "huddle" where the group establishes a "game plan" so that everyone will know his or her role for the day.

In a city where new hotels pop up every day, stiff competition inspires constant attention to detail. The Talbott, built in 1927, is kept fresh with continuous refurbishing.

The Talbott offers meeting space for small groups who might otherwise be lost in the vast resources of Chicago's major hotels. In the second floor Victoria Room, people can interact in a congenial, private

atmosphere served by the hotel's catering staff. Brides often choose the first-floor Delaware Room for their wedding receptions. The space can be combined with part of the lobby to host cocktail receptions for as many as 175 guests. A newly renovated first-floor boardroom — equipped with a custom conference cabinet housing a flip chart, screen and white board — suits executive meetings. The room seats 12 in comfortable, high-back chairs.

Upstairs in guest rooms and suites the sedate yet comfortable English décor blends nicely with modern conveniences. Nightly turndown service includes old-fashioned chocolates; every room has cable television, pay-per-view movies and three telephones. Dry-cleaning service and thick terrycloth robes contrast with voice mail and data ports. Newly renovated bathrooms with granite countertops, marble floors and Jacuzzi tubs add a touch of class. Suites with separate sleeping quarters allow corporate guests plenty of space for work and relaxation.

The bar grew out of another Kromelow dream. In 1999 he gutted the former dry-cleaning establishment, then constructed an upscale English lounge around a 13-foot-long, 11-foot-high, hand-carved, 100-year-old walnut bookcase that once graced a villa in Como, Italy. The bookcase serves as the lounge's "back bar." The lounge's front window wall opens onto a lovely sidewalk café.

Prints and memorabilia, including photos of Kromelow's wife, chanteuse Laurcanne Lemay, brighten the bar's wood-paneled walls. Kromelow met Lemay in 1961 when he was working behind the desk at The Elms and she was a guest at the apartment-hotel. Lemay,

originally from Quebec, had brought her show to America and was appearing at a nearby night spot. Kromelow went to see her sing, stayed until 5 a.m. and fell in love.

In what might be seen as an homage to those days, singers provide entertainment in "Basil's" on Friday and Saturday nights. Occasionally Lemay herself performs. On weekends the bar hums with activity as out-of-towners and Chicagoans mingle to enjoy entertainment and light food such as artichoke pizza and roasted vegetable sandwiches.

The Talbott, one of the few independent hotels in the city and the last independent hotel in downtown Chicago, draws guests from around the world. The hotel joined the Steigenberger Reservation Service in 1992 and benefits from this connection to 380 independent hotels worldwide. Membership has greatly increased The Talbott's international business.

Chicago recognizes its debt to people like Kromelow and his father who have helped make it a world-class city. Since 1995, the year Jack Kromelow died, an honorary street sign announcing "Jack Kromelow Way" has graced Delaware Place outside The Talbott, reminding residents and visitors alike of one of the area's earliest boosters.

Basil's at The Talbott features a large selection of wines and a sophisticated light menu.

Guest rooms and suites offer all the comforts of the finest European hotels.

TCA

At a summer camp in Pennsylvania, his father handed the 5-year-old a tennis racquet and began to teach him how to play. For Alan Schwartz, it was the beginning of an outstanding career as both tennis player and entrepreneur.

Years later, father and son would make tennis history on Fullerton Avenue in Chicago. By 1968 Alan Schwartz had carved out a career in real estate and his father, Kevie, had an engineering degree and construction experience. With their love of tennis as a starting point, they decided to pool their human resources and create the world's largest indoor tennis facility, Mid-Town Tennis Club®. According to tennis legend Billie Jean King, it is "the best indoor facility in the country."

It was just the beginning of the company the Schwartz family named Tennis Corporation of America (TCA). The only differences between then and now are that a different Schwartz is making history and the emphasis stresses fitness and wellness in addition to tennis. Alan, now chairman of the board, has passed the torch to son Steven, president and COO, who has used his well-honed business skills to push TCA to the top of the industry.

In 30 years TCA has grown from that single Chicago tennis facility to an industry leader, owning and/or managing 48 fitness, racquet and multisport facilities in the United States and Canada, including 18 in the Chicago area. The clubs range from amenity clubs in office, hotel or apartment complexes to free-standing, multisport clubs and corporate fitness centers including General Motors, Sam Zell's Equity Group, Kraft Foods, The Travelers insurance companies, McDonald's and Computer Discount Warehouse.

Rick Wagoner, president of General Motors, understands the value of TCA: "Congratulations on being selected to handle our new fitness center — a tribute to TCA's track record of success," he wrote. And Joseph Endress, facilities director at McDonald's Corporation, echoes his praise. "This letter should serve as an overwhelming recommendation of TCA. When working relationships are first established, there is always a honeymoon. I can say that after 10 years we are still on our honeymoon."

Each TCA club is an individual creation, with special attention paid to the design, layout and decor. Wonderful color schemes, geometric shapes and spectacular artwork reinforce TCA's belief that "art feeds the soul while you build your body." Even though each club makes its own statement in appearance, "The name, the quality and the mission are the same — to offer every member the total club experience," says Steven Schwartz.

From the clubs' lounges, cafes, kids' clubs, spas, pro shops and facilities for tennis, basketball, fitness, group exercise, and indoor and outdoor swimming pools, variety at TCA clubs appeals to everyone.

But the nuts and bolts of a TCA club are just the beginning. For three decades, TCA has pioneered innovative programs. Tennis in No Time® (TNT®), which includes films and written homework and is the only lesson program ever trademarked by the U.S. Patent Office, has introduced more than 75,000 people to tennis. TCA developed the National Tennis Rating Program (NTRP), a self-rating program currently used by more than four million players.

Although TCA began with tennis, today 75 percent of TCA clubs are multisport facilities offering fitness programs, and in

The Willowbrook Athletic Club, Willowbrook, Illinois

many cases other racquet sports such as squash and platform tennis.

But TCA is more than appearance and innovative programs. Its employees provide the services members need — in some cases even car detailing, valet parking and dry cleaning services. In addition TCA has worked diligently to provide creative ways for employees to grow and develop. To address the need for continuing education, TCA instituted Professional Development Accounts, which permit employees to spend a portion of their annual salary on additional education, with two-thirds paid by TCA and one-third paid by the employee.

TCA University, an ongoing, high-quality, employee-education program with a controlled curriculum, offers employees classes in marketing, sales, member retention and industry advancements. Each year, the curriculum expands, involving more aspects of club operations. A primary part of TCA University is a series of "conventions" — meetings held throughout the year for professional and management staff that address targeted topics and general management principles. "The addition of TCA University was one of the best steps in employee advancement we have made," says Steven Schwartz.

TCA's commitment goes beyond the health and wellness of its members. The philosophy of all of TCA's clubs is to form a partnership with the local community. One club received the C. Everett Koop Award for Fitness for its innovative programming. And for more than five years, TCA has offered free tennis programs through the Chicago Park District, and has revitalized and maintained the 790 courts that are part of the district, giving both children and adults a chance to learn, play, enjoy and excel in the sport.

To continue this commitment, TCA has also partnered with health care organizations and integrated health care services into its clubs, consulted with and managed hospital fitness facilities and introduced physical therapy units in many of its clubs.

Understanding the need to provide a memorable experience each time a member enters a TCA club or corporate fitness center has always been paramount to the company. Beginning with Mid-Town Tennis Club®, TCA clubs have delivered this experience because of the company's understanding of

General Motors' FitnessWorks in Detroit, Michigan

member needs. With the awareness and dedication of TCA employees, clubs become a place that members can call their own.

In the new millennium, the evolution of health and fitness trends shows no sign of slowing down. At TCA Steven Schwartz plans to take the company to a new level. The vision includes use of the Internet as a vehicle for TCA to provide individualized health and fitness prescriptions for diet, exercise and rehab to as many people as possible.

Club Business International, the industry's leading trade publication, recently reported, "Steven's keen eye for the opportunity and his unerring ability to identify new trends have made TCA an industry leader."

The Sporting Club at Windy Hill in Atlanta, Georgia

Loyola University Health System

Loyola University Health System in Maywood is a private, Jesuit, academic health-care system and a leader in primary and specialty health care and research. "We also treat the human spirit," emphasizes its commitment beyond the treatment of disease to care for patients' emotional and spiritual well-being.

LUHS, formed as a wholly owned subsidiary of Loyola University Chicago in 1996, comprises Loyola University Medical Center; a network of primary care, specialty care and ambulatory surgery facilities in Cook and DuPage counties; an affiliation with the Rehabilitation Institute of Chicago; and co-ownership of the RML Specialty Hospital, which provides long-term acute care.

This aerial view shows a portion of the 70-acre campus of Loyola University Medical Center in Maywood, Illinois, just west of the city of Chicago. The medical center is part of Loyola University Health System.

Loyola University Medical Center was established in 1969, gaining prominence in the diagnosis, treatment and management of cancer and heart-related problems; care of high-risk mothers and children; neurology and neurological surgery; and trauma, burn care and emergency medical services. Since 1988, Loyola's Lifestar helicopter has transported critically ill patients to Foster G. McGaw Hospital. Loyola has gained worldwide attention as a solid organ transplantation center for hearts, lungs, livers and kidneys.

In 1996, after the establishment of the Ronald McDonald House, the world's first Ronald McDonald Children's Hospital opened within Loyola's Foster G. McGaw Hospital. The children's hospital provides a full range of health-care services.

Loyola's Cardinal Bernardin Cancer Center opened in 1994 as the first freestanding facility in Illinois integrating diagnosis, clinical care, prevention and research in cancer under one roof. Named in honor of the late Joseph Cardinal Bernardin, the center received the only National Cancer Institute Planning Grant in 1998.

Formation of LUHS began in the mid-1990s when the first off-campus primary-care facility opened in Glendale Heights. The network now includes 15 primary-care facilities, five specialty-care centers and two ambulatory-surgery centers. Loyola's Center for Home Care and Hospice, a Medicare-certified program licensed by the Illinois Department of Public Health, offers services to children and adults in cardiac, neonatal and psychiatric care; skilled nursing care; physical, occupational and speech therapy; and hospice care.

LUHS' partnership with the Rehabilitation Institute of Chicago began in 1997 to provide comprehensive physical medicine and rehabilitation in Chicago's western and southwestern suburbs. The partnership, RIC&LOYOLA, established a 24-bed acute rehabilitative care facility within Loyola's Foster G. McGaw Hospital and outpatient rehabilitation programs based at Loyola's Oakbrook Terrace Medical Center and the Loyola Primary Care Center at Hickory Hills. RIC&LOYOLA also operates an outpatient rehabilitation program in Forest Park.

The RML Specialty Hospital, co-owned with Rush-Presbyterian-St. Luke's Medical Center and the MacNeal Health Network, is one of three Chicago-area facilities providing long-term acute care. It cares for patients dependent on ventilators, wound-healing problems and chronic disease conditions.

Associated with LUHS and located at Loyola's Maywood medical center is the Loyola University Chicago Stritch School of Medicine. Established in 1909 and named in honor of the late Samuel Cardinal Stritch of Chicago in 1948, the school is a national model for students aspiring to become physicians. In 1996 Loyola University Chicago opened a new medical educational facility that provides instruction to an estimated 520 students.

Loyola University Medical Center also includes the graduate nursing program of the Loyola University Chicago Marcella Niehoff School of Nursing. Adjacent to the medical center is Edward Hines Jr. Veterans Affairs Hospital, which serves as a teaching site for Loyola students, residents and fellows.

Moody Bible Institute

The Moody Bible Institute has been a premier provider of Christian education, missionary training and evangelical services for more than 114 years. Through its numerous educational and outreach ministries, the Institute has brought to fruition the goal of its founder, Dwight Lyman Moody — to equip and motivate people to advance the cause of Christ.

Since its formation in 1886, the Moody Bible Institute has been responsible for training more than 30,000 Christian men and women who have served as pastors, missionaries and Christian workers throughout the world.

Located on a 23-acre site on the city's Near North Side, the Moody Bible Institute campus currently houses more than 1,500 undergraduate and graduate students. Here, students can obtain an undergraduate Christian education without paying tuition costs. Paying only room and board fees, students choose from 16 undergraduate majors, including educational ministries, missionary aviation technology, communications and pastoral studies.

The Graduate School began in 1985 and today offers five graduate programs, including a newly added master of divinity degree. As part of MBI's External Studies Division, 23 extension sites around the country offer continuing education and undergraduate level classes. For those who desire to study at their own pace, Moody Independent Studies courses offer a convenient way to obtain a Moody education at home.

In addition to education, the Moody Bible Institute has initiated numerous outreach ministries. Moody's work in publishing began in the late 1800s. Today the legacy continues through Moody Press, which publishes up to 60 new titles each year and distributes Bibles and Christian books worldwide. Other publications include *Moody* magazine, published six times a year with more than 290,000 subscribers, and *Today in the Word*, a monthly devotional guide.

The Moody Broadcasting Network, started in 1926, currently owns and operates 30 radio stations in 14 states. Through this medium, Christian-related programming is sent to more than 265 affiliate stations in the United States, and taped programs are sent to nearly 400 additional stations around the world. WMBI, which broadcasts from the downtown campus, reaches the Chicagoland area with both AM and FM programming. Moody Video has produced several award-winning productions that focus on science and God's creation, along with other videos covering children's topics. They have been translated into nearly 40 languages and are used in public schools, churches and military installations, and in homes in more than 130 countries.

In keeping with the vision to provide Christian training, Moody's Conference Ministries division holds specialty seminars and conferences around the country that focus on women's and men's issues, parenting, marriage and pastoral encouragement. Founder's Week is an annual Bible conference held in Chicago every February that features prominent Bible teachers from around the country and draws an aggregate of 40,000 attendees. Moody's retail division operates three bookstores that offer a wide selection of Christian books, Bibles, music and church supplies.

The selfless legacy that Moody left behind continues to support the Moody Bible Institute. Today, more than 125,000 active donors help financially support the institute's endeavors and underwrite its students' tuition costs. This was one of Moody's initial guidelines for the school — that graduates would not be saddled with debt upon completing their education. Instead, they could go and serve without financial hindrance.

Moody Bible Institute's mission of "Serving Christ… to Advance His Cause" continues into the 21st century. Future plans call for using emerging technology to offer a Moody education to anyone in the world who wants it.

Located on a 23-acre campus on the city's Near North Side, the Moody Bible Institute has served as a provider of Christian education, missionary training and evangelical services for more than 114 years.

Chicago Center for Surgery of the Hand and Reconstructive Microsurgery

The Windy City is home to a hand surgery school pushed to international acclaim by four Chicago surgeons who played a tremendous role in the development of hand surgery around the time of World Wars I and II.

The Chicago Center for Surgery of the Hand and Reconstructive Microsurgery, revered by many in the field, stands today just east of the Magnificent Mile. The center's foundations date to the pioneering work of Dr. Allen B. Kanavel and his colleagues Drs. Sumner L. Koch, Michael L. Mason and Harvey S. Allen.

Dr. Kanavel, a general surgeon who did an internship at Chicago's Cook County Hospital before joining the staff of Northwestern University Medical School, literally

Dr. Allen B. Kanavel

(Left to right)
Drs. Wiedrich, Harris, Nagle and Stogin

Drs. Allen B. Kanavel, Sumner L. Koch and Michael L. Mason

wrote the book on hand surgery, *Infections of the Hand*, published in 1912. This book, widely accepted throughout the world through seven editions until 1939, was the only practical textbook on hand surgery in use during World War I, a time when many soldiers were being treated for shrapnel injuries to the hand.

Toward the end of the war, Northwestern University Medical School sent Dr. Kanavel and Dr. Koch, a surgeon 14 years his junior, to Europe to treat American troops. Inspired by all he had learned from Dr. Kanavel, Dr. Koch returned from the war and set up a hand clinic in Chicago. In turn, a young sergeant who the doctors met abroad, Michael Mason, was impressed by their work and followed them back to Chicago where

he pursued his medical studies at Northwestern and joined them in practice in 1926.

Koch and Mason specialized in the treatment of burns of the hand. Dr. Mason authored *Rate of Healing of Tendons* with Dr. Harvey S. Allen. The landmark paper discussed the healing of lacerated tendons.

Dr. Allen spent fours years at Northwestern University Medical School under the tutelage of Kanavel, Koch and Mason. In 1936 he joined them in practice and eventually assumed charge of the hand clinic where his experience in the care of burn wounds brought about the still-used practice of early excision of burn tissue to cut short the healing phase.

Although their hand clinic was not an official school, doctors from all over the world flocked to Chicago to learn the techniques of Drs. Kanavel, Koch, Mason and Allen. In fact the office was one of four regional hand centers developed at the end of World War II. These hand centers were designed to treat the hand injuries of the World War II veterans. The legacy of the Chicago School of Hand Surgery continues this day under the direction of Drs. Harris, Nagle, Wiedrich and Stogin, who were inspired by the founding doctors.

It is difficult to estimate how many hands have been saved and restored to useful function because of the work of these doctors or the work of those who studied their techniques. Chicago is fortunate that the tradition of the Chicago Hand Surgery School continues to this day.

Photo by Russell Lee of the Farm Security Administration. Library of Congress

Diverse businesses have gathered to make Chicago one of the country's leading centers of technology innovation, development, manufacturing and employment.

TECHNOLOGY

Motorola

Since 1928 Motorola has been committed to creating innovative products and technologies that enhance the way people live and work. A fearless, pioneering spirit and deep respect for both employees and customers highlight Motorola's history.

Motorola got its start in 1928 when Paul V. Galvin and his brother Joseph E. Galvin purchased a battery eliminator business from the bankrupt Stewart Storage Battery Company in Chicago. The brothers incorporated

Manufacturing and headquarters facility, c. 1940. The first facility built and owned by Galvin Manufacturing Corporation was located on West Augusta Boulevard, Chicago, Illinois. Construction was completed in 1937.

as the Galvin Manufacturing Corporation on September 25, 1928.

The Galvin Manufacturing Corporation rented space on Chicago's West Side. The business consisted of five employees, assets of $565 in cash and $750 in tools, and a design for the company's first product — a battery eliminator. The eliminator enabled battery-operated home radios to operate on ordinary household current.

The small company faced its first test when the battery eliminator business ground to a halt in 1929 due to the widespread introduction of non-battery home radios and the onset of the Great Depression. Determined to renew their company, in 1930 Galvin and his associates designed and produced the first practical and affordable car radios. At the time radios were not directly available from automobile manufacturers. Galvin auto radios were sold and installed as accessories by independent distributors and dealers. Liking the idea of motion and radio, Paul Galvin coined the name Motorola for the company's new product.

A national advertising campaign used printed media, billboards and a famous roadside sign campaign to link the new car radio with the name Motorola. In 1937 Galvin built a new, modern headquarters and manufacturing facility not far from its original location and drew many of its employees from the surrounding neighborhoods.

By the mid-1930s more than half of all American households owned radios. Each night millions of Americans listened to Fred Allen, Jack Benny, Little Orphan Annie and hosts of big bands. In its "Golden Age," radio became the primary means of mass communication. The Galvin brothers established their own line of home radios in 1937.

Galvin next turned its attention to the new and growing field of radio communication products. The Police Cruiser — an AM auto radio pre-set to a single frequency that received police broadcasts — was the company's first such product.

Daniel E. Noble, a pioneer in FM radio communications and semiconductor technology, joined Galvin as director of research in 1940. That year the first complete Motorola two-way AM police radio system was put into use by the police department in Bowling Green, Kentucky. But innovative Motorola researchers recognized that FM radio communication — with greater range and quieter operation — had an edge over AM equipment. With this in mind, the company soon introduced the first commercial line of two-way FM radio communications products.

During World War II Galvin Manufacturing focused its energy on the war effort. Noble designed the first portable FM two-way radio for use by the military. Known as the "Walkie-Talkie" backpack radio, it and the "Handie-Talkie" handheld radio became vital to battlefield communications throughout Europe and the South Pacific.

Following the war, the company resumed the manufacture of electronics equipment for civilian use. By 1947 the Motorola trademark was so widely recognized that the company changed its name officially from the Galvin Manufacturing Corporation to Motorola, Inc.

Auto radios continued to be a major product for the company. In the late 1940s Motorola began supplying auto radios to Ford and Chrysler plants for direct installation in cars. With a contract to produce radios for other auto manufacturers, Motorola opened an auto radio manufacturing facility in Quincy, Illinois.

Anticipating the enormous potential of the newly invented transistor, Noble then launched a Motorola transistor research and development facility in Phoenix, Arizona. Motorola's first mass-produced commercial product incorporating transistors was a new type of auto radio. Smaller and more durable than previous auto radios, this model required less power from the car's battery. An all-transistor auto radio, introduced in 1959, was considered the most reliable in the industry. Motorola also introduced the shirt-pocket-sized X11, its first all-transistor pocket-sized radio.

At the same time Motorola was developing a new radio communications product — a small radio receiver called a pager. The pager was designed to deliver a radio

Motorola, Inc. was a recipient of the first Malcolm Baldrige National Quality Award, established by the U.S. Congress to recognize and inspire the pursuit of quality in American business. Robert W. Galvin is shown here accepting the Malcolm Baldrige Quality Award in 1988.

message selectively to a particular individual carrying the device. Hospitals were among the first industries to supply their employees with pagers.

Work by engineers at Motorola's Phoenix research center led to the company becoming one of the world's largest manufacturers of semiconductors. The Semiconductor Products Division was established in 1958 and headquartered in Phoenix, Arizona. Having first manufactured semiconductors for exclusive use in its own radios, televisions and communications products, in 1959 Motorola became a commercial producer and supplier of semiconductors for sale to other manufacturers.

As the cost of semiconductors continued to decline, their application in consumer electronic products increased, creating a major market. Motorola responded with a full line of low-cost, plastic-encapsulated transistors. Its design for these devices eventually was adopted by the entire semiconductor industry.

At the same time, Motorola continued its work in the automotive arena. As the company developed various low-cost techniques for making the silicon rectifiers used in automobile alternators, the alternator became an economical replacement for the less-durable auto generator. The Automotive Products Division began producing alternators, inaugurating the company's role as a supplier of "under the hood" electronics.

In a joint program with Ford and RCA in 1965, Motorola helped design and manufactured the first 8-track tape players for the automotive market. The players became a major product line for the Automotive Product Division, second only to auto radios. Several domestic and foreign auto manufacturers soon became customers for tape players.

Motorola also actively participated in the U.S. space program. On its 1962 flight to Venus, Mariner II carried a Motorola transponder that provided a radio link spanning 54 million miles. Images of Mars were relayed to Earth by similar equipment aboard Mariner IV in 1964. Motorola also supplied transponders for the Gemini manned-space program. In 1969 astronaut Neil Armstrong's first words from the Moon were relayed to Earth by a transponder designed and manufactured by Motorola's Government Electronics Division.

Semiconductor production, 1990. Semiconductors are packaged onto reels so machines can automatically place the devices onto circuit boards.

When the Lunar Roving Vehicle traversed the moon, a Motorola FM radio receiver provided the voice link that sped its messages across 240,000 miles of outer space. The receiver was 100 times more sensitive than a standard car radio, yet it weighed only 1.5 pounds. In 1976 Motorola equipment relayed to Earth detailed color photographs of the surface of Mars taken by Viking 2.

Motorola also tackled the timepiece industry, adding the manufacture of components for battery powered quartz watches to its range of skills. Between 1971 and 1979 the company gained critical experience in producing and supplying integrated circuits, quartz crystals, and miniature motors to manufacturers like Timex, Benrus and Bulova.

Always on the cutting edge, in 1974 Motorola introduced its first microprocessor, the 6800. It contained 4,000 transistors, used a single, 5-volt power supply and was supported by a range of devices. The earliest customers for the 6800 came from the automotive, communications, industrial, and business-machine market sectors.

Five years later Motorola introduced its first 16-bit microprocessor, the 68000. Capable of completing two million calculations per second, it was efficient at running and writing programs for scientific, data processing and business applications.

Motorola's next entry into the computer field was the first true 32-bit microprocessor, the MC68020. Its 200,000 transistors were able to access up to four billion bytes of memory. By 1986 more than 125 companies were producing systems that used this device. The MC68HC11 — an advanced microcomputer adjustable to specific applications — was also introduced.

Television was another area of development at Motorola. In 1967 the company introduced its "Quasar" line of color receivers. America's first all-transistor color television sets, they were designed to be easy to repair, a feature stressed in their "Works in a Drawer" trademark. But by 1974 Motorola was once again reinventing itself, this time with an increased focus on the development of microprocessors. Quasar and all other aspects of Motorola's home television business were sold to Matsushita Electric Industrial Company, Ltd., along with the Motorola facility in Quincy, Illinois.

After years of development, Motorola's cellular business really took off in 1983 when the company's first "Dyna-TAC" cellular system began commercial operation. In paging more than 43,000 Pocket Bell pagers were supplied to Nippon Telegraph and Telephone of Japan. Motorola created a new, convenient "Sensar" pager less than six inches long. By 1984 200,000 Motorola pagers were being used in Japan. The Motorola Paging Division moved into a new plant in Boynton Beach, Florida.

In 1985 Motorola formed its General Systems Group, combining Motorola Computer Systems, Inc. (formerly Four-Phase Systems, Inc.) with the company's Cellular group. Contracts for cellular systems soon were received from New York, Philadelphia, Beijing and Hong Kong, along with system expansion contracts from the United Kingdom, Scandinavia and Japan.

Over the years employee education had always been of major importance at Motorola. In 1986 the company invested a considerable sum in employee education. A companywide Motorola Training and Education Center (MTEC) was created and headquartered in Schaumburg, Illinois, within the company's Galvin Center for Continuing Education. In 1990 MTEC became Motorola University. The school now has 101 sites worldwide.

Times changed and Motorola's direction continued to change with them. In 1987 the company produced its last auto radio and divested itself of its display systems business as well as its automotive alternator and electro-mechanical meter product lines. New products included instrumentation for cars and trucks, and control modules for engine transmissions.

Effort has its rewards. In 1988 Motorola won the first Malcolm Baldrige National Quality Award, given by Congress to recognize and inspire the pursuit of quality in American business.

For Motorola the 1990s was a decade of continued pioneering in the communications industry. The company's Government Electronics Group supplied radio equipment for the Galileo, Magellan and Hubble Space Telescope missions, and introduced a new 8.5-pound portable Lightweight Satellite Terminal radio.

Motorola's ever-expanding Communications Sector was divided into the Paging and Telepoint Systems Group, and the Land Mobile Products Sector. Focusing on the growth of wireless technologies, the Land Mobile Products sector developed and produced both two-way and data communications radio equipment and systems.

Motorola's third-generation 32-bit microprocessor, the 68040, was adopted by more than 100 customers for applications in their product lines. The "040" contained 1.2 million transistors, was able to process 20 million instructions per second and was compatible with existing software developed for the 68000 family of microprocessors.

Also in the 1990s, the Motorola Museum of Electronics opened in Schaumburg, Illinois. Exhibits chronicled the closely intertwined evolution of Motorola and the electronics industry.

A fearless, pioneering spirit and deep respect for both employees and customers highlight Motorola's history.

"It is the voice of our past," says Robert W. Galvin, son of company founder Paul Galvin. "But through the lessons and examples contained in this museum, we are better prepared to address our future."

Today, Motorola is composed of three basic business groups: Communications Enterprise, Semiconductor Products Sector and Integrated Electronic Systems Sector.

Communications Enterprise (CE) aligns all of the company's communications businesses into an actively managed and coordinated unit that provides integrated communications solutions to a variety of customers and consumers around the world. CE handles approximately 70 percent of Motorola's global business.

Personal Communications Sector delivers integrated solutions that enable consumers to take their world with them, fulfilling the promise that they can carry voice, data or video communication systems anywhere and use them at anytime. A major component — the Consumer Solutions Group — ensures that Motorola understands and answers consumers' needs.

Commercial, Government and Industrial Solutions serves three distinct global markets, providing integrated communications solutions that include systems, equipment, software, services, applications and content. These solutions involve Motorola and, where necessary, non-Motorola products and services.

Network Solutions Sector is responsible for manufacturing, sales and integration of Motorola's cellular infrastructure. The group works closely with the Global

Motorola founder Paul V. Galvin (left) and his son, Robert W. Galvin, review the benefits of plated circuitry used in the Roto-tenna portable radio, c. 1956. Plated circuit boards helped make Motorola radios smaller and more reliable.

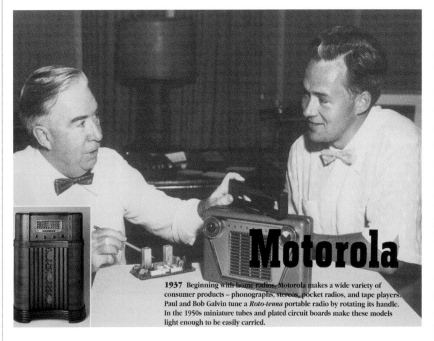

Motorola

1937 Beginning with home radios, Motorola makes a wide variety of consumer products – phonographs, stereos, pocket radios, and tape players. Paul and Bob Galvin tune a *Roto-tenna* portable radio by rotating its handle. In the 1950s miniature tubes and plated circuit boards make these models light enough to be easily carried.

Telecom Solutions Group to ensure an infrastructure that gives network operators an expanded range of services. Within NSS, the satellite communications group is a developer, system integrator and prime contractor for satellite-based communications networks.

Global Telecom Solutions Group understands the requirements of large global network operators and coordinates the delivery of solutions from other Motorola businesses to meet their needs. The group works closely with the Personal Communications Sector and the Network Solutions Group to deliver total customer solutions.

Internet and Networking Group combines Motorola's Internet, data networking and software capabilities to develop servers, applications and Internet solutions. The group launches innovative new products and services through Motorola's customer-focused businesses.

As the world's No. 1 producer of embedded processors, Motorola's Semiconductor Products Sector offers multiple DigitalDNA solutions which enable customers to create new business opportunities in the consumer, networking and computing, transportation and wireless communications markets.

The Integrated Electronic Systems Sector designs and manufactures a broad range of electronic components, modules and integrated electronic systems and products for automotive, computer, industrial, transportation, navigation, energy systems, consumer and lighting markets.

Since its earliest days Motorola has been cognizant of its place in the world and the need to take care of the earth. The company's Environmental, Health and Safety (EHS) organizations provide a critical support function for all company operations around the globe. Assuring that its workplaces are safe, assisting in the design of new facilities and negotiating with government agencies for permits, EHS professionals influence Motorola policy and contribute directly toward Motorola's bottom line.

Recognizing that Motorola's business success is entwined with its EHS performance, Motorola has embarked on a challenging journey — the journey to become a company that fully supports a sustainable use of the earth's resources. Motorola envisions a future in which its factories are accident-free, create zero waste, emit only benign emissions, use energy in highly efficient ways and utilize their discarded products as feed for new products. The company seeks to design all of its products for innovative performance and low environmental impact, and to have superb benefits for the environmental quality and the safety of their users.

> Motorola believes that part of doing business is being a good neighbor. Across the world Motorola has taken an active role to protect the environment in the communities where its employees and customers live and work.

It is the policy of Motorola to conduct all business activities in a responsible manner, free from recognized hazards; to respect the environment, health and safety of its employees, customers, suppliers, partners and community neighbors; to foster the sustainable use of the earth's resources; and to comply with all applicable environmental, health and safety laws and regulations of the countries where it operates, while committing itself to continuous improvement in its EHS management systems, pollution prevention practices and safety programs.

Motorola sites around the world operate under a common EHS Management Systems (MS) framework. All Motorola manufacturing sites are staffed with EHS professionals who are responsible for developing and implementing site-specific programs to comply with the EHS MS requirements.

The number of EHS employees corporatewide and their role in the company has grown tremendously over the years. Twenty or more years ago, EHS activities were predominantly reactive. Today, to achieve its challenging vision, much of its work is proactive, and includes partnering with manufacturing, facilities, finance, business planning, human relations and other divisions inside and outside of Motorola to assure continual improvement of worker, asset and environmental protection.

Motorola believes that part of doing business is being a good neighbor. Across the world Motorola has taken an active role to protect the environment in the communities where its employees and customers live and work. For instance, the company donates funds generated by internal recycling programs to various charities and community environmental projects.

Motorola considers its customers' needs, too. It offers them creative solutions through its Consulting and Training Services (CTS) team. The team works with Motorola departments, selected customers, suppliers and other external organizations to improve their business performance. Services include quality and cycle time analyses, customized education and training programs and application consulting to ensure implementation and continuous performance improvement.

Each CTS team member has over 20 years of experience either with Motorola or with other major global organizations. Team members combine consulting, teaching and facilitating to help clients apply in their own organizations what has successfully been incorporated into Motorola's culture.

The team's consulting extends beyond the classroom to help each organization that uses CTS services gain a distinctive competitive advantage. Motorola's consultants have proven skills in a variety of areas including business needs analysis, cross-functional process mapping, cycle time reduction, quality improvement processes, benchmarking,

> Since its earliest days Motorola has been cognizant of its place in the world and the need to take care of the earth.

strategic planning, advanced tools and techniques and quality system review processes.

Today Motorola responds quickly to the rapidly changing global marketplace by stepping up its comprehensive renewal programs. These are based on four key objectives.

The company's primary goal is to attain global leadership in its core businesses. To make the company more competitive, Motorola's management team is committed to investing in brand marketing, advanced digital technology, software and continuous business model modification.

A second objective is to provide total solutions through partnerships. Because Motorola views its business world as an ecosystem, the company enters new and innovative partnerships and aligns itself with best-of-breed providers in multiple industries, even with its competitors.

Developing new "platforms" for future global leadership is a third objective. Researchers sustain an intensive effort to find new products and services.

The company's fourth objective is performance excellence. The Motorola-designed Six Sigma quality process has provided the foundation for much of the company's progress over the last decade and is applied to the realm of consumer preferences.

Motorola continues to pursue a rigorous focus on improving financial results. Balanced with the necessary business and technology investments to earn leadership in its market segments, the company is building long-term shareholder value and maintaining customer respect for its name.

"People have an insatiable desire to communicate. Demand remains strong for wireless communications. Additionally, Motorola is positioned to make billions of things smarter with our embedded silicon and software solutions," CEO Christopher B. Galvin says. "Motorola is focused on performance-improvement and continuing-change management, which is intended to please our customers, consumers and stockholders worldwide."

Abbott Laboratories

Headquartered in north suburban Chicago, Abbott Laboratories is a *Fortune* 150 corporation and one of the world's largest health care manufacturers.

Abbott Laboratories began in the apartment of a young Chicago physician, Dr. Wallace C. Abbott, more than a century ago. Since then, this *Fortune* 150 corporation has evolved into one of the world's leading health care companies, with a presence in more than 130 countries. Headquartered in north suburban Chicago, Abbott discovers, develops, manufactures and markets an array of innovative products that span the health care spectrum and continually advance the practice of medicine. Worldwide, the company employs more than 57,000 people, about a third of whom work in the Chicago area.

In addition to being one of Illinois' largest employers, Abbott is one of the state's largest investors. The company performs more research and development in Illinois — and commits more capital — than any other company in the state. In the past five years, Abbott has dedicated $3 billion to scientific research and development in Illinois, where it has more than 3,500 high-quality jobs dedicated to the research and development of advanced health care products and technologies.

SPANNING THE HEALTH CARE SPECTRUM

The diversity of its health care businesses makes Abbott Laboratories a powerful and comprehensive provider in a growing number of medical markets throughout the world. The company's four major businesses — pharmaceuticals, nutritionals, diagnostics and hospital products — are all focused on the discovery, development and marketing of products that address some of the world's most prevalent medical conditions, including AIDS, cancer and diabetes.

Abbott's aim is to provide total, integrated solutions across the health care continuum for these and other medical conditions. To achieve this goal, the company combines the strengths found across all of its businesses: leading-edge science, extensive manufacturing expertise, well-developed distribution channels and superior sales organizations. Abbott continues to build on its broad business diversity, expanding in new directions and into new markets throughout the world.

Led by a management team dedicated to accelerating the company's growth, Abbott has initiated internal and external expansion efforts that have delivered both financial success and medical breakthroughs. *Fortune* magazine has heralded the company for its financial performance, hiring practices, development programs and employee benefits. In fact, Abbott has been an innovator and leader in offering employee benefits throughout its history. *Industry Week* has consistently identified it as one of the world's best-managed companies.

As for financial performance, Abbott has achieved double-digit, year-over-year growth in earnings per share for more than 25 consecutive years and has paid dividends to its stockholders for more than 75 consecutive years. The company has consistently been listed in the book *The 100 Best Stocks to Own in America*.

A SUCCESS STORY BASED ON SCIENCE

Although no single factor is responsible for Abbott's growth and success over the past century, the catalyst, certainly, is science. Abbott's commitment to research and development began with Dr. Abbott and through the years has remained the company's top priority.

Abbott creates new health care technologies through both internal and external efforts. The company relies on its corps of world-class research scientists to discover and develop products internally, while leveraging its powerful research, manufacturing, marketing and distribution capabilities to form technology alliances with other companies.

Abbott continually adds new technologies through acquisitions, as well as through partnerships, in-licensing agreements and alliances with some of the world's leading companies. These give Abbott access to both innovative products and technologies to enhance ongoing research.

A TRADITION OF INNOVATION

As a pioneer in health care, Abbott has created a number of medical breakthroughs throughout its history, including the development, in 1936, of the anesthetic Pentothal; early mass production of penicillin and development of other antibiotics; the introduction, in 1985, of the world's first diagnostic test for AIDS; and the development, in 1996, of Norvir, one of the world's first protease inhibitors to fight HIV, the virus that causes AIDS.

The company's tradition of innovation started more than 100 years ago with Dr. Abbott himself. In 1888 the then 30-year-old physician purchased a medical practice and drugstore in Chicago's Ravenswood neighborhood. From this operation, which he named the People's Drug Store, Dr. Abbott made house calls and sold the common medical treatments of the day. However, Dr. Abbott wasn't satisfied with the medicines available to his practice, many of which consisted of alcoholic extracts or crude waters drawn from medicinal plants. These treatments required large doses, were nauseating in taste and were hit-and-miss in their effectiveness.

Instead, Dr. Abbott advocated a new scientific theory of pharmacy based upon the alkaloid, or active part, of a drug plant for medicinal purposes. This alkaloid could be compressed into a tiny granule or pill form and then taken orally for treatment. Dr. Abbott began to offer some of these granule medicines at the People's Drug Store, but found them unsatisfactory in treating his patients.

In search of a better alternative for his patients, he began producing his own. His kitchen sink became the original production center of his new enterprise, which he called the Abbott Alkaloidal Company. Using spatulas and molds of hard rubber, Dr. Abbott, along with his family members, worked around-the-clock forming the tiny granules. He found his new formulations to be far more dependable than older preparations. Dosages were more accurate and uniform. Their ease of use helped his patients to comply with treatment regimens, resulting in better medical outcomes. The company's first-year sales: $2,000.

Dr. Abbott continued to research new treatments and remedies using the alkaloids of drug plants and created an arsenal of medicines for physicians to choose from. The early success of these medicines and the circulation of *The Alkaloidal Clinic*, a medical journal published by Dr.

Abbott Laboratories' commitment to advancing the practice of medicine began with Dr. Wallace C. Abbott more than a century ago.

Abbott's commitment to research began with Dr. Abbott and through the years has remained the company's top priority.

Abbott Laboratories was a pioneer in the introduction of anesthetics and anti-infective medicines, including penicillin.

Abbott, firmly established the Abbott Alkaloidal Company as an innovative leader in the medical community.

By 1915 the market for alkaloidal remedies had peaked, with a number of competitors entering the market. Advances in chemistry and medicine allowed for a new pharmaceutical field — synthetic drugs. These medicines were made from synthetic chemicals rather than the alkaloids of plants. Recognizing this evolution, the Abbott Alkaloidal Company shifted its focus and became an early leader in synthetic treatments. In 1915 the company changed its name to Abbott Laboratories, reflecting its emphasis on scientific research.

As a consequence of its new direction, the company doubled its revenues and created a need for larger production facilities. In 1920 construction began on a new manufacturing and headquarters facility in the city of North Chicago, about 30 miles north of Ravenswood. Unfortunately, in 1921, just as the new site of Abbott Laboratories neared completion, Dr. Abbott died at the age of 63. The company was 33 years old, growing robustly and firmly rooted in science. Its commitment to research and development would only grow in the years ahead.

A LEGACY OF MEDICAL BREAKTHROUGHS

An early focus of Abbott's research and development was anesthesia, a field in which the company has been a leader since its creation of Nembutal. This sedative quickly became widely used to ease childbirth, control convulsions, relieve insomnia and alleviate disorders ranging from seasickness to delirium. Today, Nembutal continues to be a part of Abbott Laboratories' extensive portfolio of anesthesia products.

To build on the success of Nembutal, its creators, Drs. Ernest Volwiler and Donalee Tabern, drove forward to develop a new formulation of the drug that could be used as an intravenous anesthetic. At the time several of the anesthetics available were ineffective, rendering patients unconscious for either too little or too much time. Volwiler's and Tabern's research led to the introduction, in 1936, of Pentothal, an anesthetic still widely used today. Its introduction was timely, as Pentothal played a major role in saving lives in World War II by allowing wounded soldiers to be treated before they got to a hospital. For this important achievement, Volwiler and Tabern were inducted into the National Inventors Hall of Fame in 1986.

Another treatment area in which Abbott has long specialized is anti-infective drugs. In 1941 Abbott Laboratories became one of the first companies in the United States to commercially produce penicillin, contributing to the U.S. effort in World War II. This antibiotic had been discovered in London 13 years prior; however, the war had stalled Great Britain's research efforts. Thus, British officials came to the United States looking for companies that could produce penicillin on a large scale. Abbott welcomed this opportunity and constructed a new facility in North Chicago to research and create the most effective strain of penicillin possible.

Through its extensive research, Abbott found the most effective mold strain on an overripe cantaloupe in a Peoria, Illinois, fruit stand and successfully mass-produced the antibiotic. This discovery would eventually lead to one of Abbott's most successful and long-term franchises, anti-infective medicines, with widely used products like PCE (erythromycin) and Biaxin (clarithromycin).

WORLDWIDE EXPANSION

By the mid-1950s Abbott Laboratories had surpassed the $100 million mark in sales and had introduced hundreds of pharmaceutical and health care products. While the company had begun doing business outside the United States in 1931, it now shifted to a true global, multinational focus and continued to expand by offering its products throughout the world. Today the company has 54 international affiliates and manufacturing sites in 30 countries and markets products in every region of the world.

Abbott was also growing through acquisitions that diversified its product line but focused its drive to improve the quality of health care. The acquisition of M&R Dietetic Laboratories in 1964 was one of the company's largest. The deal led to its long-term leadership position in nutritional products. This business, which became the company's Ross Products Division, has allowed Abbott to expand its presence in the consumer market by offering products such as Similac, the best-selling infant formula in the United States, and Ensure, one of the world's leading brands of adult nutritional products.

To keep up with the company's dynamic growth, Abbott purchased 420 acres of farmland in Lake County, Illinois, in 1961. This site, known as Abbott Park, would become Abbott Laboratories' world headquarters and today houses numerous research, manufacturing and administrative facilities that involve all of the company's health care businesses.

The 1970s saw Abbott Laboratories officially launch its diagnostics division, which was devoted to developing instruments and tests to detect diseases in their early stages and prevent their spread. This division streamlined many of the diagnostic products and services already being offered by the company.

In 1977 Abbott expanded its pharmaceuticals business by launching TAP Pharmaceutical Products Inc., a joint venture with Japan's Takeda Chemical Industries Inc. TAP would later become one of the world's fastest-growing and most successful pharmaceutical companies.

A number of medical breakthroughs defined the 1980s for Abbott. In 1983 the company received approval to market Depakote, a new treatment for epilepsy that is also used to control bipolar disorder and to prevent migraine headaches. In 1985 the company received approval from the Food and Drug Administration to produce the world's first blood test to detect the AIDS virus. The test proved to be extremely accurate, and the company worked tirelessly to produce enough tests to support the medical community's worldwide effort to fight this then-new disease.

Abbott Laboratories' goal is to provide total, integrated solutions across the health care continuum for some of the world's most pressing health care needs.

Abbott Laboratories' leading-edge research focuses on providing innovative therapeutics for a broad range of medical conditions, including respiratory distress syndrome, a serious lung disorder that affects premature babies.

Additional achievements by Abbott in the 1980s included the introduction of the ADD-Vantage intravenous drug delivery system, which allows potent drugs with short-term stability in solutions to be easily and efficiently mixed just before they are administered to a hospital patient. In 1988 the company introduced its IMx immunoassay system, an automated instrument with a broad menu of diagnostic tests. It would become the world's leading immunoassay system and one of the company's best-selling products.

In keeping with its tradition of innovation, Abbott used the 1990s as an opportunity to merge technology and medicine to advance the health care industry. Through its internal research and acquisitions of complementary businesses, Abbott introduced many new products during the 1990s that target not only major diseases such as AIDS, cancer, diabetes and heart disease, but also medical conditions such as ulcers and respiratory infections.

By the end of the 1990s, the company's catalogue of product introductions comprised some of the world's most important advances in medical technology and therapeutics: Norvir, an HIV protease inhibitor for the treatment of AIDS; Biaxin, a potent anti-infective for treating serious infections, including those common in

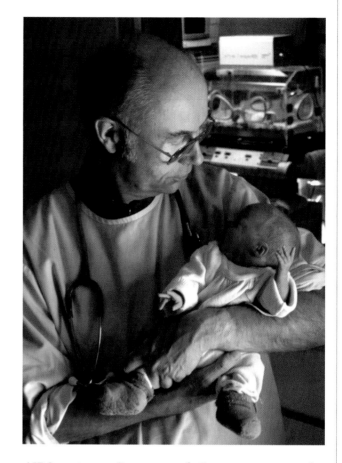

Abbott Laboratories has broad expertise in the manufacture of pharmaceuticals, diagnostics, nutritionals and hospital products, with state-of-the-art facilities in about 30 countries.

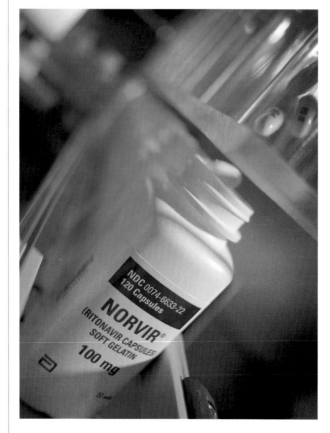

AIDS patients; Survanta and Synagis, two specialty pharmaceuticals for preventing serious respiratory conditions in infants; Ultane, a next-generation inhalation anesthetic; and AxSYM and ARCHITECT, advanced diagnostic systems for high-volume laboratory testing.

A GLOBAL COMPANY, A CHICAGO HERITAGE

As Abbott expands its worldwide presence, it remains firmly rooted in Chicago and the surrounding region, ensuring a vital place in Illinois' economy for years to come. As part of this commitment, the company plays an active role in supporting the communities in which its employees live and work. The company contributes millions of dollars annually to philanthropic organizations in Illinois and around the world, from educational initiatives, to cultural institutions, to health-related organizations.

For example, with Abbott's support, Chicago's Museum of Science and Industry became the site of the United States' first permanent museum exhibit on the science of AIDS, which was funded with a $1 million contribution from the company. As an offshoot of this exhibit, Abbott developed, in partnership with the

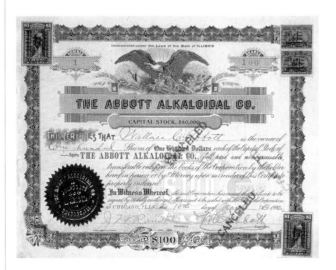

National Science Teachers Association, a unique, science-based AIDS education program for high school students.

The company also donated more than $1 million to Chicago's Field Museum to sponsor two exhibits — "Living Together: Common Concerns, Different Responses," an exhibit that educates visitors about cultural diversity; and "Underground Adventure," designed to increase public understanding about critical environmental issues.

Each year, the company contributes millions of dollars to many of Illinois' leading universities and medical and research institutions for research and development programs. These include institutions such as the University of Illinois, University of Chicago, Northwestern Memorial, Rush-Presbyterian-St. Luke's Medical Center and Argonne National Laboratories.

Through generous employee gifts and corporate funding, Abbott supports campaigns for the United Way and other health and human service organizations, and sponsors programs that enhance science education and promote environmental stewardship. While investing heavily in local communities near its major facilities, Abbott also maintains an active involvement in worldwide relief efforts, with donations of health care products estimated at more than $60 million annually for humanitarian initiatives in developing countries and to aid victims of natural and man-made disasters worldwide.

THE NEXT 100 YEARS

The year 2000 marks Abbott's 100th anniversary as a corporation and provides an occasion to celebrate its many past accomplishments. It also marks the start of a new century in which the company will build upon its strong foundation — a broad base of businesses, a strong global presence and a long tradition of innovation.

Abbott's diversified line of products — offering important therapeutics, diagnostic tests, nutritionals and medical technologies — will continue to benefit the health of the world's people. In each of its businesses, the company is poised to introduce new products to prevent, detect and treat many of the world's most urgent medical challenges. Through its innovative science and conscientious outreach efforts, Abbott Laboratories will play an active role in improving the quality of life for people in the 21st century, around the world — and, always, at home in Chicago.

Abbott Laboratories started out as the Abbott Alkaloidal Company in 1888, operating out of Dr. Abbott's Ravenswood home. The company was incorporated in 1900.

After 111 years of growth around the world, Abbott Laboratories remains rooted in Chicago and the surrounding region, ensuring a vital place in Illinois' economy for years to come.

U.S. Cellular

The innovative telecommunications services provided by U.S. Cellular have enhanced the lives of millions of wireless customers throughout the United States for nearly 20 years. Through an impressive array of wireless-communication services and an active role in customer and community service, U.S. Cellular serves not only as a leader in the telecommunications industry, but as a thriving, successful role model for other businesses to follow.

U.S. Cellular was founded in 1983 by Telephone and Data Systems Inc. and currently trades on the American Stock Exchange at AMEX:USM. Headquartered in Chicago, U.S. Cellular has become the nation's eighth-largest wireless telecommunications provider, offering services to 145 markets in 26 states throughout the country. U.S. Cellular caters to both residential and business customers with wireless communications that utilize the latest technologies, products and types of service historically available. The company has risen above the competition by providing superior wireless service to mid-sized cities

President and CEO
John E. (Jack)
Rooney

and small markets and has enjoyed explosive national growth. In 1998 the company received the Bain Award for Strategy Excellence in the technology and information category. This award was created by Bain & Company, a global consulting firm, to honor high-growth midsize Midwest companies that have translated breakthrough strategy into superior financial results.

Today, this tradition of excellence and growth continues through the efforts of John E. (Jack) Rooney, who became president and CEO of U.S. Cellular in April 2000. Rooney, who earned a B.S. in business administration from John Carroll University in Ohio and an M.B.A. in finance from Loyola University, brought to U.S. Cellular 35 years of business experience — the last 10 of which were in the fast-paced telecommunications industry. Rooney is transforming the company's culture with his vision of U.S. Cellular as a completely customer-focused company dedicated to building its customer base.

SUPERIOR SERVICES

U.S. Cellular strives for ongoing customer loyalty and satisfaction by providing digital and analog services with a variety of features designed to meet the needs of its customers. The company's digital service provides customers with increased clarity, longer battery life and better roaming capabilities, along with access to additional features not available with analog service, such as caller ID, short messaging service and access to the Internet.

The company has launched other innovative, successful products targeted to specific customer segments. These include TalkTracker℠ prepaid service, which benefits customers who can simply prepay their usage and avoid contracts or monthly bills. The success of this service has shown that U.S. Cellular is in tune with the needs of its customers who have teen-age children or those who prefer to prepay their usage in cash. U.S. Cellular also offers its ShareTalk℠ service, which allows customers to add a second wireless phone and have both lines share a single package of minutes on one bill. Through these services, U.S. Cellular develops personalized relationships based on customer needs.

Some products and services complement basic calling plans and are aimed at customer convenience. One of these products is called BillTracker℠, an electronic billing solution that offers corporate customers a simplified way to manage wireless phone service billing data. U.S. Cellular also offers Messaging Suite, which provides messaging, news and other information services to customer handsets; and Directory Assistance with Call Completion[SM], a safe and convenient way for customers to complete directory service calls automatically. For larger business customers, U.S. Cellular has designed customized wireless solutions such as Wireless PBX, a technology that facilitates communication within companies, hospitals and other institutions, and also specialized wireless solutions for hotels and campus environments.

U.S. Cellular also offers customized service plans to customers with specific or unusual needs. For example, the company's FarmFlex[SM] price plan enables farmers and agribusiness users to adjust their rate plans to accommodate calling volume variations between peak season and off-season months without having to change their contracts.

INNOVATIVE BUSINESS SOLUTIONS

U.S. Cellular's extensive portfolio of wireless communication solutions includes innovative business solutions. The company is committed to addressing the needs of businesses of all sizes in order to improve communication and increase access to information through its business services division.

For example, when St. Clare Hospital and Health Services, a 100-bed facility in Baraboo, Wisconsin, launched an overall redesign initiative two years ago, all incoming calls for nurses were being handled by unit clerks on the patient floors, who would then have to track down the nurse being called.

The solution: a wireless PBX (WPBX) system, utilizing small, portable phone handsets. Wireless phones would give nurses and other key hospital personnel more flexibility for making and taking phone calls.

The new wireless phones are also used by the plant operations department, administrators, MIS staffers and other departments. In addition to convenience and improved efficiency, the wireless system has reduced noise levels by cutting overhead paging approximately 70 percent, and also has reduced the hospital's dependency on pagers.

Cellular technology can help farmers be more efficient. With 10,000 acres of cropland spread over three counties in eastern Idaho, brothers Boyd and Brad Foster would drive hundreds of miles each day to turn their irrigation systems on or off or adjust the flow and rate of water and fertilizer being applied.

The U.S. Cellular sales team in Idaho partnered with Valmont Corporation, manufacturer of the Valley Brand pivots used on the Foster farmlands, to create a remote wireless solution.

The irrigation process for the Foster Company of Rigby, Idaho, growers of seed potatoes, grains and alfalfa, has been drastically simplified. Using ordinary cellular

phones to communicate with the wireless circuitry in the control panel of each "pivot" (the large circular irrigation systems used by the Fosters and many other agricultural enterprises), the Fosters can control irrigation from anywhere — in the field, at their office, at home or even on vacation. They can also program the computerized pivots to dial out to notify them in the event of any malfunction.

Another valuable application for their wireless technology is monitoring conditions in their storage facilities after the potatoes are harvested. Air temperature is a critical factor for seed potatoes in storage, because temperatures exceeding 40 degrees Fahrenheit will break the dormancy of the potatoes.

The Fosters are enthusiastic about the efficiencies provided by their new application of wireless communication. Farmers must be efficient to survive, and that requires better use of equipment and better time management. Wireless technology helps the Fosters achieve both.

CUSTOMER SERVICE

One of the key components of U.S. Cellular's vision statement is founded on its associates' commitment to customers and community. U.S. Cellular communicates with its customers through five regional customer care centers located in Knoxville, Tennessee; Medford, Oregon; Madison, Wisconsin; Cedar Rapids, Iowa; and Tulsa, Oklahoma. By simply dialing U.S. Cellular's toll-free number, customers are connected with friendly, knowledgeable customer service representatives who can handle any question, problem or request.

Consumers who prefer to contact the company online can visit the U.S. Cellular Web site to activate their cellular service or rate plan, get answers to questions about their bills, phones, roaming or other wireless issues, and buy accessories. U.S. Cellular maintains a prominent presence throughout its markets with more than 500 retail stores and kiosks across the country and more than 2,000 agent and dealer locations in the communities it provides wireless service.

COMMUNITY SERVICE

Not only is U.S. Cellular well regarded within the telecommunications industry for the services it provides, but it is also recognized for its commitment to its communities throughout the country. It actively encourages its 5,000 associates to be committed to both customer and community. For years U.S. Cellular has played an active role in community service, donating products and initiating programs to assist those in need. As a result, U.S. Cellular has helped fight crime, reduce homelessness, protect children and make neighborhoods safer places.

• Through its Community Action Life Line[SM] (C.A.L.L.[SM]) program, U.S. Cellular donates wireless phones preprogrammed to emergency 9-1-1 to groups that can impact public safety, such as neighborhood watch organizations, park patrols, postal carriers and school crossing guards.

• As part of its national domestic violence prevention program, U.S. Cellular provides wireless communications assistance to women who are victims of domestic abuse through its award-winning Stop Abuse From Existing℠ (S.A.F.E.℠) program. The company's unprecedented public-service efforts have been recognized by the Cellular Telecommunications Industry Association, which presented U.S. Cellular with its top honor for the S.A.F.E.℠ program.

• To assist the more than 7 million homeless people in the United States today, U.S. Cellular offers its Opportunity Calls℠ program, which works with homeless shelters to provide cellular voice mailboxes to homeless and underprivileged individuals. U.S. Cellular also assists the homeless through its Homeless Outreach Phone Effort℠ (H.O.P.E.℠) program, which provides the homeless and underprivileged with a way to talk to their families and friends on Thanksgiving.

• Through its Hometown Emergency Loaner Phones℠ (H.E.L.P.℠) program, U.S. Cellular provides local emergency organizations with wireless phones and services during times of disaster, such as tornadoes, floods, hurricanes and blizzards.

• U.S. Cellular's Cellular STARS℠ program teaches elementary school students how to dial emergency 9-1-1 on a wireless phone. To date more than 20,000 students nationwide have participated in the program.

LOOKING AHEAD

U.S. Cellular posted outstanding results in 1999. Its customer base grew by more than 400,000; at year end it had more than 2.6 million customers.

This strong customer growth generated impressive gains in service revenues and operating cash flow. A 22-percent increase in revenues and 27-percent jump in operating cash flow surpassed targets for the year.

As U.S. Cellular heads into the future, it will carry out CEO Jack Rooney's vision of a customer-oriented company developing whatever services, products and programs its customers need — a national company with a local and personal touch.

Blackwell Consulting Services

When Robert D. (Bob) Blackwell Sr. set out to start a new business, it was with the goal of creating an organization that would be internationally recognized, trusted and respected as an information technology firm providing complete management and technology solutions to complex business problems. Now, not quite eight years and some 150 consultant employees later, much of that goal has been realized. All but perhaps the international recognition (though it does have many global clients) can already be claimed by this young, dynamic, highly credible yet unique consulting company. That may be due in part to the clarity, simplicity and especially the focus of its mission: to enable the growth and success of its clients through innovative and creative business and technology solutions.

Since the beginning, Blackwell Consulting Services (BCS) has focused strongly on its clients, always striving

Robert D. (Bob) Blackwell Sr.

for the best solutions to meet client needs, to take them to greater levels of efficiency, effectiveness or profitability. Its vision has been to be thought of first when a client has a problem in its area of expertise. And that vision appears to have taken life. Its clients often think of BCS first, repaying its dedication and focus with loyalty, repeat business, and broader, stronger relationships. Those relationships grow from the inventive approach employees take to working with clients. Rather than staying strictly

> Since the beginning, Blackwell Consulting Services (BCS) has focused strongly on its clients, always striving for the best solutions to meet client needs, to take them to greater levels of efficiency, effectiveness or profitability.

at the boardroom level, BCS prefers to work at the operational level where its people's remarkable technical capabilities come to the fore. It works to understand the strengths of client teams, then frequently recommends adding to those teams with its own people in ways that complement the client, rather than coming in and taking over. The result has been rapid growth. In terms of employees the firm has gone from a core startup group of five people to more than 150. In revenue, growth has been eight fold in eight years.

But to discuss BCS in terms of numbers does not do it justice. Above all, BCS is about people — working with and supporting people. BCS serves its clients well by finding and hiring the best and the brightest — extraordinary, highly skilled and talented people — then by providing them with a work environment that's at the same time challenging and supportive: in short, by creating an environment in which people can grow and thrive — an environment where they want to stay. When appropriate it will even engage clients in developing growth opportunities for employees that provide win/win situations for all concerned. In this industry where people normally change companies every few years as a means of achieving upward mobility, BCS has an extremely low turnover rate, and that is not by accident.

Blackwell Consulting's quest for the best and the brightest has taken it in widely varied directions resulting in a remarkably diverse employee population. This reflects Bob Blackwell's belief that only a truly diverse work force can bring the creative, breakthrough solutions the firm's varied clients deserve and demand. In fact BCS currently has an employee population representing seven different countries, with nearly one-fourth being natives of countries other than the United States. At one point in its early history, with more Spanish speakers than those whose native tongue was English, the firm's principal language almost became Spanish, but stopped short in recognition of the prevailing language of its clients. This diverse group brings with it the original perspectives and solutions that are the norm at BCS — much to its clients' benefit and satisfaction.

Because the firm aggressively seeks highly talented and skilled people capable of delivering high-quality, project-based services to clients, BCS finds the work it performs demands much of its employees. And it gives much to support them in return. Employees who do their best, whether as practice leaders or receptionists, share in the firm's profits. And when someone faces a personal challenge, as most do from time to time, BCS is there to support them, working side by side to help them through it or provide the resources that may make the crucial difference.

As CEO, Bob Blackwell brings some unique practices to the firm, not the least of which is leading by example, not by pronouncement. Many claim to operate this way. But few take it to the extent he has — abandoning his corner office for a tiny space when the company's rapid growth caused tight quarters, or washing coffee cups at the end of the day to show the value of a hands-on approach. And these lessons have not been lost. A highly egalitarian atmosphere pervades the business: the kind of atmosphere in which it's easy for all to volunteer good ideas, regardless of their title or position.

It's easy for employees to volunteer in other contexts as well. Just as BCS gives much to its employees, it supports them giving to their communities, enabling them to make contributions of their own time and talents to the many worthy community organizations that can so richly benefit from abilities of the caliber BCS employees have to offer.

Typical of Bob Blackwell's style of leading by example, he has a long history of extensive and intensive involvement in various community organizations. Perhaps his most notable volunteer efforts have been 15-year relationships with the ETA Creative Arts Foundation, a group that helps communicate African-American culture and experience through artistic expression, and the Arts and Business Council (ABC), originally known as Business Volunteers for the Arts, an organization widely known for its assistance to other Chicago-area arts organizations. Bob has long been a member of the ETA board of directors and currently heads its Capital Campaign. ETA Director Abena Joan Brown says of Bob, "He's shared his vision of the importance of the arts in helping young people, especially those who are sometimes lacking in opportunities, develop fully. That vision is central to our organization. And beyond that, he's brought energy, enthusiasm and very practical resources that have been tremendously valuable to us."

He has an equally long history with the ABC. In fact it was during Bob's chairmanship of the board that it took the bold step to change its name and expand its vision. According to ABC Executive Director Joan Gunzberg, "Bob has always played a visionary role for the group, providing a guiding hand, while at the same time asking tough questions and helping us think strategically and take bold steps."

Other organizations have similarly benefited from Bob's support and involvement on their boards and beyond, including the Joel Hall Dance Company (JHDC). Because many BCS employees share his dedication to the community, they have followed in his footsteps,

> In this industry where people normally change companies every few years as a means of achieving upward mobility, BCS has an extremely low turnover rate, and that is not by accident.

providing their own support and guidance to various organizations. When time and travel constraints interfered with Bob's ability to meet his commitments to the Joel Hall group, Alesa Wilson, who had a long-standing relationship with JHDC both as a volunteer and dance student, stepped up and took over. When JHDC moved to new quarters, BCS employees provided assistance to get their new phone system in operation, then BCS added a gift of computer equipment.

Orville Wilson has become heavily involved volunteering his much-needed technical skills to aid the ETA. Blackwell has provided employee time and talents of software customization support to the Chicago Symphony Orchestra, enabling staff members to do their jobs more efficiently and effectively. Alex Bell is another BCS volunteer. For an extended period of time, she taught computer classes for adults at a major area high school. Warren Harrington recently accepted the post of chairman of the board of the Center for Research in Information Management (CRIM) of the UIC, which fosters linkage and coalition-building among the university, the business community, government and the nonprofit sector. He also chairs the finance committee and serves on other CRIM committees as well. In addition, when the city launched its Blue Bag recycling program, several BCS

employees joined in to support this major initiative. And the list could go on.

But clearly, none of these activities could benefit from the talents of these skilled employees, were it not for the company's philosophy that these are important and worthwhile efforts, and its willingness to provide them the time and flexibility to give back to the community in ways they feel are most important and beneficial. And Chicagoland is stronger as a result.

Throughout, a prime consideration for this young but well-proven and much-trusted firm is relationships: relationships among employees that facilitate exemplary teamwork; relationships with the community that provide so much gain to recipient organizations; and most of all, relationships with clients. As Bob Blackwell puts it, and his team often echoes, "There is no excuse for a client not to be happy with our services to them. If there's a problem, we must expend every effort to make it right." And they do.

Reflecting the BCS belief in a diverse workforce, nearly one quarter of its employees are natives of foreign countries. This group represents seven different nations.
Photo by Brad Baskin

Anixter
Family Enterprises

The Anixter name has become synonymous with leadership in the Chicagoland community through the family's numerous business, philanthropic and civic endeavors. From the turn of the 19th century to the end of the 20th, the family has moved from the Torah to technology. As descendants of a revered orthodox Rabbi in Chicago, they have produced many distinguished and respected community leaders in business and the professions.

Rabbi Yitzak Isaac Anixter and Rashee Ettel, of Poniemon, Russia, had five children; the eldest was Yehuda Eliezer. He earned the distinction of being the first documentably ordained Rabbi of Russian birth in Chicago, at Beth Hamidrash Hachodesh in 1879. When Rabbi Yehuda Eliezer Anixter died in Chicago in 1914, more than 10,000 people attended his funeral.

In the world of business, the Anixter impact reaches far beyond Chicago. From electrical to electronic, from the dawn of television to the cable era and now the Internet explosion, the Anixters have played a major role as specialists in the distribution of multimedia technology products throughout the country and the world. The companies have grown to billions of dollars in revenues and three have evolved into public corporations.

After decades of religious teaching and study, when World War I drew to a close the Anixter family began its Chicago business career servicing the community with the creation by Arthur Anixter and his partner of Englewood Electric Supply Company. He was later joined by his two sons, Edward and Lester. Bernard Horwich, a Chicago community leader in the first half of the 20th century, married May Anixter, Rabbi Eliezer's daughter. His company, General Felt Industries, became one of the largest manufacturers of carpet padding and related products in the country.

Another successful venture, founded in 1957, was Anixter Bros., Inc., a distribution specialist of wire and cable under the direction of brothers Alan and William. Today, this multigenerational family is riding the tidal wave of technology through Anicom, Inc., a North American leader and specialist in the distribution of multimedia wiring products. As the new millennium begins, family members are still creating and developing companies across a broad spectrum of American business and industry.

The Anixter family has long been involved in many philanthropic activities, generously supporting a cross section of charities and organizations. They credit their many successful endeavors to hard work, maintaining their religious identity and a willingness to listen and be part of the community. In their seventh generation in Chicago, from the Torah to a reel of cable, they have donated their resources and their time, with over a century of giving quietly and anonymously. Their foresight, generosity, patience and desire to serve have left their mark and helped to create a better place to live and work.

(Left to right)
Alan B. Anixter,
William R. Anixter

Anicom

Englewood Electric
Supply, 1929

549

ACS Technology Solutions

ACS Technology Solutions, a national provider of innovative Information Technology outsourcing and software consulting services, has distinguished itself as one of the most prominent Chicago-area businesses of its kind. In the late 90s the company was ranked by the prestigious *Crain's Chicago Business* as one of the top 20 management consulting groups, putting it alongside such well-known competitors as Andersen Consulting and Deloitte & Touche LLP.

ACS Technology Solutions has earned its reputation through nearly three decades of solid business growth and an impressive, ever-expanding client list that includes other Chicago success stories such as McDonald's Corporation, Kraft Foods, BP-Amoco Corporation, Motorola, Inc. and Discover Financial Services. The company maintains branch offices in several U.S. cities: Atlanta, Chicago, Denver, Houston, Philadelphia, Phoenix, Portland, Raleigh, San Diego, Seattle and Tulsa.

Formerly known as CARA Corporation, ACS Technology Solutions was founded in 1975. It originally established its corporate headquarters in Chicago and soon gained a reputation for unsurpassed technology consulting and a client-friendly corporate philosophy. The founders of CARA Corporation were a group of Irish businessmen who believed that the client should also be a trusted partner and friend, a philosophy that they built into the company's original name. "Cara" is a Gaelic term meaning "friend."

The company's name was changed to ACS Technology Solutions in 1999 after being acquired by Affiliated Computer Services in 1997. Headquartered in Dallas, Texas, Affiliated Computer Services is one of the world's largest Information Technology outsourcing companies. With this new affiliation came an exciting expansion of services and a continued commitment to working as a partner with each client.

As a means to enhance their already-strong customer commitment, ACS Technology Solutions and its parent company adhere to a corporate principle they call the "Hustle philosophy." To ACS Technology Solutions, this means that the company is intent on serving its clients by taking a proactive approach and making sure it provides solutions that meet clients' exact specifications — whether they be simple or complex. The company strives to maintain an atmosphere of personal attention to each client as well as creativity and flexibility when addressing each client's individual requirements for success. And as ACS Technology Solutions has grown, it is increasingly able to offer clients more and better services. This combination of professional growth and commitment to quality has helped to make the "Hustle philosophy" an everyday reality among the ACS staff and with its high-profile clientele.

One of ACS Technology Solutions' primary service offerings is providing expert Information Technology consulting to a large pool of corporate clients. In its efforts to find superior consultants, ACS recruits and screens Information Technology professionals using an extremely rigorous and selective process. Once placed at a company, the progress and expertise of an ACS consultant is continually measured through a two-tiered feedback-and-rewards system known as "Service

Professionals at a busy data center

ACS corporate headquarters

with PRIDE." Because of its consistently high success rate, ACS considers its exclusive recruitment strategy to be one of its biggest strengths.

ACS Technology Solutions was built on three service areas that at one time provided the basis for the company. While ACS has expanded to include a much broader range of technology services, the company has its roots in these three divisions. One vital artery of the company is the Business Systems Division, which provides high-quality staff augmentation and project management services. The Business Systems Division relies upon information systems that provide thorough application-development services for both client/server and mainframe environments.

The Engineering and Scientific Services Division is also a legacy of ACS Technology Solutions' early corporate offerings. This division is staffed with electrical engineers, physicists and mathematicians who work with the design and implementation of software real-time data acquisition and control. They also interface with monitoring systems and embedded microprocessor control, switching, communications, applications and drivers.

Since the company's inception, ACS' Training Services Division has provided clients with custom performance support and training-development services. This dynamic division provides training and documentation solutions as well as many services that help companies to support and enhance the performance of their end users.

When CARA Corporation was acquired by Affiliated Computer Services in 1997, this new partnership made it possible for the Chicago-based ACS Technology Solutions to provide clients with a wider range of service areas than ever before. Affiliated Computer Services operates more than 250 offices throughout the United States, Europe, Central and South America and the Middle East. The company and its associates serve more than 10,000 clients worldwide.

One of ACS Technology Solutions' more recent service offerings is Business Process Outsourcing. For example, the company handles various computerized processes for Blockbuster, UPS and the U.S. Senate. Clients call upon ACS for a diverse range of activities, including order entry and tracking, customer billing, call center operations, desktop services, account payable services, telemarketing, claims administration, image archival, Web site development and other essential business functions.

Clients of ACS Technology Solutions also benefit from its Professional Services and Systems Integration division. This division includes consulting services, strategic planning, system design and applications support. The company has also been able to offer its clients improved Information Technology outsourcing services, providing expert consultants skilled in Web site design, mainframe computing, desktop and client/server management, network management, help desks and more.

Another point of expansion for ACS Technology Solutions is in the area of e-commerce. Depending upon the client, ACS may assist in improving the system of receiving payment, developing a more efficient consumer Web site or updating the site's internal structure to ensure better quality control.

As ACS Technology Solutions experiences continued expansion and looks to the future, it foresees even more demand for its services. While technology becomes an increasingly important component of nearly every business process, the multilayered expertise offered by ACS and its affiliates has become necessary to the operation of a successful contemporary business. By helping clients obtain greater success and maintaining a tradition of friendly partnerships and long-standing business relationships, the staff at ACS and its affiliates will keep the company moving forward by seeking excellence from within.

Andrew Corporation

Since 1937 excellence in engineering capabilities and products has made Andrew Corporation a leader in the communications world. Its systems and services improve the speed, quality and reliability with which individuals, businesses and governments can transmit voice, video and data signals.

A ham radio operator at 15, Victor Andrew went into business as a teenager by setting up shop in the back seat of his car.

Andrew was founded by Dr. Victor J. Andrew in the basement of a modest bungalow near Chicago's Midway Airport. Dr. Andrew — affectionately referred to by employees as "Doc" — was a true entrepreneur. In his company's basement headquarters, he made custom-designed phasing, tuning and transmission line equipment required by AM broadcasters for directional antenna systems. He also offered consulting engineering services. Sales for the first year, translated into today's dollar value, were about $12,000. By the beginning of the new millennium the company was approaching $1 billion in sales.

Strong leadership is a continuing hallmark of Andrew. Doc Andrew was ably supported in his efforts by native Chicagoan C. Russell Cox. In a career spanning 54 years, Cox was a driving force in turning Andrew into a global player in the world of telecommunications; he also took the company public in 1980. In 1983 Dr. Floyd L. English picked up the reins of command. Dr. English continued to pursue international expansion; the company now has 70 locations in 27 countries on the continents of North and South America, Europe, Africa, Asia and Australia. He also repositioned Andrew, setting its people, its systems and its products on a path to keep pace with the communications changes driven by quantum leaps in computer chip technology and satellite and wireless communications.

Since its inception Andrew has been at the forefront of many major technological developments. At first the company's customers were broadcast stations and the communications departments of commercial airlines. During World War II Andrew supplied coaxial cables and other telecommunications components to the U.S. military.

After the war Andrew began a long relationship with the Department of Energy, providing coaxial cable for use in the underground testing of nuclear devices, and continued its involvement in the field of broadcasting. The end of wartime restrictions on radio station construction — and a belief in the potential of commercial television — resulted in a broadcast boom that spurred the sales of rigid coaxial transmission lines then used by FM broadcasters to carry radio frequency to an antenna.

In 1947 expansion led to the purchase of land in Orland Park, Illinois, and in 1953 a manufacturing facility was constructed and company headquarters were moved there.

In 1949 Andrew entered the microwave antenna field and quickly found markets in both civilian and military communications. In 1953 the company introduced the HELIAX® line of semiflexible coaxial cables. This product line is a major contributor to the company's sales.

The 1950s was a time of great expansion. Andrew opened a branch in California and went international with a Canadian facility near Toronto. The Cold War led to sizable military contracts for high-power coaxial transmission lines, waveguides and switching devices for strategic radar systems.

In the 1960s — stimulated by the opportunity of large microwave antenna systems contracts — Andrew opened facilities in Lochgelly, Scotland, and Campbellfield, Australia. By 1971 the company had 700 employees at plants in four countries.

The 1970s and 1980s were transition periods for the company. The core of its business changed from a focus on government and military contracts and private communications to a market dominated by inter-city telephone operations.

Andrew Corporation's Orland Park, Illinois, Headquarters. Today Andrew employs 4,500 people worldwide.

Government action had much to do with this change. In 1982 the U.S. Department of Justice settled its 1974 antitrust suit against AT&T. In the wake of the decision, new telephone companies formed and competitors hurried to build microwave antenna systems. They sought Andrew terrestrial microwave antennas, waveguide, coaxial cable and related products plus installation services to stretch their systems across the country.

During the 1980s Andrew Corporation's consolidated sales exceeded $200 million. In the 1990s the age of wireless communications dawned. This revolution in the telecommunications industry was led by cellular technology and fed by the global demand for instant, reliable communications and data exchange, and the acceleration of high-technology products and systems.

Over the past 10 years being global has given Andrew a great advantage. As the company received large contracts in widespread parts of the world, international facilities were added. Today major operators and governments view wireless network services as the least expensive and quickest way to get communications into less-developed areas of the world. Andrew shares this view, positioning itself and its products in this competitive market as a full RF communications solutions provider.

International business is a source of growth for Andrew, and the company believes that the best way to service its global customers is to be close to them. To that end it has expanded its global network of manufacturing facilities to countries such as China and India. In 2000 Andrew had 11 domestic and seven international manufacturing plants along with 13 distribution facilities and 40 sales and engineering offices.

This worldwide network ensures timely response and cost-effective delivery of the highest-quality products and services; 24-hour, seven-day technical information; and custom training and consultation.

Today with 4,500 people worldwide and products and services geared to the wireless age, Andrew is positioned to support the explosive and highly competitive wireless market and is recognized around the world as a leading manufacturer.

Although the company has grown impressively since it was founded, the corporate culture of the early days remains. Externally the Andrew culture is manifested in a commitment to industry leadership, technical superiority, focused growth and fiscal conservatism.

Excellent employees have always been a vital element of the company's success. This is expressed in the philosophy — if you want to sell the best products, you must attract, develop and retain the best people.

Internally Andrew Corporation's culture emphasizes honesty, fairness, dignity and respect in relations with people. The corporation believes that its employees are its most valuable asset, and every employee is an equal partner in the company's effort to nurture its growth and success. A vigorous team spirit pervades the company, yet the company is also firm in its insistence on maximum personal effort.

Andrew has also remained close to its Chicago origins. In March 1999 it manufactured and supplied the first TRASAR® High Power digital television antenna installed in Chicago for FOX Television Station Inc.'s Channel 32, Station WFLD-DT. The 30-foot antenna was airlifted to the top of the Sears Tower and provides digital television transmission in the Chicago area.

Andrew Corporation is a truly global company that remains true to its Midwest roots.

An Andrew digital television antenna being airlifted to the top of Chicago's Sears Tower

divine interVentures, inc.

Thriving and diverse, Chicago's economy always has been a source of strength for the city and a point of envy for the nation as sure as its stunning architecture and Lake Michigan views. As the nation's transportation hub and food processing center, Chicago first linked the harvests of Midwest farms to dinner tables across the country. Later, the city established itself as the leader in a vibrant brew of industries, from manufacturing and telecommunications to financial services and transportation. Today, Chicago is drawing on its vast and deep reservoir of industry expertise to lead the nation's next economic engine — business-to-business commerce on the Internet.

Mayor Richard M. Daley has set forth his vision of Chicago as a technology economy leader among U.S. cities, just as it became a dominant player in the nation's agriculture, transportation, financial services, telecommunications and manufacturing industries. Chicago's Internet startups are leveraging the city's wealth of opportunity and home-grown industry expertise to quickly become Internet commerce leaders as the nation's corporations increasingly conduct business online.

"The qualities that propelled Chicago to prominence in a host of industries — its strong leadership, tremendous

The divine interVentures Web site

CEO Andrew "Flip" Filipowski

talent, great educational institutions, balanced economy, strong work force and prevailing work ethic — are now powering the city's development into a new economy leader," says Andrew "Flip" Filipowski, a prominent technology visionary and one of the leaders of the city's transformation into a technology powerhouse. "We have the passion, the capital, the ideas and the programs in place to ensure Chicago builds a strong Internet economy."

divine interVentures, inc., founded by Filipowski, is at the forefront of Chicago's transformation into a Midwestern Mecca of Internet commerce and a national hub of the new economy. divine interVentures is an Internet operating company actively engaged in business-to-business e-commerce.

Filipowski brings established technology credentials to divine interVentures and Chicago. He founded PLATINUM *technology, inc.*, in 1987 and built it into one of the top 10 global software companies in record time. Now Filipowski has turned his attention to building divine interVentures.

divine interVentures has created a next-generation business model to promote the fast-paced growth of Internet companies. The divine interVentures' Internet Zaibatsu™ is a synergistic community of more than 50 Internet companies that share a common vision and can leverage collective strengths. Its inspiration comes from the Japanese concept zaibatsu, which refers to a group of family-owned

companies that work together and share resources and customers. "The power of the zaibatsu is its ability to leverage the relationships and resources of each of the member companies," Filipowski says.

The model empowers startups and corporate Internet spin-offs alike to grow and get to market quickly. Through the Internet Zaibatsu, young companies gain access to capital, managerial expertise, operating services, networking resources, incubation space and industry knowledge. Some members of this economic network create the Internet marketplaces that enable business-to-business commerce on the Internet. Other members develop commerce-enabling technologies, while others provide professional services such as marketing and public relations, accounting, human resources, legal counsel, accounting, and Web design and development.

divine interVentures has gained the support of a legion of business, technology and community leaders. Technology giants such as Microsoft Corp. and Dell Computer Co. have formed strategic relationships with and invested in divine interVentures. Its board boasts some of the nation's most dynamic and influential corporate, technology and communications leaders, including top executives from Tellabs, Inc.; Goldman Sachs & Co.; Tribune Co.; HARPO Entertainment Group, producer of "The Oprah Winfrey Show"; University of Chicago Graduate School of Business; Bank One Equity Capital; The Levy Organization; Chicago Title Corp.; Northwestern University, Kellogg Graduate School of Management; Wm. Wrigley Jr. Co.; and former National Basketball Association superstar Michael Jordan.

divine interVentures is working side-by-side with city, state and high-tech leaders in Illinois to foster the conditions that will make technology companies thrive. Besides acting as an evangelist for Chicago's technology community, Filipowski serves as a counsel to Mayor Daley and Gov. George Ryan's initiatives to promote the state's technology economy.

With the city of Chicago, divine interVentures is working to develop a state-of-the-art incubator campus for Internet businesses at the northern edge of the city's Goose Island Industrial Park. Filipowski expects the project will serve not only as a model technology development

In Chicago, but also for the rest of the nation — forever changing the way communities foster economic growth in the digital world. Providing leading-edge technology, operational support and a highly collaborative environment, the Goose Island campus will foster the growth of its resident Internet businesses.

To further promote the growth of the region's technology economy, divine interVentures has joined a collaborative effort with the city of Chicago and Mesirow Financial, a Chicago-based financial services firm, to spur technology economy development by directing capital at startup and early-stage technology companies. This effort, called Skyscraper Ventures and managed by divine interVentures, will focus its investments on Chicago and Illinois technology companies, though it also will invest nationally.

Initiatives to promote Chicago's technology economy build on a strong base. Already, Illinois is home to hundreds of budding and established Internet companies. The state is the fourth-largest region in the nation in high-tech employment and home to more than 8,000 technology-based businesses. Chicago and its surrounding suburbs have the essential ingredients for new economy success: outstanding universities, a broad and diverse business base, wealth of talent, and political and industry leadership focused on building the city's technology base.

With all the components now in place, Chicago is turning the inherent advantages of its vast industry dominance into a prescription for fast growth as an Internet commerce leader.

In December 1999, Chicago Mayor Richard M. Daley announced a partnership between the city of Chicago and divine interVentures to fund technology startups in the Chicagoland area.

Illinois Superconductor Corp.

What happens when a cell phone reverts to a noisy static box? Why does a call suddenly just disappear? How can video and the Internet work on a system that can't even handle a simple phone call?

Illinois Superconductor Corporation (ISC), located in the high-tech corridor of Chicago's northwest suburbs, has pioneered a new technology to help solve these problems. ISC is a leader in the commercialization of high-temperature superconducting technology for the wireless telecommunications industry.

Wireless networks originally carried only telephone services, but in just a few years there has been exponential growth in new features available on cellular phones. Now it is common for a cell phone to also function as a pager, a message board, a calendar and an address book. Wireless messaging is quickly graduating to full Internet and video service. When integrated with a cellular phone, it will produce the next generation of "can't live without" devices. These third-generation, or 3G, multipurpose personal-communication devices will again redefine global communications. Keeping interference out of this highly sensitive digital transmission is essential for 3G wireless systems to operate effectively.

This is where ISC's superconducting filters play an important role. High-temperature superconducting filters reject unwanted signals by filtering out interference, thereby allowing the desired signals to be received clearly. The filters extend signal range, improve clarity and minimize the number of dropped calls.

Incidentally, the term "high-temperature" is a bit misleading, since the technology relies on super-cold temperatures to function. When originally discovered, superconductors operated at temperatures too cold to be commercially viable. The breakthrough allowing commercialization to proceed occurred when superconducting was discovered for materials at liquid nitrogen temperatures — a "balmy" minus 200 degrees centigrade, hence the term, "high-temperature" superconductors.

Recognizing the commercial potential of superconducting, Arch Development Corp. formed ISC in 1989 as a spinoff of Argonne National Laboratories. The founding management team was Ora Smith, attorney and graduate engineer from Harvard and MIT; James Hodge, scientist and engineer; Lewis Erwin, professor at Northwestern University; and Steve Wasko, financier.

ISC got its first real commercial break when it received an award of $2 million from the Advanced Technology Program of the National Institute of Standards and Technology. This investment led to the

> **ISC is a leader in the commercialization of high-temperature superconducting technology for the wireless telecommunications industry.**

development of superconducting filter technology that was subsequently used in the first live trials.

ISC subsequently went public with an IPO, drawing enthusiastic investors who saw the commercial promise of the technology.

With their first hand-crafted filter, company engineers ventured off to a trade show in San Diego, California. Since it was a prototype and too fragile to ship in one piece, they disassembled the filter and carried it by hand onto the airplane. After they reassembled it in a San Diego lab, they rented a car and headed for the show.

As luck would have it, a second vehicle collided with the rental car. Gratefully, damage was minimal and no one was hurt, but the team wasn't sure about the filter. Continuing on to the show, they used liquid nitrogen to cool the cryo-chamber and crossed their fingers. They plugged in the device and found that the filter worked! It drew such large crowds to ISC's booth that the fire marshal had to clear the aisles. This filter was a unique product and clearly capable of high performance. Although ISC generated a lot of excitement in San Diego, stellar technical performance doesn't necessarily translate into immediate market success.

Why? Because carriers didn't recognize yet that they had a systemwide problem this filter could solve. Nonetheless, by 1996 ISC had begun to earn some revenue from its filter products. *Microwaves & RF* magazine, a leading trade publication, selected the company's

SpectrumMaster filter from among 5,000 new products for a top product award that year.

Sales tripled in 1998, and the company was able to reduce its product cost by 40 percent. It also began a relationship with Southwestern Bell Mobile Systems that represented the first commercial deployment with a major carrier.

On a roll, ISC understood that superior performance alone was not going to be enough. Carriers objected to the large size required by the company's cryo-chamber and worried that they would lose operation of a cell site if the chamber warmed up. Inspired by their early success, ISC engineers designed an ultra-small cryo-chamber to house the filter. The real breakthrough, however, came when ISC engineers discovered a now-patented formula to build a filter that can warm up to room temperature and still function. The performance is not at superconducting levels, but the cell site still operates at conventional levels. The new product is called ATP™ or All Temperature Performance. Poised to create an array of ATP™ products, ISC now offers the smallest superconducting filter with no risk of failure to the operator. Now that the product is small, easy to deploy, reliable and cost effective, are the carriers lined up at the door to buy them? Well, not quite yet.

1998 and 1999 were watershed years for carriers signing up new customers. They discovered, however, that there was a limit to the capacity of the system to support the business. An interesting paradox developed. More customers resulted in more interference on the line (for many reasons), which caused unhappy customers.

In August 1999 the pace quickened again with the announcement of test agreements with four original equipment manufacturers (OEMs) that were building systems for Japan's 3G cellular telecommunications systems. ISC's advanced RangeMaster filters were designed for use in a 3G wireless system to minimize interference with voice, high-speed data and video applications.

Finally, in early 2000, with Internet access on wireless devices becoming a reality, the U.S. carriers started crying "uncle!" Not only was there more demand for service, but for greater accuracy as well. Highly sensitive digital systems simply couldn't handle all of the interference created by the competition. At last, customer demand and not just scientific theory created the commercial opportunity. High-temperature superconductivity was finally recognized as a viable option.

Dr. George M. Calhoun, CEO of ISC, anticipates that the company's superconducting technology will become the central enabling technology of the 3G wireless industry. To that end, ISC continues to develop strategic initiatives and product innovations that will keep them on the crest of the new wave of global communications.

3G Wireless Communication will fundamentally change global communication. ISC filters are an enabling technology in this new system.

Moore Corporation

Samuel Moore's idea, which led to a multibillion-dollar industry, was to let one writing serve many purposes.

Samuel J. Moore was a young partner in a printing company when he came upon an idea that was simplicity itself — a fixed sheet of reusable carbon paper that could be placed between two pages of a salesbook to offer the seller and buyer identical records of a transaction. It was an innovative concept that led, 118 years ago, to the formation of a company and the beginning of an industry.

Young Moore knew he had a winner, so he developed the idea, secured a patent and launched the business forms industry — total startup cost: $2,500.

That may have been one of Moore's first innovations but not his last. These days, Moore Corporation has annual revenues of $2.4 billion and thousands of products and services offered around the world. Typically all those products and services have something in common with the Paragon Black Leaf Counter Check Book, as he called the salesbook — they all help Moore customers work more efficiently.

The Corporation's vision today — to be a high-growth, technology-based leader in the management and communications of customer information — is consistent with the objectives and vision of Samuel Moore.

"Let one writing serve many purposes," Moore said over and over in those early years. That's exactly what the patented salesbook accomplished, and many subsequent products too. He was of course referring to putting numbers and letters on pieces of paper. When technology changed and all of a sudden "writing" meant parking those numbers and letters, now called data, on hard drives and other magnetic media, Moore Corporation led the industry into the new era. And when all that magnetic media got wired up to create the Internet, Moore moved into new challenges and opportunities with it.

One of the key ways Moore is maximizing the opportunities of the Internet is through high-tech and proprietary products developed at its research center located in Grand Island, New York. Moore's integrated systems have created various one-to-one communications tools — available over the Internet — that drive customer loyalty and retention.

Moore's research center is the technological hub of Moore and the birthplace for many of the solutions that drive the company's most lucrative products. Home to a number of the company's technical, engineering, electronic, chemical, software and manufacturing specialists, the research center has registered more than 2,000 patents.

It's not that paper and paper forms have gone the way of the dinosaur. Even now, paper products make up a substantial share of Moore's total sales. The "paperless society," much ballyhooed in the early 1980s, has yet to materialize, even though the world is moving in that direction.

Actually, Moore's century of experience with paper business forms came in handy when the electronics era arrived. Moore people were skilled at organizing information, moving it, presenting it and storing it. The traits of good paper-forms management are not entirely different from effective electronic-forms management, even though the technology is vastly different.

Moore's sales representatives gain detailed knowledge of the customer's business communication needs and then apply company resources to help meet those needs. Technical capabilities have been enhanced through acquisitions and numerous strategic alliances through the years. Moore's customer list includes many Fortune 1000 companies, and some not-so-big companies, not-for-profit organizations and governmental agencies at the local, state and federal levels.

Because Moore has retained its traditional paper-forms business while migrating into high-tech digital services, the company has grown into a multi-division organization serving customer needs both technologically and geographically.

For example, Moore has expanded its paper-forms business to develop products that enhance the way companies manage and communicate customer information. Its proprietary pressure-seal product line allows companies access to high-speed, low-cost options to mail its customer information. Moore has led the industry in variable-imaged statements — allowing for more customized, personalized statements. Moore's unique label adhesives have revolutionized everyday tasks from the way mail is delivered to how data is collected.

Beyond Moore's forms/labels business, Moore addresses the communication of customer information through its customer communications services group. This group focuses on areas such as billing statement re-engineering, personalized direct-marketing programs and customer-relationship management.

The corporation's executive offices are located in the village of Bannockburn, north of Chicago, minutes away from O'Hare International Airport. When the Bannockburn offices were opened at the turn of the 21st century, Moore was able to centralize three divisions and a sales office in one location and reaffirm its commitment to the Chicago area.

Moore's reach, however, is worldwide, and changing rapidly as technology opens new ways of communicating and doing business. Due to its reputation and embedded customer base, the company is in a unique position to serve the burgeoning Internet and e-commerce phenomena.

The company is committed to guiding its customers into this new era and helping them gain the efficiencies possible from it. Moore stands ready to offer customers assistance in electronic procurement systems, data-asset management, electronic data interchange and electronic forms and fulfillment.

The potential for cost reduction through e-commerce is truly mind boggling. Moore customers are realizing great savings through Moore's capabilities in electronic bill and statement presentation. Bills and statements travel at the speed of light, and printing and postage costs are either eliminated or dramatically reduced. Customer

The Moore Research Center, the technological hub of Moore, has registered more than 2,000 patents.

satisfaction is enhanced, too, because bills and statements are easily understood, thanks to online help tools built into these systems to answer questions automatically. Obviously this reduces a great many customer service calls.

While the potential of the Internet is still unfolding, Moore continues to offer customers a full plate of more-traditional products, services and solutions, many of them industry-leading. These include:

- Document-management solutions that are dedicated to helping customers leverage today's technology to migrate from paper-based to digital forms environment.
- Consulting, re-engineering, project management and multimedia distribution of critical business-to-consumer communications, such as billing statements and other personalized applications.
- Bar code-based data capture, printing and service solutions.
- Database marketing, research and analysis, creative and program administration.
- Direct-marketing strategy and direct-mail communications.
- Teleservicing and warehouse and distribution services.
- Personalized, one-to-one print and fulfillment solutions.

Moore's list of products and services grows daily as new technology applications unfold. If Samuel Moore could come back and take a look at his company now, he would certainly be thunderstruck. He might rephrase his original perception: "Let one writing — and one bit — serve many purposes."

Rand McNally

When William Rand and Andrew McNally first met in 1858, they could hardly have imagined where their association would lead. Today, nearly a century and a half later, the partnership that began in Rand's small Chicago print shop has evolved into an internationally renowned company offering an extensive line of travel- and geography-related products.

Rand had come to Chicago from Boston in 1856, opening a shop at 148 West Lake Street that advertised "every description of printing, on the most advantageous terms." McNally had emigrated from County Armagh, Ireland, after serving a seven-year indentured apprenticeship at a printing house. Soon after arriving in Chicago, he entered Rand's shop and inquired about a job; Rand hired him on the spot at a salary of $9 a week.

In 1859 Rand was asked by the *Chicago Daily Press Tribune* (soon to become the *Chicago Tribune*) to manage its printing shop, and McNally became shop foreman. Nine years later, Rand and McNally bought out the Tribune Company's contracts and established their own company. The new partners agreed to focus their business on the booming railroad industry — Chicago had already become the greatest rail hub in the nation — and soon they were printing passenger tickets, timetables and even the annual reports of railroad companies. In 1870 they expanded into publishing, introducing a series of business directories as well as railroad guides and an illustrated newspaper, the *People's Weekly*.

But the company and its promising future nearly went up in smoke — literally — on October 8th and 9th, 1871, when the great Chicago fire swept through the city.

As the flames neared the Rand McNally building, William Rand rescued two of the company's ticket-printing machines and transported them to McNally's house three miles to the north. McNally took the machines to the beach along Lake Michigan and buried them in the sand to protect them from the intense heat, falling debris, and swirling ashes. Three days after the fire, the salvaged machines were up and running in rented space on Wabash Street — in one of the few buildings left standing — and Rand McNally was back in business.

Over the last decades of the 19th century, the company celebrated a number of milestones. The first-ever Rand McNally map appeared in the December 1872 issue of the *Railway Guide*. Four years later came the *Business Atlas*, later renamed the *Commercial Atlas & Marketing Guide*. In 1880 the company ventured into educational publishing, offering a line of globes, maps, and geography textbooks. Around this same time, the first Rand McNally world atlas made its appearance.

Rand sold his shares of the company stock to the other officers in 1899, and McNally became president. The former partners died within a year of each other — Andrew McNally in 1904 and William Rand in 1905. Leadership of the company passed to Andrew's son, Frederick. Rand McNally's long and eventful first chapter came to an end, but an exciting new chapter, heralded by the coming of the automobile, was about to begin.

In 1907 Rand McNally introduced its first "photo-auto guide," a product that combined route maps with photos of intersections and forks in the road. Arrows overprinting the photos indicated the correct directions and turns. The photos in the *Chicago-to-Milwaukee Photo-Auto Guide* were taken by Andrew McNally II (the son of Frederick) as he and his bride drove the route on their honeymoon in 1907.

During the following decade, as Rand McNally's output of road maps increased, its cartographers struggled with a significant problem: many roads and highways had long, cumbersome names that were difficult to fit onto

the maps. The company decided to sponsor a contest among its employees to see who could come up with the best solution. The winner was a draftsman named John Brink, who proposed using symbols to designate major highways. For Brink's idea to work, the actual highways would have to be marked with the same symbols that were printed on the maps. To this end, the company hired drivers to fan out over the entire country, posting signs along the highways or painting symbols on telephone poles. A few years later, Brink developed a numbering system to replace the symbols; its debut on a 1917 map of Peoria, Illinois, marked the origin of the highway numbering system used across the United States today.

In 1924 the company introduced its first road atlas, the *Rand McNally Auto Chum*, which eventually became the *Rand McNally Road Atlas*. This breakthrough product was destined to become not only a perennial best-seller but an icon of American culture. Today it ranks as the best-selling annually published travel guide in the world.

Within 24 hours of Germany's invasion of Poland in 1939, stores across the United States had sold out of Rand McNally's map of Europe. Throughout the long years of World War II, Americans continued to look to Rand McNally for maps of the theaters of battle, and the company's presses operated around the clock to meet the overwhelming demand.

In 1952, having outgrown its Chicago offices, Rand McNally moved to larger quarters in the suburb of Skokie. Under the direction of Andrew McNally III, who became president in 1948, printing and book-manufacturing operations were greatly expanded, eventually making Rand

McNally one of the largest commercial printers in the world.

In 1974 Andrew McNally IV succeeded his father as president. Among the biggest developments of his 25-year tenure was the 1989 launching of a dramatic expansion of the Rand McNally Map & Travel Stores. Within a decade the company would boast 29 stores and a coast-to-coast retail presence. Even more significant was Rand McNally's full-scale entrance into the worlds of digital technology and electronic media. Its first consumer software products, *TripMaker*® and *StreetFinder*®, immediately became market leaders in their categories. The company expanded onto the Internet in 1997. Today's Web site offers online shopping, address-to-address routing, travel planning and information, construction updates and world mapping.

The increasing focus on publishing and electronic media meant that Rand McNally's traditional printing and ticket-manufacturing businesses were becoming more and more peripheral; in 1997 the company announced the sale of these businesses. The following year brought an even bigger announcement: the McNally family had decided to sell the company to a private investment group. Under its new owners, the company quickly moved forward with ambitious plans for growth and expansion.

The dawn of the new millennium finds Rand McNally streamlined, reinvigorated and charged with a new sense of purpose. The company that began as a small Chicago printing shop is now the premier global provider of travel and geographic information and services in print and electronic media. William Rand and Andrew McNally would be proud.

The Rand McNally Road Atlas in 1926 (left) and 2001 (far left)

Rand McNally's popular *StreetFinder*® software

Tellabs

Founder, Chairman
and CEO
Michael J. Birck

When Tellabs started doing business as a supplier of telecommunications equipment in 1975, the business was relatively simple. The now-ubiquitous cell phones were unheard of, and the Internet meant nothing to most people. Cable television was more of a concept than a convenience.

The company was founded in Lisle, Illinois, a western Chicago suburb. That year the company's 20 employees were proud of sales of $312,000. Tellabs was in Lisle long before the stretch along I-88 was aptly named "the high-tech corridor."

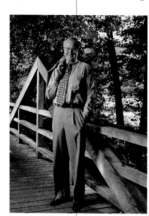

"Nothing happened very quickly back in the mid-70s, or so it seems from today's perspective," says Michael J. Birck, chairman and CEO. "Much has changed since that era of relative calm, including the variety and complexity of products and services, the very structure of the industry, and certainly the incredible growth of business and consumer communications needs."

In those early years, Tellabs manufactured a growing array of analog-based products mostly for the domestic telecommunications industry. Today those products would not seem very high-tech, but they paved the way for modern-day Tellabs.

Then came the 1990s. Demand for Tellabs products and services soared as telecommunications technology and services grew explosively, boosted largely by competition created by deregulation of the U.S. telecommunications industry. Tellabs was in a great position to profit from this

dramatic growth. Sales are now in the billions, and the company is a leading global solutions provider with leading-edge technology that meets worldwide communications needs. Recognition of just how much Tellabs has grown has also come from outside the industry. In 1999, *Fortune* magazine named Tellabs as one of "America's 100 Fastest Growing Companies."

But the company is much more than that. It is also a workplace for more than 7,000 people around the world, including many with advanced technical and scientific training. These people look to Tellabs for growth opportunities, and they find them. In 1999, Tellabs was also named to another prestigious *Fortune* magazine list, "The 100 Best Places to Work in America," premiering on the list at No. 62.

Tellabs is also a well-regarded investment for thousands of shareholders. The company's mission statement stresses management's conviction that "the key to profits is value," and adds, "actions that enhance near-term profits at the expense of future profitability are unacceptable." Tellabs has been named by *Business Week* and *Investors' Business Daily* as one of the best-performing stocks of the S&P 500. Tellabs' shares are traded on NASDAQ under the TLAB symbol.

Employee opportunities and a reasonable shareholder return are, of course, made possible by a portfolio of successful products. Tellabs is committed to being a technology-focused, market-oriented company with an emphasis on quality products and supporting services that meet the business needs of its customers. The company's products are used worldwide by the providers of communications services such as local and long-distance carriers, competitive service providers, wireless operators and multiple system operators (MSOs) in the United States and abroad, and a variety of corporations, government agencies, utility companies and system integrators.

As a telecommunications infrastructure builder, the company is an important partner with communications service providers around the world, enabling them to provide their customers with new and differentiated services. Tellabs' product lines include:

- The TITAN® families of digital cross-connect and optical networking systems
- The FOCUS™ family of SDH transport and access solutions

Tellabs' 544,500-square-foot, state-of-the-art facility located in Bolingbrook, Illinois, houses manufacturing, marketing, and research and development.

• The AN2100® Gateway Exchange™ (GX) System, which enables service providers to consolidate circuit-switched and variable-bit-rate data services over a single broadband network

• The Everest™ 9500 Integrated Switch, which combines Internet Protocol (IP) routing and Asynchronous Transfer Mode (ATM) switching into a single multilayer device to carry Internet, virtual private network and other business services on a single platform

• The ETX5000™, which enables service providers worldwide to offer next-generation, converged services such as voice over ATM and voice over IP, over any network infrastructure.

• The MartisDXX® managed access and transport network system to help service providers manage wireless voice and wired data networks

• The CABLESPAN® 2300 Universal Telephony Distribution system for delivery of voice and data services over cable networks

• The VERITY™ family of voice-quality enhancement solutions for wireless and long-distance carriers

• Element Management Systems that provide a centralized point for configuration and network management

• Tellabs' Global Solutions and Services, which provide an array of services from designing next-generation networks to helping carriers implement new revenue-generating solutions that increase their speed to market

Tellabs' products help its customers build, manage and migrate to the new public network –– a next-generation, multiservice network that integrates data, voice and video. Tellabs' service and support offerings combined with access, switching/routing, transport and voice-quality enhancement solutions enable communications service providers to deliver new revenue-generating services while reducing their operating costs.

As the company's customer base and product lines have broadened, Tellabs has grown from a Midwestern American company with mostly domestic customers to a worldwide organization. Customers are served through 14 development centers and six manufacturing facilities, as well as 35 regional sales-and-service centers around the world. Four regional headquarters coordinate Tellabs' global operations: Lisle corporate headquarters; London;

Singapore; and Fort Lauderdale, Florida. An international network of distributors, sales and support services is also employed. To accommodate continuing growth, Tellabs is expanding along Illinois' high-tech corridor in the Naperville area to an 800,000-square-foot facility that will be completed in 2001.

Tellabs uses its considerable in-house technical capabilities to generate new growth, but does not hesitate to aggressively pursue acquisitions to accelerate its progress into new markets. In 1998, the company acquired Coherent Communications Systems of Ashburn, Virginia, a major force in the global echo cancellation market. In 1999, the company acquired DSC Communications' European businesses for $110 million in cash. During the same year, Tellabs also acquired NetCore Systems of Wilmington, Massachusetts, for about $575 million in stock; select assets of DSP Software Engineering in Bedford, Massachusetts, for $35 million in cash; and SALIX Technologies in Gaithersburg, Maryland, for $300 million in stock.

Tellabs expects that the industry changes and growth that prompted the company's internal growth and acquisitions will continue.

"The forces of technology, deregulation and competition are creating an era of unprecedented opportunity for the telecommunications industry. For those involved, the change is fundamental in nature and worldwide in scope," Birck says. "The ultimate result of all this change is still uncertain. Two things are certain, however — it's coming and Tellabs will be there."

Tellabs provides the network infrastructure solutions for communication service providers.

Cobra Electronics Corporation

James R. Bazet, president and CEO

Based on the northwest side of Chicago, Cobra Electronics Corporation designs and markets consumer electronics products. Over 200 professionals in Chicago and at offices in Hong Kong and Dublin produce and

> Cobra is the leading two-way communications company in the consumer electronics industry, and a strong second in the Family Radio Service (FRS) market.

market products that have become an important part of people's lives: products including Citizen Band (CB) radios, radar detectors, Family Radio Service (FRS) and inverters. Cobra is the No. 1 seller of Citizen Band radios and radar detectors in the United States.

The company got its start in 1948 when Carl Korn — now chairman of the board of Cobra Electronics — founded Central Television Service Company to provide television-repair service. Since adequate equipment to service televisions was unavailable, Korn and his associates designed, produced and marketed their own test equipment, and the company B&K was formed. During the 1950s and 1960s B&K acquired other firms, including Precision Apparatus, Mark Products and Telemotive, a manufacturer of radio remote-control devices for overhead cranes. In 1962 this collection of companies became the Dynascan Corporation.

Dynascan produced the first single sideband Citizen Band radio, the "Sidewinder," and chose

"COBRA" to represent the symbol and brand of all of its Citizen Band products. The company moved to a larger location in 1975, and in 1979 Cobra added cordless phones to its product line.

Today, the company now known as Cobra Electronics is a leader in the consumer electronics industry and continues to design and market communications products that promote safety and convenience. By identifying four key areas — distribution, market share, the reshaping of new and existing products and entry into foreign markets — Cobra's goal is to deliver the best-quality products to the largest segments of the market.

The company aims to sell its products in an even greater number of retail outlets. Many of its leading products, including its Family Radio Service devices (FRS), radar detectors and Citizen Band radios are already sold in major consumer electronics outlets such as Best Buy and Circuit City, as well as Sears, Kmart and numerous office supply stores.

Cobra is the leading two-way communications company in the consumer electronics industry, and a strong second in the Family Radio Service (FRS) market. Its MicroTALK™ line of Family Radio Service (FRS) two-way radios is reaching new markets including families, businesses and outdoor and leisure enthusiasts, and the company's MicroTALK PRO™ is a long-range, two-way radio targeting professional, business and industrial users.

The company continually strives to enhance its offerings. This includes adding new colors and redesigning products, including its radar detectors, which feature sleek, curved designs and the industry's first nine-band radar, and its NightWatch™ line of Citizen Band radios, which have illuminated front panels. Its Safety Alert™ transmitter has been placed in police, fire and emergency vehicles in all 50 states.

Exploring foreign markets is a top priority, and the firm is experiencing growth in almost 30 international markets. By expanding throughout the world, Cobra Electronics will continue to be a major leader in the consumer electronics industry.

Chicago Park District Special Collections

Bibliography

AIA Guide to Chicago. Ed. Alice Sinkevitch. New York: Harcourt Brace, 1993.

Altgeld, John P. *Reasons For Pardoning the Haymarket Anarchists*. Chicago: Charles H. Kerr Publishing Company, 1986.

Anderson, Margaret. *My Thirty Years' War*. New York: Covici, Friede Inc., 1930.

Andreas, Alfred T. *History of Chicago from the Earliest Period to the Present Time*. 3 vols. Chicago: Alfred T. Andreas, 1884-86.

Andrews, Clarence A. *Chicago in Story: A Literary History*. Iowa City: Midwest Heritage Publishing Co., 1982.

Brown, Dee. *Hear That Lonesome Whistle Blow: Railroads in the West*. New York: Holt, Rinehart and Winston, 1977.

Browne, Waldo R. *Altgeld of Illinois: A Record of His Life and Work*. New York: B. W. Huebsch, Inc., 1924.

Cahan, Richard. *Landmark Neighborhoods in Chicago*. Chicago: The Commission on Chicago Historical and Architectural Landmarks, 1981.

Cahan, Richard. *They All Fall Down: Richard Nickel's Struggle to Save America's Architecture*. Washington: The Preservation Press, 1994.

Crombie, Robert. *The Great Chicago Fire*. Nashville: Rutledge Hill Press, 1994.

Danckers, Ulrich and Meredith, Jane. *Early Chicago: A Compendium of the Early History of Chicago to the Year 1835 When the Indians Left*. River Forest, Ill: Early Chicago, Inc., 1999.

Dedmon, Emmett. *Fabulous Chicago*. New York: Atheneum, 1981.

Duis, Perry R. *Challenging Chicago: Coping With Everyday Life, 1837-1920*. Urbana and Chicago: University of Illinois Press, 1998.

Duis, Perry, and La France, Scott. *We've Got a Job to Do: Chicagoans and World War II*. Chicago: Chicago Historical Society, 1992.

Farr, Finis. *Chicago: A Personal History of America's Most American City*. New Rochelle, N.Y.: Arlington House, 1973.

Flynn, John J. *Chicago, The Marvelous City of the West: A History, An Encyclopedia and A Guide*. Chicago: Flinn & Sheppard, 1890.

Ginger, Ray. *Altgeld's America: The Lincoln Ideal Versus Changing Realities*. New York: Funk & Wagnalls Company, 1958.

Hayes, Dorsha B. *Chicago: Crossroads of American Enterprise.* New York: Julian Messner Inc., 1944.

Hayner, Don, and McNamee, Tom. *Metro Chicago Almanac.* Chicago: Chicago Sun-Times, Inc., and Bonus Books, Inc., 1993.

Hayner, Don, and McNamee, Tom. *Streetwise Chicago.* Chicago: Loyola University Press, 1988.

Heise, Kenan and Edgerton, Michael. *Chicago: Center for Enterprise, Volumes I and II.* Woodland Hills, Calif.: Windsor Publications Inc., 1982.

Heise, Kenan. *The Chicagoization of America 1893-1917.* Evanston, Ill.: Chicago Historical Bookworks, 1990.

Historic City: The Settlement of Chicago. Chicago: City of Chicago, 1976.

Hubbard, Gurdon. *The Autobiography of Gurdon Saltonstall Hubbard.* New York: The Citadel Press, Inc., 1969.

Johnson, Curt, and Sautter, R. Craig. *Wicked City: From Kenna to Capone.* Highland Park, Ill.: December Press, 1994.

Johnson, Paul. *A History of the American People.* New York: HarperCollins Publishers, 1997.

Karamanski, Theodore J. *Rally 'Round the Flag: Chicago and the Civil War.* Chicago: Nelson-Hall Publishers, 1993.

Kogan, Herman and Wendt, Lloyd: *Chicago: A Pictorial History.* New York: E.P. Dutton and Company, Inc., 1958.

Lewis, Lloyd and Smith, Henry Justin. *Chicago: The History of Its Reputation*, New York: Blue Ribbon Books, 1929.

Lindberg, Richard. *Chicago Ragtime: Another Look at Chicago 1880-1920.* South Bend, Ind.: Icarus Press, 1985.

Lindberg, Richard C. *Quotable Chicago.* Chicago: Wild Onion Books, 1996.

Mayer, Harold M. and Wade, Richard C. *Chicago: Growth of a Metropolis.* Chicago and London: The University of Chicago Press, 1969.

Miller, Donald L. *City of the Century.* New York: Touchstone, 1997.

Ottley, Roi. *The Lonely Warrior: The Life and Times of Robert S. Abbott.* Chicago: Henry Regnery Company, 1955.

Redd, Jim. *The Illinois and Michigan Canal: A Contemporary Perspective in Essays and Photographs.* Carbondale and Edwardsville, Ill.: Southern Illinois University Press, 1993.

Sandburg, Carl. *The Chicago Race Riots July, 1919.* New York: Harcourt, Brace and Howe, 1919.

Sawislak, Karen. *Smoldering City: Chicagoans and the Great Fire, 1871-1874.* Chicago and London: The University of Chicago Press, 1995.

Smith, Alson J. *Chicago's Left Bank.* Chicago: Henry Regnery Company, 1953.

Spear, Allan H. *Black Chicago: The Making of a Negro Ghetto 1890-1920.* Chicago and London: The University of Chicago Press, 1967.

Swanson, Stevenson, editor. *Chicago Days: 150 Defining Moments in the Life of a Great City.* Wheaton Ill.: Cantigny First Division Foundation, 1997.

Tuttle, William M. Jr. *Race Riot: Chicago in the Red Summer of 1919.* New York: Atheneum, 1970.

20th Century Chicago: 100 Years 100 Voices. Ed. Adrienne Drell. Springfield, Ill.: Sports Publishing, Inc., 2000.

Winslow, Charles S. *Historical Events of Chicago.* 3 vols. Chicago: Winslow, 1933.

Young, David M. *Chicago Transit: An Illustrated History.* DeKalb Ill.: Northern Illinois University Press, 1998.

Index

Partners & Web Site Index

Corporate profiles also appear on bookofbusiness.com

Special thanks to Julia Sniderman Bachrach for providing Chicago Park District photos